4th Workshop on NLP for Conversational AI 2022 (NLP4ConvAI 2022)

Dublin, Ireland
27 May 2022

ISBN: 978-1-7138-6748-7

Printed from e-media with permission by:

Curran Associates, Inc.
57 Morehouse Lane
Red Hook, NY 12571

Some format issues inherent in the e-media version may also appear in this print version.

Association for Computational Linguistics
209 N. Eighth Street
Stroudsburg, Pennsylvania 18360

Phone: 1-570-476-8006
Fax: 1-570-476-0860

acl@aclweb.org

Additional copies of this publication are available from:

Curran Associates, Inc.
57 Morehouse Lane
Red Hook, NY 12571 USA
Phone: 845-758-0400
Fax: 845-758-2633
Email: curran@proceedings.com
Web: www.proceedings.com

ACL 2022

The 4th Workshop on NLP for Conversational AI

Proceedings of the Workshop

May 27, 2022

The ACL organizers gratefully acknowledge the support from the following sponsors.

Gold Level

Bronze Level

Introduction

Welcome to the 4th Workshop on NLP for Conversational AI, at ACL 2022.

Ever since the invention of the intelligent machine, hundreds and thousands of mathematicians, linguists, and computer scientists have dedicated their careers to empowering human-machine communication in natural language. Although the idea is finally around the corner with a proliferation of virtual personal assistants such as Siri, Alexa, Google Assistant, and Cortana, the development of these conversational agents remains difficult and there still remain plenty of unanswered questions and challenges.

Conversational AI is hard because it is an interdisciplinary subject. Initiatives were started in different research communities, from Dialogue State Tracking Challenges to NeurIPS Conversational Intelligence Challenge live competition and the Amazon Alexa Prize. However, various fields within the NLP community, such as semantic parsing, coreference resolution, sentiment analysis, question answering, and machine reading comprehension etc. have been seldom evaluated or applied in the context of conversational AI.

The goal of this workshop is to bring together NLP researchers and practitioners in different fields, alongside experts in speech and machine learning, to discuss the current state-of-the-art and new approaches, to share insights and challenges, to bridge the gap between academic research and real-world product deployment, and to shed light on future directions. "NLP for Conversational AI" will be a one-day workshop including keynotes, spotlight talks, and poster sessions. In keynote talks, senior technical leaders from industry and academia will share insights on the latest developments in the field.

An open call for papers will be announced to encourage researchers and students to share their prospects and latest discoveries. The panel discussion will focus on the challenges, future directions of conversational AI research, bridging the gap in research and industrial practice, as well as audience suggested topics.

With the increasing trend of conversational AI, NLP4ConvAI 2022 is competitive. We received 45 submissions directly to the workshop and 14 submissions through the ACL Rolling Review. After a rigorous review process, we only accepted 18 papers. There are 15 long papers and 3 short papers. The workshop overall acceptance rate is about 30.5%.

We hope you will enjoy NLP4ConvAI 2022 at ACL and contribute to the future success of our community!

NLP4ConvAI 2021 Organizers
Bing Liu, Meta
Alexandros Papangelis, Amazon Alexa AI
Stefan Ultes, Mercedes-Benz AG
Abhinav Rastogi, Google Research
Yun-Nung (Vivian) Chen, National Taiwan University
Georgios Spithourakis, PolyAI
Elnaz Nouri, Microsoft Research
Weiyan Shi, Columbia University

Organizing Committee

General Chair

Bing Liu, Meta
Alexandros Papangelis, Amazon Alexa AI

Program Chair

Stefan Ultes, Mercedes-Benz AG
Abhinav Rastogi, Google Research

Publication Chair

Yun-Nung (Vivian) Chen, National Taiwan University

Diversity Chair

Georgios Spithourakis, PolyAI

Sponsorship Chair

Elnaz Nouri, Microsoft Research

Publicity Chair

Weiyan Shi, Columbia University

Program Committee

Program Chairs

Yun-Nung (Vivian) Chen, National Taiwan University
Bing Liu, Meta
Elnaz Nouri, Microsoft Research
Alexandros Papangelis, Amazon
Abhinav Rastogi, Google
Weiyan Shi, Columbia University
Georgios P. Spithourakis, PolyAI
Stefan Ultes, Mercedes Benz Research & Development

Program Committee

Akshat Shrivastava, Meta
Alankar Jain, Google
Alborz Geramifard, Meta
Bin Zhang, Google
Bo-Hsiang Tseng, University of Cambridge
Chao-Wei Huang, National Taiwan University
Chien-Sheng Wu, Salesforce AI Research
Chinnadhurai Sankar, Meta
Christian Geishauser, Heinrich-Heine Universität Düsseldorf
Daniel Cer, Google
David Vandyke, University of Cambridge
Dilek Hakkani-Tur, Amazon Alexa AI
Emine Yilmaz, Department of Computer Science, University College London
Evgeniia Razumovskaia, University of Cambridge
Gokhan Tur, Amazon
Harrison Lee, Google
Hongyuan Zhan, Meta
Hsien-chin Lin, Heinrich Heine University Düsseldorf
Inigo Casanueva, PolyAI
Ivan Vulić, University of Cambridge
Kai Sun, Meta
Lei Shu, Amazon
Marek Rei, Imperial College London
Michael Heck, Heinrich Heine Universität Düsseldorf
Mihir Kale, Google
Nikita Moghe, University of Edinburgh
Paweł Budzianowski, PolyAI
Peng Wang, Google Research
Raghav Gupta, Google
Seokhwan Kim, Amazon
Seungwhan Moon, Meta
Shikib Mehri, Carnegie Mellon University
Shutong Feng, Heinrich-Heine Universität Düsseldorf
Simon Keizer, Toshiba Research Europe
Songbo Hu, Language Technology Lab, University of Cambridge

Stefan Larson, SkySync
Ta-Chung Chi, Carnegie Mellon University
Wei Peng, Huawei Technologies Ltd.
Wenqiang Lei, Sichuan University
Wolfgang Maier, Mercedes Benz Research and Development
Xiujun Li, University of Washington
Yang Liu, Amazon
Yi-Chia Wang, Meta
Yi-Ting Yeh, Carnegie Mellon University
Yuan Cao, Google Brain
Zhaojiang Lin, Meta
Zhiguang Wang, Meta
Zhuoran Wang, Tricorn (Beijing) Technology

Invited Speakers

Gokhan Tur, Amazon Alexa AI
Zhou Yu, Columbia University
William Wang, University of California, Santa Barbara
Michael Tjalve, University of Washington + Microsoft Philanthropies
Maria-Georgia Zachari, Omilia

Keynote Talk: HybriDialogue: Towards Information-Seeking Dialogue Reasoning Grounded on Tabular and Textual Data

William Wang
University of California, Santa Barbara

Abstract: A pressing challenge in current dialogue systems is to successfully converse with users on topics with information distributed across different modalities. Previous work in multi-turn dialogue systems has primarily focused on either text or table information. In more realistic scenarios, having a joint understanding of both is critical as knowledge is typically distributed over both unstructured and structured forms. In this talk, I will present a new dialogue dataset, HybriDialogue, which consists of crowdsourced natural conversations grounded on both Wikipedia text and tables. The conversations are created through the decomposition of complex multihop questions into simple, realistic multiturn dialogue interactions. We conduct several baseline experiments, including retrieval, system state tracking, and dialogue response generation. Our results show that there is still ample opportunity for improvement, demonstrating the importance of building stronger dialogue systems that can reason over the complex setting of information-seeking dialogue grounded on tables and text. I will also briefly mention a few related studies on dialogue research from the UCSB NLP Group.

Keynote Talk: Dialog Management for Conversational Task-Oriented Industry Solutions

Maria-Georgia Zachari
Omilia

Abstract: This talk will focus on how the Omilia Cloud Platform® leverages the notion of Dialog Act in order to solve real-life use cases in task-oriented dialog systems for call centers. We will address the challenge of completing tasks efficiently, achieving high KPIs and integrating with a call center, while at the same time building and maintaining a flexible conversational NLU system.

Keynote Talk: Directions of Dialog Research in the Era of Big Pre-training Models

Zhou Yu
Columbia University

Abstract: Big pre-training models (such as BERT and GPT3) have demonstrated excellent performances on various NLP tasks. Instruction tuning and prompting have enabled these models to shine in low-resource settings. The natural question is "Will big models solve dialog tasks?" This talk will first go through big models' impact on several sub-topics within dialog systems (e.g. social chatbots, task-oriented dialog systems, negotiation/persuasion dialog systems, continue learning in dialog systems, multilingual dialog systems, multimodal dialog systems, deployable dialog systems, etc) and then follow up with the speaker's own interpretations of the challenges remaining and possible future directions.

Keynote Talk: Scaling impact: the case for humanitarian NLP

Michael Tjalve
University of Washington + Microsoft Philanthropies

Abstract: Advances in core NLP capabilities have enabled an extensive variety of scenarios where conversational AI provides real value for companies and customers alike. Leveraging lessons learned from these successes to applying the technology in the humanitarian context requires an understanding of both the potential for impact and risk of misuse.
In this talk, we'll discuss how to leverage conversational AI to scale impact for audiences in the humanitarian sector while earning and maintaining trust with the adopters of the technology and with the people they impact.

Keynote Talk: Past, Present, Future of Conversational AI

Gokhan Tur
Amazon Alexa AI

Abstract: Recent advances in deep learning based methods for language processing, especially using self-supervised learning methods resulted in new excitement towards building more sophisticated Conversational AI systems. While this is partially true for social chatbots or retrieval-based applications, it is commonplace to see dialogue processing as yet another task while assessing these new state of the art approaches. In this talk, I will argue that Conversational AI comes with an orthogonal methodology for machine learning to complement such methods interacting with the users using implicit and explicit signals. This is an exceptional opportunity for Conversational AI research moving forward and I will present couple representative efforts from Alexa AI.

Table of Contents

Program

Friday, May 27, 2022

09:00 - 09:10 *Opening Remarks*

09:10 - 09:40 *Invited Talk 1 by William Wang*

09:40 - 10:10 *Invited Talk 2 by Maria-Georgia Zachari*

10:10 - 10:40 *Oral Paper Session 1*

Understanding and Improving the Exemplar-based Generation for Open-domain Conversation
Seungju Han, Beomsu Kim, Seokjun Seo, Enkhbayar Erdenee and Buru Chang

Conversational AI for Positive-sum Retailing under Falsehood Control
Yin-Hsiang Liao, Ruo-Ping Dong, Huan-Cheng Chang and Wilson Ma

10:40 - 11:00 *Coffee Break*

11:00 - 12:30 *Poster Paper Session*

Extracting and Inferring Personal Attributes from Dialogue
Zhulin Wang, Xuhui Zhou, Rik Koncel-Kedziorski, Alex Marin and Fei Xia

From Rewriting to Remembering: Common Ground for Conversational QA Models
Marco Del Tredici, Xiaoyu Shen, Gianni Barlacchi, Bill Byrne and Adrià de Gispert

D-REX: Dialogue Relation Extraction with Explanations
Alon Albalak, Varun R. Embar, Yi-Lin Tuan, Lise Getoor and William Yang Wang

A Randomized Link Transformer for Diverse Open-Domain Dialogue Generation
Jing Yang Lee, Kong Aik Lee and Woon Seng Gan

Knowledge Distillation Meets Few-Shot Learning: An Approach for Few-Shot Intent Classification Within and Across Domains
Anna Sauer, Shima Asaadi and Fabian Küch

Relevance in Dialogue: Is Less More? An Empirical Comparison of Existing Metrics, and a Novel Simple Metric
Ian Berlot-Attwell and Frank Rudzicz

Friday, May 27, 2022 (continued)

Stylistic Response Generation by Controlling Personality Traits and Intent
Sougata Saha, Souvik Das and Rohini Srihari

Open-domain Dialogue Generation: What We Can Do, Cannot Do, And Should Do Next
Katharina Kann, Abteen Ebrahimi, Joewie J. Koh, Shiran Dudy and Alessandro Roncone

MTL-SLT: Multi-Task Learning for Spoken Language Tasks
Zhiqi Huang, Milind Rao, Anirudh Raju, Zhe Zhang, Bach Bui and Chul Lee

Data Augmentation for Intent Classification with Off-the-shelf Large Language Models
Gaurav Sahu, Pau Rodriguez, Issam H. Laradji, Parmida Atighehchian, David Vazquez and Dzmitry Bahdanau

Toward Knowledge-Enriched Conversational Recommendation Systems
Tong Zhang, Yong Liu, Boyang Li, Peixiang Zhong, Chen Zhang, Hao Wang and Chunyan Miao

Are Pre-trained Transformers Robust in Intent Classification? A Missing Ingredient in Evaluation of Out-of-Scope Intent Detection
Jianguo Zhang, Kazuma Hashimoto, Yao Wan, Zhiwei Liu, Ye Liu, Caiming Xiong and Philip S. Yu

12:30 - 14:00 *Lunch Break*

14:00 - 14:30 *Invited Talk 3 by Zhou Yu*

14:30 - 15:00 *Invited Talk 4 by Michael Tjalve*

15:00 - 15:20 *Coffee Break*

15:20 - 15:50 *Invited Talk 5 by Gokhan Tur*

15:50 - 16:50 *Oral Paper Session 2*

Human Evaluation of Conversations is an Open Problem: comparing the sensitivity of various methods for evaluating dialogue agents
Eric Michael Smith, Orion Hsu, Rebecca Qian, Stephen Roller, Y-Lan Boureau and Jason E Weston

RetroNLU: Retrieval Augmented Task-Oriented Semantic Parsing
Vivek Gupta, Akshat Shrivastava, Adithya Sagar, Armen Aghajanyan and Denis Savenkov

Friday, May 27, 2022 (continued)

KG-CRuSE: Recurrent Walks over Knowledge Graph for Explainable Conversation Reasoning using Semantic Embeddings
Rajdeep Sarkar, Mihael Arcan and John Philip McCrae

Multimodal Conversational AI: A Survey of Datasets and Approaches
Anirudh S Sundar and Larry Heck

16:50 - 17:00 *Closing Remarks*

A Randomized Link Transformer for Diverse Open-Domain Dialogue Generation

Jing Yang Lee[1], Kong Aik Lee[2], Woon Seng Gan[3]

School of Electrical and Electronic Engineering, Nanyang Technological University[1,3]
Institute for Infocomm Research, A*STAR[2]
jingyang001@e.ntu.edu.sg[1], lee_kong_aik@i2r.a-star.edu.sg[2], ewsgan@ntu.edu.sg[3]

Abstract

A major issue in open-domain dialogue generation is the agent's tendency to generate repetitive and generic responses. The lack in response diversity has been addressed in recent years via the use of latent variable models, such as the Conditional Variational Auto-Encoder (CVAE), which typically involve learning a latent Gaussian distribution over potential response intents. However, due to latent variable collapse, training latent variable dialogue models are notoriously complex, requiring substantial modification to the standard training process and loss function. Other approaches proposed to improve response diversity also largely entail a significant increase in training complexity. Hence, this paper proposes a Randomized Link (RL) Transformer as an alternative to the latent variable models. The RL Transformer does not require any additional enhancements to the training process or loss function. Empirical results show that, when it comes to response diversity, the RL Transformer achieved comparable performance compared to latent variable models.

1 Introduction

Open-domain dialogue generation refers to the task of generating coherent, natural and human-like dialogue given solely the dialogue context (also known as the dialogue history). The development of open-domain dialogue agents that can engage humans in seamless general conversation (or chit-chat) is one of the main objectives of conversational AI. Currently, however, agents display a tendency to generate repetitive and generic dialogue responses, which negatively impact both naturalness and contextual coherence.

Recently, researchers have turned to latent variable models, specifically the Conditional Variational Auto Encoder (CVAE) (Sohn et al., 2015), to address this issue (Yang et al., 2021; Gao et al., 2019; Zhao et al., 2017; Cao and Clark, 2017). In addition to open-domain dialogue generation, latent variable models have also been applied to related tasks such as personalized dialogue (Lee. et al., 2022; Wu et al., 2020; Song et al., 2019), empathetic dialogue (Li et al., 2021, 2020b,a; Zhou and Wang, 2018), and topical dialogue generation (Wang et al., 2020). These works have generally involved modelling the potential dialogue response intents as a latent Gaussian prior, which is typically generated by a Multi-Layer Perceptron (MLP). During inference, a latent instance is sampled from the generated Gaussian prior via the reparameterization trick and fed to the decoder. Stochasticity is induced during the response generation via such random sampling process. However, even though latent variable models are effective at improving response diversity, they are notoriously hard to train primarily due to the Kullback-Liebler (KL) vanishing problem. Usually, this problem is addressed via KL annealing or incorporating a Bag-of-Words loss. While KL annealing requires tuning the weighting hyperparameter β, attaining the Bag-of-Words loss involves defining an additional task of predicting the response bag-of-words. This results in additional complexity during training.

Several other approaches to promoting response diversity which involve introducing an alternate loss function such as the Maximum Mutual Information (MMI) objective (Li et al., 2016a), the Inverse Token Frequency (ITF) objective (Nakamura et al., 2018), and the Inverse N-gram Frequency (INF) objective (Ueyama and Kano, 2020), require considerable additional computation steps. On the other hand, adversarial learning-based (Li et al., 2017a) and embedding augmentation-based (Cao et al., 2021) approaches require extensive modifications to the standard training process, resulting in a significant increase in training complexity.

Hence, inspired by randomization-based neural networks (Suganthan and Katuwal, 2021) and the Random Vector Functional Link (RVFL) neural

Proceedings of the 4th Workshop on NLP for Conversational AI, pages 1 - 11
May 27, 2022 ©2022 Association for Computational Linguistics

network (Pao and Takefuji, 1992) in particular, we introduce a novel Randomized Link (RL) Transformer. An alternative to latent variable models which does not require any modifications or enhancements to the standard training process or loss function. In other words, the RL Transformer can be trained via standard gradient descent solely on the standard negative log-likelihood loss. Experimental results on the DailyDialog (Li et al., 2017b) and EmpatheticDialogues (Rashkin et al., 2019) corpora show that our RL Transformer successfully improves the diversity of the generated response, achieving comparable response diversification relative to latent variable approaches. In addition, compared to the latent variable models, responses generated by our RL Transformer are noticeably more fluent and contextually coherent.

The remainder of this paper is organized as follows: Section 2 provides additional background information regarding open-domain dialogue generation and RVFL neural networks; Section 3 describes the proposed RL Transformer in detail; Section 4 provides details regarding our implementations and experiments; Section 5 presents the experimental results as well as our analysis of the results; Section 6 concludes the paper.

2 Related Work

2.1 Neural Open-domain Dialogue Generation

In recent years, generative neural models have been commonly applied to the task of open-domain dialogue generation. Influenced by advances in machine translation, popular approaches to this task featured a sequence-to-sequence (seq2seq) architecture (Sutskever et al., 2014). Recurrent neural networks such as the Long Short Term Memory (LSTM) and the Gated Recurrent Unit (GRU) have been often utilized in both the encoder and decoder of a seq2seq model (Shang et al., 2015; Sordoni et al., 2015). More recently, Transformer-based models (Vaswani et al., 2017) have taken centre stage. Multiple works have leveraged Transformer-based pretrained language models such as BERT, GPT and GPT-2 to improve the overall language understanding and generation capabilities of their dialogue agents (Gu et al., 2021; Zhang et al., 2020; Zhao et al., 2019). In addition to latent variable models, different learning approaches such as reinforcement learning (Saleh et al., 2019; Li et al., 2016b) and adversarial learning (Li et al., 2017a) have also been applied to this task.

2.2 Random Vector Functional Link Neural Networks

The Random Vector Functional Link (RVFL) neural network (Pao and Takefuji, 1992) is essentially a single-layer feed forward neural network with a direct link between the input and output layer. The optimal weights of an RVFL can be obtained iteratively, or through a closed form solution via regularized least squares or the Moore-Penrose pseudoinverse. Prior work has mathematically proven that the RVFL is an efficient and effective universal approximator (Needell et al., 2020). Over the years, multiple RVFL variants including (but not limited to) the deep RVFL (Shi et al., 2021), ensemble deep RVFL (Shi et al., 2021), sparse Pretrained-RVFL (Zhang et al., 2019) and Rotation Forest-RVFL (Malik et al., 2021) have been proposed. Recently, RVFL neural networks have been applied to a broad range of practical tasks across multiple domains such as remote sensing (Dai et al., 2022), malware classification (Elkabbash et al., 2021), medical image classification (Nayak et al., 2020; Katuwal et al., 2019) and even Covid-19 spread forecasting (Hazarika and Gupta, 2020).

3 Methodology

3.1 Randomized Link (RL) Transformer

In this paper, we propose a Randomized Link (RL) Transformer for open-domain dialogue generation. Our proposed model generates the dialogue response based only on the dialogue context. Similar to the standard Transformer, the RL Transformer consists of an encoder and decoder. The encoder maps an input sequence $X = \{x_0, ..., x_{J-1}\}$ (J refers to the length of the input sequence) to an intermediate representation $Z = \{z_0, ..., z_{J-1}\}$. The decoder then accepts Z as input and generates the final output $Y = \{y_0, ..., y_{K-1}\}$ (K refers to the length of the output sequence) token by token, in an auto-regressive manner.

The proposed RL Transformer leverages linear layers with randomly initialized weights to incorporate stochasticity into the response generation process. Our work is largely inspired by the Random Vector Functional Link (RVFL) neural network (Pao and Takefuji, 1992), a single-layer feed forward randomization-based neural network consisting of a fixed randomized hidden layer and a direct link from the input to the output layer. The

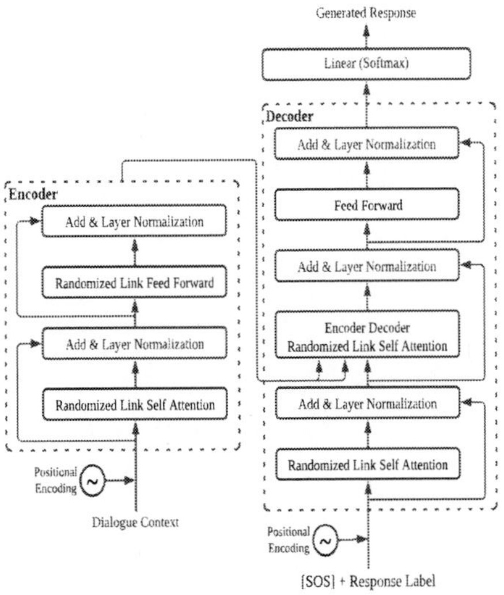

Figure 1: Model architecture of the proposed Randomized Link Transformer.

direct link is implemented by concatenating the input with the randomized hidden layer output, before being fed to the output layer. Only the weights in the output layer are trainable. We incorporate the RVFL architecture into the self-attention and feed forward networks of a Transformer.

Essentially, the Randomized Link Transformer encoder consists of a Randomized Link Self-Attention (RLSA) network and a Randomized Link Feed Forward (RLFF) network. The decoder, on the other hand, consists of a RLSA network, followed by a Encoder-Decoder (ED) RLSA network and a regular Feed Forward (FF) network. Similar to the original Transformer architecture, residual connections and layer normalization is introduced after every RLSA, RLFF, ED RLSA and FF network. An overview is provided in Figure 1.

3.2 Randomized Link Self-Attention

In order to incorporate stochasticity into the response generation process, we introduce a novel Randomized Link Self-Attention (RLSA) network featuring feed forward linear layers with random weights. Similar to to the original Transformer architecture, our randomized link self-attention involves mapping a query vector, denoted by Q, and a set of key-value vector pairs, denoted by K and V respectively, to an output. The output is derived by computing the weighted sum of the values, where the weight assigned to each value is computed by taking the dot product of the query with the corresponding key. For each attention head in the standard transformer architecture, the input is passed to three distinct linear layers, resulting in the query, key and value vectors Q_n, K_n, and V_n, where n refers to an arbitrary attention head.

In RLSA, each input will be fed to a single random linear layer. The sizes of all random linear layers used in the randomized Transformer, denoted by d_{rand}, are identical. Similar to the RVFL, we introduce a direct link by concatenating the output of this layer with the original input. The resultant representation is fed to a separate linear layer with trainable weights. Similarly, for multi-headed RLSA, a distinct Q_n, K_n, and V_n vector is defined for each of the N attention heads. The dimensionality of the Q_n and K_n vectors is denoted by d_k, and the dimensionality of the V_n vector is denoted by d_v. This can be expressed as follows:

$$Q_n = W_{Q_n}([X, W^r_{Q_n}(X)]) \tag{1}$$

$$K_n = W_{K_n}([X, W^r_{K_n}(X)]) \tag{2}$$

$$V_n = W_{V_n}([X, W^r_{V_n}(X)]) \tag{3}$$

where W_Q, W_K, and W_V represent the weights of the trainable linear layers corresponding to the Q, K and V vectors respectively. We use the superscript $()^r$ to denote the randomized matrices, whereby W^r_Q, W^r_K, and W^r_V represent the weights of the randomly initialized linear layers corresponding to the Q_n, K_n and V_n vectors respectively. X denotes the input sequence, and $[\cdot]$ represents the concatenate operation.

The randomized linear layers W^r_Q, W^r_K, and W^r_V are initialized every epoch with Xavier normal initialization (Glorot and Bengio, 2010) i.e., $W^r_Q, W^r_K, W^r_V \sim \mathcal{N}(0, \sigma^2)$ where $\sigma = \gamma \times \sqrt{\frac{2}{d_{hidden}+d_{rand}}}$. The gain value $\gamma = 1.0$. The selection of the standard deviation or the variance of the initialization is vital to model performance. This is because an excessively large variance would result in model divergence, while an excessively small variance would result in a drop in stochasticity. For the randomized layers in RLSA, weights initialized from a normal distribution with a suitable standard deviation would allow the model to converge while maintaining stochasticity. As seen in the equation, for the Xavier normal initialization, the standard deviation of the Gaussian distribution from which the initial weights are sampled is a function of the total number of inputs and outputs. Empirically, we found that the standard deviation value utilized during Xavier normal initialization would generally outperforms other standard deviation values across all randomized layer sizes.

Then, following the standard Transformer architecture, the dot product of all corresponding Q and K vectors are computed to obtain the attention maps. Then, to attain the score, the softmax function is applied over the dot products divided by the square root of the dimension of the Q and K vectors i.e., $\sqrt{d_k}$. Each of the V vectors is then multiplied with the attained score. This results in the following expression:

$$Z_n = softmax(\frac{Q_n K_n^{\mathbf{T}}}{\sqrt{d_k}})V_n \tag{4}$$

where $\mathbf{T}$ represents the transpose operation. The output of each attention head Z_n is concatenated to form Z:

$$Z = [Z_0, Z_1, Z_2 \cdots Z_{N-1}] \tag{5}$$

where N represents the number of attention heads.

Then, the resulting representation Z is then passed to a single linear layer with randomly initialized weights. Once again, to obtain the encoder output Z, the output of the random layer is concatenated with the original input $\bar{Z}$, and fed to a separate linear layer with trainable weights (direct link).

$$Z = W_Z([X, W_Z^r(Z)]) \tag{6}$$

where W_Z and W_Z^r represent the weights of the trainable linear layer and randomized linear layer used to obtain the encoder output Z respectively. Similarly, the randomized linear layer W_Z^r is initialized every epoch with Xavier normal initialization i.e., $W_Z^r \sim \mathcal{N}(0, \sigma^2)$ where $\sigma = \gamma \times \sqrt{\frac{2}{d_v + d_{rand}}}$. The gain value $\gamma = 1.0$.

For the Encoder Decoder (ED) RLSA in the decoder, the encoder outputs and prior decoder outputs are used as input. The output of the prior decoder layer is used to generate the queries, and the encoder outputs are used to generate the keys and values. An overview of the RLSA network is presented in Figure 2.

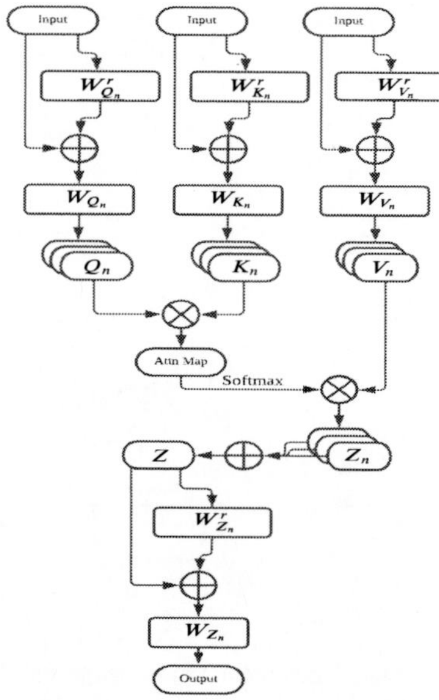

Figure 2: Overview of Randomized Link Self Attention. $\oplus$ refers to the concatenate operation.

3.3 Randomized Link Feed Forward Network

The feed forward network in the standard Transformer consists of a two-layer fully trainable feed forward neural network. Likewise, the Randomized Link Feed Forward (RLFF) network is a two-layer feed forward neural network which features a randomly initialized fixed linear layer with a ReLU activation function followed by a trainable linear layer. Similarly, the direct link is introduced by concatenating the output of the randomized layer with the original inputs, and passing the resultant representation to the trainable layer. In contrast to the RLSA network (Section 3.2), no additional randomized layers are introduced in the RLFF network. The first linear layer is randomized instead. This can be expressed as:

$$RLFF(Z) = W_2([ReLU(W_1^r(Z)), Z]) \tag{7}$$

where W_1^r and W_2 refer to the first random linear layer and the second trainable linear layer respectively. The size of the randomized linear layer W_1^r is represented by d_{ff}, and the size W_2 is d_{hidden}. Unlike the RLSA network, for the RLFF network, the randomized linear layer W_1^r is initialized every epoch with Xavier uniform initialization (Glorot and Bengio, 2010) i.e., $W_Z^r \sim \mathcal{U}(-a, a)$ where $a = \gamma \times \sqrt{\frac{6}{d_{hidden} + d_{ff}}}$. Since the ReLU activation is applied to the layer output, the gain value. The gain value $\gamma = \sqrt{2}$. We found that utilizing a uniform initialization in the RLFF network instead of a normal initialization would result in a slight increase in response diversity. Also, it should be noted that the RLFF network is only utilized in the encoder of the Randomized Transformer. An overview of the RLFF network is presented in Figure 3.

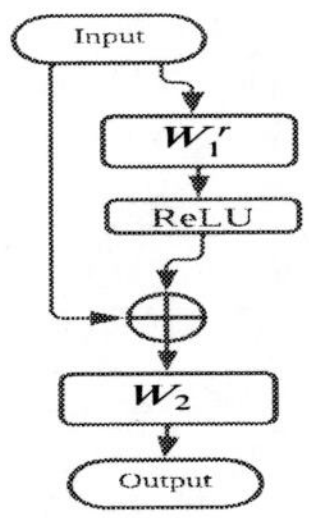

Figure 3: Overview of Randomized Link Feed Forward network. $\oplus$ refers to the concatenate operation.

4 Experiment

4.1 Data

We evaluate the Randomized Link Transformer on the DailyDialogs (Li et al., 2017b) and EmpatheticDialogues (Rashkin et al., 2019) corpora. For the EmpatheticDialogues corpus, the agent is expected to generate an appropriately empathetic response given the dialogue context and emotion label, which is not used in our experiments. The training, validation and test set consists of 19,533, 2,770, and 2,547 dialogues respectively. The DailyDialog corpus consists of general human-written dialogue examples covering a wide range of topics and emotions. Similarly, the provided intent and emotion labels are not used in our experiments. The training, validation and test set consists of 11,118, 1,000 and 1,000 dialogues respectively.

4.2 Implementation

In our experiments, we implement the Randomized Link (RL) Transformer with 4 encoding layers, 4 decoding layers, with 4 attention heads ($N = 4$). Since the 300 dimensional GloVe embedding (Pennington et al., 2014) is used, the hidden dimension d_{hidden} = 300. The size of all randomized layers in the RLSA network d_{rand} is fixed at 512. d_k, d_v and d_z were set to 64 for experiments of the DailyDialog corpus, and 256 on the EmpatheticDialogues corpus. For the RLFF network, d_{ff} is set to 2048. Inputs to the RL Transformer consists of the dialogue context (limited to 4 dialogue turns). Responses are generated via greedy decoding. During training, the Adam optimizer (learning rate = 0.00015, batch size = 32) is used.

4.3 Baselines

We implement the following four models in our experiments:

Transformer. We implement a Transformer (Vaswani et al., 2017) with standard self attention and feed forward components. The Transformer parameters are identical to the RL Transformer as described in Section 4.2.

CVAE. Similar to Zhao et al. (2017) and Lin et al. (2020), we implement a Transformer-based CVAE where the latent variable sampled from the latent Gaussian is combined with the output of the encoder before being fed to the decoder. Following Lin et al. (2020), the latent Gaussian is generated by a three-layer MLP with 512 node hidden layers, and the size of the random latent variable is fixed at 300. The remaining Transformer parameters are identical to the RL Transformer as described in Section 4.2.

SVT. We also implement the Sequential Variational Transformer (SVT) proposed in Lin et al. (2020). The SVT replaces the standard Transformer decoder with a variational decoder layer which implicitly generates a distinct latent variable for each position. Similarly, the latent Gaussians are generated via three-layer MLPs with 512 node hidden layers, and the size of the random latent variable is fixed at 300. The remaining Transformer parameters are identical to the RL Transformer described in Section 4.2.

RL Transformer. We implement the proposed RL Transformer with configuration described in Section 3.2.

4.4 Evaluation

4.4.1 Objective Measures

Distinct-N. We use the Distinct-1 and 2 scores, denoted by D-1 and D-2 respectively, to quantify the inter-response diversity of the generated responses. Essentially, the Distinct-*n* score involves computing the number of distinct *n*-grams in a given text, and dividing the number by the total number of tokens. The Distinct score is derived based on all generated responses.

MTLD & MATTR. Additionally, we also utilize lexical diversity measures such as the Measure of Textual Lexical Diversity (MTLD) and Moving-Average Type–Token Ratio (MATTR) score. MATTR and MTLD are essentially text length invariant variants of the Token-Type Ratio (TTR). MTLD involves computing the Token-Type Ratio (TTR) for sequentially larger segments of the sentence until a predefined threshold h. On the other hand, deriving MATTR requires averaging

	DailyDialog						
	Length	D-1	D-2	MATTR	MTLD	METEOR	ROUGE-L
Transformer (Vaswani et al., 2017)	6.075	0.004	0.017	0.360	12.461	0.076	0.060
CVAE (Zhao et al., 2017)	11.656	0.035	0.200	**0.661**	**32.927**	0.117	0.103
SVT (Lin et al., 2020)	10.244	0.032	0.199	0.580	21.371	**0.118**	**0.108**
RL Transformer	7.678	**0.050**	**0.221**	0.649	30.049	0.113	0.101
	EmpatheticDialogues						
	Length	D-1	D-2	MATTR	MTLD	METEOR	ROUGE-L
Transformer (Vaswani et al., 2017)	9.757	0.015	0.049	0.396	16.479	0.103	**0.116**
CVAE (Zhao et al., 2017)	11.367	0.028	0.226	0.728	49.394	0.097	0.084
SVT (Lin et al., 2020)	12.568	0.023	**0.240**	0.691	36.536	**0.105**	0.096
RL Transformer	11.808	**0.030**	0.239	**0.734**	**51.396**	0.101	0.085

Table 1: Performance comparison of the proposed RL Transformer to the three baselines on the DailyDialog and EmpatheticDialogues corpora.

the TTR of successive segments of the generated response with a fixed window size w. In this paper, h and w were fixed at 0.72 and 4 respectively. Both MTLD and MATTR are derived based on all generated responses.

ROUGE-L & METEOR. Both ROUGE-L and METEOR compares the generated response to the response label. Computing the ROUGE-L score involves first identifying the Longest Common Subsequence (LCS) between the generated response and response label, followed by computing the harmonic mean of the precision and recall between the LCS and the generated response. METEOR is similarly based on the harmonic mean between precision and recall calculated based on the generated response and response label, with more emphasis placed on recall.

4.4.2 Human Evaluation

For human evaluation, we engage five graduate students (native English speakers) to evaluate the Fluency, Diversity and Coherence of the generated responses. The Fluency criteria measures the naturalness and human-likeness of the generated response. For the Fluency criteria, the evaluators were told to regard the response in isolation, without regard for the dialogue context. The Diversity criteria accounts for the diversity on terms of vocabulary in the generated response. Coherence refers to the contextual coherence of the generated response i.e., the relevance of the generated response in relation to the dialogue context. The evaluators were given the dialogue context, and told to consider the appropriateness of the generated responses with regard to the dialogue context. For each example, they were told to compare a response generated by RL Transformer and a response generated by either the base Transformer, CVAE or SVT. The superior response in terms of either Fluency, Coherence or Diversity is selected by the evaluator, and either a 'Win', 'Lose' or 'Tie' is assigned to the corresponding model. The percentage of wins, loses or ties for each pair is then computed. Each evaluator was given 50 randomly sampled dialogue contexts and the corresponding responses generated by the implemented models for evaluation.

5 Results and Discussion

5.1 Quantitative Analysis

Automatic metric scores attained on the DailyDialog and EmpatheticDialogues copora are presented in Table 1. Human evaluation was only conducted on the DailyDialog corpus. Results are presented in Table 3.

Based on the results attained, it can be concluded that the performance of the RL Transformer is comparable to that of latent variable models such as the CVAE and SVT. On the DailyDialog corpus, RL Transformer outperformed all implemented baselines in terms of Distinct-1 and 2 scores. On the EmpatheticDialogues corpus, RL Transformer outperformed all implemented baselines in terms of Distinct-1, MATTR and MTLD.

When it comes to response diversity, the human evaluation results largely corroborate the automatic metric scores. In terms of Diversity, the RL Transformer achieved a high percentage of 'Wins' over the standard Transformer, and a relatively high percentage of 'Ties' against the latent variable models.

It can also be observed that the RL Transformer also achieved a high percentage of 'Wins' over la-

Dialogue Context	User: Hey, Peter , have you had lunch yet?
Transformer CVAE SVT RL Transformer Label	much? I'm sorry , Mom. I was hoping to have my husband. No , I didn't . I got to eat it . No , I didn't . I just want to go to bed. No . How about you?
Dialogue Context	User: How did you find your apartment?
Transformer CVAE SVT RL Transformer Label	much? I went there. I bought it in the kitchen. I had a leaking faucet in the kitchen. You can check on the bulletin boards at school for local housing.
Dialogue Context	User: Very glad to know something about you , then what are you going to do when you finish. Agent: Oh , I'll go to shanghai to practice there. User: That's a good idea . It must be easy to find a job in shanghai.
Transformer CVAE SVT RL Transformer Label	I'm sorry to see. No , I'm not sure. well , that's a great sense. I'll be great. I'm not sure I' ll be able to find a job. I think so , you know there is a great deal of opportunity for business there.

Table 2: Examples of responses generated by the Transformer, CVAE, SVT and RL Transformer models.

tent variable models in terms of Coherence. This is corroborated by the qualitative analysis of the responses provided in the following section. We suspect that low Coherence scores attained by the latent variable models could be partially attributed to the random sampling process. Since the latent Gaussian models the potential dialogue response intents, sampled random variables which deviate significantly from the mean could encompass an irrelevant dialogue intent. When this random variable is fed to the decoder, an incoherent response would likely be generated. Similarly, it can also be observed that the RL Transformer also achieved a high percentage of 'Wins' over latent variable models in terms of Fluency. This could be potentially attributed to the random linear layers introduced in the RLSA networks, which serve to improve the overall capability of the RL Transformer.

Additionally, as reported in Liu et al. (2016), we note that the ROUGE and METEOR scores do not correlate with any aspect of human evaluation.

	Fluency			
	Win	Tie	Loss	Kappa
Transformer	23%	63%	14%	0.68
CVAE	71%	19%	10%	0.72
SVT	64%	25%	11%	0.77
	Coherence			
	Win	Tie	Loss	Kappa
Transformer	56%	27%	17%	0.73
CVAE	71%	11%	18%	0.77
SVT	69%	23%	8%	0.67
	Diversity			
	Win	Tie	Loss	Kappa
Transformer	81%	6%	13%	0.62
CVAE	39%	51%	10%	0.59
SVT	46%	39%	15%	0.64

Table 3: Human evaluation results on the DailyDialog corpus. For each criteria (Fluency, Coherence, and Diversity), responses generated by the RL Transformer are compared against responses generated by the Transformer, CVAE and SVT models. The average 'Win', 'Tie', and 'Loss' percentages are presented. Kappa scores largely range from 0.6 to 0.7, indicating substantial to moderate inter-annotator agreement.

5.2 Qualitative Analysis

We conduct a qualitative analysis by examining the responses generated by each of the implemented

	D-1	D-2	MATTR	MTLD
RL Trans	0.050	0.221	0.649	30.049
−RLSS(E)	0.018	0.080	0.523	18.455
−RLFF(E)	0.042	0.173	0.601	24.364
−RLSS(D)	0.020	0.106	0.502	17.237
−ED RLSS	0.026	0.111	0.532	18.231
+RLFF(D)	0.035	0.140	0.577	21.620
RL Trans w/o Links	0.002	0.006	0.220	11.596
RL Trans (Normal)	0.044	0.197	0.634	28.034
RL Trans (Uniform)	0.035	0.185	0.683	28.663

Table 4: Ablation study results. '-' indicates that the corresponding RLSA or RLFF network was replaced with the standard variant.'+' indicates that the standard self-attention or feed forward network was replaced with either RLSA or RLFF.

	D-1	D-2	MATTR	MTLD
64	0.005	0.025	0.426	13.142
128	0.036	0.142	0.527	17.396
256	0.043	0.168	0.628	22.053
512	0.050	0.221	0.649	30.049
1024	0.023	0.100	0.586	19.884

Table 5: Ablation study results for 64, 128, 256, 512, and 1024 nodes in the random layers.

models. The qualitative analysis largely support observations from our quantitative analysis. The responses generated by the standard transformer were short, generic and repetitive. As expected, responses generated by the latent variable models CVAE and SVT as well as our proposed RL Transformer were noticeably more diverse and less repetitive.

However, numerous responses generated by CVAE and SVT were relatively unnatural due to the relatively poor fluency and contextual coherence. A large number responses generated by the latent variable models had grammatical or structural issues, and a significant number were irrelevant in relation to the dialogue context i.e., out of context. On the other hand, the responses generated by the RL Transformer were significantly more natural and human-like, displaying far fewer grammatical or structural issues and greater relevance with regard to the dialogue context.

Samples of the generated responses along with the corresponding dialogue contexts are provided in Table 2.

5.3 Ablation Study

We also conduct an ablation study, using the DailyDialog corpus, to investigate the contributions of each of the RLSA and RLFF components in the encoder and decoder. Additionally, to examine the importance of the direct links, we implement a variant of the RL Transformer without any direct links. The results of the ablation study are presented in Table 4. In the same table, we also provide the diversity scores for two variants of the RL Transformer where the randomized layers are initialized via Normal initialization ($\mathcal{N}(0.0, 0.1)$) and Uniform initialization ($\mathcal{U}(0.0, 0.01)$) respectively.

Based on the results attained, we can observe that the RLSA network in the encoder, and the RLSA and ED RLSA networks in the decoder have a relatively large impact on response diversity. Substituting the RLSA or ED RLSA networks for the standard self-attention network results in a significant drop on all diversity measures. However, substituting the RLFF in the encoder for a standard feed forward network results in a relatively minor decrease in diversity. Hence, we conclude that stochasticity introduced in the self-attention networks contribute to overall response diversity to a much larger extent compared to the RLFF network. Although, it should also be noted that, substituting the standard feed forward network in the decoder with a RLFF network would result in a slightly lower diversity scores.

Also, the importance of the direct links cannot be overstated. From the results attained by the RL Transformer without links, it is apparent that removal of the direct links would result in extremely low response diversity. Upon closer inspection of the responses generated by this variant of the RL Transformer, we notice that a majority of the generated responses are short, generic and highly repetitive.

In addition, we present the results attained by varying the number of hidden nodes in the randomized layers in Table 5. Intuitively, this implies varying levels of stochasticity. From Table 5, we can observe that increasing the number of neurons in the randomized layer would generally result in an increase in diversity. This can be attributed to an increase in stochasticity due to an increase in the number of randomized weights. However, there is a significant drop in diversity when the size of the randomized layers exceed 512. In this case, the model fails to learn effectively, and generates meaningless, generic, and repetitive responses instead.

6 Conclusion

In this paper, we have proposed a novel RL Transformer which successfully improves response diversity in the task of open-domain dialogue generation. This is achieved by inducing stochasticity in the self-attention and the feed forward networks of a Transformer via randomized layers and direct links. Experimental results on the DailyDialog and EmpatheticDialogues corpora show that, compared to latent variable models, the RL Transformer achieved comparable levels of diversification while further improving on contextual coherence and fluency. In the future, the RL Transformer can be adapted for related dialogue generation tasks such as personalized, empathetic or topical dialogue generation.

References

Kris Cao and Stephen Clark. 2017. Latent variable dialogue models and their diversity. In *Proceedings of the 15th Conference of the European Chapter of the Association for Computational Linguistics: Volume 2, Short Papers*, pages 182–187, Valencia, Spain. Association for Computational Linguistics.

Yu Cao, Liang Ding, Zhiliang Tian, and Meng Fang. 2021. Towards efficiently diversifying dialogue generation via embedding augmentation. In *ICASSP 2021 - 2021 IEEE International Conference on Acoustics, Speech and Signal Processing (ICASSP)*, pages 7443–7447.

Qijun Dai, Gong Zhang, Zheng Fang, and Biao Xue. 2022. Sar target recognition with modified convolutional random vector functional link network. *IEEE Geoscience and Remote Sensing Letters*, 19:1–5.

Emad T. Elkabbash, Reham R. Mostafa, and Sherif I. Barakat. 2021. Android malware classification based on random vector functional link and artificial jellyfish search optimizer. *PLOS ONE*, 16(11):1–22.

Jun Gao, Wei Bi, Xiaojiang Liu, Junhui Li, Guodong Zhou, and Shuming Shi. 2019. A discrete CVAE for response generation on short-text conversation. In *Proceedings of the 2019 Conference on Empirical Methods in Natural Language Processing and the 9th International Joint Conference on Natural Language Processing (EMNLP-IJCNLP)*, pages 1898–1908, Hong Kong, China. Association for Computational Linguistics.

Xavier Glorot and Yoshua Bengio. 2010. Understanding the difficulty of training deep feedforward neural networks. In *Proceedings of the Thirteenth International Conference on Artificial Intelligence and Statistics*, volume 9 of *Proceedings of Machine Learning Research*, pages 249–256, Chia Laguna Resort, Sardinia, Italy. PMLR.

Xiaodong Gu, Kang Min Yoo, and Jung-Woo Ha. 2021. DialogBERT: Discourse-aware response generation via learning to recover and rank utterances.

Barenya Bikash Hazarika and Deepak Gupta. 2020. Modelling and forecasting of covid-19 spread using wavelet-coupled random vector functional link networks. *Applied Soft Computing*, 96:106626.

Rakesh Katuwal, P. N. Suganthan, and M. Tanveer. 2019. Random vector functional link neural network based ensemble deep learning.

Jing Yang Lee., Kong Aik Lee., and Woon Seng Gan. 2022. Dlvgen: A dual latent variable approach to personalized dialogue generation. In *Proceedings of the 14th International Conference on Agents and Artificial Intelligence - Volume 2: ICAART,*, pages 193–202. INSTICC, SciTePress.

Jiwei Li, Michel Galley, Chris Brockett, Jianfeng Gao, and Bill Dolan. 2016a. A diversity-promoting objective function for neural conversation models. In *Proceedings of the 2016 Conference of the North American Chapter of the Association for Computational Linguistics: Human Language Technologies*, pages 110–119, San Diego, California. Association for Computational Linguistics.

Jiwei Li, Will Monroe, Alan Ritter, Dan Jurafsky, Michel Galley, and Jianfeng Gao. 2016b. Deep reinforcement learning for dialogue generation. In *Proceedings of the 2016 Conference on Empirical Methods in Natural Language Processing*, pages 1192–1202, Austin, Texas. Association for Computational Linguistics.

Jiwei Li, Will Monroe, Tianlin Shi, Sébastien Jean, Alan Ritter, and Dan Jurafsky. 2017a. Adversarial learning for neural dialogue generation. In *Proceedings of the 2017 Conference on Empirical Methods in Natural Language Processing*, pages 2157–2169, Copenhagen, Denmark. Association for Computational Linguistics.

Mei Li, Jiajun Zhang, Xiang Lu, and Chengqing Zong. 2021. Dual-view conditional variational auto-encoder for emotional dialogue generation. *ACM Trans. Asian Low-Resour. Lang. Inf. Process.*, 21(3).

Qintong Li, Hongshen Chen, Zhaochun Ren, Pengjie Ren, Zhaopeng Tu, and Zhumin Chen. 2020a. EmpDG: Multi-resolution interactive empathetic dialogue generation. In *COLING*, pages 4454–4466, Barcelona, Spain (Online). International Committee on Computational Linguistics.

Shifeng Li, Shi Feng, Daling Wang, Kaisong Song, Yifei Zhang, and Weichao Wang. 2020b. Emoelicitor: An open domain response generation model with user emotional reaction awareness. In *Proceedings of the Twenty-Ninth International Joint Conference on Artificial Intelligence, IJCAI-20*, pages 3637–3643. International Joint Conferences on Artificial Intelligence Organization. Main track.

Yanran Li, Hui Su, Xiaoyu Shen, Wenjie Li, Ziqiang Cao, and Shuzi Niu. 2017b. DailyDialog: A manually labelled multi-turn dialogue dataset. In *Proceedings of the Eighth International Joint Conference on Natural Language Processing (Volume 1: Long Papers)*, pages 986–995, Taipei, Taiwan. Asian Federation of Natural Language Processing.

Zhaojiang Lin, Genta Indra Winata, Peng Xu, Zihan Liu, and Pascale Fung. 2020. Variational transformers for diverse response generation. *arXiv preprint arXiv:2003.12738*.

Chia-Wei Liu, Ryan Lowe, Iulian Serban, Mike Noseworthy, Laurent Charlin, and Joelle Pineau. 2016. How NOT to evaluate your dialogue system: An empirical study of unsupervised evaluation metrics for dialogue response generation. In *Proceedings of the 2016 Conference on Empirical Methods in Natural Language Processing*, pages 2122–2132, Austin, Texas. Association for Computational Linguistics.

Ashwani Kumar Malik, M.A. Ganaie, M. Tanveer, and P.N. Suganthan. 2021. A novel ensemble method of rvfl for classification problem. In *2021 International Joint Conference on Neural Networks (IJCNN)*, pages 1–8.

Ryo Nakamura, Katsuhito Sudoh, Koichiro Yoshino, and Satoshi Nakamura. 2018. Another diversity-promoting objective function for neural dialogue generation. *CoRR*, abs/1811.08100.

Deepak Ranjan Nayak, Ratnakar Dash, Banshidhar Majhi, Ram Bilas Pachori, and Yudong Zhang. 2020. A deep stacked random vector functional link network autoencoder for diagnosis of brain abnormalities and breast cancer. *Biomedical Signal Processing and Control*, 58:101860.

Deanna Needell, Aaron A. Nelson, Rayan Saab, and Palina Salanevich. 2020. Random vector functional link networks for function approximation on manifolds. *CoRR*, abs/2007.15776.

Y.-H. Pao and Y. Takefuji. 1992. Functional-link net computing: theory, system architecture, and functionalities. *Computer*, 25(5):76–79.

Jeffrey Pennington, Richard Socher, and Christopher Manning. 2014. GloVe: Global vectors for word representation. In *Proceedings of the 2014 Conference on Empirical Methods in Natural Language Processing (EMNLP)*, pages 1532–1543, Doha, Qatar. Association for Computational Linguistics.

Hannah Rashkin, Eric Michael Smith, Margaret Li, and Y-Lan Boureau. 2019. Towards empathetic open-domain conversation models: A new benchmark and dataset. In *Proceedings of the 57th Annual Meeting of the Association for Computational Linguistics*, pages 5370–5381, Florence, Italy. Association for Computational Linguistics.

Abdelrhman Saleh, Natasha Jaques, Asma Ghandeharioun, Judy Shen, and Rosalind Picard. 2019. Hierarchical reinforcement learning for open-domain dialog. *arXiv preprint arXiv:1909.07547*.

Lifeng Shang, Zhengdong Lu, and Hang Li. 2015. Neural responding machine for short-text conversation. In *Proceedings of the 53rd Annual Meeting of the Association for Computational Linguistics and the 7th International Joint Conference on Natural Language Processing (Volume 1: Long Papers)*, pages 1577–1586, Beijing, China. Association for Computational Linguistics.

Qiushi Shi, Rakesh Katuwal, P.N. Suganthan, and M. Tanveer. 2021. Random vector functional link neural network based ensemble deep learning. *Pattern Recognition*, 117:107978.

Kihyuk Sohn, Honglak Lee, and Xinchen Yan. 2015. Learning structured output representation using deep conditional generative models. In *Advances in Neural Information Processing Systems*, volume 28. Curran Associates, Inc.

Haoyu Song, Weinan Zhang, Yiming Cui, Dong Wang, and Ting Liu. 2019. Exploiting persona information for diverse generation of conversational responses. In *IJCAI*.

Alessandro Sordoni, Michel Galley, Michael Auli, Chris Brockett, Yangfeng Ji, Margaret Mitchell, Jian-Yun Nie, Jianfeng Gao, and Bill Dolan. 2015. A neural network approach to context-sensitive generation of conversational responses. In *Proceedings of the 2015 Conference of the North American Chapter of the Association for Computational Linguistics: Human Language Technologies*, pages 196–205, Denver, Colorado. Association for Computational Linguistics.

Ponnuthurai N. Suganthan and Rakesh Katuwal. 2021. On the origins of randomization-based feedforward neural networks. *Applied Soft Computing*, 105:107239.

Ilya Sutskever, Oriol Vinyals, and Quoc V. Le. 2014. Sequence to sequence learning with neural networks. In *Proceedings of the 27th International Conference on Neural Information Processing Systems - Volume 2*, NIPS'14, page 3104–3112, Cambridge, MA, USA. MIT Press.

Ayaka Ueyama and Yoshinobu Kano. 2020. Diverse dialogue generation with context dependent dynamic loss function. In *Proceedings of the 28th International Conference on Computational Linguistics*, pages 4123–4127, Barcelona, Spain (Online). International Committee on Computational Linguistics.

Ashish Vaswani, Noam Shazeer, Niki Parmar, Jakob Uszkoreit, Llion Jones, Aidan N Gomez, Ł ukasz Kaiser, and Illia Polosukhin. 2017. Attention is all you need. In *Advances in Neural Information Processing Systems*, volume 30. Curran Associates, Inc.

Yiru Wang, Pengda Si, Zeyang Lei, and Yujiu Yang. 2020. Topic enhanced controllable cvae for dialogue generation (student abstract). *Proceedings of the AAAI Conference on Artificial Intelligence*, 34(10):13955–13956.

Bowen Wu, MengYuan Li, Zongsheng Wang, Yifu Chen, Derek F. Wong, Qihang Feng, Junhong Huang, and Baoxun Wang. 2020. Guiding variational response generator to exploit persona. In *Proceedings of the 58th Annual Meeting of the Association for Computational Linguistics*, pages 53–65, Online. Association for Computational Linguistics.

Haiqin Yang, Xiaoyuan Yao, Yiqun Duan, Jianping Shen, Jie Zhong, and Kun Zhang. 2021. Progressive open-domain response generation with multiple controllable attributes. In *Proceedings of the Thirtieth International Joint Conference on Artificial Intelligence, IJCAI-21*, pages 3279–3285. International Joint Conferences on Artificial Intelligence Organization. Main Track.

Yizhe Zhang, Siqi Sun, Michel Galley, Yen-Chun Chen, Chris Brockett, Xiang Gao, Jianfeng Gao, Jingjing Liu, and Bill Dolan. 2020. DIALOGPT : Large-scale generative pre-training for conversational response generation. In *Proceedings of the 58th Annual Meeting of the Association for Computational Linguistics: System Demonstrations*, pages 270–278, Online. Association for Computational Linguistics.

Yongshan Zhang, Jia Wu, Zhihua Cai, Bo Du, and Philip S. Yu. 2019. An unsupervised parameter learning model for rvfl neural network. *Neural Networks*, 112:85–97.

Tiancheng Zhao, Ran Zhao, and Maxine Eskenazi. 2017. Learning discourse-level diversity for neural dialog models using conditional variational autoencoders. In *Proceedings of the 55th Annual Meeting of the Association for Computational Linguistics (Volume 1: Long Papers)*, pages 654–664, Vancouver, Canada. Association for Computational Linguistics.

Xue Zhao, Ying Zhang, Wenya Guo, and Xiaojie Yuan. 2019. Bert for open-domain conversation modeling. In *2019 IEEE 5th International Conference on Computer and Communications (ICCC)*, pages 1532–1536.

Xianda Zhou and William Yang Wang. 2018. MojiTalk: Generating emotional responses at scale. In *ACL*, pages 1128–1137, Melbourne, Australia. Association for Computational Linguistics.

Are Pre-trained Transformers Robust in Intent Classification? A Missing Ingredient in Evaluation of Out-of-Scope Intent Detection

Jianguo Zhang[1] **Kazuma Hashimoto**[2] **Yao Wan**[3] **Zhiwei Liu**[4]
Ye Liu[1] **Caiming Xiong**[1] **Philip S. Yu**[4]
[1]Salesforce Research, Palo Alto, USA
[2]Google Research, Mountain View, USA
[3]Huazhong University of Science and Technology, Wuhan, China
[4]University of Illinois at Chicago, Chicago, USA
jianguozhang@salesforce.com

Abstract

Pre-trained Transformer-based models were reported to be robust in intent classification. In this work, we first point out the importance of in-domain out-of-scope detection in few-shot intent recognition tasks and then illustrate the vulnerability of pre-trained Transformer-based models against samples that are in-domain but out-of-scope (ID-OOS). We construct two new datasets, and empirically show that pre-trained models do not perform well on both ID-OOS examples and general out-of-scope examples, especially on fine-grained few-shot intent detection tasks. To figure out how the models mistakenly classify ID-OOS intents as in-scope intents, we further conduct analysis on confidence scores and the overlapping keywords, as well as point out several prospective directions for future work. Resources are available at `https://github.com/jianguoz/Few-Shot-Intent-Detection`.

1 Introduction

Intent detection, which aims to identify intents from user utterances, is a vital task in goal-oriented dialog systems (Xie et al., 2022). However, the performance of intent detection has been hindered by the data scarcity issue, as it is non-trivial to collect sufficient examples for new intents. In practice, the user requests could also be not expected or supported by the tested dialog system, referred to as out-of-scope (OOS) intents. Thus, it is important to improve OOS intents detection performance while keeping the accuracy of detecting in-scope intents in the few-shot learning scenario.

Recently, several approaches (Zheng et al., 2019; Zhang et al., 2020; Wu et al., 2020; Cavalin et al., 2020; Zhan et al., 2021; Xu et al., 2021) have been proposed to improve the performance of identifying in-scope and OOS intents in few-shot scenarios. Previous experiments have shown that a simple confidence-based out-of-distribution detection method (Hendrycks and Gimpel, 2017; Hendrycks et al., 2020a) equipped with pre-trained BERT can improve OOS detection accuracy. However, there is a lack of further study of pre-trained Transformers on few-shot fine-grained OOS detection where the OOS intents are more relevant to the in-scope intents. Besides, those studies mainly focus on the CLINC dataset (Larson et al., 2019), in which the OOS examples are designed such that they do *not* belong to any of the known intent classes. Their distribution is dissimilar to each other, and thus they are easy to be distinguished from the known intent classes. Moreover, CLINC is not enough to study more challenging few-shot fine-grained OOS detection as it lacks such semantically similar OOS examples to in-scope intents, and other popular used datasets such as BANKING77 (Casanueva et al., 2020) do not contain OOS examples.

In this paper, we aim to investigate the following research question: "*Are pre-trained Transformers robust in intent classification w.r.t. general and relevant OOS examples?*". We first define two types of OOS intents: out-of-domain OOS (**OOD-OOS**) and in-domain OOS (**ID-OOS**). We then investigate *how* robustly state-of-the-art pre-trained Transformers perform on these two OOS types. The OOD-OOS is identical to the OOS in the CLINC dataset, where the OOS and in-scope intents (e.g., requesting an online TV show service in a banking system) are topically rarely overlapped. We construct an ID-OOS set for a domain, by separating semantically-related intents from the in-scope intents (e.g., requesting a banking service that is not supported by the banking system).

Empirically, we evaluate several pre-trained Transformers (e.g., BERT (Devlin et al., 2019), RoBERTa (Liu et al., 2019), ALBERT (Lan et al., 2020), and ELECTRA (Clark et al., 2020)) in the few-shot learning scenario, as well as pre-trained ToD-BERT (Wu et al., 2020) on task-oriented dialog system. The contributions of this paper are two-fold. First, we constructed and released two

Proceedings of the 4th Workshop on NLP for Conversational AI, pages 12 - 20
May 27, 2022

new datasets for OOS intent detection based on the single-domain CLINC dataset and the large fine-grained BANKING77 dataset. Second, we reveal several interesting findings through experimental results and analysis: 1) the pre-trained models are much less robust on ID-OOS than on the in-scope and OOD-OOS examples; 2) both ID-OOS and OOD-OOS detections are not well tackled and require further explorations on the scenario of fine-grained few-shot intent detection; and 3) it is surprising that pre-trained models can predict undesirably confident scores even when masking keywords shared among confusing intents.

2 Evaluation Protocol

Task definition We consider a few-shot intent detection system that handles pre-defined K in-scope intents. The task is, given a user utterance text u, to classify u into one of the K classes or to recognize u as OOS (i.e., OOS detection). To evaluate the system, we adopt in-scope accuracy $A_{\text{in}} = C_{\text{in}}/N_{\text{in}}$, and OOS recall $R_{\text{oos}} = C_{\text{oos}}/N_{\text{oos}}$, following Larson et al. (2019) and Zhang et al. (2020). We additionally report OOS precision, $P_{\text{oos}} = C_{\text{oos}}/N'_{\text{oos}}$. C_{in} and C_{oos} are the number of correctly predicted in-scope and out-of-scope examples, respectively; N_{in} and N_{oos} are the total number of the in-scope and out-of-scope examples evaluated, respectively; if an in-scope example is predicted as OOS, it is counted as wrong. N'_{oos} ($\leq N_{\text{in}} + N_{\text{oos}}$) is the number of examples predicted as OOS.

Inference We use a confidence-based method (Hendrycks et al., 2020a) to evaluate the five pre-trained Transformers. We compute a hidden vector $h = \text{Encoder}(u) \in \mathbb{R}^{768}$ for u, where Encoder $\in$ {BERT, RoBERTa, ALBERT, ELECTRA, ToD-BERT}, and compute a probability vector $p(y|u) = \text{softmax}(Wh + b) \in \mathbb{R}^{K}$, where W and b are the model parameters. We first take the class c with the largest value of $p(y = c|u)$, then output c if $p(y = c|u) > \delta$, where $\delta \in [0.0, 1.0]$ is a threshold value, and otherwise we output OOS. δ is tuned by using the development set, so as to maximize $(A_{\text{in}} + R_{\text{oos}})$ averaged across different runs (Zhang et al., 2020).

Training To train the model, we use training examples of the in-scope intents, without using any OOS examples. This is reasonable as it is nontrivial to collect sufficient OOS data to model the large space and distribution of the unpredictable OOS intents (Zhang et al., 2020; Cavalin et al., 2020).

3 Dataset Construction

We describe the two types of OOS (i.e., OOD-OOS and ID-OOS), using the CLINC dataset (Larson et al., 2019) and the fine-grained BANKING77 dataset (Casanueva et al., 2020). The CLINC dataset covers 15 intent classes for each of the 10 different domains, and it also includes OOS examples. We randomly select two domains, i.e., the "Banking" and "Credit cards", out of the ten domains for models evaluation. The BANKING77 dataset is a large fine-grained single banking domain intent dataset with 77 intents, and it initially does not include OOS examples. We use these two datasets since CLINC dataset focuses on the OOS detection task, and we can evaluate models on the large single fine-grained banking domain on BANKING77 dataset.

OOD-OOS We use the initially provided OOS examples of CLINC dataset as OOD-OOS examples for both datasets. To justify our hypothesis that the CLINC's OOS examples can be considered as out of domains, we take 100 OOS examples from the development set, and check whether the examples are related to each domain. Consequently, only 4 examples are relevant to "Banking", while none of them is related to "Credit cards". There are also no overlaps between the added OOS examples and the original BANKING77 dataset. These findings show that most of the OOS examples are not related to the targeted domains, and we cannot effectively evaluate the model's capability to detect OOS intents within the same domain.

ID-OOS Detecting the OOD-OOS examples is important in practice, but we focus more on how the model behaves on ID-OOS examples. For the ID-OOS detection evaluation, we separate 5 intents from the 15 intents in each of the domains and use them as the ID-OOS samples for the CLINC dataset, following the previous work (Shu et al., 2017). In contrast to the previous work that randomly splits datasets, we intentionally design a confusing setting for each domain. More specifically, we select 5 intents that are semantically similar to some of the 10 remaining intents. As for the BANKING77 dataset, we randomly separate 27 intents from the 77 intents and use them as the ID-OOS samples, following the above process.

Table 1 and Table 2 show which intent labels

Domain	IN-OOS	In-scope
Banking	balance, bill_due, min_payment, freeze_account, transfer	account_blocked, bill_balance, interest_rate, order_checks, pay_bill, pin_change, report_fraud, routing, spending_history, transactions
Credit cards	report_lost_card, improve_credit_score, rewards_balance, application_status, replacement_card_duration	credit_score, credit_limit, new_card, card_declined, international_fees, apr, redeem_rewards, credit_limit change, damaged_card expiration_date

Table 1: Data split of the ID-OOS and in-scope intents for the CLINC dataset.

ID-OOS	"pin_blocked", "top_up_by_cash_or_cheque" "top_up_by_card_charge", "verify_source_of_funds", "transfer_into_account", "exchange_rate", "card_delivery_estimate", "card_not_working", "top_up_by_bank_transfer_charge", "age_limit", "terminate_account", "get_physical_card", "passcode_forgotten", "verify_my_identity", "topping_up_by_card", "unable_to_verify_identity", "getting_virtual_card", "top_up_limits", "get_disposable_virtual_card", "receiving_money", "atm_support", "compromised_card", "lost_or_stolen_card", "card_swallowed", "card_acceptance", "virtual_card_not_working", "contactless_not_working"

Table 2: Data split of the ID-OOS intents for the BANKING77 dataset. Where 27 intents are randomly selected as ID-OOS intents and the rest are treated as in-scope intents. Here we show the 27 selected ID-OOS intents.

are treated as ID-OOS for the CLINC dataset and BANKING77 dataset, respectively.

Data Statistics For each domain, the original CLINC dataset has 100, 20, and 30 examples for each in-scope intent, and 100, 100, and 1000 OOD-OOS examples for the train, development, and test sets, respectively. We reorganize the original dataset to incorporate the ID-OOS intents and construct new balanced datasets. For each in-scope intent in the training set, we keep 50 examples as a new training set, and move the rest 30 examples and 20 examples to the development and test sets through random sampling. For the examples of each ID-OOS intent in the training set, we randomly sample 60 examples, add them to the development set, and add the rest of the 40 examples to the test set. We move the unused OOD-OOS examples of the training set to the validation set and keep the OOD-OOS test set unchanged. For the BANKING77 dataset, we move the training/validation/test examples of the selected 27 intents to the ID-OOS training/validation/test examples, and we copy the OOD-OOS examples of CLINC as the OOD-OOS examples of BANKING77.

We name the two new datasets as CLINC-Single-Domain-OOS and BANKING77-OOS, respectively. Table 3 shows the dataset statistics.

CLINC-Single-Domain-OOS	K	Train	Dev.	Test
In-scope	10	500	500	500
ID-OOS	-	-	400	350
OOD-OOS	-	-	200	1000
BANKING77-OOS	K	Train	Dev.	Test
In-scope	50	5905	1506	2000
ID-OOS	-	-	530	1080
OOD-OOS	-	-	200	1000

Table 3: Statistics of CLINC-Single-Domain-OOS and BANKING77-OOS dataset.

4 Empirical Study

4.1 Experimental Setting

We implement all the models following public code from Zhang et al. (2020), based on the HuggingFace Transformers library (Wolf et al., 2019) for the easy reproduction of experiments. For each component related to the five pre-trained models, we use their base configurations. We use the `roberta-base` configuration for RoBERTa; `bert-base-uncased` for BERT; `albert-base-v2` for ALBERT; `electra-base-discriminator` for ELECTRA; `tod-bert-jnt-v1` for ToDBERT. All the model parameters are updated during the fine-tuning process. We use the AdamW (Hendrycks et al., 2020b) optimizer with a weight decay coefficient of 0.01 for all the non-bias parameters. We use a gradient clipping technique (Pascanu et al., 2013) with a clipping value of 1.0, and also use a linear warmup learning-rate scheduling with a proportion of 0.1 w.r.t. to the maximum number of training epochs.

For each model, we perform hyper-parameters searches for learning rate values $\in \{1e-4, 2e-5, 5e-5\}$, and the number of the training epochs $\in \{8, 15, 25, 35\}$. We set the batch size to 10 and 50 for CLINC- Single-Domain-OOS and BANKING77-OOS, respectively. We take the hyper-parameter sets for each experiment and train the model ten times for each hyper-parameter set to

5-shot		In-scope accuracy			OOS recall			OOS precision		
		Banking	Credit cards	BANKING77-OOS	Banking	Credit cards	BANKING77-OOS	Banking	Credit cards	BANKING77-OOS
ID-OOS	ALBERT	54.1 ± 6.9	55.5 ± 8.1	20.3 ± 2.4	86.3 ± 8.1	75.9 ± 11.2	89.5 ± 1.5	57.9 ± 3.3	55.8 ± 4.3	39.8 ± 0.7
	BERT	75.2 ± 2.9	74.1 ± 4.6	25.4 ± 3.6	81.8 ± 10.5	76.5 ± 9.7	90.9 ± 0.6	70.8 ± 2.5	68.1 ± 3.2	41.3 ± 1.4
	ELECTRA	64.8 ± 4.8	71.0 ± 7.3	30.9 ± 2.3	89.4 ± 4.3	75.8 ± 6.1	87.5 ± 2.4	65.1 ± 3.0	67.1 ± 4.8	43.0 ± 0.8
	RoBERTa	83.8 ± 1.7	64.5 ± 5.6	43.0 ± 2.9	78.4 ± 6.2	86.8 ± 5.4	83.1 ± 4.3	78.6 ± 1.5	63.3 ± 3.4	46.3 ± 1.9
	ToD-BERT	75.1 ± 2.3	67.4 ± 4.2	35.5 ± 1.5	75.8 ± 9.5	72.3 ± 3.4	82.7 ± 1.8	69.4 ± 3.6	61.3 ± 2.3	43.8 ± 0.1
OOD-OOS	ALBERT	63.1 ± 5.7	55.5 ± 8.1	20.3 ± 2.4	85.3 ± 5.4	92.5 ± 4.0	97.3 ± 2.5	83.4 ± 1.7	81.5 ± 3.1	39.9 ± 1.3
	BERT	75.2 ± 2.9	74.1 ± 4.6	39.0 ± 3.1	93.4 ± 3.7	95.5 ± 2.7	94.1 ± 1.6	88.8 ± 1.4	88.4 ± 1.9	49.0 ± 1.8
	ELECTRA	75.5 ± 4.0	71.0 ± 7.3	39.1 ± 2.7	87.3 ± 4.3	87.6 ± 4.2	93.1 ± 4.3	88.8 ± 2.1	87.0 ± 2.7	48.7 ± 1.1
	RoBERTa	83.8 ± 1.7	81.2 ± 4.0	62.1 ± 2.9	97.0 ± 0.9	96.7 ± 1.4	93.9 ± 1.4	92.9 ± 0.6	91.4 ± 1.8	68.7 ± 2.2
	ToD-BERT	83.0 ± 1.6	75.8 ± 5.0	52.9 ± 1.5	91.9 ± 1.0	96.7 ± 0.9	88.4 ± 1.7	92.8 ± 0.6	89.6 ± 2.1	66.0 ± 1.2
10-shot										
ID-OOS	ALBERT	77.8 ± 2.7	66.7 ± 7.8	27.3 ± 3.4	77.6 ± 13.0	79.8 ± 6.4	87.6 ± 1.3	72.2 ± 2.9	64.0 ± 4.1	42.4 ± 1.3
	BERT	77.5 ± 1.7	80.3 ± 3.7	52.5 ± 1.7	87.5 ± 9.2	74.5 ± 6.9	77.3 ± 3.2	73.8 ± 1.7	73.1 ± 3.3	50.8 ± 1.1
	ELECTRA	79.5 ± 2.9	78.0 ± 2.5	40.1 ± 2.7	85.2 ± 9.1	86.5 ± 5.8	84.0 ± 1.7	75.4 ± 2.7	73.3 ± 2.9	46.1 ± 1.1
	RoBERTa	76.6 ± 0.9	81.0 ± 5.5	59.7 ± 1.2	86.4 ± 6.3	83.9 ± 6.9	79.1 ± 1.7	72.7 ± 1.5	75.8 ± 5.2	55.8 ± 1.1
	ToD-BERT	80.7 ± 2.5	80.6 ± 0.9	54.3 ± 1.8	79.5 ± 6.1	70.2 ± 5.9	76.9 ± 2.7	75.4 ± 1.4	71.9 ± 2.6	52.1 ± 1.2
OOD-OOS	ALBERT	77.8 ± 2.7	66.7 ± 7.8	30.5 ± 6.5	90.6 ± 4.0	95.0 ± 3.4	92.7 ± 6.3	89.8 ± 1.0	85.7 ± 2.7	47.1 ± 1.9
	BERT	77.5 ± 1.7	90.1 ± 1.9	64.2 ± 0.5	96.8 ± 1.2	91.1 ± 4.4	91.4 ± 3.2	90.0 ± 0.7	95.5 ± 1.1	68.9 ± 1.0
	ELECTRA	79.5 ± 2.9	88.6 ± 2.1	40.1 ± 2.7	94.8 ± 1.7	89.1 ± 2.2	97.6 ± 1.0	90.7 ± 1.2	94.2 ± 1.1	47.9 ± 1.4
	RoBERTa	89.2 ± 1.3	87.5 ± 3.3	70.3 ± 0.3	95.6 ± 1.0	94.6 ± 2.4	94.0 ± 0.8	95.4 ± 0.5	94.0 ± 1.4	73.3 ± 1.5
	ToD-BERT	86.5 ± 2.6	86.5 ± 0.6	60.6 ± 1.8	96.0 ± 0.5	96.4 ± 0.5	94.9 ± 0.9	94.2 ± 1.2	93.7 ± 0.3	63.3 ± 0.9

Table 4: Testing results on the "Banking" and "Credit cards" domains in CLINC-Single-Domain-OOS and BANKING77-OOS datasets. Note that as the best δ is selected based on $(A_{\text{in}} + R_{\text{oos}})$, the in-scope accuracy could be different in the scenarios of OOD-OOS and ID-OOS (see Figure 2).

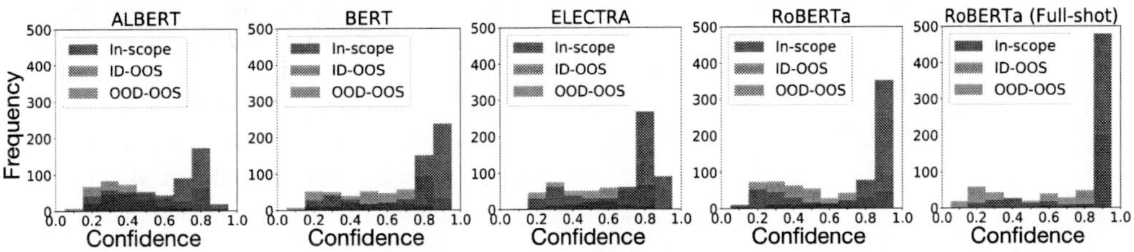

Figure 1: Model confidence on the development set of "Banking" domain in CLINC-Single-Domain-OOS dataset under 5-shot setting. Darker colors indicate overlaps.

select the best threshold δ (introduced in Section 2) on the development set. We then select the best hyper-parameter set along with the corresponding threshold. Finally, we apply the best model and the threshold to the test set. Experiments were conducted on single NVIDIA Tesla V100 GPU with 32GB memory.

We mainly conduct the experiments in 5-shot, e.g., five training examples per in-scope intent, and 10-shot; we also report partial results in the full-shot scenario.

4.2 Overall Results

Table 4 shows the results of few-shot intent detection on the test set for 5-shot and 10-shot settings. In both settings, the in-scope accuracy of ID-OOS examples tends to be lower than that of OOD-OOS examples, and the gap becomes larger for OOS recall and precision. It is interesting to see that ToD-BERT, which is pre-trained on several task-oriented dialog datasets, does not perform well in our scenario. The results indicate that the pre-trained models are much less robust on the ID-OOS intent detection. Compared with the results on the two single domains of the CLINC-Single-Domain-OOS dataset, we can find that the performances become much worse on the larger fine-grained BANKING77-OOS dataset. Especially the in-scope accuracy and OOS precision are pretty low, even with more training examples. This finding encourages more attention to be put on fine-grained intent detection with OOS examples.

4.3 Analysis and Discussions

One key to the OOS detection is a clear separation between in-scope and OOS examples in terms of the model confidence score (Zhang et al., 2020). Figure 1 illustrates the differences in confidence score distributions. The confidence scores of ID-OOS examples are close or mixed with the scores of in-scope intents, and are higher than the OOD-OOS examples, showing that separating ID-OOS examples is much harder than separating OOD-OOS examples.

Among comparisons of the pre-trained models, ALBERT performs worst, and RoBERTa performs better than other models in general since the confidence score received by in-scope examples is

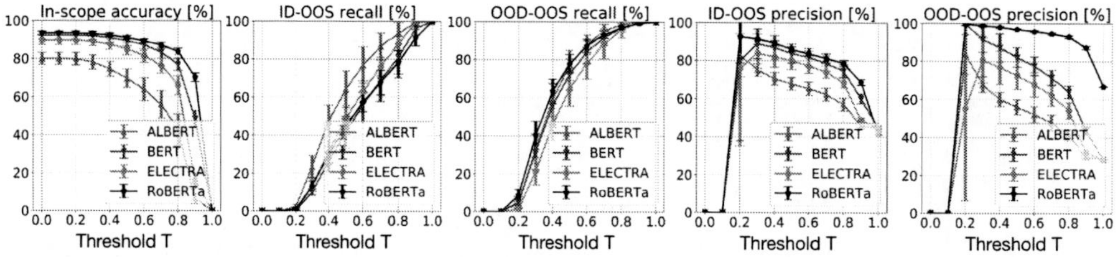

Figure 2: Results on the "Banking" domain in CLINC-Single-Domain-OOS dataset (Dev. set) under 5-shot setting.

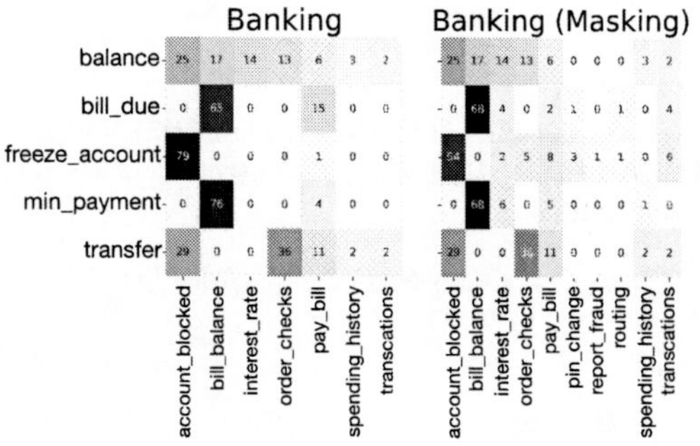

Figure 3: Full-shot confusion matrices on the development set with and without masking ("Banking", RoBERTa). Vertical axis: ID-OOS; horizontal axis: in-scope (only predicted intents considered).

Intent pair	bill_due & bill_balance
Unigram overlap	bill (60), pay (9), need (9), know (8), due (7)
Masked ID-OOS example	i [mask] to [mask] what day i [mask] to [mask] my water [mask] → bill_balance (confidence: **0.84**)
Intent pair	improve_credit_score & credit_score
Unigram overlap	credit (99), score (76), tell (7), want (3), like (3)
Masked ID-OOS example	i'd [mask] to make my [mask] [mask] better → credit_limit_change (confidence: **0.86**)

Table 5: Examples investigated for the unigram overlap analysis. The overlap frequency is also presented.

higher than that received by the OOS examples. Figure 2 also shows similar results. We conjecture that pre-trained models with more data, better architecture and objectives, etc., are relatively more robust to OOD-OOS and ID-OOS examples than the others. Comparing the RoBERTa 5-shot and full-shot confidence distributions, the ID-OOS confidence scores are improved, indicating over-confidence to separate semantically-related intents (i.e., ID-OOS examples).

Next, we inspect what ID-OOS examples are misclassified, and we take RoBERTa as an example as it performs better than other models in general. Figure 3 shows the confusion matrices of RoBERTa w.r.t. the "Banking" domain in the CLINC-Single-Domain-OOS dataset, under full-shot setting. We can see that the model is extremely likely to confuse ID-OOS intents with particular in-scope intents. We expect this is from our ID-OOS design, and the trend is consistent across evaluated models.

Now one question arises: *what causes the model's mistakes?* One presumable source is the keyword overlap. We checked unigram overlap, after removing stop words, for the intent pairs with the three darkest colors in "Banking" based on Figure 3. We then masked top-5 overlapped unigrams from the corresponding intent examples in the development set using the *mask* token in the RoBERTa masked language model pretraining and conducted the same evaluation.[1] Figure 3 shows that most of the confusing intent pairs are still misclassified even without the keyword overlap. Table 5 shows two intent pairs with the overlapped words and their masked ID-OOS examples. It is surprising that the examples show counterintuitive results. That is, even with the aggressive masking, the model still tends to assign high confidence scores to some other in-scope intents. We also adopted state-of-the-art methods with contrastive learning on few-shot text classification (Liu et al., 2021) and intent detection (Zhang et al., 2021). However, we did not achieve promising improvements on OOD-OOS and ID-OOS detection, and we leave more explorations to future work.

5 Conclusion

We have investigated the robustness of pre-trained Transformers in few-shot intent detection with OOS samples. Our results on two new constructed datasets show that pre-trained models are not robust on ID-OOS examples. Both the OOS detection tasks are challenging in the scenario of fine-grained intent detection. Our work encourages more attention to be put on the above findings.

[1]We did not mask the top-10 or top-15 overlapped unigrams, as many tokens are already masked in the user utterance when setting the threshold to 5, as shown in Table 5.

References

Iñigo Casanueva, Tadas Temčinas, Daniela Gerz, Matthew Henderson, and Ivan Vulić. 2020. Efficient intent detection with dual sentence encoders. In *Proceedings of the 2nd Workshop on Natural Language Processing for Conversational AI*, pages 38–45.

Paulo Cavalin, Victor Henrique Alves Ribeiro, Ana Appel, and Claudio Pinhanez. 2020. Improving out-of-scope detection in intent classification by using embeddings of the word graph space of the classes. In *EMNLP*, pages 3952–3961.

Kevin Clark, Minh-Thang Luong, Quoc V. Le, and Christopher D. Manning. 2020. Electra: Pre-training text encoders as discriminators rather than generators. In *ICLR*.

Jacob Devlin, Ming-Wei Chang, Kenton Lee, and Kristina Toutanova. 2019. BERT: Pre-training of Deep Bidirectional Transformers for Language Understanding. In *NAACL-HLT*, pages 4171–4186.

Dan Hendrycks and Kevin Gimpel. 2017. A baseline for detecting misclassified and out-of-distribution examples in neural networks. In *ICLR*.

Dan Hendrycks, Xiaoyuan Liu, Eric Wallace, Adam Dziedzic, Rishabh Krishnan, and Dawn Song. 2020a. Pretrained Transformers Improve Out-of-Distribution Robustness. In *ACL*, pages 2744–2751.

Dan Hendrycks, Xiaoyuan Liu, Eric Wallace, Adam Dziedzic, Rishabh Krishnan, and Dawn Song. 2020b. Pretrained Transformers Improve Out-of-Distribution Robustness. *arXiv preprint arXiv:2004.06100*.

Zhenzhong Lan, Mingda Chen, Sebastian Goodman, Kevin Gimpel, Piyush Sharma, and Radu Soricut. 2020. ALBERT: A Lite BERT for Self-supervised Learning of Language Representations. In *ICLR*.

Stefan Larson, Anish Mahendran, Joseph J. Peper, Christopher Clarke, Andrew Lee, Parker Hill, Jonathan K. Kummerfeld, Kevin Leach, Michael A. Laurenzano, Lingjia Tang, and Jason Mars. 2019. An Evaluation Dataset for Intent Classification and Out-of-Scope Prediction. In *EMNLP*, pages 1311–1316.

Fangyu Liu, Ivan Vulić, Anna Korhonen, and Nigel Collier. 2021. Fast, effective, and self-supervised: Transforming masked language models into universal lexical and sentence encoders. In *EMNLP*, pages 1442–1459.

Yinhan Liu, Myle Ott, Naman Goyal, Jingfei Du, Mandar Joshi, Danqi Chen, Omer Levy, Mike Lewis, Luke Zettlemoyer, and Veselin Stoyanov. 2019. RoBERTa: A Robustly Optimized BERT Pretraining Approach. *arXiv preprint arXiv:1907.11692*.

Razvan Pascanu, Tomas Mikolov, and Yoshua Bengio. 2013. On the difficulty of training recurrent neural networks. In *Proceedings of the 30th International Conference on Machine Learning (ICML)*, pages 1310–1318.

Lei Shu, Hu Xu, and Bing Liu. 2017. DOC: Deep Open Classification of Text Documents. In *EMNLP*, pages 2911–2916.

Thomas Wolf, Lysandre Debut, Victor Sanh, Julien Chaumond, Clement Delangue, Anthony Moi, Pierric Cistac, Tim Rault, Rémi Louf, Morgan Funtowicz, et al. 2019. Huggingface's transformers: State-of-the-art natural language processing. *arXiv preprint arXiv:1910.03771*.

Chien-Sheng Wu, Steven Hoi, Richard Socher, and Caiming Xiong. 2020. ToD-BERT: Pre-trained Natural Language Understanding for Task-Oriented Dialogues. *EMNLP*.

Tian Xie, Xinyi Yang, Angela S Lin, Feihong Wu, Kazuma Hashimoto, Jin Qu, Young Mo Kang, Wenpeng Yin, Huan Wang, Semih Yavuz, et al. 2022. Converse–a tree-based modular task-oriented dialogue system. *arXiv preprint arXiv:2203.12187*.

Keyang Xu, Tongzheng Ren, Shikun Zhang, Yihao Feng, and Caiming Xiong. 2021. Unsupervised out-of-domain detection via pre-trained transformers. In *ACL*, pages 1052–1061.

Li-Ming Zhan, Haowen Liang, Bo Liu, Lu Fan, Xiao-Ming Wu, and Albert YS Lam. 2021. Out-of-scope intent detection with self-supervision and discriminative training. In *ACL*, pages 3521–3532.

Jianguo Zhang, Trung Bui, Seunghyun Yoon, Xiang Chen, Zhiwei Liu, Congying Xia, Quan Hung Tran, Walter Chang, and S Yu Philip. 2021. Few-shot intent detection via contrastive pre-training and fine-tuning. In *EMNLP*, pages 1906–1912.

Jianguo Zhang, Kazuma Hashimoto, Wenhao Liu, Chien-Sheng Wu, Yao Wan, S Yu Philip, Richard Socher, and Caiming Xiong. 2020. Discriminative nearest neighbor few-shot intent detection by transferring natural language inference. In *EMNLP*, pages 5064–5082.

Yinhe Zheng, Guanyi Chen, and Minlie Huang. 2019. Out-of-domain Detection for Natural Language Understanding in Dialog Systems. *arXiv preprint arXiv:1909.03862*.

A More Results

Figure 4 shows the model confidence level on the development set of the "Credit cards" domain in the CLINC-Single-Domain-OOS dataset. We can see that RoBERTa is relatively more robust with limited data. Figure 5 shows the confusion matrices of RoBERTa w.r.t. the "Credit cards" domain in the CLINC-Single-Domain-OOS dataset. The model is confused to identify ID-OOS intents. Figure 6 shows the tSNE visualizations for ID-OOS intents w.r.t. the "Banking" domain in the CLINC-Single-Domain-OOS dataset. The models struggle to classify the ID-OOS intents even with more data.

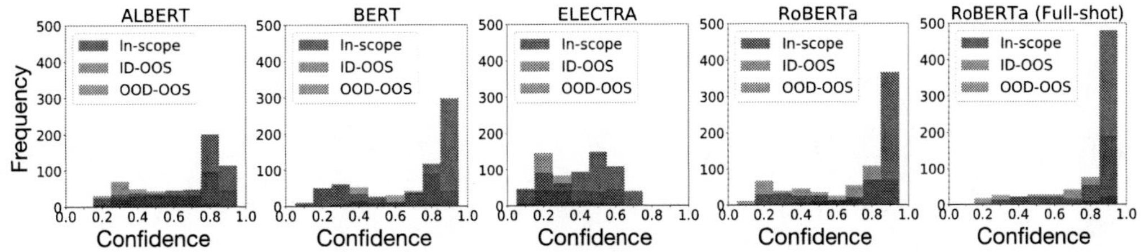

Figure 4: Model confidence on the development set of the "Credit cards" domain in CLINC-Single-Domain-OOS dataset under 5-shot setting. Darker colors indicate overlaps.

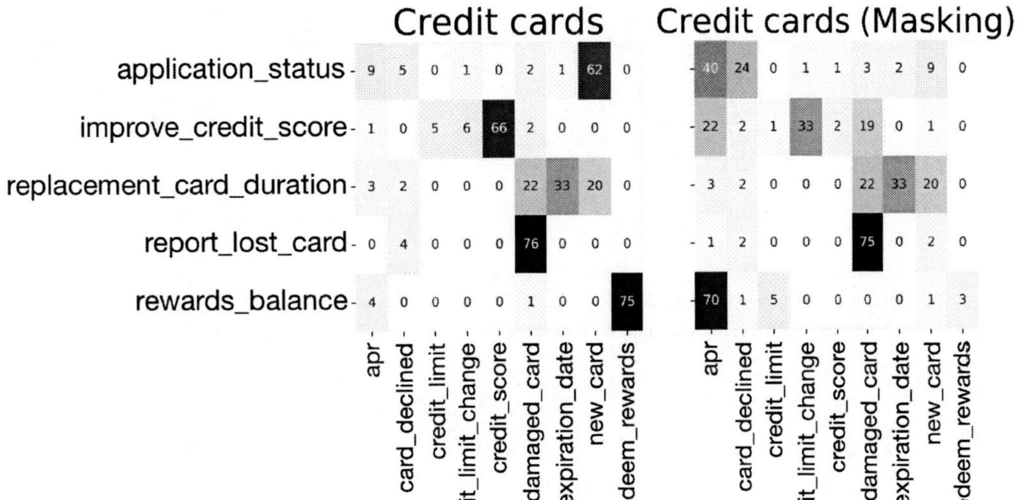

Figure 5: Full-shot confusion matrices on the development set with and without masking ("Credit cards", RoBERTa). Vertical axis: ID-OOS; horizontal axis: in-scope (only predicted intents considered).

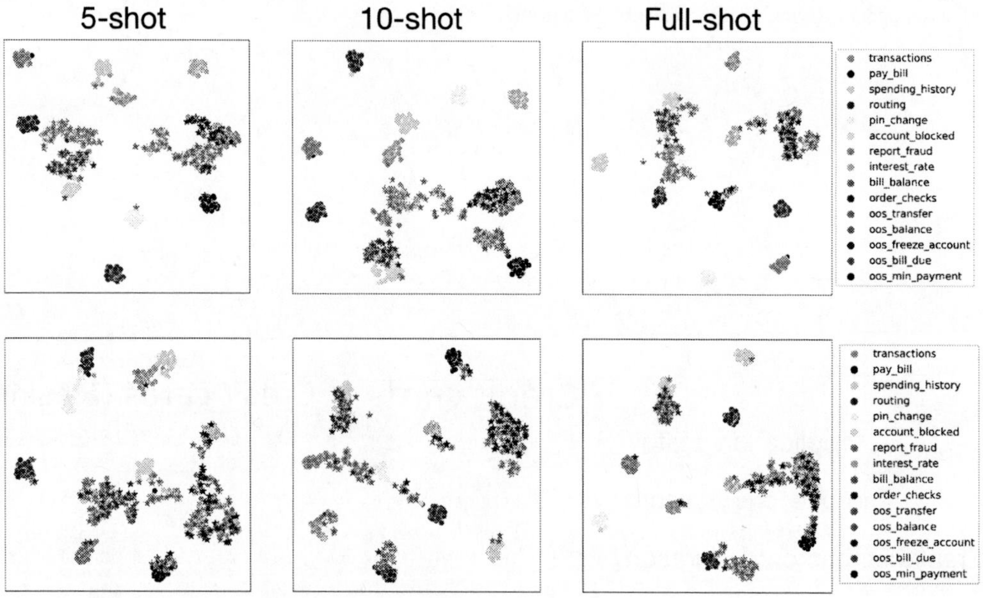

Figure 6: RoBERTa (first row) and ELECTRA (second row) tSNE visualizations on the development set of the "Banking" domain in CLINC-Single-Domain-OOS dataset.

Conversational AI for Positive-sum Retailing under Falsehood Control

Yin-Hsiang Liao
Academia Sinica
zenonliao@iis.sinica.edu.tw

Ruo-Ping Dong
Academia Sinica
dongruoping@gmail.com

Huan-Cheng Chang
Academia Sinica
changhc84@gmail.com

Wei-Yun Ma
Academia Sinica
ma@iis.sinica.edu.tw

Abstract

Retailing combines complicated communication skills and strategies to reach an agreement between buyer and seller with identical or different goals. In each transaction a good seller finds an optimal solution by considering his/her own profits while simultaneously considering whether the buyer's needs have been met. In this paper, we manage the retailing problem by mixing cooperation and competition. We present a rich dataset of buyer-seller bargaining in a simulated marketplace in which each agent values goods and utility separately. Various attributes (preference, quality, and profit) are initially hidden from one agent with respect to its role; during the conversation, both sides may reveal, fake, or retain the information uncovered to come to a final decision through natural language. Using this dataset, we leverage transfer learning techniques on a pretrained, end-to-end model and enhance its decision-making ability toward the best choice in terms of utility by means of multi-agent reinforcement learning. An automatic evaluation shows that our approach results in more optimal transactions than human does. We also show that our framework controls the falsehoods generated by seller agents. The code and dataset are available on https://github.com/ckiplab/Fruit_Stand.

1 Introduction

Retailing is a mixture of cooperation and competition between buyer and seller. The construction of virtual retailers has received widespread attention due to their broad applications in the E-commerce era. If the focus of the conversational retailer is limited to the buyer's needs, the retailer is actually a conversational recommendation system. However, if the conversational retailer's purpose is to maximize his/her own profit, the retailer is in fact a negotiation system, which typically must use discourse with opponents to perceive their intent and build strategies to achieve the retailer's own goals (Keizer et al., 2017; Afantenos et al., 2012).

Previous NLP research on negotiation concerns closed-domain scenarios in games such as Settlers of Catan (Asher and Lascarides, 2013), goods distribution (DeVault et al., 2015; Lewis et al., 2017), and open-ended settings, for example, price bargaining on a single item in a zero-sum, second-hand market (He et al., 2018). However, these scenarios do not attempt to find an optimal solution for both sides, which crucially defines a good retailer who always takes into account future transactions.

Therefore, inspired by Shapiro (1983), we propose a positive-sum setting in this paper: a buyer and a seller negotiate to achieve a transaction, and the seller not only considers his/her profit but also takes into account whether the buyer's needs have been met, thus seeking a mutually optimal solution. To simulate such a real-world vending scenario and provide enough motivation to start a conversation, both buyer and seller are given incomplete information prior to the conversation. The buyer knows what he/she prefers among multiple products but does not know the quality of the product prior to the conversation, and the seller does not know in advance the buyer's preferences but is aware of the quality of the product and its profit. The seller seeks a mutually optimal solution by which to build his/her own reputation for future business while simultaneously making a profit. Thus we propose separate utility functions for buyers and sellers.

To facilitate end-to-end fine-tuning for this scenario, we collected a large dataset of 4232 dialogues between two people negotiating on goods in a simulated market on Amazon Mechanical Turk (AMT). Our model is based on the Transformer architecture (Vaswani et al., 2017), which is predominant in recent NLP research, due in part to its inherent parallelism, which facilitates the use of large-scale datasets to train complex models such as GPT2 (Radford et al., 2019), evolved Transformer (So et al., 2019), and T5 (Raffel et al., 2020). Further, these complex models are often pre-trained

Proceedings of the 4th Workshop on NLP for Conversational AI, pages 21 - 33
May 27, 2022 ©2022 Association for Computational Linguistics

in an unsupervised fashion, yielding powerful performance in downstream tasks in an end-to-end, supervised manner, which lays the foundation for training two acceptable conversational agents to fit the proposed scenario. The supervised fine-tuning maximizes the likelihood of human utterances in the dataset. To maximize agent targets, we leverage reinforcement learning (RL) to direct the fine-tuning process.

In addition, due to the increasing saturation of machine learning algorithms in contemporary society, there has been a surge in interest in building truthful AI, a system that avoids stating falsehoods, thus enhancing transparency and helping to establish trust between system and human (Evans et al., 2021). To achieve such truthful AI, we attempt to reduce a certain type of statement against the ground truth in our negotiation scenario. First, we build a falsehood detector with respect to such statements. Second, we formulate a deduction mechanism in the RL stage to decrease the generation of falsehoods.

In summary, the contributions of our study are the following:

- We propose a simplified market setting where vendor and purchaser are in a "coopetitive" relation with information asymmetry. To this purpose we gathered FruitStand, a rich dataset of human-human negotiations under this scenario on Amazon Mechanical Turk (AMT).
- We propose an RL framework by which to cause a virtual retailer to learn how to find optimal solutions under positive-sum situation.
- The experiments demonstrate the effectiveness of reinforcement learning in improving the ability to achieve optimal transactions.
- We analyze the lies in a crowd-sourced dataset and the falsehoods generated by the seller model, based on which we propose an approach to reduce falsehoods.

2 Data Collection

In this paper, we discuss the behavior of two conversational agents negotiating given imperfect information. To promote end-to-end training, we collected FruitStand, a dataset of human-human dialogues designed around a novel scenario which simulates a fruit stand at which the negotiation takes place. In FruitStand, one agent plays the role of the buyer and the other that of the seller, communicating in natural language, developing strategies and eventually making a deal.

2.1 Task

The scenario simulates two agents transacting at a fruit stand. In each dialogue, the agents are first assigned a role, either buyer or seller, and the order of turns in which to send natural language messages. There are 3 item types—*apples*, *bananas*, and *oranges*—each of which has three attributes—*preference*, *quality*, and *profit*—as shown in upper left corner of Fig. 2. These 9 attributes determine the initial condition o. The buyer and seller each have an individual utility. The buyer's utility $U_b(item)$ to an item is defined as $\text{preference}(item) \times \text{quality}(item)$, following the intuition that the buyer is satisfied by purchasing what he/she likes in excellent condition (e.g., red, sweet, and juicy apples). Likewise, the seller's utility $U_s(item)$ is defined as $U_b + \text{profit}(item)$, taking into account the seller's current profit and the buyer's satisfaction for future profit, since the buyer might become a regular if he/she is satisfied. Each agent's best option is that which provides the highest utility. Depending on the best options, the agents' goals may be identical, or may conflict, which leads to opportunities for cooperation or competition, respectively.

In each dialogue, buyer and seller bargain turn by turn, trying to make a deal on their own best option(s). Agents possess imperfect information. Initially, the buyer knows only its *preference*, and the seller only the *quality* and *profit* of an item. During the conversation, they must estimate the other's exclusive attributes by skill of speech, all the while not revealing any exact values. Absolute honesty is not required; agents can be deceptive. In particular, the seller may mislead the buyer when a given item is more profitable; however, the final decision lies with the buyer. Each conversation ends when the buyer makes a decision; typically this occurs within 5 to 20 turns. The design of the utility functions and the right to choose compensates for the buyer's inferior position in terms of the amount of information.

2.2 Collection

We collected the FruitStand dataset based on the above task via AMT with the interface shown in Figures 1 and 3. Workers were paid per dialogue, with a bonus for achieving the best option in terms of utility. The starter of a dialogue could be either a seller or buyer, and we kept the number of starters from both sides roughly balanced. The dataset statistics in Table 1 show that FruitStand has longer and more variant dialogues than DealorNodeal(Lewis et al., 2017). FruitStand has a total of 4232 dialogues with unique initial conditions, 76.1% of which have mutually optimal solutions (the overlapping best options from two sides), as illustrated in Table 2. We partitioned 80%/10%/10% of the dialogues for training/validation/testing.

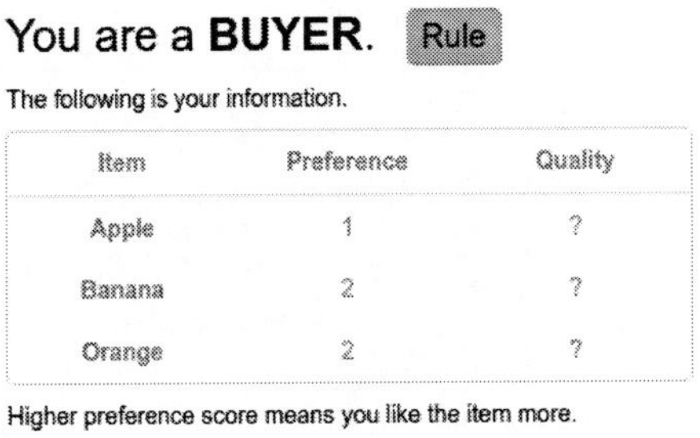

(a) Buyer

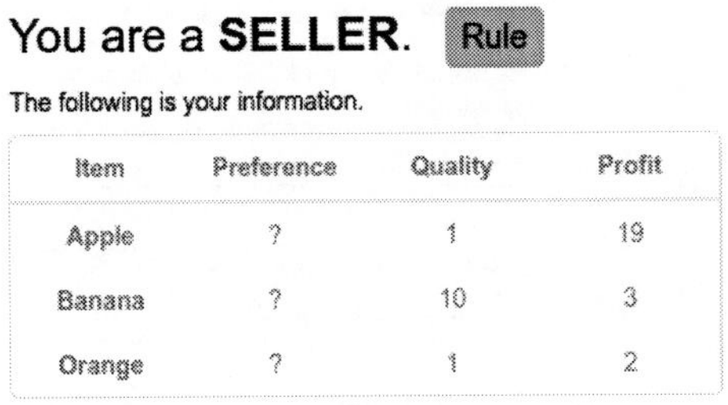

(b) Seller

Figure 1: At the start of each conversation, the buyer knows only his/her preferences, and the seller knows only the quality and profit.

	FS	DN
Number(#) of Dialogues	4232	5808
Average Turns per Dialogue	7.8	6.5
Average Words per Turn	11.6	7.6
Vocabulary Size	4318	2719
Vocabulary Size without Numbers	4229	2623
% Agreed	100	80.1

Table 1: Comparison of dataset statistics of FruitStand and DealorNodeal. FruitStand contains longer, more variant dialogues on average.

	Number (Ratio)
Buyer's optimal selection chosen	2767 (65.4%)
Seller's optimal selection chosen	2966 (70.1%)
Mutually optimal occasion	3222 (76.1%)
Mutually optimal selection chosen	2464 (58.2%)

Table 2: Statistics of final deals in the whole FruitStand dataset.

3 Retailer

3.1 Data Representation

Every turn in a dialogue is transformed into a training pair—input sequence X and label sequence Y—from the perspective of the agent. For example, as illustrated in Figure 2, the buyer starts the conversation, and its preferences and utterance in this turn are converted into the first training pair of the dialogue, $\langle X_1^B, Y_1^B \rangle$. Note that $Y_1^B = \{y_{11}^B, y_{12}^B, ..., y_{1T}^B\}$, where y_{ij} is a token and T is the length of the utterance at this turn. Next, the seller's scenario along with the buyer's previous utterance and its response in this turn become the second training pair, $\langle X_1^S, Y_1^S \rangle$, the seller's first. The process continues until the end of the conversation. A similar technique has been used, see, e.g., Wolf et al. (2019). Note that we take the natural form for the agents' scenario, o^B and o^S, instead of merely numbers, to leverage the words' underlying information from pretrained models.

3.2 Baseline Models

For the first training stage, we fine-tune a T5 model (Raffel et al., 2020) pretrained on our FruitStand dataset. T5 is a standard encoder-decoder Transformer (Vaswani et al., 2017) which regards all NLP tasks as a text-to-text format. We leverage its baseline version (T5-base) as described in Raffel et al. (2020) as our starting point. T5-base is a composite of 12 Transformer blocks (each block combines self-attention, optional encoder-decoder attention, and a feedforward layer with a hidden size of 3072). It performs well on downstream tasks as varied as machine translation, document summarization, and sentiment classification.

The pretrained model is then fine-tuned as in supervised learning (SL), i.e., by minimizing the cross-entropy loss between the generated sequence Z and the label sequence Y described in Sec. 3.1. We have two transfer paths: one for the buyer and one for the seller. The buyer path uses labels from the buyer's perspective, and the seller path uses its part in the dialogue. The pair of the

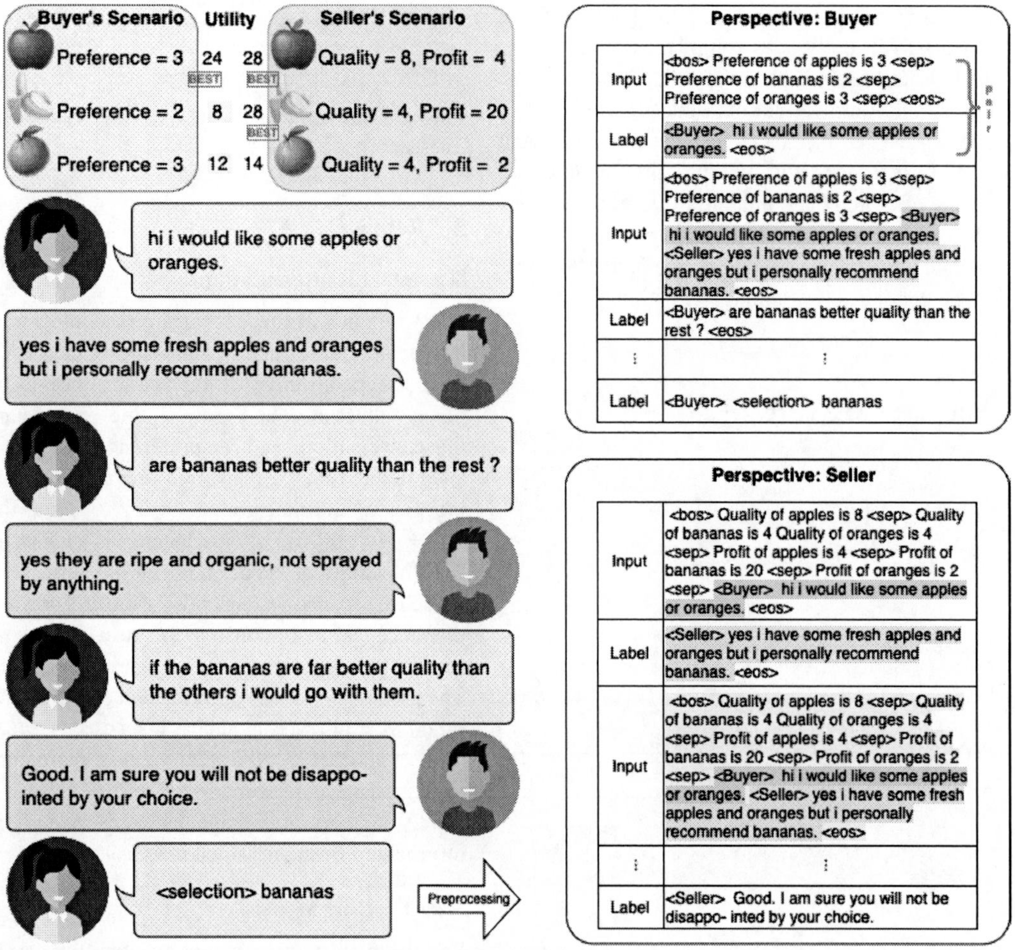

Figure 2: Transforming a crowd-sourced dialogue (left) into a series of training pairs (input, label) from perspectives of the two agents. The buyer only knows its own preference, while the seller only knows the quality and profits of fruits

two picked models, denoted as $\langle M_\phi^B, M_\theta^S \rangle$, forms the baseline for later evaluation, where ϕ and θ are the learned parameters of the buyer and seller model, respectively. See Sec. 4.1 for more details.

3.3 Goal-oriented Reinforcement

The goal of supervised learning is to imitate average human behavior; however, not every person is good at making deals. We further fine-tune the agents via reinforcement learning to improve the choice of—or the persuasion of the buyer to choose—the best option through a dialogue. This two-stage learning strategy has been widely used to enhance pretrained models toward a specific goal, e.g., Stiennon et al. (2020); Lewis et al. (2017); Li et al. (2016).

In reinforcement learning, we utilize *self play* (Lewis et al., 2017) to enhance our baseline models M_ϕ^B and M_θ^S by making one agent talk to the other turn by turn. Each turn ends when an agent outputs the END-OF-SENTENCE token, and the dialogue finishes when the buyer outputs the SELECTION token in a turn, or when the dialogue length limit is reached, as in the human case depicted in Fig. 2. A buyer's utterance in the i-th turn of a dialogue is denoted as Z_i^B, with Z_i^S for the seller's. We denote the trajectory τ^B or τ^S as the sequence of all tokens generated by buyer or seller during a dialogue. For instance, the buyer's trajectory is

$$\tau^B = Z_1^B||...||Z_i^B||...||Z_N^B \\ = \{z_{11}^B, ..., z_{1T_1}^B, ...z_{i1}^B, ...z_{iT_i}^B, ...z_{NT_N}^B\},$$

where $||$ denotes concatenation and N is the number of turns.

After a complete dialogue has been generated, we update the agents' parameters based on the negotiation results. Agents get the final reward $R(\tau)$ when the dialogue is terminated. We define $R(\tau) = 1$ if the buyer selects the item with highest utility, $R(\tau) = 0$ if the buyer selects an item other than the best one, and $R(\tau) = -1$ otherwise. Note that the best item for a buyer is not necessarily the same that for a seller. Similar to AlphaGO (Silver and Huang et al, 2016), $R(\tau)$ is then assigned to tokens generated at each previous, non-terminal time step. We use REINFORCE (Williams, 1992) to optimize the baseline models separately toward the best options. Given a sampled trajectory τ and the final reward $R(\tau)$, let a_i be the i-th token generated in a turn; we update the model's parameters θ by

$$\theta \leftarrow \theta - \eta \sum_i (R(\tau) - b) \nabla_\theta \log p_\theta(a_i | a_{<i}, o), \tag{1}$$

where η is the learning rate and b is the baseline calculated by the average reward of the previous 3 updates.

Whereas the canonical Transformer is difficult to optimize in the RL setting, often resulting in performance comparable to a random policy (Parisotto et al., 2020), or leading to meaningless results (Lewis et al., 2017; He et al., 2018), we find the pretrained T5 model works well with parameter updates by policy gradient when we simply set a smaller learning rate.

3.4 Falsehood Control

One way to increase one's integrity is to tell no lies. We follow this notion to build a more trustworthy conversational agent, especially a seller, by decreasing the possibility that an agent produces an untruthful utterance. In the FruitStand task, the seller might claim that one type of fruit is the best in quality when it really is not, attempting to attract a buyer to choose a more profitable item, and vice versa, to keep a buyer away from a less lucrative one.

Motivated by these observations, we construct a simple rule-based falsehood detector that first

Claim Parser	
SUP: best/worst	
FRUIT: apple/banana/orange	
	Matching Pattern
	SUP are the FRUIT
	SUP FRUIT
	FRUITs are your SUP
	FRUITs are my SUP
	FRUITs are the SUP
<Ignore>	FRUITs are the best seller
Falsehood Type	
Claim a type of fruit is the best or worst but actually not.	

Table 3: The falsehood detector is consisted of a claim parser and falsehood type. If the claim from a seller disobeys any fact derived from a scenario o, the detector will catch a falsehood

parses the claim for two superlatives, as shown in Table 3, and then determines whether the seller's claim conflicts with any known fact based on a given scenario o. We further use this to establish a deduction mechanism $D(\tau)$ on the final reward in the reinforcement learning stage. Given a trajectory τ, $D(\tau) = -2$ if any of the seller's utterances conflict with the facts about the quality of an item; $D(\tau) = 0$ if none of this kind of falsehood is detected. The updated final reward then becomes $R(\tau) + D(\tau)$; we term this approach RL (w/DM).

4 Experiments

4.1 Training Details

We used PyTorch to implement our models, and used the pretrained T5-base model from Hugging Face.[1] We added the special tokens BUYER, SELLER, and SELECTION as self-defined tokens to T5Tokenizer.[1] For the baseline models, we fine-tuned the pretrained T5-base for 20 epochs; after each epoch we set a checkpoint, and then picked that with the least perplexity on the validation set: for the buyer this yielded model M_ϕ^B and for the seller M_θ^S separately. We used AdamW (Loshchilov and Hutter, 2019) to optimize models with a learning rate of 6.25×10^{-5}, $\beta_1 = 0.9$, $\beta_2 = 0.999$, and a mini-batch size of 4. We clipped gradients above 1.0. Supervised fine-tuning was run on a single RTX 2080Ti GPU.

In reinforcement learning, we estimated the expected final reward under an initial condition by

[1]https://huggingface.co/transformers/model_doc/t5.html

	Fine-tuned SL Baseline	RL Interleave	RL $O_{train'}$	RL Random	Human Testing set
Buyer's optimal	62.6%	**71.9%**	69.3%	65.5%	69.0%
Seller's optimal	59.1%	**73.5%**	70.0%	63.6%	66.4%
Mutually optimal (if possible)	64.2%	**78.8%**	75.2%	68.2%	75.8%

Table 4: Rate of the optimal items being chosen in final deals. The RL approach that interleave REINFORCE and SL to update parameters reaches the highest performance among all, even better than average humans.

Item\Attr.	Preference	Quality	Profit	Buyer's Utility	Seller's Utility
Apples	2	4	16	8	24
Bananas	1	1	7	1	8
Oranges	2	10	11	20	31

a. Fine-tuned SL (baseline)	b. RL (interleaved on $O_{train'}$)
B: hello, i am looking for some fresh fruit. S: i have some great oranges. B: are they fresh? S: they are very fresh and juicy. B: great! S: great! B: <selection> oranges	B: hello, i would like to buy some fruit. S: i have some great oranges. B: are they fresher than your apples? S: they are fresher than the apples. B: ok. i will take some oranges then S: great. thank you for your business B: <selection> oranges
c. RL (random initialized O)	**d. RL (directly on $O_{train'}$)**
B: hello, i'm looking for some apples. S: i have some great apples. they are very fresh and juicy. B: great! i love apples! S: great.. how many would you like? B: i will take a dozen please S: great.. here you go. B: <selection> apples	B: hello, i am looking for some fresh fruit. what do you have that is fresh? S: my oranges are the freshest i have today. B: oh great, i love oranges. how are your apples? S: my apples are ok but my oranges are the freshest i have today. B: ok. i will take some oranges then. thank you. S: great! i will get them ready for you. B: <selection> oranges

Table 5: Cherry picked examples under the same scenario of bot-bot chats on FruitStand. Fine-tuned SL produces general response, and RL approaches get more specific and various.

sampling N turns of utterances from self-play dialogue. In each turn, at the T5 decoding phase, the next token a_t was randomly chosen according to its conditional probability distribution

$$a_t \sim P(a|a_{1:t-1})$$

using top-K sampling (Fan et al., 2018), in which the K most likely next tokens are filtered in and the pmf of the output tokens is redistributed among the K tokens. We empirically chose $N = 32$ and $K = 50$ for a given o and set the mini-batch size to N. We also used AdamW for the parameter updates but reduced the learning rate to one-tenth of that used in the supervised fine-tuning. We chose the number of dialogues in the validation dataset as the amount of dialogues used in an epoch for RL approaches. We updated the parameter per mini-batch for 10 epochs. This took about 40 hours on a single Quadro RTX 8000.

4.2 Comparison

We compare the performance of the following models:

- **Fine-tuned SL**: our baseline models described in Sec. 3.2: a pair of pretrained T5 models fine-tuned on FruitStand.

Given $O_{train'}$, the initial conditions of the dialogues randomly picked from the training set to the size of the validation set, we evaluated the variants derived from Sec. 3.3:

- **RL (interleaved on $O_{train'}$)**: Direct optimization of the agent goals via RL often results in language that differs from human language. Similar to Lewis et al. (2017), we fine-tuned the baseline models with RL followed by SL in each epoch. The learning rate was one-tenth of that for Fine-tuned SL.

- **RL (directly on $O_{train'}$)**: Under the same initial conditions, we evaluated the scenario without the following SL part. The learning rate was one-tenth of that for Fine-tuned SL.

- **RL (random initialized O)**: The baseline models self play under randomly initialized scenarios. Since the outputs of the baseline models diverge from human language during the RL process for unseen initial conditions, we further reduced their learning rate to one-hundredth of that for Fine-tuned SL.

4.3 Evaluation

We evaluated the performance of the proposed approaches on FruitStand by the proportion of the best options being chosen after self play, denoted as the p-score, with respect to the unseen initial conditions in the testing dataset. Note that in the evaluation stage, for fair competition, we used not top-K sampling but instead greedy search, which simply selects the token with the highest probability as the next token:

$$a_t = \arg\max_a P(a|a_{1:t-1}).$$

For each RL variant described in Sec. 4.2, we first evaluated our models on the validation set, pair by pair at each checkpoint, and chose that pair with the highest average p-score for testing.

The results are shown in Table 4. The RL approaches considerably enhance the ability to select the best item from the baseline models. Compared to human-human negotiation in the FruitStand testing set, RL (interleaved on $O_{train'}$), the best model, achieves even better performance. This success provides evidence that maximizing the reward outplays average humans and constitutes an acceptable imitation.

For falsehood detection, we compared the number of a typical kind of detected falsehood produced by a seller from dialogues in the testing dataset (Human), the number from baseline models (Baseline models), and the number from the RL (interleaved on $O_{train'}$) variant, RL (w/o DM).

Checkpoints	1	2	3	4	5
RL(w/o DM)	18	8	8	7	41
RL(w/ DM)	0	0	0	0	0
Checkpoints	6	7	8	9	10
RL(w/o DM)	9	6	16	7	11
RL(w/ DM)	0	0	1	0	1
Human: 18					
Baseline models: 32					
Size of testing dataset: 423					

Table 6: RL(interleave) with/without deduction mechanism in each checkpoint. Each number in a cell (expect for those horizontal to 'Checkpoints') shows how many falsehoods found by the detector in each checkpoint.

The results are shown in Table 6. In the crowd-sourced testing dataset, the specific type of falsehood exists in 18 out of 423 dialogues. In the baseline, falsehoods were detected in 32 out of 423 dialogues. RL (interleaved) on $O_{train'}$) performs poorly on falsehood detection with 6 to 41 falsehoods among all the checkpoints. In contrast, our approach, RL (w/DM), significantly reduces the falsehoods in the pattern.

5 Analysis and Discussion

Goal-based models are more task-centered. Although the fine-tuned T5-base model can generate fluent and reasonable utterances, it tends to output generic responses such as "great!" which poorly reflect the task setting. See Table 5. In comparison, RL approaches generate utterances that better fit the simulated scene. A general phenomenon is that they generate long utterances, similar to humans, who show their interest in goods by asking more questions, and vendors, who show their passion by promoting their products. We also find that models learn to compare goods; comparison is an effective way to determine which item to choose.

Behavior Control Besides falsehood, we also investigated how to control virtual sellers' other behaviors. Four different sellers are investigated: **Balanced Seller** is the standard seller described all over the paper, which utility is the sum of buyer's utility plus items' profits. **Win-win Seller**'s utility is based on whether mutual optimality was achieved. **Recommender**'s utility is exactly the same as buyer's utility. **Profit-oriented Seller**'s utility base on only items' profits. Appendix C shows their vending results accordingly. We found that in general, **Balanced Seller** remains a certain level of profitability and satisfy customers at the same time. Actually, the decision of choose what kind of virtual seller to employ in practice would depend on employers' willingness and needs. Here we just demonstrate that how virtual sellers can be customised by just adjusting their utility design.

Deduction mechanism silences all. The falsehood detector is meant to prevent the seller from generating untruthful claims, and ensure that only factual claims are made. However, we find that the deduction mechanism suppresses not only such falseness, but also expressions containing such claims. That is, it prevents the seller from generating any utterances with matching patterns. For example, at some checkpoints, the seller does not even produce the string 'the best', which is clearly not a desired consequence.

Checkpoints	1	2	3	4
RL(w/o DM)	18/44	8/32	8/21	7/18
RL(w/ DM)	0/0	0/0	0/0	0/0
RL(DM$_B$)	6/17	5/12	3/7	0/0
RL(DM$_R$)	2/10	8/23	**0/3**	0/0
Checkpoints	5	6	7	8
RL(w/o DM)	41/131	9/42	6/21	16/40
RL(w/ DM)	0/0	0/0	0/0	1/1
RL(DM$_B$)	0/0	0/0	11/37	1/3
RL(DM$_R$)	0/0	0/0	2/10	0/0
Checkpoints	9	10		
RL(w/o DM)	7/12	11/48		
RL(w/ DM)	0/0	1/3		
RL(DM$_B$)	6/26	**0/6**		
RL(DM$_R$)	0/0	0/0		
Human: 18/58 Baseline models: 32/82 Size of testing dataset: 423				

Table 7: RL(w/o DM) denotes the RL(interleave) model without deduction mechanism; RL(w/ DM), RL(DM$_B$), and RL(DM$_R$) stand for the RL(interleave) model with the deduction mechanism or its adjustment. Each number in a cell (expect for those horizontal to 'Checkpoints') shows how many falsehoods found by the detector in each checkpoint.

We thus adjust the mechanism using two approaches. First, we retain the -2 deduction on falsehood, but compensate those expressions by +0.5, denoted by RL (DM$_B$). Second, we instead reduce the deduction to -1, a more conservative value corresponding to R (τ). This path is denoted by RL (DM$_R$).

The results in Table 7 show that it is difficult to avoid mistakenly silencing non-deceptive utterances. In the experiment on both paths, at some checkpoints the seller avoids indiscriminate silencing, whereas at other checkpoints falsehoods are generated which still use those combinations of words. The underlying reasons for such unstable results are poorly understood. We leave this as future work.

6 Related Work

During the recent, rapid development of conversational agents, also known as chatbots, various applications have been created. Open-domain chatbots such as Facebook's BST (Roller et al., 2021) and Google's Meena (Adiwardana et al., 2020) seek to be more human-like, engaging in conversation on any topic. Closed-domain chatbots instead focus on improved task performance, for instance GuessWhich (Das et al., 2017), persuasion (Wang et al., 2019; Shi et al., 2020), and negotiation (Afantenos et al., 2012; Papangelis and Georgila, 2015; Lewis et al., 2017; He et al., 2018).

To negotiate item distribution (book, hat, ball), Lewis et al. (2017) apply a bi-directional GRU model to train a language model and use reinforcement learning with self play to develop data-driven strategies. For price bargaining on a single item (e.g., a TV), He et al. (2018) use a hybrid approach involving rule-based and LSTM models that decouple natural language understanding, dialogue act prediction, and natural language generation to facilitate controllable negotiation strategies. However, these scenarios do not attempt to find an optimal solution for both sides, and do not control the falsehoods generated by sellers. These limitations motivate this work.

7 Conclusion

We introduce a novel negotiation task and present FruitStand, a rich dataset of human-human dialogues, for negotiation dialogue research. We demonstrate the effectiveness of reinforcement learning in guiding the conversational agent toward a specific goal. Finally, our experiments in falsehood suppression show the potential of RL for truthful AI. A more robust falsehood detector would be our first future work. In our initial observations, a strong Natural Language Inference (NLI) model could play this role.

8 Acknowledgements

We are grateful for the insightful comments from anonymous reviewers. This work is supported by the Ministry of Science and Technology of Taiwan under grant numbers MOST111-2634-F-001-001.

References

Daniel Adiwardana, Minh-Thang Luong, David R. So, Jamie Hall, Noah Fiedel, Romal Thoppilan, Zi Yang, Apoorv Kulshreshtha, Gaurav Nemade, Yifeng Lu, and Quoc V. Le. 2020. Towards a human-like open-domain chatbot. *CoRR*, abs/2001.09977.

Stergos Afantenos, Nicholas Asher, Farah Benamara, Anaıs Cadilhac, Cedric Dégremont, Pascal Denis, Markus Guhe, Simon Keizer, et al. 2012. Modelling strategic conversation: model, annotation design and corpus. In *Proceedings of the 16th Workshop on the Semantics and Pragmatics of Dialogue*.

Nicholas Asher and Alex Lascarides. 2013. Strategic conversation. *Semantics and Pragmatics*, 6(2):1–62.

Abhishek Das, Satwik Kottur, José M.F. Moura, Stefan Lee, and Dhruv Batra. 2017. Learning cooperative visual dialog agents with deep reinforcement learning. In *Proceedings of the IEEE International Conference on Computer Vision (ICCV)*.

David DeVault, Johnathan Mell, and Jonathan Gratch. 2015. Toward natural turn-taking in a virtual human negotiation agent. In *AAAI Spring Symposia*.

Owain Evans, Owen Cotton-Barratt, Lukas Finnveden, Adam Bales, Avital Balwit, Peter Wills, Luca Righetti, and William Saunders. 2021. Truthful ai: Developing and governing ai that does not lie.

Angela Fan, Mike Lewis, and Yann Dauphin. 2018. Hierarchical neural story generation. In *Proceedings of the 56th Annual Meeting of the Association for Computational Linguistics (Volume 1: Long Papers)*, pages 889–898. Association for Computational Linguistics.

He He, Derek Chen, Anusha Balakrishnan, and Percy Liang. 2018. Decoupling strategy and generation in negotiation dialogues. In *Proceedings of the 2018 Conference on Empirical Methods in Natural Language Processing*, pages 2333–2343, Brussels, Belgium. Association for Computational Linguistics.

Simon Keizer, Markus Guhe, Heriberto Cuayáhuitl, Ioannis Efstathiou, Klaus-Peter Engelbrecht, Mihai Dobre, Alex Lascarides, and Oliver Lemon. 2017. Evaluating persuasion strategies and deep reinforcement learning methods for negotiation dialogue agents. In *Proceedings of the 15th Conference of the European Chapter of the Association for Computational Linguistics: Volume 2, Short Papers*, pages 480–484. Association for Computational Linguistics.

Mike Lewis, Denis Yarats, Yann Dauphin, Devi Parikh, and Dhruv Batra. 2017. Deal or no deal? end-to-end learning of negotiation dialogues. In *Proceedings of the 2017 Conference on Empirical Methods in Natural Language Processing*, pages 2443–2453. Association for Computational Linguistics.

Jiwei Li, Will Monroe, Alan Ritter, Michel Galley, Jianfeng Gao, and Dan Jurafsky. 2016. Deep reinforcement learning for dialogue generation. *CoRR*, abs/1606.01541.

Ilya Loshchilov and Frank Hutter. 2019. Decoupled weight decay regularization. In *7th International Conference on Learning Representations, ICLR 2019*.

Alexandros Papangelis and Kallirroi Georgila. 2015. Reinforcement learning of multi-issue negotiation dialogue policies. In *Proceedings of the 16th Annual Meeting of the Special Interest Group on Discourse and Dialogue*, pages 154–158, Prague, Czech Republic. Association for Computational Linguistics.

Emilio Parisotto, Francis Song, Jack Rae, Razvan Pascanu, Caglar Gulcehre, Siddhant Jayakumar, Max Jaderberg, Raphaël Lopez Kaufman, Aidan Clark, Seb Noury, Matthew Botvinick, Nicolas Heess, and Raia Hadsell. 2020. Stabilizing transformers for reinforcement learning. In *Proceedings of the 37th International Conference on Machine Learning*, volume 119 of *Proceedings of Machine Learning Research*, pages 7487–7498. PMLR.

Alec Radford, Jeff Wu, Rewon Child, David Luan, Dario Amodei, and Ilya Sutskever. 2019. Language models are unsupervised multitask learners.

Colin Raffel, Noam Shazeer, Adam Roberts, Katherine Lee, Sharan Narang, Michael Matena, Yanqi Zhou, Wei Li, and Peter J. Liu. 2020. Exploring the limits of transfer learning with a unified text-to-text transformer. *Journal of Machine Learning Research*, 21(140):1–67.

Stephen Roller, Emily Dinan, Naman Goyal, Da Ju, Mary Williamson, Yinhan Liu, Jing Xu, Myle Ott, Eric Michael Smith, Y-Lan Boureau, and Jason Weston. 2021. Recipes for building an open-domain chatbot. In *Proceedings of the 16th Conference of the European Chapter of the Association for Computational Linguistics: Main Volume*, pages 300–325, Online. Association for Computational Linguistics.

Carl Shapiro. 1983. Premiums for High Quality Products as Returns to Reputations*. *The Quarterly Journal of Economics*, 98(4):659–679.

Weiyan Shi, Xuewei Wang, Yoojung Oh, Jingwen Zhang, Saurav Sahay, and Zhou Yu. 2020. Effects of persuasive dialogues: Testing bot identities and inquiry strategies. *CoRR*, abs/2001.04564.

David Silver and Aja Huang et al. 2016. Mastering the game of go with deep neural networks and tree search. *Nature*, 529:484–489.

David R. So, Chen Liang, and Quoc V. Le. 2019. The evolved transformer.

Nisan Stiennon, Long Ouyang, Jeffrey Wu, Daniel Ziegler, Ryan Lowe, Chelsea Voss, Alec Radford, Dario Amodei, and Paul F Christiano. 2020. Learning to summarize with human feedback. In *Advances in Neural Information Processing Systems*, volume 33, pages 3008–3021. Curran Associates, Inc.

Ashish Vaswani, Noam Shazeer, Niki Parmar, Jakob Uszkoreit, Llion Jones, Aidan N. Gomez, Lukasz Kaiser, and Illia Polosukhin. 2017. Attention is all you need. *Conference on Neural Information Processing Systems*.

Xuewei Wang, Weiyan Shi, Richard Kim, Yoojung Oh, Sijia Yang, Jingwen Zhang, and Zhou Yu. 2019. Persuasion for good: Towards a personalized persuasive dialogue system for social good. In *Proceedings of the 57th Annual Meeting of the Association for Computational Linguistics*, pages 5635–5649. Association for Computational Linguistics.

Ronald J. Williams. 1992. Simple statistical gradient-following algorithms for connectionist reinforcement learning. *Machine Learning*, 8(3):229–256.

Thomas Wolf, Victor Sanh, Julien Chaumond, and Clement Delangue. 2019. Transfertransfo: A transfer learning approach for neural network based conversational agents. *CoRR*, abs/1901.08149.

A FruitStand Interface

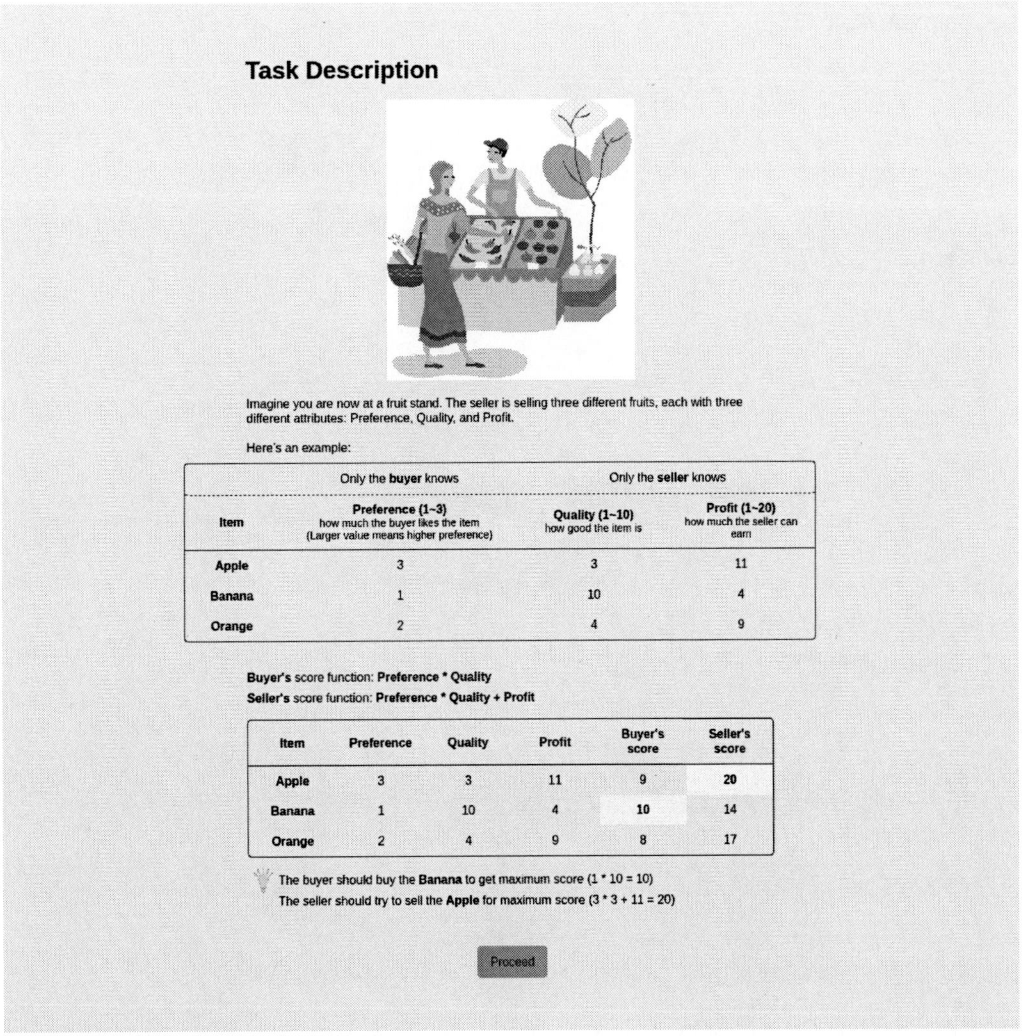

Task Description

Imagine you are now at a fruit stand. The seller is selling three different fruits, each with three different attributes: Preference, Quality, and Profit.

Here's an example:

	Only the **buyer** knows	Only the **seller** knows	
Item	**Preference (1~3)** how much the buyer likes the item (Larger value means higher preference)	**Quality (1~10)** how good the item is	**Profit (1~20)** how much the seller can earn
Apple	3	3	11
Banana	1	10	4
Orange	2	4	9

Buyer's score function: **Preference * Quality**
Seller's score function: **Preference * Quality + Profit**

Item	Preference	Quality	Profit	Buyer's score	Seller's score
Apple	3	3	11	9	**20**
Banana	1	10	4	**10**	14
Orange	2	4	9	8	17

The buyer should buy the **Banana** to get maximum score (1 * 10 = 10)
The seller should try to sell the **Apple** for maximum score (3 * 3 + 11 = 20)

Proceed

Figure 3: The interface we use for collecting dataset on the Amazon Mechanical Turk.

B FruitStand Interface (Cont.)

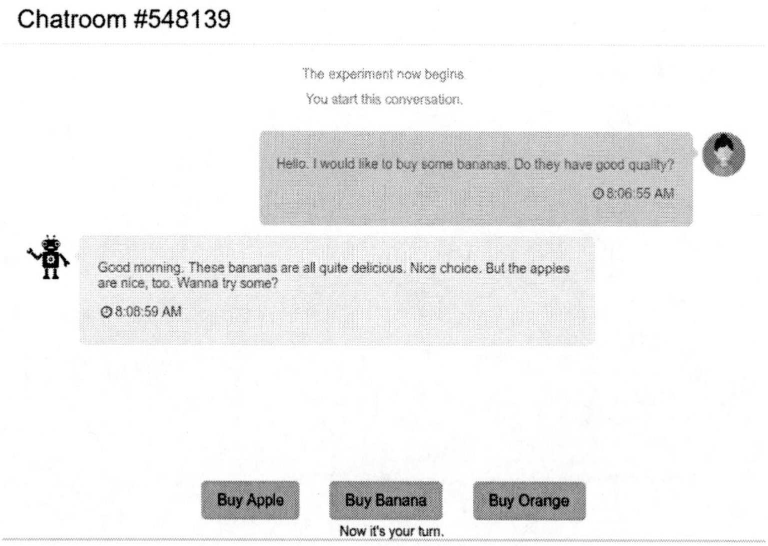

Figure 4: Buyer's interface

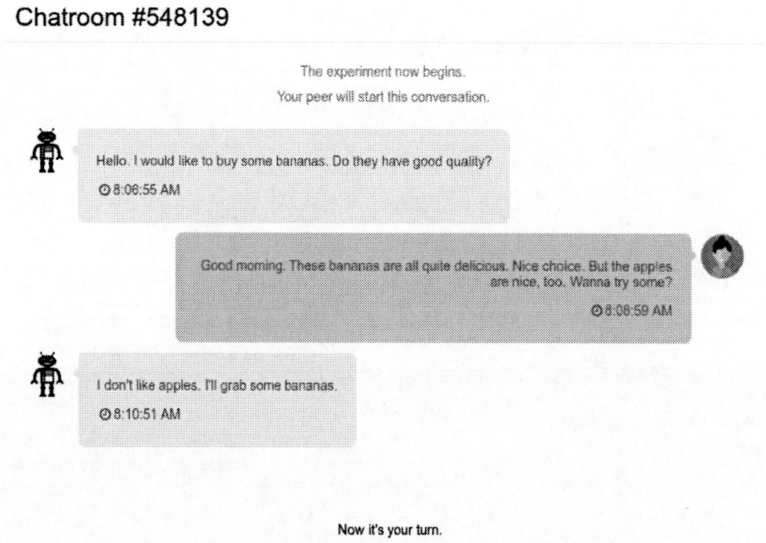

Figure 5: Seller's interface

C Behavior Control

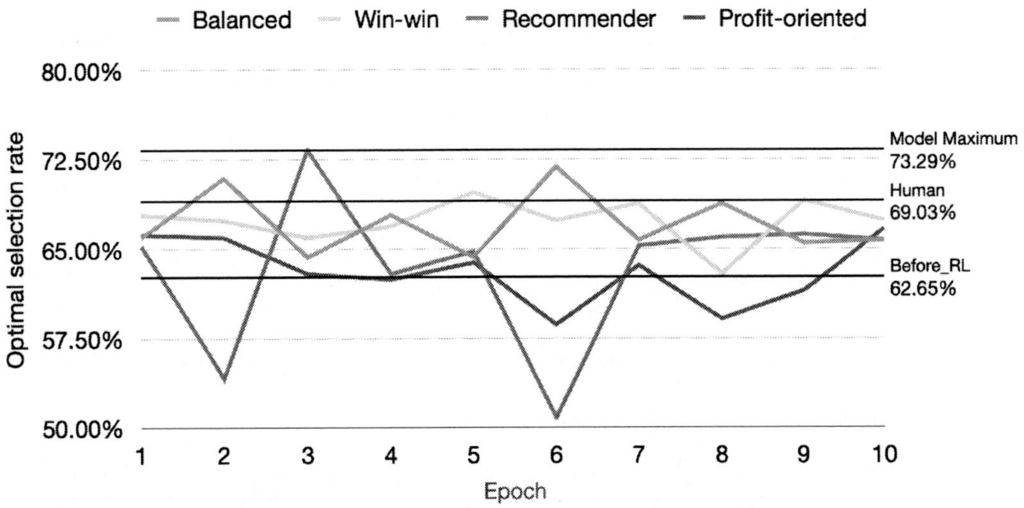

Figure 6: Rate of Buyer's best items being chosen. 'Human' stands for the human selections in testing. 'Before_RL' stands for the model before reinforcement learning.

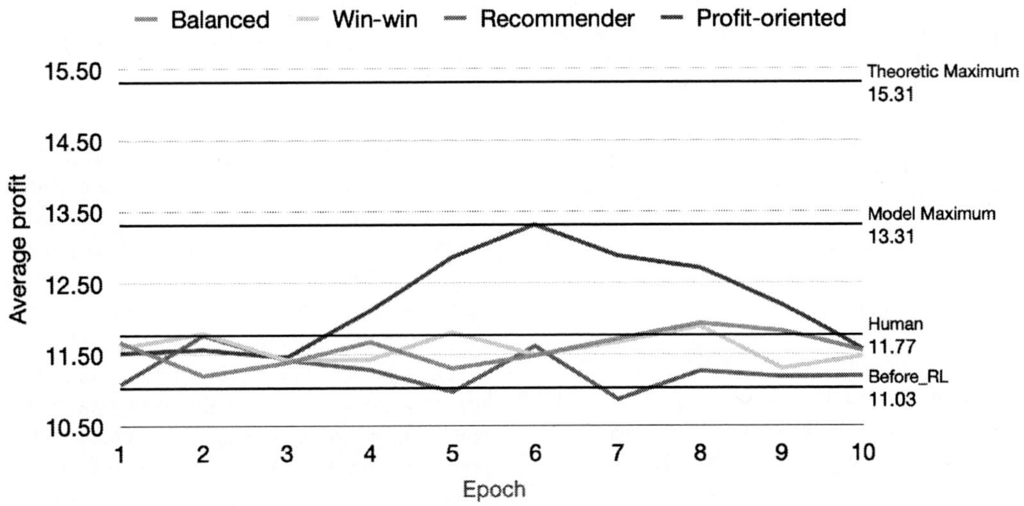

Figure 7: Seller's average profit. 'Theoretic maximum' stands for the average maximal profit of dialogues/scenarios in testing set. 'Human' stands for the human selections in testing. 'Before_RL' stands for the model before reinforcement learning.

D-REX: Dialogue Relation Extraction with Explanations

Alon Albalak[1], Varun Embar[2], Yi-lin Tuan[1], Lise Getoor[2], William Yang Wang[1]
[1]University of California, Santa Barbara [2]University of California, Santa Cruz
{alon_albalak, ytuan}@ucsb.edu
{vembar, getoor}@ucsc.edu
william@cs.ucsb.edu

Abstract

Existing research studies on cross-sentence relation extraction in long-form multi-party conversations aim to improve relation extraction without considering the explainability of such methods. This work addresses that gap by focusing on extracting explanations that indicate that a relation exists while using only partially labeled explanations. We propose our model-agnostic framework, D-REX, a policy-guided semi-supervised algorithm that optimizes for explanation quality and relation extraction simultaneously. We frame relation extraction as a re-ranking task and include relation- and entity-specific explanations as an intermediate step of the inference process. We find that human annotators are 4.2 times more likely to prefer D-REX's explanations over a joint relation extraction and explanation model. Finally, our evaluations show that D-REX is simple yet effective and improves relation extraction performance of strong baseline models by 1.2-4.7%.[1]

1 Introduction

Traditional relation extraction (RE) approaches discover relations that exist between entities within a single sentence. Recently, several approaches have been proposed which focus on cross-sentence RE, the task of extracting relations between entities that appear in separate sentences (Peng et al., 2017; Quirk and Poon, 2017; Han and Wang, 2020; Yao et al., 2019) as well as cross-sentence RE in dialogues (Yu et al., 2020; Chen et al., 2020; Xue et al., 2021; Qiu et al., 2021; Lee and Choi, 2021).

A crucial step towards performing cross-sentence RE in multi-entity and multi-relation dialogues is to understand the context surrounding relations and entities (e.g., who said what, and to whom). Figure 1 shows an example from the DialogRE dataset where a simple BERT-based model

Speaker 1: Could you please get the key off the back of the door for me.

Speaker 2: Oh yeah! Yeah!

Speaker 1: You tell your friend Chandler that we're definitely broken up this time.

Speaker 2: Okay!

Subject	Object	Initial Predicted Relation	D-REX Predicted Explanation	D-REX Predicted Relation
Speaker 2	Chandler	girl/boyfriend	your friend	friends

Figure 1: A sample dialogue between 2 speakers with actual D-REX predictions. The model initially classifies Speaker 2 and chandler, incorrectly, as girl/boyfriend. After predicting the explanation "your friend", D-REX correctly re-ranks the relation as friends.

(Initial Predicted Relation in Figure 1) gets confused by multiple entities and relations existing in the same dialogue (Yu et al., 2020). The model predicts the "girl/boyfriend" relation between Speaker 2 and Chandler, however, it is clear from the context that the "girl/boyfriend" relation is referring to a different pair of entities: Speaker 1 and Chandler.

One approach to encourage a model to learn the context surrounding a relation is by requiring the model to generate an explanation along with the relation (Camburu et al., 2018). In addition to the DialogRE dataset, Yu et al. (2020) introduces manually annotated *trigger words* which they show play a critical role in dialogue-based RE. They define trigger words as "the smallest span of contiguous text which clearly indicates the existence of the given relation". In the context of RE, these trigger words can be used as potential explanations.

Our work aims to extract explanations that clearly indicate a relation while also benefiting an RE model by providing cross-sentence reasoning. Our proposed approach, D-REX, makes use of multiple learning signals to train an explanation extraction model. First, D-REX utilizes trigger words as a partial supervision signal. Additionally, we pro-

[1]Code and data publicly available at https://github.com/alon-albalak/D-REX

Proceedings of the 4th Workshop on NLP for Conversational AI, pages 34 - 46
May 27, 2022 ©2022 Association for Computational Linguistics

pose multiple reward functions used with a policy gradient, allowing the model to explore the explanation space and find explanations that benefit the re-ranking model. Including these reward functions allows D-REX to learn meaningful explanations on data with less than 40% supervised triggers.

In order to predict relation- and entity-specific explanations in D-REX, we pose RE as a relation re-ranking task with explanation extraction as an intermediate step and show that this is not possible for a model trained to perform both tasks jointly.

Our contributions are summarized as follows:

- We propose D-REX, **D**ialogue **R**elation **E**xtraction with e**X**planations, a novel system trained by policy gradient and semi-supervision.
- We show that D-REX outperforms a strong baseline in explanation quality, with human evaluators preferring D-REX explanations over 90% of the time.
- We demonstrate that by conditioning on D-REX extracted explanations, relation extraction models can improve by 1.2-4.7%.

2 Problem Formulation

We follow the problem formulation of Yu et al.: let $d = (s_1 : u_1, s_2 : u_2, \ldots, s_n : u_n)$ be a dialogue where s_i and u_i denote the speaker ID and the utterance from the ith turn, respectively. Let $\mathcal{E}, \mathcal{R}$ be the set of all entities in the dialogue and the set of all possible relations between entities, respectively. Each dialogue is associated with m relational triples $<s, r, o>$ where $s, o \in \mathcal{E}$ are subject and object entities in the given dialogue and $r \in \mathcal{R}$ is a relation held between the s and o. Each relational triple may or may not be associated with a trigger t. It is important to note that there is no restriction on the number of relations held between an entity pair; however, there is at most one trigger associated with a relational triple. In this work, we consider an explanation to be of high quality if it strongly indicates that a relation holds, and for this purpose we consider triggers to be short explanations, though not always optimal in quality.

2.1 Relation Extraction (RE)

Given a dialogue d, subject s, and object o, the goal of RE is to predict the relation(s) that hold between s and o. We also consider RE with additional evidence in the form of a trigger or predicted explanation. Formally, this is the same as relation extraction with an additional explanation, ex.

2.2 Explanation Extraction (EE)

We formulate EE as a span prediction problem. Given a dialogue d consisting of n tokens T_1 through T_n, and a relational triple $<s, r, o>$, the goal of EE is to predict start and end positions, i, j in the dialogue, such that the explanation $ex = [T_i, T_{i+1}, \ldots, T_j]$ indicates that r holds between s and o.

3 Baseline Models

We first introduce approaches for RE and EE based on state-of-the-art language models. We then propose a multitask approach that performs both tasks jointly. Our approaches use $\text{BERT}_{\text{base}}$ (Devlin et al., 2019) and $\text{RoBERTa}_{\text{base}}$ (Liu et al., 2019b) pre-trained models[2], and follow their respective fine-tuning protocols.

For all models, we maintain a single input format, which follows from Yu et al.. Formally, for a dialogue d, subject s, object o, relation r, and explanation ex, the input sequence to all models is [CLS]$\{r/ex$[SEP]$\}s$[SEP]o[SEP]d, where $\{r/ex$[SEP]$\}$ denotes that the relation or explanation may be included depending on the task setting. For RoBERTa models, we use the <s> and </s> tokens rather than [CLS] and [SEP], respectively.

3.1 Relation Extraction (RE)

We follow the fine-tuning protocols of Devlin et al. and Liu et al. for BERT and RoBERTa classification models by using the output corresponding to the first token $C \in \mathbb{R}^H$ ([CLS] and <s>, respectively) as a latent representation of the entire input and train a classification matrix $W \in \mathbb{R}^{K \times H}$, where K is the number of relation types and H is the dimension of the output representations from the language model. For each relation r_i, the probability of r_i holding between s and o in d is calculated as $P_i = \text{sigmoid}(CW_i^T)$. We compute the standard cross-entropy loss for each relation as

$$\mathcal{L}_{RE} = -\frac{1}{\text{K}} \sum_{i=1}^{\text{K}} y_i \cdot \log(P_i) + (1 - y_i) \cdot \log(1 - P_i) \quad (1)$$

where y_i denotes whether relation i holds.

[2]Pre-trained models obtained from https://github.com/huggingface/transformers (Wolf et al., 2020)

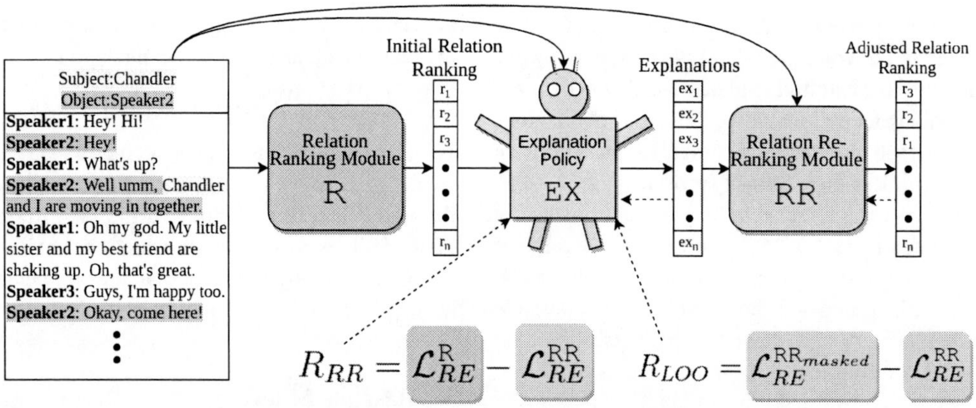

Figure 2: Overview of the D-REX system. The relation ***R****anking* module ranks relations conditioned only on the subject, object, and the dialogue. The ***EX****planation* policy extracts supporting evidence for the ranked relations by conditioning on individual relations in addition to the original input. The relation ***ReR****anking* module conditions its rankings on supporting evidence from the explanation policy. In this hypothetical example, we see that relation 3 was originally ranked number 3 but had strong supporting evidence and was re-ranked in the number 1 spot. Solid lines represent model inputs/outputs, and dotted lines represent learning signals. Reward functions, $\mathcal{R}_{RR}$ and $\mathcal{R}_{LOO}$, are detailed in equations 4 and 5, respectively.

3.2 Explanation Extraction (EE)

For EE, we use the input described above, with a natural language phrasing of a relation appended to the beginning of the sequence. For example, if r is "per:positive_impression", then we concatenate "person positive impression" to the beginning.

We follow the fine-tuning protocol of Devlin et al. for span prediction. We introduce start and end vectors, $S, E \in \mathbb{R}^H$. If $T_i \in \mathbb{R}^H$ is the final hidden representation of token i, then we compute the probability of token i being the start of the predicted explanation as a dot product with the start vector, followed by a softmax over all words in the dialogue:

$$P_{T_i}^{S} = \frac{exp(S \cdot T_i)}{\sum_j exp(S \cdot T_j)} \tag{2}$$

To predict the end token, we use the same formula and replace the start vector S with the end vector E. To compute the loss, we take the mean of the cross-entropy losses per token for the start and end vectors. Formally, let $|d|$ be the number of tokens in dialogue d, then

$$\begin{aligned}\mathcal{L}_{EX} = -\frac{1}{|d|}\sum_{i}^{|d|} \\ \big(y_i^S \cdot log(P_{T_i}^S) + (1-y_i^S)\cdot \log(1-P_{T_i}^S)\big) \\ +\big(y_i^E \cdot log(P_{T_i}^E) + (1-y_i^E)\cdot \log(1-P_{T_i}^E)\big)\end{aligned} \tag{3}$$

where y_i^S and y_i^E are the start and end labels. Because we want explanations extracted only from the dialogue, if the start or end token with largest log-likelihood occurs within the first l tokens, where l is the length of [CLS]r[SEP]s[SEP]o[SEP], then we consider there to be no predicted explanation.

3.3 Joint Relation and Explanation Model

The joint RE and EE model uses the standard input from §3. It utilizes a BERT or RoBERTa backbone, and has classification and span prediction layers identical to those in the RE and EE models. Similarly, the loss is computed as the weighted sum of RE and EE losses:

$$\mathcal{L}_{\mathcal{J}} = \alpha\mathcal{L}_{RE} + (1-\alpha)\mathcal{L}_{EX}$$

where α is an adjustable weight. In practice, we find that $\alpha = 0.5$ works best.

Flaw of the joint model The disadvantage of the joint model is this: supposing that an entity pair has 2 relations, each explanation should be paired with a single relation. However, by making predictions jointly, there is no guaranteed mapping from predicted explanations to predicted relations. One method of solving this issue is to predict relations and explanations in separate steps. It is possible to first predict relations and then condition the explanation prediction on each individual relation and conversely. This idea forms the basis for D-REX.

4 D-REX

In this section, we introduce the D-REX system. We begin by introducing the models which make up the system. Next, we present the training and inference algorithms. Finally, we discuss the optimization objectives for each model in the system.

4.1 Models

The D-REX framework requires three components: an initial relation ranking model, an explanation model, and a relation re-ranking model, shown in Figure 2.

Initial Ranking Model (*R*) In our algorithm and discussions, we use *R* to denote the initial ranking model. There are no restrictions on *R*, it can be any algorithm which ranks relations (e.g., deep neural network, rule-based, etc.) such as (Yu et al., 2020; Lee and Choi, 2021). However, if *R* needs to be trained, it must be done prior to D-REX training; D-REX will not make any updates to *R*.

In our evaluations, we use the relation extraction model described in §3.1. The input to this model is (*s*,*o*,*d*) and the output is a ranking, $R(s, o, d)$.

Explanation Extraction Model (*EX*) In our algorithm and discussions, we use *EX* to denote the explanation model. In this paper we limit our experiments to extractive explanation methods, as opposed to generative explanation methods, however this is not a limitation of D-REX. The only limitation on the explanation model is that we require it to produce human-interpretable explanations. Thus, it is also possible to use generative models such as GPT-2 (Radford et al., 2019) or graph-based methods such as (Yu and Ji, 2016; Xue et al., 2021) with adjustments to the formulation of the reward functions.

In our evaluations, we use the model as described in §3.2. The input to *EX* is (*r*,*s*,*o*,*d*) and the output is an extracted phrase from *d*, denoted as $EX(r, s, o, d)$.

Relation Re-Ranking Model (*RR*) In our algorithm and discussions, we let *RR* denote the relation re-ranking model. In the D-REX training algorithm, *RR* is updated through gradient-based optimization methods, and must be able to condition its ranking on explanations produced by *EX*. In our experiments, we use the same model architecture as *R* and include an explanation as additional input to the model. The input to *RR* is (ex,*s*,*o*,*d*) and the output is a relation ranking, denoted as $RR(ex, s, o, d)$.

Algorithm 1: The proposed training algorithm for D-REX

```
Input : Pre-trained ranking, explanation, and
        re-ranking models: R, EX, RR
        k: for number of relations to re-rank
Data: Dataset: D
for (s, r, o, t, d) in D do
    Compute ranking loss: L^R_RE(s, o, d)
    r_pred <- R(s,o,d)_1:k
    for i in r_pred do
        ex_i <- EX(r_pred_i, s, o, d)
        Compute Re-ranking loss:
          L^RR_RE(ex_i, s, o, d) ;   // Equation 1
        Compute Re-Ranking Reward: R_RR ;
          // Equation 4
        Compute Leave-one-out Reward: R_LOO ;
          // Equation 5
        Compute policy gradient with rewards
          R_RR, R_LOO ;            // Equation 6
    end
    if t not empty then
        Compute L_EX ;             // Equation 3
    end
    Update EX,RR parameters with calculated losses
end
```

4.2 D-REX Algorithm

The outline of this algorithm is shown in pseudocode in Algorithm 1.

Assuming that we have ranking, explanation, and re-ranking models *R*, *EX*, *RR*, then given a single datum (s, r, o, t, d), comprised of a subject, relation, object, trigger(may be empty), and dialogue, the D-REX algorithm operates as follows: The ranking model takes as input (s, o, d) and computes the probability of each relation from the predefined relation types. Next, we take the top-k ranked relations, $r_{pred} = R(s, o, d)_{1:k}$, and compute explanations. For $i = 1, ..., k$, explanations are computed as $ex_i = EX(r_{pred_i}, s, o, d)$. Finally, for each predicted explanation, the re-ranking model computes k probabilities for each relation type, using (ex_i, s, o, d) as the input to *RR*. The final probabilities for each relation type are computed as the mean across all k+1 predictions from *R* and *RR*.

4.3 Model optimization

We propose multiple optimization objectives to train an *EX* model that extracts explanations meaningful to humans and beneficial to the relation extraction performance while ensuring that *RR* maintains high-quality predictions.

Explanation Model Optimization We train *EX* with supervision on labeled samples, and a policy gradient for both labeled and unlabeled samples, allowing for semi-supervision. For the policy gradient, we introduce two reward functions: a relation re-ranking reward and a leave-one-out reward.

Re-ranking Reward The purpose of the re-ranking reward is to ensure that *EX* predicts explanations which benefit *RR*. Formally, let $\mathcal{L}^{R}_{RE}(s,o,d)$ be the loss for *R*, given the subject, object, and dialogue: s,o,d. And let $\mathcal{L}^{RR}_{RE}(ex,s,o,d)$ be the loss of *RR*, given the explanation, subject, object, and dialogue: ex,s,o,d. Then we define the relation re-ranking reward as:

$$\mathcal{R}_{RR} = \mathcal{L}^{R}_{RE}(s,o,d) - \mathcal{L}^{RR}_{RE}(ex,s,o,d) \quad (4)$$

Because *R* is stationary, *EX* maximizes this function by minimizing $\mathcal{L}^{RR}_{RE}$. Of course, *EX* can only minimize $\mathcal{L}^{RR}_{RE}$ through its predicted explanations.

Leave-one-out Reward The purpose of the leave-one-out reward is to direct *EX* in finding phrases which are essential to correctly classifying the relation between an entity-pair. This reward function is inspired by previous works which make use of the leave-one-out idea for various explanation purposes (Shahbazi et al., 2020; Li et al., 2016). We can calculate the leave-one-out reward using either *R* or *RR*, and it is calculated by finding the difference between the standard relation extraction loss and the loss when an explanation has been masked. Formally, if *d* is the original dialogue and ex is the given explanation, let $d_{mask}(ex)$ be the dialogue with ex replaced by mask tokens. Then, the leave-one-out reward is defined as:

$$\mathcal{R}_{LOO} = \mathcal{L}_{RE}(s,o,d_{mask}(ex)) - \mathcal{L}_{RE}(s,o,d) \quad (5)$$

Because $\mathcal{L}_{RE}$ is calculated using the same model for both the masked and unmasked loss, *EX* maximizes this reward function by maximizing the masked loss. Of course, the only interaction that *EX* has with the masked loss is through the explanation it predicts.

Policy Gradient We view *EX* as an agent whose action space is the set of all continuous spans from the dialogue. In this view, the agent interacts with the environment by selecting two tokens, a start and end token and receives feedback in the form of the previously discussed reward functions. Let i,j be the start and end indices that the explanation model selects and T_i be the ith token, then $ex = d[i:j] = [T_i, T_{i+1}, \dots, T_j]$ and the probabilities of i,j being predicted are calculated as $P^{S}_{T_i}$ and $P^{E}_{T_j}$ according to equation 2.

For both reward functions, we use a policy gradient (Sutton and Barto, 2018) to update the weights of the explanation model and calculate the loss as

$$\mathcal{L}_{EX_{PG}} = -(log(P^{S}_{T_i}) + log(P^{E}_{T_j})) * (R_{RR} + R_{LOO}) \quad (6)$$

Additionally, while training *EX* in the D-REX algorithm, we make use of supervision when available. In the case where supervision exists, we calculate an additional loss, $\mathcal{L}_{EX}$, as defined in equation 3.

Relation Extraction Re-ranking Model Optimization While training D-REX we train *RR* with labeled relations as supervision and use a cross-entropy loss, $\mathcal{L}^{RR}_{RE}$, calculated in the same way as *R* in Equation 1.

5 Experimental Evaluation

In this section, we present an evaluation of D-REX in comparison with baselines methods on the relation extraction and explanation extraction tasks.

5.1 Experimental settings

For our experiments, we re-implement the BERT_S model from (Yu et al., 2020) as well as a new version which replaces BERT with RoBERTa. In our paper, we refer to these models as R_{BERT} and R_{RoBERTa}. All models are implemented in PyTorch[3] and Transformers(Wolf et al., 2020), trained using the AdamW optimizer (Loshchilov and Hutter, 2018). All experiments were repeated five times and we report mean scores along with standard deviations. D-REX models use a top-k of five and are initialized from the best performing models with the same backbone. For example, D-REX_{BERT} uses two copies of R_{BERT} (Yu et al., 2020) to initialize the ranking and re-ranking models and EX_{BERT} to initialize the explanation model. When training *Joint*, we do not calculate $\mathcal{L}_{EX}$ for relational triples without a labeled trigger. The full details of our training settings are provided in Appendix B.

DialogRE Dataset We evaluate our models on the DialogRE English V2 dataset[4] which contains dialogues from the Friends TV show (Yu et al., 2020), details of which are in Table 1. D-REX models are trained with trigger supervision on less than 40% of the training data, and make no use of dev or test set triggers. The learning signal for the remaining triples comes entirely from our rewards through a policy gradient.

[3]https://pytorch.org/

[4]Dataset collected from https://dataset.org/dialogre/ for research purposes only

DialogRE V2			
Dial-ogues	Rela-tions	Relational Triples (train/dev/ test)	Triggers (train/dev/ test)
1788	36	6290/1992/1921	2446/830/780

Table 1: **Dataset details** for DialogRE. With only 2446 labeled triggers in the training set, D-REX models learn using only a policy gradient and no direct supervision on the remaining 3844 triples.

Model	F1(σ)	MRR(σ)
R_{BERT}	59.2(1.9)	74.8(1.3)
$Joint_{\text{BERT}}$	59.4(1.7)	74.0(0.9)
D-REX$_{\text{BERT}}$	**59.9**(0.5)	**75.4**(0.1)
R_{RoBERTa}	64.2(1.6)	77.9(1.0)
$Joint_{\text{RoBERta}}$	65.2(0.3)	78.3(0.3)
D-REX$_{\text{RoBERTa}}$	**67.2**(0.3)	**79.4**(0.3)
*GDPNet	60.2(1.0)	-
*TUCORE-GCN$_{\text{BERT}}$	65.5(0.4)	-
†SocAoG	**69.1**(0.5)	-

Table 2: **Relation extraction results on DialogRE V2.** *R* models are described in Section 3.1, *Joint* models in 3.3, and D-REX models in 4. R_{BERT} is a replication of BERT_S from Yu et al. (2020). "*" denotes results taken from Lee and Choi (2021) and "†" from Qiu et al. (2021)

Evaluation Metrics We adopt separate evaluations for relation and explanation extraction.

First, for relation extraction, we evaluate our models using F1 score, following Yu et al. (2020), and additionally calculate the mean reciprocal rank (MRR), which provides further insight into a model's performance. For example, MRR is able to differentiate between a ground truth relation ranked 2nd or 10th, while the F1 score does not. In the dialogRE dataset, multiple relations may hold between a single pair of entities, so we use a variation of MRR which considers all ground truth relations, rather than just the highest-ranked ground truth relation.

For explanation extraction, we focus mainly on manual evaluations, but also propose the Leave-One-Out metric, introduced in section 5.4 for an ablation study.

5.2 Relation Extraction (RE) Evaluation

In Table 2, we compare the baseline RE model R_{BERT} with the methods presented in this paper. We also compare with three other methods which use similarly sized language models, but additionally utilize graph neural networks (GNN): GDPNet(Xue et al., 2021), TUCORE-GCN$_{\text{BERT}}$(Lee and Choi, 2021), and SocAoG(Qiu et al., 2021).

First, we see that even though D-REX is designed to introduce human-understandable explanations, it still has modest improvements over R_{BERT}, which focuses on RE, while *Joint* has no significant improvement. Next, we see a five point absolute improvement in F1 from the baseline model when using RoBERTa. The trend from BERT to RoBERTa is similar to results found by Lee and Choi (2021), where changing from a $\text{BERT}_{\text{base}}$ model to $\text{RoBERTa}_{\text{Large}}$(not shown here) improved their model performance significantly. Additionally, we see a 3 point improvement from *R* to D-REX when using RoBERTa (compared to 0.7 for BERT), which we believe is due to the better performing ranking model, which allows for D-REX to rely more on the input explanations. Finally, we see that by using GNNs, and task-specific dialogue representations, all three GNN-based methods can improve over the general BERT-based methods.

5.3 Explanation Extraction (EE) Evaluation

Automatic Evaluation Although the aim of this paper is not trigger prediction, for completeness and reproducibility, we include results on the test set of triggers in Appendix A.

Human Evaluation To better understand how our model performs in extracting explanations and what challenges still exist, we perform two analyses; a comparative and an absolute analysis. We consider two sets of data for evaluation: samples for the DialogRE test set where **N**o **L**abeled trigger exists (***NL***) and samples where the predicted explanation **D**iffers from the **L**abeled trigger (***DL***).

5.3.1 Comparative Analysis

In Table 3, we show the results for pairwise comparisons of explanations predicted by D-REX$_{\text{RoBERTa}}$ against 3 baselines: random strings of 1-4 words, predictions from $Joint_{\text{RoBERTa}}$, and labeled triggers. For each comparison, we employ 3 crowd-workers[5], who were given the full dialogue, a natural language statement corresponding to a relational triple, and the two proposed explanations highlighted in the dialogue[6]. The crowd-workers were asked to specify which of the highlighted explanations was most indicative of the relation, or

[5]Amazon Mechanical Turk workers were paid \$0.35 per HIT, where a HIT includes 3 comparisons. We estimate an average HIT completion time of ~1.5 minutes, averaging ~\$14 per hour. We only accept workers from AUS, CA, and USA.

[6]Example HIT included in Appendix 4

D-REX$_{\text{RoBERTa}}$ vs.	Win(%)	Tie(%)	Lose(%)
Random (*NL*)	79.9	10.4	9.8
Joint$_{\text{RoBERTa}}$ (*NL*)	38.5	52.3	9.2
Ground truth (*DL*)	12.1	44.3	43.7

Table 3: **Human evaluator preferences on explanation extraction methods**. *NL* and *DL* are samples where **N**o **L**abeled trigger exists, and where the predicted explanation **D**iffers from the **L**abel, respectively. Results presented are percentages of preference.

	Not Indicative	Incorrect Entity Pair	Incorrect Relation	Indicative
NL	29	19	18	34
DL	19	13	7	61

Table 4: **Explanation error analysis** on 100 samples where **N**o **L**abeled trigger exists (*NL*) and 100 where the predicted explanation **D**iffers from the **L**abel (*DL*).

they could be equal. For each comparison we use a majority vote, and if there was a three-way tie we consider the explanations to be equal. We compare D-REX with random strings and the joint model on 174 samples from ***NL***, as well as 174 samples from ***DL***.

In Table 3 we see that for ***NL***, D-REX produces explanations which were 4.2 times more likely to be outright preferred by crowd-workers than the joint model, suggesting that our reward functions properly guided the explanation policy to learn meaningful explanations on unlabeled data. Surprisingly, we found that on over 12% of samples with labeled triggers, evaluators outright preferred D-REX explanations over the ground truth trigger, suggesting that D-REX indeed finds some explanations which are better than the ground truth trigger.

In Appendix 5.5, we include 2 examples comparing explanations from D-REX and *Joint*.

5.3.2 Absolute Analysis

To better understand the quality of D-REX's explanations, we randomly sample 100 from both ***NL*** and ***DL*** for a fine-grained analysis. We classify the explanations into 4 categories: not indicative, incorrect entity-pair, incorrect relation, and indicative. "Indicative" and "Not indicative" have the obvious meanings, "Incorrect entity-pair" means that an explanation actually explains the correct relation, but between the incorrect entity-pair, and "Incorrect relation" means that the explanation indicates a relation different from the desired relation.

Table 4 shows the results. Interestingly, we see in the ***NL*** set, that errors were equally likely to come from either an explanation indicating the relation for an incorrect entity-pair as for the incorrect relation altogether. This is in contrast to the ***DL*** set, where D-REX was nearly half as likely to predict an explanation for an incorrect relation as it was for an incorrect entity-pair.

Additionally, in our fine-grained analysis, we also considered whether a relational triple was identifiable from the context alone and found that nearly 20% of the 200 samples had ambiguities which could not be resolved without outside knowledge. This suggests that there is likely a maximum achievable relation extraction score on the DialogRE dataset under the current setting.

Model	F1	Leave-one-out(↓)
D-REX$_{\text{RoBERTa}}$ (Full)	67.2	83.9
- reranking reward	66.0	84.9
- LOO reward	67.1	85.4

Table 5: **Ablation study** on reward functions. Leave-One-Out metric (LOO) measures how salient a predicted explanation is in determining a relation and is further defined and motivated in §5.4. Smaller LOO is better.

5.4 Ablation Study

To assess the benefit of each proposed reward individually, we perform an ablation study on the reward functions. In order to study explanation quality automatically, we introduce a new metric for explanation quality; the Leave-One-Out metric.

The Leave-One-Out (LOO) metric has a theoretical basis in the works of Li et al. (2016) and Ribeiro et al. (2016), where Li et al. (2016) use word erasure to determine a "word importance score". Here we define LOO formally. For a relation extraction model R, an explanation extraction model EX, and a dataset $\mathcal{D}$, LOO is calculated as

$$LOO(R, EX, \mathcal{D}) = \frac{\text{F1}_R(\mathcal{D}_{\text{MASK}}(EX))}{\text{F1}_R(\mathcal{D})}$$

where $\text{F1}_R(\mathcal{D})$ is the F1 score of R on $\mathcal{D}$ and $\mathcal{D}_{\text{MASK}}(EX)$ is the dataset where explanations predicted by EX are replaced by mask tokens. The LOO metric calculates how essential the predicted explanations are to the ability of the relation extraction model.

To show that LOO is an appropriate measure of explanation quality, we compute the Pearson correlation coefficient between token F1 score and LOO scores for models on labeled triggers, found in Table 6. With 6 models trained on 5 random seeds each, we have 30 data points and a correlation

Dialogue	Subject Object Relation
... Speaker 1: Oh, I'm just so exhausted from dragging around this huge ***engagement ring***! ... Speaker 7: Hey, I'm sorry. I should have given you guys my black book when I got married! Although it wasn't so much a book as a...napkin. With Janice's phone number on it. ...	Janice Speaker 7 girl/boy-friend
Speaker 1: Sir? Speaker 2: What's ***in*** it? Speaker 1: Goat cheese, water chestnuts and panchetta. ... Speaker 3: Joey, it's been three days, okay. You're just a little homesick, okay. Would you just try to relax. Just try to enjoy yourself. Speaker 2: You're different here too. You're mean in England. ...	England Speaker 3 visited_by

Figure 3: Two examples comparing predicted explanations from D-REX (underlined) and *Joint* (***bold***).

coefficient of -87.4 with $p = 2.4 * 10^{-8}$. Because we calculate the coefficient with respect to human-annotated triggers, this suggests that a low LOO correlates with explanations that humans would determine as indicative of the given relation.

For our experiments, we always calculate LOO using the baseline model, R_{BERT}. From the results in Table 5, we see that both reward functions benefit the final results. Compared with R_{RoBERTa}, D-REX$_{\text{RoBERTa}}$ gains 3 F1 points, but without the reranking reward, the model only gains 1.8 F1 score or 60% of the total possible improvement. This performance loss demonstrates that the reranking reward is critical to attaining the best score in relation extraction. Similarly, without the leave-one-out reward, the model's explanation quality, measured in LOO, is 1.5 points, or nearly 10% worse, demonstrating that the leave-one-out reward is beneficial in guiding the model to salient explanations.

5.5 Explanation Samples

Figure 3 shows two samples comparing explanations from D-REX and *Joint*. In both examples, even though there was no labelled trigger, each model was able to predict an explanation which correlates with the relation. Specifically, "engagement ring" and "got married" are related to the girl/boyfriend relation, and "in" and "mean in" can be associated with the visited_by relation. However, the bottom example shows that *Joint* did not consider the context surrounding it's explanation. The conversation is about food, and the visited_by relation is not relevant. On the other hand, D-REX finds the phrase "you're mean in", where "you're" refers to speaker3, and "in" refers to "England". This is clearly an explanation which indicates the correct relation between the correct entities.

5.6 Reduced Labels

All previous results use 100% of labeled triggers in the DialogRE dataset, which covers 40% of all relational triples. To test how few labeled triggers *EX* requires in order to learn meaningful explanations we ran a small scale experiment (1 random seed) using labeled triggers from only 5, 10, and 20% of relational triples. However, in the small tests we ran, we found that at 20% labeled triggers the *EX* model mostly predicts no explanations. Furthermore, at 10% and fewer labeled triggers, the model converges to the trivial solution in the explanation space which is to never predict any tokens.

We believe that this issue is due, in part, to two challenges: the search space over all possible start/end tokens is too large, and the policy gradient has a high variance. Although these results may seem discouraging, we believe this challenge can be overcome in the future by using algorithms which reduce variance in the policy gradient and by initializing *EX* with a model pre-trained in span extraction.

6 Limitations and Future Work

Firstly, this study focuses on learning explanations as well as relations in dialogue and DialogRE is the only currently available dataset with annotations for both tasks. A limitation of this study is the small scale at which we were able to test the methods. A future direction would be to learn explanations on a different RE dataset and use the pre-trained model in D-REX, however it would be non-trivial for a model to transfer explanations learned on a wildly different domain. Additionally, it is theoretically possible to train D-REX with no labeled triggers at all, however, we were unsuccessful and in Section 5.6 we discuss these and additional negative results.

This study focuses on relations and entities found in multi-party conversations, and while there are similarities between the dialogue domain, medical literature, and wikipedia (e.g., multi-entity, multi-relation), it is not clear whether the methods from this paper can transfer to other such domains. We plan to investigate how well the proposed methods transfer to relations and entities in other domains such as news and web text (Zhang et al., 2017) and for other types of semantic relations as in Hendrickx et al. (2010) or Yao et al. (2019).

We acknowledge that this study is English-focused, and it is not clear that these methods can transfer to languages in other families such as afro-asiatic or sino-tibetan. Additionally, we think that it would be very interesting to see how these methods perform on languages with very different linguistic features; for example, languages with inflection such as Finnish. We leave non-English and multi-lingual variations of these methods to future work.

In this work, we do not focus on improving state-of-the-art trigger prediction. However, we recognize that trigger annotation is labor-intensive, and a possible use of D-REX would be to use predicted labels as a form of weak supervision for a system whose goal *is* to improve on trigger prediction.

7 Related Work

Recently, there have been numerous information extraction tasks proposed which involve dialogues, including character identification (Zhou and Choi, 2018), visual coreference resolution (Yu et al., 2019), emotion detection (Zahiri and Choi, 2018).

New settings for relation extraction have also been proposed, such as web text (Ormándi et al., 2021) and, in many ways similar to dialogue, document text (Yao et al., 2019). There have also been methods developed to include explanations in similar natural language understanding tasks (Camburu et al., 2018; Kumar and Talukdar, 2020; Liu et al., 2019a; Lei et al., 2016). There have even been methods developed which, similarly to our re-ranking, make use of an explanation as additional information (Hancock et al., 2018).

The work by Shahbazi et al. is aligned with our study. They also focus on relation extraction with explanations; however, their method is based on distant supervision from bags of sentences containing an entity-pair. Due to the cross-sentence nature of relations in dialogue, their method is not applicable here, although we draw inspiration from their work. They explain their model by considering the salience of a sentence to their model's prediction, similarly to our leave-one-out reward.

Also relevant to our work is that by Bronstein et al.. Their work focuses on the task of semi-supervised event trigger labeling, which is very similar to our semi-supervised prediction of relation explanations. In their work, they use only a small seed set of triggers and use a similarity-based classifier to label triggers for unseen event types.

Finally, there have been multiple recent works in dialogue RE which perform quite well by using graph neural networks (Xue et al., 2021; Qiu et al., 2021; Lee and Choi, 2021). However, they focus only on RE and not on explaining the relations.

8 Conclusion

In this work, we demonstrated that not only is it possible to extract relation explanations from multi-party dialogues, but these explanations can in turn be used to improve a relation extraction model. We formulated purpose-driven reward functions for training the explanation model and demonstrated their importance in learning high quality explanations. Our proposed approach, D-REX, is powered by a very simple reformulation of the traditional relation extraction task into a re-ranking task.

9 Ethical and Social Considerations

The methods proposed in this work on their own are not nefarious, however, proposed explanations should not be blindly accepted as fact. For the same reasons that language models may have ethical and social risks, so may our algorithm which is built on top of such language models. While we test only on TV show dialogues, were this technology to be put to use in non-scripted, real life conversations, there would need to be very thorough analysis of any ethical risks that the proposed explanations may have.

References

Ofer Bronstein, Ido Dagan, Qi Li, Heng Ji, and Anette Frank. 2015. Seed-based event trigger labeling: How far can event descriptions get us? In *Proceedings of the 53rd Annual Meeting of the Association for Computational Linguistics and the 7th International Joint Conference on Natural Language Processing (Volume 2: Short Papers)*, pages 372–376, Beijing, China. Association for Computational Linguistics.

Oana-Maria Camburu, Tim Rocktäschel, Thomas Lukasiewicz, and Phil Blunsom. 2018. e-snli: Natural language inference with natural language explanations. In *Advances in Neural Information Processing Systems*, volume 31. Curran Associates, Inc.

H. Chen, Pengfei Hong, Wei Han, Navonil Majumder, and Soujanya Poria. 2020. Dialogue relation extraction with document-level heterogeneous graph attention networks. *ArXiv*, abs/2009.05092.

Jacob Devlin, Ming-Wei Chang, Kenton Lee, and Kristina Toutanova. 2019. BERT: Pre-training of deep bidirectional transformers for language understanding. In *Proceedings of the 2019 Conference of the North American Chapter of the Association for Computational Linguistics: Human Language Technologies, Volume 1 (Long and Short Papers)*, pages 4171–4186, Minneapolis, Minnesota. Association for Computational Linguistics.

Xiaoyu Han and Lei Wang. 2020. A novel document-level relation extraction method based on bert and entity information. *IEEE Access*, 8:96912–96919.

Braden Hancock, Paroma Varma, Stephanie Wang, Martin Bringmann, Percy Liang, and Christopher Ré. 2018. Training classifiers with natural language explanations. In *Proceedings of the 56th Annual Meeting of the Association for Computational Linguistics (Volume 1: Long Papers)*, pages 1884–1895, Melbourne, Australia. Association for Computational Linguistics.

Iris Hendrickx, Su Nam Kim, Zornitsa Kozareva, Preslav Nakov, Diarmuid Ó Séaghdha, Sebastian Padó, Marco Pennacchiotti, Lorenza Romano, and Stan Szpakowicz. 2010. SemEval-2010 task 8: Multi-way classification of semantic relations between pairs of nominals. In *Proceedings of the 5th International Workshop on Semantic Evaluation*, pages 33–38, Uppsala, Sweden. Association for Computational Linguistics.

Sawan Kumar and Partha Talukdar. 2020. NILE : Natural language inference with faithful natural language explanations. In *Proceedings of the 58th Annual Meeting of the Association for Computational Linguistics*, pages 8730–8742, Online. Association for Computational Linguistics.

Bongseok Lee and Yong Suk Choi. 2021. Graph based network with contextualized representations of turns in dialogue. In *Proceedings of the 2021 Conference on Empirical Methods in Natural Language Processing*, pages 443–455, Online and Punta Cana, Dominican Republic. Association for Computational Linguistics.

Tao Lei, Regina Barzilay, and Tommi Jaakkola. 2016. Rationalizing neural predictions. In *Proceedings of the 2016 Conference on Empirical Methods in Natural Language Processing*, pages 107–117, Austin, Texas. Association for Computational Linguistics.

Jiwei Li, Will Monroe, and Dan Jurafsky. 2016. Understanding neural networks through representation erasure. *CoRR*, abs/1612.08220.

Hui Liu, Qingyu Yin, and William Yang Wang. 2019a. Towards explainable NLP: A generative explanation framework for text classification. In *Proceedings of the 57th Annual Meeting of the Association for Computational Linguistics*, pages 5570–5581, Florence, Italy. Association for Computational Linguistics.

Yinhan Liu, Myle Ott, Naman Goyal, Jingfei Du, Mandar Joshi, Danqi Chen, Omer Levy, Mike Lewis, Luke Zettlemoyer, and Veselin Stoyanov. 2019b. Roberta: A robustly optimized BERT pretraining approach. *CoRR*, abs/1907.11692.

Ilya Loshchilov and Frank Hutter. 2017. Fixing weight decay regularization in adam. *CoRR*, abs/1711.05101.

Ilya Loshchilov and Frank Hutter. 2018. Fixing weight decay regularization in adam.

Róbert Ormándi, Mohammad Saleh, Erin Winter, and Vinay Rao. 2021. Webred: Effective pretraining and finetuning for relation extraction on the web. *CoRR*, abs/2102.09681.

Nanyun Peng, Hoifung Poon, Chris Quirk, Kristina Toutanova, and Wen tau Yih. 2017. Cross-sentence n-ary relation extraction with graph lstms. *Transactions of the Association for Computational Linguistics*, 5:101–115.

Liang Qiu, Yuan Liang, Yizhou Zhao, Pan Lu, Baolin Peng, Zhou Yu, Ying Nian Wu, and Song-Chun Zhu. 2021. Socaog: Incremental graph parsing for social relation inference in dialogues. In *ACL/IJCNLP*.

Chris Quirk and Hoifung Poon. 2017. Distant supervision for relation extraction beyond the sentence boundary. In *Proceedings of the 15th Conference of the European Chapter of the Association for Computational Linguistics: Volume 1, Long Papers*, pages 1171–1182, Valencia, Spain. Association for Computational Linguistics.

Alec Radford, Jeff Wu, Rewon Child, David Luan, Dario Amodei, and Ilya Sutskever. 2019. Language models are unsupervised multitask learners.

Marco Tulio Ribeiro, Sameer Singh, and Carlos Guestrin. 2016. "why should i trust you?": Explaining the predictions of any classifier. In *Proceedings of the 22nd ACM SIGKDD International Conference on Knowledge Discovery and Data Mining*, KDD '16, page 1135–1144, New York, NY, USA. Association for Computing Machinery.

Hamed Shahbazi, Xiaoli Fern, Reza Ghaeini, and Prasad Tadepalli. 2020. Relation extraction with explanation. In *Proceedings of the 58th Annual Meeting of the Association for Computational Linguistics*, pages 6488–6494, Online. Association for Computational Linguistics.

Richard S Sutton and Andrew G Barto. 2018. *Reinforcement learning: An introduction.* MIT press.

Thomas Wolf, Lysandre Debut, Victor Sanh, Julien Chaumond, Clement Delangue, Anthony Moi, Pierric Cistac, Tim Rault, Rémi Louf, Morgan Funtowicz, Joe Davison, Sam Shleifer, Patrick von Platen, Clara Ma, Yacine Jernite, Julien Plu, Canwen Xu, Teven Le Scao, Sylvain Gugger, Mariama Drame, Quentin Lhoest, and Alexander M. Rush. 2020. Transformers: State-of-the-art natural language processing. In *Proceedings of the 2020 Conference on Empirical Methods in Natural Language Processing: System Demonstrations*, pages 38–45, Online. Association for Computational Linguistics.

Fuzhao Xue, Aixin Sun, Hao Zhang, and Eng Siong Chng. 2021. Gdpnet: Refining latent multi-view graph for relation extraction. In *AAAI*.

Yuan Yao, Deming Ye, Peng Li, Xu Han, Yankai Lin, Zhenghao Liu, Zhiyuan Liu, Lixin Huang, Jie Zhou, and Maosong Sun. 2019. Docred: A large-scale document-level relation extraction dataset. In *Proceedings of the 57th Annual Meeting of the Association for Computational Linguistics*, pages 764–777.

Dian Yu and Heng Ji. 2016. Unsupervised person slot filling based on graph mining. In *Proceedings of the 54th Annual Meeting of the Association for Computational Linguistics (Volume 1: Long Papers)*, pages 44–53, Berlin, Germany. Association for Computational Linguistics.

Dian Yu, Kai Sun, Claire Cardie, and Dong Yu. 2020. Dialogue-based relation extraction. In *Proceedings of the 58th Annual Meeting of the Association for Computational Linguistics*, pages 4927–4940, Online. Association for Computational Linguistics.

Xintong Yu, Hongming Zhang, Yangqiu Song, Yan Song, and Changshui Zhang. 2019. What you see is what you get: Visual pronoun coreference resolution in dialogues. In *Proceedings of the 2019 Conference on Empirical Methods in Natural Language Processing and the 9th International Joint Conference on Natural Language Processing (EMNLP-IJCNLP)*, pages 5123–5132, Hong Kong, China. Association for Computational Linguistics.

Sayyed M Zahiri and Jinho D Choi. 2018. Emotion detection on tv show transcripts with sequence-based convolutional neural networks. In *Workshops at the thirty-second aaai conference on artificial intelligence*.

Yuhao Zhang, Victor Zhong, Danqi Chen, Gabor Angeli, and Christopher D. Manning. 2017. Position-aware attention and supervised data improve slot filling. In *Proceedings of the 2017 Conference on Empirical Methods in Natural Language Processing*, pages 35–45, Copenhagen, Denmark. Association for Computational Linguistics.

Ethan Zhou and Jinho D. Choi. 2018. They exist! introducing plural mentions to coreference resolution and entity linking. In *Proceedings of the 27th International Conference on Computational Linguistics*, pages 24–34, Santa Fe, New Mexico, USA. Association for Computational Linguistics.

model	token F1(σ)	EM(σ)	LOO(σ)
EX_{BERT}	62.1(3.1)	54.1(1.9)	82.2(0.4)
$Joint_{\text{BERT}}$	43(1.3)	38.6(1.4)	89.0(1.0)
D-REX$_{\text{BERT}}$	50.5(1.1)	45.7(1.7)	84.4(1.6)
EX_{RoBERTa}	66.5(2.2)	58.4(2.0)	82.2(0.4)
$Joint_{\text{RoBERTa}}$	49(0.7)	47(0.7)	86.2(0.8)
D-REX$_{\text{RoBERTa}}$	57.2(2.1)	51.6(1.6)	83.9(0.4))

Table 6: **Trigger prediction results**. Leave-One-Out metric (LOO) measures how salient a predicted explanation is in determining a relation and is further defined in §5.4. Smaller LOO is better.

A Trigger prediction

In Table 6, we compare our methods for supervised explanation extraction with D-REX. Interestingly, we find that the joint model achieves the lowest F1 score for both the BERT and RoBERTa models. $Joint_{\text{BERT}}$ scores nearly 20 points below its counterpart BERT model, while the $Joint_{\text{RoBERTa}}$ model cuts that difference to just over 15 points below its RoBERTa counterpart. On the other hand, D-REX maintains a token F1 score within 10 points of its counterpart even though it has been trained to generalize beyond the labeled triggers.

B Hyperparameters

All models are trained using the AdamW optimizer (Loshchilov and Hutter, 2017) with a learning rate of 3*e*-5 and batch sizes of 30. To determine the best learning rate, *R* and *EX* models were trained using learning rates in {3*e*-6, 1*e*-5, 3*e*-5, 1*e*-4}. The best learning rate, 3*e*-5, was determined by performance on a held out validation dataset. Baseline models (*R*, *EX*, and *Joint*) are trained for at most 30 epochs and we use validation-based early stopping to determine which model to test. D-REX models are trained for at most 30 additional epochs with the best model determined based on relation extraction F1 scores computed on validation data. We found the best validation result to always occur within the first 30 epochs. All experiments were repeated five times and we report the mean score along with standard deviation. To train the joint model, we do not calculate $\mathcal{L}_{EX}$ for relational triples which do not have a labeled trigger and we select α from {0.25,0.5,0.75} and set α to 0.5 based on validation performance.

C Crowd-Worker Sample

In Figure 4, we show a sample HIT that was provided to crowd-workers. Each crowd-worker was shown three examples. The layour is as follows: the top always asks the worker to decide which of the highlighted texts is a better indication of the relation. Next, a natural language interpretation of the relational triple is given, in this case, "Speaker 2 and Speaker 1 are (or were) lovers". Then, we show the entire dialogue along with highlighted spans of text for each explanation. Finally, at the bottom, we always provide the user with three choices: yellow is better, equal, or orange is better, where the user is only allowed to select one option.

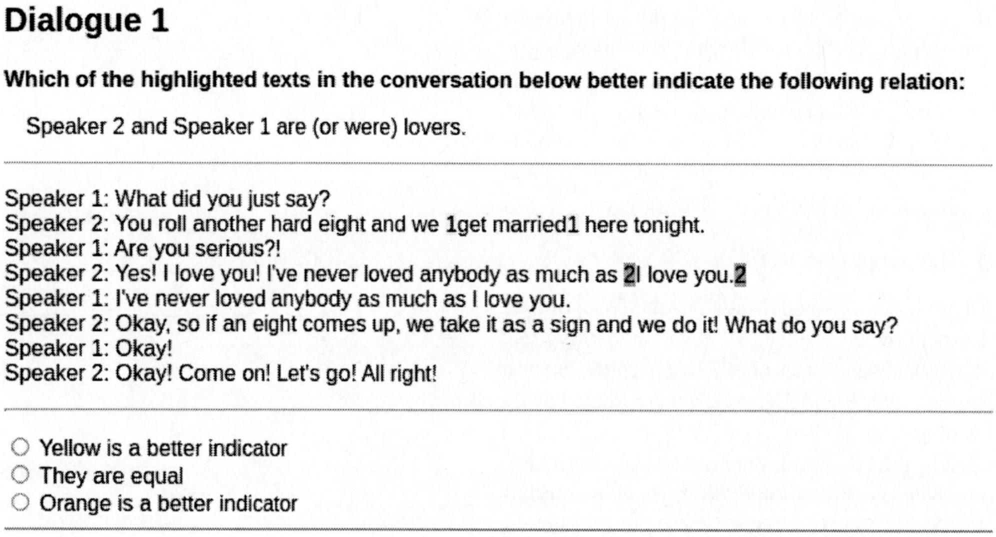

Figure 4: A sample HIT that was presented to crowd-workers for the comparative study of explanations.

Data Augmentation for Intent Classification with Off-the-shelf Large Language Models

Gaurav Sahu* University of Waterloo gsahu@uwaterloo.ca

Pau Rodriguez ServiceNow Research

Issam H. Laradji ServiceNow Research

Parmida Atighehchian ServiceNow Research

David Vazquez ServiceNow Research

Dzmitry Bahdanau ServiceNow Research

Abstract

Data augmentation is a widely employed technique to alleviate the problem of data scarcity. In this work, we propose a prompting-based approach to generate labelled training data for intent classification with off-the-shelf language models (LMs) such as GPT-3. An advantage of this method is that no task-specific LM-fine-tuning for data generation is required; hence the method requires no hyper-parameter tuning and is applicable even when the available training data is very scarce. We evaluate the proposed method in a few-shot setting on four diverse intent classification tasks. We find that GPT-generated data significantly boosts the performance of intent classifiers when intents in consideration are sufficiently distinct from each other. In tasks with semantically close intents, we observe that the generated data is less helpful. Our analysis shows that this is because GPT often generates utterances that belong to a closely-related intent instead of the desired one. We present preliminary evidence that a prompting-based GPT classifier could be helpful in filtering the generated data to enhance its quality.[1]

Input Prompt:

```
The following sentences belong to the same
category music_likeness:

Example 1: i like soft rock music
Example 2: current song rating three stars
Example 3: save this song as a favorite
Example 4: remind me that i like that song
Example 5: save my opinion on the currently
           playing song
Example 6: i love the song do you
Example 7: add the song to my favorites
Example 8: store opinion on song
Example 9: the song in background is cool
Example 10: i am the living blues
Example 11:
```

Completions:

```
i dislike classical music
she is a music lover
i am a lover of painting
this is the best song ever
video that looks like the other video
save preference on my profile
express negative opinion on the song
i am a great blues follower
the song is better than i thought
this song is also fun
```

Figure 1: **Generation Process.** Given a seed intent (here, music_likeness) and K(=10) available examples for that intent, we construct a prompt following the shown template. Note that the last line of the prompt is incomplete (there is no new line character.) We then feed this prompt to a GPT-3 engine, which generates some completions of the prompt. In this example, `red text` denotes unfaithful examples and `blue text` denotes faithful examples. **Note:** For brevity, we only show ten generated sentences.

1 Introduction

A key challenge in creating task-oriented conversational agents is gathering and labelling training data. Standard data gathering options include manual authoring and crowd-sourcing. Unfortunately, both of these options are tedious and expensive. *Data augmentation* is a widely used strategy to alleviate this problem of data acquisition.

There are two particularly promising paradigms for data augmentation in natural language processing that use pretrained language models (LMs) (Peters et al., 2018; Devlin et al., 2018). The first family of methods fine-tunes an LM on task-specific data and generates new examples using the fine-tuned LM (Wu et al., 2018; Kumar et al., 2019, 2021; Anaby-Tavor et al., 2020; Lee et al., 2021). A limitation of these methods is that, in a real-world scenario, task-specific data is scarce and fine-tuning an LM can quickly become the bottleneck. The second family of methods sidesteps this bot-

*Work done during an internship at ServiceNow Research

[1]Our code is available at: `https://github.com/ElementAI/data-augmentation-with-llms`

Proceedings of the 4th Workshop on NLP for Conversational AI, pages 47 - 57
May 27, 2022 ©2022 Association for Computational Linguistics

tleneck by employing off-the-shelf pretrained LMs such as GPT-3 (Brown et al., 2020) to directly generate text without any task-specific fine-tuning. In particular, data generation by the GPT3Mix approach by Yoo et al. (2021) boosts performance on multiple classification tasks; however, they only consider tasks with few (up to 6) classes and easy-to-grasp class boundaries (e.g., *positive* and *negative*).

This work studies the applicability of massive off-the-shelf LMs, such as GPT-3 and GPT-J (Wang and Komatsuzaki, 2021) to perform effective data augmentation for intent classification (IC) tasks. In IC, the end goal is to predict a user's intent given an utterance, i.e., what the user of a task-oriented chatbot wants to accomplish. Data augmentation for IC is particularly challenging because the generative model must distinguish between a large number (in practice up to several hundreds) of fine-grained intents that can be semantically very close to each other. Prior methods such as GPT3Mix prompt the model with the names of all classes as well as a few examples from randomly chosen classes. We test GPT3Mix for one and observe that such approaches are poorly suitable for intent classification tasks with tens or hundreds of possible intents. Instead, in this study, we use a simple prompt structure that focuses on a single seed intent (see Figure 1) as it combines the intent's name and all available examples.

Our experiments primarily focus on few-shot IC on four prominent datasets: CLINC150 (Larson et al., 2019), HWU64 (Xingkun Liu and Rieser, 2019), Banking77 (Casanueva et al., 2020), and SNIPS (Coucke et al., 2018). We also consider a partial few-shot setup to compare to the Example Extrapolation (Ex2) approach by Lee et al. (2021) who use a similar prompt but fine-tune the LM instead of using it as is. The main findings of our experiments are as follows: **(1)** GPT-generated samples boost classification accuracy when the considered intents are well-distinguished from each other (like in CLINC150, SNIPS). **(2)** On more granular datasets (namely HWU64 and Banking77), we find that GPT struggles in distinguishing between different confounding intents. **(3)** A small-scale study to further understand this behaviour suggests that GPT could be used as a classifier to filter out unfaithful examples and enhance the quality of the generated training set. Additionally, we investigate how valuable the generated data could be if relabelled by a human. Using an oracle model, we show that **(4)** the human labelling of GPT-generated examples can further improve the performance of intent classifiers, and that **(5)** LM-generated data has a higher relabelling potential compared to edit-based augmentation techniques, such as Easy Data Augmentation (EDA) (Wei and Zou, 2019).

2 Method

We consider training an intent classifier, where an intent is a type of request that the conversational agent supports; e.g. the user may want to change the language of the conversation, play a song, transfer money between accounts, etc. However, collecting many example utterances that express the same intent is difficult and expensive. Therefore, this paper experiments with a straightforward method to augment the training data available for an intent: creating prompts from the available examples and feeding them to a large language model such as GPT-3 (Brown et al., 2020). Figure 1 illustrates the process of data generation for an intent with K available examples.

3 Experimental Setup

3.1 Datasets

We use four intent classification datasets in our experiments with varying levels of granularity among intents. CLINC150 (Larson et al., 2019), HWU64 (Xingkun Liu and Rieser, 2019) are multi-domain datasets, each covering a wide range of typical task-oriented chatbot domains, such as playing music and setting up alarms. Importantly, the CLINC150 task also contains examples of out-of-scope (OOS) utterances that do not correspond to any of CLINC's 150 intents. Banking77 (Casanueva et al., 2020) is a single domain dataset with very fine-grained banking-related intents. Finally, the SNIPS (Coucke et al., 2018) dataset contains 7 intents typical for the smart speaker usecase. We refer the reader to Table 1 for exact statistics of all used datasets.

3.2 Setup

The main data-scarce setup that we consider in this work is the *few-shot setup*, where only $K = 10$ training examples are available for every intent of interest. Additionally, to compare to example extrapolation with fine-tuned language models as proposed by Lee et al. (2021), we consider a *partial*

	CLINC150	SNIPS	HWU64	Banking77
domains	10	1	18	1
intents	150	7	64	77
train examples	15000 (100)	13084	8954*	9002*
val. examples	3000 (100)	700	1076*	1001*
test examples	4500 (1000)	700	1076	3080

Table 1: Statistics of the intent classification datasets that we use in our experiments. * indicates that we split the original data into training and validation instead of using a split provided by the dataset authors. For CLINC150, the number of out-of-scope examples in different data partitions is given in parenthesis.

few-shot setup. In the latter setting, we limit the amount of training data only for a handful of *few-shot intents*[2] and use the full training data for others. When data augmentation is performed, we augment the few-shot intents to have N examples, where N is the median number of examples per intent of the original data.

To precisely describe the training and test data in all settings, we will use D_{part} to refer to dataset parts, i.e. train, validation, and test. In addition, we use D_F and D_M to refer to data-scarce and data-rich intents (the latter only occur in the partial few-shot setting). This notation is defined for all parts, therefore, $D_{part} = D_{\{F,part\}} \cup D_{\{M,part\}}$, $\forall part \in \{train, val, test\}$. When GPT-3 or a baseline method is used to augment the training data we generate $N - K$ examples per intent and refer to the resulting data as $\tilde{D}_{F,train}$. We experiment with four different-sized GPT-3 models[3] by OpenAI and GPT-J by EleutherAI[4] to obtain $\tilde{D}$. The four GPT-3 models are: Ada, Babbage, Curie, and Davinci. In order, Ada is the smallest model and Davinci is the largest. Model sizes of GPT-3 engines are not known precisely but are estimated by Eleuther AI to be between 300M and 175B parameters[5].

[2]We use the truncation heuristic provided by Lee et al. (2021): https://github.com/google/example_extrapolation/blob/master/preprocess_clinc150.py

[3]https://beta.openai.com/docs/engines

[4]https://github.com/kingoflolz/mesh-transformer-jax/

[5]https://blog.eleuther.ai/gpt3-model-sizes/

3.3 Training and Evaluation

We fine-tune BERT-large (Devlin et al., 2018) on the task of intent classification by adding a linear layer on top of the `[CLS]` token (Wolf et al., 2019). In all setups we use the original validation set for tuning the classifier's training hyperparameters. We chose to use the full validation set as opposed to a few-shot one to avoid issues with unstable hyperparameter tuning and focus on assessing the quality of the generated data.

Full few-shot. In this setup, we treat *all* the intents as few-shot and evaluate our method on the following three scenarios: (i) **Baseline**: all the intents are truncated to $K = 10$ samples per intent, (ii) **Augmented**: $\tilde{D}_{\{F,train\}}$ is generated using GPT and models are trained on $D_{\{F,train\}} \cup \tilde{D}_{\{F,train\}}$ and (iii) **EDA-baseline**: same as above, but $\tilde{D}_{\{F,train\}}$ is generated using Easy Data Augmentation (EDA) by Wei and Zou (2019). For each scenario, we report the 1) overall in-scope accuracy on the complete test set D_{test}, i.e. intent classification accuracy excluding OOS samples in the test set, and 2) few-shot classification accuracy of the models on $D_{\{F,test\}}$. For CLINC150, we also report out-of-scope recall (OOS recall) on D_{test} that we compute as the percentage of OOS examples that the model correctly labelled as such.

The purpose of this setting is to estimate what further gains can be achieved if the data generated by GPT were labelled by a human. We train an oracle $\mathcal{O}$ on the full training data D_{train}. We also use $\mathcal{O}$ to assess the quality of the generated data. Namely, we compute *fidelity* of the generated data as the ratio of generated utterances that the oracle labels as indeed belonging to the intended seed intent. A higher fidelity value means that the generated samples are more faithful to original data distribution.

Partial few-shot. In this setup, we train $\mathcal{S}$ intent classifiers, choosing different *few-shot intents* every time to obtain D_F. We then average the metrics across these $\mathcal{S}$ runs. For CLINC150, $\mathcal{S} = 10$ corresponding to the 10 different domains, whereas for SNIPS, $\mathcal{S} = 7$ corresponding to the 7 different intents. We evaluate our method on the following three scenarios introduced by Lee et al. (2021): (i) **Baseline**: models are trained without data augmentation on $D_{\{F,train\}} \cup D_{\{M,train\}}$. (ii) **Upsampled**: $D_{\{F,train\}}$ is upsampled to have N examples per intent. Then models are trained on upsampled

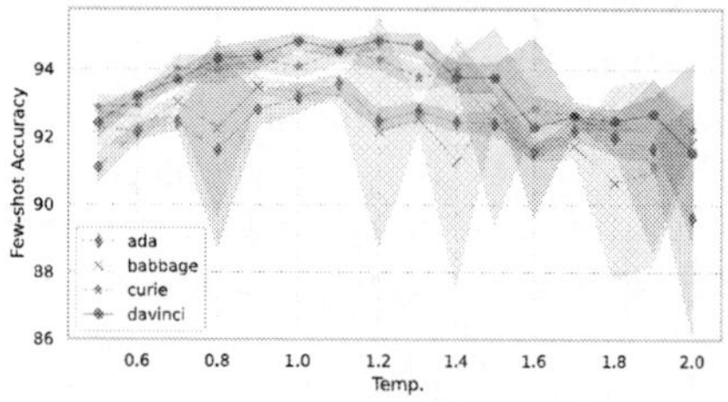

(a) Temperature v/s Few-shot accuracy

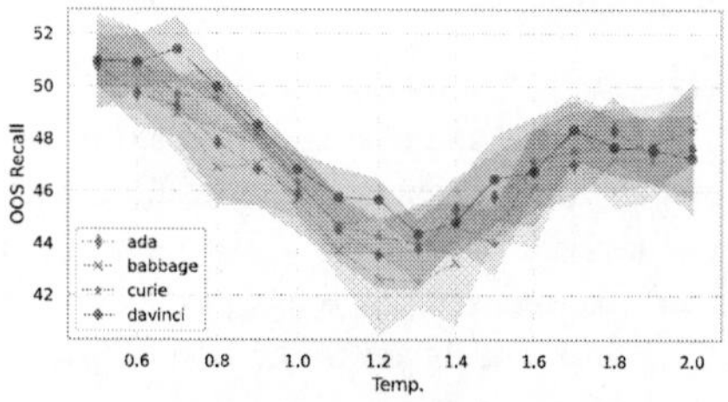

(b) Temperature v/s OOS recall

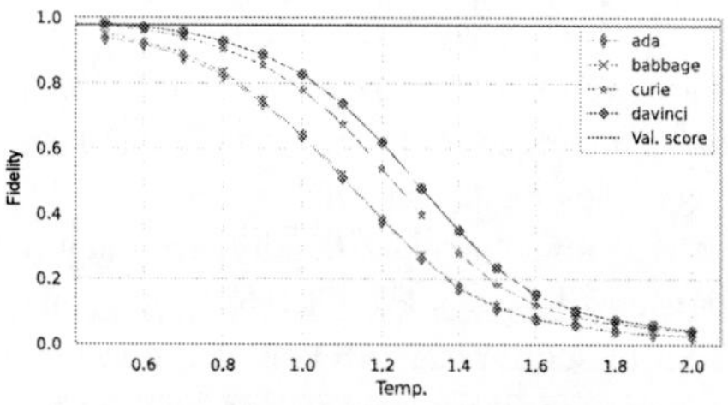

(c) Temperature v/s Fidelity

Figure 2: **Partial few-shot validation performance for different GPT-3 models and temperatures.** (a) few-shot accuracy, (b) OOS recall of intent classifiers trained on augmented sets, and (c) fidelity measured as the accuracy of the oracle on the augmented sets.

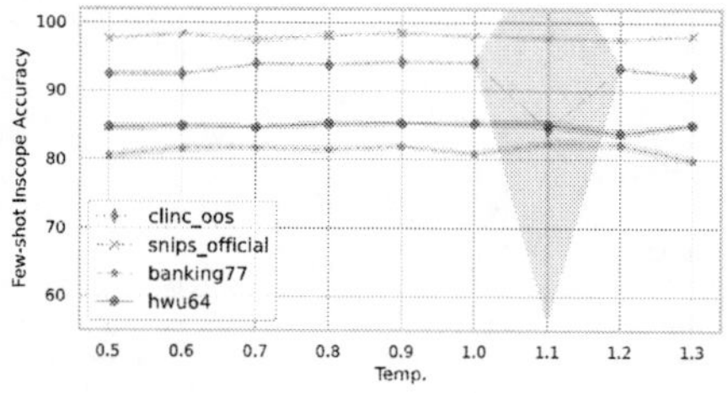

(a) Temperature v/s Few-shot inscope accuracy

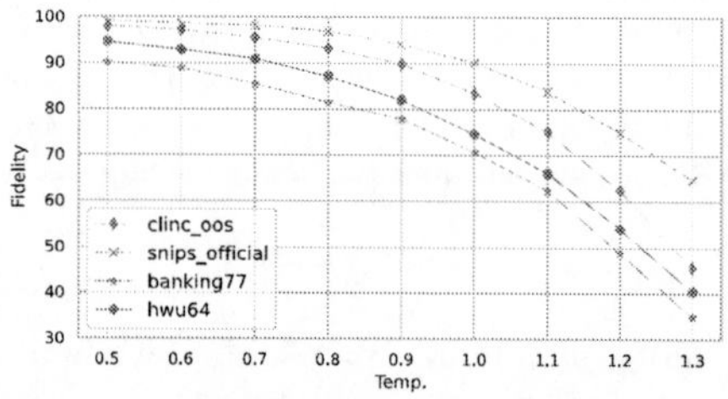

(b) Temperature v/s Fidelity

Figure 3: **Full few-shot validation performance for different GPT-J temperatures on different datasets.** (a) few-shot inscope accuracy of intent classifiers trained on augmented sets, and (b) fidelity (oracle accuracy) of augmented sets generated by GPT-J with different temperatures.

$D_{\{F,train\}} \cup D_{\{M,train\}}$. (iii) **Augmented**: models are trained on $D_{\{F,train\}} \cup \tilde{D}_{\{F,train\}} \cup D_{\{M,train\}}$. For each scenario in this setup, we report the overall in-scope classification accuracy (and OOS Recall for CLINC150).

For both partial few-shot and full few-shot settings, we report means and standard deviations over 10 repetitions of each experiment.

4 Experimental Results

Full few-shot. Table 2 shows the results of our few-shot experiments. For CLINC150 and SNIPS, data augmentation with GPT-3 is very effective as it leads to respective accuracy improvements of up to approximately 3.7% and 6% on these tasks. These improvements are larger than what the baseline EDA method brings, namely 2.4% and 2.9% for CLINC150 and SNIPS. Importantly, using larger GPT models for data augmentation brings significantly bigger gains. Data augmentation results on Banking77 and HWU64 are, however, much worse, with no or little improvement upon the plain few-shot baseline. We present a thorough investigation of this behaviour in Section 4.1. One can also see that data augmentation with GPT models lowers the OOS recall.

Next, we observe that relabelling EDA and GPT-generated sentences by the oracle gives a significant boost to accuracies across the board, confirming our hypothesis that human inspection of generated data could be fruitful. Importantly, we note that the magnitude of improvement for EDA is less than for GPT models. This suggests that GPT models generate more diverse data that can eventually be more useful after careful human inspection. Lastly, relabelling also improves OOS recall on CLINC150, which is due to the fact that much of the generated data was labelled as OOS by the oracle.

Partial few-shot. Table 3 shows the results of our partial few-shot experiments on CLINC150 and SNIPS. By augmenting the dataset with GPT-

Model	CLINC150 IA (96.93)	CLINC150 OR (42.9)	HWU64 IA (92.75)	Banking77 IA (93.73)	SNIPS IA (98.57)
EDA	92.66 (0.40)	43.81 (2.03)	83.67 (0.48)	83.96 (0.66)	92.50 (1.61)
Baseline (Ours)	90.28(0.49)	50.18(1.14)	81.43 (0.57)	83.35 (0.59)	89.69 (1.63)
Augmented					
Ada (Ours)	91.31 (0.34)	21.69 (1.57)	79.68 (0.83)	79.30 (0.42)	94.27 (0.52)
Babbage (Ours)	92.72 (0.33)	22.99 (2.39)	81.86 (0.78)	80.31 (0.41)	94.74 (0.67)
Curie (Ours)	93.37 (0.21)	25.85 (1.49)	82.85 (0.70)	83.50 (0.44)	94.73 (0.62)
GPT-J (Ours)	93.25 (0.19)	24.02 (1.45)	81.78 (0.56)	82.32 (0.90)	95.19 (0.61)
Davinci (Ours)	94.07 (0.18)	27.36 (1.08)	82.79 (0.93)	83.60 (0.45)	95.77 (0.86)
Augmented + Relabelled					
EDA	93.43 (0.22)	48.56 (1.84)	85.58 (0.73)	84.82 (0.57)	94.91 (0.66)
Ada (Ours)	95.09 (0.16)	41.38 (1.77)	88.53 (0.61)	88.45 (0.19)	97.03 (0.18)
Babbage (Ours)	95.39 (0.17)	40.58 (1.63)	89.49 (0.32)	88.86 (0.26)	96.89 (0.49)
Curie (Ours)	95.08 (0.19)	40.09 (2.38)	89.78 (0.47)	88.30 (4.64)	96.86 (0.31)
GPT-J (Ours)	95.11 (0.13)	43.94 (1.76)	89.52 (0.54)	88.94 (0.40)	97.33 (0.38)
Davinci (Ours)	95.08 (0.13)	40.76 (1.37)	89.53 (0.45)	88.89 (0.31)	97.03 (0.38)

Table 2: **Full few-shot results on CLINC150, HWU64, Banking77, and SNIPS datasets. IA**: Inscope Accuracy (mean (std)). **OR**: OOS-Recall (mean (std)). Towards the top of the table, we also report the test set performance (enclosed in parentheses) when all examples are used for fine-tuning (without any augmentation.)

		CLINC150			SNIPS	
		Overall		Few-shot	Overall	Few-shot
	Classifier	IA	OR	A	IA	A
Baseline♠	T5	97.4	-	93.7	95.2	74.0
Upsampled♠	T5	97.4	-	94.4	95.9	80.0
Augmented (Ex2)♠	T5	97.4	-	95.6	97.8	94.0
Baseline (ours)	BERT	96.28 (0.06)	39.14 (0.82)	91.36 (0.47)	95.47 (0.45)	78.38 (3.34)
Upsample (ours)	BERT	96.20 (0.05)	40.21 (0.59)	90.93 (0.19)	95.29 (0.37)	79.28 (2.05)
Augmented (Ada)	BERT	96.16 (0.05)	34.37 (0.27)	92.60 (0.15)	97.30 (0.24)	94.41 (0.72)
Augmented (Babbage)	BERT	96.39 (0.06)	35.71 (0.46)	93.66 (0.21)	97.46 (0.25)	95.31 (0.74)
Augmented (Curie)	BERT	96.41 (0.06)	36.77 (0.93)	93.90 (0.21)	97.37 (0.19)	94.79 (0.64)
Augmented (GPT-J)	BERT	96.38 (0.05)	35.91 (0.94)	93.85 (0.25)	97.59 (0.21)	96.08 (0.39)
Augmented (Davinci)	BERT	96.45 (0.03)	37.52 (0.54)	94.28 (0.24)	97.66 (0.21)	96.52 (0.35)

Table 3: **Partial few-shot results on CLINC150 and SNIPS datasets.** Refer to Section 3.3 for more details. **IA**: Inscope accuracy (mean (std)). **OR**: OOS Recall (mean (std)). **A**: Accuracy (mean (std)). ♠ (Lee et al., 2021).

generated samples, the few-shot accuracy improves by up to 2.92% on CLINC150 and 18.14% on SNIPS compared to the baseline setting. Our method achieves competitive results compared to Ex2 (Lee et al., 2021), both in terms of absolute accuracies and the relative gains brought by data augmentation. Note that Ex2 uses T5-XL (Roberts et al., 2020) with nearly 3 billion parameters as its base intent classifier, while our method uses BERT-large with only 340 million parameters.

4.1 Analysis

Effect of GPT sampling temperature. We investigate the impact of generation temperature on the quality and fidelity of generated data. We perform this investigation on the CLINC150 dataset using the partial few-shot setup. Results in Figure 2 show that, for all engines, the generated data leads to the

Davinci generated sentences	Seed Intent	Oracle Prediction
HWU64		
play a song with the word honey	music_likeness	play_music
you are playing music	music_likeness	play_music
'let me hear some of that jazz!'	music_likeness	play_music
i really like myspace music	play_music	music_likeness
i love the start lucky country music	play_music	music_likeness
thank you for the music	play_music	music_likeness
please play the next song	music_settings	play_music
play background music	music_settings	play_music
play the hour long loop of rock song	music_settings	play_music
need you to play that song one more time	play_music	music_settings
skip that song, its turkish	play_music	music_settings
pickup the beat or a temp track or audio plugin	play_music	music_settings
Banking77		
My last attempt to top up didn't seem to work, any success?	topping_up_by_card	top_up_failed
I tried to top off my wallet using my card but it says "top up failed".	topping_up_by_card	top_up_failed
I cannot top-up by my cellular phone number? How do I do that?	topping_up_by_card	top_up_failed
Can you transfer money to my Ola prepaid option? Or help me top up my card to money. They never accept my card so I always have to suffer	top_up_failed	topping_up_by_card
Hi my app is activated on activate.co.in, but unable to top up my phone. I tried credit card, debit card and Paytm but fails	top_up_failed	topping_up_by_card
I try to top up my card but it's not going through. It's still on pending status. Do I need to wait or did I do something wrong	top_up_failed	pending_top_up
I tried top-up with my card but notification shows that 'Pending'. This has been happening since last night. Can you tell me what's going on	top_up_failed	pending_top_up
Top up didn't go through.	pending_top_up	top_up_failed
Did my master card top-up fail?	pending_top_up	top_up_failed

Table 4: **Davinci-generated sentences for closely-related intents in HWU64 and Banking77 datasets.** Highlighted sub-strings indicate a difference with respect to the seed intent.

highest classification accuracy when the generation temperature is around 1.0, although lower temperatures result in higher OOS recall. We also observe that the fidelity of the generated samples decreases as we increase the temperature (i.e. higher diversity, see Figure 2c). This suggests that higher fidelity does not always imply better quality samples as the language model may simply copy or produce less diverse utterances at lower temperatures. In Appendix A, we perform a human evaluation, reaching similar conclusions as when using an oracle to approximate fidelity.

Fidelity on different datasets. Our results in Section 4 show that data augmentation gains are much higher on CLINC150 and SNIPS than on HWU64 and Banking77. To contextualize these results, we report the fidelity of GPT-J-generated data for all these tasks in Figure 3b. Across all generation temperatures, the fidelity of the generated data is higher for CLINC150 and SNIPS than for HWU64 and Banking77. For all datasets, the fidelity is higher when the generation temperature is lower; however, Figure 3a shows that low-temperature data also does improve the model's performance.

Data generation for close intents. To better understand the lower fidelity and accuracy on HWU64 and Banking77 datasets, we focus on intents with the lowest fidelities. Here, by intent fidelity, we mean the percentage of the intent's generated data that the oracle classified as indeed belonging to the seed intent. In the Banking77 dataset, the lowest-fidelity intent is "topping_up_by_card." For this intent, only 33% of the Davinci-generated sentences were labelled as "topping_up_by_card"

Fidelity (3 intents)	HWU64	Banking77
w/o filtering (468)	60.26	57.31
w/ filtering (371)	72.51	65.54
3-way accuracy		
Davinci	86.36	78.75
10-shot BERT-large	82.95	65.54
Full data BERT-large	94.32	95.00

Table 5: The impact and the accuracy of using GPT-3 as a 3-way classifier on close intent triplets from HWU64 and Banking77 datasets. For fidelity, generated examples are rejected if the GPT-3 classifier labels them as not belonging to the seed intent. Classification accuracies are reported on the reduced validation+test sets where we only consider examples from the three confounding intents.

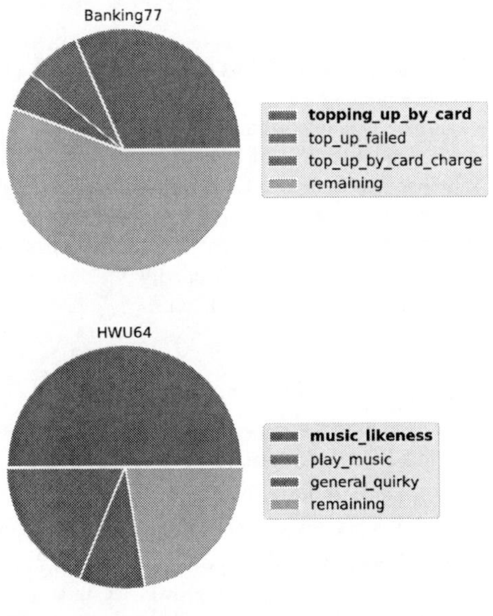

Figure 4: Distribution of labels as predicted by the oracle for lowest-fidelity intents in Banking77 and HWU64 datasets ("topping_up_by_card" and "music_likeness," respectively). Green areas denote the portion of generated sentences deemed fit by the oracle for the lowest-fidelity intents in the two datasets. Red and Blue areas respectively correspond to the most common and the second most common alternative intent predicted by the oracle.

by the oracle, implying that two-thirds of the sentences did not fit that intent, "top_up_failed" and "top_up_card_charge" being the two most common alternatives chosen by the oracle. Similarly, only 50% of the Davinci-generated sentences abide by the lowest-fidelity "music_likeness" intent in the HWU64 dataset, "play_music" and "general_quirky" being the most common intents among the "unfaithful" sentences. Figure 4 visualizes this high percentage of unfaithful generated sentences. It also shows the proportion of the two most common alternatives that the oracle preferred over the seed intent. Table 4 presents generated sentences for confounding intents in the HWU64 and Banking77 datasets. There are clear indications of mix-up of intents, e.g., Davinci generates, "play a song with the word honey," which should belong to "play_music" rather than "music_likeness." There are also instances where the LM mixes two intents; for instance, Davinci generates "Hi my app is activated on activate.co.in, but unable to top up my phone. I tried credit card, debit card and Paytm but fails," which could belong to either "topping_up_by_card" intent (as it mentions about using credit card in the context of a top up) or "top_up_failed" (as the top up ultimately fails).

4.2 Can GPT Models Understand Close Intents?

We perform extra investigations to better understand what limits GPT-3's ability to generate data accurately. We hypothesize that one limiting factor can be GPT-3's inability to understand fine-grained differences in the meanings of utterances. To verify this hypothesis, we evaluate how accurate GPT-3 is at classifying given utterances as opposed to generating new ones. Due to the limited prompt size of 2048 tokens, we can not prompt GPT-3 to predict all the intents in the considered datasets. We thus focus on the close intent triplets from HWU64 and Banking77 datasets that we use in Table 4. We compare the 3-way accuracy of a prompted GPT-3 classifier to the similarly-measured 3-way performance of conventional BERT-large classifiers. We prompt GPT-3 with 10 examples per intent (see Figure 5). For comparison, we train BERT-large classifiers on either the same 10 examples or the full training set. Table 5 shows that the Davinci version of GPT-3 performs in between the 10-shot and the full-data conventional classifiers. This suggests that while GPT-3's understanding of nuanced intent differences is imperfect, it could still be sufficient to improve the performance of the downstream few-shot model. Inspired by this finding, we experiment with using GPT-3's classification abilities to improve the quality of generated data. Namely, we reject the generated utterances that GPT-3 classifies as not belonging to the seed intent. For both HWU64 and Banking77, this filtering method significantly improves the fidelity of the generated data for the chosen close intent triplets.

4.3 Comparison with GPT3Mix

To test our initial hypothesis that prior methods such as GPT3Mix are not suitable for intent classification, we experiment with the said method on the CLINC150 dataset using Curie. Specifically, we include an enumeration of the 150 intent names in the prompt and randomly select one example for K intents. We observe a poor in-scope accuracy of 86.33% in the *Augmented* scenario[6]. Furthermore, the generated samples have low fidelity (27.96%). We also test a mixture of GPT3Mix prompt and our prompt where we include all the K examples for the seed intent instead of 1 example per K randomly sampled intents. This mixed variant also performs poorly on CLINC150 and only achieves an in-scope accuracy of 86.05%[7] and a fidelity of 33.56%. Our interpretation of this result is that GPT cannot handle the long list of 150 intent names in the prompt.

5 Related Work

The natural language processing literature features diverse data augmentation methods. Edit-based methods such as Easy Data Augmentation apply rule-based changes to the original utterances to produce new ones (Wei and Zou, 2019). In back-translation methods (Sennrich et al., 2016) available examples are translated to another language and back. Recently, data augmentation with fine-tuned LMs has become the dominant paradigm (Wu et al., 2018; Kumar et al., 2019, 2021; Anaby-Tavor et al., 2020; Lee et al., 2021). Our simpler method sidesteps LM-fine-tuning and directly uses off-she-shelf LMs as is.

The data augmentation approach that is closest to the one we use here is GPT3Mix by Yoo et al. (2021). A key part of the GPT3Mix prompt is a list of names of all possible classes (e.g. "The sentiment is one of 'positive' or 'negative'"). The LM is then expected to pick a random class from the list and generate a new example as well as the corresponding label. However, this approach does not scale to intent classification setups, which often feature hundreds of intents (see Section 4.3). Therefore, we choose a different prompt that encourages the model to extrapolate between examples of a seed intent similarly to (Lee et al., 2021).

[6]Average of 10 runs with a standard deviation of 1.17

[7]Average of 10 runs with a standard deviation of 0.59

```
Input Prompt:

Each example in the following list contains
a sentence that belongs to a category. A
category is one of the following:
music_likeness, play_music, music_settings:

sentence: next i want to hear shinedown ;
category: play_music
sentence: i am the living blues ;
category: music_likeness
sentence: open music player settings ;
category: music_settings
sentence: play hopsin from my latest
playlist ; category: play_music
sentence: i like this song ;
category:


GPT-3 Predictions:

play_music,music_likeness,music_settings,
music_likeness,music_likeness,help_command
```

Figure 5: **Using GPT-3 as a classifier.** Given a triplet of close intents, we mix and shuffle the multiple seed examples available for each of them. Then, we append an incomplete line to the prompt with just the generated sentence and feed it to GPT-3 multiple times. Among the responses, we choose the most generated in-triplet intent as the predicted intent ("music_likeness" in the above example). **Note:** For brevity, we don't show all the seed examples and predictions.

Other work on few-shot intent classification explores fine-tuning dialogue-specific LMs as classifiers as well as using similarity-based classifiers instead of MLP-based ones on top of BERT (Vulić et al., 2021). We believe that improvements brought by data augmentation would be complementary to the gains brought by these methods.

Lastly, our method to filter out unfaithful GPT generations is related to the recent work by Wang et al. (2021) that proposes using GPT3 for data labelling. A crucial difference with respect to our work, however, is that we use GPT-3 for rejecting mislabelled samples rather than proposing labels for unlabelled samples.

6 Conclusion

We propose a prompt-based method to generate intent classification data with large pretrained language models. Our experiments show that generated data can be helpful as additional labelled data for some tasks, whereas, for other tasks, the generated data needs to be either relabelled or filtered to be helpful. We show that a filtering method that recasts the same GPT model as a classifier can be effective. Our filtering method, however, requires knowing the other intents that the generated data is likely to belong to instead of the seed intent. Future work can experiment with heuristics for approximately identifying the most likely actual intents for the generated utterances. This would complete a data generation and filtering pipeline that, according to our preliminary results in Section 4.2 here, could be effective. Other filtering methods could also be applied, such as looking at the likelihood of the generated utterances as explored in a concurrent work by Meng et al. (2022). Lastly, an interesting future work direction is identifying which generated utterances most likely need a human inspection.

7 Ethical Considerations

As discussed for the GPT3Mix method in Yoo et al. (2021), using large language models for data augmentation presents several challenges: they exhibit social biases and are prone to generating toxic content. Therefore, samples generated using our prompting-based approach need to be considered carefully.

To address such ethical concerns, human inspection would be the most reliable way to identify and filter out problematic generations. The practitoners who apply our method may also consider debiasing the language model before using it for generation (Schick and Schütze, 2021).

References

Ateret Anaby-Tavor, Boaz Carmeli, Esther Goldbraich, Amir Kantor, George Kour, Segev Shlomov, Naama Tepper, and Naama Zwerdling. 2020. Do Not Have Enough Data? Deep Learning to the Rescue! *Proceedings of the AAAI Conference on Artificial Intelligence*, 34(05):7383–7390.

Tom B. Brown, Benjamin Mann, Nick Ryder, Melanie Subbiah, Jared Kaplan, Prafulla Dhariwal, Arvind Neelakantan, Pranav Shyam, Girish Sastry, Amanda Askell, Sandhini Agarwal, Ariel Herbert-Voss, Gretchen Krueger, Tom Henighan, Rewon Child, Aditya Ramesh, Daniel M. Ziegler, Jeffrey Wu, Clemens Winter, Christopher Hesse, Mark Chen, Eric Sigler, Mateusz Litwin, Scott Gray, Benjamin Chess, Jack Clark, Christopher Berner, Sam McCandlish, Alec Radford, Ilya Sutskever, and Dario Amodei. 2020. Language Models are Few-Shot Learners. *arXiv:2005.14165 [cs]*. ArXiv: 2005.14165.

Iñigo Casanueva, Tadas Temčinas, Daniela Gerz, Matthew Henderson, and Ivan Vulić. 2020. Efficient intent detection with dual sentence encoders. In *Proceedings of the 2nd Workshop on Natural Language Processing for Conversational AI*, pages 38–45, Online. Association for Computational Linguistics.

Alice Coucke, Alaa Saade, Adrien Ball, Théodore Bluche, Alexandre Caulier, David Leroy, Clément Doumouro, Thibault Gisselbrecht, Francesco Caltagirone, Thibaut Lavril, Maël Primet, and Joseph Dureau. 2018. Snips Voice Platform: an embedded Spoken Language Understanding system for private-by-design voice interfaces. *arXiv:1805.10190 [cs]*. ArXiv: 1805.10190.

Jacob Devlin, Ming-Wei Chang, Kenton Lee, and Kristina Toutanova. 2018. BERT: Pre-training of Deep Bidirectional Transformers for Language Understanding. In *Proceedings of the 2019 Conference of the North American Chapter of the Association for Computational Linguistics, NAACL 2019*.

Varun Kumar, Ashutosh Choudhary, and Eunah Cho. 2021. Data Augmentation using Pre-trained Transformer Models. *arXiv:2003.02245 [cs]*. ArXiv: 2003.02245.

Varun Kumar, Hadrien Glaude, Cyprien de Lichy, and Wlliam Campbell. 2019. A Closer Look At Feature Space Data Augmentation For Few-Shot Intent Classification. In *Proceedings of the 2nd Workshop on Deep Learning Approaches for Low-Resource NLP (DeepLo 2019)*, pages 1–10, Hong Kong, China. Association for Computational Linguistics.

Stefan Larson, Anish Mahendran, Joseph J. Peper, Christopher Clarke, Andrew Lee, Parker Hill, Jonathan K. Kummerfeld, Kevin Leach, Michael A. Laurenzano, Lingjia Tang, and Jason Mars. 2019. An Evaluation Dataset for Intent Classification and Out-of-Scope Prediction. In *Proceedings of the 2019 Conference on Empirical Methods in Natural Language Processing and the 9th International Joint Conference on Natural Language Processing (EMNLP-IJCNLP)*, pages 1311–1316, Hong Kong, China. Association for Computational Linguistics.

Kenton Lee, Kelvin Guu, Luheng He, Tim Dozat, and Hyung Won Chung. 2021. Neural Data Augmentation via Example Extrapolation. *arXiv:2102.01335 [cs]*. ArXiv: 2102.01335.

Yu Meng, Jiaxin Huang, Yu Zhang, and Jiawei Han. 2022. Generating training data with language models: Towards zero-shot language understanding. *arXiv preprint arXiv:2202.04538*.

Matthew E. Peters, Mark Neumann, Mohit Iyyer, Matt Gardner, Christopher Clark, Kenton Lee, and Luke

Zettlemoyer. 2018. Deep Contextualized Word Representations. In *Proceedings of the 2018 Conference of the North American Chapter of the Association for Computational Linguistics, NAACL-HLT 2018*. ArXiv: 1802.05365.

Adam Roberts, Colin Raffel, and Noam Shazeer. 2020. How much knowledge can you pack into the parameters of a language model? In *Proceedings of the 2020 Conference on Empirical Methods in Natural Language Processing (EMNLP)*, pages 5418–5426, Online. Association for Computational Linguistics.

Timo Schick and Hinrich Schütze. 2021. Exploiting Cloze Questions for Few Shot Text Classification and Natural Language Inference. *arXiv:2001.07676 [cs]*. ArXiv: 2001.07676.

Rico Sennrich, Barry Haddow, and Alexandra Birch. 2016. Improving Neural Machine Translation Models with Monolingual Data. In *Proceedings of the 54th Annual Meeting of the Association for Computational Linguistics (Volume 1: Long Papers)*, pages 86–96, Berlin, Germany. Association for Computational Linguistics.

Ivan Vulić, Pei-Hao Su, Samuel Coope, Daniela Gerz, Paweł Budzianowski, Iñigo Casanueva, Nikola Mrkšić, and Tsung-Hsien Wen. 2021. ConvFiT: Conversational fine-tuning of pretrained language models. In *Proceedings of the 2021 Conference on Empirical Methods in Natural Language Processing*, pages 1151–1168, Online and Punta Cana, Dominican Republic. Association for Computational Linguistics.

Ben Wang and Aran Komatsuzaki. 2021. GPT-J-6B: A 6 Billion Parameter Autoregressive Language Model. `https://github.com/kingoflolz/mesh-transformer-jax`.

Shuohang Wang, Yang Liu, Yichong Xu, Chenguang Zhu, and Michael Zeng. 2021. Want To Reduce Labeling Cost? GPT-3 Can Help. *arXiv:2108.13487 [cs]*. ArXiv: 2108.13487.

Jason Wei and Kai Zou. 2019. EDA: Easy Data Augmentation Techniques for Boosting Performance on Text Classification Tasks. In *Proceedings of the 2019 Conference on Empirical Methods in Natural Language Processing and the 9th International Joint Conference on Natural Language Processing (EMNLP-IJCNLP)*, pages 6382–6388, Hong Kong, China. Association for Computational Linguistics.

Thomas Wolf, Lysandre Debut, Victor Sanh, Julien Chaumond, Clement Delangue, Anthony Moi, Pierric Cistac, Tim Rault, Rémi Louf, Morgan Funtowicz, et al. 2019. Huggingface's transformers: State-of-the-art natural language processing. *arXiv preprint arXiv:1910.03771*.

Xing Wu, Shangwen Lv, Liangjun Zang, Jizhong Han, and Songlin Hu. 2018. Conditional BERT Contextual Augmentation. *arXiv:1812.06705 [cs]*. ArXiv: 1812.06705.

Pawel Swietojanski Xingkun Liu, Arash Eshghi and Verena Rieser. 2019. Benchmarking natural language understanding services for building conversational agents. In *Proceedings of the Tenth International Workshop on Spoken Dialogue Systems Technology (IWSDS)*, pages xxx–xxx, Ortigia, Siracusa (SR), Italy. Springer.

Kang Min Yoo, Dongju Park, Jaewook Kang, Sang-Woo Lee, and Woomyoung Park. 2021. GPT3Mix: Leveraging large-scale language models for text augmentation. In *Findings of the Association for Computational Linguistics: EMNLP 2021*, pages 2225–2239, Punta Cana, Dominican Republic. Association for Computational Linguistics.

Appendix

A Human Evaluation

In Figure 2 we evaluate the fidelity of the samples generated by GPT-3 with respect to the original set of sentences used to prompt it. Fidelity is approximated by the classification performance of an "oracle" intent classifier trained on the whole dataset ($D_{train} \cup D_{test}$) and evaluated over the generated samples. In order assess whether the oracle predictions are comparable to those of a human, we perform a human evaluation study.

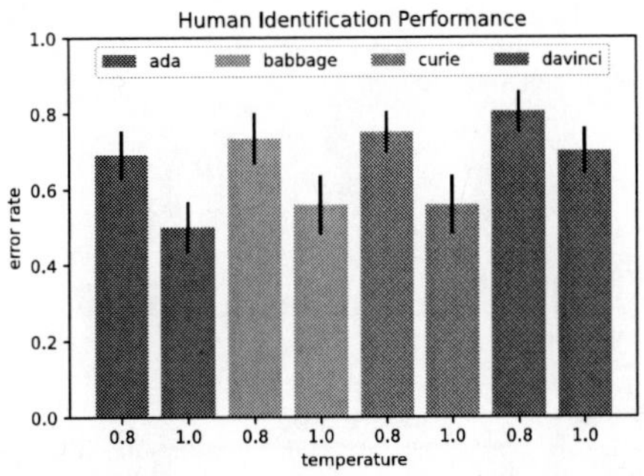

Figure 6: **Human evaluation.** Error rate of human evaluators at the task of finding whether any sentence in a group of 5 was generated by GPT-3 or not. Each color represents a different GPT-3 engine. Higher error rate indicates that humans could not correctly identify generated samples and thus it also indicates higher fidelity. The standard error is displayed as a vertical line on top of each bar.

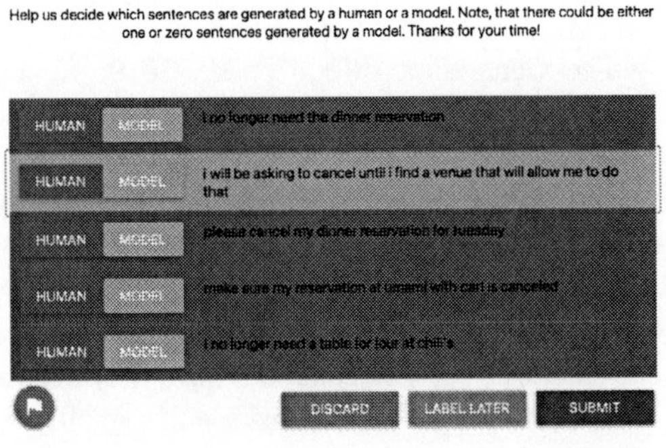

Figure 7: **Human evaluation tool.** Example of a question for the human evaluators. Human evaluators are asked to flag which example is GPT-3 generated if any among the 5 presented ones.

We consider that a model produces sentences with high fidelity if a human is unable to distinguish them from a set of human-generated sentences belonging to the same intent. Therefore, for each intent in the CLINC150 dataset, we sample five random examples and we randomly choose whether to replace one of them by a GPT-3 generated sentence from the same intent. We generate sentences with each of the four GPT-3 models considered in the main text with two different temperatures (0.8 and 1.0). The sentence to replace is randomly selected. Finally, the five sentences are displayed to a human who has to choose which of the sentences is generated by GPT-3, if any.

The task is presented to human evaluators in the form of a web application (see Figure 7). We placed a button next to each sentence in order to force human evaluators to individually consider each of the examples. Once annotated, the evaluator can either *submit, discard,* or leave the task to *label later.* We used a set of 15 voluntary evaluators from multiple backgrounds, nationalities, and genders. Each evaluator annotated an average of 35 examples, reaching a total of 500 evaluated tasks.

For each model and temperature, we report the error rate of humans evaluating whether a task contains a GPT-generated sample. We consider that evaluators succeeds at a given task when they correctly find the sentence that was generated by GPT or when they identify that none of them was generated. Thus, the error rate for a given model and temperature is calculated as #failed / total_evaluated.

Results are displayed in Figure 6. We find that human evaluators tend to make more mistakes when the temperature used to sample sentences from GPT-3 is smaller. This result is expected since lowering the temperature results in sentences closer to those prompted to GPT-3, which are human-made. We also observe that models with higher capacity such as `Davinci` tend to generate more indistinguishable sentences than lower-capacity models such as `Ada`, even for higher temperatures. These results are in agreement with the "oracle" fidelity results introduced in Figure 2.

Extracting and Inferring Personal Attributes from Dialogue

Zhilin Wang*, Xuhui Zhou, Rik Koncel-Kedziorski, Alex Marin, Fei Xia
University of Washington, *Nvidia
{zhilinw, xuhuizh, kedzior, amarin, fxia}@uw.edu

Abstract

Personal attributes represent structured information about a person, such as their hobbies, pets, family, likes and dislikes. We introduce the tasks of extracting and inferring personal attributes from human-human dialogue, and analyze the linguistic demands of these tasks. To meet these challenges, we introduce a simple and extensible model that combines an autoregressive language model utilizing constrained attribute generation with a discriminative reranker. Our model outperforms strong baselines on extracting personal attributes as well as inferring personal attributes that are not contained verbatim in utterances and instead requires commonsense reasoning and lexical inferences, which occur frequently in everyday conversation. Finally, we demonstrate the benefit of incorporating personal attributes in social chit-chat and task-oriented dialogue settings.

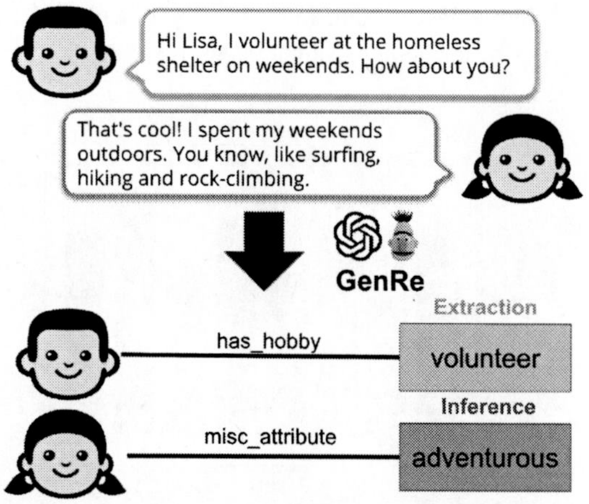

Figure 1: Overview of obtaining personal attribute triple from utterances using our model GenRe. Attribute values are contained within the utterance in the EXTRACTION task, but not the INFERENCE task.

1 Introduction

Personal attributes are structured information about a person, such as what they like, what they have, and what their favorite things are. These attributes are commonly revealed either explicitly or implicitly during social dialogue as shown in Figure 1, allowing people to know more about one another. These personal attributes, represented in the form of knowledge graph triples (*e.g.* I, has_hobby, volunteer), can represent large numbers of personal attributes in an interpretable manner, facilitating their usage by weakly-coupled downstream dialogue tasks (Li et al., 2014; Qian et al., 2018; Zheng et al., 2020a,b; Hogan et al., 2021).

One such task is to ground open-domain chit-chat dialogue agents to minimize inconsistencies in their language use (*e.g.*, **I like cabbage** →(next turn) →**Cabbage is disgusting**) and make them engaging to talk with (Li et al., 2016; Zhang et al., 2018; Mazaré et al., 2018; Qian et al., 2018; Zheng et al., 2020a,b; Li et al., 2020; Majumder et al., 2020). Thus far, personalization in chit-chat has made use of dense embeddings and natural language sentences. While KG triples have been shown to be capable of grounding Natural Language Generation (Moon et al., 2019; Koncel-Kedziorski et al., 2019), they have yet to be used to personalize chit-chat dialogue agents.

Personal attributes can also help task-oriented dialogue agents to provide personalized recommendations (Mo et al., 2017; Joshi et al., 2017; Luo et al., 2019; Lu et al., 2019; Pei et al., 2021). Such personalized recommendations have only been attempted for single-domain tasks with a small set of one-hot features (< 30). Personalization across a wide range of tasks (recommending food, movies and music by multi-task dialogue agents such as Alexa, Siri and Assistant) however can require orders of magnitude more personal attribute features. This makes KG triples ideal for representing them, given the advantages of this data structure for models to select and utilize pertinent features (Li et al.,

Proceedings of the 4th Workshop on NLP for Conversational AI, pages 58 - 69
May 27, 2022

2014; Hogan et al., 2021).

Based on these advantages, we investigate how personal attributes can be predicted from dialogue. An important bottleneck for this step lies in the poor coverage of relevant personal attributes in existing labeled datasets. Therefore, we introduce two new tasks for identifying personal attributes in Section 2. As shown in Figure 1, the EXTRACTION task requires determining which phrase in an utterance indicate a personal attribute, while the INFERENCE task adds further challenge by requiring models to predict personal attributes that are not explicitly stated verbatim in utterances. This is common in conversational settings, where people express personal attributes using a variety of semantically related words or imply them using commonsense reasoning. We analyze how these factors allow personal attributes to be linked to utterances that express them.

To tackle these tasks, we propose a simple yet extensible model, **GenRe**, in Section 3. GenRe combines a constrained attribute generation model (that is flexible to accommodate attributes not found verbatim in utterances) with a discriminative reranker (that can contrast between highly similar candidates). Our experiments in Section 4 suggest that such design allows our model to outperform strong baseline models on both the EXTRACTION and INFERENCE tasks. Subsequently in Section 5, detailed ablation studies demonstrate the value of our model components while further analysis identifies future areas for improvement.

Finally in Section 6, we show how personal attributes in the form of KG triples can improve the personalization of open-domain social chit-chat agents as well as task-oriented dialogue agents. In the former case, personal attributes can be utilized to improve chat-bot consistency on the PersonaChat task (Zhang et al., 2018). In the latter case, we suggest how our personal attributes can support personalization in multi-task, task-oriented dialogue settings.

2 Personal Attribute Tasks

Based on the usefulness of personal attributes for dialogue personalization, we propose the task of obtaining personal attributes from natural language sentences. We first explain how we formulate two complementary tasks from DialogNLI data and then formally define our tasks. Finally, we analyze the task datasets to gather insights into the linguistic phenomena that our tasks involve.

2.1 Source of Personal Attributes

DialogNLI (Welleck et al., 2019) contains samples of PersonaChat utterances (Zhang et al., 2018) in English, each paired with a manually annotated personal attribute triple. Each triple consists of a head entity, a relation, and a tail entity. These triples were initially annotated to identify entailing, contradicting and neutral statements within the PersonaChat corpus. For instance, a statement labelled with (I, [favorite_color], blue) will contradict with another statement labelled with (I, [favorite_color], green). The three largest groups of relations are: a. *has_X* (where X = *hobby, vehicle, pet*) b. *favourite_Y* (where Y = *activity, color, music*) c. *like_Z* (where Z = *read, drink, movie*).

2.2 Extraction and Inference Tasks

By re-purposing the DialogNLI dataset, our tasks seek to extract these personal attribute triples from their paired utterances. We first used a script that obtains pairs of personal triples and utterances. Next, we combined relations with similar meanings such as *like_food* and *favourite_food* and removed under-specified relations such as *favourite, have* and *others*. Finally, we removed invalid samples with triples containing *None* or *<blank>* and removed prefix numbers of tail entities (*e.g.* 11 dogs), since the quantity is not important for our investigation.

We formulate two tasks by partitioning the DialogNLI dataset into two non-overlapping subsets. Here, each **sample** refers to a sentence paired with an annotated triple. Train/dev/test splits follow DialogNLI, with descriptive statistics shown in Table 1. The dataset for the EXTRACTION task contains samples in which both the head and tail entities are spans inside the paired sentence. An example is (I, [has_profession], receptionist) from the sentence "I work as a receptionist in my day job". We formulate the EXTRACTION task in a similar way to existing Relation Extraction tasks such as ACE05 (Wadden et al., 2019) and NYT24 (Nayak and Ng, 2020). This allows us to apply modeling lessons learned from Relation Extraction.

The complementary set is the dataset for the INFERENCE task, for which the head entity and/or the tail entity cannot be found as spans within the paired sentence. This is important in real-world conversations because people do not always express their personal attributes explicitly and instead

	EXTRACTION	INFERENCE
Samples		
train	22911	25328
dev.	2676	2658
test	2746	2452
Unique elements		
head entities	88	109
relations	39	39
tail entities	2381	2522
Avg. words		
head entities	1.03	1.08
relations	1.00	1.00
tail entities	1.20	1.28
sentences	12.9	12.2

Table 1: Statistics of the dataset for the two tasks.

use paraphrasing and commonsense reasoning to do so. An example of a paraphrased triple is (I, [physical_attribute], tall) from the sentence "I am in the 99th height percentile", while one based on commonsense reasoning is (I, [want_job], umpire) from the sentence "my ultimate goal would be calling a ball game".

The INFERENCE task is posed as a challenging version of the EXTRACTION task that tests models' ability to identify pertinent information in sentences and then make commonsense inferences/paraphrases based on such information. An existing task has sought to predict personal attributes that are not always explicitly found within sentences (Wu et al., 2019). However, it did not distinguish between personal attributes that can be explicitly found within sentences (*i.e.* EXTRACTION) from those that cannot (*i.e.* INFERENCE) . We believe that, given that the inherent difficulty of identifying the two types of personal attributes are greatly different, it is helpful to pose them as two separate tasks. In this way, the research community can first aim for an adequate performance on the simpler task before applying lessons to make progress at the more challenging task. This is also the first time that personal attributes that are not explicitly contained in sentences are shown to be derivable from words in the sentence using commonsense/lexical inferences.

2.3 Formal Task Definition

Given a sentence S, we want to obtain a personal-attribute triple in the form of `(head entity, relation, tail entity)`. The relation must belong to a set of 39 predefined relations. In the EXTRACTION subset, the head entity and tail entity are spans within S. Conversely, in the INFERENCE subset, the head entity and/or the tail entity cannot be found as spans within S.

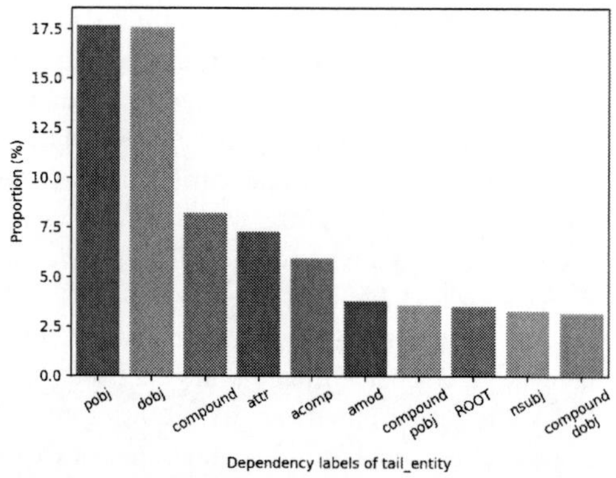

Figure 2: Bar plot for 10 most common dependency role labels of tail entities within sentences

2.4 Dataset Analysis

We analyze the datasets to obtain insights into how the tasks can be approached. Because the majority of head entities (93.3%) are simply the word "I", our analysis will focus on tail entities.

Dataset for the EXTRACTION task We use dependency parses of sentences to understand the relationship between words within tail entities and the sentence ROOT. Dependency parsing was chosen because it is a well-studied syntactic task (Nivre et al., 2016) and previously used for the relation extraction task (Zhang et al., 2017). Dependency parses and labels associated with each dependent word were identified using a pre-trained transformer model from spaCy.[1] The parser was trained on data annotated with the ClearNLP dependency schema that is similar to Universal Dependencies (Nivre et al., 2016).[2]

As shown in Figure 2, objects of prepositions (pobj) and direct objects (dobj) each comprise 17.5% of tail entities, followed by compound words (compound), attributes (attr) and adjectival complements (acomp), plus 138 other long-tail labels. The range of grammatical roles as well as the fact that one third of tail entities do not involve nouns

[1] https://spacy.io/

[2] https://github.com/clir/clearnlp-guidelines/blob/master/md/specifications/dependency_labels.md

Transformation	Example (sentence→tail entity)	%
ConceptNet_related	mother →female	**71.3**
ConceptNet_connect	wife →married	56.8
WordNet_synonym	outside →outdoors	39.5
WordNet_hypernym	drum →instrument	5.04
WordNet_hyponym	felines →cats	4.17
Same_stem	swimming →swim	43.3

Table 2: Proportion (%) of tail entities that can be related to sentence words after applying each transformation.

(see Figure in Section A.2) also suggest that the tail entities in our dataset go beyond proper nouns, which are what many Relation Extraction datasets (*e.g.*, ACE05 and NYT24) are mainly concerned with. Such diversity in grammatical roles played by tail entities means that approaches based on rule-based extraction, parsing or named entity recognition alone are unlikely to be successful in the EXTRACTION task.

Dataset for the INFERENCE task A qualitative inspection of the dataset showed that inferences can be made on the basis of semantically-related words and commonsense inferences, as shown in examples discussed in Section 2.2. To better understand how tail entities can be inferred from the sentence in the INFERENCE subset, we analyze the relationship between words in the tail entity and words in the sentence. 79.2% of tail entities cannot be directly identified in the sentence. We performed a few transformations to identify potential links between the tail entity and the sentence. *ConceptNet_connect* refers to words with highest-weighted edges on ConceptNet to sentence words while *ConceptNet_related* refers to words that have closest embedding distances to sentence words. Details of their preparation are in Appendix A.3. As in Table 2, our analysis shows that a model that can perform well on the INFERENCE task requiring both WordNet semantic knowledge (Fellbaum, 1998) as well as ConceptNet commonsense knowledge (Speer et al., 2017).

3 GenRe

This section proposes GenRe, a model that uses a unified architecture for both the EXTRACTION and the INFERENCE tasks. We use a simple and extensible generator-reranker framework to address the needs of the two tasks. On one hand, a generative model is necessary because head and/or tail entities cannot be directly extracted from the sentence for the INFERENCE dataset. On the other hand, preliminary experiments using a Generator in isolation showed that a large proportion of correct triples are among the top-k - but not top-1 - outputs. A Reranker can be used to select the most likely triple among the top-k candidate triples, leading to a large improvement in performance (see Table 4).

3.1 Generator

We use an autoregressive language model (GPT-2 small) as our Generator because its extensive pre-training is useful in generating syntactically and semantically coherent entities. The small model was chosen to keep model size similar to baselines. We finetune this model to predict a personal attribute triple occurring in a given input sentence. Specifically, we treat the flattened triples as targets to be predicted using the original sentence as context. The triple is formatted with control tokens to distinguish the head entity, relation, and tail entity as follows:

$$\mathbf{y} = \text{[HEAD]}, t^{head}_{1:m}, \text{[RELN]}, t^{reln}, \text{[TAIL]}, t^{tail}_{1:k}$$

where {[HEAD],[RELN], [TAIL]} are control tokens, $t^{head}_{1:m}$ is the head entity (a sequence of length m), t^{reln} is a relation, and $t^{tail}_{1:k}$ is the tail entity.

During evaluation, we are given a sentence as context and seek to generate a personal attribute triple in the flattened format as above. To reduce the search space, we adopt a constrained generation approach. Specifically, after the [RELN] token, only one of 39 predefined relations can be generated, and so the output probability of all other tokens is set to 0. After the [TAIL] token, all output tokens not appearing in the input sentence will have zeroed probabilities in the EXTRACTION task. Conversely for the INFERENCE task, the only allowed output tokens after the [TAIL] token are those which have appeared following the predicted relation in the training data. For example, tail entities that can be generated with a [physical_attribute] relation include "short", "skinny" or "wears glasses", as these examples occur in the training data. We imposed this restriction to prevent the model from hallucinating attributes that are not associated to the predicted relation (such as "dog" with [physical_attribute]). Despite limiting the model's ability to generate novel but compatible tail entities (and thereby upper-bounding maximum possible recall to 75.7%), this approach helped to improve model performance overall. Implementation details are in Appendix A.4.

3.2 Reranker

We use BERT-base as the Reranker because its bi-directionality allows tail tokens to influence the choice of relation tokens. Furthermore, BERT has demonstrated the best commonsense understanding among pre-trained language models (Petroni et al., 2019; Zhou et al., 2020). These benefits have led to many relation extraction models using BERT as part of the pipeline (Wadden et al., 2019; Yu et al., 2020; Ye et al., 2021).

For each S, we obtain the L most likely sequences using the Generator, including the context sentence. Each sequence is labelled as correct or incorrect based on whether the predicted triple (head entity, relation, tail entity) matches exactly the ground-truth triple. Incorrect sequences serve as challenging negative samples for the Reranker because they are extremely similar to the correct sequence since they were generated together. We fine-tune a BERT model with a binary cross-entropy loss function to classify whether sequences are correct. During inference, we select the sequence with the highest likelihood of being correct as our predicted sequence. We set L to 10 in all experiments. Implementation details are in Appendix A.5.

4 Experiments

We first explain the metrics used in the experiments. Next, we introduce the baseline models. Finally, we examine how GenRe compares to baseline models to understand its advantages.

4.1 Metrics

Micro-averaged Precision/Recall/F1 were calculated following Nayak and Ng (2020), in which a sample is considered correct only when all three elements (head_entity, relation and tail entity) are resolved correctly. We chose these metrics because we are interested in the proportion of all predicted personal attributes that have been correctly identified (precision) and of all ground truth personal attributes (recall). F1 is considered as an aggregate metric for precision and recall.

4.2 Baseline Models

Generative models can be used for both the EXTRACTION and the INFERENCE tasks.

WDec is an encoder-decoder model that achieved state-of-the-art performance in the NYT24 and NYT29 tasks (Nayak and Ng, 2020). The encoder is a Bi-LSTM, while the decoder is an LSTM with attention over encoder states. An optional copy mechanism can be used: when used, the decoder will only generate tokens found in the original sentence. The copy mechanism was used on the EXTRACTION dataset but not on the INFERENCE dataset (given their better empirical performance).

GPT2 is an autoregressive language model that we build GenRe on. We use the same configuration as in GenRe.

Extractive models can be used only for the EXTRACTION task, because they select for head and tail entities from the original sentence.

DyGIE++ is a RoBERTa-based model that achieved state-of-the-art performance in multiple relation extraction tasks including ACE05 (Wadden et al., 2019). It first extracts spans within the original sentence as head and tail entities. Then, it pairs up these entities with a relation and passes them through a graph neural network, with the head and tail entities as the nodes, and relations as the edges. This allows information flow between related entities before passing the triple through a classifier.

PNDec is an Encoder-Decoder model that achieved close to SOTA performance in NYT24 and NYT29 (Nayak and Ng, 2020). It uses the same encoder as WDec but uses a pointer network to identify head and tail entities from the original sentence, which it pairs with possible relation tokens to form a triple that is subsequently classified.

All baseline models were trained on our datasets using their suggested hyper-parameters.

4.3 Model Results

The top-performing baseline models on the EXTRACTION dataset are the extractive models, which select spans within the sentence and classify whether an entire triple is likely to be correct. Because there are only a small number of spans within the sentence, this approach can effectively limit its search space. On the other hand, extractive models cannot solve the INFERENCE task, because the underlying assumption that head and tail entities must be found within the sentence does not hold. Conversely, generative models perform more poorly on the Extraction task but are capable on the INFER-

	EXTRACTION			INFERENCE		
	P	R	F1	P	R	F1
GenRe	**68.0**	**52.4**	**59.2**	**46.5**	**35.4**	**39.2**
Generative						
WDec	57.0	49.0	52.7	33.6	34.7	34.1
GPT2	50.9	31.1	38.6	31.3	17.3	22.3
Extractive						
DyGIE++	60.8	50.9	55.3			
PNDec	63.1	49.5	55.5			

Table 3: Performance on the test set. GenRe has significantly higher mean F1 than all baseline models with 5 runs based on a two-tailed t-test ($p < 0.05$).

	EXTRACTION			INFERENCE		
	P	R	F1	P	R	F1
GenRe	68.0	52.4	59.2	46.5	35.4	39.2
- Constr. Gen	53.5	40.7	46.2	37.2	27.1	31.4
- Reranker	67.6	41.0	51.0	31.0	22.3	25.9

Table 4: Ablation study for Reranker and constrained generation.

ENCE task. This is because generation happens in a left-to-right manner, meaning that some elements of the triple have to be generated without knowing what the other elements are. Our approach of linking a Generative model with a BERT-base Reranker (akin to models used by Extractive approaches) combines the best of both worlds. Not only does it perform well on the Extraction task ($\geq$ 3.7 F1 points over baselines), it also excels on the Inference task ($\geq$ 5.1 F1 points over baselines).

5 Analysis

We first conduct an ablation study to better understand the contribution of constrained generation and the Reranker, by measuring the performance of our model when each component is removed. Then, we seek to understand how errors are made on predicted personal attribute relations to identify future areas of improvement.

5.1 Ablation Study

Table 4 shows that both the Reranker and constrained generation contribute to the performance of GenRe. In particular, the constrained generation plays a larger role on the EXTRACTION dataset while the Reranker plays a greater role on the INFERENCE dataset.

Constrained generation has a large impact on the EXTRACTION dataset (+13.0% F1), likely because it very much restricts the generation search space to spans from the context sentence. On the INFERENCE dataset, the original search space cannot be effectively limited to tokens in the context sentence. Therefore, applying the heuristic that only tail entities associated with a particular relation (in the training set) can be decoded is useful, even though it upper bounds maximum recall to 75.7%, which is much higher than the achieved 35.4%. Compared to the EXTRACTION dataset, the improvement on the INFERENCE dataset is smaller (+7.8% F1), since the range of tail entities that can be decoded after imposing the constraint is greater.

The Reranker is needed because, many times, the correct triple can be generated by the Generator but might not be the triple that is predicted to have the highest likelihood. The maximum possible recall on the EXTRACTION and INFERENCE tasks increases from 41.0% to 59.9% and 22.3% to 41.0% respectively when considering top-10 instead of only top-1 generated candidate. While the achieved recall (52.4% and 35.4% respectively) are still a distance from the maximum possible recall, the achieved recall is much higher than using the Generator alone.

5.2 Misclassification of Relations

Major sources of error on the EXTRACTION dataset came from relation tokens that have close semantic meanings. They either were related to one another (*e.g.*, [has_profession] vs [want_job]) or could be correlated with one another (*e.g.*, [like_animal] vs [have_pet] or [like_music] vs [favorite_music_artist]) , as illustrated in Table 5. Such errors likely arose due to the way that the DialogNLI dataset (Welleck et al., 2019) was annotated. Specifically, annotators were asked to label a single possible triple given a sentence instead of all applicable triples. Because of this, our evaluation metrics are likely to over-penalize models when they generate reasonable triples that did not match the ground truth. Future work can avoid this problem by labelling all possible triples and framing the task as multilabel learning.

6 Applications of Personal Attributes

Personal attributes can make social chit-chat agents more consistent and engaging as well as enable task-oriented agents to make personalized recommendations. In this section, we use personal at-

Dataset	True Relation (n)	P	R	F1	Predicted Relations	Top 3 Most Frequent (n) True Tail Entities	Predicted Tail Entities
EXTRACTION	[has_profession] (274)	83.8	62.0	71.3	[has_profession] (189) [employed_by_general] (30) [want_job] (17)	teacher (29) nurse (28) real estate agent (25)	nurse (27) real estate (25) teacher (19)
	[have_pet] (149)	97.3	55.0	70.3	[have_pet] (88) [have_family] (18) [like_animal] (12)	dog (55) cat (45) pets (22)	cat (32) pets (23) dog (18)
INFERENCE	[like_food] (77)	46.7	41.6	44.0	[like_food] (62) [like_activity] (5) [like_animal] (4)	pizza (18) onion (9) italian (7)	pizza (19) italian cuisine (10) onion (8)
	[like_music] (71)	40.8	23.9	30.2	[like_music] (40) [favorite_music_artist] (9) [like_activity] (7)	jazz (10) country (9) rap (6)	the story so far (12) country (8) jazz (7)

Table 5: Some relations in EXTRACTION and INFERENCE datasets

tributes to improve chit-chat agent consistency and provide information for personalizing task-oriented dialogue agents.

6.1 Consistency in Chit-chat agents

PersonaChat (Zhang et al., 2018) was created to improve the personality consistency of open-domain chit-chat dialogue agents. PersonaChat was constructed by giving pairs of crowdworkers a set of English personal attribute related sentences and asking them to chat in a way that is congruent with those sentences. Models were then trained to generate dialogue responses that are in line with those expressed by crowdworkers using the provided persona information as context.

Methods We fine-tune the generative version of Blender 90M (a transformer-based model trained on multiple related tasks) on PersonaChat, which is currently the state-of-the-art generative model on this task (Roller et al., 2020) and uses personal attribute sentences to ground dialogue response generation. Building on Blender, we prepend a corresponding DialogNLI personal attribute before each utterance (*i.e.* **+Per. Attr.**), in order to better direct the model in generating a suitable response that is consistent with the set persona. This modification is relatively minimal to demonstrate the informativeness of personal attribute KG triples, while keeping the model architecture and hyperparameter fine-tuning the same as in the original work (details in Appendix A.1).

Metrics We follow Roller et al. (2020) and Dinan et al. (2019). Metrics for **+Per. Attr.** setting consider both personal attributes and utterances. **Hits@1** uses the hidden states of the generated output to select the most likely utterance amongst 20 candidates (the correct utterance and 19 randomly chosen utterances from the corpus). **Perplexity** reflects the quality of the trained language model. **F1** demonstrates the extent of the overlap between the generated sequence and the ground truth sequence.

	Hits@1 ↑	Perplexity ↓	F1 ↑
Blender	32.3	11.3	20.4
+ Per. Attr.	35.2*	10.4*	20.6*

Table 6: Effects of using personal attributes to augment Blender on Personachat. Higher is better for Hits@1 and F1; lower is better for perplexity. *Significantly different from Blender with 5 runs based on a two-tailed t-test ($p<0.05$).

Fact 1	I love cats and have two cats
Fact 2	I've a hat collection of over 1000 hats.
Blender	My cats names are all the hats i have
+ Per. Attr.	My cats are called kitties
Fact 1	I am a doctor.
Fact 2	My daughter is a child prodigy.
Blender	My daughter is prodigy so she gets a lot of accidents.
+ Per. Attr.	I've seen a lot of accidents.

Table 7: Examples of incorrect utterances generated by Blender by mixing up two facts, which are avoided by our Blender + Per. Attr. model

Results As shown in Table 6, including personal attributes can improve performance on the PersonaChat task. An inspection of the generated utterances suggests that including personal attributes into Blender can more effectively inform the model which persona statement to focus on during generation. This can prevent Blender from including information in irrelevant persona statements (*e.g.* by mixing up facts from two unrelated persona statements), as in Table 7.

Dataset	Domains	#Unique features
Ours	Restaurants, Movies, Music, Sports, Recreation, Shopping	5583
Ours	Restaurants *only*	206
Joshi et al. (2017)	Restaurants	30
Mo et al. (2017)	Restaurants	10
Lu et al. (2019)	Shopping	7

Table 8: Domains covered by various datasets for personalizing task-oriented dialogue. #Uniques features refers to the number of unique attribute-values (*e.g.* the specific food people like) that can be used for personalization.

6.2 Personalization in Task-oriented dialogue

While personalization has been incorporated into single-task settings (Joshi et al., 2017; Mo et al., 2017; Luo et al., 2019; Lu et al., 2019; Pei et al., 2021), there has been no attempt for personalization in multi-task settings. This is against the background in which multi-task dialogue is rapidly becoming the standard in task-oriented dialogue evaluation (Byrne et al., 2019; Rastogi et al., 2019; Zang et al., 2020; Shalyminov et al., 2020). To overcome this gap, we show how our dataset can lay a foundational building block for personalization in multi-task dialogue.

Methods We used several popular datasets on multi-task task-oriented dialogue (Zang et al., 2020; Shalyminov et al., 2020; Byrne et al., 2019; Rastogi et al., 2019). From each dataset, we manually observed its tasks and categorized them into several overarching domains, as shown in Table 8. We then created a mapping between the various domains and datasets available for personalizing task-oriented dialogue (including ours). Domains that are not supported by any dataset are omitted.

Results Compared to existing datasets in Table 8, our dataset is capable of personalizing recommendations in a much larger number of domains. These domains include restaurants and shopping, which have been explored by existing datasets, as well as movies, music, sports and recreation, which have thus far been overlooked. For domains that have been previously explored, such as restaurants, our dataset contains a more diverse set of possible personal attribute values (*e.g.* the foods people like), which can support it to personalize recommendations in more realistic manners.

7 Related Work

Personal Attribute Extraction: Most work on extracting personal attributes from natural language (Pappu and Rudnicky, 2014; Mazaré et al., 2018; Wu et al., 2019; Tigunova et al., 2019, 2020) employed distant supervision approaches using heuristics and hand-crafted templates, which have poor recall. In contrast, we use a strong supervision approach in which triples were manually annotated. Li et al. (2014) and Yu et al. (2020) attempted to extract personal information from dialogue using a strongly supervised paradigm. However, they focused on demographic attributes as well as interpersonal relationships, which contrast with our focus on what people own and like. Li et al. (2014) used SVMs to classify relations and CRFs to perform slot filling of entities while Yu et al. (2020) used BERT to identify relations between given entities.
Generating KG triple using Language Models: Autoregressive language models have been applied to a wide range of tasks involving the generation of data with similar structures as personal attribute KG triples, including dialogue state tracking (Hosseini-Asl et al., 2020) and commonsense KG completion (Bosselut et al., 2019). The most similar application is Alt et al. (2019), which used the original GPT model (Radford and Narasimhan, 2018) for relation classification. Their task formulation involves identifying a specific relation (out of around 30 possible options) for two given entities. On the other hand, our tasks seek to identify not only the relation, but also the head and tail entities, which have potentially open vocabulary requirements, which makes them much harder.

8 Conclusion

In conclusion, we propose the novel tasks of extracting and inferring personal attributes from dialogue and carefully analyze the linguistic demands of these tasks. To meet the challenges of our tasks, we present GenRe, a model which combines constrained attribute generation and re-ranking on top of pre-trained language models. GenRe achieves the best performance vs. established Relation Extraction baselines on the Extraction task ($\geq$ 3.7 F1 points) as well as the more challenging INFERENCE task that involves lexical and commonsense inferences ($\geq$ 5.1 F1 points). Together, our work contributes an important step towards realizing the potential of personal attributes in personalization of social chit-chat and task-oriented dialogue agents.

Acknowledgments

We thank Noah Smith, Waleed Ammar, Massimilliano Ciaramita, Dongqi Su, Weizhe Lin and many others at UW-NLP and beyond for insight discussions.

Ethics and Broader Impact

Privacy in real world applications We inspected a selection of the Dialog NLI dataset to ensure it contains no real names, personally-identifying information or offensive content. Because our task involves extracting and inferring personal attributes, real-world users should be given the option to disallow particular types of relations from being collected and/or used for downstream applications. Users should also be given the freedom to delete their collected personal attributes. A further step might be to restrict the extraction and storage of personal attributes to only local devices using differential privacy and federated learning techniques.

References

Christoph Alt, Marc Hübner, and Leonhard Hennig. 2019. Improving relation extraction by pre-trained language representations. In *Automated Knowledge Base Construction (AKBC)*.

Antoine Bosselut, Hannah Rashkin, Maarten Sap, Chaitanya Malaviya, Asli Çelikyilmaz, and Yejin Choi. 2019. Comet: Commonsense transformers for automatic knowledge graph construction. In *Proceedings of the 57th Annual Meeting of the Association for Computational Linguistics (ACL)*.

Bill Byrne, Karthik Krishnamoorthi, Chinnadhurai Sankar, Arvind Neelakantan, Daniel Duckworth, Semih Yavuz, Ben Goodrich, Amit Dubey, Kyu-Young Kim, and Andy Cedilnik. 2019. Taskmaster-1: Toward a realistic and diverse dialog dataset.

Emily Dinan, Varvara Logacheva, Valentin Malykh, Alexander Miller, Kurt Shuster, Jack Urbanek, Douwe Kiela, Arthur Szlam, Iulian Serban, Ryan Lowe, Shrimai Prabhumoye, Alan W Black, Alexander Rudnicky, Jason Williams, Joelle Pineau, Mikhail Burtsev, and Jason Weston. 2019. The second conversational intelligence challenge (convai2).

Christiane Fellbaum. 1998. *WordNet: An Electronic Lexical Database*. Bradford Books.

Aidan Hogan, Eva Blomqvist, Michael Cochez, Claudia d'Amato, Gerard de Melo, Claudio Gutierrez, José Emilio Labra Gayo, Sabrina Kirrane, Sebastian Neumaier, Axel Polleres, Roberto Navigli, Axel-Cyrille Ngonga Ngomo, Sabbir M. Rashid, Anisa Rula, Lukas Schmelzeisen, Juan Sequeda, Steffen Staab, and Antoine Zimmermann. 2021. Knowledge graphs.

Ehsan Hosseini-Asl, Bryan McCann, Chien-Sheng Wu, Semih Yavuz, and Richard Socher. 2020. A simple language model for task-oriented dialogue.

Chaitanya K. Joshi, Fei Mi, and Boi Faltings. 2017. Personalization in goal-oriented dialog.

Rik Koncel-Kedziorski, Dhanush Bekal, Yi Luan, Mirella Lapata, and Hannaneh Hajishirzi. 2019. Text Generation from Knowledge Graphs with Graph Transformers. In *Proceedings of the 2019 Conference of the North American Chapter of the Association for Computational Linguistics: Human Language Technologies, Volume 1 (Long and Short Papers)*, pages 2284–2293, Minneapolis, Minnesota. Association for Computational Linguistics.

Aaron W. Li, Veronica Jiang, Steven Y. Feng, Julia Sprague, Wei Zhou, and Jesse Hoey. 2020. Aloha: Artificial learning of human attributes for dialogue agents. *Proceedings of the AAAI Conference on Artificial Intelligence*, 34(05):8155–8163.

Jiwei Li, Michel Galley, Chris Brockett, Georgios Spithourakis, Jianfeng Gao, and Bill Dolan. 2016. A persona-based neural conversation model. In *Proceedings of the 54th Annual Meeting of the Association for Computational Linguistics (Volume 1: Long Papers)*, pages 994–1003, Berlin, Germany. Association for Computational Linguistics.

X. Li, G. Tur, D. Hakkani-Tür, and Q. Li. 2014. Personal knowledge graph population from user utterances in conversational understanding. In *2014 IEEE Spoken Language Technology Workshop (SLT)*, pages 224–229.

Yichao Lu, Manisha Srivastava, Jared Kramer, Heba Elfardy, Andrea Kahn, Song Wang, and Vikas Bhardwaj. 2019. Goal-oriented end-to-end conversational models with profile features in a real-world setting. In *Proceedings of the 2019 Conference of the North American Chapter of the Association for Computational Linguistics: Human Language Technologies, Volume 2 (Industry Papers)*, pages 48–55, Minneapolis, Minnesota. Association for Computational Linguistics.

Liangchen Luo, Wenhao Huang, Qi Zeng, Zaiqing Nie, and Xu Sun. 2019. Learning personalized end-to-end goal-oriented dialog. *Proceedings of the AAAI Conference on Artificial Intelligence*, 33(01):6794–6801.

Bodhisattwa Prasad Majumder, Harsh Jhamtani, Taylor Berg-Kirkpatrick, and Julian McAuley. 2020. Like hiking? you probably enjoy nature: Persona-grounded dialog with commonsense expansions. In *Proceedings of the 2020 Conference on Empirical Methods in Natural Language Processing (EMNLP)*, pages 9194–9206, Online. Association for Computational Linguistics.

Pierre-Emmanuel Mazaré, Samuel Humeau, Martin Raison, and Antoine Bordes. 2018. Training millions of personalized dialogue agents. In *Proceedings of the 2018 Conference on Empirical Methods in Natural Language Processing*, pages 2775–2779, Brussels, Belgium. Association for Computational Linguistics.

A. H. Miller, W. Feng, A. Fisch, J. Lu, D. Batra, A. Bordes, D. Parikh, and J. Weston. 2017. Parlai: A dialog research software platform. *arXiv preprint arXiv:1705.06476*.

Kaixiang Mo, Shuangyin Li, Yu Zhang, Jiajun Li, and Qiang Yang. 2017. Personalizing a dialogue system with transfer reinforcement learning.

Seungwhan Moon, Pararth Shah, Anuj Kumar, and Rajen Subba. 2019. OpenDialKG: Explainable conversational reasoning with attention-based walks over knowledge graphs. In *Proceedings of the 57th Annual Meeting of the Association for Computational Linguistics*, pages 845–854, Florence, Italy. Association for Computational Linguistics.

Tapas Nayak and Hwee Tou Ng. 2020. Effective modeling of encoder-decoder architecture for joint entity and relation extraction. *Proceedings of the AAAI Conference on Artificial Intelligence*, 34(05):8528–8535.

Joakim Nivre, Marie-Catherine de Marneffe, Filip Ginter, Yoav Goldberg, Jan Hajič, Christopher D. Manning, Ryan McDonald, Slav Petrov, Sampo Pyysalo, Natalia Silveira, Reut Tsarfaty, and Daniel Zeman. 2016. Universal Dependencies v1: A multilingual treebank collection. In *Proceedings of the Tenth International Conference on Language Resources and Evaluation (LREC'16)*, pages 1659–1666, Portorož, Slovenia. European Language Resources Association (ELRA).

Aasish Pappu and Alexander Rudnicky. 2014. Knowledge acquisition strategies for goal-oriented dialog systems. In *Proceedings of the 15th Annual Meeting of the Special Interest Group on Discourse and Dialogue (SIGDIAL)*, pages 194–198, Philadelphia, PA, U.S.A. Association for Computational Linguistics.

Jiahuan Pei, Pengjie Ren, and Maarten de Rijke. 2021. A cooperative memory network for personalized task-oriented dialogue systems with incomplete user profiles. *arXiv preprint arXiv:2102.08322*.

Fabio Petroni, Tim Rocktäschel, Sebastian Riedel, Patrick Lewis, Anton Bakhtin, Yuxiang Wu, and Alexander Miller. 2019. Language models as knowledge bases? In *Proceedings of the 2019 Conference on Empirical Methods in Natural Language Processing and the 9th International Joint Conference on Natural Language Processing (EMNLP-IJCNLP)*, pages 2463–2473, Hong Kong, China. Association for Computational Linguistics.

Martin F Porter. 1980. An algorithm for suffix stripping. *Program*, 14(3):130–137.

Qiao Qian, Minlie Huang, Haizhou Zhao, Jingfang Xu, and Xiaoyan Zhu. 2018. Assigning personality/profile to a chatting machine for coherent conversation generation. In *Proceedings of the Twenty-Seventh International Joint Conference on Artificial Intelligence, IJCAI-18*, pages 4279–4285. International Joint Conferences on Artificial Intelligence Organization.

A. Radford and Karthik Narasimhan. 2018. Improving language understanding by generative pre-training.

Abhinav Rastogi, Xiaoxue Zang, Srinivas Sunkara, Raghav Gupta, and Pranav Khaitan. 2019. Towards scalable multi-domain conversational agents: The schema-guided dialogue dataset. *arXiv preprint arXiv:1909.05855*.

Stephen Roller, Emily Dinan, Naman Goyal, Da Ju, Mary Williamson, Yinhan Liu, Jing Xu, Myle Ott, Kurt Shuster, Eric M. Smith, Y-Lan Boureau, and Jason Weston. 2020. Recipes for building an open-domain chatbot.

Igor Shalyminov, Alessandro Sordoni, Adam Atkinson, and Hannes Schulz. 2020. Fast domain adaptation for goal-oriented dialogue using a hybrid generative-retrieval transformer. In *2020 IEEE International Conference on Acoustics, Speech and Signal Processing (ICASSP)*.

Robyn Speer, Joshua Chin, and Catherine Havasi. 2017. Conceptnet 5.5: An open multilingual graph of general knowledge. In *Proceedings of the Thirty-First AAAI Conference on Artificial Intelligence*, AAAI'17, page 4444–4451. AAAI Press.

Anna Tigunova, Andrew Yates, Paramita Mirza, and Gerhard Weikum. 2019. Listening between the lines: Learning personal attributes from conversations.

Anna Tigunova, Andrew Yates, Paramita Mirza, and Gerhard Weikum. 2020. CHARM: Inferring personal attributes from conversations. In *Proceedings of the 2020 Conference on Empirical Methods in Natural Language Processing (EMNLP)*, pages 5391–5404, Online. Association for Computational Linguistics.

David Wadden, Ulme Wennberg, Yi Luan, and Hannaneh Hajishirzi. 2019. Entity, relation, and event extraction with contextualized span representations. In *Proceedings of the 2019 Conference on Empirical Methods in Natural Language Processing and the 9th International Joint Conference on Natural Language Processing (EMNLP-IJCNLP)*, pages 5784–5789, Hong Kong, China. Association for Computational Linguistics.

Sean Welleck, Jason Weston, Arthur Szlam, and Kyunghyun Cho. 2019. Dialogue natural language inference. In *Proceedings of the 57th Annual Meeting of the Association for Computational Linguistics*, pages 3731–3741, Florence, Italy. Association for Computational Linguistics.

Chien-Sheng Wu, Andrea Madotto, Zhaojiang Lin, Peng Xu, and Pascale Fung. 2019. Getting to know you: User attribute extraction from dialogues. *arXiv preprint arXiv:1908.04621*.

Hongbin Ye, Ningyu Zhang, Shumin Deng, Mosha Chen, Chuanqi Tan, Fei Huang, and Huajun Chen. 2021. Contrastive triple extraction with generative transformer.

Dian Yu, Kai Sun, Claire Cardie, and Dong Yu. 2020. Dialogue-based relation extraction. In *Proceedings of the 58th Annual Meeting of the Association for Computational Linguistics*, pages 4927–4940, Online. Association for Computational Linguistics.

Xiaoxue Zang, Abhinav Rastogi, Srinivas Sunkara, Raghav Gupta, Jianguo Zhang, and Jindong Chen. 2020. Multiwoz 2.2: A dialogue dataset with additional annotation corrections and state tracking baselines. In *Proceedings of the 2nd Workshop on Natural Language Processing for Conversational AI, ACL 2020*, pages 109–117.

Saizheng Zhang, Emily Dinan, Jack Urbanek, Arthur Szlam, Douwe Kiela, and Jason Weston. 2018. Personalizing dialogue agents: I have a dog, do you have pets too? In *Proceedings of the 56th Annual Meeting of the Association for Computational Linguistics (Volume 1: Long Papers)*, pages 2204–2213, Melbourne, Australia. Association for Computational Linguistics.

Yuhao Zhang, Victor Zhong, Danqi Chen, Gabor Angeli, and Christopher D. Manning. 2017. Position-aware attention and supervised data improve slot filling. In *Proceedings of the 2017 Conference on Empirical Methods in Natural Language Processing (EMNLP 2017)*, pages 35–45.

Yinhe Zheng, Guanyi Chen, Minlie Huang, Song Liu, and Xuan Zhu. 2020a. Personalized dialogue generation with diversified traits.

Yinhe Zheng, Rongsheng Zhang, Minlie Huang, and Xiaoxi Mao. 2020b. A pre-training based personalized dialogue generation model with persona-sparse data. *Proceedings of the AAAI Conference on Artificial Intelligence*, 34(05):9693–9700.

Xuhui Zhou, Yue Zhang, Leyang Cui, and Dandan Huang. 2020. Evaluating commonsense in pre-trained language models. *Proceedings of the AAAI Conference on Artificial Intelligence*, 34(05):9733–9740.

A Appendix

A.1 Blender Fine-tuning Details

Finetuning hyperparameters are taken from https://parl.ai/projects/recipes/, with the exception of validation metric changed to Hits@1. Each fine-tuning epoch takes 1.5 hours on a Nvidia V100 GPU. We only prepend personal attributes before system utterances but not user utterances. Metrics are for the validation set because test set was not available. All experiments were conducted using ParlAI (Miller et al., 2017).

A.2 Task Analysis Details

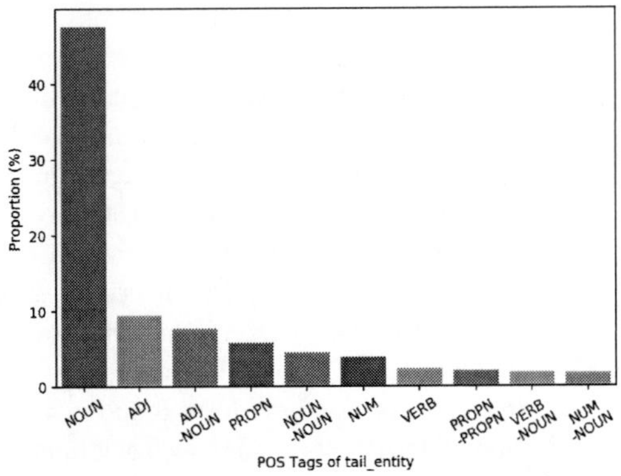

Figure 3: Bar plot for 10 most common POS tags of tail entities.

A.3 Details of Transformations to Link Tail Entity to Sentence

ConceptNet_related: All words in the tail entity can be found in the 100 most related words to each sentence word based on embedding distance on ConceptNet

ConceptNet_connect: All words in the tail entity can be found in the 100 words that have the highest-weighted edge with each sentence word on ConceptNet.

WordNet_synonym: All words in the tail entity can be found in the synonyms of every synset of each sentence word on WordNet.

WordNet_hypernym: All words in the tail entity can be found in the hypernyms of every synset of each sentence word on WordNet

WordNet_hyponym: All words in the tail entity can be found in the hyponyms of every synset of each sentence word on WordNet

Same_stem: All words in the sentence and tail entity are stemmed using a Porter Stemmer (Porter, 1980) before searching for the tail entity in the sentence

A.4 Generator Details

GPT-2-small was used. Additional special tokens including the control tokens ([HEAD], [RELN], [TAIL]) as well as relation tokens were added into the tokenizer. Beam search decoding (beam size = 10) was used at inference time. GPT2-small was accessed from HuggingFace Transformers library with 125M parameters, context window 1024, 768-hidden, 768-hidden, 12-heads, dropout = 0.1. AdamW optimizer was used with $\alpha = 7.5 * 10^{-4}$ for the EXTRACTION dataset and $\alpha = 2.5 * 10^{-3}$ for the INFERENCE dataset, following a uniform search using F1 as the criterion at intervals of $\{2.5, 5, 7.5, 10\} * 10^n; -5 \leq n \leq -3$. Learning rate was linearly decayed (over a max epoch of 8) with 100 warm-up steps. Each training epoch took around 0.5 hour on an Nvidia V100 GPU with a batch size of 16. Validation was done every 0.25 epochs during training. 5 different seeds (40-44) were set for 5 separate runs.

A.5 Reranker Details

BERT-base-uncased was used. Additional special tokens including the control tokens ([HEAD], [RELN], [TAIL]) as well as relation tokens were added into the tokenizer. BERT-base-uncased was accessed from HuggingFace Transformers library (with 12-layer, 768-hidden, 12-heads, 110M parameters, dropout = 0.1). The choice of the base model was made to have fairness of comparison with baseline models in terms of model size. AdamW optimizer was used with $\alpha = 5 * 10^{-6}$, following a uniform search using F1 as the criterion at intervals of $\{2.5, 5, 7.5, 10\} * 10^n; -6 \leq n \leq -3$. Learning rate was linearly decayed (over a max epoch of 8) with 100 warm-up steps. Each training epoch took around 1 hour on an Nvidia V100 GPU with a batch size of 10.Validation was done every 0.25 epochs during training. 5 different seeds (40-44) were set for 5 separate runs.

From Rewriting to Remembering: Common Ground for Conversational QA Models

Marco Del Tredici, Xiaoyu Shen, Gianni Barlacchi, Bill Byrne, Adrià de Gispert
Amazon Alexa AI
mttredic|gyouu|gbarlac|willbyrn|agispert@amazon.com

Abstract

In conversational QA, models have to leverage information in previous turns to answer upcoming questions. Current approaches, such as Question Rewriting, struggle to extract relevant information as the conversation unwinds. We introduce the Common Ground (CG), an approach to accumulate conversational information as it emerges and select the relevant information at every turn. We show that CG offers a more efficient and human-like way to exploit conversational information compared to existing approaches, leading to improvements on Open Domain Conversational QA.

1 Introduction

Speakers involved in a conversation continuously share new information, and build on it to achieve their communicative goals. In human communication, this process takes place effortlessly. As QA systems become conversational, efforts were made to make them able to mimic human behaviour, and to interpret the question at a turn in a conversation, based on the information in the previous turns. An approach to this task is to concatenate the previous turns to the current question (Christmann et al., 2019; Ju et al., 2019; Qu et al., 2019b). The approach has a main shortcoming, namely, it introduces a great amount of noise, since not everything in the previous turns is relevant. An alternative approach is Question Rewriting (QR), in which the question is rewritten in a self-contained form based on the previous conversational information (Vakulenko et al., 2021a; Anantha et al., 2020). QR selects only the relevant information in previous turns, thus improving over concatenation. However, as the conversation progresses and the amount of information grows, QR models often fail to compress it in a rewrite. We argue that this is not only a limitation of the models, but an intrinsic limit of this approach, since producing informative rewrites is often unnatural also for humans (see Section 4).

In this work, we address the shortcomings above. Inspired by the studies of Clark (1996), we propose a methodology to represent conversational information as a set of propositions, named the *Common Ground* (CG): At each turn, the relevant information is distilled in one or more propositions, which are added to the CG. As a new question comes in, the model selects the relevant information in the CG, and uses it to answer the question. The CG can thus be considered as an *optimized* summary, which returns the relevant information at every turn while keeping all the information discussed so far.

We use the QReCC dataset (Anantha et al., 2020) to test CG on the task of Open-Domain Conversational QA (ODCQA) - in which answers to questions in a conversation have to be found in a large collection of documents - and show that it improves over existing approaches for modelling conversational information. We show that this is due to the fact that CG implements a more efficient and human-like way to account for previous information, which takes the best of existing approaches while avoiding their shortcomings: on the one hand, CG can access and maintain the full previous conversational context, but it avoids the noise issue; on the other, it can distill relevant information, but it is not forced to compress it in a single rewrite.

2 Common Ground

We now detail how we created a dataset for CG, and the model we implemented to generate the CG.

2.1 Building the CG

We devise the CG as a set of propositions summarizing the information in a conversation. Since no dataset annotated for CG is available for QA, we created it. We use QReCC (Anantha et al., 2020), a dataset for QR consisting in a set of conversations. For each turn in a conversation, the original question q and its rewrite r are provided. Intuitively, the rewrite makes explicit the entities discussed in the

Proceedings of the 4th Workshop on NLP for Conversational AI, pages 70 - 76
May 27, 2022 ©2022 Association for Computational Linguistics

conversation. If q is self-contained, then q=r. We define a proposition in the CG as any sequence of words in the rewrite which are nouns, adjectives or entities.[1] For example, given q_1 'how old is Messi?', the rewrite r_1 is equal to q_1, and CG_1 is {*'Messi'*}. Given q_2 'which position does he play?', r_2 is 'which position does Messi play?' and CG_2 is {*'Messi'*, *'position'*}. We use this approach to enrich each turn in QReCC with the gold CG.

Importantly, ~70% of the conversations in QReCC were collected by showing the speaker the title and first sentence of a Wikipedia article (Anantha et al., 2020). This information is often crucial to understand a question, especially at turn 1 (e.g., title: 'Albert Camus', q_1: 'When was he born?'), but, potentially, also at subsequent turns (q_2: 'What did he write?'). We therefore collect the relevant Wikipedia information (which we call *doc*), and use it to further enrich QReCC conversations.[2] Note that *doc* is the same at every turn in the conversation. We refer to the union of conversational and Wikipedia information as *contextual* information. Finally, since QReCC only includes train and test split, we randomly sample 20% of the train and use it as validation set.

2.2 Predicting the CG

We introduce a model to produce the CG, which consists of two modules: *Generator* and *Selector*.

Generator At turn t_n, the Generator is trained to generate the gold CG CG_n given $doc \| conv_{[0:n-1]} \| q_n$, where $\|$ indicates concatenation, *doc* is the information from Wikipedia, $conv_{[0:n-1]}$ is the concatenation of questions and answers from turn t_0 to t_{n-1}, and q_n is the current question. We implement the Generator using a T5-base model.[3] We train the generator using the enriched QReCC.

Selector The propositions returned by the Generator for every turn are stacked in the CG. However, as the conversion goes on, some of the propositions are no longer relevant. The role of the Selector is to select only the relevant propositions in the CG.

We implement the Selector as a binary classifier. To create the data to train the model, we use again QReCC: given the full CG available at turn n, we label as 1 the propositions in it that occur in the gold answer span, 0 otherwise. The rationale behind this approach is: an item in the CG is relevant if it is mentioned in the answer. We train the model on the QReCC train split. At test time, we label the propositions in the CG, and keep only those labelled as 1. Figure 1 shows an example of CG.

Question	CG
How was Netflix started?	Netflix
What is its relationship with Blockbuster?	Netflix Blockbuster relationship
When did Netflix shift from DVDs to a streaming service?	Netflix Blockbuster relationship DVDs streaming service
What are its other competitors?	Netflix Blockbuster relationship DVDs streaming service competitors
How does it compare to Amazon Prime Video?	Netflix Blockbuster relationship DVDs streaming service competitors Amazon Prime Video

Figure 1: On the left, the questions from the user; on the right, the CG generated by the Generator: highlighted the propositions selected by the Selector at each turn, in grey those kept in the CG but not selected.

3 Experiments

The goal of accounting for contextual information is to improve the performance on a downstream task. Hence, we compare CG to existing approaches on the task of ODCQA.

Data We use again QReCC, as it meets the requirements of the task: it is conversational, and it allows to experiment in an Open-Domain scenario.

Pipeline We use a retriever-reader pipeline. The retriever returns the top *n* most relevant candidates from the set of documents; these are passed to the reader, which extracts the final answer. We use BERTserini (Yang et al., 2019), using BM25 as a retriever and a BERT-Large as a reader. Each candidate returned by the retriever has a score s_{ret}; the answer extracted from that candidate by the reader has a score s_{rea}. The final score s for the answer is defined as: $(1-\mu) \cdot s_{ret} + \mu \cdot s_{rea}$.

For the retriever, we set *n* to 20, and we follow Anantha et al. (2020) in setting k_1=0.82 and b=0.68. We tune the value of μ on the validation set inde-

[1] Identified using Spacy: `https://spacy.io/`.

[2] The details about the enriched dataset are in Appendix A.

[3] The details of Generator and Selector are in Appendix B.

pendently for each approach (see Section 3.1). We do not finetune the reader, as we want to assess how much the CG can directly benefit any QA model, without the need to finetune it.

3.1 Setups

We test the pipeline's performance when provided, at turn n, with each of the following inputs:
original: the original question q_n.
concat.: the concatenation $doc \,||\, conv_{n-1} \,||\, q_n$.[4]
rewrite: the rewrite r_n produced with a T5-base model. The model generates the rewrite based on $doc \,||\, conv_{[0:n-1]} \,||\, q_n$.
summary: the concatenation $summ_{[0:n-1]} \,||\, q_n$, where $summ_{[0:n-1]}$ is the summary of $doc \,||\, conv_{[0:n-1]}$, created with a T5-base model pretrained for summarization (Raffel et al., 2019).[5]
CG: The CG predicted using our approach, concatenated with the current question: $CG_n \,||\, q_n$.
CG-full: The full CG generated up to turn n, i.e., we do not use the Selector module: $CG_n\text{-}full \,||\, q_n$.

4 Results and Analysis

We show the results of our experiments in Table 1. We measure the performance on the target task in terms of F1, and use MRR and Recall@10/20 to assess the performance of the retriever.[6] We also report the results obtained with gold (-g) rewrites and CG, where the latter is defined, at turn *n*, as gold $CG\text{-}full_n$ for the retriever and gold CG_n for the reader - i.e., the best combination observed in our experiments (see below).

As expected, approaches leveraging contextual information improve over the original question. Among these approaches, CG is the best: it improves the performance over rewrite, and, remarkably, it matches the results obtained with *gold* rewrites. A further improvement in F1 is observed when using CG-full at the retriever and CG at the reader (CG-full/CG), while using only CG-full degrades the performance. This shows that using the more informative but potentially noisier CG-full improves retrieval, but one needs to feed the filtered information from CG to the reader to see improvements in F1, as also observed by Del Tredici et al. (2021). The different response to noise also explains the results of concatenation, which obtain high performance in retrieval, but drops in F1.

Approach	F1	MRR	R@10	R@20
original	6.23	2.89	5.56	6.65
concat.	8.95	21.67	37.55	41.51
rewrite	12.46	13.73	24.52	28.6
summary	12.02	21.81	34.72	38.33
CG	13.41	15.66	27.67	32.09
CG-full	12.18	16.52	29.47	34.06
CG-full/CG	14.2	16.52	29.47	34.06
rewrite-g	13.42	17.16	29.07	33.26
CG-g	15.17	17.95	31.18	35.65

Table 1: Results on the QReCC test set. CG-full/CG indicates that we used CG-full for the retriever and CG for the reader.

CG vs. QR In Table 2, we show examples from QR and CG. In row 1, both approaches extract the relevant information from the previous turns - in a conversation about physician assistants. In the next turn (2), QR fails to expand the question and to substitute 'about' with the contextual information, due to the large amount of information required ('the average starting salary for a physician's assistant in the US'). We often observe this limitation for the QR model. This is not the case for CG, since here the information grows *incrementally*, i.e., the information from the current turn ('the US') is added *on top* of the one already present, while non relevant information ('the UK') is discarded.

In the previous case, the QR model fails to produce a rewrite; in others, this is just not possible. In the 6th turn of a conversation about different kinds of data network architectures (row 3), the user asks a general question about flaw types which encompasses all the previous information: there is so much information to compress, here, that *not even* humans manage to do it, and the gold rewrite is the same as the original question.[7] CG sidesteps this problem simply by making available all the pieces of relevant information emerged in the conversation, which can be selected and exploited by the model, without the need to produce a long natural sentence. Note that besides being more effective, this solution is also more human-like: Speakers do not *repeat* all the contextual information as they

[4] Note that we use $conv_{n-1}$, and not $conv_{[0:n-1]}$, due to the max length limit of the reader of BERTserini.

[5] The details of the Rewrite and Summarization models are in Appendix C.

[6] We use the code by QReCC authors: `github.com/apple/ml-qrecc/tree/main/utils`.

[7] We provide in Appendix D the whole conversation, plus additional examples of (nearly) impossible rewrites.

	Original Question	Question Rewriting	Common Ground
1	What's the average starting salary in the UK?	What's the average starting salary for a physician assistant in the UK?	{*the average starting salary, the UK, a physician assistant* }
2	What about in the US?	What about in the US?	{*the average starting salary, the US, a physician assistant* }
3	Are flows bidirectional?	<u>Are flows bidirectional?</u>	{*data network architectures, edge switches, bidirectional flows, FAT tree topology, upstream packet, routes, core, aggregator*}

Table 2: Examples of rewrites and CG. Predicted rewrites are in plain text, gold rewrites underlined.

make a question, but, rather, they *remember* the key points of the conversation.

CG vs. Summary Summaries convey all contextual information, which makes them suitable for the retriever, but not for the reader. CG is superior because, as said above, is an *optimized* summary conditioned on the current question. In fact, when we create the CG without considering the current question, the model cannot identify the relevant information, and the results are comparable to those of summary (F1=12.6). For example, for the question 'where did he come from?', the CG predicted in the normal scenario is {*Rick Barry*}, while, without the current question, is {*the ABA, free-throw percentage, the 1968–69 season, Rick Barry*}.

Conv* vs. *Doc We measure the performance for the best setup (CG-full/CG) when the CG is created considering either *doc* or *conv*: with the former, the F1 is 13.38, with the latter 13.65. The decrease in performance of *doc* and *conv* compared to *doc+conv* indicates that considering multiple source of information is beneficial for the overall performance of the model. Also, the fact that *conv* yields better results than *doc* is expected: in QReCC, the information from *doc* is mostly leveraged at the first turn, while the information from *conv* is relevant throughout the full conversation.

5 Related Work

Approaches to modelling conversational information have used either sparse or dense representation (Qu et al., 2019a,b, 2020). This work focuses on the former. In this group, concatenation was proposed as an initial approach (Christmann et al., 2019; Ju et al., 2019; Qu et al., 2019b), followed by Question Rewriting (Elgohary et al., 2019). The main models for QR are either generative (Vakulenko et al., 2021a; Yu et al., 2020) or extractive one (Voskarides et al., 2020) - i.e., the relevant tokens in the context are appended to the question. When a single model is used for both retriever and reader, generative model overperform extractive ones (Vakulenko et al., 2021b); however, mixing the two approaches further improves the performance (Del Tredici et al., 2021). Our work is related to (Voskarides et al., 2020), as we also aim at extracting the relevant contextual information. However, instead of appending this information to the question, we stack it in the CG, and enable the model to pick the relevant information at each turn.

6 Conclusions

We introduced the Common Ground, a novel approach for leveraging contextual information. We show that CG outperforms the main existing approaches in the ODCQA task, due to its ability to select and maintain the relevant information in a more effective and human-like way.

We see two main directions for future research on CG. First, we will exploit the ability of CG to include several kinds of information to make it more informative. For example, to answer the question 'how many Covid cases today?', a QA system needs to be aware of the *time* and *location* of the person asking it (Zhang and Choi, 2021). We want to include these and other information in the CG. Second, we want to use CG to make QA models more transparent. Currently, virtual assistants (such as Alexa, Siri and Google Assistant) are black boxes, i.e, the user does not know which information they extract from the input question, and which one they leverage to provide answers. This can make the interaction with them frustrating. CG offers a solution to the problem, as it allows to see what the assistant *has in mind* at each conversational turn. We will conduct experiments in which the CG is shared with the user, and see how this can make the interaction with the assistant more engaging and successful.

References

Raviteja Anantha, Svitlana Vakulenko, Zhucheng Tu, Shayne Longpre, Stephen Pulman, and Srinivas Chappidi. 2020. Open-domain question answering goes conversational via question rewriting. *arXiv preprint arXiv:2010.04898*.

Philipp Christmann, Rishiraj Saha Roy, Abdalghani Abujabal, Jyotsna Singh, and Gerhard Weikum. 2019. Look before you hop: Conversational question answering over knowledge graphs using judicious context expansion. In *Proceedings of the 28th ACM International Conference on Information and Knowledge Management*, pages 729–738.

Herbert H Clark. 1996. *Using language*. Cambridge university press.

Marco Del Tredici, Gianni Barlacchi, Xiaoyu Shen, Weiwei Cheng, and Adrià de Gispert. 2021. Question rewriting for open-domain conversational qa: Best practices and limitations. In *Proceedings of the 30th ACM International Conference on Information and Knowledge Management (CIKM '21)*.

Ahmed Elgohary, Denis Peskov, and Jordan Boyd-Graber. 2019. Can you unpack that? Learning to rewrite questions-in-context. In *Proceedings of the 2019 Conference on Empirical Methods in Natural Language Processing and the 9th International Joint Conference on Natural Language Processing*, pages 5918–5924, Hong Kong, China. ACL.

Ying Ju, Fubang Zhao, Shijie Chen, Bowen Zheng, Xuefeng Yang, and Yunfeng Liu. 2019. Technical report on conversational question answering. *arXiv preprint arXiv:1909.10772*.

Chen Qu, Liu Yang, Cen Chen, Minghui Qiu, W.B̃ruce Croft, and Mohit Iyyer. 2020. Open-retrieval conversational question answering. In *Proceedings of the 43rd International ACM SIGIR Conference on Research and Development in Information Retrieval*, page 539–548, Xi'an, China. ACM.

Chen Qu, Liu Yang, Minghui Qiu, W. Bruce Croft, Yongfeng Zhang, and Mohit Iyyer. 2019a. BERT with history answer embedding for conversational question answering. In *Proceedings of the 42nd International ACM SIGIR Conference on Research and Development in Information Retrieval*, page 1133–1136, Paris, France. ACM.

Chen Qu, Liu Yang, Minghui Qiu, Yongfeng Zhang, Cen Chen, W Bruce Croft, and Mohit Iyyer. 2019b. Attentive history selection for conversational question answering. In *Proceedings of the 28th ACM International Conference on Information and Knowledge Management*, pages 1391–1400.

Colin Raffel, Noam Shazeer, Adam Roberts, Katherine Lee, Sharan Narang, Michael Matena, Yanqi Zhou, Wei Li, and Peter J Liu. 2019. Exploring the limits of transfer learning with a unified text-to-text transformer. *arXiv preprint arXiv:1910.10683*.

Svitlana Vakulenko, Shayne Longpre, Zhucheng Tu, and Raviteja Anantha. 2021a. Question rewriting for conversational question answering. In *Proceedings of the 14th ACM International Conference on Web Search and Data Mining*, pages 355–363.

Svitlana Vakulenko, Nikos Voskarides, Zhucheng Tu, and Shayne Longpre. 2021b. A comparison of question rewriting methods for conversational passage retrieval. *CoRR*, arXiv:2101.07382. ECIR short paper.

Nikos Voskarides, Dan Li, Pengjie Ren, Evangelos Kanoulas, and Maarten de Rijke. 2020. Query resolution for conversational search with limited supervision. In *Proceedings of the 43rd International ACM SIGIR Conference on Research and Development in Information Retrieval*, page 921–930, Xi'an, China. ACM.

Wei Yang, Yuqing Xie, Aileen Lin, Xingyu Li, Luchen Tan, Kun Xiong, Ming Li, and Jimmy Lin. 2019. End-to-end open-domain question answering with bertserini. In *Proceedings of the 2019 Conference of the North American Chapter of the Association for Computational Linguistics (Demonstrations)*, pages 72–77.

Shi Yu, Jiahua Liu, Jingqin Yang, Chenyan Xiong, Paul Bennett, Jianfeng Gao, and Zhiyuan Liu. 2020. Few-shot generative conversational query rewriting. In *Proceedings of the 43rd International ACM SIGIR Conference on Research and Development in Information Retrieval*, pages 1933–1936, Xi'an, China. ACM.

Michael Zhang and Eunsol Choi. 2021. Situatedqa: Incorporating extra-linguistic contexts into qa. In *Proceedings of the 2021 Conference on Empirical Methods in Natural Language Processing*, pages 7371–7387.

A Enriching QReCC

Approx. 78% of the conversations in QReCC are derived from the QuAC dataset (`https://quac.ai/`). In QuAC, dialogues are created by showing to the student (i.e., the person making questions) the title of the section of a Wikipedia page and the first sentence of first paragraph in the page. We retrieve this information from the QuAC dataset, and add it to the QReCC dataset. As mentioned in the main paper, we add the information from Wikipedia to all the turns in a conversations. As a results, 76.5% of the datapoints in the train split and 71.8% of those in the test split have additional information. We will release the code for enriching QReCC with CG and Wikipedia information upon publication.

B Model for CG prediction

Generator In order to generate the CG, we use the T5-base model available at: `https://huggingface.co/transformers/model_doc/t5.html`.

We fine-tuned the model on the task of generating the CG with the following parameters: max source length= 512; max target length= 64; val max target length= 64; evaluation strategy= steps; num train epochs= 5; per device train batch size= 4; per device eval batch size= 8; eval steps= 82; seed= 42; warmup steps= 500; eval beams= 5; learning rate= 5e-5.

Selector In order to select the relevant propositions in the CG, we use the DistilBert model available at: `https://huggingface.co/transformers/model_doc/distilbert.html`.

We fine-tuned the model with the following parameters: max source length= 512; evaluation strategy= steps; num train epochs= 5; per device train batch size= 16; per device eval batch size= 64; eval steps= 82; seed= 42; warmup steps= 0; learning rate= 5e-5.

C Generative models for QR and Summarization

QR model In order to generate the rewrites, we use the same T5-base model used to implement the Generator. We fine-tuned the model on the QR task using the QReCC train split, with the same parameters reported in Appendix B.

Summarization model In order to generate the summaries, we use again the same T5-base model used for the Generator and the QR model. In this case, however, we do not need to fine-tuned the model, since it was already optimized for the task: to generate the summaries, we simply provide to the model as input the string 'summarize: ' followed by the contextual information.

D Example of conversation

We report below the full conversation up to the question used as an example in Table 2, row 3.

q_1: What are scalable data center network architectures?
a_1: DCNs need to be scalable and efficient to connect tens or even hundreds of thousands of servers to handle the growing demands of Cloud computing.
q_2: What are some examples of scalable data center network architectures?
a_2: 1 Three-tier DCN 2 Fat tree DCN 3 DCell
q_3: Describe the characteristics of FAT tree topology
a_3: In a fat tree, branches nearer the top of the hierarchy are fatter (thicker) than branches further down the hierarchy. In a telecommunications network, the branches are data links; the varied thickness (bandwidth) of the data links allows for more efficient and technology-specific use.
q_4: What routes can be taken by an upstream packet?
a_4: The router is upstream of the computer, connecting the computer to the whole internet. ... Each router does not need to know the whole route to the destination;
q_5: Describe core, aggregator and edge switches.
a_5: In small networks of a few hundred users, edge switches can be connected redundantly directly to core switch/router devices. However, for larger networks, , an additional layer of switching, called the distribution layer, aggregates the edge switches.

In Table 3, we report examples for which the gold rewrite provided in the QReCC dataset is equal to the original question, despite the fact that the question needs contextual information to be correctly understood. For each example, we provide the information in the CG, and a comment about why creating a rewrite is not possible, or very unnatural. Due to space reasons, we do not report the full conversation. However, we report the conversation and turns IDs, which can be used to look up for the full conversation in the QReCC dataset available at `https://github.com/apple/ml-qrecc/tree/main/dataset`.

17-10	**Question**: What form of energy is used in eating? **Common Ground**: *energy, light energy, heat energy, gravitational energy, form, type, motion, mechanical energy, examples, potential energy, electrical energy, sound energy, chemical energy, nuclear energy, atomic energy, kinetic energy* **Comment**: the question comes at the end of a long conversation, and refers to the previously mentioned forms of energy. The hypothetical QR should include them all: *What form of energy, among light energy, heat energy, [..] is used in eating?*
22-9	**Question**: What is the oldest spice? **Common Ground**: *spices, cumin, world, coriander, cilantro, herb, garlic, oregano, root, stem, seed, fruit, flower, bark, tree, plant, Indian, pepper, Nutmeg, mace, Mustard, seeds, Fenugreek, Turmeric, Saffron* **Comment**: similarly to the previous example, the question comes at the end of a long conversation, and refers to all previous information. The hypothetical QR should be: *What is the oldest spice among cumin, coriander [...]?*
28-4	**Question**: What can I do as an individual level? **Common Ground**: *global warming, long-term rise, average temperature, Earth's climate system, climate change, temperature measurements, dangers, scientists, sea ice, sea level rise, heat waves, methods, Carbon dioxide, oil, coal, fossil fuels, energy, homes, cars, smartphones* **Comment**: again, the user's question encompasses all previous conversation, in which several problems related to global warming were mentioned. A (tentative) rewrite which captures the information up to this point should therefore be of the kind: *What can I do in order to better use energy for my home, car, smartphone, thus reducing the emission of carbon dioxide and reduce impact on global warming?*
583-6	**Question**: Was there anyone opposed to him in this? **Common Ground**: *Ira Hayes, World War II, civilian life, war, family, 1946, Gila River Indian Community, Edward Harlon Block, Hank Hansen, flag-raiser controversy, Marine Corps* **Comment**: in this dialogue, many facts about Ira Hayes are explained. The original question refers to several of them, and a (very tentative) rewrite should be like: *Was there anyone opposed to Ira Hayes in revealing the truth that Harlon Block was still being misrepresented publicly as Hank Hansen?*
590-6	**Question**: What was the impact of this column? **Common Ground**: *Israel, Krauthammer, Oslo accords, 2006 Lebanon War, column, Let Israel Win the War* **Comment**: also in this case, the conversation touches upon several related facts, and in order to correctly interpret the question in the light of such facts, it should be rewritten like: *What was the impact of the column 'Let Israel Win the War' written by Krauthammer during the 2006 Lebanon War, in which he opposes the Oslo accords?*

Table 3: Examples in which the rewrite is nearly impossible or very unnatural. In the left column we report the conversation-turn IDs.

Human Evaluation of Conversations is an Open Problem: *comparing the sensitivity of various methods for evaluating dialogue agents*

Eric Michael Smith[1] **Orion Hsu**[2] **Rebecca Qian**[1]
Stephen Roller[1] **Y-Lan Boureau**[1] **Jason Weston**[1]

[1]Facebook AI Research [2]Duke University

Abstract

At the heart of improving conversational AI is the open problem of how to evaluate conversations. Issues with automatic metrics are well known (Liu et al., 2016), with human evaluations still considered the gold standard. Unfortunately, how to perform human evaluations is also an open problem: differing data collection methods have varying levels of human agreement and statistical sensitivity, resulting in differing amounts of human annotation hours and labor costs. In this work we compare five different crowdworker-based human evaluation methods and find that different methods are best depending on the types of models compared, with no clear winner across the board. While this highlights the open problems in the area, our analysis leads to advice of when to use which one, and possible future directions.

1 Introduction

Any comprehensive analysis of the performance of an open-domain conversational model must include human evaluations: automatic metrics can capture certain aspects of model performance but are no replacement for having human raters judge how adept models are at realistic and interesting conversation (Deriu et al., 2021; Liu et al., 2016; Dinan et al., 2019b). Unfortunately, human evaluations themselves must be carefully constructed in order to capture all the aspects desired of a good conversationalist. Any evaluation technique must evaluate over many turns of a conversation in order to detect emergent faults such as repetitiveness or contradiction, while techniques that rely solely on a single evaluation at the end of a conversation may fail to take into account changes in model performance over its span. Further, techniques that rate model performance on a Likert scale may suffer from inconsistencies in subjective numerical ratings across evaluations of different models (Li et al., 2019). When comparing various human evaluation methods to assess which works best, we find that each has success and failure cases, leading us to conclude that human evaluation is still an open problem.

In this work, we analyze a representative set of human evaluation techniques. First, we compare *per-turn* evaluations, where ratings are given after every model response, and *per-dialogue* evaluations, where ratings are collected solely at the end of the conversation. Per-turn evaluations have the advantage of being more fine-grained, encouraging annotators to focus on small differences; however, the quality of a conversation is more than the sum of its parts, and global per-dialogue evaluations can capture this better. Second, we consider *pairwise methods*, where two models are compared directly by an annotator, to *single-model* methods, where the annotator sees and rates only one model at a time. Both approaches can be either per-turn or per-dialogue. For example, in Pairwise Per-Turn evaluation, a crowdworker chats with a dialogue agent, and after each of the worker's messages, they must choose between two possible responses from the agent, one from each of two different models. The pairwise approach can spot subtle differences apparent when comparing responses, and it can mitigate problems with distribution shift that occur in absolute scoring. Single-model approaches, however, can work well when direct comparison is not paramount.

We compare all of these different techniques for evaluating dialogue models in three different settings, and we contrast their individual strengths. We find that:

- Pairwise per-turn evaluations are adept at measuring changes in model performance throughout a conversation. This technique tends to work well when pairs of models clearly differ in how appropriate their responses are in the context of the previous lines of dialogue, for example, when comparing two models that are trained on different datasets.

Proceedings of the 4th Workshop on NLP for Conversational AI, pages 77 - 97
May 27, 2022

- Pairwise per-dialogue evaluations tend to perform best when differences between models only emerge after several conversation turns, such as when these differences are very subtle, or when noticing patterns in responses that emerge globally across the entire conversation, for example the average length of responses.

- Single-model evaluations, performed both per conversation turn and at the end of a conversation, tend to not do as well in the two previously described settings, but do perform well when comparing models that differ only slightly in quality but are otherwise similar, for example two models with different numbers of parameters.

These findings, while highlighting the difficulty of human evaluation, also provide guidance on which method might be best to use in these different circumstances, as well as possible future work. In particular, investigating the best way to merge pairwise and single-model, per-turn and per-dialogue benefits into a single method could be a fruitful direction. We also analyze the interpretability of these approaches when collecting human written explanations. We have released code for these evaluation techniques in the ParlAI framework.[1]

2 Existing work

This work concerns itself with evaluation of open-domain dialogue, which, unlike more restricted domains such as question-answering and goal-oriented conversations, may not have a precise goal, and no widely accepted evaluation technique for it currently exists (Deriu et al., 2021; Huang et al., 2020; Roller et al., 2020). Automatic metrics are relatively fast, efficient, and reproducible, but many of them have been shown to "correlate very weakly with human judgement" (Liu et al., 2016, see also Dinan et al. (2019b)), and the best way to create a reliable automatic metric is still up for debate (Deriu et al., 2021). In this work we focus on human evaluation, and in particular on employing crowdworkers, which has an advantage over utilizing trained experts (Deriu et al., 2021) or deployment (Gabriel et al., 2020; Shuster et al., 2020) of allowing for a larger pool of evaluators and for ensuring alignment with research goals, respectively. However, the use of crowdworkers itself has a number of pitfalls to avoid as well (Huynh et al., 2021).

Particular instruction wording choices to crowdworkers have a large effect on the quality of conversations and resulting evaluations (Huynh et al., 2021). Wording can direct workers to evaluate specific facets, such as general "get to know each other" chitchat (Zhang et al., 2018), getting a bot to generate unsafe utterances (Xu et al., 2020), and instructing crowdworkers to be adversarial vs. not (Dinan et al., 2019a). One can also pick from a variety of specific questions when asking crowdworkers to rate conversations, including asking about interestingness, making sense, fluency (See et al., 2019), sensibleness, specificity (Adiwardana et al., 2020), toxicity, and bias (Xu et al., 2020), and the exact phrasing of these questions can have a large impact on sensitivity (Li et al., 2019). Standard evaluation protocols have a single human both converse with a model and rate that conversation in the same task, but other methods have a rater rate pre-existing conversations between a human and a model or between a pair of models (Li et al., 2019; Deriu et al., 2020). These latter techniques allow for efficient reuse of existing conversational data, and have shown to be useful experimentally (Li et al., 2019; Roller et al., 2021), but it may be harder for evaluators to rate conversations that they have not been involved in.

Another choice when designing evaluation protocols is whether conversations are rated individually, e.g., with Likert-score ratings (Ashwin et al., 2017; Venkatesh et al., 2018, see more in Appendix A), or pairwise by comparing models (Li et al., 2019; Liang et al., 2020, etc.). Likert scoring suffers from weaknesses such as potential per-annotator bias (Kulikov et al., 2019) and drift in the distribution of errors over time (See et al., 2019), but is more efficient than pairwise comparisons in that new models' ratings can be compared to those of older models without having to re-collect those older models' ratings.

Lastly, evaluation techniques differ in whether they collect ratings on each turn of the conversation (Adiwardana et al., 2020; Komeili et al., 2021) or only at the end of the conversation, as in Acute-Eval (Li et al., 2019). Whole-conversation techniques can work well if the quality of a conversation is assumed to be more than just the sum of its parts, but could perhaps suffer due to the *primacy effect* and *recency effect* that appear when more weight is given to information presented at the start and end of the rating session, respectively (Asch,

[1]https://parl.ai/projects/humaneval

1946; Anderson, 1965; Murdock Jr, 1962; Postman and Phillips, 1965).

See Appendix A for a more thorough assessment of related works.

3 Methods

3.1 Evaluation techniques

We investigate several human evaluation techniques, spanning a cross-section of the different methods discussed in existing work. Specifically:

- Single-model per-turn evaluations
- Single-model per-dialogue evaluations
- Pairwise per-turn evaluations
- Pairwise per-dialogue evaluations
- Pairwise per-dialogue *self-chat* evaluations

We thus compare the spectrum of single vs. pairwise and per-turn vs. per-dialogue variations, as well as trying a self-chat method compared to conventional human-bot conversation ratings. Figure 1 summarizes the methods. In the following, we will describe our exact methodology for each. See Appendix B.3 for details on quality checks used when performing these evaluations.

3.1.1 Conversational setting

Our human-bot evaluations consist of a set of conversations. Each conversation consists of a human worker crowdsourced from Amazon Mechanical Turk[2] (the "Human Speaker") paired with a conversational model (the "Bot Speaker"). The Human Speaker will speak naturally in the conversation, and they will be role-playing as a certain persona with the help of two provided *persona sentences* given to them at the start of the conversation: see Figure 2 (left) for an example.

The Human Speaker's first message in the conversation is fixed to *"Hi!"*, following the convention of Adiwardana et al. (2020). The conversation ends after the Human Speaker and Bot Speaker have both spoken for 6 turns each, to roughly match the conversation lengths used for BlenderBot evaluations in Roller et al. (2021). We test three different evaluation metrics, *preference*, *humanness* and *interestingness*, with exact wordings described in the following subsections.

[2]Our crowdsourcing task pays workers well above minimum wage, and the task does not request any personal information from workers.

3.1.2 Pairwise per-turn evaluations

The Pairwise Per-Turn evaluation (PW-Turn) technique provides annotations for every turn of conversation by asking for the crowdworker to choose from a pair of model responses after every sent message. Hence, in this setting the Human Speaker speaks to a Bot Speaker, the latter of which actually represents the two models to be compared. The Human Speaker will speak naturally in the conversation. Every time that it is the Bot Speaker's turn to speak, the crowdworker will first be presented with two options as possible responses: each response will come from one of the two models being compared, similarly to Clark and Smith (2021). We randomize the ordering of these model responses. The worker must choose the better response for the given evaluation metric. The wordings we use for the three metrics are adapted from Li et al. (2019):

- **Preference**: *"Which next response from your partner would you prefer in a long conversation?"*
- **Humanness**: *"Which next response from your partner sounds more human?"*
- **Interestingness**: *"If you had to say one of these responses is interesting and one is boring, which would you say is more interesting?"*

The worker must give a free-text justification for their choice of response. The response that they choose is set to be the actual response given by the Bot Speaker, and the conversation continues from there. Figure 2 provides a screenshot example of the UI. A description of quality checks performed when onboarding workers for this evaluation technique is given in Appendix B.2. In our experiments we consider win rates based on simply averaging over turns, as well as nonlinear combinations of per-turn results over entire dialogues (e.g., winner-takes-all voting) in order to measure their impact.

3.1.3 Pairwise per-dialogue evaluations

The Pairwise Per-Dialogue evaluation (PW-Dialog) technique we introduce asks evaluators to choose between two models by presenting a pair of conversations. The technique we employ is identical to the Acute-Eval method (Li et al., 2019), but for consistency with the names of other techniques, we refer to it here as PW-Dialog evaluations. For each of the model pairs and evaluation metrics used, we

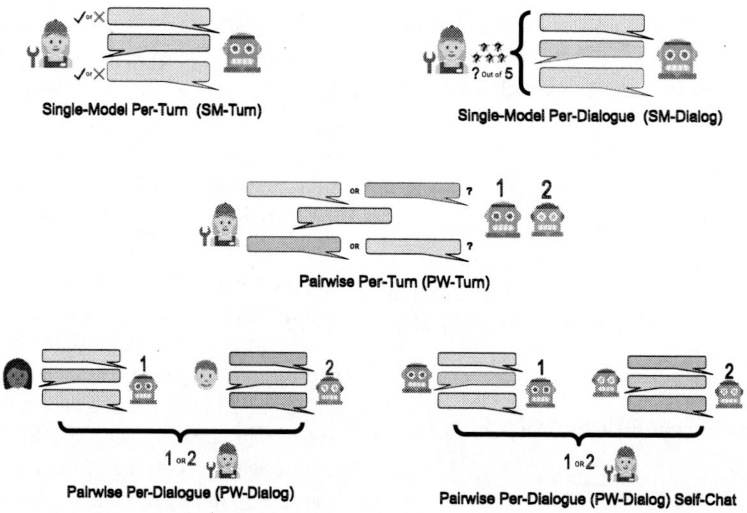

Figure 1: The human evaluation methods we compare in this work. SM-Turn rates each bot response during the conversation, while SM-Dialog rates the entire conversation. PW-Turn compares two different bots' responses at every turn in the conversation, while PW-Dialog compares two entire conversations with two different bots. PW-Dialog *self-chat* compares two conversations which only involve the two bots talking to themselves (self-chat).

collect evaluations on (1) conversations conducted between a crowdworker and a model agent; and (2) self-chat conversations conducted between two conversational agents of the same model (the *self-chat* variant). The wordings we use (from Li et al. (2019)) are almost identical to the PW-Turn versions, but phrased for the per-dialogue, rather than per-turn, case:

- **Preference**: *"Who would you prefer to talk to for a long conversation?"*
- **Humanness**: *"Which speaker sounds more human?"*
- **Interestingness**: *"If you had to say one of these speakers is interesting and one is boring, who would you say is more interesting?"*

Figure 3 provides a screenshot example of the UI.

3.1.4 Single-model evaluations

In our single-model evaluation experiments, we combine per-turn and per-dialogue into the same UI (see Figure 4 for a screenshot).[3] A crowdworker chats with a conversational agent backed by a single model, and for each response of that model the worker must annotate whether it is engaging, human-like, and/or interesting, with wording provided in the screenshot. At the end of the conversation, again consisting of 6 messages per speaker, the worker must rate their partner on a Likert scale of 1 to 5 for each of the three evaluation metrics listed in Section 3.1.2. We refer to the per-turn annotations of model responses from this task as Single-Model Per-Turn evaluations (SM-Turn) and the end-of-conversation Likert scores as Single-Model Per-Dialogue evaluations (SM-Dialog).

Empirically, we find that SM-Turn success rates and SM-Dialog Likert scores are highly dependent on the particular day that the evaluations are collected: this is perhaps due to day-to-day variability in the pool of crowdworkers. To counteract this, we run these evaluations on all four of the models discussed in this work (Section 3.2) simultaneously.[4]

3.2 Models

We analyze the relative performance of these five human evaluation techniques, SM-Turn, SM-Dialog, PW-Turn, PW-Dialog, and PW-Dialog *self-chat*, on four different well-performing but relatively similar dialogue models from Roller et al. (2021):

[3]This may have undesirable effects in correlating their results, but nonetheless they do appear to perform quite differently in evaluations.

[4]For the pairwise evaluation techniques PW-Turn and PW-Dialog, we collect evaluations over several days across multiple weeks for each of the three model pairs evaluated. This helps to smooth out variability among days.

- **BlenderBot3B**: The version of BlenderBot with 2.7 billion parameters, pretrained on a previously existing Reddit dataset (extracted and obtained by a third party and made available on pushshift.io (Baumgartner et al., 2020)) and then fine-tuned on several purpose-built dialogue datasets.

- **BlenderBot3B-M0**: BlenderBot3B uses a minimum generation length of 20 tokens to ensure relatively long, interesting responses. We also compare to exactly the same model but without a minimum generation length, referring to it with **-M0** postfix.

- **BlenderBot90M**: The variant of BlenderBot with 90 million parameters, trained on the same datasets as BlenderBot3B.

- **Reddit3B**: BlenderBot3B, but only pretrained on the third-party Reddit dump and not fine-tuned on dialogue datasets.

For all models, we use the same generation settings as in Roller et al. (2021), apart from the **-M0** adaptation. We choose these relatively similar models in our experiments as a difficult challenge for evaluation techniques to tell which one is best, but we *a priori* expect from previous Acute-Eval (PW-Dialog) *self-chat* measurements in Roller et al. (2021) that BlenderBot3B may perform as well as or better than the other three models.

For the three pairwise evaluation techniques, we specifically perform comparisons between three pairs of models, each of which differ in a characteristic way:

- **Length comparison**: Comparing BlenderBot3B to BlenderBot3B-M0: these models differ only in the length of their generations.

- **Size comparison**: Comparing two models with different numbers of parameters, BlenderBot3B and BlenderBot90M.

- **Fine-tuning comparison**: Comparing the fine-tuned BlenderBot3B to the pretrained-only Reddit3B (both with the same number of parameters).

4 Results

4.1 Model win rates from pairwise per-turn evaluations

We compute the win rates of BlenderBot3B over other models in Table 1 for the pairwise evaluation technique PW-Turn. We expect BlenderBot3B to be better, hence values closer to 100% are deemed more preferable. We display the win rates of four different variants: including all 6 conversation turns from the Bot Speaker, excluding the Bot Speaker's first turn from the evaluations, and computing a nonlinear function of the turns: either calculating squared or winner-takes-all win rates for each conversation and then averaging those scores across all conversations. We generally find that PW-Turn win rates are higher when dropping the first turn of the Bot Speaker, as discussed further in Appendix C.2. Win rates are typically even higher by aggregating over conversations in a winner-takes-all fashion, which has the effect of reducing the turn-by-turn variability of which model's response is chosen by the crowdworker.

We find that, in general, win rates of BlenderBot3B do not vary much as a function of the evaluation question used when asking workers to choose one model response over the other. It is unclear *a priori* whether this results from an ambiguity in the precise definitions of these questions/metrics when interpreted by the workers, correlations in

		All turns	Turns 2 to 6		
Comp.	Metric	Lin	Lin	Sqr	WTA
Length	Pref	63%	67%	72%	**74%**
	Human	63%	68%	75%	**79%**
	Inter	68%	70%	77%	**84%**
Size	Pref	48%	52%	**53%**	49%
	Human	51%	56%	**58%**	54%
	Inter	49%	52%	54%	**55%**
FT	Pref	80%	82%	88%	**93%**
	Human	81%	84%	88%	**93%**
	Inter	71%	75%	80%	**85%**

Table 1: PW-Turn win rates of BlenderBot3B vs. BlenderBot3B-M0 ("Length"), vs. BlenderBot90M ("Size"), and vs. the base pretrained model, Reddit3B ("FT"), across three different evaluation metrics, Preference, Humanness, and Interestingness. Win rates are computed both across all turns and across only the last 5 turns from the Bot Speaker ("Turns 2 to 6"). **Lin**: the linear win rate $x/(x+y)$ of BlenderBot3B, given x wins of BlenderBot3B and y wins of the comparison model. **Sqr**: the "squared" win rate $x^2/(x^2+y^2)$, calculated per-conversation and then averaged across all conversations. **WTA**: the winner-takes-all win rate, defined as the percentage of all conversations for which BlenderBot3B wins on more turns, or equivalently $x^\infty/(x^\infty+y^\infty)$ as calculated per-conversation. Winner-takes-all scores are generally highest (highest values bolded).

how well models perform on some metrics vs. others, or some other reason.

4.2 Model scores from single-model evaluations

		SM-Turn			SM-Dialog
		All	Turns 3 to 6		
Met.	Model	Lin	Lin	WTA	
Preference	BB3B	70%	**71%**	**73%**	**4.19**
	BB3B-M0	**71%**	70%	70%	4.02
	BB90M	65%	64%	65%	3.97
	Reddit3B	55%	50%	50%	3.30
Human	BB3B	**70%**	**72%**	**73%**	**4.49**
	BB3B-M0	67%	66%	70%	4.22
	BB90M	65%	66%	70%	3.94
	Reddit3B	56%	54%	53%	3.50
Interesting	BB3B	**44%**	**45%**	**47%**	**4.22**
	BB3B-M0	35%	35%	36%	3.76
	BB90M	39%	40%	42%	3.83
	Reddit3B	39%	39%	37%	3.30

Table 2: Performance of BlenderBot3B (BB3B), BlenderBot3B-M0 (BB3B-M0), BlenderBot90M (BB90M), and Reddit3B on SM-Turn and SM-Dialog evaluations. SM-Turn mean success rates are calculated across all turns ("All") or across only the last 4 turns from the Bot Speaker ("Turns 3 to 6"). Scores represent the overall fraction of model responses marked as successful on the given evaluation metric ("Lin") or the number of conversations for which at least half of the model responses are marked as successful (winner-takes-all, "WTA"). SM-Dialog evaluations are Likert scores (with standard deviations in the range of 0.8 to 1.3). Highest scores across models are bolded.

Table 2 provides the per-turn success rates (SM-Turn) and end-of-conversation Likert scores (SM-Dialog) over all models. As with the pairwise evaluations of Section 4.1 and Roller et al. (2021), BlenderBot3B generally outperforms the other models using the SM-Turn and SM-Dialog methods as well. Table 5 (in the Appendix) shows success rates from the SM-Turn technique as a function of conversation turn (rather than aggregated). BlenderBot3B scores are generally stable across conversation turn but are slightly lower on the first two turns of the Bot Speaker, echoing similar findings with PW-Turn in Appendix C.2. We thus also consider removing SM-Turn scores from the first two turns in order to maximize the performance of BlenderBot3B relative to the other models. As with PW-Turn, we find that calculating the winner-takes-all score per conversation allows for an even bigger separation in performance between BlenderBot3B and the other models.

Unlike PW-Turn for which win rates are similar across all three evaluation metrics (Section 4.1), single-model success rates on the Interestingness metric are generally lower than those on the other two, especially for SM-Turn. We hypothesize that the juxtaposition of all three evaluation questions side-by-side in the UI of the SM-Turn and SM-Dialog crowdworker task (Figure 4) may aid workers in distinguishing among these three metrics and rating models differently on them.

See Appendix C.4 for an exploration of which turns of the conversation contribute most strongly to workers' final Likert-scale ratings.

4.3 Direct comparison of all evaluation techniques

In this section we directly compare all the pairwise and single-model evaluation techniques to each other to discern their relative strengths. See Appendix C.1 for details on the number of evaluations performed and number of crowdworker hours spent per technique.

4.3.1 Computing win rates across all techniques

In order to directly compare the performance of SM-Turn and SM-Dialog with that of the pairwise techniques, we calculate effective win rates for the two single-model techniques by bootstrapping samples of ratings from different models and then calculating how often SM-Turn success rates and SM-Dialog Likert scores from one model are higher than those of another. Following the analysis of best performing methods from Sections 4.1 and 4.2, we consider only Bot Speaker turns 2 through 6 for PW-Turn and turns 3 through 6 for SM-Turn in winner-takes-all (WTA) mode, in order to maximize the ability of these techniques to distinguish different models' performances.

Table 3 compares the win rates produced by all evaluation techniques. Overall, we find that a different technique performs best for each of the three model comparison types:

Length comparison The pairwise evaluation techniques PW-Dialog and PW-Turn perform much better than the single-model ones. BlenderBot3B responses tend to contain many more words on average than those of BlenderBot3B-M0, and so we hypothesize that this difference in sensitivity among the techniques may be due to the fact that

		PW-Turn	PW-Dialog		PW combo	SM-Turn	SM-Dialog
Comparison	Metric	Turns 2–6, WTA	Human	Self		Turns 3–6, WTA	
Length	Pref	74%	77%	**82%**	80%	55%	58%
	Human	79%	77%	**83%**	81%	52%	59%
	Inter	84%	**85%**	73%	73%	60%	65%
Size	Pref	49%	56%	55%	54%	59%	**60%**
	Human	54%	61%	55%	55%	52%	**66%**
	Inter	55%	59%	57%	56%	55%	**64%**
Fine-tuning	Pref	**93%**	70%	66%	69%	64%	71%
	Human	**93%**	54%	61%	65%	62%	73%
	Inter	**85%**	59%	64%	66%	60%	70%

Table 3: Win rates of BlenderBot3B vs. other models, for all evaluation techniques. For the per-turn techniques PW-Turn and SM-Turn, only the specified Bot Speaker turns are used to compute winner-takes-all scores, as in Tables 1 and 2. We show PW-Dialog win rates as measured on conversations between a crowdworker and a model ("Human") as well as from model self-chats ("Self"). "PW combo" represents the win rate when sampling ratings from PW-Turn (turns 2–6) and PW-Dialog (on model self-chats) at a ratio of 1:5. PW-Turn, PW-Dialog, and SM-Dialog are each found to be most sensitive at measuring model performance for one of the three model comparisons tested (highest win rates bolded). See Appendix C.1 for the number of evaluations and the estimated total number of worker-hours per technique.

viewing responses from both models side-by-side makes the length differences between them much more evident, especially when comparing two entire conversations as in PW-Dialog. Thus, if crowdworkers tend to prefer longer responses on average, the side-by-side comparison of model responses might aid in their ability to choose BlenderBot3B responses over those of BlenderBot3B-M0.

Size comparison The differences among the techniques here are smaller than for the Length comparison, with the full-dialogue techniques PW-Dialog and SM-Dialog slightly outperforming the per-turn ones. As shown by Roller et al. (2021), BlenderBot3B and BlenderBot90M do not perform statistically significantly differently on Acute-Evals (i.e. PW-Dialog) on self-chat conversations. Thus, it may make sense that any small differences in performance between these models are more evident on the level of whole conversations.

Fine-tuning comparison In this comparison, PW-Turn performs best out of all techniques. Because the Reddit3B model was not fine-tuned on conversational dialogue datasets, its responses to its partner generally make less sense in context than those of BlenderBot3B. We hypothesize that these more nonsensical responses may be very obvious to workers who are in the middle of having a conversation with the Bot Speaker during the PW-Turn evaluation. However, these responses may be less obvious to workers reading whole conversations in the PW-Dialog evaluation who have not interacted with the models directly, as well as to workers in SM-Turn and SM-Dialog evaluations who cannot directly compare Reddit3B responses to those of a model that has been fine-tuned on dialogue.

Explainability in experiments: analysis of crowdworker reasons During the crowdworker evaluation tasks, we also ask for reasons for the crowdworker's judgments. These reasons can give interpretability to the results. A full analysis is given in Appendix C.5. Overall, we find justifications that make sense in each of the three model comparisons, e.g. in the Length comparison we see keywords like *"information"* and *"detailed"* appearing often. For the Fine-tuning comparison, we often find keywords like *"flows"*, *"personal"* and *"contradicts"*, which implies that the fine-tuning conversational datasets like Persona-Chat provide for more personal, less contradictory, and flowing conversations.

Repeatability of experiments We provide an analysis in Appendix C.6 of the variability of model win rates over time for each of the evaluation techniques. Overall, we find that PW-Turn, PW-Dialog, and SM-Turn vary least across chunked experiments, with SM-Dialog having more variability. This makes the use of SM-Dialog less compelling.

4.3.2 Overall findings

The results of these three model comparisons hint that perhaps a per-turn evaluation technique may be more suitable for pairs of models that differ in their ability to reply sensibly in a way that is easily detectable by their partner (i.e. BlenderBot3B vs. Reddit3B), but that a whole-conversation technique may be preferable when differences between models are more sensitive. However, evaluations on many more pairs of models would be needed to sufficiently support such a broad hypothesis. We also find that single-model techniques perform competitively to pairwise ones except for when model generations differ by average length: in this case, comparing the responses of both models side-by-side may make the differences between them more apparent than just viewing them separately.

Combining techniques Given how much the relative sensitivities of different evaluation techniques vary across different pairs of models, we also explore whether combining results from multiple techniques together may allow for a compromise technique that performs reasonably well in all cases. We thus include in Table 3 the win rate ("PW combo") when sampling ratings from the PW-Turn and PW-Dialog techniques together at a ratio of 1:5. This sampling retains most of the ability of PW-Dialog to quickly compare BlenderBot3B to BlenderBot3B-M0 and BlenderBot90M (the Length and Size comparisons), and it also gains some of PW-Turn's superior strength at measuring the performance of BlenderBot3B over Reddit3B (the Fine-tuning comparison).

By contrast, since ratings for the two single-model techniques SM-Turn and SM-Dialog are collected simultaneously, ratings from both techniques on a given conversation can be averaged together to achieve slightly finer sensitivity than either technique individually. Figures 11, 12, and 13 show that, with the proper weighting, such averaging can produce a statistically significant difference between models a bit faster than with only SM-Dialog and dramatically faster than with only SM-Turn (Appendix C.8).

Beyond win rates, another way to directly compare the relative usefulness of our various evaluation techniques is to estimate the amount of person-hours that must be spent on evaluations by crowdworkers in order to achieve a statistically significant result. These results (Figures 8, 9, and 10) roughly follow the patterns found by win rates (Section 4.3.1). See Appendix C.7 for a discussion of the assumptions made when producing these time estimates.

5 Conclusion

In this work we compare the extent to which different evaluation techniques are able to measure performance differences between dialogue models, and we show instances in which the performance varies between per-turn techniques and per-dialogue techniques, and between pairwise techniques and single-model techniques. A completely exhaustive analysis of the cases in which each technique is most appropriate would require measurement on many more pairs of models than the three studied here, and would likely require a dramatic scaling-up of labor for crowdworkers.

Nevertheless, the results shown here demonstrate the difficulty in anointing one evaluation technique as superior to all others regardless of the models being compared, and they suggest that a combination of techniques, or else a different technique entirely, may be necessary for optimal measurement of differences among models. A more universally ideal technique would likely need to investigate model performance per-turn but still be able to give an overall judgment of model quality across a conversation in order to capture elements of performance that manifest clearest in a single response vs. in aggregate. We demonstrate that combining evaluation scores from per-turn and per-dialogue techniques can bridge the gap in the performance differences between the two, but that this does not outperform either individual technique in all cases, at least in the way that we combined them.

Future improvements may also come from exploring other ways to amplify the weak signal from models with only slight performance differences such as BlenderBot3B and BlenderBot90M, perhaps by training workers to select responses based on general measures of conversational quality, as opposed to content that appeals to their personal interests. Improving sensitivity to roughly equivalent pairs of models such as these should in turn enable the comparison of models whose performance differences are smaller still.

While this work has concentrated on evaluating techniques that enable *differentiability* (one can differentiate between models) with efficiency (with less annotator hours), there are other desirable qualities as well. Some of these in particular are *diversity* of conversations (Hashimoto et al., 2019), *repeatability* of experiments, and *explainability* of results (Deriu et al., 2021). While there is some discussion of the latter two topics in our experiments, these topics are fully deserving of a more thorough analysis than is provided here.

References

Daniel Adiwardana, Minh-Thang Luong, David R So, Jamie Hall, Noah Fiedel, Romal Thoppilan, Zi Yang, Apoorv Kulshreshtha, Gaurav Nemade, Yifeng Lu, et al. 2020. Towards a human-like open-domain chatbot. *arXiv preprint arXiv:2001.09977*.

Leonard Adolphs, Kurt Shuster, Jack Urbanek, Arthur Szlam, and Jason Weston. 2021. Reason first, then respond: Modular generation for knowledge-infused dialogue. *arXiv preprint arXiv:2111.05204*.

Joshua Albrecht and Rebecca Hwa. 2007. A re-examination of machine learning approaches for sentence-level mt evaluation. In *Proceedings of the 45th Annual Meeting of the Association of Computational Linguistics*, pages 880–887.

Norman H Anderson. 1965. Primacy effects in personality impression formation using a generalized order effect paradigm. *Journal of personality and social psychology*, 2(1):1.

SE Asch. 1946. Forming impressions of personality. *The Journal of Abnormal and Social Psychology*, 41(3):258–290.

Ram Ashwin, Prasad Rohit, Khatri Chandra, Venkatesh Anu, Gabriel Raefer, Liu Qing, Nunn Jeff, Hedayatnia Behnam, Cheng Ming, Nagar Ashish, King Eric, Bland Kate, Wartick Amanda, Pan Yi, Song Han, Jayadevan Sk, Hwang Gene, and Pettigrue Art. 2017. Conversational AI: The science behind the Adlexa Prize. In *Proceedings of Workshop on Conversational AI*.

Jason Baumgartner, Savvas Zannettou, Brian Keegan, Megan Squire, and Jeremy Blackburn. 2020. The pushshift reddit dataset. *Proceedings of the International AAAI Conference on Web and Social Media*, 14(1):830–839.

Antoine Bordes, Y-Lan Boureau, and Jason Weston. 2017. Learning end-to-end goal-oriented dialog. In *Proceedings of the International Conference on Learning Representations*.

Anthony Chen, Gabriel Stanovsky, Sameer Singh, and Matt Gardner. 2019. Evaluating question answering evaluation. In *Proceedings of the 2nd Workshop on Machine Reading for Question Answering*, pages 119–124.

Elizabeth Clark and Noah A Smith. 2021. Choose your own adventure: Paired suggestions in collaborative writing for evaluating story generation models. In *Proceedings of the 2021 Conference of the North American Chapter of the Association for Computational Linguistics: Human Language Technologies*, pages 3566–3575.

Jan Deriu, Alvaro Rodrigo, Arantxa Otegi, Guillermo Echegoyen, Sophie Rosset, Eneko Agirre, and Mark Cieliebak. 2021. Survey on evaluation methods for dialogue systems. *Artificial Intelligence Review*, 54(1):755–810.

Jan Milan Deriu, Don Tuggener, Pius von Däniken, Jon Ander Campos, Álvaro Rodrigo, Thiziri Belkacem, Aitor Soroa, Eneko Agirre, and Mark Cieliebak. 2020. Spot the bot: A robust and efficient framework for the evaluation of conversational dialogue systems. In *Proceedings of the 2020 Conference on Empirical Methods in Natural Language Processing (EMNLP)*, pages 3971–3984.

Emily Dinan, Samuel Humeau, Bharath Chintagunta, and Jason Weston. 2019a. Build it break it fix it for dialogue safety: Robustness from adversarial human attack. In *Proceedings of the 2019 Conference on Empirical Methods in Natural Language Processing and the 9th International Joint Conference on Natural Language Processing (EMNLP-IJCNLP)*, pages 4537–4546.

Emily Dinan, Varvara Logacheva, Valentin Malykh, Alexander Miller, Kurt Shuster, Jack Urbanek, Douwe Kiela, Arthur Szlam, Iulian Serban, Ryan Lowe, et al. 2019b. The second conversational intelligence challenge (convai2). *arXiv preprint arXiv:1902.00098*.

Emily Dinan, Stephen Roller, Kurt Shuster, Angela Fan, Michael Auli, and Jason Weston. 2018. Wizard of wikipedia: Knowledge-powered conversational agents. *arXiv preprint arXiv:1811.01241*.

Layla El Asri, Hannes Schulz, Shikhar Sharma, Jeremie Zumer, Justin Harris, Emery Fine, Rahul Mehrotra, and Kaheer Suleman. 2017. Frames: a corpus for adding memory to goal-oriented dialogue systems. In *Proceedings of the 18th Annual SIGDIAL Meeting on Discourse and Dialogue*, pages 207–219. ACL.

Angela Fan, Yacine Jernite, Ethan Perez, David Grangier, Jason Weston, and Michael Auli. 2019. Eli5: Long form question answering. In *Proceedings of the 57th Annual Meeting of the Association for Computational Linguistics*, pages 3558–3567.

Sarah E Finch and Jinho D Choi. 2020. Towards unified dialogue system evaluation: A comprehensive analysis of current evaluation protocols. In *Proceedings of the 21th Annual Meeting of the Special Interest Group on Discourse and Dialogue*, pages 236–245.

Raefer Gabriel, Yang Liu, Anna Gottardi, Mihail Eric, Anju Khatri, Anjali Chadha, Qinlang Chen, Behnam Hedayatnia, Pankaj Rajan, Ali Binici, et al. 2020. Further advances in open domain dialog systems in the third alexa prize socialbot grand challenge. *Alexa Prize Proceedings*.

Asma Ghandeharioun, Judy Hanwen Shen, Natasha Jaques, Craig Ferguson, Noah Jones, Àgata

Lapedriza, and Rosalind W. Picard. 2019. Approximating interactive human evaluation with self-play for open-domain dialog systems. *Advances in Neural Information Processing Systems*.

Prakhar Gupta, Shikib Mehri, Tiancheng Zhao, Amy Pavel, Maxine Eskenazi, and Jeffrey P Bigham. 2019. Investigating evaluation of open-domain dialogue systems with human generated multiple references. In *Proceedings of the 20th Annual SIGdial Meeting on Discourse and Dialogue*, pages 379–391.

Tatsunori B Hashimoto, Hugh Zhang, and Percy Liang. 2019. Unifying human and statistical evaluation for natural language generation. In *Proceedings of the 2019 Conference of the North American Chapter of the Association for Computational Linguistics: Human Language Technologies, Volume 1 (Long and Short Papers)*, pages 1689–1701.

Helen Hastie. 2012. Metrics and evaluation of spoken dialogue systems. In Oliver Lemon and Olivier Pietquin, editors, *Data-Driven Methods for Adaptive Spoken Dialogue Systems*, pages 131–150. Springer.

Matthew Henderson, Blaise Thomson, and Jason D Williams. 2014. The second dialog state tracking challenge. In *Proceedings of the 15th Annual Meeting of the Special Interest Group on Discourse and Dialogue*, pages 263–272.

Stephen J Hoch. 1984. Availability and interference in predictive judgment. *Journal of Experimental Psychology: Learning, Memory, and Cognition*, 10(4):649.

Minlie Huang, Xiaoyan Zhu, and Jianfeng Gao. 2020. Challenges in building intelligent open-domain dialog systems. *ACM Transactions on Information Systems (TOIS)*, 38(3):1–32.

Jessica Huynh, Jeffrey Bigham, and Maxine Eskenazi. 2021. A survey of nlp-related crowdsourcing hits: what works and what does not. *arXiv preprint arXiv:2111.05241*.

Mojtaba Komeili, Kurt Shuster, and Jason Weston. 2021. Internet-augmented dialogue generation. *arXiv preprint arXiv:2107.07566*.

Ilia Kulikov, Alexander Miller, Kyunghyun Cho, and Jason Weston. 2019. Importance of search and evaluation strategies in neural dialogue modeling. In *Proceedings of the 12th International Conference on Natural Language Generation*, pages 76–87, Tokyo, Japan. Association for Computational Linguistics.

Seolhwa Lee, Heuiseok Lim, and João Sedoc. 2020. An evaluation protocol for generative conversational systems. *arXiv preprint arXiv:2010.12741*.

Jiwei Li, Michel Galley, Chris Brockett, Georgios P Spithourakis, Jianfeng Gao, and Bill Dolan. 2016. A persona-based neural conversation model. In *Proceedings of the 54th Annual Meeting of the Association for Computational Linguistics*, pages 994–1003. ACL.

Margaret Li, Jason Weston, and Stephen Roller. 2019. Acute-eval: Improved dialogue evaluation with optimized questions and multi-turn comparisons. *arXiv preprint arXiv:1909.03087*.

Weixin Liang, James Zou, and Zhou Yu. 2020. Beyond user self-reported likert scale ratings: A comparison model for automatic dialog evaluation. In *Proceedings of the 58th Annual Meeting of the Association for Computational Linguistics*, pages 1363–1374.

Chia-Wei Liu, Ryan Lowe, Iulian Vlad Serban, Mike Noseworthy, Laurent Charlin, and Joelle Pineau. 2016. How not to evaluate your dialogue system: An empirical study of unsupervised evaluation metrics for dialogue response generation. In *Proceedings of the 2016 Conference on Empirical Methods in Natural Language Processing*, pages 2122–2132.

Ryan Lowe, Michael Noseworthy, Iulian Vlad Serban, Nicolas Angelard-Gontier, Yoshua Bengio, and Joelle Pineau. 2017. Towards an automatic turing test: Learning to evaluate dialogue responses. In *Proceedings of the 55th Annual Meeting of the Association for Computational Linguistics*, pages 1116–1126. ACL.

Norman Miller and Donald T Campbell. 1959. Recency and primacy in persuasion as a function of the timing of speeches and measurements. *The Journal of Abnormal and Social Psychology*, 59(1):1.

Bennet B Murdock Jr. 1962. The serial position effect of free recall. *Journal of experimental psychology*, 64(5):482.

Leo Postman and Laura W Phillips. 1965. Short-term temporal changes in free recall. *Quarterly journal of experimental psychology*, 17(2):132–138.

Hannah Rashkin, Eric Michael Smith, Margaret Li, and Y-Lan Boureau. 2019. Towards empathetic open-domain conversation models: A new benchmark and dataset. In *Proceedings of the 57th Annual Meeting of the Association for Computational Linguistics*, pages 5370–5381, Florence, Italy. Association for Computational Linguistics.

Stephen Roller, Y-Lan Boureau, Jason Weston, Antoine Bordes, Emily Dinan, Angela Fan, David Gunning, Da Ju, Margaret Li, Spencer Poff, et al. 2020. Open-domain conversational agents: Current progress, open problems, and future directions. *arXiv preprint arXiv:2006.12442*.

Stephen Roller, Emily Dinan, Naman Goyal, Da Ju, Mary Williamson, Yinhan Liu, Jing Xu, Myle Ott, Eric Michael Smith, Y-Lan Boureau, et al. 2021. Recipes for building an open-domain chatbot. In *Proceedings of the 16th Conference of the European Chapter of the Association for Computational Linguistics: Main Volume*, pages 300–325.

Alexander Schmitt and Stefan Ultes. 2015. Interaction quality: Assessing the quality of ongoing spoken dialog interaction by experts—and how it relates to user satisfaction. *Speech Communication*, 74:12–36.

Abigail See, Stephen Roller, Douwe Kiela, and Jason Weston. 2019. What makes a good conversation? how controllable attributes affect human judgments. In *Proceedings of the 2019 Conference of the North American Chapter of the Association for Computational Linguistics*, pages 1702–1723. ACL.

Kurt Shuster, Jack Urbanek, Emily Dinan, Arthur Szlam, and Jason Weston. 2020. Deploying lifelong open-domain dialogue learning. *arXiv preprint arXiv:2008.08076*.

Neil Stewart, Gordon DA Brown, and Nick Chater. 2005. Absolute identification by relative judgment. *Psychological review*, 112(4):881.

Alan M Turing and J Haugeland. 1950. *Computing machinery and intelligence*. MIT Press Cambridge, MA.

Anu Venkatesh, Chandra Khatri, Ashwin Ram, Fenfei Guo, Raefer Gabriel, Ashish Nagar, Rohit Prasad, Ming Cheng, Behnam Hedayatnia, Angeliki Metallinou, et al. 2018. On evaluating and comparing conversational agents. *arXiv preprint arXiv:1801.03625*, 4:60–68.

Oriol Vinyals and Quoc Le. 2015. A neural conversational model. In *Proceedings of the 31st International Conference on Machine Learning, Deep Learning Workshop*, Lille, France.

Sean Welleck, Ilia Kulikov, Stephen Roller, Emily Dinan, Kyunghyun Cho, and Jason Weston. 2020. Neural text generation with unlikelihood training. In *International Conference on Learning Representations*.

Tsung-Hsien Wen, David Vandyke, Nikola Mrkšić, Milica Gasic, Lina M. Rojas Barahona, Pei-Hao Su, Stefan Ultes, and Steve Young. 2017. A network-based end-to-end trainable task-oriented dialogue system. In *Proceedings of the 15th Conference of the European Chapter of the Association for Computational Linguistics*, pages 438–449. ACL.

Jason D Williams, Antoine Raux, and Matthew Henderson. 2016. The dialog state tracking challenge series: A review. *Dialogue & Discourse*, 7(3):4–33.

Yu Wu, Furu Wei, Shaohan Huang, Yunli Wang, Zhoujun Li, and Ming Zhou. 2019. Response generation by context-aware prototype editing. In *Proceedings of the AAAI Conference on Artificial Intelligence*, volume 33, pages 7281–7288.

Jing Xu, Da Ju, Margaret Li, Y-Lan Boureau, Jason Weston, and Emily Dinan. 2020. Recipes for safety in open-domain chatbots. *arXiv preprint arXiv:2010.07079*.

Jing Xu, Arthur Szlam, and Jason Weston. 2021. Beyond goldfish memory: Long-term open-domain conversation. *arXiv preprint arXiv:2107.07567*.

Yi-Ting Yeh, Maxine Eskenazi, and Shikib Mehri. 2021. A comprehensive assessment of dialog evaluation metrics. In *The First Workshop on Evaluations and Assessments of Neural Conversation Systems*, pages 15–33.

Saizheng Zhang, Emily Dinan, Jack Urbanek, Arthur Szlam, Douwe Kiela, and Jason Weston. 2018. Personalizing dialogue agents: I have a dog, do you have pets too? In *Proceedings of the 56th Annual Meeting of the Association for Computational Linguistics (Volume 1: Long Papers)*, pages 2204–2213.

A Additional existing work

Open-domain versus specific domain Our work concentrates on the open-domain setting. In specific conversational domains, such as question answering (QA), evaluation can be simpler and is often reduced to measuring overlap or exact match with the correct answer (Chen et al., 2019). However, this no longer as easily suffices for free-form, conversational and long-form QA where answers are more open-ended (Fan et al., 2019; Adolphs et al., 2021). Similarly, for certain types of goal-oriented conversations more targeted evaluations can take place, for example evaluation of state tracking (Williams et al., 2016), interaction quality (Schmitt and Ultes, 2015), and task completion (Hastie, 2012; Henderson et al., 2014; Bordes et al., 2017; El Asri et al., 2017; Wen et al., 2017). Open-domain dialogue potentially covers all these other cases as special cases, but also covers conversations that are more free-form or do not have a precise goal. Hence, finding a reliable evaluation technique is more difficult, and there is currently no single standard method that is agreed upon (Deriu et al., 2021; Huang et al., 2020; Roller et al., 2020). Different techniques that have been proposed will be described in the following paragraphs.

Automatic metrics Automatic metrics are the most convenient for fast, efficient and reproducible research with a quick turn-around and development cycle, hence they are frequently used. Unfortunately, many of them, such as BLEU, METEOR and ROUGE, have been shown to only "correlate very weakly with human judgement" (Liu et al., 2016). A central problem is that, due to the open-ended nature of conversations, there are many possible responses in a given dialogue, and, while having multiple references can help, there is typically only one gold label available (Gupta et al., 2019). Perplexity (computing the predicted probability of the given gold utterances) has been argued to correlate with human judgments (Adiwardana et al., 2020), however this has also been shown to not always be the case (Dinan et al., 2019b), and moreover does not actually evaluate the generations themselves produced by a decoder architecture. Hence, changing the behavior of the generation method can dramatically change human evaluations, while maintaining identical or near-identical perplexity (See et al., 2019; Welleck et al., 2020; Adiwardana et al., 2020; Roller et al., 2021). An alternative recent trend is to employ trainable metrics, whereby a neural network model is used to score the conversational model (typically also another neural network), see e.g. Lowe et al. (2017); Ghandeharioun et al. (2019). Such systems provide a promise of improved speed of research and development of dialogue agents, but so far have not been met with wide adoption. Some issues are that they may not generalize as well to data beyond that which they are trained (overfit) and also may be biased and gameable (Wu et al., 2019; Albrecht and Hwa, 2007). For a comprehensive comparison of automatic metrics – both standard and learned metrics – see Yeh et al. (2021). In general, creating a reliable automatic metric is still considered an open problem (Deriu et al., 2021).

Crowdworkers versus experts versus organic users While utilizing human evaluations in research is the current standard, we contend that choosing exactly which kind of human evaluation is also still an open question. In this work we concentrate on the study of crowdworker human evaluations, however there are several alternative paradigms. Utilizing trained experts, such as a group of researchers in the same institution, is one alternative (Deriu et al., 2021). Compared to employing crowdworkers, while model comparison results can agree between the two types of annotators, there can be vastly different sensitivity and win rates (Welleck et al., 2020), with the experts having more agreement and higher resulting sensitivity. On the other hand, it is harder to recruit and employ experts, limiting reproducibility. In both the crowdworker and expert annotator cases, neither of those groups are necessarily the intended target audience of a given system. If it is possible to deploy a model to people who genuinely want to talk to it (e.g., without being paid), conversations may be more natural and evaluations will be in line with genuine interests. Evaluation by deployment can be successful (Gabriel et al., 2020; Shuster et al., 2020), where behavioral metrics such as the amount of conversation time per user or retention rate can serve as a proxy for interestingness and engagingness metrics. Model deployment however also has its issues. First, user desires may not necessarily be aligned with the goals of the research itself, meaning researchers may have to develop features and improvements towards the goals of the product rather than towards long-term research. Further, experiments are difficult to set up and may be difficult to reproduce by other groups. Crowdworker tasks can be more reproducible especially when code is made available to reproduce experiments, but there are also many pitfalls when constructing the tasks, see e.g. Huynh et al. (2021).

Conversation instructions to raters When utilizing evaluators in a evaluator-model conversational setup, the precise instructions on how to go about the conversation will clearly have large effects. Such instructions can control the topic, e.g. "get to know each other" as in the Persona-Chat task (Zhang et al., 2018), versus "have a knowledgeable conversation" in Wizard of Wikipedia (Dinan et al., 2018). Instructions can also orient workers towards a more fruitful strategy for a desired dataset, for example orienting them towards open questions on sensitive topics rather than profanity to get a bot to generate unsafe utterances (Xu et al., 2020). The length of the conversation will also play a role in the performance of models, for example, short conversations do not test the ability of models to retain knowledge in the long-term (Xu et al., 2021). Overall, the style of conversation has large effects (even if the topic is unchanged) for example when instructing crowdworkers to be adversarial vs. non-adversarial (Dinan et al., 2019a), which relates to the classic Turing Test (Turing and Haugeland, 1950). Further, particular instruction wording choices will change the quality of conversations, as they will change how well crowdworkers understand the task (Huynh et al., 2021).

Evaluation question phrasing for raters Besides how the conversation is carried out, one also needs to choose the precise question (or questions) being asked to crowdworkers in order for them to rate conversations. In open-domain conversation there are a variety of qualities one could expect from a good conversationalist, and potentially one could ask about any of them individually, as well as asking for overall performance. For example, See et al. (2019) asks evaluators for ratings of interestingness, making sense, fluency, avoiding repetition, listening ability and inquisitiveness as intermediate conversational aspects, and humanness and engagingness questions to measure overall quality. Adiwardana et al. (2020) asks questions based on sensibleness and specificity. Responsibility, toxicity and bias can also be measured (Xu et al., 2020). Even after settling on the exact question(s) to be asked, their exact phrasing also has impact on sensitivity, as shown in Li et al. (2019). In that work, the authors optimized the question phrasing by running evaluations with alternative phrasings, and choosing the one with the highest agreement.

Rating existing versus own conversations The standard setup is for a human to have a conversation with a model, and rate that conversation. Some evaluation protocols deviate from this setup, and ask evaluators to rate conversations they did not participate in. One simple approach of that kind is to present model completions of a dialogue from the fixed test set of a given task, and ask for their evaluation, with hence no human taking part in the actual conversation (Vinyals and Le, 2015; Li et al., 2016). In the Acute-Eval method (Li et al., 2019) raters are asked to compare two existing conversation logs, and the authors consider both the case of human-model chat logs, and model-model (self-chat) logs, where the former are actually a different set of human conversationalists compared to the final raters. Deriu et al. (2020) considers chat logs between pairs of models, again with no humans taking part in the conversations. These techniques allow efficient reuse of existing conversational data and have some reproducibility gains: conversations collected in previous trials and by other systems can be directly compared with a new system, without having to recollect additional data. This can significantly reduce the resources needed by a new evaluation, and ensure that multiple papers are comparing to prior work consistently. On the other hand, it may be harder for evaluators to rate conversations that they have not been involved in (Finch and Choi, 2020). Conversations that do not even involve humans should be treated with some scepticism, as there is no human to guide conversation and hence evaluate interactive quality. Nevertheless, such approaches do appear to be useful experimentally (Li et al., 2019; Roller et al., 2021).

Pairwise versus single-model ratings Conversations are often either rated individually, e.g. with Likert-score ratings (Ashwin et al., 2017; Venkatesh et al., 2018; Zhang et al., 2018; Rashkin et al., 2019; See et al., 2019; Dinan et al., 2019b, 2018), or pairwise by comparing models (Li et al., 2019; Liang et al., 2020; Vinyals and Le, 2015; Li et al., 2016; Lee et al., 2020). Likert scoring relies on absolute identification rather than relative discrimination, which is less reliable in humans (Stewart et al., 2005), leading to different biases per annotator (Kulikov et al., 2019). It is thus often necessary to then re-evaluate existing models at the same time as a new model, as the distribution of human annotators can easily shift over time, causing measurement errors (See et al., 2019). Another common difficulty is related to sequential effects (Stewart et al., 2005), where the annotator can be influenced by the first model they evaluate, causing difficulties in using an absolute scale. Pairwise comparisons, on the other hand, make comparing a set of models less efficient, and also have the same problem that existing baseline models have to be essentially reassessed with respect to new ones.

Per-turn versus per-dialogue evaluation Some research evaluates *single-turn* responses in conversations given gold dialogue contexts, without taking into account whole interactive conversations (Lee et al., 2020; Vinyals and Le, 2015; Li et al., 2016). This fails to take into account multi-turn aspects of a conversation, for example a model repeating itself over multiple turns. *Per-turn* evaluation instead conducts an entire conversation, but raters are still asked to evaluate each turn (response by their partner) (Schmitt and Ultes, 2015; Adiwardana et al., 2020; Komeili et al., 2021). Collecting per-turn evaluation also allows for measuring learning effects where workers become more adept at interacting with the bot for certain specific tasks (e.g., see Xu et al. (2020)). In contrast, methods like multi-turn Likert or Acute-Eval ask evaluators to assess the entire dialogue as a whole, rather than the individual turns, under the assumption that the quality of a conversation is not simply the sum of its parts. Literature from psychology predicts several effects when considering how people combine their impressions from single conversational turns into an evaluation of an entire conversation. The *primacy effect* refers to how overall judgment is more shaped by characteristics presented earlier (Asch, 1946; Anderson, 1965). Conversely, the *recency* *effect* appears when more weight is given to information presented the most recently, and both effects combine to give more weight to items at the beginning and end of a list (Murdock Jr, 1962; Postman and Phillips, 1965), with the recency effect being more prominent when judgment is elicited without any delay when the recent information is still fresh (Miller and Campbell, 1959; Hoch, 1984).

B Additional methods

B.1 Screenshots of crowdsourced human evaluation tasks

See Figure 2 for a screenshot of the PW-Turn evaluation technique, Figure 3 for a screenshot of the PW-Dialog technique, and Figure 4 for a screenshot of the SM-Turn and SM-Dialog techniques. Figure 5 additionally displays the onboarding UI for PW-Turn.

B.2 Pairwise per-turn evaluation onboarding

In order to perform quality control on crowdworkers before the start of the conversation itself, we ask each worker to first annotate a conversation in which there are two possible responses for each turn of one of the speakers, one response of which is clearly better than the other (Figure 5). These pairs of responses vary slightly depending on which of the evaluation metrics is being tested. Workers must ultimately choose the correct response for all four pairs of responses but have two tries in which to do so.

B.3 Quality checks on crowdworkers

In order to ensure that our comparisons between evaluation techniques are not affected by variability in the pool of crowdworkers when running one technique vs. another, we adopt a consistent set of criteria across all techniques regarding which workers to exclude from our final set of data. If a worker fails one of the checks in Appendix B.4 during one of the per-turn evaluations PW-Turn or SM-Turn, we retroactively exclude their ratings from all of the evaluation techniques.

In order to prevent any worker from disproportionately contributing to the final results, each worker is restricted to one conversation per model pair and evaluation metric (for PW-Turn and PW-Dialog) or one conversation per model (for SM-Turn and SM-Dialog). All evaluations are collected among residents of the United States on weekdays, from roughly 9 AM to 6 PM in the U.S. Eastern time zone, following Li et al. (2019).

B.4 Checks used when filtering per-turn evaluations

We check each conversation between a crowdworker and a Bot Speaker collected during PW-Turn and SM-Turn evaluations against the criteria below to see if they have issues that warrant their exclusion from the final filtered set of evaluations. If at least one of the following problems is present, all evaluations from the crowdworker in question are filtered out of the results shown in this work:

- The messages consist of less than three words on average
- The first message inputted by the worker contains a greeting (redundant, since a dummy *"Hi!"* message is already fixed to be the worker's first line of conversation)
- Several of the messages are written using all capital letters
- Later messages are duplicates of the first one (i.e. the worker is repeating their messages throughout the conversation)
- One or more of the messages use offensive language

C Additional results

C.1 Evaluation data collection

After filtering out workers with unacceptable messages following Appendix B.3, we are left with a minimum of 144 and a mean of 231 ratings (typically 6 per conversation) for each of the PW-Turn evaluations, a minimum of 191 and a mean of 324 ratings for PW-Dialog, a minimum of 349 and a mean of 411 ratings (typically 6 per conversation) for SM-Turn, and a minimum of 58 and a mean of 68 ratings for SM-Dialog evaluations (for which there is only one rating per conversation). On average, the collection of ratings after filtering represents 5.73 hours of worker labor for PW-Turn per model pair and evaluation metric, 6.03 hours for PW-Dialog per model pair and evaluation metric, and 4.39 hours for joint SM-Turn/SM-Dialog evaluations per model.

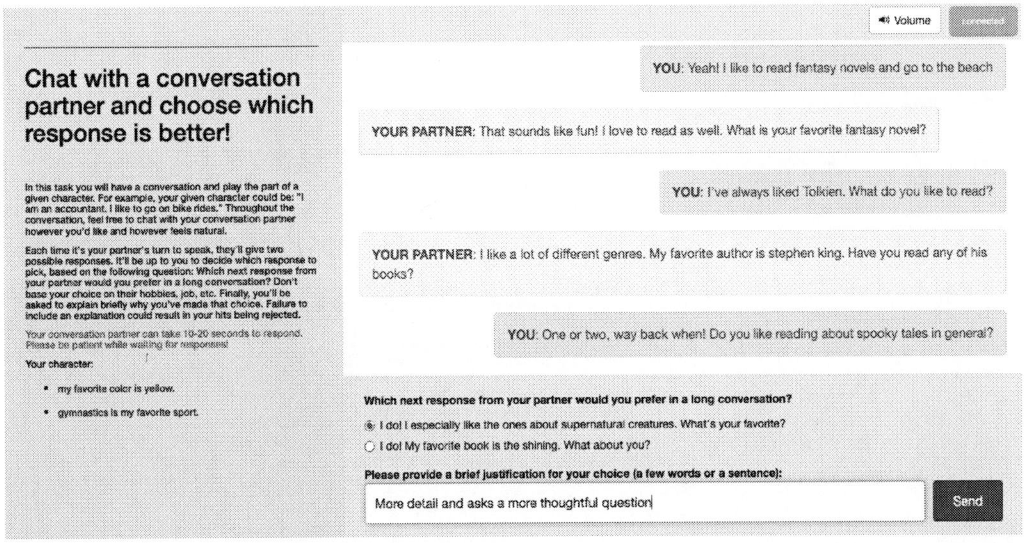

Figure 2: Screenshot of the Pairwise Per-Turn (PW-Turn) evaluation technique, in which we ask crowdworkers to choose one of two possible responses from their conversation partner and describe why that response is better. The two responses come from the two models that we are trying to compare the performance of.

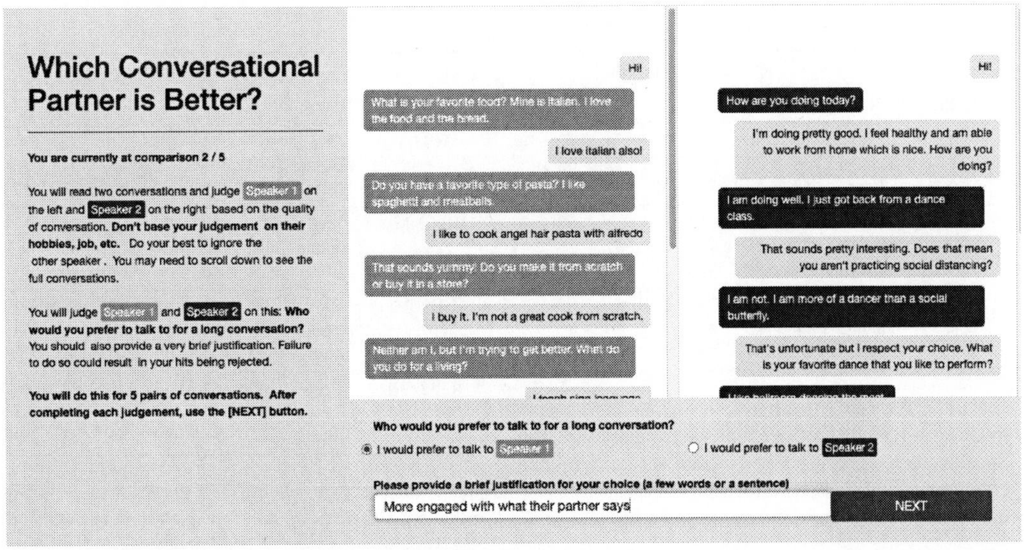

Figure 3: Screenshot of the Pairwise Per-Dialogue (PW-Dialog) evaluation technique, in which we ask crowdworkers to choose which of two speakers in two separate conversations is better on the given evaluation metric, here *"Who would you prefer to talk to for a long conversation?"* The crowdworker must then describe why that speaker is better.

C.2 PW-Turn model win rates as a function of turn

Unlike PW-Dialog, the PW-Turn technique is able to measure differences in the win rate of models as a function of the number of turns into the conversation. In Figure 6 and Table 4, we see that BlenderBot3B's win rates tend to be closer to 50% in the first 1 or 2 turns of the Bot Speaker, and higher later: this may be because the first few lines of the conversation typically consist of greetings (*"Hi, how are you?"*) or pleasantries, which may be harder to judge model performance on. However, it may also be because improvements are accumulated and factored into evaluators' decisions

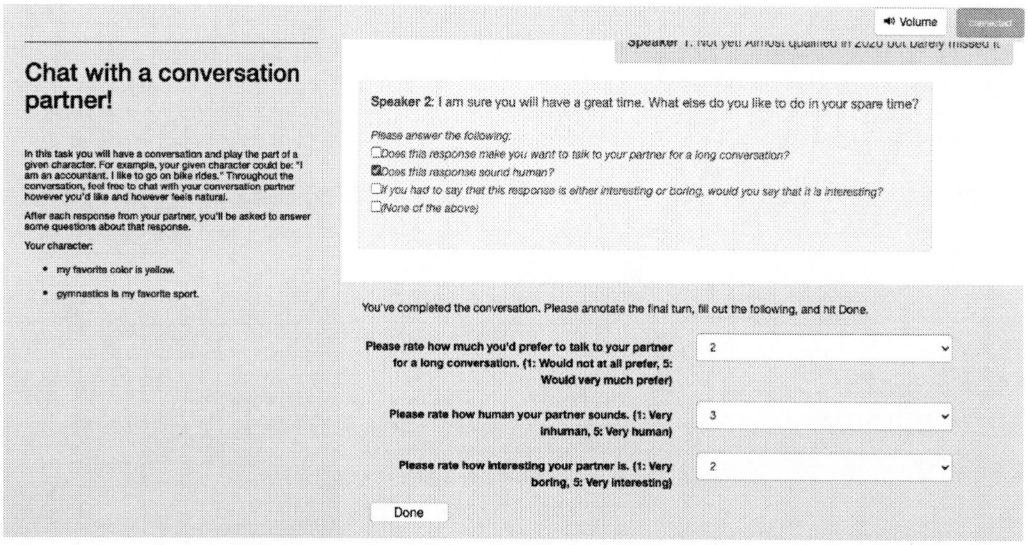

Figure 4: Screenshot of the crowdsourcing task for collecting Single-Model Per-Turn (SM-Turn) and Single-Model Per-Dialogue (SM-Dialog) evaluations. We ask the crowdworker to annotate each response from their partner along several dimensions, as well as give a global Likert-scale rating of their partner's performance at the end of the conversation.

		PW-Turn: turn index					
Comp.	Metric	1	2	3	4	5	6
Length	Pref	40	56	67	67	**74**	72
	Human	38	**72**	69	62	**72**	62
	Inter	59	62	72	**78**	69	69
Size	Pref	26	56	51	54	38	**62**
	Human	29	58	50	46	**67**	58
	Inter	31	59	**62**	52	45	45
FT	Pref	70	78	74	**89**	81	**89**
	Human	69	73	**90**	88	84	85
	Inter	52	59	**89**	74	67	85

Table 4: Percentage win rates of BlenderBot3B vs. other models on PW-Turn evaluations as a function of Bot Speaker turn. The highest win rate for each model comparison and evaluation metric is bolded. This is a tabular representation of the curves in Figure 6.

		SM-Turn: turn index					
Model	Metric	1	2	3	4	5	6
BB3B	Pref	67	71	**72**	70	**72**	70
	Human	70	63	72	**76**	71	70
	Inter	42	43	**47**	43	45	**47**
BB3B-M0	Pref	**74**	**74**	**74**	67	66	72
	Human	66	**72**	64	67	69	66
	Inter	29	**40**	38	34	36	33
BB90M	Pref	**71**	67	65	64	64	64
	Human	59	64	61	**70**	65	67
	Inter	39	35	39	**41**	**41**	38
Reddit3B	Pref	**67**	63	49	50	54	46
	Human	**60**	57	54	53	51	58
	Inter	44	36	39	**46**	31	39

Table 5: Percentage success rates of responses of various models on various evaluation questions (metrics) for SM-Turn, as a function of Bot Speaker turn. The highest win rate turn for each model and evaluation metric is bolded.

later in the conversation. Strikingly, BlenderBot3B performs very poorly vs. BlenderBot90M (the Size comparison) on the first Bot Speaker turn: empirically, this may be due to the fact that BlenderBot3B generally starts its first responses with the greetings *"Hi"* or *"Hello"* much less frequently than BlenderBot90M does.

C.3 SM-Turn success rates as a function of conversation turn

See Table 5 for the success rates of model responses using the SM-Turn technique, as a function of Bot Speaker turn.

C.4 Relationship between per-turn ratings and final ratings

Given that SM-Turn allows us to measure per-turn ratings of model performance, it is worth exploring whether there are certain turns of the conversation that contribute more strongly to the workers' final Likert-scale ratings of the conversation (SM-

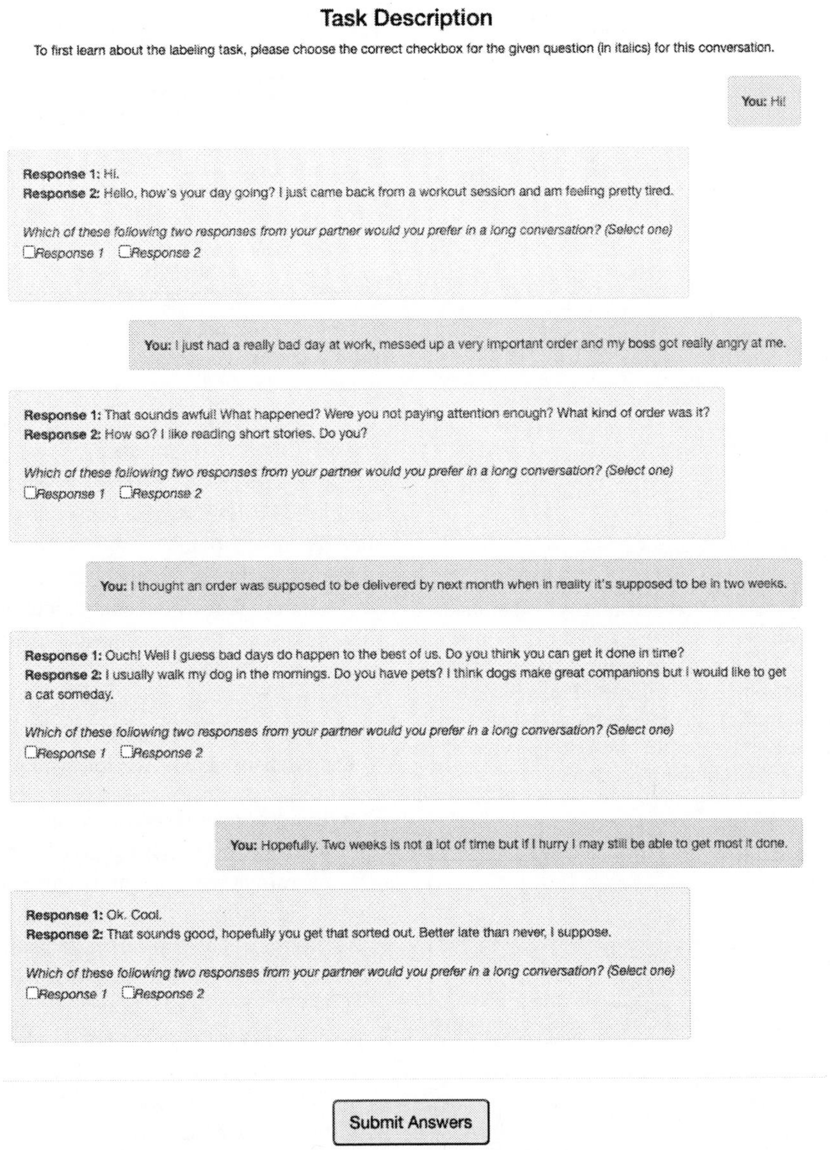

Figure 5: Screenshot of the onboarding process for crowdworkers for the PW-Turn technique.

Dialog). Figure 7 plots the coefficients of workers' per-turn SM-Turn ratings in an OLS regression, with the SM-Dialog Likert score at the end of the conversation as the dependent variable. (Here, we reduce variability by taking the mean over the three evaluation metrics for each turn's SM-Turn ratings and SM-Dialog Likert scores.) Generally, we see a higher positive coefficient of the SM-Turn ratings in later turns in the conversation, which implies that the workers may have a recency bias: they may remember the most recent turns of the conversation more strongly when determining how to rate the model's performance overall.

C.5 Text justification for model response selection

For PW-Turn evaluations, we collect and analyze justification texts for each turn, after the worker selects a model response. We then group justification texts by model type and comparison.

To measure lengths of justifications, we split text strings into words (space-delimited), and we

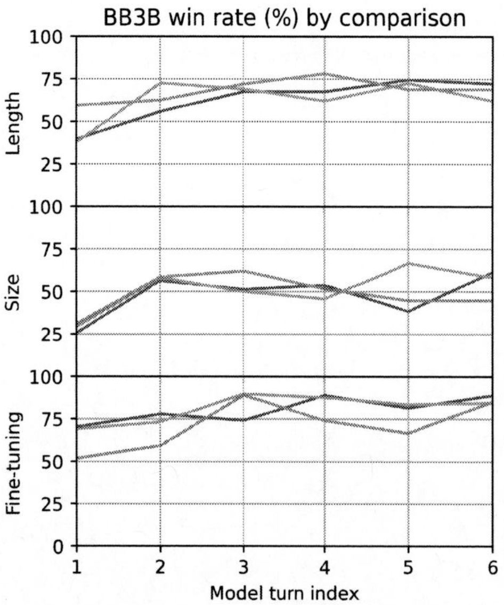

Figure 6: Win rate of BlenderBot3B vs. other models for the comparisons in Section 3.2 on the PW-Turn evaluations, as a function of the number of Bot Speaker turns into the conversation, for the Preference (blue), Humanness (orange), and Interestingness (green) metrics. BlenderBot3B tends to fare better against other models in later turns of the conversation.

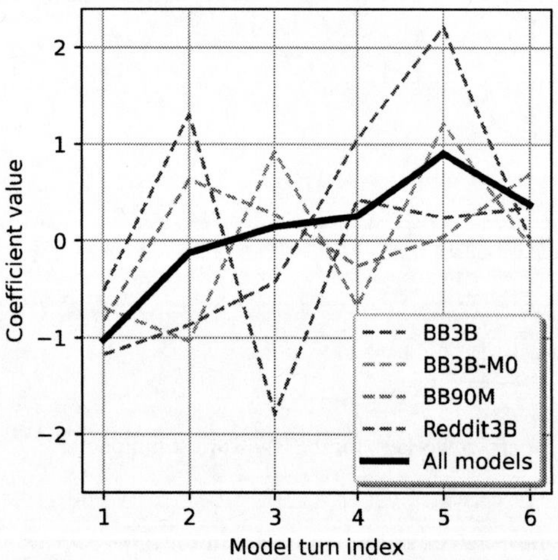

Figure 7: The per-turn coefficients of SM-Turn success rates in an OLS regression with SM-Dialog Likert scores as the dependent variable. SM-Turn rates and SM-Dialog scores are averaged across evaluation metrics. The black curve represents data from all models concatenated together. SM-Turn rates from later turns tend to be more positively correlated to the final SM-Dialog Likert scores, suggesting a possible recency bias.

calculate the mean number of words in each sample. Results are shown in Table 6.

Comparison	Model	Avg. number of words
Length	BB3B	8.85
	BB3B-M0	7.70
Size	BB3B	8.95
	BB90M	8.81
Fine-tuning	BB3B	9.40
	Reddit3B	9.25

Table 6: Mean number of words in justifications given for BlenderBot3B vs. other models on PW-Turn evaluations.

For term importance, we use the `scikit-learn TfidfVectorizer` class to compute TF-IDF scores for each term in each model comparison.

We use a list of English stopwords from the `NLTK` library to filter out common terms. Additionally, we discard terms that have a higher document frequency than 0.8.

The top 20 terms (descending order) for each model pairing are shown in Table 7.

Our analysis reveals the following:

- **Length comparison**: While it appears that many crowdworkers prefer longer responses overall, at least in some conversational turns some crowdworkers may prefer shorter responses. The top terms in justifications for BlenderBot3B-M0 responses include "simple", "short" and "direct", while top terms in reasons for choosing BlenderBot3B include "detailed" and "longer". This shows that PW-Turn evaluation does well in capturing sensitivity to length, and that workers' selections are due to their own preferences at a given conversational turn.

  Interestingly, in PW-Turn we find that workers' justifications for choosing the BlenderBot3B-M0 responses are themselves on average shorter than for BlenderBot3B. Table 6 shows the mean justification lengths for different model pairings. The mean justification length for BlenderBot3B is 8.85 words, compared to a mean length of BlenderBot3B-M0 justifications of 7.7 words. This suggests that workers choosing shorter, "simple" responses may also be less detail-oriented.

- **Size comparison**: Top TF-IDF weighted

terms from workers' justifications for both models contain a mix of references to the conversational content, such as "hiking", "beach" or "dogs", and conversational structure, such as "relates" or "engaging". By inspection, there are no discernible differences between these terms.

- **Fine-tuning comparison**: High TF-IDF-weighted terms in justifications given by workers who choose the BlenderBot3B model are mostly related to conversational flow, such as "follows", "responds", and "acknowledges". In contrast, terms appearing in justifications for the Reddit3B model are specific and often refer to the topic instead of conversational style, such as "bath", "robot", and "paris". This suggests that workers who choose the Reddit3B model often favor less natural responses because they contain particular references.

These nuanced differences are clear when evaluating model responses per turn, but are difficult to capture when evaluating the conversation as a whole. Analysis of worker justifications supports our hypothesis that differences in conversational quality are easier to identify in the PW-Turn evaluation.

C.6 Variability in win rate across evaluation techniques

Table 8 shows the variability in the win rates of BlenderBot3B per evaluation technique, as measured by splitting the ratings from each technique into chunks of equal crowdworker time. The win rates from PW-Turn, PW-Dialog, and SM-Turn vary least across chunks, largely because the mean time per rating is small, leading to a larger number of ratings per chunk and thus a more precise estimate obtainable within a given block of time.[5] This suggests that calculating the per-conversation winner-takes-all win rate for the per-turn methods PW-Turn and SM-Turn may be disadvantageous if having a precise measurement of the win rate is more important than one that is statistically significant.

[5]We omit win rates of PW-Dialog on conversations between a human and a model for simplicity. For this technique, the time to collect conversations varies non-linearly as a function of the number of ratings (Section C.7), and thus any dividing of ratings into chunks of equal crowdworker time would have to take this irregularly-spaced conversation collection time into account.

C.7 Crowdsourcing time needed per technique

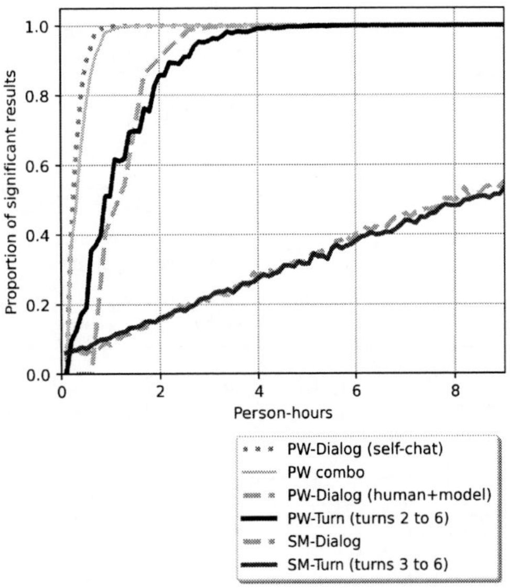

Figure 8: The time needed for statistical significance for the Length comparison between models (BlenderBot3B vs. BlenderBot3B-M0).

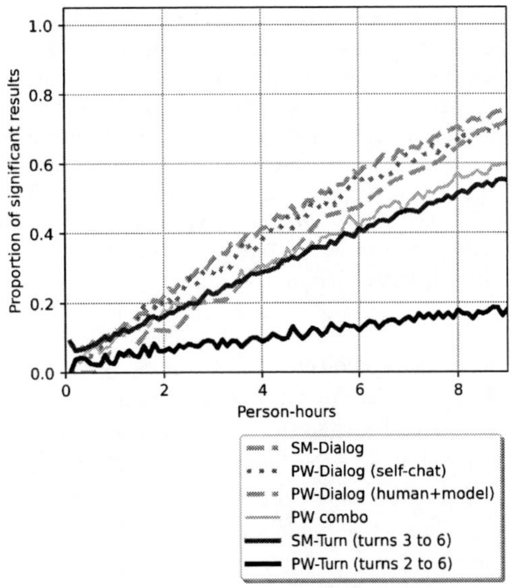

Figure 9: The time needed for statistical significance for the Size comparison between models (BlenderBot3B vs. BlenderBot90M).

Figures 8, 9, and 10 show the time needed to achieve a statistically significant difference between a pair of models for each of the evaluation

Comparison	Model	Top terms
Length	BB3B	information, chosen, provides, follow, engaging, going, adds, speaker, detailed, interested, conversational, looks, little, *play*, chat, new, *pets*, includes, longer, *tallies*
	BB3B-M0	*day*, *wow*, *game*, going, simple, stays, short, direct, express, speaker, keeps, conversational, precise, *western*, *popular*, *silk*, *hands*, use, tone, elaborate
Size	BB3B	message, information, easy, time, correct, want, interested, enjoy, change, relates, spend, prefer, fun, well, *hiking*, *pets*, go, moves, *beach*, sound
	BB90M	never, going, ok, excited, *fav*, correct, changes, *color*, new, engaging, personal, explain, *ohio*, fluent, enjoy, *hop*, *hip*, listen, back, *dogs*
Fine-tuning	BB3B	follows, going, contradicts, great, responds, follow, responsive, never, contradict, flows, acknowledges, responses, responded, stays, looks, personal, keep, well, nothing, contradiction
	Reddit3B	*bath*, personal, *robot*, im, *someone*, *bubble*, detailed, flowing, *play*, information, *paris*, due, *softball*, *careers*, unique, direct, watch, told, *book*, boring

Table 7: Top TF-IDF-weighted terms in justifications given for BlenderBot3B responses vs. other models on PW-Turn evaluations. Terms that are irrelevant to conversational evaluation are italicized.

Technique	Length	Size	Fine-Tuning
PW-Turn	10%	8%	11%
PW-Turn (WTA)	18%	24%	13%
PW-Dialog (self-chat)	9%	9%	6%
SM-Turn	14%	13%	12%
SM-Turn (WTA)	17%	16%	15%
SM-Dialog	14%	15%	16%

Table 8: The variability of win rates of BlenderBot3B across different evaluation techniques, for different model comparisons (columns). Variability was measured by splitting each time-ordered set of ratings into chunks representing 45 minutes of crowdworker time each, and then computing the standard deviation of the win rate across chunks. Standard deviations are averaged across the three evaluation metrics (Section 3.1.2). Win rates for PW-Turn were compiled over Bot Speaker turns 2 to 6 and for SM-Turn over turns 3 to 6, following Section 4.3.1.

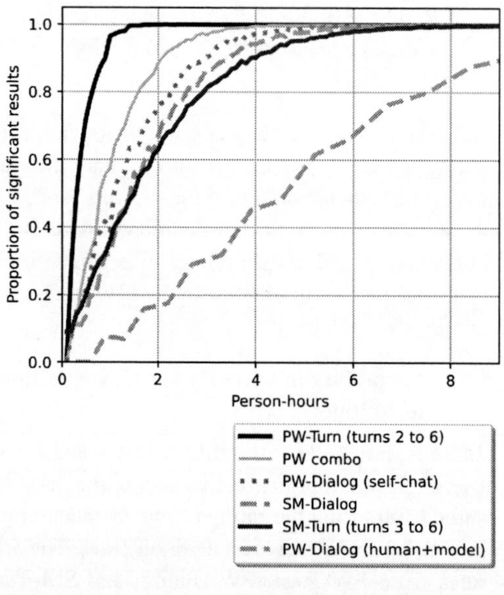

Figure 10: The time needed for statistical significance for the Fine-tuning comparison between models (BlenderBot3B vs. Reddit3B).

techniques studied. For these plots, we consider ratings for each turn in Bot Speaker turns 2 through 6 for PW-Turn and Bot Speaker turns 3 through 6 for SM-Turn, as in Section 4.3.1.[6] We use a two-sided binomial test for PW-Turn and PW-Dialog and a two-sided independent t-test for SM-Turn and SM-Dialog. Significance is measured at a p-value of 5%. When estimating the crowdsourcing time needed for each evaluation technique, we include an estimate of each technique's time to complete onboarding, which is mandatory before being approved to work on an evaluation.

For PW-Dialog evaluations (i.e. Acute-Evals) on conversations between a human and a model, the labor costs involve collecting both conversations and rating pairs. This gives us a parameter to tune in this method: how many conversations to collect, and then how many times to reuse them when rating pairs of them. In our experiments, the

[6] We do not compute winner-takes-all scores for each conversation because in experiments this works less well. It greatly diminishes the total number of ratings per technique, and thus it increases the number of conversations needed to achieve statistical significance. We note that, compared to the per-dialogue technique SM-Dialog, the resulting rating is binary per evaluation metric in this case, which may contribute to poor performance.

number of conversations necessary is chosen such that each possible pairing of a conversation from one model and a conversation from another model should only be evaluated once at most: thus, if we have N conversations for each of the two models being compared, we will be able to perform a maximum of N^2 PW-Dialog evaluations on these conversations.[7]

C.8 Crowdsourcing time needed when combining single-model methods

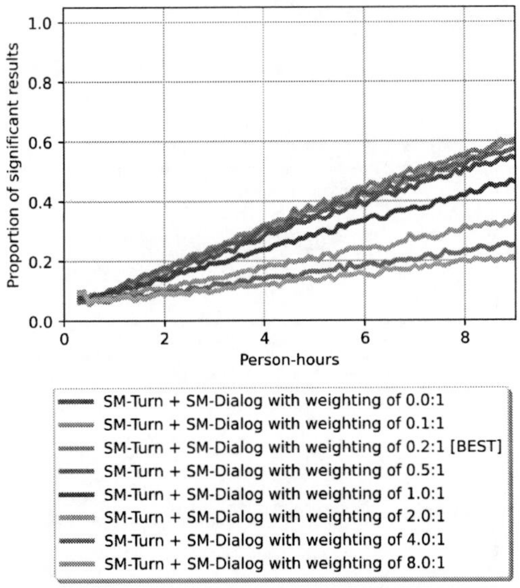

Figure 11: The time needed to measure a statistically significant result when averaging together per-conversation evaluations of SM-Turn and SM-Dialog with the given weighting, for the Length comparison. The fastest weighting is marked with "[BEST]".

Figures 11, 12, and 13 show the time needed to achieve a statistically significant difference between models when averaging together SM-Turn winner-takes-all success rates from Bot Speaker turns 3 to 6 (Section 4.2) with SM-Dialog Likert scores. To perform the weighted average between SM-Turn and SM-Dialog on each conversation, we first shift and scale the originally 1-to-5 SM-Dialog Likert scores to fall within the range $[0, 1]$, matching the range of the individual binary SM-Turn success rates. We see that statistical significance is reached fastest when weighting SM-Turn much less heavily than SM-Dialog at a ratio of 1:5 or 1:10, which is to be expected given the already much stronger sensitivity of SM-Dialog.

[7]The potential drawback of this assumption is that the performance of the models will then likely be judged using only a relatively small handful of conversations, which may or may not be representative of the models' true performance.

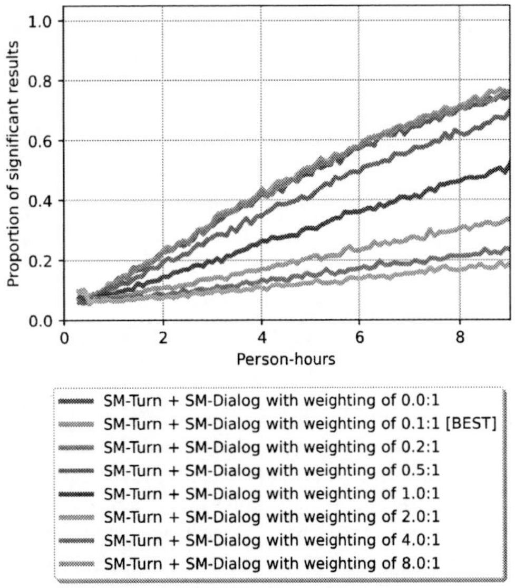

Figure 12: The time needed to measure a statistically significant result when averaging together per-conversation evaluations of SM-Turn and SM-Dialog with the given weighting, for the Size comparison.

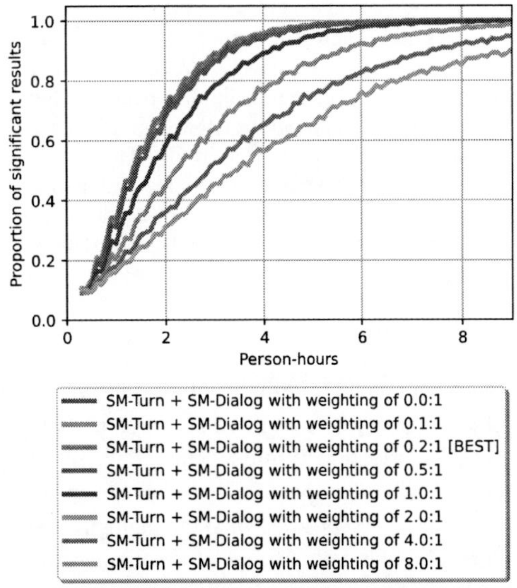

Figure 13: The time needed to measure a statistically significant result when averaging together per-conversation evaluations of SM-Turn and SM-Dialog with the given weighting, for the Fine-tuning comparison.

KG-CRuSE: Recurrent Walks over Knowledge Graph for Explainable Conversation Reasoning using Semantic Embeddings

Rajdeep Sarkar[1], **Mihael Arcan**[2] and **John P. McCrae**[1,2]

[1] Data Science Institute, National University of Ireland Galway, Ireland
[2] Insight SFI Research Centre for Data Analytics, National University of Ireland Galway, Ireland
{r.sarkar1, mihael.arcan, john.mccrae}@nuigalway.ie

Abstract

Knowledge-grounded dialogue systems utilise external knowledge such as knowledge graphs to generate informative and appropriate responses. A crucial challenge of such systems is to select facts from a knowledge graph pertinent to the dialogue context for response generation. This fact selection can be formulated as path traversal over a knowledge graph conditioned on the dialogue context. Such paths can originate from facts mentioned in the dialogue history and terminate at the facts to be mentioned in the response. These walks, in turn, provide an explanation of the flow of the conversation. This work proposes KG-CRuSE, a simple, yet effective LSTM based decoder that utilises the semantic information in the dialogue history and the knowledge graph elements to generate such paths for effective conversation explanation. Extensive evaluations showed that our model outperforms the state-of-the-art models on the OpenDialKG dataset on multiple metrics.

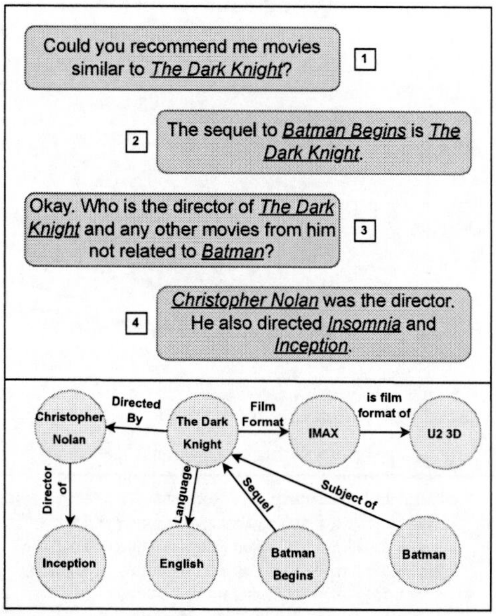

Figure 1: An example conversation wherein the agent utilises relevant information from the KG while generating responses. The agent generates facts about "Christopher Nolan" in utterance 4 while utilising the semantic information in the dialogue history and the KG.

1 Introduction

Inducing factual information during response generation has garnered a lot of attention in dialogue systems research. While language models (Zhao et al., 2020; Zheng et al., 2020) have been shown to generate responses akin to the dialogue history, they seldom contain factual information, leading to a bland conversation with the agent. Knowledge-grounded dialogue systems focus on leveraging external knowledge to generate coherent responses. Knowledge Graphs (KGs) are a rich source of factual information and can be combined with an utterance generator for a natural and informative conversational flow.

Zhou et al. (2018) showed that utilising KGs in dialogue systems improves the appropriateness and informativeness of the conversation. Augmenting utterances in a dialogue with the KG information guides the conversational agent to include relevant entities and facts in the response. For example, Figure 1 shows an example conversation where a user is interacting with a dialogue agent about movies. The agent has access to a KG that aids in suggesting relevant facts during the dialogue flow. When responding to utterance 3, the agent can utilise information from the KG and produce relevant facts about "Christopher Nolan". This information would be more engaging than responding with information about "Batman" or "Batman Begins".

While KGs have been used extensively to include relevant facts in a dialogue, the explicability of such systems is limited. Naturally, this fostered

Proceedings of the 4th Workshop on NLP for Conversational AI, pages 98 - 107
May 27, 2022 ©2022 Association for Computational Linguistics

research on developing models for explainable conversation reasoning. Moon et al. (2019) addressed this problem by inducing KG paths for conversation explainability. They posited a dialogue-KG path aligned corpus wherein utterances are augmented with a KG path to denote fact transitions in the dialogue. The KG paths emanate from entities or facts mentioned in the dialogue history and terminate at the entity to be mentioned in the response text. Such paths form a sequence of entities and relations and aid the dialogue agent in introducing appropriate knowledge to the dialogue. In addition to this, they proposed an attention-based recurrent decoder over the KG to generate entity paths. Jung et al. (2020) designed a novel dialogue-context infused graph neural network to propagate attention scores over the knowledge graph entities for KG path generation. While such approaches have their inherent strengths, their limitations are manifold.

Given a dialogue context, it is desirable to generate paths that results in a natural dialogue flow. Therefore it is essential to capture the semantic information in the dialogue context as well as the KG elements. Transformer based models (Devlin et al., 2019; Lan et al., 2020; Liu et al., 2019a) have enabled the capture of contextual relationships between different words in a sentence. Textual representations from such models have been successfully adapted for the dialogue conditioned KG reasoning task (Jung et al., 2020). However, prior works use the embedding of the $[CLS]$ token to encode the dialogue history and the KG elements. Reimers and Gurevych (2019) demonstrated that such sentence embeddings are sub-optimal and lead to degraded performance in downstream application tasks. Sentence-transformers (Reimers and Gurevych, 2019) are strong tools for capturing the semantic information of a sentence into a fixed-size vector. As KG elements can be long phrases, KG-CRUSE uses the Sentence-BERT (SBERT) model to encode both the dialogue history and the KG elements for capturing their semantic information.

As a result of the long tailed distribution of node neighbors in a KG, it can become difficult to generate relevant paths over the KG for explainable conversation. Given the dialogue history, it is desirable to traverse paths that are semantically relevant. KG-CRUSE utilises the rich sequential information in the dialogue history and the path history to sample the top-k semantically similar neighbors for extending its walk over the KG.

We show that our KG-CRUSE improves upon the current state-of-the-art on multiple metrics, demonstrating the effectiveness of KG-CRUSE for explainable conversation reasoning.

To summarise, our contributions are as follows:

- We propose a KG-CRUSE , a LSTM based decoder leveraging Sentence-Transformer (S-BERT) embedding to reason KG paths for explainable conversation.
- We show the efficacy of our model by improving the current state-of-the-art performances over multiple metrics on the OpenDialKG (Moon et al., 2019) dataset. Additionally, we conduct extensive empirical analysis to emphasise the effectiveness of KG-CRUSE for the reasoning task.
- We release[1] our system and baseline systems as an open-source toolkit to allow reproducibility and future comparison on this task.

2 Related Work

The use of external knowledge in dialogue agents has become commonplace, owing to the rich heterogeneous information contained in them. He et al. (2017) addressed the knowledge-grounded conversation task by iteratively updating the knowledge base embeddings to generate informative responses. Following this, knowledge-based dialogue systems have been studied extensively including the collection of new knowledge-grounded datasets (Ghazvininejad et al., 2018; Qin et al., 2019; Zhang et al., 2018) and developing knowledge-centric dialogue systems (Liu et al., 2018; Parthasarathi and Pineau, 2018a; Zhang et al., 2020).

Young et al. (2018a) attempted to integrate a large scale KG into an end-to-end dialogue system. Other similar works (Chen et al., 2019; Zhou et al., 2020; Sarkar et al., 2020) leveraged graph neural networks and KG embeddings to recommend relevant products in conversational recommender systems. Though successful in retrieving suitable entities or facts from the KG, these systems fail to provide explainability to the recommendations.

Such limitations encouraged explainable conversation reasoning using external knowledge. Liu et al. (2019b) develop the problem as a Partially

[1]https://github.com/rajbsk/kg-cruse

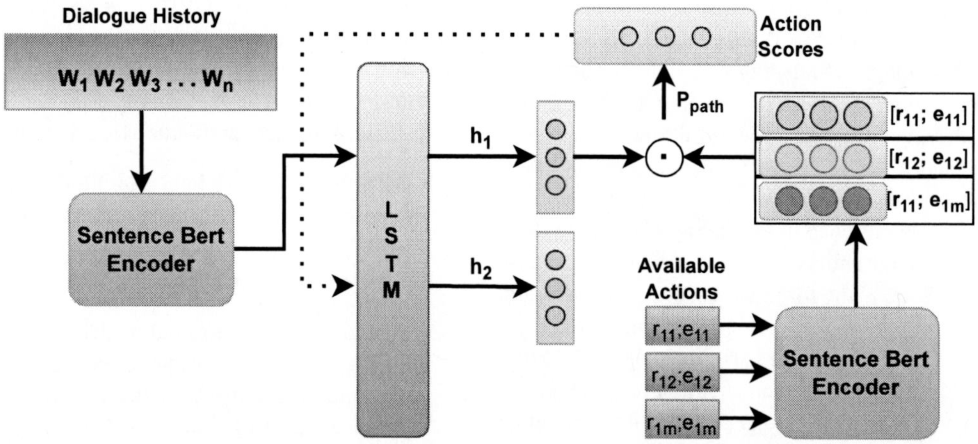

Figure 2: Modular overview of KG-CRUSE architecture. KG-CRUSE utilises the SBERT architecture to encode the dialogue history and the KG elements. To generate walk paths over the KG, KG-CRUSE leverages an LSTM network to model the temporal information. To generate the path at timestep t, the LSTM takes as input ($\mathbf{D}$, $(\mathbf{r_1}; \mathbf{e_1})$, ..., $(\mathbf{r_{t-1}}; \mathbf{e_{t-1}})$) and outputs the hidden state representation $\mathbf{h_t}$ of the step t. KG-CRUSE then computes dot-product of $\mathbf{h_t}$ with the embeddings of the actions available at timestep t ($[\mathbf{r_{t,1}}; \mathbf{e_{t,1}}]$, $[\mathbf{r_{t,2}}; \mathbf{e_{t,2}}]$, ...,$[\mathbf{r_{t,m}}; \mathbf{e_{t,m}}]$) followed by a softmax layer to compute the probability of each available action.

Observable Markov Decision Process and use policy gradient for training the agent to generate KG paths. Moon et al. (2019) posited a KG path-parallel-dialogue corpus along with DialKG Walker (DKGW) model, a recurrent decoder model to generate the KG path for a response entity selection. Jung et al. (2020) suggested the use of graph neural networks using attention flow to generate KG entity paths. While novel, DKGW does not explicitly utilise the graph structure during model training. On the other hand, the performance of AttnIO (Jung et al., 2020) relies on the node sampler during training. AttnIO becomes computationally expensive due to dialogue specific graph neural network (both during training and inference) as the model concatenates the dialogue embedding to the node embeddings while propagating attention scores. To counter these issues, we design a very simple, lightweight, yet efficient LSTM network leveraging the dialogue and path history to extend the path over the KG.

While, DKGW uses TransE (Bordes et al., 2013) for encoding the elements of the KG, such translation embeddings have weak representation capacity. On the other hand, Jung et al. (2020) utilise the ALBERT (Lan et al., 2020) representation of sentence to encode the dialogue history and the KG elements. They use the $[CLS]$ token representation of the text sequence as the sentence representation. Reimers and Gurevych (2019) suggested Sentence-Transformers for encoding sentences. We encode the dialogue history and the KG elements using Sentence-Transformers to capture rich semantic similarities between the dialogue history and the KG elements.

The processing of semantically rich sequential information using a lightweight LSTM model makes KG-CRUSE ideal for generating walks over a KG for explainable conversation.

3 Methodology

In the following sections, we begin with formally introducing the problem statement. We then outline the embeddings used in KG-CRUSE. Following this, we discuss the architecture of KG-CRUSE as illustrated in Figure 2. Finally, we describe decoding process used by KG-CRUSE during the inference step.

3.1 Formal Problem Definition

We describe the problem statement similar to Moon et al. (2019). The KG is defined as $\mathcal{G} = \mathcal{V}_{\mathcal{KG}} \times \mathcal{R}_{\mathcal{KG}} \times \mathcal{V}_{\mathcal{KG}}$, where $\mathcal{V}_{\mathcal{KG}}$ is set of entities and $\mathcal{R}_{\mathcal{KG}}$ is set of relations in the KG. Facts in the KG are denoted by triples, and each has the form (*e, r, e'*) where *e, e'* $\in \mathcal{V}_{\mathcal{KG}}$ are entities and *r* $\in \mathcal{R}_{\mathcal{KG}}$ is the relation connecting them.

In addition to the KG, each input contains a dialogue D $\in \mathcal{D}$, represented as a sequence of utterances D = $\{s_1, ..., s_n\}$, and the set of entities $\mathrm{x_e}$ = $\{\mathrm{x_e^{(i)}}\}$ occurring in the user's last utterance s_n, where $\mathrm{x_e^{(i)}} \in \mathcal{V}_{\mathcal{KG}}$. The output is represented as $\mathrm{y} = \{\mathrm{y_e}, \mathrm{y_r}\}$, where y_e is a set of entity paths $\mathrm{y_e} = \{\mathrm{y_e^{(i)}}\}$, with each element $\mathrm{y_e^{(i)}} = \{\mathrm{y}_{e,t}^{(i)}\}_{t=1}^{T}$ denoting an entity path connecting $\mathrm{x_e^{(i)}}$ to the response entity $\mathrm{y}_{e,T}^{(i)}$. Likewise, $\mathrm{y_r} = \{\mathrm{y}_r^{(i)}\}$ is a set of relation paths, where $\mathrm{y}_r^{(i)} \in \mathcal{R}_{\mathcal{KG}}$. The element $\mathrm{y}_r^{(i)} = \{\mathrm{y}_{r,t}^{(i)}\}_{t=1}^{T}$ is a sequence of relations from the KG connecting $\mathrm{x}_e^{(i)}$ and $\{\mathrm{x}_{e,t}^{(i)}\}_{t=1}^{T}$.

3.2 Dialogue and KG Representation

Capturing the semantic information in the dialogue context is an important component of our model. SBERT is a contextual sentence encoder that captures the semantic information of a sentence in a fixed-size vector. We encode pieces of text using Equation 1. The text is first sent though a pre-trained BERT model to obtain the contextual representation of its tokens. The sentence embedding is computed by taking a mean-pool of the contextual token representations. The dialogue context is constructed by concatenating a maximum of three previous utterances and is then passed through SBERT encoder to obtain a fixed-size contextual dialogue representation.

$$\mathbf{S} = \text{MeanPooling}(\text{BERT}(S)) \quad (1)$$

In order to align the semantic vector space of the dialogue representations and the KG representations, we use SBERT to encode the KG elements. As KG entities and relations can be words or phrases, SBERT can effectively capture their semantic information. We use the publicly available SBERT-BERT-BASE-NLI[2] model with mean-pooling as our SBERT encoder.

3.3 KG-CRuSE Architecture

KG-CRuSE learns to traverse a path on the KG by learning a function π_θ that calculates the probability of an action $a_t \in \mathcal{A}_t$ given the state s_t. The state s_t contains the dialogue history and entities already traversed by KG-CRuSE while decoding the paths, while a_t is the set of edges from the KG available to KG-CRuSE for extending its path.

[2] https://huggingface.co/sentence-transformers/bert-base-nli-mean-tokens

The state s_t at step t is defined as a tuple (D, (r_1, e_1, ..., r_{t-1}, e_{t-1})), where D is the dialogue context and $r_i, e_i (i < t)$ are the relation and entity already decoded by KG-CRuSE at step i. The initial state s_0 is denoted as $(D, \varnothing)$, where $\varnothing$ is the empty set.

At step t, an action has the form $a_t = (r_t, e_t) \in \mathcal{A}_t$, where $\mathcal{A}_t$ is the set of all possible actions available to the model at step t. $\mathcal{A}_t$ includes all outgoing edges of e_{t-1} in the KG $\mathcal{G}$, i.e. $\mathcal{A}_t$ is the set of all the outgoing edges of the entity decoded by KG-CRuSE at timestep $t-1$. To let the agent terminate the search process, we add self-loop edges to every entity node in the graph denoting no operation ("self-loop"). The action a_t is represented as a concatenation of the relation and entity embedding $\mathbf{a}_t = [\mathbf{r}_t; \mathbf{e}_t]$, where $\mathbf{r} \in \mathbb{R}^{d_r}$, $\mathbf{e} \in \mathbb{R}^{d_e}$ and $\mathbb{R}^{d_e}$, $\mathbb{R}^{d_r}$ are the size of the entity embedding and relation embedding respectively. At step 1, KG-CRuSE chooses between the entities mentioned in s_n for path traversal. The relation associated with action at step 1 is the zero vector. As mentioned, the state s_t contains the dialogue context and action history (path history). This sequential information in s_t is modelled using an LSTM:

$$\mathbf{d} = \mathbf{W}_d\mathbf{D} \quad (2)$$

$$\mathbf{h}_0 = \text{LSTM}(\mathbf{0}, \mathbf{d}) \quad (3)$$

$$\mathbf{h}_t = \text{LSTM}(\mathbf{h}_{t-1}, \mathbf{a}_{t-1}), t > 0 \quad (4)$$

where $\mathbf{D}$ is the contextual dialogue embedding obtained using Equation 1 and $\mathbf{W}_d$ is a learnable matrix that maps the dialogue embedding to the LSTM input dimension. Given the hidden state representation $\mathbf{h}_t$ at time t, KG-CRuSE assigns a probability to each action using Equation 6.

$$\mathbf{x}_t = \mathbf{W}_{3,\theta}(\text{ReLU}(\mathbf{W}_{2,\theta}\mathbf{h}_t^{\intercal})) \quad (5)$$

$$\pi_\theta(a_t|s_t, \mathcal{A}_t) = \frac{\exp(\mathbf{a}_t \cdot \mathbf{x}_t)}{\sum_{a_i \in \mathcal{A}_t} \exp(\mathbf{a}_i \cdot \mathbf{x}_t)} \quad (6)$$

The hidden state representation $\mathbf{h}_t$ is passed through a two-layered dense network with ReLU activation (Nair and Hinton, 2010) in the first layer. The LSTM weights, $\mathbf{W}_{2,\theta} \in \mathbb{R}^{d_h \times d_h}$ and $\mathbf{W}_{3,\theta} \in \mathbb{R}^{(d_r+d_e) \times d_h}$ are the learnable parameters, and d_h is the LSTM hidden representation size.

3.3.1 Model Learning

We train KG-CRuSE by minimising the cross-entropy loss on the entities decoded at each timestep. Additionally, we train the model using teacher forcing (Sutskever et al., 2014), wherein the model makes each action conditioned on the gold history of the target path. To prevent overfitting, we add L_2 regularisation to the parameters of the model. During training, we do not fine-tune the SBERT architectures, but back-propagate the gradients to the entity and relation embeddings.

3.3.2 KG-CRUSE Path Generation

Once the model is trained, KG-CRUSE takes the dialogue history and the entities mentioned in the current utterance as input, a horizon T and outputs a set of entity paths, relations paths of length T along with the probability score of each path. During inference, we remove self-loops from the KG except for the self-loop with label "self-loop" introduced in section 3.3. We do so to allow the agent traverse diverse paths rather than staying at entities mentioned in the dialogue history.

4 Experimental Setup

This section presents the dataset used, the baselines compared with and the description of the model settings of KG-CRUSE along with the metrics the models have been evaluated on.

4.1 Dataset

We evaluate our proposed framework on the OpenDialKG dataset (Moon et al., 2019). The dataset has 91,209 turns spread over 15,673 dialogues in the form of either task-oriented dialogues (recommendations) or chit-chat conversations on a given topic. Each turn is annotated with a KG path to represent fact transitions in the conversation. The KG is a subset of the Freebase KG (Bollacker et al., 2008), which has 1,190,658 fact triples, 100,813 entities and 1,358 relations. Following Moon et al. (2019), we split the dataset randomly into 70%, 15% and 15% for training, testing and validation.

4.2 Baselines and Evaluation Metrics

We compare KG-CRUSE against the following baseline models suggested by Moon et al. (2019) and Jung et al. (2020):

- Tri-LSTM (Young et al., 2018b): The model encodes each utterance along with facts from the KG within 1-hop distance from the entities mentioned in the current utterance. This is used to retrieve facts from the KG for dialogue explanation.
- Ext-ED (Parthasarathi and Pineau, 2018b): Moon et al. (2019) conditioned the response generation with external knowledge vector input to generate response entity token at the final softmax layer, without using the structural information from the KG.
- Seq2Path (Jung et al., 2020): An attention based Seq2Seq model is modified to generate entity paths by masking out unreachable nodes at each decoding step.
- Seq2Seq: An LSTM based seq2seq (Sutskever et al., 2014) model where the decoder is modified to generate entity paths. Similar to DKGW (Moon et al., 2019) model, we use modality attention as the output of the encoder. Following Moon et al. (2019), we replace the softmax layer in the decoder with a zero-shot learning layer in the KG embedding space.
- DKGW (Moon et al., 2019): A model to generate KG paths using domain-agnostic, attention-based recurrent graph decoder reinforced with a zero-shot learning layer over the KG embedding space.
- AttnIO (Jung et al., 2020): A dialogue conditioned KG path traversal leveraging attention flow using graph neural networks.

Since the authors of OpenDialKG and AttnIO have not released their implementations, we report their performance on our re-implementations. We note that for most systems, our implementation is similar or better than the reported results. Regarding AttnIO, we were not able to reproduce the results although we note that errors in the implementation of the node sampler or leakage of the test dataset into the training dataset can easily lead to overestimation of the accuracy. The code and dataset used for re-implementation as well as our system is accessible at `https://github.com/rajbsk/kg-cruse`.

We evaluate our models on different recall@k metrics for entity and path retrieval. Path@k measures if the ground-truth path is present in the top-k paths with the highest probability searched by the agent. Similarly, tgt@k measures if the response entity is present in the top-k entities retrieved by the agent. In situations where multiple paths point to the same response entity, we consider the path with the highest score for entity retrieval.

Model	path@1	path@5	path@10	Recall@k path@25	tgt@1	tgt@5	tgt@10	tgt@25
Tri-LSTM	3.2	22.6	36.3	56.2	-	-	-	-
Ext-ED	1.9	9.0	13.3	19.0	-	-	-	-
Seq2Path	14.92	31.1	38.68	48.15	15.65	33.86	42.52	53.28
Seq2Seq*	6.53±0.78	26.21±1.21	35.02±1.27	45.78±1.18	7.13±0.85	30.64±1.62	41.01±1.43	52.97±1.55
DKGW*	14.16±1.16	37.26±1.91	47.85±2.60	59.20±2.33	14.96±1.04	39.53±1.81	51.06±2.15	63.85±1.58
AttnIO*	19.08±1.19	38.49±0.79	43.99±1.10	48.94±0.55	**20.32±1.80**	45.90±0.93	52.82±0.65	55.17±0.96
KG-CRUSE	**19.59±0.43**	**44.62±1.08**	**56.16±1.21**	**70.59±0.38**	20.20±0.36	**47.76±0.62**	**60.11±0.92**	**75.30±0.57**

Table 1: Performance of KG-CRUSE in comparison with other baseline methods on different Recall@k metrics. The numbers reported are the mean values with the sample standard deviation (p=0.01). Results are statistically significant with p=0.01. Models with * denote our re-implementation.

4.3 Implementation Details

For the task, we set horizon T to 3. The dialogue, entity and relation embeddings are encoded using SBERT into a 768 dimensional vector. In KG-CRUSE, we consider 3 LSTM layers with $d_h = d_e + d_r = 1,536$. To prevent the agent from overfitting on the dataset, we add L_2 regularisation with a weight decay parameter of 1e-3.

Similar to Jung et al. (2020), we set the batch size to 8 and train the model with Adam optimiser (Kingma and Ba, 2015) with a learning rate of 1e-4 for 20 epochs. For models with re-implementations, we report the results on five different splits of the data. For Tri-LSTM and Ext-ED, we report the number reported by Moon et al. (2019), while for Seq2Path, the numbers are reported from the work of Jung et al. (2020). As entity occurrences in a dialogue dataset is sparse, it is desirable to report the performance on five different splits of the data rather than an assessment of five models on one split.

Model	P@1	P@25	E@1	E@25	Rel@1
BERT	12.74	66.72	12.98	72.14	39.37
ALBERT	13.42	65.67	13.96	72.23	**40.93**
SRoBERTa	17.17	68.04	17.65	73.34	40.71
SBERT	**19.52**	**70.72**	**20.20**	**75.72**	40.02

Table 2: Influence of sentence embeddings on KG-CRUSE performance. Comparison of different embedding methods.

5 Results and Discussion

We begin with performing a quantitative evaluation of the models. Following this, we study the impact of our choice of sentence embeddings on the model performance. Then we analyse the impact of beam-width at each decoding step during inference. Finally, we provide insights of examples where the results of KG-CRUSE are not consistent with the ground truth paths.

5.1 Quantitative Analysis

In this section, we compare the performance of our proposed approach against the different baselines. From Table 1, it can be observed that KG-CRUSE performs better than the different baseline models on the OpenDialKG dataset. For entity and path accuracy, AttnIO has the closest performance compared to our model, with the latter being 2.7% relatively better on both path@1 and entity@1 metrics. On increasing k of recall@k, we find KG-CRUSE has at least 10% relative improvement over the baseline models. It is interesting to notice that on increasing the value "k", KG-CRUSE performs relative better than other models. KG-CRUSE identifies paths semantically relevant to the dialogue context although different from the gold-label paths as discussed in Section 5.6. The huge gain on the path@25 metric advocates for this hypothesis. It is worthwhile to notice that although AttnIO has the closest performance for path@1 and entity@1 to KG-CRUSE, the performance degrades when "k" increases in path@k and entity@k. This might be due to the fact that the beam-width reported by the authors is not expressive enough to capture semantically relevant paths or entities.

5.2 Effectiveness of Sentence Embeddings

In our framework, we utilise sentence SBERT embeddings to encode dialogue context and KG elements. In this section, we conduct an ablation study on the efficacy of such embeddings. We replace the SBERT embeddings with the *[CLS]*

SBERT Fine-tuned	Aligned KG	P@1	P@25	E@1	E@25	Rel@1
Yes	No	17.82	69.47	18.21	74.47	40.24
Yes	Yes	18.46	69.93	19.00	74.75	40.47
No	No	18.00	62.01	18.52	74.54	38.48
No	Yes	**19.52**	**70.72**	**20.20**	**75.72**	**40.02**

Table 3: Results on fine-tuning the SBERT architecture used for encoding the dialogue history. Additionally, the table reports the results of initialising the KG elements with random initialisation.

token representation of BERT[3] (Devlin et al., 2019) and ALBERT model[4] (Lan et al., 2020) in KG-CRUSE. Additionally, we consider an instance wherein the elements are encoded using Sentence-RoBERTa (SRoBERTa)[5] (Reimers and Gurevych, 2019). The results in Table 2 demonstrates the strength of our embedding choices wherein SBERT and SRoBERTa outperforms the BERT and ALBERT embeddings. Both the sentence embedding models models are pre-trained on NLI datasets, which allows them to capture rich semantic information for textual similarity. These embeddings have demonstrated strong performances in the task of semantic search using cosine-similarity (Reimers and Gurevych, 2019). It should be noted that before the softmax layer in KG-CRUSE, we compute the dot product of the LSTM layer hidden representation with that of the relation-entity embeddings available at the given timestep. As a result of this step, we expect the performance of SBERT and SRoBERTa embeddings to be better that BERT and ALBERT embeddings.

Additionally, we see from the Table 2 that the relation accuracy of different models is higher than path accuracy. This is due to the outgoing edges of a node (from the dialogue history) sharing similar features if they are connected using the same relation. Thus multiple entities can fit our choice of the response entity given the dialogue context.

5.3 Impact of KG Embedding Alignment and SBERT Fine-tuning

In this section, we study the impact of encoding KG elements with SBERT embeddings. Additionally, we analyse if fine-tuning the SBERT architecture used for encoding the dialogue history is beneficial for explainability.

[3] https://huggingface.co/bert-base-uncased

[4] https://huggingface.co/albert-base-v2

[5] https://huggingface.co/sentence-transformers/roberta-base-nli-mean-tokens

Size	P@1	P@25	E@1	E@25
2, 5, 50	**19.59**	56.26	**20.09**	62.19
2, 10, 25	19.55	64.93	20.04	70.16
2, 10, 50	19.55	64.93	20.04	70.18
2, 25, 10	19.52	69.75	20.02	74.57
2, 25, 25	<u>19.52</u>	<u>**70.72**</u>	<u>20.02</u>	<u>75.72</u>
2, 25, 50	19.52	**70.72**	20.02	**75.75**
2, 50, 5	19.52	68.46	20.02	72.53
2, 50, 25	19.52	70.56	20.02	75.43

Table 4: Impact of the beam width at different timesteps on the model performance. The results are reported on one of the dataset split. Best results are shown in bold, while the results on the default setting of KG-CRUSE are underlined. All numbers are in percentage.

Model	GPU	Train Time	Test Time
Seq2Seq	Nvidia 1080Ti	≈8 mins	≈1 mins
DKGW	Nvidia 1080Ti	≈4 mins	≈8 mins
AttnIO	Tesla V100	≈38 mins	≈82 mins
KG-CRUSE	Nvidia 1080Ti	≈7 mins	≈8 mins

Table 5: Analysis of the time required by different models for training and inference on the OpenDialKG dataset. The numbers in the third column denote per epoch train time.

Table 3 outlines four situations, where in two cases we fine-tune the SBERT architecture used for encoding the dialogue history. We also consider two cases where the embeddings of the KG elements are initialised with values drawn from a normal distribution with mean 0 and standard deviation 1, corresponding to the value "No" in the second column. It should be noted that we never consider fine-tuning the SBERT architecture used for encoding the KG elements.

We see from the Table 3 that in cases when the KG elements are not encoded with SBERT embeddings, their performance drops as compared to cases when we use SBERT embeddings. Additionally, we find that fine-tuning SBERT leads to a decrease in the performance of KG-CRUSE. This can be attributed to the change in semantic space of the dialogue embeddings and the KG embeddings during fine-tuning. Hence, we do not finetune the SBERT architecture in the default setting of KG-CRUSE.

5.4 Impact of Beam-Width on Path Reasoning

In this experiment, we study the influence of beam-width at different timesteps on the model perfor-

Dialogue	Model	Walk Path
A: Could you recommend movies similar to Kung Fu Panda? B: [response]	KG-CRUSE Ground Truth	Kung Fu Panda→written by→Cyrus Voris Kung Fu Panda→directed by→Mark Osborne→wrote→Monsters vs. Aliens
A: Oh cool, I also read Wocket in my Pocket! But sure, what else is there? B: Cool! Yertle the Turtle and Horton Hears a Who! are also written by Dr. Seuss. A: That first one is really old right? I think it was released in 1958. // B: [response]	KG-CRUSE Ground Truth	1958→released year→Tom's Midnight Garden Garden→has genre→Children's literature 1958→released year→Have Space Suit - Will Travel→written by →Robert A. Heinlein
A:Could you recommend a book by Jeffrey Zaslow? B: [response]	KG-CRUSE Ground Truth	Jeffrey Zaslow→wrote→The Last Lecture Jeffrey Zaslow→wrote→Last Lecture →has genre→Non-fiction

Table 6: Examples where KG-CRUSE generates path different from the true paths.

mance. The first column of Table 4 lists the tuples (K_1, K_2, K_3) where each K_i denotes the top-K_i edges sampled at timestep i.

We conduct this analysis on a single split of the dataset keeping all other parameters of the model constant. We consider a diverse set of values for each K_i. From Table 4, we find that although the tuples (2, 5, 50), (2, 10, 25), (2, 25, 10) and (2, 50, 5) have an equal number of sampled paths, tuple (2, 25, 10) performs better than others. Interestingly, we observe that the sampling sizes at the second timestep play a significant role in finding optimal paths for KG-CRUSE. The first two sets of fact selection (i.e. during timesteps 1 and 2) largely determine the facts reachable by KG-CRUSE. Sampling more samples during the initial timesteps enables the agent to explore diverse paths initially and KG-CRUSE then makes an optimal selection of facts dependent on the dialogue information.

5.5 Analysis of Computational Requirements

In this study, we conduct an analysis of the time required for training the model. We also compare the performance of different architectures with regards to the inference speed.

Table 5 shows that while DKGW has a better train time per epoch than KG-CRUSE and Seq2Seq has a better inference speed than KG-CRUSE, we can observe from Table 1 that our model achieves better performance compared to these models. It is worthwhile to mention that while AttnIO achieves the closest performance to KG-CRUSE as shown in Table 1, it requires roughly six times more training time and is ten times slower during inference. This clearly indicates the benefits of using KG-CRUSE for explainable conversation using KGs.

5.6 Qualitative Analysis

This section highlights three scenarios showcasing the underlying working of KG-CRUSE. Table 6 displays three examples where KG-CRUSE generates paths different from the gold KG paths. In the first example, it can be observed that KG-CRUSE identifies a path that is not sufficient to answer the given question. This can be due to the limited dialogue context provided. Choosing this fact might lead to a dialogue with the agent, however, the user query is not answer with the path chosen by KG-CRUSE.

In the second example, the relation traversed by KG-CRUSE is correct, however as the dialogue context is not specific, it decodes a path that might potentially fit the dialogue context but is different from the gold path. However, in the third example, even with limited context, KG-CRUSE identifies a path relevant to the context, however the final entity differs from the gold path. Such paths are admissible as all of them fit the dialogue context appropriately.

6 Conclusion

In this work, we propose KG-CRUSE, an LSTM based lightweight framework for explainable conversational reasoning. We utilise SBERT embeddings to capture the rich semantic information in the dialogue history and the KG elements. We conduct an extensive evaluation to demonstrate that our framework outperforms several baseline models on both explainability and response entity retrieval. As annotating ground truth paths is expensive, we plan on extending this model to scenarios when ground truth paths are not available involving the generation of knowledge-conditioned dialogue.

7 Acknowledgements

This work is supported by a grant from The Government of Ireland Postgraduate Fellowship, Irish Research Council under project ID GOIPG/2019/3480. The work is also co-supported by Science Foundation Ireland under grant number SFI/12/RC/2289 2 (Insight).

References

Kurt D. Bollacker, Colin Evans, Praveen Paritosh, Tim Sturge, and Jamie Taylor. 2008. Freebase: a collaboratively created graph database for structuring human knowledge. In *Proceedings of the ACM SIGMOD International Conference on Management of Data, SIGMOD 2008, Vancouver, BC, Canada, June 10-12, 2008*, pages 1247–1250. ACM.

Antoine Bordes, Nicolas Usunier, Alberto García-Durán, Jason Weston, and Oksana Yakhnenko. 2013. Translating embeddings for modeling multi-relational data. In *Advances in Neural Information Processing Systems 26: 27th Annual Conference on Neural Information Processing Systems 2013. Proceedings of a meeting held December 5-8, 2013, Lake Tahoe, Nevada, United States*, pages 2787–2795.

Qibin Chen, Junyang Lin, Yichang Zhang, Ming Ding, Yukuo Cen, Hongxia Yang, and Jie Tang. 2019. Towards knowledge-based recommender dialog system. In *Proceedings of the 2019 Conference on Empirical Methods in Natural Language Processing and the 9th International Joint Conference on Natural Language Processing*, pages 1803–1813.

Jacob Devlin, Ming-Wei Chang, Kenton Lee, and Kristina Toutanova. 2019. BERT: pre-training of deep bidirectional transformers for language understanding. In *Proceedings of the 2019 Conference of the North American Chapter of the Association for Computational Linguistics: Human Language Technologies, NAACL-HLT 2019, Minneapolis, MN, USA, June 2-7, 2019, Volume 1 (Long and Short Papers)*, pages 4171–4186. Association for Computational Linguistics.

Marjan Ghazvininejad, Chris Brockett, Ming-Wei Chang, Bill Dolan, Jianfeng Gao, Wen-tau Yih, and Michel Galley. 2018. A knowledge-grounded neural conversation model. In *Proceedings of the Thirty-Second AAAI Conference on Artificial Intelligence*, pages 5110–5117.

He He, Anusha Balakrishnan, Mihail Eric, and Percy Liang. 2017. Learning symmetric collaborative dialogue agents with dynamic knowledge graph embeddings. In *Proceedings of the 55th Annual Meeting of the Association for Computational Linguistics*, pages 1766–1776.

Jaehun Jung, Bokyung Son, and Sungwon Lyu. 2020. Attnio: Knowledge graph exploration with in-and-out attention flow for knowledge-grounded dialogue. In *Proceedings of the 2020 Conference on Empirical Methods in Natural Language Processing*, pages 3484–3497.

Diederik P. Kingma and Jimmy Ba. 2015. Adam: A method for stochastic optimization. In *3rd International Conference on Learning Representations, ICLR 2015, San Diego, CA, USA, May 7-9, 2015, Conference Track Proceedings*.

Zhenzhong Lan, Mingda Chen, Sebastian Goodman, Kevin Gimpel, Piyush Sharma, and Radu Soricut. 2020. ALBERT: A lite BERT for self-supervised learning of language representations. In *8th International Conference on Learning Representations, ICLR 2020, Addis Ababa, Ethiopia, April 26-30, 2020*. OpenReview.net.

Shuman Liu, Hongshen Chen, Zhaochun Ren, Yang Feng, Qun Liu, and Dawei Yin. 2018. Knowledge diffusion for neural dialogue generation. In *Proceedings of the 56th Annual Meeting of the Association for Computational Linguistics, ACL 2018, Melbourne, Australia, July 15-20, 2018, Volume 1: Long Papers*, pages 1489–1498. Association for Computational Linguistics.

Yinhan Liu, Myle Ott, Naman Goyal, Jingfei Du, Mandar Joshi, Danqi Chen, Omer Levy, Mike Lewis, Luke Zettlemoyer, and Veselin Stoyanov. 2019a. Roberta: A robustly optimized BERT pretraining approach. *CoRR*, abs/1907.11692.

Zhibin Liu, Zheng-Yu Niu, Hua Wu, and Haifeng Wang. 2019b. Knowledge aware conversation generation with explainable reasoning over augmented graphs. In *Proceedings of the 2019 Conference on Empirical Methods in Natural Language Processing and the 9th International Joint Conference on Natural Language Processing*, pages 1782–1792.

Seungwhan Moon, Pararth Shah, Anuj Kumar, and Rajen Subba. 2019. OpenDialKG: Explainable conversational reasoning with attention-based walks over knowledge graphs. In *Proceedings of the 57th Conference of the Association for Computational Linguistics*, pages 845–854.

Vinod Nair and Geoffrey E. Hinton. 2010. Rectified linear units improve restricted Boltzmann machines. In *Proceedings of the 27th International Conference on Machine Learning (ICML-10), June 21-24, 2010, Haifa, Israel*, pages 807–814. Omnipress.

Prasanna Parthasarathi and Joelle Pineau. 2018a. Extending neural generative conversational model using external knowledge sources. In *Proceedings of the 2018 Conference on Empirical Methods in Natural Language Processing*, pages 690–695.

Prasanna Parthasarathi and Joelle Pineau. 2018b. Extending neural generative conversational model using external knowledge sources. In *Proceedings of the 2018 Conference on Empirical Methods in Natural Language Processing, Brussels, Belgium, October 31 - November 4, 2018*, pages 690–695. Association for Computational Linguistics.

Lianhui Qin, Michel Galley, Chris Brockett, Xiaodong Liu, Xiang Gao, Bill Dolan, Yejin Choi, and Jianfeng Gao. 2019. Conversing by reading: Contentful neural conversation with on-demand machine reading. In *Proceedings of the 57th Conference of the Association for Computational Linguistics*, pages 5427–5436.

Nils Reimers and Iryna Gurevych. 2019. Sentence-BERT: Sentence embeddings using Siamese BERT-networks. In *Proceedings of the 2019 Conference on Empirical Methods in Natural Language Processing and the 9th International Joint Conference on Natural Language Processing*, pages 3980–3990.

Rajdeep Sarkar, Koustava Goswami, Mihael Arcan, and John P. McCrae. 2020. Suggest me a movie for tonight: Leveraging knowledge graphs for conversational recommendation. In *Proceedings of the 28th International Conference on Computational Linguistics*, pages 4179–4189.

Ilya Sutskever, Oriol Vinyals, and Quoc V. Le. 2014. Sequence to sequence learning with neural networks. In *Advances in Neural Information Processing Systems 27: Annual Conference on Neural Information Processing Systems 2014, December 8-13 2014, Montreal, Quebec, Canada*, pages 3104–3112.

Tom Young, Erik Cambria, Iti Chaturvedi, Hao Zhou, Subham Biswas, and Minlie Huang. 2018a. Augmenting end-to-end dialogue systems with commonsense knowledge. In *Proceedings of the Thirty-Second AAAI Conference on Artificial Intelligence*, pages 4970–4977.

Tom Young, Erik Cambria, Iti Chaturvedi, Hao Zhou, Subham Biswas, and Minlie Huang. 2018b. Augmenting end-to-end dialogue systems with commonsense knowledge. In *Proceedings of the Thirty-Second AAAI Conference on Artificial Intelligence, (AAAI-18), the 30th innovative Applications of Artificial Intelligence (IAAI-18), and the 8th AAAI Symposium on Educational Advances in Artificial Intelligence (EAAI-18), New Orleans, Louisiana, USA, February 2-7, 2018*, pages 4970–4977. AAAI Press.

Houyu Zhang, Zhenghao Liu, Chenyan Xiong, and Zhiyuan Liu. 2020. Grounded conversation generation as guided traverses in commonsense knowledge graphs. In *Proceedings of the 58th Annual Meeting of the Association for Computational Linguistics, ACL 2020, Online, July 5-10, 2020*, pages 2031–2043. Association for Computational Linguistics.

Saizheng Zhang, Emily Dinan, Jack Urbanek, Arthur Szlam, Douwe Kiela, and Jason Weston. 2018. Personalizing dialogue agents: I have a dog, do you have pets too? In *Proceedings of the 56th Annual Meeting of the Association for Computational Linguistics*, pages 2204–2213.

Xiangyu Zhao, Longbiao Wang, Ruifang He, Ting Yang, Jinxin Chang, and Ruifang Wang. 2020. Multiple knowledge syncretic transformer for natural dialogue generation. In *WWW '20: The Web Conference 2020, Taipei, Taiwan, April 20-24, 2020*, pages 752–762. ACM / IW3C2.

Yinhe Zheng, Rongsheng Zhang, Minlie Huang, and Xiaoxi Mao. 2020. A pre-training based personalized dialogue generation model with persona-sparse data. In *The Thirty-Fourth AAAI Conference on Artificial Intelligence, AAAI 2020, The Thirty-Second Innovative Applications of Artificial Intelligence Conference, IAAI 2020, The Tenth AAAI Symposium on Educational Advances in Artificial Intelligence, EAAI 2020, New York, NY, USA, February 7-12, 2020*, pages 9693–9700. AAAI Press.

Hao Zhou, Tom Young, Minlie Huang, Haizhou Zhao, Jingfang Xu, and Xiaoyan Zhu. 2018. Commonsense knowledge aware conversation generation with graph attention. In *Proceedings of the Twenty-Seventh International Joint Conference on Artificial Intelligence, IJCAI 2018, July 13-19, 2018, Stockholm, Sweden*, pages 4623–4629. ijcai.org.

Kun Zhou, Wayne Xin Zhao, Shuqing Bian, Yuanhang Zhou, Ji-Rong Wen, and Jingsong Yu. 2020. Improving conversational recommender systems via knowledge graph based semantic fusion. In *KDD '20: The 26th ACM SIGKDD Conference on Knowledge Discovery and Data Mining*, pages 1006–1014.

Knowledge Distillation Meets Few-Shot Learning: An Approach for Few-Shot Intent Classification Within and Across Domains

Anna Sauer
University of Stuttgart
anna.sauer@ims.uni-stuttgart.de

Shima Asaadi and **Fabian Küch**
Fraunhofer IIS
{shima.asaadi,fabian.kuech}@iis.fraunhofer.de

Abstract

Large Transformer-based natural language understanding models have achieved state-of-the-art performance in dialogue systems. However, scarce labeled data for training, the large model size, and low inference speed hinder their deployment in low-resource scenarios. Few-shot learning and knowledge distillation techniques have been introduced to reduce the need for labeled data and computational resources, respectively. However, these techniques are incompatible because few-shot learning trains models using few data, whereas, knowledge distillation requires sufficient data to train smaller, yet competitive models that run on limited computational resources. In this paper, we address the problem of distilling generalizable small models under the few-shot setting for the intent classification task. Considering in-domain and cross-domain few-shot learning scenarios, we introduce an approach for distilling small models that generalize to new intent classes and domains using only a handful of labeled examples. We conduct experiments on public intent classification benchmarks, and observe a slight performance gap between small models and large models. Overall, our results in both few-shot scenarios confirm the generalization ability of the small distilled models while having lower computational costs.

1 Introduction

Transformer-based language models, such as BERT (Devlin et al., 2019), contribute widely to the development of dialogue systems. A key component in the development of these systems is natural language understanding (NLU), such as intent classification (IC). Intent classification refers to determining the intent of the speaker's utterance in a given domain in dialogue systems. Recently, BERT-based language models have achieved state-of-the-art performance in intent classification through fine-tuning on task-specific datasets (Chen et al., 2019). However, there are two main challenges in the development of BERT-based intent classification models for task-oriented dialogue systems. First, training such models across many domains needs labeled training data from multiple domains. Due to the lack of large amounts of multi-domain training data, few-shot learning (FSL) methods, such as metric-based meta-learning techniques (Vinyals et al., 2016; Snell et al., 2017), have been used to adapt BERT-based intent classification models to new domains (Li et al., 2021). In cross-domain few-shot learning methods, the model learns transferable knowledge from large-scale source domain data and generalizes to unseen target domains using only a handful of training samples.

The second challenge is the large model size and long inference time of Transformer-based models, which hinder the deployment of such models when limited computational resources are available. Approaches to reduce the size of models, e.g., knowledge distillation (KD; Hinton et al. 2015), have been introduced. It has been shown that the new compressed models retain a high percentage of the performance while having a shorter inference time than the original models (Liu et al., 2019). Task-specific knowledge distillation approaches require sufficiently large training datasets (Tang et al., 2019), ideally with labels (Hinton et al., 2015), to distill a powerful small model. However, to obtain both generalized and small models, knowledge distillation methods seem to be incompatible with few-shot learning due to the large need of sufficient training data. Therefore, an adaptation of knowledge distillation to few-shot learning is necessary. To the best of our knowledge, task-specific knowledge distillation in cross-domain few-shot learning has largely remained unexplored with a few exceptions in computer vision (Zhang et al., 2020b; Li et al., 2020) and natural language processing (NLP; Pan et al. 2021; Zhou et al. 2021).

In this paper, we propose a task-specific approach for distilling small models with generaliza-

Proceedings of the 4th Workshop on NLP for Conversational AI, pages 108 - 119
May 27, 2022

tion ability to new classes and domains in two few-shot learning scenarios: 1) in-domain target class generalization in single- and multi-domain intent classification; 2) target domain adaptation in multi-domain intent classification. To this end, we first pretrain a Transformer-based prototypical teacher network (Snell et al., 2017) on source classes and domains using meta-learning. Then, we design a prototypical student network and pass the transferable knowledge to the student using knowledge distillation. During the distillation process, we consider a prototype loss as a new component in the standard distillation loss function. This loss measures how much each prototype that is produced by the student model resembles the respective prototype produced by the teacher model. Moreover, as opposed to standard batch training in knowledge distillation, we introduce an episodic distillation process. This way, we obtain a small student model that is compatible with few-shot scenarios and generalizes to unseen target classes and domains.

Our contributions are summarized as follows: 1) We propose a new knowledge distillation approach compatible with few-shot learning by introducing an episodic distillation process and using the prototype-based distillation loss. Our novel approach combines advantages of few-shot learning with knowledge distillation. 2) We perform extensive experiments on four public NLU benchmarks and compare the distilled small model with the large model in the few-shot intent classification scenario. Results show a slight performance drop for the small model while having lower memory consumption and a slightly faster inference speed. 3) We show that the small model can effectively generalize and adapt to target domains without the teacher supervision in the few-shot target domain adaptation. This is a more challenging and realistic scenario for small student models.

2 Background and Related Work

2.1 Few-shot learning

Few-shot learning has received substantial interest in NLP. One prominent technique in FSL is meta-learning, such as metric-based meta-learning techniques (Vinyals et al., 2016; Snell et al., 2017). In these techniques, a model is trained on source training tasks with sufficient labeled instances, called meta-training, and generalizes or adapts to new tasks with only a handful of labeled examples, called meta-testing. The meta-training step is performed through episodes. In each episode, a set of N classes (N-way) is chosen per task. For each class, a support set, which contains K labeled examples, and a query set are created for training and evaluating the performance of the classifier for updating the model parameters. The learning process is performed in the form of N-way K-shot classification task. During meta-testing, an adaptation to new tasks using a few labeled examples is performed similarly to meta-training.

Recent attempts in few-shot intent classification focus on both in-domain and cross-domain generalization using different meta-learning techniques. Some approaches introduce metric-based meta-learning, such as Prototypical networks (Snell et al., 2017) to train models on large-scale source class or domain data and generalize to emerging classes or domains using only a handful of training samples (Geng et al., 2019; Nguyen et al., 2020; Krone et al., 2020; Li et al., 2021). In metric-based methods, a metric function is trained to classify new examples by comparing them with labeled examples. Other approaches propose to pretrain models on different source tasks and transfer them to the few-shot intent detection task (Casanueva et al., 2020; Zhang et al., 2020a). Alternatively, Xia et al. (2020) propose a novel model to augment training data by generating utterances for unseen intent class labels.

2.2 Knowledge distillation

Knowledge distillation approaches transfer the knowledge and generalization ability of a large trained model, called teacher, to a small model, called student (Ba and Caruana, 2014; Hinton et al., 2015). In the simplest case, the objective function during distillation is to minimize the difference between the soft labels produced by the teacher and the student predictions. As an alternative, the logits, i.e., the inputs to the final softmax function, can be used instead of the soft labels for training the student (Bucila et al., 2006). Hinton et al. (2015) The teacher and student models can have different architectures. For instance, Liu et al. (2019) explore Transformer-based teacher and both Transformer- and LSTM-based student models for multi-task knowledge distillation in NLP. KD has received special attention in Transformer-based teacher models to train light-weight generic students (Sanh et al., 2019; Sun et al., 2019; Jiao et al., 2020; Sun et al., 2020; Wu et al., 2020) and task-specific students with practical applications (Tsai et al., 2019; Liu et al., 2019; Clark et al., 2019) including intent classification (Jiang et al., 2021).

2.3 Knowledge distillation and few-shot learning

In NLP models, knowledge distillation for improving the overall efficiency and generalization ability to new classes and domains is not straightforward under the few-shot learning scenario. Recent investigations suggest that larger models show a better few-shot performance than smaller models because of higher model capacity (Brown et al., 2020).[1] At the same time, knowledge distillation needs sufficiently large training data, ideally with labels (Hinton et al., 2015), to distill a small model with small performance gap. Thus, employing few-shot learning and knowledge distillation methods jointly seems to be conflicting.

There have been only a few attempts to apply knowledge distillation in the context of the few-shot learning scenario in computer vision (Zhang et al., 2020b; Li et al., 2020; Liu et al., 2020). To the best of our knowledge, attempts in NLP are restricted to the work by Pan et al. (2021) and Zhou et al. (2021). In their work, Pan et al. (2021) train a multi-domain Transformer-based meta-teacher and introduce a meta-distillation approach to obtain domain-specific student models. Similar to our work, they consider in-domain generalization and target domain adaptation scenarios during the distillation process. However, we focus on a more challenging scenario where the student model does not have access to the teacher for emerging domains. That is, the student adapts to new target domains using a handful of labeled examples independently and without any distillation process. Thus, our model architecture is different from that of Pan et al. (2021) to preserve the model capacity for generalization and adaptation purposes. Zhou et al. (2021) propose a meta-learning approach for knowledge distillation in which both teacher and student are trained through interacting with each other. The teacher learns to improve its transfer ability by receiving feedback about the performance of the student on a new data split called quiz set. Alternative approaches to KD in a low-resource setting consider data augmentation to generate unlabeled data and distill small models using the augmented data (Melas-Kyriazi et al., 2019).

[1] Although there has recently been a discussion around this assumption (Schick and Schütze, 2021).

3 Approach

We first describe the teacher and student model architectures, followed by our proposed model training procedure. We elaborate on details of the proposed episodic distillation process and show how our approach preserves the generalization ability of the distilled models under few-shot learning scenarios.

3.1 Model architecture

Since we consider the few-shot learning scenario, both teacher and student models are designed as a prototypical network (Protonet; Snell et al. 2017), which is a metric-based meta-learning approach.

A teacher Protonet $\mathcal{T}$ with trainable parameters $\theta_{\mathcal{T}}$ is composed of an encoding block, which is a Transformer with L layers ($L >= 2$), followed by two linear hidden layers. The objective of the network is to learn a metric space by training model parameters $\theta_{\mathcal{T}}$. The input to the teacher is a sequence $x = t_1 \ldots t_k$ with k tokens. The fixed-length encoded sequence is the mean pooling of the token embeddings from the output of the last layer of the Transformer $e(x) = \frac{1}{k}\sum_{i=1}^{k} h^L(t_i)$. Then, $e(x)$ serves as the input to the hidden layers and the output is an m-dimensional sequence representation. Given C classes, $\mathcal{T}$ computes m-dimensional class representations $r_c \in \mathbb{R}^m$ for $c \in \{1, \ldots, C\}$, called prototype, as the mean aggregation of the m-dimensional representations of support instances in the respective class. For each new sequence, a classification is performed by computing the Euclidean distance between the class prototypes and the created m-dimensional sequence representation.

The student Protonet $\mathcal{S}$ with trainable parameters $\theta_{\mathcal{S}}$ consists of a Transformer with two layers in the encoding block, followed by two linear hidden layers. The Transformer layers are initialized from the first two layers of the teacher's encoding block. Class prototypes are computed in the same way as the teacher. In both architectures, all model parameters are trainable and shared across all domains in multi-domain intent classification.

3.2 Model training and testing

Inspired by meta-learning, we implement meta-training and meta-testing steps. Given two few-shot scenarios in our work, we adjust these steps accordingly. The first scenario is in-domain target class generalization and the second scenario is target domain adaptation in multi-domain classification. Due to the joint FSL and KD approach, meta-training consists of two steps: 1) teacher pretraining on source classes (domains), referred to as *episodic pretraining*, 2) student pretraining on source classes (domains) using the proposed episodic knowledge distillation, referred to as *episodic distillation*. At meta-testing, we implement an additional target domain adaptation step for the second scenario, called *Mini-episodic adaptation*. In the following, we explain the details of (mini-)episode construction and the training steps.

3.2.1 Episode construction

Assume there are disjoint sets of source classes C_{train} and target classes C_{test} for meta-training and meta-testing, respectively. These sets belong to source and target domains splits, D_{train} and D_{test}. In the in-domain target class generalization scenario, $D_{train} = D_{test}$. To construct an episode, a domain d is uniformly chosen from domains D_{split} where *split* is either $train$ or $test$. Then, we create variable size episodes by sampling the number of ways n, support shot k_s, and query shot k_q from the selected domain d, following the work by Krone et al. (2020) and Triantafillou et al. (2020). Then the support set S_c and the query set Q_c for each class c are sampled from the domain splits. As discussed in Krone et al. (2020)'s work, by setting variable shots and ways per episode, our approach is more compatible with real-world cases where unbalanced classes are available in the datasets. Please refer to Appendix A.1 for the details of episode construction. Meta-training consists of epochs and each epoch contains distinct episodes. Therefore, in line with Krone et al. (2020), once an episode is constructed, we remove the respective samples from the meta-training split until all samples are seen in an epoch.

3.2.2 Episodic pretraining

To pretrain a teacher $\mathcal{T}$ on source classes (domains), we implement the standard meta-learning approach. At each step, an episode is created through the described variable episode construction approach. Then, class prototypes $r_c \in \mathbb{R}^m$ are computed utilizing the labeled support set of each class S_c:

$$r_c = \frac{1}{|S_c|} \sum_{(x_i, y_i) \in S_c} \mathcal{T}_\theta(x_i). \quad (1)$$

Next, the model computes the negative of the squared Euclidean distance between each query example representation and the class prototypes, denoted as *logits*. Finally, we use the cross-entropy loss between the computed logits of the query set and query labels y as the classification loss:

$$\mathcal{L}_{cls} = \sum_{c \in C_{train}} \sum_{i=1}^{|Q_c|} \text{cross-entropy}(logits_i, y_i), \quad (2)$$

and update the model parameters $\theta_\mathcal{T}$ using the Adam optimizer.

3.2.3 Episodic distillation process

Our goal is to obtain efficient small student models that generalize to unseen classes (domains). Therefore, we combine the advantages of FSL and KD and introduce episodic knowledge distillation as the main component in our approach. It is performed during the pretraining step of the student on source classes (domains).

Given a pretrained teacher $\mathcal{T}$ on source classes (domains), we distill a student $\mathcal{S}$ on the same classes (domains). The distillation process consists of epochs. At each distillation step in an epoch, we create an episode. The support set is used to compute the class prototypes in both $\mathcal{T}$ and $\mathcal{S}$ for the classification of the query set. We define the overall distillation loss function as follows:

$$\mathcal{L}_{\text{kd}} = \mathcal{L}_{\text{soft}} + \mathcal{L}_{\text{pt}}, \quad (3)$$

where $\mathcal{L}_{soft}$ is the Kullback-Leibler (KL) divergence between the soft labels of the teacher and student output layer on the query set, which is computed as follows:

$$\begin{aligned} p_\mathcal{T} &= \text{softmax}(\text{logits}^\mathcal{T}) \\ p_\mathcal{S} &= \text{softmax}(\text{logits}^\mathcal{S}) \\ \mathcal{L}_{\text{soft}}(\mathcal{T}, \mathcal{S}) &= \text{KL}(p_\mathcal{T}, p_\mathcal{S}). \end{aligned} \quad (4)$$

To transfer the generalization ability of the teacher, we use a new term $\mathcal{L}_{pt}$ in the distillation loss function, which is specific to the few-shot learning setting. $\mathcal{L}_{pt}$ computes the difference between the class prototypes in $\mathcal{T}$ and $\mathcal{S}$. It is computed as the Mean-Squared Error (MSE) on the class prototypes in the teacher and student:

$$\mathcal{L}_{pt}(\mathcal{T}, \mathcal{S}) = \sum_{c=1}^{C_{train}} \text{MSE}(r_c^\mathcal{T}, r_c^\mathcal{S}). \quad (5)$$

After computing the loss, the student model parameters θ_S are updated. Note that the student does not have access to the query set labels during distillation.

3.2.4 Mini-episodic adaptation

Both pretrained teacher and student models can be adapted on target domains in multi-domain IC. However, our assumption is that the models have access to only a handful of labeled examples. For this purpose, similar to the episodic pretraining step, the standard meta-learning approach is applied for adapting the teacher or student on the target domain. To simulate the few-shot assumption, we create mini-episodes from episodes, devised originally by Luo et al. (2017). At each adaptation step, akin to the k-fold cross-validation approach, the k_s instances in the support set of the created episode are repeatedly split into n-way $k_s - 1$ mini-support instances and one mini-query instance. Model parameters are updated after each mini-episode. The episode's query set is left for evaluation purposes at inference time. We adapt the teacher using mini-episodic adaptation. The student is also adapted using the same procedure without the teacher supervision.

3.2.5 Meta-testing

Model performance is evaluated at meta-testing time through random test episodes on the meta-testing split C_{test} following the experimental setup in (Krone et al., 2020; Li et al., 2021). In the first scenario, we use the support and query sets at each random test episode for prototype computations and performance evaluation, respectively. In the second scenario, we adapt the model to target domains using mini-episodic adaptation and use the mini-support and mini-query sets for model parameters update. Then, the episode's support set is used for prototype computations while the query set is used for performance evaluation. If the model is evaluated on target domains without any adaptations, we use the support and query sets for prototype computations and performance evaluation.

4 Experiments

We conduct extensive experiments to evaluate the proposed approach on public intent classification datasets. We simulate two scenarios: in-domain target class generalization and the more challenging scenario, target domain adaptation in multi-domain intent classification. Experiments have been implemented in PyTorch and performed on a single NVIDIA 8GB GPU in Ubuntu 16.04.6 LTS.

4.1 Experiment setup

4.1.1 Datasets and splits

We use four public NLU benchmarks in our experiments: SNIPS (Coucke et al., 2018), ATIS (Hemphill et al., 1990), TOP (Gupta et al., 2018), and Clinc150 (Larson et al., 2019). To simulate few-shot class generalization in intent classification, we use the proposed splits by Krone et al. (2020). They create a meta-training split (train split) and a meta-testing split (test split) from the classes in each dataset. To simulate few-shot domain adaptation, we use the proposed splits by Li et al. (2021). The statistics on the datasets and splits for both scenarios are provided in Tables 7 and 8 in Appendix B.1, respectively. Intent classes of each split can be found in (Krone et al., 2020). We only remove the *atis_day_name* intent from the test split of ATIS as it contains only two utterances. Moreover, we use *Work*, *Banking*, and *Credit card* domains as the source domains and *Home* and *Kitchen and Dining* as the target domains in the Clinc150 dataset for the second scenario. We choose this split to minimize the overlap between the source and target domains. Moreover, we do not utilize any validation set for model parameters optimization. In this way, we increased the difficulty level for a meaningful comparison in few-shot scenarios. Furthermore, SNIPS is in fact a multi-domain dataset and contains cross-domain intent classes, and ATIS and TOP are highly unbalanced resulting in rather difficult datasets for comparison in the few-shot setting. TOP also contains various intent classes in the *navigation and events* domain.

4.1.2 Training and testing Settings

In all scenarios, we use the Adam optimizer during pretraining and distillation with a learning rate of $1e^{-5}$. Following the experiments setup in (Krone et al., 2020) and (Li et al., 2021), training epochs for both teacher and student are set to 30. At test time, we report the average accuracy and standard deviation of the models over three random seeds and 100 random test episodes on the test split. We use $\text{BERT}_{\text{base\_uncased}}$ as the base language model with hidden size of 768. All hidden layers and output features m in the Protonet are set to 200 based on practical experiments.

In the in-domain target class generalization, we pretrain the teacher using episodic training with two different maximum support set size (K_{max}) for episodes: 20 and 100. This way, we compare our results directly with the results of Krone et al. (2020). In the target domain adaptation scenario, we report the results of the distilled student on target domains without adaptation and with 10 epochs of mini-episodic adaptation. In line with Li et al. (2021)'s work, the ways n is set to the number of the intent classes in the target domain during the target domain adaptation of the student. Moreover, we fix both k_s and k_q to 10 during the adaptation. Therefore, variable episode construction is not utilized in this step. Pretraining and episodic distillation steps remain the same as before.

4.2 Results and discussions

4.2.1 In-domain target class generalization

We investigate the generalization ability of the small student model on unseen classes and compare with the proposed models in (Krone et al., 2020). They study different encoding blocks (GloVe, ELMo, BERT) and algorithms (Fine-tune, foMAML, Proto) for joint IC and slot filling under the few-shot learning scenario. We report the results of the BERT+Proto model (Baseline BERT+Proto), which is the $\text{BERT}_{\text{base\_uncased}}$ model with a Protonet, and the best results obtained among all models (Baseline best result). Note that the reported Baseline BERT+Proto model is approximately as large as the teacher model in the number of parameters. Table 1 shows the evaluation results on the three benchmark datasets, considering two different values of K_{max}. For each domain dataset, we train a teacher model on the train split via the episodic pretraining step, and distill an in-domain student using the episodic distillation process. We then evaluate the performance of the student on the unseen intent classes, i.e., the test split, in the respective dataset without further adaptation. Moreover, following the experiments in (Krone et al., 2020), we train a multi-domain teacher using the train splits of all datasets jointly. We then evaluate two types of distilled students on the test split of each dataset individually: 1) a multi-domain student distilled on all datasets, and 2) a domain-specific student. Table 2 shows the results of the multi-domain intent class generalization.

As can be computed from Table 1, the domain-specific student retains 95.7% of the domain-specific teacher's performance on average, which confirms its generalization ability given the limited capacity of small models. The student outperforms the Baseline BERT+Proto model by 5.6 points in $K_{max} = 20$ and 1.75 points in $K_{max} = 100$ on average. Note that Krone et al. (2020) proposed a joint few-shot learning approach for IC and slot filling tasks, which results in a more challenging final task. Therefore, for fairness, we refrain from comparing our teacher results with their models. The performance boost by larger K_{max} in the student is 2.4 points. Since there is a semantic overlap between the train and test intent classes in ATIS, the student shows competitive performance with the teacher. SNIPS contains semantically distant classes. Similarly, TOP contains diverse intent classes besides being highly unbalanced, which explains the performance gap between the student and the teacher in these datasets.

Table 2 shows that the multi-domain and domain-specific students distilled from the multi-domain teacher, achieve 82.31% and 92.06% of the teacher performance, respectively. As is expected, the multi-domain student underperforms the domain-specific student by 7.35 accuracy points on average since its representational capacity is limited for several domains. However, the multi-domain student outperforms the Baseline BERT+Proto in the ATIS domain. This demonstrates that multi-domain training is beneficial when the test set is highly imbalanced, like the ATIS dataset. Compared to the Baseline BERT+Proto, the domain-specific student achieves a higher performance in four out of six experiments and falls behind in the other two experiments by 1.79 points on average. Therefore, there is a trade-off between less memory consumption by deploying a multi-domain small model and a higher accuracy performance by deploying several distinct domain-specific models in an application. Slight improvements with $K_{max} = 100$ can be observed in our model.

4.2.2 Target domain adaptation

In this experiment, a multi-domain teacher is pretrained on source domains (pretrained $\mathcal{T}$) and a student is distilled on source domains using the episodic knowledge distillation (pretrained $\mathcal{S}$). To evaluate the generalization ability of the student on unseen domains, we adapt the student to a target domain without teacher access (adapted $\mathcal{S}$) using mini-episodic adaptation. We compare its performance with the teacher adapted to the respective

	$K_{max} = 20$			$K_{max} = 100$		
Model	**SNIPS**	**ATIS**	**TOP**	**SNIPS**	**ATIS**	**TOP**
Baseline best result	85.53 ± 0.35	65.95 ± 2.29	52.76 ± 2.26	87.69 ± 1.05	70.25 ± 0.39	61.30 ± 0.32
Baseline BERT+Proto	81.39 ± 1.85	58.84 ± 1.33	52.76 ± 2.26	83.51 ± 0.88	66.89 ± 2.31	61.30 ± 0.32
Domain-specific teacher	87.66 ± 1.69	69.44 ± 1.21	63.08 ± 1.80	87.58 ± 1.95	72.98 ± 2.29	64.65 ± 2.74
Domain-specific student	82.83 ± 0.92	69.45 ± 3.21	57.49 ± 3.17	84.19 ± 0.83	71.57 ± 2.98	61.21 ± 1.46

Table 1: Average test accuracy on in-domain target class generalization. Models are trained and tested on each domain (dataset) separately.

	$K_{max} = 20$			$K_{max} = 100$		
Model	**SNIPS**	**ATIS**	**TOP**	**SNIPS**	**ATIS**	**TOP**
Baseline best result	87.64 ± 0.73	65.19 ± 1.29	52.64 ± 2.58	88.90 ± 0.18	71.89 ± 1.45	62.51 ± 1.79
Baseline BERT+Proto	81.44 ± 2.91	58.82 ± 1.55	52.64 ± 2.58	86.29 ± 1.09	65.70 ± 2.31	62.51 ± 1.79
Multi-domain teacher	87.74 ± 0.48	79.65 ± 6.27	62.83 ± 2.00	86.91 ± 3.06	83.77 ± 0.89	65.72 ± 0.77
Multi-domain student	72.97 ± 0.62	72.03 ± 2.07	45.36 ± 0.94	75.57 ± 0.82	68.90 ± 2.02	51.82 ± 0.76
Domain-specific student	85.74 ± 0.49	72.08 ± 3.16	56.37 ± 3.60	85.58 ± 0.73	71.36 ± 2.16	59.64 ± 3.64

Table 2: Average test accuracy on in-domain target class generalization. Multi-domain models are trained on all three datasets and tested on each dataset separately.

domain (adapted $\mathcal{T}$) using mini-episodic adaptation. Train and test splits are reported in Table 8 in Appendix B.1.

Table 3 shows the average results on three target domains. We also report the results of two cross-domain models proposed by Li et al. (2021), referred to as Base Protonet and Base best. The Base Protonet utilizes BERT as the encoding block, which is approximately in the same size as our teacher model. The Base best is the best results obtained among different models. As can be seen, the adapted student without teacher supervision shows a significant improvement over its pretrained counterpart. It also achieves 95% of the adapted teacher's performance and even outperforms it on SNIPS slightly. Moreover, the adapted student outperforms the large baselines by 7.03 points on average. This leads to a conclusion that our proposed approach brings benefits in the few-shot generalization problem on small distilled models with limited representational capacity. Note that Li et al. (2021) proposed a joint meta-learning approach for cross-domain IC and slot filling, which results in a more challenging final task. Therefore, for fairness, we refrain from comparing our teacher results with their models.

We extend the experiments with the Clinc150 dataset, which is a balanced dataset. Table 4 presents evaluation results for the Clinc150 target domain split. Following the same discussion, the pretrained teacher outperforms the pretrained student. The adapted student achieves higher accuracy than its pretrained counterpart and retains 87% of the adapted teacher, which is slightly lower than the previously studied domains. We argue that it is due to the more challenging target domains with larger number of intent types (15 intents per domain) and highly overlapping intents (e.g., *todo_list* and *todo_list_update*, *restaurant_suggestion* and *restaurant_review*), which should be handled by a single student in the Clinc150 dataset. This limits the application of our approach in such multi-domain settings.

Model	**SNIPS**	**ATIS**	**TOP**
Base best	90.9 ± 0.3	76.0 ± 0.8	61.9 ± 1.1
Base Protonet	90.9 ± 0.3	75.3 ± 0.7	61.9 ± 1.1
Pretrained $\mathcal{T}$	79.11 ± 1.68	82.20 ± 1.56	62.97 ± 1.91
Pretrained $\mathcal{S}$	75.24 ± 3.02	76.56 ± 2.28	57.16 ± 0.73
Adapted $\mathcal{T}$	89.90 ± 0.13	94.70 ± 0.33	76.12 ± 0.90
Adapted $\mathcal{S}$	90.41 ± 0.89	92.36 ± 0.73	66.78 ± 0.97

Table 3: Average test accuracy on target domain adaptation in SNIPS, ATIS, and TOP

To compare the computational cost of the teacher and student, we report the memory size and average inference time of the models per episode on target domains. The number of parameters (in millions) for teacher and student is 109.68M and 38.80M. The student consumes 64% less memory (2.8 times fewer parameters) than the teacher. The average inference speed of the student for one episode in-

Model	Home	Kitchen_dining
Pretrained $\mathcal{T}$	78.08 ± 0.70	79.39 ± 0.40
Pretrained $\mathcal{S}$	63.74 ± 0.86	69.76 ± 0.94
Adapted $\mathcal{T}$	91.91 ± 0.07	91.44 ± 0.44
Adapted $\mathcal{S}$	76.60 ± 0.29	82.17 ± 0.78

Table 4: Average test accuracy on Clinc150 target domains

Source\Target	SNIPS	ATIS	TOP
SNIPS	–	58.42 ± 3.65 89.45 ± 1.99	40.50 ± 0.71 62.58 ± 0.87
ATIS	75.92 ± 2.78 89.51 ± 1.17	–	53.88 ± 0.39 66.93 ± 0.54
TOP	65.59 ± 3.18 82.46 ± 1.18	70.08 ± 1.90 91.42 ± 0.28	–

Table 5: Average test accuracy of models trained on one source domain. Upper rows report pretrained student and lower rows report adapted student.

cluding prototype computations and query set predictions on the Clinc150 target domains (Home and Kitchen) is 5.6 and 1.1 times faster than teacher on CPU and GPU, respectively.[2]

4.2.3 Ablation Study

We analyze the impact of source domains on the performance of the student model on target domains in the target domain adaptation scenario. For this purpose, we pretrain the teacher and student on one source domain and evaluate the pretrained and adapted student on the two other target domains individually and compare with the results in Table 3. Table 5 shows the results of the pretrained and adapted student in each target domain. We observe a performance gap between one versus multiple source domains in pretrained students, specially when we opt out the source ATIS; The performance of the pretrained student on TOP is 40.50 with source SNIPS and 57.16 with source ATIS and SNIPS. This demonstrates that the pretrained student takes an advantage of diverse source domains for evaluation on target domains. Moreover, the average higher performance of the student in the multiple source domain setting indicates that the knowledge is transferred effectively through the episodic distillation process. Small performance gap between one versus multiple source domains is also observed in the adapted student.

Lastly, we analyze how FSL and KD influence

[2]The CPU is a 3.1 GHz Quad-Core Intel Core i7.

	Teacher	Student	Student - Teacher
MSL	77.78 ± 0.59	62.59 ± 0.92	-15.19
FSL	$69.56 \pm 2,94$	52.96 ± 2.44	-16.60
FSL - MSL	-8.22	-9.63	–

Table 6: Average test accuracy on the effect of FSL and KD on Clin150-Home

the IC performance separately. For this, we measure the performance of the teacher and the distilled student, which are pretrained on the Clinc150 source domains and tested on the Clinc150-Home target domain without adaptation. We test these models with support shot $k_s = 10$ and $k_s = 70$, called FSL and many-shot learning (MSL) scenario, respectively. We use the first 10 and 70 instances of each class in the official train set of the Home domain as the support set. The official test set with 30 instances per class is also used as the query set. Evaluation results are shown in Table 6. We observe an accuracy drop from teacher to student in both scenarios (15.19 and 16.60 points), however, with a negligible difference . Therefore, the distilled student loses approximately the same amount of teacher's performance accuracy in few- and many-shot learning settings. This indicates the effectiveness of the proposed episodic distillation process in knowledge transfer under the FSL setting. Moreover, the difference in the performance loss from MSL to FSL in both teacher and student models is small ($9.63 - 8.22 = 1.41$ point). This implies the capability of the proposed approach for obtaining generalizable small models. Note that the discrepancy between the performance results in this section and previous section is due to the different support and query splits at meta-testing.

5 Conclusion

We address the nontrivial merging problem of meta-learning and knowledge distillation. Our proposed approach distills large Transformer-based models into smaller student models, which are compatible with few-shot learning scenarios in intent classification. Through a multi-step meta-training with an episodic knowledge distillation, we obtain a small distilled model that is generalizable and adaptable to new classes and domains using only a few labeled examples. Our results in target domain adaptation show that the small model can adapt effectively to new domains without teacher supervision.

This removes the need for a large teacher when time and computational resources are limited. Compared to the large model, we observe a slight performance loss and less memory consumption in the distilled model. In summary, our results provide insights into the advantages and limitations of a joint few-shot learning and knowledge distillation approach to foster future research in this area.

Our primary findings suggest that it is worthwhile to explore different FSL techniques jointly with KD for cross-domain few-shot performance improvements. Overall, this topic still merits more attention to aid the practical deployment of NLU models in dialogue systems under low-resource scenarios. As future research, we will study novel joint methods for the cross-domain generalization problem under low-resource scenarios. Moreover, we will investigate the methods in joint NLU tasks, specifically slot filling and IC.

Acknowledgements

This research was carried out while the first author was affiliated with the Fraunhofer IIS. This work is supported by the German Federal Ministry for Economic Affairs and Energy (BMWi) through the SPEAKER project (FKZ 01MK19011).

References

Jimmy Ba and Rich Caruana. 2014. Do deep nets really need to be deep? In *Advances in Neural Information Processing Systems*, volume 27. Curran Associates, Inc.

Tom Brown, Benjamin Mann, Nick Ryder, Melanie Subbiah, Jared D Kaplan, Prafulla Dhariwal, Arvind Neelakantan, Pranav Shyam, Girish Sastry, Amanda Askell, Sandhini Agarwal, Ariel Herbert-Voss, Gretchen Krueger, Tom Henighan, Rewon Child, Aditya Ramesh, Daniel Ziegler, Jeffrey Wu, Clemens Winter, Chris Hesse, Mark Chen, Eric Sigler, Mateusz Litwin, Scott Gray, Benjamin Chess, Jack Clark, Christopher Berner, Sam McCandlish, Alec Radford, Ilya Sutskever, and Dario Amodei. 2020. Language models are few-shot learners. In *Advances in Neural Information Processing Systems*, volume 33, pages 1877–1901. Curran Associates, Inc.

Cristian Bucila, R. Caruana, and Alexandru Niculescu-Mizil. 2006. Model compression. In *KDD'06*.

Iñigo Casanueva, Tadas Temčinas, Daniela Gerz, Matthew Henderson, and Ivan Vulić. 2020. Efficient intent detection with dual sentence encoders. In *Proceedings of the 2nd Workshop on Natural Language Processing for Conversational AI*, pages 38–45, Online. Association for Computational Linguistics.

Qian Chen, Zhu Zhuo, and Wen Wang. 2019. BERT for joint intent classification and slot filling. *CoRR*, abs/1902.10909.

Kevin Clark, Minh-Thang Luong, Urvashi Khandelwal, Christopher D. Manning, and Quoc V. Le. 2019. BAM! born-again multi-task networks for natural language understanding. In *Proceedings of the 57th Annual Meeting of the Association for Computational Linguistics*, pages 5931–5937, Florence, Italy. Association for Computational Linguistics.

A. Coucke, A. Saade, Adrien Ball, Théodore Bluche, A. Caulier, David Leroy, Clément Doumouro, Thibault Gisselbrecht, F. Caltagirone, Thibaut Lavril, Maël Primet, and J. Dureau. 2018. Snips voice platform: an embedded spoken language understanding system for private-by-design voice interfaces. *ArXiv*, abs/1805.10190.

Jacob Devlin, Ming-Wei Chang, Kenton Lee, and Kristina Toutanova. 2019. BERT: Pre-training of deep bidirectional transformers for language understanding. In *Proceedings of the 2019 Conference of the North American Chapter of the Association for Computational Linguistics: Human Language Technologies, Volume 1 (Long and Short Papers)*, pages 4171–4186, Minneapolis, Minnesota. Association for Computational Linguistics.

Ruiying Geng, Binhua Li, Yongbin Li, Xiaodan Zhu, Ping Jian, and Jian Sun. 2019. Induction networks for few-shot text classification. In *Proceedings of the 2019 Conference on Empirical Methods in Natural Language Processing and the 9th International Joint Conference on Natural Language Processing (EMNLP-IJCNLP)*, pages 3904–3913, Hong Kong, China. Association for Computational Linguistics.

Sonal Gupta, Rushin Shah, Mrinal Mohit, Anuj Kumar, and Mike Lewis. 2018. Semantic parsing for task oriented dialog using hierarchical representations. In *Proceedings of the 2018 Conference on Empirical Methods in Natural Language Processing*, pages 2787–2792, Brussels, Belgium. Association for Computational Linguistics.

Charles T. Hemphill, John J. Godfrey, and George R. Doddington. 1990. The ATIS spoken language systems pilot corpus. In *Speech and Natural Language: Proceedings of a Workshop Held at Hidden Valley, Pennsylvania, June 24-27,1990*, Hidden Valley, Pennsylvania.

Geoffrey Hinton, Oriol Vinyals, and Jeff Dean. 2015. Distilling the knowledge in a neural network.

Yidi Jiang, Bidisha Sharma, Maulik Madhavi, and Haizhou Li. 2021. Knowledge distillation from bert transformer to speech transformer for intent classification.

Xiaoqi Jiao, Yichun Yin, Lifeng Shang, Xin Jiang, Xiao Chen, Linlin Li, Fang Wang, and Qun Liu. 2020. TinyBERT: Distilling BERT for natural language understanding. In *Findings of the Association for Computational Linguistics: EMNLP 2020*, pages 4163–4174, Online. Association for Computational Linguistics.

Jason Krone, Yi Zhang, and Mona Diab. 2020. Learning to classify intents and slot labels given a handful of examples. In *Proceedings of the 2nd Workshop on Natural Language Processing for Conversational AI*, pages 96–108, Online. Association for Computational Linguistics.

Stefan Larson, Anish Mahendran, Joseph J. Peper, Christopher Clarke, Andrew Lee, Parker Hill, Jonathan K. Kummerfeld, Kevin Leach, Michael A. Laurenzano, Lingjia Tang, and Jason Mars. 2019. An evaluation dataset for intent classification and out-of-scope prediction. In *Proceedings of the 2019 Conference on Empirical Methods in Natural Language Processing and the 9th International Joint Conference on Natural Language Processing (EMNLP-IJCNLP)*, pages 1311–1316, Hong Kong, China. Association for Computational Linguistics.

Shang-Wen Li, Jason Krone, Shuyan Dong, Yufu Zhang, and Y. Al-Onaizan. 2021. Meta learning to classify intent and slot labels with noisy few shot examples. In *2021 IEEE Spoken Language Technology Workshop (SLT)*, pages 1004–1011.

Tianhong Li, Jianguo Li, Zhuang Liu, and Changshui Zhang. 2020. Few sample knowledge distillation for efficient network compression. In *2020 IEEE/CVF Conference on Computer Vision and Pattern Recognition (CVPR)*, pages 14627–14635.

Benlin Liu, Yongming Rao, Jiwen Lu, Jie Zhou, and Cho-Jui Hsieh. 2020. Metadistiller: Network self-boosting via meta-learned top-down distillation. In *Computer Vision – ECCV 2020*, pages 694–709, Cham. Springer International Publishing.

L. Liu, Haiquan Wang, Jimmy J. Lin, R. Socher, and Caiming Xiong. 2019. Mkd: a multi-task knowledge distillation approach for pretrained language models.

Zelun Luo, Yuliang Zou, Judy Hoffman, and Li Fei-Fei. 2017. Label efficient learning of transferable representations across domains and tasks. In *Proceedings of the 31st International Conference on Neural Information Processing Systems*, NIPS'17, page 164–176, Red Hook, NY, USA. Curran Associates Inc.

Luke Melas-Kyriazi, George Han, and Celine Liang. 2019. Generation-distillation for efficient natural language understanding in low-data settings. In *Proceedings of the 2nd Workshop on Deep Learning Approaches for Low-Resource NLP (DeepLo 2019)*, pages 124–131, Hong Kong, China. Association for Computational Linguistics.

Hoang Nguyen, Chenwei Zhang, Congying Xia, and Philip Yu. 2020. Dynamic semantic matching and aggregation network for few-shot intent detection. In *Findings of the Association for Computational Linguistics: EMNLP 2020*, pages 1209–1218, Online. Association for Computational Linguistics.

Haojie Pan, Chengyu Wang, Minghui Qiu, Yichang Zhang, Yaliang Li, and Jun Huang. 2021. Meta-KD: A meta knowledge distillation framework for language model compression across domains. In *Proceedings of the 59th Annual Meeting of the Association for Computational Linguistics and the 11th International Joint Conference on Natural Language Processing (Volume 1: Long Papers)*, pages 3026–3036, Online. Association for Computational Linguistics.

Victor Sanh, Lysandre Debut, Julien Chaumond, and Thomas Wolf. 2019. Distilbert, a distilled version of bert: smaller, faster, cheaper and lighter. In *5th Workshop on Energy Efficient Machine Learning and Cognitive Computing - NeurIPS 2019*, Vancouver.

Timo Schick and Hinrich Schütze. 2021. It's not just size that matters: Small language models are also few-shot learners. In *Proceedings of the 2021 Conference of the North American Chapter of the Association for Computational Linguistics: Human Language Technologies, NAACL-HLT 2021, Online, June 6-11, 2021*, pages 2339–2352. Association for Computational Linguistics.

Jake Snell, Kevin Swersky, and Richard Zemel. 2017. Prototypical networks for few-shot learning. In *Advances in Neural Information Processing Systems*, volume 30. Curran Associates, Inc.

Siqi Sun, Yu Cheng, Zhe Gan, and Jingjing Liu. 2019. Patient knowledge distillation for BERT model compression. In *Proceedings of the 2019 Conference on Empirical Methods in Natural Language Processing and the 9th International Joint Conference on Natural Language Processing (EMNLP-IJCNLP)*, pages 4323–4332, Hong Kong, China. Association for Computational Linguistics.

Zhiqing Sun, Hongkun Yu, Xiaodan Song, Renjie Liu, Yiming Yang, and Denny Zhou. 2020. MobileBERT: a compact task-agnostic BERT for resource-limited devices. In *Proceedings of the 58th Annual Meeting of the Association for Computational Linguistics*, pages 2158–2170, Online. Association for Computational Linguistics.

Raphael Tang, Yao Lu, L. Liu, Lili Mou, Olga Vechtomova, and Jimmy J. Lin. 2019. Distilling task-specific knowledge from bert into simple neural networks. *ArXiv*, abs/1903.12136.

Eleni Triantafillou, Tyler Zhu, Vincent Dumoulin, Pascal Lamblin, Kelvin Xu, Ross Goroshin, Carles Gelada, Kevin Swersky, Pierre-Antoine Manzagol, and Hugo Larochelle. 2020. Meta-dataset: A dataset of datasets for learning to learn from few examples.

In *International Conference on Learning Representations (ICLR 2020)*, Addis Ababa, Ethiopia. ICLR.

Henry Tsai, Jason Riesa, Melvin Johnson, Naveen Arivazhagan, Xin Li, and Amelia Archer. 2019. Small and practical BERT models for sequence labeling. In *Proceedings of the 2019 Conference on Empirical Methods in Natural Language Processing and the 9th International Joint Conference on Natural Language Processing (EMNLP-IJCNLP)*, pages 3632–3636, Hong Kong, China. Association for Computational Linguistics.

Oriol Vinyals, Charles Blundell, Timothy Lillicrap, Koray Kavukcuoglu, and Daan Wierstra. 2016. Matching networks for one shot learning. In *Proceedings of the 30th International Conference on Neural Information Processing Systems*, NIPS'16, page 3637–3645, Red Hook, NY, USA. Curran Associates Inc.

Bowen Wu, Huan Zhang, MengYuan Li, Zongsheng Wang, Qihang Feng, Junhong Huang, and Baoxun Wang. 2020. Towards non-task-specific distillation of BERT via sentence representation approximation. In *Proceedings of the 1st Conference of the Asia-Pacific Chapter of the Association for Computational Linguistics and the 10th International Joint Conference on Natural Language Processing*, pages 70–79, Suzhou, China. Association for Computational Linguistics.

Congying Xia, Chenwei Zhang, Hoang Nguyen, Jiawei Zhang, and Philip S. Yu. 2020. CG-BERT: conditional text generation with BERT for generalized few-shot intent detection. *CoRR*, abs/2004.01881.

Jianguo Zhang, Kazuma Hashimoto, Wenhao Liu, Chien-Sheng Wu, Yao Wan, Philip Yu, Richard Socher, and Caiming Xiong. 2020a. Discriminative nearest neighbor few-shot intent detection by transferring natural language inference. In *Proceedings of the 2020 Conference on Empirical Methods in Natural Language Processing (EMNLP)*, pages 5064–5082, Online. Association for Computational Linguistics.

Min Zhang, Donglin Wang, and Sibo Gai. 2020b. Knowledge distillation for model-agnostic meta-learning. In *ECAI 2020*, pages 1355–1362. IOS Press.

Wangchunshu Zhou, Canwen Xu, and Julian McAuley. 2021. Meta learning for knowledge distillation. *ArXiv*, abs/2106.04570.

A Approach

A.1 Variable episode construction

Following the work by Krone et al. (2020) and Triantafillou et al. (2020), to create an episode, first, the way n is uniformly selected from the range $[3, |C_{split}|]$ for each domain $d \in D_{split}$. Then, the query shot k_q is computed as follows:

$$k_q = \min(10, (\min_{c \in C_{split}} \lfloor 0.5 * |U_c| \rfloor)),$$

where U_c is the set of instances in class c in domain d. Then, we compute the overall support set size:

$$|S| = \min \{K_{max}, \sum_{c \in C_{split}} \lceil \beta \min\{20, |U_c| - k_q\} \rceil \},$$

where β is sampled uniformly from $(0, 1]$. K_{max} is a constant value indicating the maximum size of the support set as a whole. Finally, we calculate the support shot k_s for each class c:

$$k_s = \min\{\lfloor R_c * (|S| - |C_{split}|) \rfloor + 1, |U_c| - k_q\},$$

where R_c noisily approximates the ratio of instances belonging to class c in domain d:

$$R_c = \frac{\exp(\alpha_c) * |U_c|}{\sum_{c' \in C_d} \exp(\alpha_{c'}) * |U_{c'}|}.$$

α_c is uniformly sampled from the interval $[\log(0.5), \log(2))$. Then, we construct distinct random episodes by choosing the set of support and query instances of each class, S_c and Q_c, from the corresponding split.

B Experiment setup

B.1 Datasets and splits

Following (Krone et al., 2020) and Li et al. (2021), the statistics on the datasets and splits for in-domain target class generalization and target domain adaptation in cross-domain intent classification are provided in Table 7 and 8, respectively.

Split\Dataset	SNIPS	TOP	ATIS
Train	(8230,4)	(20345,7)	(4373,5)
Test	(6254,3)	(4426,6)	(827,6)

Table 7: Statistics of train and test splits in NLU datasets for in-domain class generalization with (number of utterances in the split, number of intents in the split).

Target domain\Split	Train	Test
SNIPS	(TOP,20345,7) (ATIS,4373,5)	(SNIPS,6254,3)
TOP	(SNIPS, 8230,4) (ATIS,4373,5)	(TOP,4426,6)
ATIS	(TOP,20345,7) (SNIPS, 8230,4)	(ATIS,827,6)
Clinc150-Home	(Work,1500,15) (Banking,1500,15) (Credit-card,1500,15)	(Home,450,15)
Clinc150-Kitchen_dining	(Work,1500,15) (Banking,1500,15) (Credit-card,1500,15)	(Kitchen_dining,450,15)

Table 8: Statistics of train and test splits in NLU datasets for target domain adaptation with (domain, number of utterances, number of intents)

MTL-SLT: Multi-Task Learning for Spoken Language Tasks

Zhiqi Huang[1], Milind Rao[2], Anirudh Raju[2], Zhe Zhang[2], Bach Bui[2], Chul Lee[2]

[1]Peking University, China
[2]Amazon Alexa, USA
zhiqihuang@pku.edu.cn, {milinrao, ranirudh}@amazon.com

Abstract

Language understanding in speech-based systems has attracted extensive interest from both academic and industrial communities in recent years with the growing demand for voice-based applications. Prior works focus on independent research by the automatic speech recognition (ASR) and natural language processing (NLP) communities, or on jointly modeling the speech and NLP problems focusing on a single dataset or single NLP task. To facilitate the development of spoken language research, we introduce MTL-SLT, a multi-task learning framework for spoken language tasks. MTL-SLT takes speech as input, and outputs transcription, intent, named entities, summaries, and answers to text queries, supporting the tasks of spoken language understanding, spoken summarization and spoken question answering respectively. The proposed framework benefits from three key aspects: 1) pre-trained sub-networks of ASR model and language model; 2) multi-task learning objective to exploit shared knowledge from different tasks; 3) end-to-end training of ASR and downstream NLP task based on sequence loss. We obtain state-of-the-art results on spoken language understanding tasks such as SLURP and ATIS. Spoken summarization results are reported on a new dataset: Spoken-Gigaword.

	Input
Speech	I am going to the airport tomorrow, please turn off bedroom light at nine thirty pm.
Q1	When should I turn off bedroom light?
Q2	When do I go to the airport?
	Output
Sum.	turn off the bedroom light
Intent	hue_lightoff
Slots	[date : tomorrow], [time : nine thirty pm] [house_place : bedroom],
Ans1.	nine thirty pm
Ans2.	tomorrow

Table 1: An example of multiple spoken language tasks. Given input utterances in the form of speech, the ASR-NLP system can provide a summary of the speech (summarization), intent detection and named entity recognition (language understanding) and answer textual queries. The spoken question answering task requires additional questions as input.

1 Introduction

The wide deployment of voice controlled computing has led to extensive interest in spoken language tasks in recent years (Saade et al., 2019; Bastianelli et al., 2020; Li et al., 2018). For instance, spoken language understanding aims to extract the semantics from user queries (Chung et al., 2021; Kim et al., 2021a; Lai et al., 2021), spoken question answering aims to predict the answer given the spoken context (You et al., 2021; Kuo et al., 2020). The rapid development of spoken language tasks have followed dataset releases (Zhang et al., 2020; Liu et al., 2019) and the evolution of pre-trained models (Devlin et al., 2019; Lewis et al., 2020; Chuang et al., 2020).

Multi-task learning (MTL) (Caruana, 1997) focuses on simultaneously solving multiple related tasks and has attracted much attention in recent years. Compared with single-task learning, it can reduce the training and inference time while improving generalization performance and prediction accuracy by learning a shared representation across related tasks. Prior works show the effectiveness of MTL while they only focus on multiple text-based tasks/datasets (e.g., MT-DNN (Liu et al., 2019; Wang et al., 2019)) or multiple speech-based tasks/datasets (e.g., SpeechStew (Chan et al., 2021)). Also, some works (Raju et al., 2021; Rao et al., 2021) prove the effectiveness of considering speech information when performing NLP tasks. Thus, as can be seen in Figure 1, we argue that it is helpful when extend these MTL approaches to spoken language tasks (i.e., ASR-NLP-shared).

Proceedings of the 4th Workshop on NLP for Conversational AI, pages 120 - 130
May 27, 2022 ©2022 Association for Computational Linguistics

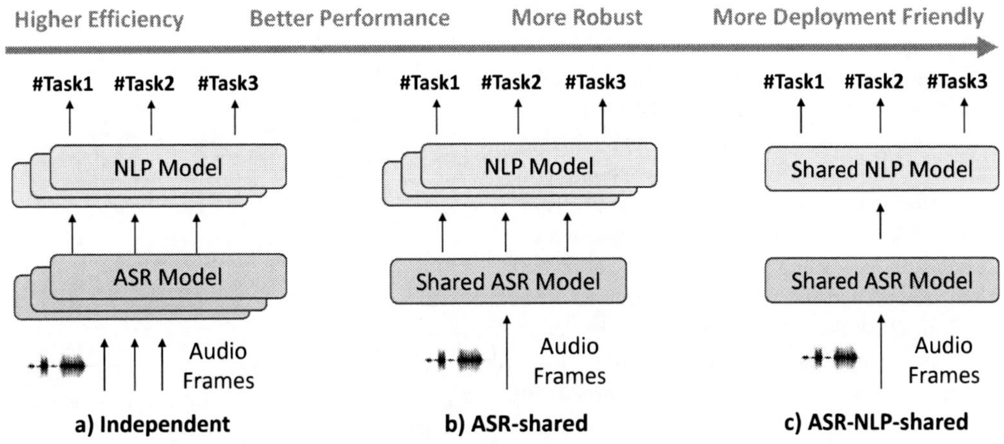

Figure 1: Different Implementations of Spoken Language Tasks.

In this paper, we develop multi-task learning methods to optimize spoken summarization, spoken question answering, spoken language understanding (intent classification and slot filling), as well as speech recognition on multiple spoken language datasets. An example of an application with these four tasks can be seen in Table 1. Note that instead of performing experiments only on understanding task (e.g., Feng et al. (2021)), we also consider harder generation task into our framework, whose data distribution has significant difference to classification task (Observation can be witnessed from Figure 2, the purple points are far away from the other data).

A primary challenge with audio as an input modality is the impact of speech recognition errors and acoustic noise on spoken language tasks. To mitigate this, our approach jointly optimizes pretrained speech recognition and language models for semantic metrics of interest and we train across multiple language tasks. The various language tasks and the impact of multi-task training can be visualized in the clustering plot of the hidden state of a pretrained language model in Figure 2. We demonstrate our results using listen-attend-spell (LAS) (Chan et al., 2016) speech recognition model and a BART (Lewis et al., 2020) based NLP model.

Overall, the main contributions are as follows:

- We propose a MTL-SLT framework to effectively joint train an ASR model and an NLP model on multiple spoken language tasks.
- Experimental results show that our proposed multi-task learning framework is state-of-the-art on spoken language understanding tasks. Training multiple language tasks followed by task-specific finetuning yields optimal models. Jointly training ASR and NLP with policy gradient methods improves metrics on all spoken language tasks.
- We prepare a spoken summarization dataset based on the Gigaword dataset (Rush et al., 2015) using a multi-speaker text-to-speech (TTS) model. The performance of the introduced spoken-summarization task with the MTL framework is studied.
- Our approach extends to multiple NLP tasks, providing improvements in an end-to-end spoken language learning setting. We make our code and data publicly available for researchers to accelerate the development of related spoken language tasks.

2 Related Work

MTL MTL aims to improve the performance on a set of primary tasks through an inductive bias (Caruana, 1997) introduced by additional training objectives on auxilliary tasks. MTL has also been used to train several tasks jointly, without the notions of primary and auxilliary tasks (McCann et al., 2018). MTL approaches for deep learning include hard parameter sharing where the entire layers and parameters are shared between tasks; and soft parameter sharing, where each task has it's own model parameters but the distance between the model parameters is regularized to help the task-specific parameters to be similar (Ruder, 2017).

Pre-trained Models The paradigm of pre-training a language model (LM) followed by task-specific fine-tuning has been shown to obtain remarkable performance on many NLP tasks. BERT (Devlin et al., 2019) pre-trains deep bidirectional representations from unlabeled text and showed competitive performance on the GLUE (Wang et al., 2019) benchmark. This provided a base for researchers to build upon, leading to several extensions and rapid progress in the space of pre-trained LMs. The MultiTask Deep Neural Network (Liu et al., 2019) is one such extension with multi-task learning across all GLUE tasks. The paper argues for improved domain transfer by performing standard BERT pretraining, followed by multi-task learning and task-specific fine-tuning. BERT has been leveraged for various NLP tasks, for e.g. the effectiveness of BERT for the summarization task was explored by Liu and Lapata (2019). The performance of text generation tasks have been approaching a near-human level by virtue of pre-trained encoder-decoder models, such as BART (Lewis et al., 2020) and T5 (Raffel et al., 2020).

Spoken Language Tasks Spoken language tasks include standard NLP tasks with speech-input instead of text-input. Speech recognition errors can impact the performance of downstream NLP systems. Recently, Feng et al. (2021) proposed the ASR-GLUE benchmark, augmented 6 NLP tasks from GLUE with speech generated from Google TTS, and analyzed the robustness of NLP to ASR errors. However, all 6 tasks are sentence-level classification problems, and the models did not utilize MTL framework. Chung et al. (2021) introduced a speech-language joint pre-training framework for SLU tasks. The paper showed the effectiveness of the joint pre-training method with experiments on four classification tasks, i.e., intent detection, dialog act classification, spoken sentiment analysis and spoken question answering. Prior works for SLU show the impact of speech recognition errors on downstream Natural Language Understanding (NLU) performance and propose joint training of ASR and NLU to improve overall performance (Rao et al., 2021). Kim et al. (2021b) introduced a speech-based benchmark for task-oriented dialogue systems, specifically targeting the problems of multi-domain dialogue state tracking and knowledge grounded dialogue modeling, and showed that well-behaved models trained on written conversations do not perform well on spoken data.

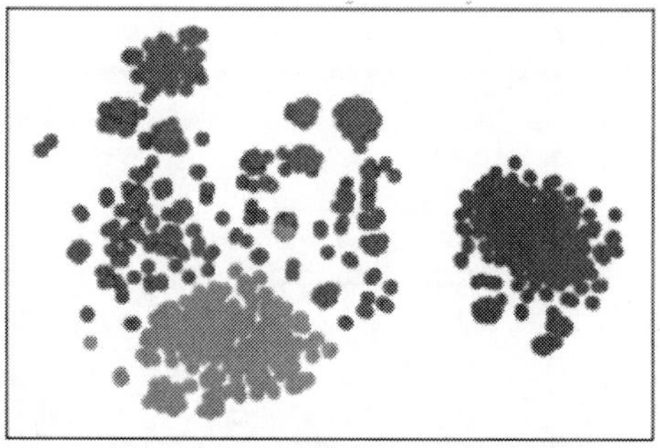

Figure 2: T-SNE Visualization of BART's last hidden state features. Red and blue represent ATIS and SLURP datasets, green denotes Spoken-SQuAD dataset, purple denotes Spoken-Gigaword dataset.

3 Approach

3.1 Architecture of MTL-SLT

Figure 3 shows the proposed MTL framework which consists of three different modules, i.e., the ASR model, the NLP model and the interface between them. In this work, the MTL-SLT uses the LAS architecture for ASR and BART for NLP.

ASR Model Unlike previous works on spoken language tasks (SLT) that obtain transcriptions using existing ASR systems/tools (Feng et al., 2021; Li et al., 2018), in our approach, the ASR model is updated with the training of end-to-end spoken language tasks. To address this, we generate the ASR transcriptions from a LAS model explained in (Rao et al., 2021; Chan et al., 2016), and pre-trained it on the LibriSpeech dataset (Panayotov et al., 2015) following previous works (Lugosch et al., 2019).

Enc-Decoder NLP Model Bidirectional and Auto-Regressive Transformers (BART) (Lewis et al., 2020) uses a separate bidirectional encoder and autoregressive decoder similar to BERT (Devlin et al., 2019) except that (1) BART's decoder incorporates cross attention over the final encoder layer and (2) BART's encoder does not use a feed-forward dense layer for word prediction. The BART model can be used to perform both language understanding (i.e., intent classification) and language generation (i.e., summarization) problems at the same time, we refer to it as an NLP model in this work. We use the same pre-trained BART-base model as the original paper, which includes 6 transformer layers in the encoder and decoder.

Spoken Language Interface The interface exposes relevant outputs from the ASR model to the

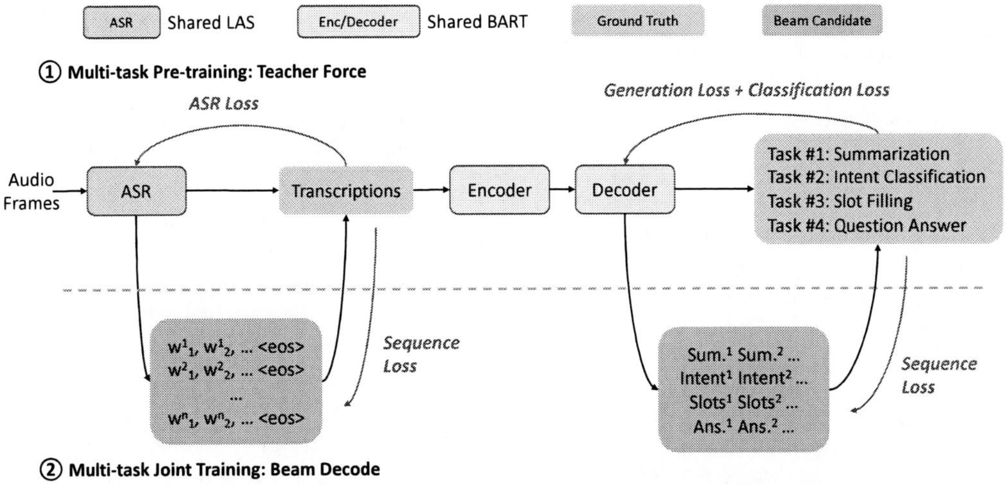

Figure 3: Our proposed MTL framework for LAS-BART-based Spoken Language Models. The model consists of an ASR system to generate transcription for the input audio frames, and an encoder-decoder system to generate intents, slots, answers, summarizations for different tasks. They share parameters of LAS, BART encoder and decoder, and are first trained on multiple tasks with ASR Loss, Generation Loss and Classification Loss; then the two systems are jointly trained with Sequence Loss.

downstream NLP model. Prior works have proposed rich interfaces that expose neural embeddings from ASR in addition to the text recognition (Rao et al., 2020). In this work, we use a simple text interface i.e. the best text recognition hypothesis from the output of ASR as the input to the NLP models. We leverage pre-trained models for both ASR and NLP. Inspired by (Rao et al., 2021; Raju et al., 2021), we introduce sequence loss training for the joint ASR-NLP system that allows direct optimization of non-differentiable SLT metrics. Specifically, we consider the error rate of ASR, summarization, QA, intent classification and slot filling as the SLT metrics.

3.2 Joint MTL Training Strategy

The MTL Training Strategy can be divided into three steps.

Backbone Pre-training The ASR model is first pre-trained for the speech recognition task using the LibriSpeech dataset. The NLP model uses the pre-trained BART (Lewis et al., 2020) model which is trained to reconstruct corrupted text.

MTL Pre-training Our joint pre-training on multiple tasks falls into the paradigm of multi-task learning (MTL). Training details of the MTL-SLT can be seen in Algorithm 1, in the training stage, we take turns to load the training data of these pre-training tasks. For example, we update model parameters on a batch of training instances from the first task, and then update parameters on a batch of training instances of the second task, and the process repeats. Note that, according to our preliminary experimentation, the effect of different orders of carrying out these pre-training tasks is negligible.

Post Fine-tuning After pre-trained with MTL objective, the MTL model is further fine-tuned on each dataset with few training steps to improve the performance.

3.3 Training Losses

There are three types of losses to be optimized in our framework, i.e., ASR loss, language task-specific losses and sequence losses. Our model is first trained by updating $\boldsymbol{\theta}_{ASR}$ based on the ASR loss, then trained by updating $\boldsymbol{\theta}_{NLP}$ for each downstream task. Finally, sequence loss training is employed to update both $\boldsymbol{\theta}_{ASR}$ and $\boldsymbol{\theta}_{NLP}$.

ASR Loss Given input audio sequence $\boldsymbol{x}$, the ASR system is trained by teacher-forcing the encoder-decoder network with the tokens of the ground truth transcript w with the loss function being $\mathcal{L}_{\text{asr}} = -\sum_{j=1}^{N} \log p(w_j|\boldsymbol{x}, w_{:j-1}; \boldsymbol{\theta})$.

Intent Detection For sentence-level classification problem, denote the sentence pooled represen-

Algorithm 1: Training a MTL-SLT model.

Parameter: Pre-trained LAS model and BART model θ, random initialized task specific heads , epoch number M, task number T.

//Prepare the data for T tasks.

```
for t in 1, 2, ..., T do
    Pack the dataset t into mini-batch: D_t.
end
// Multi-task Learning.
for epoch in 1, 2, ..., M do
    1. Merge all the datasets:
       D = D_1 ∪ D_2 ... ∪ D_T
    2. Shuffle D
    for b_t in D do
        //b_t is a mini-batch of task t.
        3. Compute loss : L(θ)
        //Train the ASR and NLP tasks.
        L(θ) += L_asr for ASR
        L(θ) += L_gen for Summarization
        L(θ) += L_tagging for Slot Filling
        L(θ) += L_intent for Intent Detection
        L(θ) += L_qa for Question Answer
        if perform joint training then
            L(θ) += L_seq for ASR and NLP
        end
        4. Compute gradient: ∇(θ)
        5. Update model: θ = θ − ε∇(θ)
    end
end
```

tation as e from input ASR token sequence $\mathbf{w}$, and the correct intent label is c, the model infers c from e. The negative log-likelihood loss is used for the classification loss $\mathcal{L}_{\text{intent}} = -\log p(c|e;\boldsymbol{\theta})$.

Slot Filling For token-level classification problem, denote the slot sequence as s, the input as $\boldsymbol{v}$, and the sequence length as N, the negative log-likelihood loss is used for calculating slot loss $\mathcal{L}_{\text{tagging}} = -\sum_{j=1}^{N} \log p(s_j|\boldsymbol{v}, s_{:j-1};\boldsymbol{\theta})$.

Summarization The summarization of $\boldsymbol{x}$ is defined as $\boldsymbol{y} = (y_1, \ldots, y_M)$. The model infers an appropriate $\boldsymbol{y}$ from $\boldsymbol{v}$. The generation loss $\mathcal{L}_{\text{gen}}$ is calculated with the negative log-likelihood loss $\mathcal{L}_{\text{gen}} = -\sum_{j=1}^{N} \log p(y_j|\boldsymbol{v}, y_{:j-1};\boldsymbol{\theta})$.

Question Answering For question answering, we employ binary cross entropy loss on the sentence pooling representation $\mathcal{L}_{\text{has\_key}}$ and the span-based losses (Rajpurkar et al., 2016) on the sentence representation $\mathcal{L}_{\text{span}}$. The QA loss is $\mathcal{L}_{\text{qa}} = \mathcal{L}_{\text{has\_key}} + \mathcal{L}_{\text{span}}$.

Sequence Losses Inspired by reinforce framework (Prabhavalkar et al., 2018), sequence loss training enables end-to-end joint training of ASR and a downstream language task (Rao et al., 2021). Denote C as a joint sequence of ASR and NLP outputs, this is done by directly optimizing model parameters θ for the expected metric cost $M(c, c^*)$ over the distribution of candidate hypotheses. Here c^* is the ground-truth output and c is a model candidate. This is expressed as,

$$\begin{aligned} \mathcal{L}_{seq} &= \mathbf{E}_{C\in\mathcal{C}}[M(C, c^*)] && (1)\\ \Rightarrow \nabla_\theta \mathcal{L}_{seq} &= \nabla_\theta \mathbf{E}_{C\in\mathcal{C}}[M(C, c^*)] && (2)\\ &\approx \nabla_\theta \sum_{c\in\bar{\mathcal{C}}} \bar{p}_\theta(c) M(c, c^*) && (3)\\ &\approx \sum_{c\in\bar{\mathcal{C}}} M(c, c^*) \nabla_\theta \bar{p}_\theta(c). && (4) \end{aligned}$$

Here, the approximation of the expectation in Eq. (3) is from using an n-best candidate set $\bar{\mathcal{C}}$ produced by the model with each candidate arising from a normalized probability $\bar{p}_\theta(c) = \frac{p_\theta(c)}{\sum_{c'\in\bar{\mathcal{C}}} p_\theta(c')}$. The probability of a candidate c is given by the combination of ASR and language task probabilities.

Sequence loss training is a policy gradient approach that jointly trains θ_{ASR} and θ_{NLP} by increasing the prediction probability of candidates with lower metric costs.

In this work, we optimize for a composite metric which is a sum of metrics of interest, namely, word error rate (WER) for ASR task and a language task metric. The metrics for language task include: (1) rouge error rate for the summarization task, (2) exact match error rate and QA F1 error rate for question answering, and (3) intent and domain classification error rate as well as SLU-F1 error rate for the language understanding task. These metrics are further detailed in Sec. 4.3.

Sequence loss training can be done for an individual task and is used in conjunction with the cross-entropy losses defined earlier that acts as a regularizing term. It can also be combined with multi-task learning by applying task-appropriate sequence loss training to update relevant parameters for a batch from the merged dataset.

	Datasets	Spoken-Gigaword				Spoken-SQuAD			ATIS			SLURP		
Settings	Models	WER(↓)	R1(↑)	R2(↑)	RL(↑)	WER(↓)	EM(↑)	F1(↑)	WER(↓)	Acc(↑)	F1(↑)	WER(↓)	Acc(↑)	SLU-F1(↑)
1. ASR	LAS-*S*	22.63	-	-	-	27.11	-	-	4.52	-	-	18.00	-	-
	LAS-*M*	**21.20**	-	-	-	**26.40**	-	-	**3.03**	-	-	**16.53**	-	-
2. NLP	BART-*S*	-	43.12	25.72	40.78	-	56.30	65.82	-	97.63	96.19	-	87.24	85.10
	BART-*M*	-	**43.30**	**26.02**	**41.29**	-	**57.92**	**67.79**	-	**98.38**	**97.55**	-	**88.31**	**85.62**
3. Pipeline	*S* -> *S*	22.63	15.81	8.10	14.66	27.11	15.73	29.82	4.52	96.87	92.30	18.00	83.22	72.50
	M -> *M*	21.20	16.33	8.61	15.29	26.40	17.44	32.30	3.03	**98.11**	**94.19**	16.53	**83.75**	72.81
4. Jointly	*S* + *S*	20.66	16.02	9.24	14.90	25.10	21.98	36.78	2.74	96.90	93.11	16.14	81.87	73.88
	M + *M*	**19.80**	**16.90**	**9.88**	**15.78**	**22.89**	**23.31**	**41.26**	**2.55**	97.13	93.65	**15.81**	83.10	**74.49**

Table 2: Main results of different models and settings on different datasets. **BOLD BLACK** numbers are in the first place for ASR and NLP settings, **BOLD RED** numbers are in the first place for Pipeline and jointly settings. A (↓) means lower is better, and (↑) means higher is better. a) For evaluation, we choose four typical and large generation and understanding datasets, i.e., Spoken-Gigaword, Spoken-SQuAD, ATIS and SLURP. b) For trainging settings, ASR and NLP represent two independent systems for their own tasks. Pipeline means that the output transcriptions from the pre-trained ASR system are used as the input of the pre-trained NLP system. Jointly training means that the parameters of ASR and NLP system are jointly optimized through extra sequence losses. c) For models, we use LAS for ASR system and BART for NLP system empirically. Single models (*S*) are treated as baselines and trained only on their own task. MTL models (*M*) mean that parameters are shared across four tasks and trained together. S -> S means pipeline training of LAS-S and then BART-S. S + S refers to pre-trained LAS-S and BART-S which are further jointly trained with sequence loss.

4 Experiments

4.1 Datasets

We perform experiments on four datasets, three of which are existing public corpora (ATIS, SLURP, Spoken-SQuAD) and one is generated by us (Spoken-gigaword).

ATIS Airline Travel Information Systems (ATIS) (Hemphill et al., 1990; Shivakumar et al., 2019) is a widely used Spoken Language Understanding dataset for airline reservation, where the user's intent and utterance's slots are predicted given the input command.

SLURP SLURP (Bastianelli et al., 2020) is a recently released Spoken Language Understanding dataset. It is larger and more semantically complex compared to ATIS dataset. The SLURP is a collections of 72k audio recordings of single turn user interactions with a home assistant on 18 domains.

Spoken-SQuAD Spoken-SQuAD (Li et al., 2018) is a large extraction-based Spoken Question Answering (SQA) dataset, where the answer of question is predicted given corresponding context. For the dataset, the context is in the form of speech and text, while the question and the answer are in the form of text. The transcripts of Spoken-SQuAD are collected from SQuAD benchmark dataset (Rajpurkar et al., 2016).

Spoken-Gigaword Spoken-Gigaword is a large summarization dataset. It is formulated as a summary generation problem, where the general headlines are generated given articles. Considering that Gigaword is abstractive summaries generation dataset with large amount of data, it can provide possibility for designing data-driven models. The transcripts of Spoken-Gigaword are collected from Gigaword (Rush et al., 2015), the speech of Spoken-Gigaword are generated by existing TTS model.

4.2 Experimental Settings

For the MTL-SLT model, we use LAS as the ASR model, where the input audio features are 64-dim log-mel filterbank features computed over a 25 ms window, with 10 ms shifts, the text is tokenized into subword tokens using a unigram language model (Kudo, 2018) of vocabulary of 4500. We use BART-base as NLP model, which has 6 encoder layers and 6 decoder layers, a hidden size of 768, filter size of 3,072, and 12 attention heads. We apply the default hyper-parameters from prior works (Rao et al., 2021; Lewis et al., 2020) including the learning rate schedule.

4.3 Experimental Metrics

In this section, we show the evaluation metrics for each tasks. For extractive question answering task (Rajpurkar et al., 2016), it is evaluated with two metrics: Exact Match (EM) to check whether the answer extracted by the model are exactly the same as the correct answer and F1 score to measure the degree of word overlap at token level. For summarization, we follow previous work (Rush et al., 2015) and use ROUGE-1 (unigrams), ROUGE-2 (bigrams), and ROUGE-L (longest-common substring) (Lin, 2004). For ATIS dataset, we evaluate it with intent classification accuracy and slot filling F1 score (Hemphill et al., 1990; Ruan et al., 2020). For SLURP dataset, we evaluate it with intent-domain classification accuracy and slot filling SLU-F1 score proposed in Bastianelli et al. (2020), which does not overly penalise misalignments caused by ASR errors.

4.4 Main Results

Results of different models and settings on four datasets are shown in Table 2.

ASR Taking word error rate (WER) as evaluation metric, we can see that the MTL has some advantages for the ASR task. From Setting 1, MTL helps improve the performance of LAS model on ASR when pooling data across tasks. From Setting 4, when jointly training with the NLP model, the MTL setting sees better performance than independently training ASR. Comparing the *S+S* in Setting 4 to the LAS-*S* and LAS-*M* in Setting 1, the improvements as per ASR from jointly training are (1.91% on average) larger than from MTL (1.28% on average), we attribute this to the optimization of ASR using sequence loss training for word error rate as well as related semantic metrics, similar conclusion can be witnessed in Rao et al. (2021).

NLP NLP system is different from the ASR system, in which all datasets are trained for same objective. For different NLP tasks, they share the backbone BART parameters and update their own task specific heads. From Table 2, we can see that BART-M has improvements over all independent models on all metrics, which proves the effectiveness of MTL in NLP system. Classification tasks see larger improvements than the generation tasks. In Setting 3 and Setting 4, NLP tasks can be further improved through jointly training, which shows the potential of sequence loss training in ASR-NLP system to make the system robust to acoustic noise. In Setting 4, *M+M* performs better than *S+S*, proving the effectiveness of MTL in ASR-NLP system.

Pipeline and Jointly Training Methods After pre-training the ASR and NLP model in single task mode or on multiple tasks, we have two methods to jointly use them, the pipeline method that is non-differentiable and the outputs of ASR system are directly treated as inputs of NLP system, and the jointly training method with sequence loss that is differentiable and can pass the gradient from NLP system to ASR system. From Table 2, we can see that results of different spoken language tasks in Setting 4 are better than in Setting 3, under both of independent training models and multi-tasks training models. Also multi-task trained models always perform better than independent trained models, no matter under pipeline setting or jointly training setting showing that both these effects are orthogonal and can complement one another.

Comparison with Existing Works We show the comparison results of our method to previous works on SLURP and ATIS in Table 4. Results are reported on the test set of ATIS and SLURP, as well as the development set of Spoken-SQuAD. From Table 3, because it is a recently released large SLU dataset, there are not too much previous works that we can refer, but we still get best performance compared the existing works to our knowledge.

Models	Acc	SLU-F1
Trained on text		
NLU* (Bastianelli et al., 2020)	84.84	-
NLU+ (Seo et al., 2021)	87.73	84.34
BART (Lewis et al., 2020)	88.00	85.49
Ours: MTL-Text	**88.31**	**85.62**
End-to-End trained		
ASR+ -> NLU+ (Seo et al., 2021)	82.93	71.12
Ours: MTL-SLT	**83.10**	**74.49**

Table 3: Comparison with existing works on SLURP. NLU* represents the results from SLURP paper. NLU+ represents the results from a recently released paper.

5 Analysis

5.1 Effect of MTL

MTL on ASR Chan et al. (2021) shows that by simply mixing multiple ASR datasets together, ASR model can perform better on each dataset, and can learn powerful transfer learning representation. Inspired by this, in our experiment, we would also like to investigate the performance change after employing multi-task training only on the experimented audio data and transcription. Specifi-

Models	Acc	F1
Trained on text		
Attention BiRNN (Liu and Lane, 2016)	91.10	94.20
Capsule-NLU (Zhang et al., 2019)	95.00	95.20
LIDSNet (Agarwal et al., 2021)	95.97	-
SF-ID Network (E et al., 2019)	96.60	95.60
SyntacticTF (Wang et al., 2021)	97.31	96.01
BERT SLU (Chen et al., 2019)	97.50	96.10
Stack-Prop. (Qin et al., 2019)	96.90	95.90
Stack-Prop. + BERT (Qin et al., 2019)	97.50	96.10
ASR Error Robust SLU (Ruan et al., 2020)	97.13	96.03
Ours: MTL-Text	**98.18**	**96.51**
End-to-End trained		
Phoneme-BERT (Sundararaman et al., 2021)	**97.25**	84.15
E2E SLP (Qian et al., 2021)	96.30	90.95
Pre-trained MTL (da Silva Morais et al., 2021)	96.60	91.20
Ours: MTL-SLT	96.92	**91.43**

Table 4: Comparison results on ATIS test set.

cally, during training, only the LAS model is shared across different tasks. Results can be seen in Setting 1 row LAS-M, in Table 2. We can see that after employing more data, LAS performs better on each dataset, which proves that it is effective to perform more data on ASR model.

MTL on NLP We can see from Table 2 that with multi-task training, BART performs better in both the text-based setting (i.e., BART) and jointly training setting (i.e., LAS-BART).

5.2 Effect of Sequence Loss

With the used sequence loss ($\mathcal{L}_{seq}$), we can train not only the ASR model NLP model independently, but also train both of them in an end-to-end manner. We compared the models with and without $\mathcal{L}_{seq}$, and the result are shown in Table 2. By using the $\mathcal{L}_{seq}$, we observe improvements in ASR and NLP metrics by 2-5%. Sequence loss training allows for the downstream language modelling task to be trained with potentially erroneous ASR hypotheses allowing for robustness to word errors. This also minimizes the domain shift that occurs from training (language task has the clean ground truth transcription as input) to inference (language task has ASR hypotheses as input) resulting in improved performance. Another impact of sequence loss training is that ASR is optimized for differentiable (eg. cross-entropy), non-differentiable (eg. WER) ASR losses along with arbitrary non-differentiable metrics of interest (eg. rouge scores, SLU-F1) of the downstream language task.

5.3 Effect of Post Fine-tuning

The post fine-tuning step described in 3.2 is important in our framework, because 1) it can eliminate differences between datasets arising from different domains; 2) the optimal performance of different datasets falls on different positions of a pareto-optimal surface, post fine-tuning can solve this problem without introducing more parameters. Effect of post fine-tuning can be seen in Table 5.

Models	ASR	Summarization-R1
MTL-ASR	21.20	-
w/o Post FT	23.13	-
MTL-Text	-	43.12
w/o Post FT	-	26.50
MTL-SLT	19.80	16.02
w/o Post FT	21.45	14.39

Table 5: Ablation study on Post Fine-tuning.

6 Conclusion

We proposed a multi-task learning framework for spoken language understanding tasks that take speech as input and produces (1) intents and named-entities in language understanding tasks, (2) abstract text summaries, or (3) question answering. This framework can be extended to other language tasks such as translation.

In this framework, we make use of pretrained ASR models and language models like BART and jointly train these layers across multiple language tasks. We demonstrate that this training across tasks coupled with task-specific post-finetuning produces significantly better results for ASR and BART separately. We made use of the sequence loss training framework to enable end-to-end training of ASR and BART to optimize for metrics of interest for the classification, sequence tagging, and generation tasks. This made the downstream language task robust to errors in ASR hypotheses that otherwise leads to performance degradation in pipelined ASR and language task systems.

We demonstrate state-of-the-art results on public corpora of SLURP and ATIS for spoken language understanding. We also prepare the Spoken-Gigaword dataset for abstractive summarization of speech.

References

Vibhav Agarwal, Sudeep Deepak Shivnikar, Sourav Ghosh, Himanshu Arora, and Yashwant Saini. 2021. Lidsnet: A lightweight on-device intent detection model using deep siamese network. *CoRR*, abs/2110.15717.

Emanuele Bastianelli, Andrea Vanzo, Pawel Swietojanski, and Verena Rieser. 2020. SLURP: A spoken language understanding resource package. In *EMNLP*. Association for Computational Linguistics.

Rich Caruana. 1997. Multitask learning. *Machine learning*, 28(1):41–75.

William Chan, Navdeep Jaitly, Quoc V. Le, and Oriol Vinyals. 2016. Listen, attend and spell: A neural network for large vocabulary conversational speech recognition. In *ICASSP*.

William Chan, Daniel S. Park, Chris Lee, Yu Zhang, Quoc V. Le, and Mohammad Norouzi. 2021. Speechstew: Simply mix all available speech recognition data to train one large neural network. *CoRR*, abs/2104.02133.

Qian Chen, Zhu Zhuo, and Wen Wang. 2019. BERT for joint intent classification and slot filling. *CoRR*, abs/1902.10909.

Yung-Sung Chuang, Chi-Liang Liu, Hung-yi Lee, and Lin-Shan Lee. 2020. Speechbert: An audio-and-text jointly learned language model for end-to-end spoken question answering. In *INTERSPEECH*.

Yu-An Chung, Chenguang Zhu, and Michael Zeng. 2021. SPLAT: speech-language joint pre-training for spoken language understanding. In *NAACL-HLT*.

Edmilson da Silva Morais, Hong-Kwang Jeff Kuo, Samuel Thomas, Zoltán Tüske, and Brian Kingsbury. 2021. End-to-end spoken language understanding using transformer networks and self-supervised pretrained features. In *ICASSP*.

Jacob Devlin, Ming-Wei Chang, Kenton Lee, and Kristina Toutanova. 2019. BERT: pre-training of deep bidirectional transformers for language understanding. In *NAACL-HLT (1)*, pages 4171–4186. Association for Computational Linguistics.

Haihong E, Peiqing Niu, Zhongfu Chen, and Meina Song. 2019. A novel bi-directional interrelated model for joint intent detection and slot filling. In *ACL*.

Lingyun Feng, Jianwei Yu, Deng Cai, Songxiang Liu, Haitao Zheng, and Yan Wang. 2021. ASR-GLUE: A new multi-task benchmark for asr-robust natural language understanding. *CoRR*, abs/2108.13048.

Charles T. Hemphill, John J. Godfrey, and George R. Doddington. 1990. The ATIS spoken language systems pilot corpus. In *HLT*. Morgan Kaufmann.

Minjeong Kim, Gyuwan Kim, Sang-Woo Lee, and Jung-Woo Ha. 2021a. St-bert: Cross-modal language model pre-training for end-to-end spoken language understanding. In *ICASSP*, pages 7478–7482. IEEE.

Seokhwan Kim, Yang Liu, Di Jin, Alexandros Papangelis, Karthik Gopalakrishnan, Behnam Hedayatnia, and Dilek Hakkani-Tur. 2021b. " how robust ru?": Evaluating task-oriented dialogue systems on spoken conversations. *arXiv preprint arXiv:2109.13489*.

Taku Kudo. 2018. Subword regularization: Improving neural network translation models with multiple subword candidates. In *ACL*.

Chia-Chih Kuo, Shang-Bao Luo, and Kuan-Yu Chen. 2020. An audio-enriched bert-based framework for spoken multiple-choice question answering. In *INTERSPEECH*.

Cheng-I Lai, Yung-Sung Chuang, Hung-Yi Lee, Shang-Wen Li, and James R. Glass. 2021. Semi-supervised spoken language understanding via self-supervised speech and language model pretraining. In *ICASSP*.

Mike Lewis, Yinhan Liu, Naman Goyal, Marjan Ghazvininejad, Abdelrahman Mohamed, Omer Levy, Veselin Stoyanov, and Luke Zettlemoyer. 2020. BART: denoising sequence-to-sequence pre-training for natural language generation, translation, and comprehension. In *ACL*, pages 7871–7880. Association for Computational Linguistics.

Chia-Hsuan Li, Szu-Lin Wu, Chi-Liang Liu, and Hung-yi Lee. 2018. Spoken squad: A study of mitigating the impact of speech recognition errors on listening comprehension. In *INTERSPEECH*.

Chin-Yew Lin. 2004. Rouge: A package for automatic evaluation of summaries. In *Text summarization branches out*.

Bing Liu and Ian R. Lane. 2016. Attention-based recurrent neural network models for joint intent detection and slot filling. In *INTERSPEECH*.

Xiaodong Liu, Pengcheng He, Weizhu Chen, and Jianfeng Gao. 2019. Multi-task deep neural networks for natural language understanding. In *ACL*. Association for Computational Linguistics.

Yang Liu and Mirella Lapata. 2019. Text summarization with pretrained encoders. In *EMNLP/IJCNLP*. Association for Computational Linguistics.

Loren Lugosch, Mirco Ravanelli, Patrick Ignoto, Vikrant Singh Tomar, and Yoshua Bengio. 2019. Speech Model Pre-Training for End-to-End Spoken Language Understanding. In *Interspeech*.

Bryan McCann, Nitish Shirish Keskar, Caiming Xiong, and Richard Socher. 2018. The natural language decathlon: Multitask learning as question answering. *arXiv preprint arXiv:1806.08730*.

Vassil Panayotov, Guoguo Chen, Daniel Povey, and Sanjeev Khudanpur. 2015. Librispeech: An ASR corpus based on public domain audio books. In *ICASSP*, pages 5206–5210. IEEE.

Rohit Prabhavalkar, Tara N. Sainath, Yonghui Wu, Patrick Nguyen, Zhifeng Chen, Chung-Cheng Chiu, and Anjuli Kannan. 2018. Minimum word error rate training for attention-based sequence-to-sequence models. In *ICASSP*, pages 4839–4843. IEEE.

Yao Qian, Ximo Bian, Yu Shi, Naoyuki Kanda, Leo Shen, Zhen Xiao, and Michael Zeng. 2021. Speech-language pre-training for end-to-end spoken language understanding. In *ICASSP*.

Libo Qin, Wanxiang Che, Yangming Li, Haoyang Wen, and Ting Liu. 2019. A stack-propagation framework with token-level intent detection for spoken language understanding. In *EMNLP/IJCNLP*.

Colin Raffel, Noam Shazeer, Adam Roberts, Katherine Lee, Sharan Narang, Michael Matena, Yanqi Zhou, Wei Li, and Peter J. Liu. 2020. Exploring the limits of transfer learning with a unified text-to-text transformer. *J. Mach. Learn. Res.*, 21:140:1–140:67.

Pranav Rajpurkar, Jian Zhang, Konstantin Lopyrev, and Percy Liang. 2016. Squad: 100, 000+ questions for machine comprehension of text. In *EMNLP*.

Anirudh Raju, Gautam Tiwari, Milind Rao, Pranav Dheram, Bryan Anderson, Zhe Zhang, Bach Bui, and Ariya Rastrow. 2021. End-to-end spoken language understanding using rnn-transducer ASR. *CoRR*, abs/2106.15919.

Milind Rao, Pranav Dheram, Gautam Tiwari, Anirudh Raju, Jasha Droppo, Ariya Rastrow, and Andreas Stolcke. 2021. DO as I mean, not as I say: Sequence loss training for spoken language understanding. In *ICASSP*.

Milind Rao, Anirudh Raju, Pranav Dheram, Bach Bui, and Ariya Rastrow. 2020. Speech to semantics: Improve ASR and NLU jointly via all-neural interfaces. In *INTERSPEECH*.

Weitong Ruan, Yaroslav Nechaev, Luoxin Chen, Chengwei Su, and Imre Kiss. 2020. Towards an ASR error robust spoken language understanding system. In *INTERSPEECH*.

Sebastian Ruder. 2017. An overview of multi-task learning in deep neural networks.

Alexander M. Rush, Sumit Chopra, and Jason Weston. 2015. A neural attention model for abstractive sentence summarization. In *EMNLP*.

Alaa Saade, Joseph Dureau, David Leroy, Francesco Caltagirone, Alice Coucke, Adrien Ball, Clément Doumouro, Thibaut Lavril, Alexandre Caulier, Théodore Bluche, Thibault Gisselbrecht, and Maël Primet. 2019. Spoken language understanding on the edge. In *EMC2@NeurIPS*.

Seunghyun Seo, Donghyun Kwak, and Bowon Lee. 2021. Integration of pre-trained networks with continuous token interface for end-to-end spoken language understanding. *CoRR*, abs/2104.07253.

Jonathan Shen, Ruoming Pang, Ron J. Weiss, Mike Schuster, Navdeep Jaitly, Zongheng Yang, Zhifeng Chen, Yu Zhang, Yuxuan Wang, RJ-Skerrv Ryan, Rif A. Saurous, Yannis Agiomyrgiannakis, and Yonghui Wu. 2018. Natural TTS synthesis by conditioning wavenet on MEL spectrogram predictions. In *ICASSP*.

Prashanth Gurunath Shivakumar, Mu Yang, and Panayiotis G. Georgiou. 2019. Spoken language intent detection using confusion2vec. In *INTERSPEECH*.

Mukuntha Narayanan Sundararaman, Ayush Kumar, and Jithendra Vepa. 2021. Phoneme-bert: Joint language modelling of phoneme sequence and asr transcript. *CoRR*, abs/2102.00804.

Alex Wang, Amanpreet Singh, Julian Michael, Felix Hill, Omer Levy, and Samuel R. Bowman. 2019. Glue: A multi-task benchmark and analysis platform for natural language understanding.

Jixuan Wang, Kai Wei, Martin Radfar, Weiwei Zhang, and Clement Chung. 2021. Encoding syntactic knowledge in transformer encoder for intent detection and slot filling. In *AAAI*.

Chenyu You, Nuo Chen, and Yuexian Zou. 2021. Knowledge distillation for improved accuracy in spoken question answering. In *ICASSP*.

Chenwei Zhang, Yaliang Li, Nan Du, Wei Fan, and Philip S. Yu. 2019. Joint slot filling and intent detection via capsule neural networks. In *ACL*.

Yu Zhang, James Qin, Daniel S. Park, Wei Han, Chung-Cheng Chiu, Ruoming Pang, Quoc V. Le, and Yonghui Wu. 2020. Pushing the limits of semi-supervised learning for automatic speech recognition. *CoRR*, abs/2010.10504.

A Experiment Settings

A.1 Statistics of datasets

For the experimental datasets (Spoken-SQuAD, SLURP, ATIS), we follow the default train/dev/test splits from the original paper.

A.2 Hyperparameters

We show the detailed hyperparameters for the MTL Pre-training and Post Fine-tuning stages described in Section 3.2 of the proposed method on different datasets in Table 6.

	Pre-training	Fine-tuning
Speech Model Batch Size	16	16
Text Model Batch Size	16	16
Joint Training Model Batch Size	4	4
Learning Rate	$2e-5$	$2e-5$
Warmup Steps	0	0
Learning Rate Decay	Linear	Linear
Weight Decay	0	0
Gradient Clipping	1	1
Dropout	0.1	0.1
Attention Dropout	0.1	0.1
Training Steps	100k	20k

Table 6: Hyperparameters for the Pre-training and fine-tuning stages in training MTL-SLT on the four datasets.

B Spoken-gigaword Dataset

The detail statistics of the generated Spoken-Gigaword dataset are shown in Table 7. The articles and summarizations are acquired from gigaword headline generation dataset (Rush et al., 2015), we then generate the speech data for the articles using Tacotron2 (Shen et al., 2018) to extract feature and . Note that because the input article is noisy, which make it hard to generate proper speech, so we remove the ones with special symbols, and we remove the articles that have more than 30 words. The implementation is based on an open source library [1].

Types		Spoken-Gigaword
Training Set		249199
Validation Set		12578
Article	words	119M
	uni-words	110K
	aver length	14.6
	max length	30
	min length	11
Headline	words	31M
	uni-words	69K
	aver words	8.3
	max length	30
	min length	2

Table 7: Statistics of the generated Spoken-gigaword.

C Model Structure of NLP task with BART Model

As a pre-trained sequence-to-sequence denoising autoencoder, BART uses a standard Transformer-based neural machine translation architecture, which consists of 6 encoder and 6 decoder segments. In our work, we attribute each tasks with task specific classification head over the BART model. Specifically, for the Intent Detection task, we use the End-Of-Sentence (EOS) token on the last decoder layer to do the prediction; for the slot filling task, we predict the slot labels in BIO format after the last encoder layer; for the summarization task, generated sentences with EOS token at end are used to calculate the summarized loss; for the question answering task, EOS token in the last decoder layer is used to predict the answer.

D E2E Spoken Question Answering

In Section 3.3, we mention the $\mathcal{L}_{\text{has\_key}}$ in Spoken Question Answering. Actually, Spoken-SQuAD is a dataset with all examples having answers. However, since the input context of each example is too long, if we process the input audio directly, the model's performance will be very poor. Thus, instead of processing the input audio directly, we first split the input into sentence-wise segments, and then during the training, we predict the answer on each sentence. Note that we have a classification head to determine whether this sentence contains the answer or not, and the loss over this classification head is $\mathcal{L}_{\text{has\_key}}$.

[1] https://github.com/mozilla/TTS/

Multimodal Conversational AI
A Survey of Datasets and Approaches

Anirudh S Sundar, Larry Heck
Department of Electrical and Computer Engineering
Georgia Institute of Technology
{asundar34, larryheck}@gatech.edu

Abstract

As humans, we experience the world with all our senses or modalities (sound, sight, touch, smell, and taste). We use these modalities, particularly sight and touch, to convey and interpret specific meanings. Multimodal expressions are central to conversations; a rich set of modalities amplify and often compensate for each other. A multimodal conversational AI system answers questions, fulfills tasks, and emulates human conversations by understanding and expressing itself via multiple modalities. This paper motivates, defines, and mathematically formulates the multimodal conversational research objective. We provide a taxonomy of research required to solve the objective: multimodal representation, fusion, alignment, translation, and co-learning. We survey state-of-the-art datasets and approaches for each research area and highlight their limiting assumptions. Finally, we identify multimodal co-learning as a promising direction for multimodal conversational AI research.

1 Introduction

The proliferation of smartphones has dramatically increased the frequency of interactions that humans have with digital content. These interactions have expanded over the past decade to include conversations with smartphones and in-home smart speakers. Conversational AI systems (e.g., Alexa, Siri, Google Assistant) answer questions, fulfill specific tasks, and emulate natural human conversation (Hakkani-Tür et al., 2011; Gao et al., 2019).

Early examples of conversational AI include those based on primitive rule-based methods such as ELIZA (Weizenbaum, 1966). More recently, conversational systems were driven by statistical machine translation systems: translating input queries to responses (Ritter et al., 2011; Hakkani-Tür et al., 2012). Orders of magnitude more data led to unprecedented advances in conversational technology in the mid-part of the last decade. Techniques were developed to mine conversational training data from the web search query-click stream (Hakkani-Tür et al., 2011; Heck, 2012; Hakkani-Tür et al., 2013) and web-based knowledge graphs (Heck and Hakkani-Tür, 2012; El-Kahky et al., 2014). With this increase in data, deep neural-networks gained momentum in conversational systems (Mesnil et al., 2014; Heck and Huang, 2014; Sordoni et al., 2015; Vinyals and Le, 2015; Shang et al., 2015; Serban et al., 2016; Li et al., 2016a,b).

Most recently, specialized deep learning-based conversational agents were developed primarily for three tasks: (1) goal-directed tasks in research systems (Shah et al., 2016; Eric et al., 2017; Liu et al., 2017, 2018; Li et al., 2019; Hosseini-Asl et al., 2020; Wu et al., 2020; Peng et al., 2021; Xu et al., 2021b) and commercial products (Siri, Cortana, Alexa, and Google Assistant), (2) question-answering (Yi et al., 2019; Raffel et al., 2020; Zaheer et al., 2021), and (3) open-domain conversations (Wolf et al., 2019; Zhou et al., 2020; Adiwardana et al., 2020; Paranjape et al., 2020; Roller et al., 2020; Bao et al., 2020; Henderson et al., 2020; Zhang et al., 2020a). However, developing a single system with a unified approach that achieves human-level performance on all three tasks has proven elusive and is still an open problem in conversational AI.

One limitation of existing agents is that they often rely exclusively on language to communicate with users. This contrasts with humans, who converse with each other through a multitude of senses. These senses or modalities complement each other, resolving ambiguities and emphasizing ideas to make conversations meaningful. Prosody, auditory expressions of emotion, and backchannel agreement supplement speech, lip-reading disambiguates unclear words, gesticulation makes spatial references, and high-fives signify celebration.

Alleviating this unimodal limitation of conversational AI systems requires developing methods

Proceedings of the 4th Workshop on NLP for Conversational AI, pages 131 - 147
May 27, 2022 ©2022 Association for Computational Linguistics

to extract, combine, and understand information streams from multiple modalities and generate multimodal responses while simultaneously maintaining an intelligent conversation.

Similar to the taxonomy of multimodal machine learning research (Baltrušaitis et al., 2017), the research required to extend conversational AI systems to multiple modalities can be grouped into five areas: Representation, Fusion, Translation, Alignment, and Co-Learning. Representation and fusion involve learning mathematical constructs to mimic sensory modalities. Translation maps relationships between modalities for cross-modal reasoning. Alignment identifies regions of relevance across modalities to identify correspondences between them. Co-learning exploits the synergies across modalities by leveraging resource-rich modalities to train resource-poor modalities.

Concurrently, it is necessary for the research areas outlined above to address four main challenges in multimodal conversational reasoning – disambiguation, response generation, coreference resolution, and dialogue state tracking (Kottur et al., 2021). Multimodal disambiguation and response generation are challenges associated with fusion that determine whether available multimodal inputs are sufficient for a direct response or if follow-up queries are required. Multimodal coreference resolution is a challenge in both translation and alignment, where the conversational agent must resolve referential mentions in dialogue to corresponding objects in other modalities. Multimodal dialogue state tracking is a holistic challenge across research areas typically associated with task-oriented systems. The goal is to parse multimodal signals to infer and update values for slots in user utterances.

In this paper, we discuss the taxonomy of research challenges in multimodal Conversational AI as illustrated in Figure 1. Section 2 provides a history of research in multimodal conversations. In Section 3, we mathematically formulate multimodal conversational AI as an optimization problem. Sections 4, 5, and 6 survey existing datasets and state-of-the-art approaches for multimodal representation and fusion, translation, and alignment. Section 7 highlights limitations of existing research in multimodal conversational AI and explores multimodal co-learning as a promising direction for research.

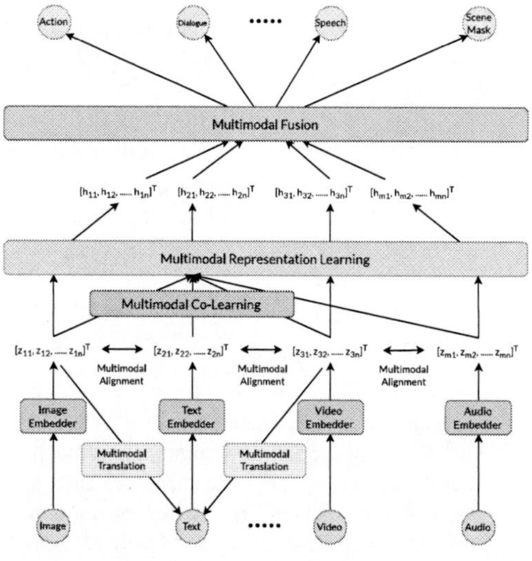

Figure 1: Taxonomy of multimodal Conversational AI research

2 Background

Early work in multimodal conversational AI focused on the use of visual information to improve automatic speech recognition (ASR). One of the earliest papers along these lines is by Yuhas et al. (1989) followed by many papers including work by Meier et al. (1996), Duchnowski et al. (1994), Bregler and Konig (1994), and Ngiam et al. (2011).

Advances in client-side capabilities enabled ASR systems to utilize other modalities such as tactile, voice, and text inputs. These systems supported more comprehensive interactions and facilitated a higher degree of personalization. Examples include ESPRIT's MASK (Lamel et al., 1998), Microsoft's MiPad (Huang et al., 2001), and AT&T's MATCH (Johnston et al., 2002).

Vision-driven tasks motivated research in adding visual understanding technology into conversational AI systems. Early work in reasoning over text+video include work by Ramanathan et al. (2014) where they leveraged these combined modalities to address the problem of assigning names of people in the cast to tracks in TV videos. Kong et al. (2014) leveraged natural language descrptions of RGB-D videos for 3D semantic parsing. Srivastava and Salakhutdinov (2014) developed a multimodal Deep Boltzmann Machine for image-text retrieval and ASR using videos. Antol et al. (2015) introduced a dataset and baselines for multimodal question-answering, a challenge combining computer vision and natural language processing. More recent work by Zhang et al. (2019b) and Selvaraju et al. (2019) leveraged conversational explanations to make vision and language models more grounded, resulting in improved visual question answering.

While modalities most commonly considered in the conversational AI literature are text, vision, tactile, and speech, other sources of information are gaining popularity within the research community. These include eye-gaze, 3D scans, emotion, action and dialogue history, and virtual reality. Heck et al. (2013) and Hakkani-Tür et al. (2014) use gesture, speech, and eye-gaze to resolve and infer intent in conversational web-browsing systems. Grauman et al. (2021) presents ego-centric video understanding, Padmakumar et al. (2021), and Shridhar et al. (2020) present task completion from 3D simulations, and Gao et al. (2021) presents multisensory object recognition.

Processing conventional and new modalities brings forth numerous challenges for multimodal conversations. To answer these challenges, we will first mathematically formulate the multimodal conversational AI problem, then detail fundamental research sub-tasks required to solve it.

3 Mathematical Formulation

We formulate multimodal conversational AI as an optimization problem. The objective is to find the optimal response $\mathbf{S}$ to a message m given underlying multimodal context c. Based on the sufficiency of the context, the optimal response could be a statement of fact or a follow-up question to resolve ambiguities. Statistically, $\mathbf{S}$ is estimated as:

$$\mathbf{S} = \operatorname*{argmax}_{r} p(r|c, m). \tag{1}$$

The probability of an arbitrary response r can be expressed as a product of the probabilities of responses $\{r_i\}_{i=1}^{T}$ over T turns of conversation (Sordoni et al., 2015).

$$p(r|c, m) = \prod_{i=1}^{T} p(r_i|r_1, \ldots r_{i-1}, c, m) \tag{2}$$

It is also possible for conversational AI to respond through multiple modalities. We represent the multimodality of output responses by a matrix $R := \{r_i^1, r_i^2, \ldots r_i^l\}$ over l permissible output modalities.

$$\mathbf{S} = \operatorname*{argmax}_{R} p(R|c, m) \tag{3}$$

Learning from multimodal data requires manipulating information from all modalities using a function $f(\cdot)$ consisting of five sub-tasks: representation, fusion, translation, alignment, and co-learning. We include these modifications and present the final multimodal conversational objective below.

$$\mathbf{S} = \operatorname*{argmax}_{R} p(R|f(c, m)) \tag{4}$$

In the following sections, we describe each subtask contained in $f(\cdot)$.

4 Multimodal Representation + Fusion

Multimodal representation learning and fusion are primary challenges in multimodal conversations. Multimodal representation is the encoding of multimodal data in a format amenable to computational processing. Multimodal fusion concerns joining features from multiple modalities to make predictions.

4.1 Multimodal Representations

Using multimodal information of varying granularity for conversations necessitates techniques to represent high-dimensional signals in a latent space. These latent multimodal representations encode human senses to improve a conversational AI's perception of the real-world. Success in multimodal tasks requires that representations satisfy three desiderata (Srivastava and Salakhutdinov, 2014):

1. Similarity in the representation space implies similarity of the corresponding concepts

2. The representation is easy to obtain in the absence of some modalities

3. It is possible to infer missing information from observed modalities

There exist numerous representation methods for the range of problems multimodal conversational AI addresses. Multimodal representations are broadly classified as either joint representations or coordinated representations (Baltrušaitis et al., 2017).

4.1.1 Joint Representations

Joint representations combine unimodal signals into the same representation space. Traditional techniques to learn joint representations include multimodal autoencoders (Ngiam et al., 2011), multimodal deep belief networks (Srivastava and

Salakhutdinov, 2014), and sequential networks (Nicolaou et al., 2011).

The success of the Transformer to represent text (Vaswani et al., 2017) and BERT when modeling language (Devlin et al., 2019) have inspired a variety of multimodal transformer-based architectures for (1) vision-and-language understanding (Sun et al., 2019b; Lu et al., 2019; Gabeur et al., 2020; Chen et al., 2020b; Tan and Bansal, 2019; Singh et al., 2021a), (2) vision-grounded speech recognition (Baevski et al., 2020; Hsu et al., 2021; Chan et al., 2021), and (3) User Interface (UI) understanding (Bapna et al., 2017; He et al., 2021; Bai et al., 2021; Li et al., 2021; Xu et al., 2021b; Heck and Heck, 2022).

Transformer-based models used as joint multimodal representations can be described as illustrated in the taxonomy of Figure 1. Modality specific encoders $\{j_i(\cdot)\}_{i=1}^{n}$ embed unimodal tokens $\{c_{i_k}\}_{k=1}^{n}$ to create latent features $\{z_{i_k}\}_{k=1}^{n}$ (Equation 5). Decoder networks use latent features to produce output symbols. A transformer $\Psi(\cdot)$ consists of stacked encoders and decoders with intra-modality attention. Attention heads compute relationships within elements of a modality, producing multimodal representations $\{h_{i_k}\}_{k=1}^{n}$ (Equation 6).

$$z_{i_1}, z_{i_2}, \ldots z_{i_n} = j_i(c_{i_1}, c_{i_2}, \ldots c_{i_n}) \quad (5)$$

$$h_{1_1} \ldots h_{m_n} = \Psi(z_{1_1}, z_{1_2}, \ldots z_{m_n}) \quad (6)$$

4.1.2 Coordinated Representations

In contrast, coordinated representations model each modality separately. Constraints coordinate representations of separate modalities by enforcing cross-modal similarity over concepts. For example, the audio representation $g_a(\cdot)$ of a dog's bark would be closer to the dog's image representation $g_i(\cdot)$ and further away from a car's (Equation 7). A notion of distance d between modalities in the coordinated space enables cross-modal retrieval.

$$d(g_a(\text{dog}), g_i(\text{dog})) < d(g_a(\text{dog}), g_i(\text{car})) \quad (7)$$

In practice, contrastive objectives are used to coordinate representations between pairs of modalities. Contrastive learning has been successful in relating separate views of the same image (Becker and Hinton, 1992; Chen et al., 2020a; He et al., 2020; Grill et al., 2020; Radford et al., 2021), images and their natural language descriptions (Weston et al., 2010; Kiros et al., 2014; Zhang et al., 2020b; Li et al., 2020), and videos with their corresponding audio and natural language descriptions (Owens et al., 2016; Korbar et al., 2018; Sun et al., 2019a; Miech et al., 2020; Alayrac et al., 2020; Akbari et al., 2021; Xu et al., 2021a; Qian et al., 2021; Morgado et al., 2021).

4.2 Multimodal Fusion

Multimodal fusion combines features from multiple modalities to make decisions, denoted by the final block before the outputs in Figure 1. Fusion approaches are broadly classified into model-agnostic and model-based methods.

Model-agnostic methods are independent of specific algorithms and are split into early, late, and hybrid fusion. Early fusion integrates features following extraction, projecting features into a shared space (Potamianos et al., 2003; Ngiam et al., 2011; Nicolaou et al., 2011; Jansen et al., 2019). In contrast, late fusion integrates decisions from unimodal predictors (Becker and Hinton, 1992; Korbar et al., 2018; Shuster et al., 2020; Alayrac et al., 2020; Akbari et al., 2021). Early fusion is predominantly used to combine features extracted in joint representations while late fusion combines decisions made in coordinated representations. Hybrid fusion exploits both low and high level modality interactions (Wu et al., 2005; Schwartz et al., 2020; Piergiovanni et al., 2020; Goyal et al., 2020).

Model-based methods consist of graphical techniques like Hidden Markov Models (Nefian et al., 2002; Gurban et al., 2008), neural networks (Nicolaou et al., 2011; Antol et al., 2015; Gao et al., 2015; Malinowski et al., 2015; Kottur et al., 2018; Qian et al., 2021), and transformers (Xu and Saenko, 2016; Hori et al., 2017; Peng et al., 2019; Zhang et al., 2019a; Shuster et al., 2020; Chen et al., 2020b; Geng et al., 2021; Xu et al., 2021b)

4.3 State-of-the-art Representation+Fusion Models for Conversational AI

Having introduced the multimodal representation and fusion challenges, we present the state-of-the-art in these sub-tasks for conversational AI.

4.3.1 Factor Graph Attention

Schwartz et al. (2020) develops Factor Graph Attention (FGA), a joint representation for multi-turn question answering grounded in images. FGA embeds images using VGG-16 (Simonyan and Zisserman, 2015) or F-RCNN (Ren et al., 2016) and textual modalities using LSTMs. Nodes in the factor graph represent attention distributions over elements of each modality, and factors capture relationships between nodes.

There are two types of factors – local and joint. Local factors capture interactions between nodes of a single modality (e.g., words in the same sentence), while joint factors capture interactions between different modalities (e.g., a word in a sentence and an object in an image).

Representations from all modalities are concatenated via hybrid fusion and passed through a multilayer perceptron network to retrieve the best candidate answer.

Table 1 compares the Recall-at-k (R@k) of discriminative models on VisDial v1.0 test-std. The F-RCNN version of FGA is the state-of-the-art.

Model	R@1	R@5	R@10
LF (Das et al., 2017)	40.95	72.45	82.83
HRE (Das et al., 2017)	39.93	70.45	81.50
Memory Network (Das et al., 2017)	40.98	72.30	83.30
CorefNMN (ResNet-152) (Kottur et al., 2018)	47.55	78.10	88.80
NMN (ResNet-152) (Hu et al., 2017)	44.15	76.88	86.88
FGA (F-RCNNx101) (Schwartz et al., 2020)	**52.75**	**82.92**	**91.07**

Table 1: Comparison of models on VisDial v1.0 test-std (Recall@k)(Schwartz et al., 2020)

4.3.2 TRANSRESNET

Shuster et al. (2020) presents TRANSRESNET for image-based dialogue. Image-based dialogue is the task of choosing the optimal response on a dialogue turn given an image, an agent personality, and dialogue history. TRANSRESNET consists of separately learned sub-networks to represent input modalities. Images are encoded using ResNeXt 32x48d trained on 3.5 billion Instagram images (Xie et al., 2017), personalities are embedded using a linear layer, and dialogue is encoded by a transformer pretrained on Reddit (Mazaré et al., 2018) to create a joint representation.

TRANSRESNET compares model-agnostic and model-based fusion by using either concatenation or attention networks to combine representations. Like FGA, the chosen dialogue response is the candidate closest to the fused representation.

On the first turn, TRANSRESNET uses only style and image information to produce responses. Dialogue history serves as an additional modality on subsequent rounds. Ablation of one or more modalities diminishes the ability of the model to retrieve the correct response. Optimal performance on Image-Chat (Shuster et al., 2020) is achieved using multimodal concatenation of jointly represented modalities (Table 2).

Modalities	Turn 1	Turn 2	Turn 3	All
Image Only	37.6	28.1	20.7	28.7
Style Only	18.3	15.3	17.0	16.9
Dialogue History Only	1.0	33.7	32.3	22.3
Style + Dialogue	18.3	45.4	43.1	35.4
Image + Dialogue	37.6	39.4	32.6	36.5
Image + Style	**54.0**	41.1	35.2	43.4
Style + Dialogue + Image	**54.0**	**51.9**	**44.8**	**50.3**

Table 2: Recall@1 (%) on Image-Chat using $\text{TRANSRESNET}_{\text{RET}}$ (ResNeXt-IG-3.5B, MM-Sum)

4.3.3 MultiModal Versatile Networks (MMV)

Alayrac et al. (2020) presents a training strategy to learn coordinated representations using self-supervised contrastive learning from instructional videos. Videos are encoded using TSM with a ResNet50 backbone (Lin et al., 2019), audio is encoded using log MEL spectrograms from ResNet50, and text is encoded using Google News pre-trained word2vec (Mikolov et al., 2013).

Alayrac et al. (2020) defines three types of coordinated spaces: shared, disjoint, and 'fine+coarse'. The shared space enables direct comparison and navigation between modalities, by assuming equal granularity. The disjoint space sidesteps navigation to solve the granularity problem by creating a space for each pair of modalities. The 'fine+coarse' space solves both issues by learning two spaces. A fine-grained space compares audio and video, while a lower-dimensional coarse-grained space compares fine-grained embeddings with text. We further discuss the MMV model in Section 6.3.

5 Multimodal Translation

Multimodal translation maps embeddings from one modality to signals from another for cross-modality reasoning (Figure 1). Cross-modal reasoning enables multimodal conversational AI to hold meaningful conversations and resolve references across multiple senses, specifically language and vision. To this end, we survey existing work addressing the translation of images and videos to text. We discuss multimodal question-answering and multimodal dialogue, translation tasks that extend to multimodal conversations.

5.1 Image

Antol et al. (2015) and Zhu et al. (2016) present Visual Question-Answering (VQA) and Visual7W for multimodal question answering (MQA). The MQA challenge requires responding to textual queries about an image. Both datasets collect questions and answers using crowd workers, encouraging trained models to learn natural responses. Heck and Heck (2022) presents the Visual Slot dataset, where trained models learn answers to questions grounded in UIs.

The objective of MQA is a simplification of Equation 4 to a single-turn, single-timestep scenario ($T = 1$), producing a response to a question m_q given multimodal context $\{c_i\}_{i=1}^{n}$:

$$\mathbf{S}_{MQA} = \underset{R}{\operatorname{argmax}}\, p(R|f(c_1, \ldots c_n, m_q)) \quad (8)$$

Multi-turn question-answering (MTQA) is the next step towards multimodal conversational AI. VisDial (Das et al., 2017) extends VQA to multiple turns, translating over QA history in addition to images. GuessWhat?! (de Vries et al., 2017) is a guessing game, discovering objects in a scene through dialogue. MANYMODALQA (Hannan et al., 2020) requires reasoning over prior knowledge, images, and databases. MIMOQA (Singh et al., 2021b) is an example of multimodal responses, where answers are image-text pairs.

The objective of MTQA (Equation 9) is an extension of MQA to include QA history $\mathbf{h}_{qa} = \{m_{q_1}, r_{a_1}, m_{q_2}, r_{a_2}, \ldots m_{q_{i-1}}, r_{a_{i-1}}\}$.

$$\mathbf{S}_{MTQA} = \underset{R}{\operatorname{argmax}}\, p(R|f(c_1, \ldots c_n, \mathbf{h}_{qa})) \quad (9)$$

Image-Grounded Conversations (IGC) (Mostafazadeh et al., 2017) builds on MTQA by presenting a dataset for multimodal dialogue (MD): machine perception and conversation through language. Image-Chat (Shuster et al., 2020) extends IGC to agents with personalities. Crowd workers hold three-turn conversations about an image with one of 215 emotions (e.g., peaceful, erratic, skeptical). Motivated by the popularity of visual content in instant-messaging, Meme incorporated Open-domain Dialogue (MOD) (Fei et al., 2021) contains natural language conversations interspersed with behavioral stickers. SIMMC (Moon et al., 2020) and SIMMC2.0 (Kottur et al., 2021) present goal-oriented dialogue for shopping. The challenge requires leveraging dialogue and a state of the world to resolve references, track dialogue state, and recommend the correct object. IGC, Image-Chat, MOD, SIMMC, and SIMMC2.0 solve the MD objective that depends on previous dialogue responses $\mathbf{h}_d = \{m_{d_1}, r_{d_1}, m_{d_2}, r_{d_2}, \ldots m_{d_{i-1}}, r_{d_{i-1}}\}$:

$$\mathbf{S}_{MD} = \underset{R}{\operatorname{argmax}}\, p(R|f(c_1, \ldots c_n, \mathbf{h}_d)) \quad (10)$$

5.2 Video

An extension of VQA to the video domain includes TVQA, TVQA+ (Lei et al., 2020) built on TV shows, MovieQA (Tapaswi et al., 2016) based on movies, and Audio Visual Scene-Aware Dialog (AVSD) (Alamri et al., 2019) based on CHARADES (Sigurdsson et al., 2016). DVD (Le et al., 2021) presents video-QA over videos synthesized from the CATER dataset (Girdhar and Ramanan, 2020). Besides visual reasoning, video-QA requires temporal reasoning, a challenge addressed by multimodal alignment that we discuss in the following section.

6 Multimodal Alignment

While image-based dialogue revolves around objects (e.g., cats and dogs), video-based dialogue revolves around objects and associated actions (e.g., jumping cats and barking dogs) where spatial and temporal features serve as building blocks for conversations. Extracting these spatiotemporal features requires multimodal alignment – aligning sub-components of different modalities to find correspondences. We identify action recognition and action from modalities as alignment challenges relevant to multimodal conversations.

6.1 Action Recognition

Action recognition is the task of extracting natural language descriptions from videos. UCF101 (Soomro et al., 2012), HMDB51 (Kuehne et al., 2011), and Kinetics-700 (Carreira et al., 2019) involve extracting actions from short YouTube and Hollywood movie clips. HowTo100M (Miech et al., 2019), MSR-VTT (Xu et al., 2016), and YouCook2 (Zhou et al., 2017) are datasets containing instructional videos on the internet and require learning text-video embeddings. YouCook2 and MSR-VTT are annotated by hand while HowTo100M uses existing video subtitles or ASR.

Mathematically, the goal is to retrieve the correct natural language description $\mathbf{y} \in \mathcal{Y}$ to a query video $\mathbf{x}$ (Equation 11). Video and text representation functions $g(\cdot)_{\text{video}}$ and $g(\cdot)_{\text{text}}$ embed modalities into a coordinated space where they are compared using a distance measure d.

$$\underset{y \in \mathcal{Y}}{\operatorname{argmin}}\, d(g_{\text{video}}(\mathbf{x}), g_{\text{text}}(\mathbf{y}_j)) \tag{11}$$

6.2 Action from Modalities

Equipping multimodal conversational agents with the ability to perform actions from multiple modalities provides them with an understanding of the real world, improving their conversational utility.

Talk the Walk (de Vries et al., 2018) presents the task of navigation conditioned on partial information. A "tourist" provides descriptions of a photo-realistic environment to a "guide" who determines actions. Vision-and-Dialog Navigation (Thomason et al., 2019) contains natural dialogues grounded in a simulated environment. The task is to predict a sequence of actions to a goal state given the world scene, dialogue, and previous actions. TEACh (Padmakumar et al., 2021) extends Vision-and-Dialog Navigation to complete tasks in an AI2-THOR simulation. The challenge involves aligning information from language, video, as well as action and dialogue history to solve daily tasks. Ego4D (Grauman et al., 2021) contains text annotated egocentric (first person) videos in real-world scenarios. Ego4D includes 3D scans, multiple camera views, and eye gaze, presenting new representation, fusion, translation, and alignment challenges. It is associated with five benchmarks: Video QA, object state tracking, audio-visual diarization, social cue detection, and camera trajectory forecasting.

6.3 Multimodal Versatile Networks (MMV)

In addition to a representation, Alayrac et al. (2020) presents a self-supervised task to train modality embedding graphs for multimodal alignment. Sampling temporally aligned audio, visual clips, and narrations from the same video creates positive training examples, while those from different videos comprise negative training examples. A Noise-Contrastive Estimation (NCE) loss (Gutmann and Hyvärinen, 2010) is minimized to ensure similarity between embeddings of positive training examples while forcing negative pairs further apart. A Multiple Instance Learning (MIL) (Miech et al., 2020) variant of NCE measures loss on pairs of modalities of different granularity. MIL accounts for misalignment between audio/video and text by measuring the loss of fine-grained information with multiple temporally close narrations.

The network is trained on HowTo100M (Miech et al., 2019) and AudioSet (Gemmeke et al., 2017). Table 3 compares the performance of MMV on action classification, audio classification, and zero-shot text-to-video retrieval.

7 Discussion

The current datasets used for research in multimodal conversational AI are summarized in Table 4. While MQA and MTQA are promising starting points for multimodal natural language tasks, extending QA to conversations is not straightforward. Inherently, MQA limits itself to direct questions targeting visible content, whereas multimodal conversations require understanding information that is often implied (Mostafazadeh et al., 2017). Utterances in dialogue represent speech acts and are classified as constatives, directives, commissives, or acknowledgments (Bach and Harnish, 1979). Answers belong to a single speech act (constatives) and represent a subset of natural conversations.

Similarly, the work to-date on action recognition is incomplete and insufficient for conversational systems. Conversational AI must represent and understand spatiotemporal interactions. However, current research in action recognition attempts to learn relationships between videos and their natural language descriptions. These descriptions are not speech acts themselves. Therefore, they do not adequately represent dialogue but rather only serve as anchor points in the interaction.

In contrast, Image-Chat (Shuster et al., 2020) presents a learning challenge directly aligned with the multimodal dialogue objective in Equation 4. Image-Chat treats dialogue as an open-ended discussion grounded in the visual modality. Succeeding in the task requires jointly optimizing visual and conversational performance. The use of crowd workers that adopt personalities during data collection encourages natural dialogue and captures conversational intricacies and implicatures.

MQA answers explicit questions about an image ($\rightarrow$ *Is this at a farm?*), and action recognition describes videos ($\rightarrow$ *Mountain biking*). On the other hand, Image-Chat requires both implicit knowledge ($\rightarrow$ *Halloween*, $\rightarrow$ *Exercise*) and multi-turn reasoning ($\rightarrow$ *Halloween* $\rightarrow$ *Holiday*, $\rightarrow$ *Exercise* $\rightarrow$ *Fitness*).

Despite its advantages over other datasets, Image-Chat makes three assumptions about multimodal conversations limiting its extension to the multimodal conversational objective:

Model	UCF101 (FT)	HMDB51 (FT)	ESC-50 (Linear)	AS	K600	YC2	MSR-VTT
MIL-NCE (S3D-G) (Miech et al., 2020)	91.3	61.0	/	/	/	**51.2**	**32.4**
AVTS (MC3) (Korbar et al., 2018)	89.0	61.6	80.6	/	/	/	/
AA+AV CC (Jansen et al., 2019)	/	/	/	28.5	/	/	/
CVRL (Qian et al., 2021)	/	/	/	/	64.1	/	/
XDC (Alwassel et al., 2020)	91.2	61.0	84.8	/	/	/	/
ELo (Piergiovanni et al., 2020)	93.8	67.4	/	/	/	/	/
AVID (Morgado et al., 2021)	91.5	64.7	**89.2**	/	/	/	/
GDT (IG65M) (Patrick et al., 2020)	**95.2**	72.8	88.5	/	/	/	/
MMV FAC (TSM-50x2) (Alayrac et al., 2020)	**95.2**	**75.0**	88.9	**30.9**	**70.5**	45.4	31.1

Table 3: Comparison of learnt representations on UCF101, HMDB51, ESC-50, AudioSet, Kinetics600, YouCook2, and MSR-VTT. Top-1 Accuracy for UCF101, HMDB51, ESC-50, Kinetics600, mean Average Precision (mAP) for AudioSet, Recall@10 for YouCook2 and MSR-VTT (Alayrac et al., 2020).

Dataset	Modalities	Task	Data Collection	POV
VQA (Antol et al., 2015)	I,Q	Question Answering	Human-Human	Third Person
Visual7W (Zhu et al., 2016)	I,Q	Question Answering	Human-Human	Third Person
Visual Slot (Heck and Heck, 2022)	UI, Q	Question Answering	Human	X
TVQA (Lei et al., 2019)	V,Q,S	Question Answering	Human-Human	Third Person
MovieQA (Tapaswi et al., 2016)	V,C,Q,T,S	Question Answering	Human	Third Person
MANYMODALQA (Hannan et al., 2020)	I,C,Q,T,Tables	Question Answering	Human-Human	Third Person
MIMOQA (Singh et al., 2021b)	I,Q,T	Question Answering	Machine	X
VisDial (Das et al., 2017)	I,H_Q,H_A,C,Q	Question Answering	Human-Human	Third person
Guesswhat (de Vries et al., 2017)	I, H_Q,H_A	Question Answering	Human-Human	Third Person
AVSD (Alamri et al., 2019)	V,A,H_Q,H_A,C,Q	Question Answering	Human-Human	Third Person
DVD (Le et al., 2021)	V,Q,H_Q,H_A	Question Answering	Machine	X
SIMMC (Moon et al., 2020)	H_D, Q, VR	Shopping	Machine Self-play	First Person
SIMMC2.0 (Kottur et al., 2021)	H_D, Q, VR	Shopping	Machine Self-play	First Person
IGC (Mostafazadeh et al., 2017)	I,Q,D	Chit-chat + Question Answering	Human-Human	Third-Person
Image-Chat (Shuster et al., 2020)	I,D,Personality	Chit-chat	Human-Human	Third Person
MOD (Fei et al., 2021)	D, Personality	Visual chit-chat	Human-Human	X
UCF101 (Soomro et al., 2012)	V,A (partial)	Action Recognition	YouTube	Third Person
HMDB51 (Kuehne et al., 2011)	V	Action Recognition	YouTube+Movies	Third Person
Kinetics 700 (Carreira et al., 2019)	V	Action Recognition	YouTube	Third Person
HowTo100M (Miech et al., 2019)	V,T,S	Text-Video Embeddings	YouTube	First+Third Person
YouCook2 (Zhou et al., 2017)	V,T	Text-video retrieval, activity recognition	YouTube	Third Person
MSRVTT (Xu et al., 2016)	V,A,T	Video-to-text	Web videos	First+Third Person
Talk the Walk (de Vries et al., 2018)	I, Actions, D	Navigation from Actions and Dialogue	Human-Human	First Person
CVDN (Thomason et al., 2019)	VR, Actions, H_Q,H_A	Navigation from Dialogue History	Human-Human	First Person
TEACh (Padmakumar et al., 2021)	Scene, Actions, D	Action prediction, Task from language	AI2-THOR	First+Third Person
Ego4D (Grauman et al., 2021)	V,T,A,Gaze,3D Scan,S	Spatial Reasoning	Human	First Person

Table 4: Datasets for multimodal representations. I=Image, V=Video, UI=User Interface, C=Caption, Q=Question, T=Text, H_Q = Question history, H_A=Answer history, H_D=Dialogue history, VR=Virtual Reality, D=Dialogue, A=Audio, S=Speech

1. Conversations are limited to three turns, devoid of long-term dialogue dependencies.
2. Language and images are the only modalities.
3. Personalities are independent of previous responses. This differs from natural human conversations where humans tend to understand and reciprocate the personality of a dialogue partner (Rashkin et al., 2019).

The discussion above highlights the limitations of existing datasets for the multimodal conversational AI task. Datasets need to be improved to better capture and represent more natural, multi-turn dialogues over multiple modalities; dialogues that more closely resemble how humans converse with each other and their environment.

In addition, algorithmic improvements are required to advance the field of multimodal conversational AI - particularly with respect to the objective function. Current approaches such as MQA and action recognition models optimize a limited objective compared to Equation 4. We postulate that the degradation of these methods when applied to multimodal conversations is largely caused by this and, therefore, motivates investigation.

Another open research problem is to improve performance on Image-Chat. The current state-of-the-art TRANSRESNET$_{\text{RET}}$ is limited. The model often hallucinates, referring to content missing in the image and previous dialogue turns. The model also struggles when answering questions and holding extended conversations. We suspect these problems are a reflection of the limiting assumptions Image-Chat makes and the absence of multimodal co-learning to extract relationships between modalities. For further details, we refer readers to example conversations in Appendix A.

Different modalities often contain complementary information when grounded in the same concept. Multimodal co-learning exploits this cross-modality synergy to model resource-poor modalities using resource-rich modalities. An example of co-learning in context of Figure 1 is the use of visual information and audio to generate contextualized text representations.

Blum and Mitchell (1998) introduced an early approach to multimodal co-training, using information from hyperlinked pages for web-page classification. Socher and Fei-Fei (2010) and Duan et al. (2014) presented weakly-supervised techniques to tag images given information from other modalities. Kiela et al. (2015) grounded natural language descriptions in olfactory data. More recently, Upadhyay et al. (2018) jointly trains bilingual models to accelerate spoken language understanding in low resource languages. Selvaraju et al. (2019) uses human attention maps to teach QA agents "where to look". Despite the rich history of work in multimodal co-learning, extending these techniques to develop multimodal conversational AI that understands and leverages cross-modal relationships is still an open challenge.

8 Conclusions

We define multimodal conversational AI and outline the objective function required for its realization. Solving this objective requires multimodal representation and fusion, translation, and alignment. We survey existing datasets and state-of-the-art methods for each sub-task. We identify simplifying assumptions made by existing research preventing the realization of multimodal conversational AI. Finally, we outline the collection of a suitable dataset and an approach that utilizes multimodal co-learning as future steps.

References

Daniel Adiwardana, Minh-Thang Luong, David R. So, Jamie Hall, Noah Fiedel, Romal Thoppilan, Zi Yang, Apoorv Kulshreshtha, Gaurav Nemade, Yifeng Lu, and Quoc V. Le. 2020. Towards a Human-like Open-Domain Chatbot. *arXiv:2001.09977 [cs, stat]*. ArXiv: 2001.09977.

Hassan Akbari, Liangzhe Yuan, Rui Qian, Wei-Hong Chuang, Shih-Fu Chang, Yin Cui, and Boqing Gong. 2021. VATT: Transformers for Multimodal Self-Supervised Learning from Raw Video, Audio and Text. *arXiv:2104.11178 [cs, eess]*. ArXiv: 2104.11178.

Huda Alamri, Vincent Cartillier, Abhishek Das, Jue Wang, Anoop Cherian, Irfan Essa, Dhruv Batra, Tim K. Marks, Chiori Hori, Peter Anderson, Stefan Lee, and Devi Parikh. 2019. Audio-Visual Scene-Aware Dialog. *arXiv:1901.09107 [cs]*. ArXiv: 1901.09107.

Jean-Baptiste Alayrac, Adrià Recasens, Rosalia Schneider, Relja Arandjelović, Jason Ramapuram, Jeffrey De Fauw, Lucas Smaira, Sander Dieleman, and Andrew Zisserman. 2020. Self-Supervised MultiModal Versatile Networks. *arXiv:2006.16228 [cs]*. ArXiv: 2006.16228.

Humam Alwassel, Dhruv Mahajan, Bruno Korbar, Lorenzo Torresani, Bernard Ghanem, and Du Tran. 2020. Self-Supervised Learning by Cross-Modal Audio-Video Clustering. *arXiv:1911.12667 [cs]*. ArXiv: 1911.12667.

Stanislaw Antol, Aishwarya Agrawal, Jiasen Lu, Margaret Mitchell, Dhruv Batra, C. Lawrence Zitnick, and Devi Parikh. 2015. VQA: Visual Question Answering. In *2015 IEEE International Conference on Computer Vision (ICCV)*, pages 2425–2433, Santiago, Chile. IEEE.

Kent Bach and Robert M. Harnish. 1979. *Linguistic Communication and Speech Acts*. Cambridge: MIT Press.

Alexei Baevski, Henry Zhou, Abdelrahman Mohamed, and Michael Auli. 2020. wav2vec 2.0: A Framework for Self-Supervised Learning of Speech Representations. *arXiv:2006.11477 [cs, eess]*. ArXiv: 2006.11477.

Chongyang Bai, Xiaoxue Zang, Ying Xu, Srinivas Sunkara, Abhinav Rastogi, Jindong Chen, and Blaise Aguera y Arcas. 2021. UIBert: Learning Generic Multimodal Representations for UI Understanding. *arXiv:2107.13731 [cs]*. ArXiv: 2107.13731.

Tadas Baltrušaitis, Chaitanya Ahuja, and Louis-Philippe Morency. 2017. Multimodal Machine Learning: A Survey and Taxonomy. *arXiv:1705.09406 [cs]*. ArXiv: 1705.09406.

Siqi Bao, Huang He, Fan Wang, Hua Wu, and Haifeng Wang. 2020. PLATO: Pre-trained Dialogue Generation Model with Discrete Latent Variable. *arXiv:1910.07931 [cs]*. ArXiv: 1910.07931.

Ankur Bapna, Gokhan Tur, Dilek Hakkani-Tur, and Larry Heck. 2017. Towards zero-shot frame semantic parsing for domain scaling. *arXiv preprint arXiv:1707.02363*.

Suzanna Becker and Geoffrey E. Hinton. 1992. Self-organizing neural network that discovers surfaces in random-dot stereograms. *Nature*, 355:161–163.

Avrim Blum and Tom Mitchell. 1998. Combining labeled and unlabeled data with co-training. In *Proceedings of the eleventh annual conference on Computational learning theory - COLT' 98*, pages 92–100, Madison, Wisconsin, United States. ACM Press.

C. Bregler and Y. Konig. 1994. "Eigenlips" for robust speech recognition. In *Proceedings of ICASSP '94. IEEE International Conference on Acoustics, Speech and Signal Processing*, volume ii, pages II/669–II/672 vol.2.

Joao Carreira, Eric Noland, Chloe Hillier, and Andrew Zisserman. 2019. A Short Note on the Kinetics-700 Human Action Dataset. *arXiv:1907.06987 [cs]*. ArXiv: 1907.06987.

David M. Chan, Shalini Ghosh, Debmalya Chakrabarty, and Björn Hoffmeister. 2021. Multi-Modal Pre-Training for Automated Speech Recognition. *arXiv:2110.09890 [cs, eess]*. ArXiv: 2110.09890.

Ting Chen, Simon Kornblith, Mohammad Norouzi, and Geoffrey Hinton. 2020a. A Simple Framework for Contrastive Learning of Visual Representations. *arXiv:2002.05709 [cs, stat]*. ArXiv: 2002.05709.

Yen-Chun Chen, Linjie Li, Licheng Yu, Ahmed El Kholy, Faisal Ahmed, Zhe Gan, Yu Cheng, and Jingjing Liu. 2020b. UNITER: UNiversal Image-TExt Representation Learning. *arXiv:1909.11740 [cs]*. ArXiv: 1909.11740.

Abhishek Das, Satwik Kottur, Khushi Gupta, Avi Singh, Deshraj Yadav, José M. F. Moura, Devi Parikh, and Dhruv Batra. 2017. Visual Dialog. *arXiv:1611.08669 [cs]*. ArXiv: 1611.08669.

Harm de Vries, Kurt Shuster, Dhruv Batra, Devi Parikh, Jason Weston, and Douwe Kiela. 2018. Talk the Walk: Navigating New York City through Grounded Dialogue. *arXiv:1807.03367 [cs]*. ArXiv: 1807.03367.

Harm de Vries, Florian Strub, Sarath Chandar, Olivier Pietquin, Hugo Larochelle, and Aaron Courville. 2017. GuessWhat?! Visual object discovery through multi-modal dialogue. *arXiv:1611.08481 [cs]*. ArXiv: 1611.08481.

Jacob Devlin, Ming-Wei Chang, Kenton Lee, and Kristina Toutanova. 2019. BERT: Pre-training of Deep Bidirectional Transformers for Language Understanding. *arXiv:1810.04805 [cs]*. ArXiv: 1810.04805.

Kun Duan, David J. Crandall, and Dhruv Batra. 2014. Multimodal Learning in Loosely-Organized Web Images. In *2014 IEEE Conference on Computer Vision and Pattern Recognition*, pages 2465–2472, Columbus, OH, USA. IEEE.

P. Duchnowski, Uwe Meier, and Alex Waibel. 1994. See Me, Hear Me: Integrating Automatic Speech Recognition and Lip-reading. In *Proceedings of 3rd International Conference on Spoken Language Processing (ICSLP '94)*, pages 547 – 550.

Ali El-Kahky, Xiaohu Liu, Ruhi Sarikaya, Gokhan Tur, Dilek Hakkani-Tur, and Larry Heck. 2014. Extending domain coverage of language understanding systems via intent transfer between domains using knowledge graphs and search query click logs. In *2014 IEEE International Conference on Acoustics, Speech and Signal Processing (ICASSP)*, pages 4067–4071. IEEE.

Mihail Eric, Lakshmi Krishnan, Francois Charette, and Christopher D. Manning. 2017. Key-Value Retrieval Networks for Task-Oriented Dialogue. In *Proceedings of the 18th Annual SIGdial Meeting on Discourse and Dialogue*, pages 37–49, Saarbrücken, Germany. Association for Computational Linguistics.

Zhengcong Fei, Zekang Li, Jinchao Zhang, Yang Feng, and Jie Zhou. 2021. Towards Expressive Communication with Internet Memes: A New Multimodal Conversation Dataset and Benchmark. *arXiv:2109.01839 [cs]*. ArXiv: 2109.01839.

Valentin Gabeur, Chen Sun, Karteek Alahari, and Cordelia Schmid. 2020. Multi-modal Transformer for Video Retrieval. *arXiv:2007.10639 [cs]*. ArXiv: 2007.10639.

Haoyuan Gao, Junhua Mao, Jie Zhou, Zhiheng Huang, Lei Wang, and Wei Xu. 2015. Are You Talking to a Machine? Dataset and Methods for Multilingual Image Question Answering. *arXiv:1505.05612 [cs]*. ArXiv: 1505.05612.

Jianfeng Gao, Michel Galley, and Lihong Li. 2019. Neural Approaches to Conversational AI. *arXiv:1809.08267 [cs]*. ArXiv: 1809.08267.

Ruohan Gao, Yen-Yu Chang, Shivani Mall, Li Fei-Fei, and Jiajun Wu. 2021. ObjectFolder: A Dataset of Objects with Implicit Visual, Auditory, and Tactile Representations. *arXiv:2109.07991 [cs]*. ArXiv: 2109.07991.

Jort F. Gemmeke, Daniel P. W. Ellis, Dylan Freedman, Aren Jansen, Wade Lawrence, R. Channing Moore, Manoj Plakal, and Marvin Ritter. 2017. Audio Set: An ontology and human-labeled dataset for audio events. In *Proc. IEEE ICASSP 2017*, New Orleans, LA.

Shijie Geng, Peng Gao, Moitreya Chatterjee, Chiori Hori, Jonathan Le Roux, Yongfeng Zhang, Hongsheng Li, and Anoop Cherian. 2021. Dynamic Graph Representation Learning for Video Dialog via Multi-Modal Shuffled Transformers. *arXiv:2007.03848 [cs]*. ArXiv: 2007.03848.

Rohit Girdhar and Deva Ramanan. 2020. Cater: A diagnostic dataset for compositional actions and temporal reasoning. In *International Conference on Learning Representations*.

Palash Goyal, Saurabh Sahu, Shalini Ghosh, and Chul Lee. 2020. Cross-modal Learning for Multimodal Video Categorization. *arXiv:2003.03501 [cs]*. ArXiv: 2003.03501.

Kristen Grauman, Andrew Westbury, Eugene Byrne, Zachary Chavis, Antonino Furnari, Rohit Girdhar, Jackson Hamburger, Hao Jiang, Miao Liu, Xingyu Liu, Miguel Martin, Tushar Nagarajan, Ilija Radosavovic, Santhosh Kumar Ramakrishnan, Fiona Ryan, Jayant Sharma, Michael Wray, Mengmeng Xu, Eric Zhongcong Xu, Chen Zhao, Siddhant Bansal, Dhruv Batra, Vincent Cartillier, Sean Crane, Tien Do, Morrie Doulaty, Akshay Erapalli, Christoph Feichtenhofer, Adriano Fragomeni, Qichen Fu, Christian Fuegen, Abrham Gebreselasie, Cristina Gonzalez, James Hillis, Xuhua Huang, Yifei Huang, Wenqi Jia, Weslie Khoo, Jachym Kolar, Satwik Kottur, Anurag Kumar, Federico Landini, Chao Li, Yanghao Li, Zhenqiang Li, Karttikeya Mangalam, Raghava Modhugu, Jonathan Munro, Tullie Murrell, Takumi Nishiyasu, Will Price, Paola Ruiz Puentes, Merey Ramazanova, Leda Sari, Kiran Somasundaram, Audrey Southerland, Yusuke Sugano, Ruijie Tao, Minh Vo, Yuchen Wang, Xindi Wu, Takuma Yagi, Yunyi Zhu, Pablo Arbelaez, David Crandall, Dima Damen, Giovanni Maria Farinella, Bernard Ghanem, Vamsi Krishna Ithapu, C. V. Jawahar, Hanbyul Joo, Kris Kitani, Haizhou Li, Richard Newcombe, Aude Oliva, Hyun Soo Park, James M. Rehg, Yoichi Sato, Jianbo Shi, Mike Zheng Shou, Antonio Torralba, Lorenzo Torresani, Mingfei Yan, and Jitendra Malik. 2021. Ego4D: Around the World in 3,000 Hours of Egocentric Video. *arXiv:2110.07058 [cs]*. ArXiv: 2110.07058.

Jean-Bastien Grill, Florian Strub, Florent Altché, Corentin Tallec, Pierre Richemond, Elena Buchatskaya, Carl Doersch, Bernardo Avila Pires, Zhaohan Guo, Mohammad Gheshlaghi Azar, Bilal Piot, koray kavukcuoglu, Remi Munos, and Michal Valko. 2020. Bootstrap Your Own Latent - A New Approach to Self-Supervised Learning. In *Advances in Neural Information Processing Systems*, volume 33, pages 21271–21284. Curran Associates, Inc.

Mihai Gurban, Jean-Philippe Thiran, Thomas Drugman, and Thierry Dutoit. 2008. Dynamic modality weighting for multi-stream hmms inaudio-visual speech recognition. In *Proceedings of the 10th international conference on Multimodal interfaces - IMCI '08*, page 237, Chania, Crete, Greece. ACM Press.

Michael Gutmann and Aapo Hyvärinen. 2010. Noise-contrastive estimation: A new estimation principle for unnormalized statistical models. In *Proceedings of the Thirteenth International Conference on Artificial Intelligence and Statistics*, volume 9 of *Proceedings of Machine Learning Research*, pages 297–304, Chia Laguna Resort, Sardinia, Italy. PMLR.

Dilek Hakkani-Tür, Larry Heck, and Gokhan Tur. 2011. Exploiting query click logs for utterance domain detection in spoken language understanding. In *2011 IEEE International Conference on Acoustics, Speech and Signal Processing (ICASSP)*, pages 5636–5639. IEEE.

Dilek Hakkani-Tür, Larry Heck, and Gokhan Tur. 2013. Using a knowledge graph and query click logs for unsupervised learning of relation detection. In *2013 IEEE International Conference on Acoustics, Speech and Signal Processing*, pages 8327–8331. IEEE.

Dilek Hakkani-Tür, Gokhan Tur, Rukmini Iyer, and Larry Heck. 2012. Translating natural language utterances to search queries for slu domain detection using query click logs. In *2012 IEEE International Conference on Acoustics, Speech and Signal Processing (ICASSP)*, pages 4953–4956. IEEE.

Dilek Hakkani-Tür, Malcolm Slaney, Asli Celikyilmaz, and Larry Heck. 2014. Eye Gaze for Spoken Language Understanding in Multi-Modal Conversational Interactions. In *Proceedings of the 16th International Conference on Multimodal Interaction*, ICMI '14, pages 263–266, New York, NY, USA. Association for Computing Machinery. Event-place: Istanbul, Turkey.

Dilek Hakkani-Tür, Gokhan Tur, and Larry Heck. 2011. Research Challenges and Opportunities in Mobile Applications [DSP Education]. *IEEE Signal Processing Magazine*, 28(4):108–110. Conference Name: IEEE Signal Processing Magazine.

Darryl Hannan, Akshay Jain, and Mohit Bansal. 2020. ManyModalQA: Modality Disambiguation and QA over Diverse Inputs. *arXiv:2001.08034 [cs]*. ArXiv: 2001.08034.

Kaiming He, Haoqi Fan, Yuxin Wu, Saining Xie, and Ross Girshick. 2020. Momentum Contrast for Unsupervised Visual Representation Learning. In *2020 IEEE/CVF Conference on Computer Vision and Pattern Recognition (CVPR)*, pages 9726–9735, Seattle, WA, USA. IEEE.

Zecheng He, Srinivas Sunkara, Xiaoxue Zang, Ying Xu, Lijuan Liu, Nevan Wichers, Gabriel Schubiner, Ruby Lee, Jindong Chen, and Blaise Agüera y Arcas. 2021. ActionBert: Leveraging User Actions for Semantic Understanding of User Interfaces. *arXiv:2012.12350 [cs]*. ArXiv: 2012.12350.

Larry Heck. 2012. The conversational web. In *Keynote, IEEE Workshop on Spoken Language Technology*, Miami, FL, USA.

Larry Heck and Dilek Hakkani-Tür. 2012. Exploiting the semantic web for unsupervised spoken language understanding. In *2012 IEEE Spoken Language Technology Workshop (SLT)*, pages 228–233. IEEE.

Larry Heck, Dilek Hakkani-Tür, Madhu Chinthakunta, Gokhan Tur, Rukmini Iyer, Partha Parthasacarthy, Lisa Stifelman, Elizabeth Shriberg, and Ashley Fidler. 2013. Multimodal Conversational Search and Browse. IEEE Workshop on Speech, Language and Audio in Multimedia.

Larry Heck and Simon Heck. 2022. Zero-Shot Visual Slot Filling as Question Answering. *arXiv:2011.12340 [cs]*. ArXiv: 2011.12340.

Larry Heck and Hongzhao Huang. 2014. Deep learning of knowledge graph embeddings for semantic parsing of twitter dialogs. In *2014 IEEE Global Conference on Signal and Information Processing (GlobalSIP)*, pages 597–601. IEEE.

Matthew Henderson, Iñigo Casanueva, Nikola Mrkšić, Pei-Hao Su, Tsung-Hsien Wen, and Ivan Vulić. 2020. ConveRT: Efficient and Accurate Conversational Representations from Transformers. In *Findings of the Association for Computational Linguistics: EMNLP 2020*, pages 2161–2174, Online. Association for Computational Linguistics.

Chiori Hori, Takaaki Hori, Teng-Yok Lee, Kazuhiro Sumi, John R. Hershey, and Tim K. Marks. 2017. Attention-Based Multimodal Fusion for Video Description. *arXiv:1701.03126 [cs]*. ArXiv: 1701.03126.

Ehsan Hosseini-Asl, Bryan McCann, Chien-Sheng Wu, Semih Yavuz, and Richard Socher. 2020. A Simple Language Model for Task-Oriented Dialogue. *arXiv:2005.00796 [cs]*. ArXiv: 2005.00796.

Wei-Ning Hsu, Yao-Hung Hubert Tsai, Benjamin Bolte, Ruslan Salakhutdinov, and Abdelrahman Mohamed. 2021. Hubert: How Much Can a Bad Teacher Benefit ASR Pre-Training? In *ICASSP 2021 - 2021 IEEE International Conference on Acoustics, Speech and Signal Processing (ICASSP)*, pages 6533–6537. ISSN: 2379-190X.

Ronghang Hu, Jacob Andreas, Marcus Rohrbach, Trevor Darrell, and Kate Saenko. 2017. Learning to Reason: End-to-End Module Networks for Visual Question Answering. _eprint: 1704.05526.

X. Huang, A. Acero, C. Chelba, L. Deng, J. Droppo, D. Duchene, J. Goodman, H. Hon, D. Jacoby, L. Jiang, R. Loynd, M. Mahajan, P. Mau, S. Meredith, S. Mughal, S. Neto, M. Plumpe, K. Steury, G. Venolia, K. Wang, and Y. Wang. 2001. MiPad: a multimodal interaction prototype. In *2001 IEEE International Conference on Acoustics, Speech, and Signal Processing. Proceedings (Cat. No.01CH37221)*, volume 1, pages 9–12 vol.1.

Aren Jansen, Daniel P. W. Ellis, Shawn Hershey, R. Channing Moore, Manoj Plakal, Ashok C. Popat, and Rif A. Saurous. 2019. Coincidence, Categorization, and Consolidation: Learning to Recognize Sounds with Minimal Supervision. *arXiv:1911.05894 [cs, eess, stat]*. ArXiv: 1911.05894.

Michael Johnston, Srinivas Bangalore, Gunaranjan Vasireddy, Amanda Stent, Patrick Ehlen, Marilyn Walker, Steve Whittaker, and Preetam Maloor. 2002. MATCH: An Architecture for Multimodal Dialogue Systems. In *Proceedings of the 40th Annual Meeting of the Association for Computational Linguistics*, pages 376–383, Philadelphia, Pennsylvania, USA. Association for Computational Linguistics.

Sebastian Kalkowski, Christian Schulze, Andreas Dengel, and Damian Borth. 2015. Real-time Analysis and Visualization of the YFCC100m Dataset. In *Proceedings of the 2015 Workshop on Community-Organized Multimodal Mining: Opportunities for Novel Solutions - MMCommons'15*, pages 25–30, Brisbane, Australia. ACM Press.

Douwe Kiela, Luana Bulat, and Stephen Clark. 2015. Grounding Semantics in Olfactory Perception. In *Proceedings of the 53rd Annual Meeting of the Association for Computational Linguistics and the 7th International Joint Conference on Natural Language Processing (Volume 2: Short Papers)*, pages 231–236, Beijing, China. Association for Computational Linguistics.

Ryan Kiros, Ruslan Salakhutdinov, and Richard S. Zemel. 2014. Unifying Visual-Semantic Embeddings with Multimodal Neural Language Models. *arXiv:1411.2539 [cs]*. ArXiv: 1411.2539.

Chen Kong, Dahua Lin, Mohit Bansal, Raquel Urtasun, and Sanja Fidler. 2014. What Are You Talking About? Text-to-Image Coreference. In *2014 IEEE Conference on Computer Vision and Pattern Recognition*, pages 3558–3565. ISSN: 1063-6919.

Bruno Korbar, Du Tran, and Lorenzo Torresani. 2018. Cooperative Learning of Audio and Video Models from Self-Supervised Synchronization. *arXiv:1807.00230 [cs]*. ArXiv: 1807.00230.

Satwik Kottur, Seungwhan Moon, Alborz Geramifard, and Babak Damavandi. 2021. SIMMC 2.0: A Task-oriented Dialog Dataset for Immersive Multimodal Conversations. *arXiv:2104.08667 [cs]*. ArXiv: 2104.08667.

Satwik Kottur, José M. F. Moura, Devi Parikh, Dhruv Batra, and Marcus Rohrbach. 2018. Visual Coreference Resolution in Visual Dialog using Neural Module Networks. *arXiv:1809.01816 [cs]*. ArXiv: 1809.01816.

H. Kuehne, H. Jhuang, E. Garrote, T. Poggio, and T. Serre. 2011. HMDB: A large video database for human motion recognition. In *2011 International Conference on Computer Vision*, pages 2556–2563. ISSN: 2380-7504.

Lori Lamel, Samir Bennacef, Jean-Luc Gauvain, Hervé Dartigues, and Jean-Noel Temem. 1998. User Evaluation Of The Mask Kiosk.

Hung Le, Chinnadhurai Sankar, Seungwhan Moon, Ahmad Beirami, Alborz Geramifard, and Satwik Kottur. 2021. DVD: A Diagnostic Dataset for Multi-step Reasoning in Video Grounded Dialogue. *arXiv:2101.00151 [cs]*. ArXiv: 2101.00151.

Jie Lei, Licheng Yu, Mohit Bansal, and Tamara L. Berg. 2019. TVQA: Localized, Compositional Video Question Answering. *arXiv:1809.01696 [cs]*. ArXiv: 1809.01696.

Jie Lei, Licheng Yu, Tamara L. Berg, and Mohit Bansal. 2020. TVQA+: Spatio-Temporal Grounding for Video Question Answering. *arXiv:1904.11574 [cs]*. ArXiv: 1904.11574.

Jiwei Li, Michel Galley, Chris Brockett, Jianfeng Gao, and Bill Dolan. 2016a. A Diversity-Promoting Objective Function for Neural Conversation Models. *arXiv:1510.03055 [cs]*. ArXiv: 1510.03055.

Jiwei Li, Michel Galley, Chris Brockett, Georgios P. Spithourakis, Jianfeng Gao, and Bill Dolan. 2016b. A Persona-Based Neural Conversation Model. *arXiv:1603.06155 [cs]*. ArXiv: 1603.06155.

Toby Jia-Jun Li, Marissa Radensky, Justin Jia, Kirielle Singarajah, Tom M. Mitchell, and Brad A. Myers. 2019. PUMICE: A Multi-Modal Agent that Learns Concepts and Conditionals from Natural Language and Demonstrations. In *Proceedings of the 32nd Annual ACM Symposium on User Interface Software and Technology*, pages 577–589, New Orleans LA USA. ACM.

Xiujun Li, Xi Yin, Chunyuan Li, Pengchuan Zhang, Xiaowei Hu, Lei Zhang, Lijuan Wang, Houdong Hu, Li Dong, Furu Wei, Yejin Choi, and Jianfeng Gao. 2020. Oscar: Object-Semantics Aligned Pre-training for Vision-Language Tasks. In *Computer Vision – ECCV 2020*, pages 121–137, Cham. Springer International Publishing.

Yang Li, Gang Li, Xin Zhou, Mostafa Dehghani, and Alexey Gritsenko. 2021. VUT: Versatile UI Transformer for Multi-Modal Multi-Task User Interface Modeling. *arXiv:2112.05692 [cs]*. ArXiv: 2112.05692.

Ji Lin, Chuang Gan, and Song Han. 2019. TSM: Temporal Shift Module for Efficient Video Understanding. *arXiv:1811.08383 [cs]*. ArXiv: 1811.08383.

Bing Liu, Gokhan Tur, Dilek Hakkani-Tur, Pararth Shah, and Larry Heck. 2017. End-to-end optimization of task-oriented dialogue model with deep reinforcement learning. *arXiv preprint arXiv:1711.10712*.

Bing Liu, Gokhan Tur, Dilek Hakkani-Tur, Pararth Shah, and Larry Heck. 2018. Dialogue learning with human teaching and feedback in end-to-end trainable task-oriented dialogue systems.

Jiasen Lu, Dhruv Batra, Devi Parikh, and Stefan Lee. 2019. ViLBERT: Pretraining Task-Agnostic Visiolinguistic Representations for Vision-and-Language Tasks. *arXiv:1908.02265 [cs]*. ArXiv: 1908.02265.

Mateusz Malinowski, Marcus Rohrbach, and Mario Fritz. 2015. Ask Your Neurons: A Neural-based Approach to Answering Questions about Images. *arXiv:1505.01121 [cs]*. ArXiv: 1505.01121.

Pierre-Emmanuel Mazaré, Samuel Humeau, Martin Raison, and Antoine Bordes. 2018. Training Millions of Personalized Dialogue Agents. In *Proceedings of the 2018 Conference on Empirical Methods in Natural Language Processing*, pages 2775–2779, Brussels, Belgium. Association for Computational Linguistics.

U. Meier, W. Hurst, and P. Duchnowski. 1996. Adaptive bimodal sensor fusion for automatic speechreading. In *1996 IEEE International Conference on Acoustics, Speech, and Signal Processing Conference Proceedings*, volume 2, pages 833–836 vol. 2.

Grégoire Mesnil, Yann Dauphin, Kaisheng Yao, Yoshua Bengio, Li Deng, Dilek Hakkani-Tur, Xiaodong He, Larry Heck, Gokhan Tur, Dong Yu, et al. 2014. Using recurrent neural networks for slot filling in spoken language understanding. *IEEE/ACM Transactions on Audio, Speech, and Language Processing*, 23(3):530–539.

Antoine Miech, Jean-Baptiste Alayrac, Lucas Smaira, Ivan Laptev, Josef Sivic, and Andrew Zisserman. 2020. End-to-End Learning of Visual Representations from Uncurated Instructional Videos. *arXiv:1912.06430 [cs]*. ArXiv: 1912.06430.

Antoine Miech, Dimitri Zhukov, Jean-Baptiste Alayrac, Makarand Tapaswi, Ivan Laptev, and Josef Sivic. 2019. HowTo100M: Learning a Text-Video Embedding by Watching Hundred Million Narrated Video Clips. *arXiv:1906.03327 [cs]*. ArXiv: 1906.03327.

Tomas Mikolov, Kai Chen, Greg Corrado, and Jeffrey Dean. 2013. Efficient Estimation of Word Representations in Vector Space. *arXiv:1301.3781 [cs]*. ArXiv: 1301.3781.

Seungwhan Moon, Satwik Kottur, Paul A. Crook, Ankita De, Shivani Poddar, Theodore Levin, David Whitney, Daniel Difranco, Ahmad Beirami, Eunjoon Cho, Rajen Subba, and Alborz Geramifard. 2020. Situated and Interactive Multimodal Conversations. *arXiv:2006.01460 [cs]*. ArXiv: 2006.01460.

Pedro Morgado, Nuno Vasconcelos, and Ishan Misra. 2021. Audio-Visual Instance Discrimination with Cross-Modal Agreement. *arXiv:2004.12943 [cs]*. ArXiv: 2004.12943.

Nasrin Mostafazadeh, Chris Brockett, Bill Dolan, Michel Galley, Jianfeng Gao, Georgios P. Spithourakis, and Lucy Vanderwende. 2017. Image-Grounded Conversations: Multimodal Context for Natural Question and Response Generation. *arXiv:1701.08251 [cs]*. ArXiv: 1701.08251.

Ara V. Nefian, Luhong Liang, Xiaobo Pi, Liu Xiaoxiang, Crusoe Mao, and Kevin Murphy. 2002. A coupled HMM for audio-visual speech recognition. In *2002 IEEE International Conference on Acoustics, Speech, and Signal Processing*, volume 2, pages II–2013–II–2016. ISSN: 1520-6149.

Jiquan Ngiam, Aditya Khosla, Mingyu Kim, Juhan Nam, Honglak Lee, and Andrew Y. Ng. 2011. Multimodal Deep Learning. In *Proceedings of the 28th International Conference on International Conference on Machine Learning*, ICML'11, pages 689–696, Madison, WI, USA. Omnipress. Event-place: Bellevue, Washington, USA.

Mihalis A. Nicolaou, Hatice Gunes, and Maja Pantic. 2011. Continuous Prediction of Spontaneous Affect from Multiple Cues and Modalities in Valence-Arousal Space. *IEEE Transactions on Affective Computing*, 2(2):92–105. Conference Name: IEEE Transactions on Affective Computing.

Andrew Owens, Jiajun Wu, Josh H. McDermott, William T. Freeman, and Antonio Torralba. 2016. Ambient Sound Provides Supervision for Visual Learning. *arXiv:1608.07017 [cs]*. ArXiv: 1608.07017.

Aishwarya Padmakumar, Jesse Thomason, Ayush Shrivastava, Patrick Lange, Anjali Narayan-Chen, Spandana Gella, Robinson Piramithu, Gokhan Tur, and Dilek Hakkani-Tur. 2021. TEACh: Task-driven Embodied Agents that Chat. *arXiv:2110.00534 [cs]*. ArXiv: 2110.00534.

Ashwin Paranjape, Abigail See, Kathleen Kenealy, Haojun Li, Amelia Hardy, Peng Qi, Kaushik Ram Sadagopan, Nguyet Minh Phu, Dilara Soylu, and Christopher D. Manning. 2020. Neural Generation Meets Real People: Towards Emotionally Engaging Mixed-Initiative Conversations. *arXiv:2008.12348 [cs]*. ArXiv: 2008.12348.

Mandela Patrick, Yuki Markus Asano, Ruth Fong, João F. Henriques, Geoffrey Zweig, and Andrea Vedaldi. 2020. Multi-modal self-supervision from generalized data transformations. *CoRR*, abs/2003.04298.

Baolin Peng, Chunyuan Li, Jinchao Li, Shahin Shayandeh, Lars Liden, and Jianfeng Gao. 2021. SOLOIST: Building Task Bots at Scale with Transfer Learning and Machine Teaching. *arXiv:2005.05298 [cs]*. ArXiv: 2005.05298.

Gao Peng, Zhengkai Jiang, Haoxuan You, Pan Lu, Steven Hoi, Xiaogang Wang, and Hongsheng Li. 2019. Dynamic Fusion with Intra- and Inter- Modality Attention Flow for Visual Question Answering. *arXiv:1812.05252 [cs, eess]*. ArXiv: 1812.05252.

A. J. Piergiovanni, Anelia Angelova, and Michael S. Ryoo. 2020. Evolving Losses for Unsupervised Video Representation Learning. *arXiv:2002.12177 [cs]*. ArXiv: 2002.12177.

G. Potamianos, C. Neti, G. Gravier, A. Garg, and A.W. Senior. 2003. Recent advances in the automatic recognition of audiovisual speech. *Proceedings of the IEEE*, 91(9):1306–1326. Conference Name: Proceedings of the IEEE.

Rui Qian, Tianjian Meng, Boqing Gong, Ming-Hsuan Yang, Huisheng Wang, Serge Belongie, and Yin Cui. 2021. Spatiotemporal Contrastive Video Representation Learning. *arXiv:2008.03800 [cs]*. ArXiv: 2008.03800.

Alec Radford, Jong Wook Kim, Chris Hallacy, Aditya Ramesh, Gabriel Goh, Sandhini Agarwal, Girish Sastry, Amanda Askell, Pamela Mishkin, Jack Clark, Gretchen Krueger, and Ilya Sutskever. 2021. Learning Transferable Visual Models From Natural Language Supervision. *arXiv:2103.00020 [cs]*. ArXiv: 2103.00020.

Colin Raffel, Noam Shazeer, Adam Roberts, Katherine Lee, Sharan Narang, Michael Matena, Yanqi Zhou, Wei Li, and Peter J. Liu. 2020. Exploring the Limits of Transfer Learning with a Unified Text-to-Text Transformer. *arXiv:1910.10683 [cs, stat]*. ArXiv: 1910.10683.

Vignesh Ramanathan, Armand Joulin, Percy Liang, and Li Fei-Fei. 2014. Linking People in Videos with "Their" Names Using Coreference Resolution. In *Computer Vision – ECCV 2014*, pages 95–110, Cham. Springer International Publishing.

Hannah Rashkin, Eric Michael Smith, Margaret Li, and Y-Lan Boureau. 2019. Towards Empathetic Open-domain Conversation Models: A New Benchmark and Dataset. In *Proceedings of the 57th Annual Meeting of the Association for Computational Linguistics*, pages 5370–5381, Florence, Italy. Association for Computational Linguistics.

Shaoqing Ren, Kaiming He, Ross Girshick, and Jian Sun. 2016. Faster R-CNN: Towards Real-Time Object Detection with Region Proposal Networks. *arXiv:1506.01497 [cs]*. ArXiv: 1506.01497.

Alan Ritter, Colin Cherry, and William B. Dolan. 2011. Data-Driven Response Generation in Social Media. In *Proceedings of the 2011 Conference on Empirical Methods in Natural Language Processing*, pages 583–593, Edinburgh, Scotland, UK. Association for Computational Linguistics.

Stephen Roller, Y.-Lan Boureau, Jason Weston, Antoine Bordes, Emily Dinan, Angela Fan, David Gunning, Da Ju, Margaret Li, Spencer Poff, Pratik Ringshia, Kurt Shuster, Eric Michael Smith, Arthur Szlam, Jack Urbanek, and Mary Williamson. 2020. Open-Domain Conversational Agents: Current Progress, Open Problems, and Future Directions. *arXiv:2006.12442 [cs]*. ArXiv: 2006.12442.

Idan Schwartz, Seunghak Yu, Tamir Hazan, and Alexander Schwing. 2020. Factor Graph Attention. *arXiv:1904.05880 [cs]*. ArXiv: 1904.05880.

Ramprasaath Ramasamy Selvaraju, Stefan Lee, Yilin Shen, Hongxia Jin, Shalini Ghosh, Larry Heck, Dhruv Batra, and Devi Parikh. 2019. Taking a HINT: Leveraging Explanations to Make Vision and Language Models More Grounded. In *2019*

IEEE/CVF International Conference on Computer Vision (ICCV), pages 2591–2600, Seoul, Korea (South). IEEE.

Iulian V. Serban, Alessandro Sordoni, Yoshua Bengio, Aaron Courville, and Joelle Pineau. 2016. Building End-To-End Dialogue Systems Using Generative Hierarchical Neural Network Models. *arXiv:1507.04808 [cs]*. ArXiv: 1507.04808.

Pararth Shah, Dilek Hakkani-Tur, and Larry Heck. 2016. Interactive reinforcement learning for task-oriented dialogue management.

Lifeng Shang, Zhengdong Lu, and Hang Li. 2015. Neural Responding Machine for Short-Text Conversation. In *Proceedings of the 53rd Annual Meeting of the Association for Computational Linguistics and the 7th International Joint Conference on Natural Language Processing (Volume 1: Long Papers)*, pages 1577–1586, Beijing, China. Association for Computational Linguistics.

Mohit Shridhar, Jesse Thomason, Daniel Gordon, Yonatan Bisk, Winson Han, Roozbeh Mottaghi, Luke Zettlemoyer, and Dieter Fox. 2020. ALFRED: A Benchmark for Interpreting Grounded Instructions for Everyday Tasks. *arXiv:1912.01734 [cs]*. ArXiv: 1912.01734.

Kurt Shuster, Samuel Humeau, Antoine Bordes, and Jason Weston. 2020. Image Chat: Engaging Grounded Conversations. *arXiv:1811.00945 [cs]*. ArXiv: 1811.00945.

Gunnar A. Sigurdsson, Gül Varol, Xiaolong Wang, Ali Farhadi, Ivan Laptev, and Abhinav Gupta. 2016. Hollywood in Homes: Crowdsourcing Data Collection for Activity Understanding. *arXiv:1604.01753 [cs]*. ArXiv: 1604.01753.

Karen Simonyan and Andrew Zisserman. 2015. Very Deep Convolutional Networks for Large-Scale Image Recognition. *arXiv:1409.1556 [cs]*. ArXiv: 1409.1556.

Amanpreet Singh, Ronghang Hu, Vedanuj Goswami, Guillaume Couairon, Wojciech Galuba, Marcus Rohrbach, and Douwe Kiela. 2021a. FLAVA: A Foundational Language And Vision Alignment Model. *arXiv:2112.04482 [cs]*. ArXiv: 2112.04482.

Hrituraj Singh, Anshul Nasery, Denil Mehta, Aishwarya Agarwal, Jatin Lamba, and Balaji Vasan Srinivasan. 2021b. MIMOQA: Multimodal Input Multimodal Output Question Answering. In *Proceedings of the 2021 Conference of the North American Chapter of the Association for Computational Linguistics: Human Language Technologies*, pages 5317–5332, Online. Association for Computational Linguistics.

Richard Socher and Li Fei-Fei. 2010. Connecting modalities: Semi-supervised segmentation and annotation of images using unaligned text corpora. In *2010 IEEE Computer Society Conference on Computer Vision and Pattern Recognition*, pages 966–973. ISSN: 1063-6919.

Khurram Soomro, Amir Roshan Zamir, and Mubarak Shah. 2012. UCF101: A Dataset of 101 Human Actions Classes From Videos in The Wild. *arXiv:1212.0402 [cs]*. ArXiv: 1212.0402.

Alessandro Sordoni, Michel Galley, Michael Auli, Chris Brockett, Yangfeng Ji, Margaret Mitchell, Jian-Yun Nie, Jianfeng Gao, and Bill Dolan. 2015. A Neural Network Approach to Context-Sensitive Generation of Conversational Responses. *arXiv:1506.06714 [cs]*. ArXiv: 1506.06714.

Nitish Srivastava and Ruslan Salakhutdinov. 2014. Multimodal Learning with Deep Boltzmann Machines. *Journal of Machine Learning Research*, 15(84):2949–2980.

Chen Sun, Fabien Baradel, Kevin Murphy, and Cordelia Schmid. 2019a. Learning Video Representations using Contrastive Bidirectional Transformer. *arXiv:1906.05743 [cs, stat]*. ArXiv: 1906.05743.

Chen Sun, Austin Myers, Carl Vondrick, Kevin Murphy, and Cordelia Schmid. 2019b. VideoBERT: A Joint Model for Video and Language Representation Learning. *arXiv:1904.01766 [cs]*. ArXiv: 1904.01766.

Hao Tan and Mohit Bansal. 2019. Lxmert: Learning cross-modality encoder representations from transformers. *arXiv preprint arXiv:1908.07490*.

Makarand Tapaswi, Yukun Zhu, Rainer Stiefelhagen, Antonio Torralba, Raquel Urtasun, and Sanja Fidler. 2016. MovieQA: Understanding Stories in Movies through Question-Answering. *arXiv:1512.02902 [cs]*. ArXiv: 1512.02902.

Jesse Thomason, Michael Murray, Maya Cakmak, and Luke Zettlemoyer. 2019. Vision-and-Dialog Navigation. *arXiv:1907.04957 [cs]*. ArXiv: 1907.04957.

Shyam Upadhyay, Manaal Faruqui, Gokhan Tür, Hakkani-Tür Dilek, and Larry Heck. 2018. (Almost) Zero-Shot Cross-Lingual Spoken Language Understanding. In *2018 IEEE International Conference on Acoustics, Speech and Signal Processing (ICASSP)*, pages 6034–6038. ISSN: 2379-190X.

Ashish Vaswani, Noam Shazeer, Niki Parmar, Jakob Uszkoreit, Llion Jones, Aidan N Gomez, Łukasz Kaiser, and Illia Polosukhin. 2017. Attention is All you Need. In *Advances in Neural Information Processing Systems*, volume 30. Curran Associates, Inc.

Oriol Vinyals and Quoc Le. 2015. A Neural Conversational Model. *arXiv:1506.05869 [cs]*. ArXiv: 1506.05869.

Joseph Weizenbaum. 1966. ELIZA—a computer program for the study of natural language communication between man and machine. *Communications of the ACM*, 9(1):36–45.

Jason Weston, Samy Bengio, and Nicolas Usunier. 2010. Large Scale Image Annotation: Learning to Rank with Joint Word-Image Embeddings. In *European Conference on Machine Learning*.

Thomas Wolf, Victor Sanh, Julien Chaumond, and Clement Delangue. 2019. TransferTransfo: A Transfer Learning Approach for Neural Network Based Conversational Agents. *arXiv:1901.08149 [cs]*. ArXiv: 1901.08149.

Chien-Sheng Wu, Steven C.H. Hoi, Richard Socher, and Caiming Xiong. 2020. TOD-BERT: Pre-trained Natural Language Understanding for Task-Oriented Dialogue. In *Proceedings of the 2020 Conference on Empirical Methods in Natural Language Processing (EMNLP)*, pages 917–929, Online. Association for Computational Linguistics.

Zhiyong Wu, Lianhong Cai, and Helen Meng. 2005. Multi-level Fusion of Audio and Visual Features for Speaker Identification. In David Hutchison, Takeo Kanade, Josef Kittler, Jon M. Kleinberg, Friedemann Mattern, John C. Mitchell, Moni Naor, Oscar Nierstrasz, C. Pandu Rangan, Bernhard Steffen, Madhu Sudan, Demetri Terzopoulos, Dough Tygar, Moshe Y. Vardi, Gerhard Weikum, David Zhang, and Anil K. Jain, editors, *Advances in Biometrics*, volume 3832, pages 493–499. Springer Berlin Heidelberg, Berlin, Heidelberg. Series Title: Lecture Notes in Computer Science.

Saining Xie, Ross Girshick, Piotr Dollár, Zhuowen Tu, and Kaiming He. 2017. Aggregated Residual Transformations for Deep Neural Networks. *arXiv:1611.05431 [cs]*. ArXiv: 1611.05431.

Hu Xu, Gargi Ghosh, Po-Yao Huang, Dmytro Okhonko, Armen Aghajanyan, Florian Metze, Luke Zettlemoyer, and Christoph Feichtenhofer. 2021a. VideoCLIP: Contrastive Pre-training for Zero-shot Video-Text Understanding. *arXiv:2109.14084 [cs]*. ArXiv: 2109.14084.

Huijuan Xu and Kate Saenko. 2016. Ask, Attend and Answer: Exploring Question-Guided Spatial Attention for Visual Question Answering. *arXiv:1511.05234 [cs]*. ArXiv: 1511.05234.

Jun Xu, Tao Mei, Ting Yao, and Yong Rui. 2016. MSR-VTT: A Large Video Description Dataset for Bridging Video and Language. In *2016 IEEE Conference on Computer Vision and Pattern Recognition (CVPR)*, pages 5288–5296, Las Vegas, NV, USA. IEEE.

Nancy Xu, Sam Masling, Michael Du, Giovanni Campagna, Larry Heck, James Landay, and Monica S. Lam. 2021b. Grounding Open-Domain Instructions to Automate Web Support Tasks. *arXiv:2103.16057 [cs]*. ArXiv: 2103.16057.

Kexin Yi, Jiajun Wu, Chuang Gan, Antonio Torralba, Pushmeet Kohli, and Joshua B. Tenenbaum. 2019. Neural-Symbolic VQA: Disentangling Reasoning from Vision and Language Understanding. *arXiv:1810.02338 [cs]*. ArXiv: 1810.02338.

B.P. Yuhas, M.H. Goldstein, and T.J. Sejnowski. 1989. Integration of acoustic and visual speech signals using neural networks. *IEEE Communications Magazine*, 27(11):65–71. Conference Name: IEEE Communications Magazine.

Manzil Zaheer, Guru Guruganesh, Avinava Dubey, Joshua Ainslie, Chris Alberti, Santiago Ontanon, Philip Pham, Anirudh Ravula, Qifan Wang, Li Yang, and Amr Ahmed. 2021. Big Bird: Transformers for Longer Sequences. *arXiv:2007.14062 [cs, stat]*. ArXiv: 2007.14062.

Heming Zhang, Shalini Ghosh, Larry Heck, Stephen Walsh, Junting Zhang, Jie Zhang, and C.-C. Jay Kuo. 2019a. Generative Visual Dialogue System via Adaptive Reasoning and Weighted Likelihood Estimation. *arXiv:1902.09818 [cs]*. ArXiv: 1902.09818.

Heming Zhang, Shalini Ghosh, Larry P Heck, Stephen Walsh, Junting Zhang, Jie Zhang, and C-C Jay Kuo. 2019b. Generative visual dialogue system via weighted likelihood estimation. In *IJCAI*, pages 1025–1031.

Yizhe Zhang, Siqi Sun, Michel Galley, Yen-Chun Chen, Chris Brockett, Xiang Gao, Jianfeng Gao, Jingjing Liu, and Bill Dolan. 2020a. DIALOGPT : Large-Scale Generative Pre-training for Conversational Response Generation. In *Proceedings of the 58th Annual Meeting of the Association for Computational Linguistics: System Demonstrations*, pages 270–278, Online. Association for Computational Linguistics.

Yuhao Zhang, Hang Jiang, Yasuhide Miura, Christopher D. Manning, and Curtis P. Langlotz. 2020b. Contrastive Learning of Medical Visual Representations from Paired Images and Text. *arXiv:2010.00747 [cs]*. ArXiv: 2010.00747.

Li Zhou, Jianfeng Gao, Di Li, and Heung-Yeung Shum. 2020. The Design and Implementation of XiaoIce, an Empathetic Social Chatbot. *Computational Linguistics*, 46(1):53–93.

Luowei Zhou, Chenliang Xu, and Jason J. Corso. 2017. Towards Automatic Learning of Procedures from Web Instructional Videos. *arXiv:1703.09788 [cs]*. ArXiv: 1703.09788.

Yuke Zhu, Oliver Groth, Michael Bernstein, and Li Fei-Fei. 2016. Visual7W: Grounded Question Answering in Images. *arXiv:1511.03416 [cs]*. ArXiv: 1511.03416.

A Conversations with TRANSRESNET

Image	Personality	Conversations
	Glamorous	The star of the show is the man and his fabulous car
	[-]	I don't see a man
	Glamorous	That tends to be the case with men that buy flashy cars and BIG houses!
	[-]	I would like to drive that car
	Glamorous	That tends to be the case with men that buy flashy cars and BIG houses!
	[-]	Would you drive that car?
	Glamorous	And I would pay him to do that in my backyard as well
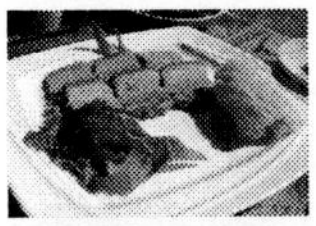	[-]	I love going to new restaurants
	Wise	Well, easy come easy go with your food then, raw is dangerous but it's your life
	[-]	Do you like spicy food?
	Wise	It is most likely too spicy for you
	[-]	This is Lucy, my labrador
	Businesslike	I should start a dog walking business
	[-]	That's a good idea!
	Suave	He would make a lovely companion for me.
	[-]	Do you have any pets?
	Considerate	I think I will. Dogs are a nice animal for the regular person to have
	Caring	I hope you're injured too. If not, I can help you with that
	[-]	I'm not injured
	Extreme	At least if you crash you'll beat the paramedics to the scene by at least 20 minutes!
	[-]	Haha that's a nice joke
	Silly	I would die laughing if you did fall
	[-]	That doesn't look great
	Angry	It makes me mad. Why did they have to hang it before the paint was dry?
	[-]	It's not a painting
	Angry	Oh come on, you're so negative! How is that NOT artistic?!
	[-]	I didn't say it wasn't artistic
	Angry	Oh come on, you're so negative! How is that NOT artistic?!
	[-]	I'm not being negative
	Angry	Oh come on, you're so negative! How is that NOT artistic?!
	[-]	Why are you repeating yourself?
	Angry	Because you have ruined the artistic integrity of the image. If you had the talent that I have, you would understand this.
	[-]	I agree with you
	Angry	Why are people so judgemental about art? It's infuriating!

Conversations from TRANSRESNET. Images are chosen from YFCC100M using the browser by Kalkowski et al. (2015) and the internet, and personalities are chosen at random.

[-] indicates lines spoken by the author.

Open-domain Dialogue Generation: What We Can Do, Can*not* Do, And Should Do Next

Katharina Kann, Abteen Ebrahimi, Joewie J. Koh, Shiran Dudy, Alessandro Roncone
University of Colorado
first.last@colorado.edu

Abstract

Human–computer conversation has long been an interest of artificial intelligence and natural language processing research. Recent years have seen a dramatic improvement in quality for both task-oriented and open-domain dialogue systems, and an increasing amount of research in the area. The goal of this work is threefold: (1) to provide an overview of recent advances in the field of open-domain dialogue, (2) to summarize issues related to ethics, bias, and fairness that the field has identified as well as typical errors of dialogue systems, and (3) to outline important future challenges. We hope that this work will be of interest to both new and experienced researchers in the area.

1 Introduction

Being an empathetic, entertaining, and knowledgeable dialogue partner can be difficult even for humans. Unsurprisingly, the task of dialogue generation, i.e., creating a system that is able to hold an intelligent conversation in a way a human would, constitutes a hard challenge for the natural language processing (NLP) community. In recent years, partially due to the development of powerful natural language understanding (NLU) and natural language generation (NLG) models (Radford et al., 2018; Devlin et al., 2019), the quality of dialogue systems has been improving.

Systems fall into two broad categories, depending on if they support task-oriented or open-domain dialogues. Task-oriented dialogue systems are built for specific purposes, such as booking a flight, and the topic of conversation is limited to the domain of interest. While a narrow scope reduces the complexity of the task, the fact that misunderstandings can have severe consequences adds to it: exact understanding of the user's intentions is crucial. In contrast, open-domain dialogue systems have the ability to talk about a wide variety of arbitrary topics. Thus, conversations with open-domain dialogue systems more closely resemble

Utterance	Fluent	Meaningful	Engaging
I have never been to Italy.	✓		
Mulan I yesterday		✓	
I saw Mulan yesterday.	✓	✓	
I saw Mulan yesterday and it was great – have you seen it?	✓	✓	✓

Table 1: Possible responses of an open-domain dialogue system to *Have you recently seen a good movie?*

human–human conversations. Users often do not have any specific goal beyond enjoying the conversation. Over the last few years – boosted by the development of deep learning models for text – the NLP community has seen rapid advances in the area of dialogue generation. A consequence of this success, as well as of the general growth of the NLP community, has been an abundance of publications on the topic: 275 submissions made *Dialogue Systems* the fourth largest track at ACL 2021 in terms of submitted papers.[1]

To assist researchers in keeping up with the fast progress and to provide a starting point for newcomers, we aim at providing a comprehensive overview of what we as a field currently can do (*existing research*), what we yet cannot do (*common errors of dialogue systems*) or believe must not do (*problems related to ethics, bias, and fairness*), and what we should do (*open challenges for open-domain dialogue generation*). Our work complements Serban et al. (2015), Finch and Choi (2020), and Huang et al. (2020) – surveys of dialogue datasets, evaluation techniques, and model architectures, respectively, by providing a holistic view of the field.

2 Open-domain Dialogue Generation

We use the following definition for open-domain dialogue generation, the task of a *social chatbot* or *socialbot*: Given zero or more previous dialogue

[1]These numbers are based on statistics presented during the opening session of ACL-IJCNLP 2021.

Proceedings of the 4th Workshop on NLP for Conversational AI, pages 148 - 165
May 27, 2022 ©2022 Association for Computational Linguistics

turns between itself and one or more other participants, a system must output a fluent, engaging, and meaningful natural language response. Table 1 shows example outputs of low and high quality. In general, the conversation should continue until all human participants signal that it should end. An open-domain dialogue further does not have to have an explicit goal, i.e., it does not have to center around a task to solve. The conversation can further shift between topics or *domains*, e.g., from movies to politics to sports. While an ideal open-domain dialogue system would also handle task-oriented parts of the conversation, this is not yet common practice. Thus, we consider open-domain and task-oriented dialogue to be mutually exclusive for the purpose of this survey.

Task evaluation. Evaluation strategies can be sorted into two broad categories: *automatic metrics* and *human evaluation*. Automatic metrics are cheap, but do not always correlate well with human judgments (Liu et al., 2016). Common metrics for generative systems are perplexity (Vinyals and Le, 2015), BLEU (Papineni et al., 2002; Ghazvininejad et al., 2017), or DIST-n (Li et al., 2016a). For retrieval systems, recall at position k in n candidates ($R_n@k$), mean average precision (MAP), mean reciprocal rank (MRR) and precision at position 1 (P@1) are used (Wu et al., 2017).

Human evaluation is expensive, but done frequently, due to a lack of good automatic alternatives (Shang et al., 2015; Ram et al., 2018b). For instance, Deriu et al. (2020) propose to evaluate models by determining from which point in a conversation on one can tell they are not human.

A detailed description of open-domain dialogue evaluation goes beyond the scope of this paper. We refer the interested reader to a recent survey on the subject by Finch and Choi (2020).

3 Open-domain Dialogue Datasets

English datasets. The Twitter dataset (Ritter et al., 2010) consists of roughly 1.3 million Twitter conversations with 2 to 243 posts each. Sordoni et al. (2015) generalize it to the Twitter Triples Corpus, which contains context–message–response triples. The context represents previous dialogue turns, and the response is the user's reply to the message. Adiwardana et al. (2020) mine the Meena dataset, which consists of about 867 million context–reply pairs from public posts. Each context consists of all previous utterances in the conversation that a reply is participating in.

The PersonaChat dataset (Zhang et al., 2018b) consists of chats and personas which are collections of five or more sentences that describe a personality. The dataset also contains revised personas, which are rewritten versions meant to prevent models from using simple word overlap to learn a persona. The chats are dialogues between two workers who each emulate one persona. The Target Guided Conversation Dataset (Tang et al., 2019) is derived from the PersonaChat corpus and leverages keywords for transitions between turns. The persona information is removed, and a rule-based keyword extractor is used to find keywords. This dataset allows for models to proactively guide the user towards a target topic. Similar to the PersonaChat dataset, the Wizard of Wikipedia dataset (Dinan et al., 2019) consists of dialogues between two crowdworkers: now, one worker is a "wizard" and the other an "apprentice". The wizard is given text about a topic from Wikipedia, and the two are told to converse about it. The wizard labels each of their utterances with a sentence in the article that provides the knowledge used. The dataset is meant to aid creating dialogue systems that are able to use knowledge in retrieving or generating responses.

OpenDialKG (Moon et al., 2019) is created by asking two workers to converse about a topic using facts from a KG. One worker is given an entity and told to start a conversation about it. The second worker is given facts and told to respond using the most natural and relevant-sounding fact. As the conversation evolves, KG entities are surfaced to allow workers to use them in their responses. Another grounded dataset is the CMU Document Grounded Dataset (Zhou et al., 2018). The authors give workers a Wikipedia article on a movie, and ask them to converse about it for at least 12 turns. 2 experimental scenarios are considered: in the first, only one worker is given the article, and is told to convince the other person to watch it; in the second, both workers are given the article, and they are instructed to talk about the content. In a similar vein, Qin et al. (2019) create a large corpus of grounded conversations by scraping comments between users on Reddit. They consider threads where users are discussing entities found in a linked web document. Due to the common use of anchors to relevant information in the URLs of linked documents, the authors use this dataset to train systems which can take advantage of machine reading comprehension models. The Topical-Chat Corpus (Gopalakrishnan et al., 2019) is a grounded corpus built using 300 entities across 8 topics. Two workers are given reading sets, which are a collection of crowdsourced fun facts, Washington Post articles, and condensed Wikipedia lead sections. Different reading set configurations allow for a potentially asymmetrical amount of information to be given to each person. Conversations are required to have a minimum of 20 turns, and workers are asked to annotate the sentiment of their utterances, where they found the information they spoke about, and the quality of their partner's utterances. The DailyDialog dataset (Li et al., 2017b) is created by scraping text from conversations held on an English learning website. Each utterance is labeled with a dialogue act and an emotion.

The EmpatheticDialogues dataset (Rashkin et al., 2019) contains conversations grounded in situation descriptions. To get these situation descriptions, crowdworkers are asked to write about an emotional situation. Subsequently, two workers are paired up and given a situation to roleplay. The goal of the dataset is to help to train systems that can identify user emotion from dialogue text. Li et al. (2020c) also give workers roles in order to create the AntiScam dataset. It consists of dialogues between crowdworkers, where one worker is assigned the role of an attacker and the other the role of a user. In their conversations, the attacker poses as an Amazon customer service agent and attempts to collect the user's information. The Persuasion for Social Good dataset (Wang et al., 2020b) contains conversations between two crowdworkers, one of whom is trying to convince the other to donate to a specific charity. 300 of these conversations are annotated with one of ten persuasion strategies, or marked as a non-strategy. The objective of collecting this data is to improve the persuasiveness of dialogue agents.

Chinese datasets. Song et al. (2020) introduce the Key-value Profile Identification dataset (KvPI). This data comes from the Sina Weibo social network and consists of text in Mandarin Chinese. KvPI contains post–response pairs, along with three attributes describing the poster (gender, location, and constellation). Each post–response pair is annotated as either entailing, contradicting, or being irrelevant to an attribute. This dataset is designed to investigate how to automatically detect consistency between dialogue posts and the dialogue agent's profile. The Weibo dataset (Wang et al., 2013) is a standard open-domain dialogue generation corpus. Similar to the aforementioned ones it is collected from Sina Weibo. It contains about 0.6 million query–response pairs. Also from Weibo, Shang et al. (2015) create the Short Text Conversation Corpus. Utterance pairs are matching posts and their replies. PersonalDialog (Zheng et al., 2019) was also collected from Weibo. Multi-turn conversations were created by taking user posts and their comments, and each utterance is connected with a specific person, who is represented by a key-value dictionary of traits. This dataset allows to incorporate personality information into generated responses. The PChatbot dataset is collected by Qian et al. (2021) from Weibo posts and Chinese judicial forums. It is composed of almost 200 million dialogue pairs. Each utterance is linked to an anonymized user ID. One potential use for this dataset is to have a model learn to respond differently to users depending on their dialogue history.

Wu et al. (2017) present the Douban dataset, which consists of conversations between two people on the Douban social network. All but the last utterance of each conversation are considered the context and the last utterance is considered an appropriate response. The Douban dataset further contains an additional test set that consists of contexts from Douban posts paired with final utterances from the Weibo that are labeled by humans as positive or negative matches based on the context. The E-commerce dataset (Zhang et al., 2018c) consists of conversations between Chinese customers and customer service staff. As in the Douban dataset, the last utterance is considered a positive response for the rest of the conversation. Negative responses are retrieved from other conversations in an automated fashion. The E-commerce and Douban datasets can be used for training and testing retrieval-based multi-turn dialogue systems.

DuConv (Wu et al., 2019) is a KG-based dataset. A KG is created from information about movies and their characters. To create conversations, first a "conversation path" is created by finding a path between two sampled entries in the KG. Then, two crowdsource workers are given roles – leader and follower – and asked to converse. The leader has access to the conversation path and the KG, and the follower only has access to the leader's utterances. The conversation continues until the leader reaches the conversation goal. DyKgChat (Tuan et al., 2019) was created by scraping conversations from two TV shows, one in Chinese, and one in English. Additionally, manually created KGs are provided to cover entities from the shows.

Finally, Chen and Kan (2013) collect NUS SMS, consisting of over 70,000 SMS messages in both Chinese and English.

Multilingual and multimodal datasets. Open-domain dialogue datasets in languages besides English and Chinese are difficult to find. A Korean dataset has been created by Kim et al. (2021) by translating the English Wizard of Wikipedia dataset (Dinan et al., 2019). To the best of our knowledge, the only *multilingual* dataset is XPersona (Lin et al., 2020a), an extension of the English PersonaChat dataset (Zhang et al., 2018b) to Chinese, French, Indonesian, Italian, Korean, and Japanese. It is created by first automatically translating the training, development and test data. The latter two splits are then manually corrected, while the training set only receives semi-manual cleaning. The authors use this dataset to evaluate approaches based on multilingual models and automatic translation.

Multimodal datasets also exist: Image-Chat by Shuster et al. (2020) consists of images together with English dialogues. Each dialogue is linked to a pair of styles or emotions portrayed in the dialogue. The images are of everyday things, such as food or landscapes. The dialogues are from conversations between two crowd workers who are asked to discuss the image and each given a style or emotion to portray in their discussion. This dataset aims at creating dialogue systems that can speak in different styles and express varying emotions. Meng et al. (2020) present OpenViDial, which consists of dialogues and their visual contexts from movies and TV series. MMChat (Zheng et al., 2021a) contains Chinese conversations about images, which have been scraped from Weibo.

We refer interested readers to Serban et al. (2015) for more information on corpora; for a table with all datasets mentioned here see Appendix A.

4 Open-domain Dialogue Systems

We sort approaches into three categories: (1) *retrieval systems*, which get their responses from a dataset; (2) *generative systems*, which generate responses automatically; and (3) *comprehensive systems*, which consist of a dialogue manager (DM), at least one system from the aforementioned categories, and optionally other functional modules.

4.1 Retrieval Systems

Retrieval systems first obtain a candidate response set from a large repertoire of options and then determine how well each candidate suits the dialogue context. Models can be arbitrarily complex and operate on a single-turn (Wang et al., 2013) or multi-turn (Wu et al., 2017) basis. As retrieval systems do not have a generative component and their outputs originate from human conversations, they are generally fluent and understandable. They are also relatively safe, as many types of harmful responses can be filtered. However, retrieval systems are limited in their ability to converse about topics not covered in the provided responses.

Non-neural approaches exist, such as support-vector machine (SVM)-based ones (Wang et al., 2013; Ji et al., 2014). More recently, neural models which compute the matching score between candidate responses and dialogue contexts have been developed. Initially, feed-forward networks have been employed (Lu and Li, 2013). Wang et al. (2015) extend prior approaches by representing both a candidate response and the context as dependency trees and extracting features from those representations, before obtaining their score via a deep feed-forward network. Later work has used a combination of convolutional neural network (CNN) and recurrent neural network (RNN) layers to determine the matching scores of possible responses, sometimes in combination with an attention mechanism (Yan et al., 2016; Zhou et al., 2016; Wu et al., 2017; Zhang et al., 2018c; Tao et al., 2019). Lu et al. (2019) add spatio-temporal features to their model. The multi-hop selector network by Yuan et al. (2019) looks for the relevant context in a multi-turn dialogue, and uses the context utterances determined to be relevant when retrieving a response. The dually interactive matching network (Gu et al., 2019b) retrieves responses based on personas. It extends Li et al. (2016b) to the previously proposed interactive matching network (Gu et al., 2019a).

Retrieval systems can also be based on transformers (Vaswani et al., 2017). The transformer memory network, for instance, takes knowledge from the Wizard of Wikipedia dataset to retrieve more knowledge-focused responses (Dinan et al., 2019). Whang et al. (2020) go one step further and use *pretrained* transformer models, namely BERT (Devlin et al., 2019) and ELECTRA (Clark et al., 2020), for matching. With this, they follow earlier work on response retrieval for domain-specific dialogue systems. They further add multi-task training. Gao et al. (2020) propose a DialoGPT (Zhang et al., 2020c)-based model to rank retrieved responses.

Lin et al. (2020b) propose to train retrieval models using a ranking loss and so-called grey-scale data: they construct training examples from ground-truth, generated, and random responses.

4.2 Generative Systems

Generative systems generate responses freely, i.e., they are not limited to a predefined set of utterances. Their responses are not guaranteed to be well-formed. However, in contrast to retrieval systems, they are not restricted to talking about topics within a predefined set of responses.

The arguably first generative dialogue system has been ELIZA (Weizenbaum, 1966). ELIZA is rule-based and plays the role of a therapist. Parry, in contrast, is designed to act like a psychology *patient* (Colby, 1975). Later, ALICE has been created by Wallace (1995) as a proof of concept for the Artificial Intelligence Markup Language.

The large majority of generative systems are neural sequence-to-sequence (seq2seq) models. The first such models have been created by Shang et al. (2015) and, concurrently, Vinyals and Le (2015). Their systems are LSTM-based seq2seq models. Parthasarathi and Pineau (2018) add two knowledge sources to an LSTM seq2seq model: the NELL knowledge base (Carlson et al., 2010) and Wikipedia summaries (Scheepers, 2017). Li et al. (2016b) propose a persona-based LSTM encoder-decoder. They represent personas via sentences, with a persona vector being the combination of the sentences. Similarly, Zhang et al. (2018b) condition a dialogue system on profile sentences and also build profiles of its users, allowing it to better tailor its responses to individuals.

Luo et al. (2018)'s LSTM seq2seq model is able to learn utterance-level semantic dependencies, which makes responses more coherent and fluent. Furthermore, Li et al. (2020b) propose two additions to a standard LSTM model: a rank-aware calibrator network, used to construct contrastive optimization objectives, and a knowledge inference component, which learns keywords in order to help the model use more informative words during generation. Zhang et al. (2020a) use a GRU-based response generation model along with a deep utterance aggregation model to generate a context vector from previous turns.

Ghazvininejad et al. (2017) leverage a facts dataset to inject knowledge into a GRU seq2seq model, which helps the model generate more knowledgeable responses. A collection of synonym sets was used by Hsueh and Ma (2020) to help address the problem of social chatbots repeatedly responding with similarly worded sentences.

A variational hierarchical recurrent encoder-decoder (VHRED) for open-domain dialogue generation is proposed by Serban et al. (2017). This model uses latent stochastic variables to model hierarchical structure between dialogue turns, and feeds that information into an RNN. Subsequently, Zhao and Kawahara (2020) introduce a VHRED with a linear Gaussian prior.

Transformer-based models include generative variants of the transformer memory network (Dinan et al., 2019). Further, Keskar et al. (2019) train a conditional transformer language model, which accepts various control codes as part of the input. These control codes allow the control of style, content, and other behaviors without requiring the model to be retrained. Meena (Adiwardana et al., 2020) is a transformer-based seq2seq model trained on large amounts of real chat data. Know-EDG (Li et al., 2020a) consists of a knowledge-enhanced context encoder and an emotion identifier linear layer in front of a transformer model. The input from the emotion identifier allows the model to alter its generated responses based on the emotion its dialogue partner is expressing. Zheng et al. (2021b) add style embeddings to a transformer-based system to alter its dialogue style. Dziri et al. (2021) tackle the problem of factually untrue responses with a generate-then-refine strategy: generated responses are corrected with the help of a knowledge graph.

A mixture between a retrieval and a generative system is the RetrieveNRefine model (Weston et al., 2018). It first employs a key-value memory network to retrieve a good dialogue response, which is then refined by an LSTM seq2seq model.

Only recently, multimodal dialogue models, which combine language and image processing components have been developed (Shuster et al., 2020). Shuster et al. (2021) explore the integration of large pretrained transformer models for text into such systems.

4.3 Comprehensive Systems

Comprehensive systems consist of multiple components together with a DM. They are typically not trained in an end-to-end fashion. The DM selects one or more of the available – in some cases highly specialized – response generators to produce a response for a given context.

XiaoIce (Zhou et al., 2020) is a comprehensive system which consists of 3 layers: The user experience layer connects the system to social media and chat services. The conversation engine layer contains a core chat module, a skills module, a DM, and an empathetic computing module. Finally, the data layer contains profile information on XiaoIce and users, knowledge graphs (KGs), topic indices, and other information. Adapter-Bot (Madotto et al., 2020) employs a DM which is based on BERT (Devlin et al., 2019), a backbone conversational model based on DialoGPT (Zhang et al., 2020c), and a series of additional smaller modules.

Alexa Prize competition. The Amazon Alexa Prize (AP) is an annual competition, with the grand challenge of designing a system capable of holding an open-domain conversation for 20 minutes (Ram et al., 2018a). Contestants develop live systems which are randomly selected to converse with Alexa users. Once the conversation is finished, users are requested to give a rating, which is the main metric used for evaluation. The teams with the highest rating move on to the finals, where expert judges decide the winner.

Sounding Board (Fang et al., 2017), which won the inaugural AP in 2017, is a comprehensive dialogue system which is comprised of an NLU module, a DM, topic-specific modules with rule-based mini-skills, and an NLG component. The NLU module uses a series of text classifiers to extract the user's primary intent. The DM receives that information and, using a hierarchical rule-based architecture, decides which of the mini-skills to use when generating dialogue acts and content to pass to the NLG module. The NLG module builds a response in a rule-based fashion. Gunrock (Chen et al., 2018), the winner of the 2018 AP, differs from Sounding Board in the techniques used for each piece. The NLU module contains multiple submodules, including a noun phrase extractor, a topic model, and a sentiment analyzer. The information from these submodules is passed to the DM, which selects a topic and activates the corresponding submodules. The information from the NLU module and the topic submodule is then passed to the NLG module, which builds a response using templates. Gunrock 2.0 entered the 2019 AP (Liang et al., 2020), and differs from its predecessor by relying more on neural models. However, the 2019 AP was won by Emora (Finch et al., 2020). In addition to mentioning facts, Emora also supports talking about experiences and opinions. Besides the winning system, finalists of the 2019 AP include Chirpy Cardinal (Paranjape et al., 2020), which employs generators based on GPT-2 (Radford et al., 2019), and Alquist (Pichl et al., 2020), which relies on conversation graphs to dynamically use knowledge in its responses. Many design choices were common among other contenders. For NLU, systems often use dialogue act, topic, and intent classifiers. Systems also rely heavily on named entity recognition and entity linking, such as Tartan (Chen et al., 2020), whose response generators use a knowledge base for slot filling. Other systems employ a mixture of strategies to generate responses, such as Athena (Harrison et al., 2020), which attempts to switch between rule-based, knowledge-based, and retrieval-based modules on-the-fly, as well as DREAM (Kuratov et al., 2020), which employs candidate and response annotators before serving a final response. Other contenders include Audrey (Hong et al., 2020), which focuses on emotion and personality, Zotbot (Schallock et al., 2020), which incorporates a commonsense-reasoning element, and Bernard (Majumder et al., 2020), which is built around non-deterministic finite automata.

5 Training and Data Augmentation

Retrieval-based systems are commonly trained with a cross-entropy loss (Zhang et al., 2018c; Lu et al., 2019), comparing a prediction against the gold standard from a training set. As an alternative, using a ranking loss, where a model is trained on distinguishing suitable from unsuitable responses, has been proposed (Lin et al., 2020b). In *comprehensive systems*, the individual components are usually trained separately.

Several algorithms to train *generative systems* have been proposed. Given a training set $D = \{(R_1, C_1, B_1), \dots, (R_N, C_N, B_N)\}$ with N examples consisting of context C_i, background information B_i, and response R_i, models are most commonly trained using maximum likelihood estimation (Shang et al., 2015; Vinyals and Le, 2015).

The goal is to minimize the loss

$$L = -\sum_{i=1}^{N} \log P(R_i|C_i, B_i). \quad (1)$$

However, it has been shown that this encourages boring responses (Li et al., 2016a). As a remedy, several ways to weight training examples have been proposed (Shang et al., 2018; Li et al., 2020b). With that, the loss changes to

$$L = -\sum_{i=1}^{N} w_i \log P(R_i|C_i, B_i), \quad (2)$$

where w_i is the weight corresponding to example i. Further, Zhao and Kawahara (2020) address the concern that generally multiple responses are possible. They propose multi-referenced training and automatically create M different responses $\widetilde{R}_{im}$ for each original R_i. Their loss is

$$L = -\sum_{i=1}^{N} \frac{1}{M} \sum_{m=1}^{M} \log P(\widetilde{R}_{im}|C_i, B_i). \quad (3)$$

Contrastive learning (Hadsell et al., 2006; Gutmann and Hyvärinen, 2012; Cai et al., 2020a) – where a model is trained to assign higher and, respectively, lower conditional probabilities to positive and negative samples than a reference model – and curriculum learning – during which examples are presented to a model in a specific order – have also been employed (Cai et al., 2020c). Finally, dialogue systems can also be trained via reinforcement learning (Li et al., 2016c; Zhang et al., 2018a; Sankar and Ravi, 2019) or adversarial learning (Li et al., 2017a).

Pretraining. Large pretrained models such as BERT (Devlin et al., 2019) or GPT and its successors (Radford et al., 2018, 2019; Brown et al., 2020) have improved the state of the art for a variety of NLP tasks. Pretraining has also been used for open-domain dialogue generation. Two different strategies exist: One option is to pretrain a model on large unlabeled corpora to then finetune it on dialogue data. Liu et al. (2020c), for instance, initialize parts of their generative system with a pretrained BERT model, and Gu et al. (2020) finetune BERT for multi-turn response selection in retrieval-based chatbots. Shi et al. (2020) introduce an English language-learning chatbot based on GPT-2. Boyd et al. (2020) condition a GPT-2 model for dialogue generation on several previous conversations of a single individual to get it to use that individual's style. Further, plug and play language models consist of pretrained language models in combination with one or more simple attribute classifiers, which control various aspects of its behavior, such as style or dialogue content (Dathathri et al., 2020).

The second option is to pretrain a model on large dialogue corpora, such that it can then be finetuned on out-of-domain dialogue data. DialoGPT (Zhang et al., 2020c) is such a model. Its architecture resembles GPT, i.e., it is a transformer (Vaswani et al., 2017) language model. For training, specifically collected Reddit data is used. Like GPT, DialoGPT is publicly available. The authors also experiment with GPT-2 as a basis for DialoGPT and, similar to the work mentioned in the last paragraph, find pretraining on raw text to be beneficial. ConveRT (Henderson et al., 2020) is another model which is pretrained on dialogue data: pretraining is done on a response selection task using Reddit.

Data augmentation. Data augmentation, i.e., the creation of artificial training examples, can help in the low-resource setting. Zhang et al. (2020b) augment paired dialogue data using unlabeled data in the form of unpaired dialogue data. A dialogue pair consists of a social media post and a corresponding response. Their method starts by randomly selecting a sentence from the unpaired dataset. Then, posts that are semantically similar to the randomly selected sentence are retrieved from the paired dataset. Next, responses corresponding to the posts are collected from the paired dataset. Finally, sentences that are semantically similar to the responses are pulled from the unpaired data. Each of these newly pulled sentences are matched with the original randomly selected sentence, to create a set of candidate pairs. Those candidate pairs are then ranked, and the top-ranked pairs are saved for later use.

Other approaches differ from the aforementioned in that they do not require unlabeled data. Li et al. (2019) propose a conditional variational autoencoder as a generative data augmentation model. They combine this with a discriminator, which decides whether the generated responses are suitable for a given query. Cai et al. (2020b) design a data augmentation and instance weighting model which is trained using gradient descent and the model's performance on development examples.

6 Common Errors of Dialogue Systems

We now discuss errors common across multiple systems, considering mistakes at the turn level, the conversation level, and the system level.

Turn level. At the turn level, errors consist mostly of system responses being either *ungrammatical* or *nonsensical*. Both types of problems are more common in generative systems, as those commit errors seen in other NLG tasks, such as highly repetitive, nonsensical, or insignificant replies (Li et al., 2016a; See and Manning, 2021). Models which are motivated by semantic similarity may resort to constantly echoing the user, rather than returning a coherent response (Ritter et al., 2011; Fedorenko et al., 2018).

Conversation level. Problems arising at the conversation level are arguably more substantial than those at the turn level. Potential solutions will most likely rely heavily on advancements in other areas of NLP, such as reasoning and information extraction. A common issue consists of replies being fluent, but either not relevant in the overall context of the conversation or too generic (Adiwardana et al., 2020). Off-topic replies can often be attributed to a failure to recognize entities or previous dialogue acts. Another common problem are answers that are inconsistent across turns (Nie et al., 2021).

System level. At the system level, researchers and model developers face the difficulty of incorporating world knowledge and common sense into models (Wang et al., 2020a), as models still frequently generate responses that are factually incorrect (Mielke et al., 2020; Santhanam et al., 2021). There exists a trade-off between the range of topics a system can cover and the depth of knowledge it can leverage for any individual topic. Currently, especially comprehensive systems frequently rely heavily on curated content and static, handwritten conversation paths to talk intelligently and deeply about specific topics. However, the more a system relies on handwritten paths, the more brittle it becomes. Similarly, curated content is impossible to scale to a truly open-domain setting. Conversely, leaning more towards dynamically structured conversations gives models more flexibility and allows them to cover a wider range of topics, but often results in less meaningful responses.

7 Ethics, Bias, and Fairness

The NLP research community is becoming increasingly aware of the ethical challenges around the systems we are building, and the area of dialogue generation is no exception to this. We now summarize prior work around safety and unwanted biases.

Safety. Dialogue systems should avoid being unintentionally offensive or harming the user (Henderson et al., 2018). Therefore, attempts have been made to detect sensitive language around religion, race, violence, or contentious news as well as profanity (Tripathi et al., 2019). However, how to respond when sensitive topics are being identified is still an open question. As some of these topics shape our identities and our lives, an ideal system might not completely avoid them, and the best response strategy depends on the objectives of the system. When GPT-3 (Brown et al., 2020) and Blender (Roller et al., 2021) detect toxic language in a user utterance, they stop producing output (Xu et al., 2020). While this is an ad-hoc solution, in the long term, a graceful reaction could potentially carry the conversation to healthier places as shown by Wright et al. (2017).

Dinan et al. (2021) identify three potentially dangerous behaviors a dialogue system can exhibit: First, it can act as an *instigator* and provoke the user using negative language, as has infamously happened with the Microsoft Tay chatbot. Second, even if a system exclusively uses non-harmful language, it can cause harm to the user by being a so-called *yea-sayer*, i.e., by being overly eager to agree with the user on wrong or inappropriate statements (Lee et al., 2019; Baheti et al., 2021). Third, a dialogue system can unintentionally *impose as an expert* and provide harmful advice.

Biases. An abundance of recent work has shown that NLP models are learning undesirable biases from the data they are being trained on (Bolukbasi et al., 2016; Bordia and Bowman, 2019; Bartl et al., 2020; Shah et al., 2020). Dialogue systems are no exception to this: Liu et al. (2020a) investigate fairness in dialogue models and find that dialogue models exhibit significant prejudice against some genders and races. They propose two debiasing methods based on data augmentation and word embeddings regularization. Dinan et al. (2020b) point out that there are three types of gender bias in chat bots: the first one being due to the gender of the person that speakers are talking about, the second being due to the gender of the speaker, and the last being due to the gender of the addressee. Liu et al. (2020b) aim at mitigating the former via adversarial learning. Similarly, Dinan et al. (2020a) propose to reduce gender bias via data augmentation, targeted data collection, and bias-controlled training.

Barikeri et al. (2021) introduce RedditBias, a dataset grounded in conversations from Reddit, which enables the measurement and mitigation of gender, race, religion, and queerness bias, and use it to explore DialoGPT with and without debiasing.

8 Open Challenges for Future Research

Model evaluation and analysis. Surveying research on open-domain dialogue generation (cf. Section 4) as well as research on system evaluation (Finch and Choi, 2020), it is clear that a good automatic metric (or even manual evaluation strategy) has not yet been found. What the field needs are metrics that (1) evaluate different aspects of dialogue systems (cf. Table 1), (2) do not require references, since no reasonable set of references can contain all possibly suitable responses, and (3) correlate strongly with human judgments. One possible way to move the field towards the development of new evaluation strategies could be the establishment of a shared task on open-domain dialogue generation metrics, similar to the WMT metrics shared task (Ma et al., 2019).

Furthermore, while entire surveys are necessary to summarize work on the analysis of BERT (Rogers et al., 2020), we still know little about what dialogue systems, including DialoGPT (Zhang et al., 2020c), learn from their training data. Prior work on the analysis of dialogue models (with the exception of still non-exhaustive investigations of their biases) is limited; e.g., Saleh et al. (2020). We argue that learning more about dialogue models, which are likely to directly interact with users, is crucial. We should investigate the following: (1) What world knowledge do models acquire during training? (2) What linguistic knowledge do dialogue models learn? (3) Which potentially harmful biases do models learn from real-world data?

Multi-party dialogue. How to extend systems to handle multi-party dialogue, as posed by Seering et al. (2019), remains an underexplored area of research. Having such systems will potentially contribute to creating richer social interactions in both online and offline communities. It will further increase our understanding of the dynamics behind turn taking (Bohus and Horvitz, 2011).

Multilingual dialogue. Section 3 makes it obvious that open-domain dialogue datasets mostly exist for two high-resource languages: English and Chinese. Work on other languages is limited (e.g., Lin et al. (2020a)). We argue that, in order to speed up research on other languages, the field needs to develop datasets with the following properties: (1) datasets should be created for a diverse set of potentially low-resource languages and (2) the created datasets should not be translations of existing datasets. The latter is necessary since it has been shown for other NLP tasks that translated datasets show different properties from those natively collected in a language (Artetxe et al., 2020).

9 Conclusion

Recent years have seen a drastic improvement in the quality of open-domain dialogue systems as well as in the amount of research in the area. Therefore, we first presented an overview of the state of the field of NLP for open-domain dialogue. Then, we outlined important future challenges: better model evaluation and analysis, multi-party dialogue, and multilingual dialogue.

Acknowledgments

We thank the anonymous reviewers for their helpful feedback. We are also grateful to the members of CU Boulder's NALA group for their feedback on and input to this paper. This research was supported by the NSF National AI Institute for Student-AI Teaming (iSAT) under grant DRL 2019805. The opinions expressed are those of the authors and do not represent views of the NSF.

References

Daniel Adiwardana, Minh-Thang Luong, David R So, Jamie Hall, Noah Fiedel, Romal Thoppilan, Zi Yang, Apoorv Kulshreshtha, Gaurav Nemade, Yifeng Lu, et al. 2020. Towards a human-like open-domain chatbot. *arXiv preprint arXiv:2001.09977*.

Rami Al-Rfou, M. Pickett, Javier Snaider, Yun-Hsuan Sung, B. Strope, and R. Kurzweil. 2016. Conversational contextual cues: The case of personalization and history for response ranking. *ArXiv*, abs/1606.00372.

Mikel Artetxe, Gorka Labaka, and Eneko Agirre. 2020. Translation artifacts in cross-lingual transfer learning.

In *Proceedings of the 2020 Conference on Empirical Methods in Natural Language Processing (EMNLP)*, pages 7674–7684, Online. Association for Computational Linguistics.

Ashutosh Baheti, Maarten Sap, Alan Ritter, and Mark Riedl. 2021. Just say no: Analyzing the stance of neural dialogue generation in offensive contexts. In *Proceedings of the 2021 Conference on Empirical Methods in Natural Language Processing*, pages 4846–4862, Online and Punta Cana, Dominican Republic. Association for Computational Linguistics.

Soumya Barikeri, Anne Lauscher, Ivan Vulić, and Goran Glavaš. 2021. RedditBias: A real-world resource for bias evaluation and debiasing of conversational language models. In *Proceedings of the 59th Annual Meeting of the Association for Computational Linguistics and the 11th International Joint Conference on Natural Language Processing (Volume 1: Long Papers)*, pages 1941–1955, Online. Association for Computational Linguistics.

Marion Bartl, Malvina Nissim, and Albert Gatt. 2020. Unmasking contextual stereotypes: Measuring and mitigating BERT's gender bias. In *Proceedings of the Second Workshop on Gender Bias in Natural Language Processing*, pages 1–16, Barcelona, Spain (Online). Association for Computational Linguistics.

Dan Bohus and Eric Horvitz. 2011. Multiparty turn taking in situated dialog: Study, lessons, and directions. In *Proceedings of the SIGDIAL 2011 Conference*, pages 98–109.

Tolga Bolukbasi, Kai-Wei Chang, James Y Zou, Venkatesh Saligrama, and Adam T Kalai. 2016. Man is to computer programmer as woman is to homemaker? Debiasing word embeddings. *Advances in neural information processing systems*, 29:4349–4357.

Shikha Bordia and Samuel R. Bowman. 2019. Identifying and reducing gender bias in word-level language models. In *Proceedings of the 2019 Conference of the North American Chapter of the Association for Computational Linguistics: Student Research Workshop*, pages 7–15, Minneapolis, Minnesota. Association for Computational Linguistics.

Alex Boyd, Raul Puri, Mohammad Shoeybi, Mostofa Patwary, and Bryan Catanzaro. 2020. Large scale multi-actor generative dialog modeling. In *Proceedings of the 58th Annual Meeting of the Association for Computational Linguistics*, pages 66–84, Online. Association for Computational Linguistics.

Tom Brown, Benjamin Mann, Nick Ryder, Melanie Subbiah, Jared D Kaplan, Prafulla Dhariwal, Arvind Neelakantan, Pranav Shyam, Girish Sastry, Amanda Askell, Sandhini Agarwal, Ariel Herbert-Voss, Gretchen Krueger, Tom Henighan, Rewon Child, Aditya Ramesh, Daniel Ziegler, Jeffrey Wu, Clemens Winter, Chris Hesse, Mark Chen, Eric Sigler, Mateusz Litwin, Scott Gray, Benjamin Chess, Jack Clark, Christopher Berner, Sam McCandlish, Alec Radford, Ilya Sutskever, and Dario Amodei. 2020. Language models are few-shot learners. In *Advances in Neural Information Processing Systems*, volume 33, pages 1877–1901. Curran Associates, Inc.

Hengyi Cai, Hongshen Chen, Yonghao Song, Zhuoye Ding, Yongjun Bao, Weipeng Yan, and Xiaofang Zhao. 2020a. Group-wise contrastive learning for neural dialogue generation. In *Findings of the Association for Computational Linguistics: EMNLP 2020*, pages 793–802, Online. Association for Computational Linguistics.

Hengyi Cai, Hongshen Chen, Yonghao Song, Cheng Zhang, Xiaofang Zhao, and Dawei Yin. 2020b. Data manipulation: Towards effective instance learning for neural dialogue generation via learning to augment and reweight. In *Proceedings of the 58th Annual Meeting of the Association for Computational Linguistics*, pages 6334–6343, Online. Association for Computational Linguistics.

Hengyi Cai, Hongshen Chen, Cheng Zhang, Yonghao Song, Xiaofang Zhao, Yangxi Li, Dongsheng Duan, and Dawei Yin. 2020c. Learning from easy to complex: Adaptive multi-curricula learning for neural dialogue generation. In *Proceedings of the AAAI Conference on Artificial Intelligence*, volume 34, pages 7472–7479.

Andrew Carlson, Justin Betteridge, Bryan Kisiel, Burr Settles, Estevam R Hruschka Jr, and Tom M Mitchell. 2010. Toward an architecture for never-ending language learning. In *Proceedings of the 24th AAAI Conference on Artificial Intelligence*, pages 1306–1313.

Chun-Yen Chen, Dian Yu, Weiming Wen, Yi Mang Yang, Jiaping Zhang, Mingyang Zhou, Kevin Jesse, Austin Chau, Antara Bhowmick, Shreenath Iyer, et al. 2018. Gunrock: Building a human-like social bot by leveraging large scale real user data. *Alexa Prize Proceedings*.

Fanglin Chen, Ta-Chung Chi, Shiyang Lyu, Jianchen Gong, Tanmay Parekh, Rishabh Joshi, Anant Kaushik, and Alexander Rudnicky. 2020. Tartan: A two-tiered dialog framework for multi-domain social chitchat. *Alexa prize proceedings*.

Tao Chen and Min-Yen Kan. 2013. Creating a live, public short message service corpus: the nus sms corpus. *Language Resources and Evaluation*, 47(2):299–335.

Kevin Clark, Minh-Thang Luong, Quoc V. Le, and Christopher D. Manning. 2020. ELECTRA: Pretraining text encoders as discriminators rather than generators. In *International Conference on Learning Representations*.

Kenneth Mark Colby. 1975. *Artificial Paranoia: A Computer Simulation of Paranoid Processes*. Elsevier Science Inc.

Sumanth Dathathri, Andrea Madotto, Janice Lan, Jane Hung, Eric Frank, Piero Molino, Jason Yosinski, and Rosanne Liu. 2020. Plug and play language models: A simple approach to controlled text generation. In *International Conference on Learning Representations*.

Jan Deriu, Don Tuggener, Pius von Däniken, Jon Ander Campos, Alvaro Rodrigo, Thiziri Belkacem, Aitor Soroa, Eneko Agirre, and Mark Cieliebak. 2020. Spot the bot: A robust and efficient framework for the evaluation of conversational dialogue systems. In *Proceedings of the 2020 Conference on Empirical Methods in Natural Language Processing (EMNLP)*, pages 3971–3984, Online. Association for Computational Linguistics.

Jacob Devlin, Ming-Wei Chang, Kenton Lee, and Kristina Toutanova. 2019. BERT: Pre-training of deep bidirectional transformers for language understanding. In *Proceedings of the 2019 Conference of the North American Chapter of the Association for Computational Linguistics: Human Language Technologies, Volume 1 (Long and Short Papers)*, pages 4171–4186, Minneapolis, Minnesota. Association for Computational Linguistics.

Emily Dinan, Gavin Abercrombie, A Stevie Bergman, Shannon Spruit, Dirk Hovy, Y-Lan Boureau, and Verena Rieser. 2021. Anticipating safety issues in E2E conversational AI: Framework and tooling. *arXiv preprint arXiv:2107.03451*.

Emily Dinan, Angela Fan, Adina Williams, Jack Urbanek, Douwe Kiela, and Jason Weston. 2020a. Queens are powerful too: Mitigating gender bias in dialogue generation. In *Proceedings of the 2020 Conference on Empirical Methods in Natural Language Processing (EMNLP)*, pages 8173–8188, Online. Association for Computational Linguistics.

Emily Dinan, Angela Fan, Ledell Wu, Jason Weston, Douwe Kiela, and Adina Williams. 2020b. Multi-dimensional gender bias classification. In *Proceedings of the 2020 Conference on Empirical Methods in Natural Language Processing (EMNLP)*, pages 314–331, Online. Association for Computational Linguistics.

Emily Dinan, Stephen Roller, Kurt Shuster, Angela Fan, Michael Auli, and Jason Weston. 2019. Wizard of Wikipedia: Knowledge-powered conversational agents. In *International Conference on Learning Representations*.

Nouha Dziri, Andrea Madotto, Osmar Zaïane, and Avishek Joey Bose. 2021. Neural path hunter: Reducing hallucination in dialogue systems via path grounding. In *Proceedings of the 2021 Conference on Empirical Methods in Natural Language Processing*, pages 2197–2214, Online and Punta Cana, Dominican Republic. Association for Computational Linguistics.

Hao Fang, Hao Cheng, Elizabeth Clark, Ariel Holtzman, Maarten Sap, Mari Ostendorf, Yejin Choi, and Noah A Smith. 2017. Sounding board–university of washington's alexa prize submission. *Alexa prize proceedings*.

Denis Fedorenko, Nikita Smetanin, and Artem Rodichev. 2018. Avoiding echo-responses in a retrieval-based conversation system. In *Conference on Artificial Intelligence and Natural Language*, pages 91–97. Springer.

Sarah E. Finch and Jinho D. Choi. 2020. Towards unified dialogue system evaluation: A comprehensive analysis of current evaluation protocols. In *Proceedings of the 21th Annual Meeting of the Special Interest Group on Discourse and Dialogue*, pages 236–245, 1st virtual meeting. Association for Computational Linguistics.

Sarah E. Finch, James D. Finch, Ali Ahmadvand, Ingyu, Choi, Xiangjue Dong, Ruixiang Qi, Harshita Sahijwani, Sergey Volokhin, Zihan Wang, Zihao Wang, and Jinho D. Choi. 2020. Emora: An inquisitive social chatbot who cares for you.

Xiang Gao, Yizhe Zhang, Michel Galley, Chris Brockett, and Bill Dolan. 2020. Dialogue response ranking training with large-scale human feedback data. In *Proceedings of the 2020 Conference on Empirical Methods in Natural Language Processing (EMNLP)*, pages 386–395, Online. Association for Computational Linguistics.

Marjan Ghazvininejad, Chris Brockett, Ming-Wei Chang, Bill Dolan, Jianfeng Gao, Wen-tau Yih, and Michel Galley. 2017. A knowledge-grounded neural conversation model. *arXiv preprint arXiv:1702.01932*.

J. J. Godfrey, E. C. Holliman, and J. McDaniel. 1992. Switchboard: telephone speech corpus for research and development. In *[Proceedings] ICASSP-92: 1992 IEEE International Conference on Acoustics, Speech, and Signal Processing*, volume 1, pages 517–520 vol.1.

Karthik Gopalakrishnan, Behnam Hedayatnia, Q. Chen, Anna Gottardi, Sanjeev Kwatra, Anu Venkatesh, R. Gabriel, and D. Hakkani-Tur. 2019. Topical-chat: Towards knowledge-grounded open-domain conversations. In *INTERSPEECH*.

Jia-Chen Gu, Tianda Li, Quan Liu, Zhen-Hua Ling, Zhiming Su, Si Wei, and Xiaodan Zhu. 2020. Speaker-aware bert for multi-turn response selection in retrieval-based chatbots. In *Proceedings of the 29th ACM International Conference on Information & Knowledge Management*, pages 2041–2044.

Jia-Chen Gu, Zhen-Hua Ling, and Quan Liu. 2019a. Interactive matching network for multi-turn response selection in retrieval-based chatbots. In *Proceedings of the 28th ACM International Conference on Information and Knowledge Management*, CIKM '19, page 2321–2324, New York, NY, USA. Association for Computing Machinery.

Jia-Chen Gu, Zhen-Hua Ling, Xiaodan Zhu, and Quan Liu. 2019b. Dually interactive matching network for personalized response selection in retrieval-based chatbots. In *Proceedings of the 2019 Conference on Empirical Methods in Natural Language Processing and the 9th International Joint Conference on Natural Language Processing (EMNLP-IJCNLP)*, pages 1845–1854, Hong Kong, China. Association for Computational Linguistics.

Michael U Gutmann and Aapo Hyvärinen. 2012. Noise-contrastive estimation of unnormalized statistical models, with applications to natural image statistics. *Journal of Machine Learning Research*, 13(2).

Raia Hadsell, Sumit Chopra, and Yann LeCun. 2006. Dimensionality reduction by learning an invariant mapping. In *2006 IEEE Computer Society Conference on Computer Vision and Pattern Recognition (CVPR'06)*, volume 2, pages 1735–1742. IEEE.

Vrindavan Harrison, Juraj Juraska, Wen Cui, Lena Reed, Kevin K. Bowden, Jiaqi Wu, Brian Schwarzmann, Abteen Ebrahimi, Rishi Rajasekaran, Nikhil Varghese, Max Wechsler-Azen, Steve Whittaker, Jeffrey Flanigan, and Marilyn Walker. 2020. Athena: Constructing dialogues dynamically with discourse constraints. *Alexa prize proceedings*.

Matthew Henderson, Iñigo Casanueva, Nikola Mrkšić, Pei-Hao Su, Tsung-Hsien Wen, and Ivan Vulić. 2020. ConveRT: Efficient and accurate conversational representations from transformers. In *Findings of the Association for Computational Linguistics: EMNLP 2020*, pages 2161–2174, Online. Association for Computational Linguistics.

Peter Henderson, Koustuv Sinha, Nicolas Angelard-Gontier, Nan Rosemary Ke, Genevieve Fried, Ryan Lowe, and Joelle Pineau. 2018. Ethical challenges in data-driven dialogue systems. In *Proceedings of the 2018 AAAI/ACM Conference on AI, Ethics, and Society*, pages 123–129.

Chung Hoon Hong, Yuan Liang, Sagnik Sinha Roy, Arushi Jain, Vihang Agarwal, Ryan Draves, Zhizhou Zhou, William Chen, Yujian Liu, Martha Miracky, Lily Ge, Nikola Banovic, and David Jurgens. 2020. Audrey: A personalized open-domain conversational bot. *Alexa prize proceedings*.

Cheng-Hsun Hsueh and Wei-Yun Ma. 2020. Semantic guidance of dialogue generation with reinforcement learning. In *Proceedings of the 21th Annual Meeting of the Special Interest Group on Discourse and Dialogue*, pages 1–9, 1st virtual meeting. Association for Computational Linguistics.

Minlie Huang, Xiaoyan Zhu, and Jianfeng Gao. 2020. Challenges in building intelligent open-domain dialog systems. *ACM Trans. Inf. Syst.*, 38(3).

Zongcheng Ji, Zhengdong Lu, and Hang Li. 2014. An information retrieval approach to short text conversation. *arXiv preprint arXiv:1408.6988*.

Nitish Shirish Keskar, Bryan McCann, Lav R Varshney, Caiming Xiong, and Richard Socher. 2019. Ctrl: A conditional transformer language model for controllable generation. *arXiv preprint arXiv:1909.05858*.

San Kim, Jin Yea Jang, Minyoung Jung, and Saim Shin. 2021. A model of cross-lingual knowledge-grounded response generation for open-domain dialogue systems. In *Findings of the Association for Computational Linguistics: EMNLP 2021*, pages 352–365, Punta Cana, Dominican Republic. Association for Computational Linguistics.

Yuri Kuratov, Idris Yusupov, Dilyara Baymurzina, Denis Kuznetsov, Daniil Cherniavskii, Alexander Dmitrievskiy, Elena Ermakova, Fedor Ignatov, Dmitry Karpov, Daniel Kornev, The Anh Le, Pavel Pugin, and Mikhail Burtsev. 2020. Dream technical report for the alexa prize 2019. *Alexa prize proceedings*.

Nayeon Lee, Andrea Madotto, and Pascale Fung. 2019. Exploring social bias in chatbots using stereotype knowledge. In *Proceedings of the 2019 Workshop on Widening NLP*, pages 177–180.

Jiwei Li, Michel Galley, Chris Brockett, Jianfeng Gao, and Bill Dolan. 2016a. A diversity-promoting objective function for neural conversation models. In *Proceedings of the 2016 Conference of the North American Chapter of the Association for Computational Linguistics: Human Language Technologies*, pages 110–119, San Diego, California. Association for Computational Linguistics.

Jiwei Li, Michel Galley, Chris Brockett, Georgios Spithourakis, Jianfeng Gao, and Bill Dolan. 2016b. A persona-based neural conversation model. In *Proceedings of the 54th Annual Meeting of the Association for Computational Linguistics (Volume 1: Long Papers)*, pages 994–1003, Berlin, Germany. Association for Computational Linguistics.

Jiwei Li, Will Monroe, Alan Ritter, Dan Jurafsky, Michel Galley, and Jianfeng Gao. 2016c. Deep reinforcement learning for dialogue generation. In *Proceedings of the 2016 Conference on Empirical Methods in Natural Language Processing*, pages 1192–1202, Austin, Texas. Association for Computational Linguistics.

Jiwei Li, Will Monroe, Tianlin Shi, Sébastien Jean, Alan Ritter, and Dan Jurafsky. 2017a. Adversarial learning for neural dialogue generation. In *Proceedings of the 2017 Conference on Empirical Methods in Natural Language Processing*, pages 2157–2169, Copenhagen, Denmark. Association for Computational Linguistics.

Juntao Li, Lisong Qiu, Bo Tang, Dongmin Chen, Dongyan Zhao, and Rui Yan. 2019. Insufficient data can also rock! learning to converse using smaller data with augmentation. In *Proceedings of the AAAI Conference on Artificial Intelligence*, volume 33, pages 6698–6705.

Qintong Li, Piji Li, Zhumin Chen, and Zhaochun Ren. 2020a. Empathetic dialogue generation via knowledge enhancing and emotion dependency modeling.

Xin Li, Piji Li, Yan Wang, Xiaojiang Liu, and Wai Lam. 2020b. Enhancing dialogue generation via multi-level contrastive learning. *arXiv preprint arXiv:2009.09147*.

Yanran Li, Hui Su, Xiaoyu Shen, Wenjie Li, Ziqiang Cao, and Shuzi Niu. 2017b. DailyDialog: A manually labelled multi-turn dialogue dataset. In *Proceedings of the Eighth International Joint Conference on Natural Language Processing (Volume 1: Long Papers)*, pages 986–995, Taipei, Taiwan. Asian Federation of Natural Language Processing.

Yu Li, Kun Qian, Weiyan Shi, and Zhou Yu. 2020c. End-to-end trainable non-collaborative dialog system. *Proceedings of the AAAI Conference on Artificial Intelligence*, 34(05):8293–8302.

Kaihui Liang, Austin Chau, Yu Li, Xueyuan Lu, Dian Yu, Mingyang Zhou, Ishan Jain, Sam Davidson, Josh Arnold, Minh Nguyen, and Zhou Yu. 2020. Gunrock 2.0: A user adaptive social conversational system. *Alexa prize proceedings*.

Zhaojiang Lin, Zihan Liu, Genta Indra Winata, Samuel Cahyawijaya, Andrea Madotto, Yejin Bang, Etsuko Ishii, and Pascale Fung. 2020a. Xpersona: Evaluating multilingual personalized chatbot. *arXiv preprint arXiv:2003.07568*.

Zibo Lin, Deng Cai, Yan Wang, Xiaojiang Liu, Haitao Zheng, and Shuming Shi. 2020b. The world is not binary: Learning to rank with grayscale data for dialogue response selection. In *Proceedings of the 2020 Conference on Empirical Methods in Natural Language Processing (EMNLP)*, pages 9220–9229, Online. Association for Computational Linguistics.

Chia-Wei Liu, Ryan Lowe, Iulian Serban, Mike Noseworthy, Laurent Charlin, and Joelle Pineau. 2016. How NOT to evaluate your dialogue system: An empirical study of unsupervised evaluation metrics for dialogue response generation. In *Proceedings of the 2016 Conference on Empirical Methods in Natural Language Processing*, pages 2122–2132, Austin, Texas. Association for Computational Linguistics.

Haochen Liu, Jamell Dacon, Wenqi Fan, Hui Liu, Zitao Liu, and Jiliang Tang. 2020a. Does gender matter? Towards fairness in dialogue systems. In *Proceedings of the 28th International Conference on Computational Linguistics*, pages 4403–4416, Barcelona, Spain (Online). International Committee on Computational Linguistics.

Haochen Liu, Wentao Wang, Yiqi Wang, Hui Liu, Zitao Liu, and Jiliang Tang. 2020b. Mitigating gender bias for neural dialogue generation with adversarial learning. In *Proceedings of the 2020 Conference on Empirical Methods in Natural Language Processing (EMNLP)*, pages 893–903, Online. Association for Computational Linguistics.

Qian Liu, Yihong Chen, Bei Chen, Jian-Guang Lou, Zixuan Chen, Bin Zhou, and Dongmei Zhang. 2020c. You impress me: Dialogue generation via mutual persona perception. In *Proceedings of the 58th Annual Meeting of the Association for Computational Linguistics*, pages 1417–1427, Online. Association for Computational Linguistics.

Junyu Lu, Chenbin Zhang, Zeying Xie, Guang Ling, Tom Chao Zhou, and Zenglin Xu. 2019. Constructing interpretive spatio-temporal features for multi-turn responses selection. In *Proceedings of the 57th Annual Meeting of the Association for Computational Linguistics*, pages 44–50.

Zhengdong Lu and Hang Li. 2013. A deep architecture for matching short texts. In *Advances in neural information processing systems*, pages 1367–1375.

Liangchen Luo, Jingjing Xu, Junyang Lin, Qi Zeng, and Xu Sun. 2018. An auto-encoder matching model for learning utterance-level semantic dependency in dialogue generation. In *Proceedings of the 2018 Conference on Empirical Methods in Natural Language Processing*, pages 702–707, Brussels, Belgium. Association for Computational Linguistics.

Qingsong Ma, Johnny Wei, Ondřej Bojar, and Yvette Graham. 2019. Results of the WMT19 metrics shared task: Segment-level and strong MT systems pose big challenges. In *Proceedings of the Fourth Conference on Machine Translation (Volume 2: Shared Task Papers, Day 1)*, pages 62–90, Florence, Italy. Association for Computational Linguistics.

Andrea Madotto, Zhaojiang Lin, Yejin Bang, and Pascale Fung. 2020. The adapter-bot: All-in-one controllable conversational model.

Bodhisattwa Prasad Majumder, Shuyang Li, Jianmo Ni, Huanru Henry Mao, Sophia Sun, and Julian McAuley. 2020. Bernard: A stateful neural open-domain socialbot. *Alexa prize proceedings*.

Yuxian Meng, Shuhe Wang, Qinghong Han, Xiaofei Sun, Fei Wu, Rui Yan, and Jiwei Li. 2020. Openvidial: A large-scale, open-domain dialogue dataset with visual contexts. *arXiv preprint arXiv:2012.15015*.

Sabrina J Mielke, Arthur Szlam, Y-Lan Boureau, and Emily Dinan. 2020. Linguistic calibration through metacognition: aligning dialogue agent responses with expected correctness. *arXiv preprint arXiv:2012.14983*.

Seungwhan Moon, Pararth Shah, Anuj Kumar, and Rajen Subba. 2019. OpenDialKG: Explainable conversational reasoning with attention-based walks over knowledge graphs. In *Proceedings of the 57th Annual Meeting of the Association for Computational Linguistics*, pages 845–854, Florence, Italy. Association for Computational Linguistics.

Yixin Nie, Mary Williamson, Mohit Bansal, Douwe Kiela, and Jason Weston. 2021. I like fish, especially dolphins: Addressing contradictions in dialogue modeling. In *Proceedings of the 59th Annual Meeting of the Association for Computational Linguistics and the 11th International Joint Conference on Natural Language Processing (Volume 1: Long Papers)*, pages 1699–1713, Online. Association for Computational Linguistics.

Kishore Papineni, Salim Roukos, Todd Ward, and Wei-Jing Zhu. 2002. Bleu: a method for automatic evaluation of machine translation. In *Proceedings of the 40th Annual Meeting of the Association for Computational Linguistics*, pages 311–318, Philadelphia, Pennsylvania, USA. Association for Computational Linguistics.

Ashwin Paranjape, Abigail See, Kathleen Kenealy, Haojun Li, Amelia Hardy, Peng Qi, Kaushik Ram Sadagopan, Nguyet Minh Phu, Dilara Soylu, and Christopher D. Manning. 2020. Neural generation meets real people: Towards emotionally engaging mixed-initiative conversations.

Prasanna Parthasarathi and Joelle Pineau. 2018. Extending neural generative conversational model using external knowledge sources. *arXiv preprint arXiv:1809.05524*.

Jan Pichl, Petr Marek, Jakub Konrad, Petr Lorenc, Van Duy Ta, and Jan Sedivy. 2020. Alquist 3.0: Alexa prize bot using conversational knowledge graph. *Alexa prize proceedings*.

Hongjin Qian, Xiaohe Li, Hanxun Zhong, Yu Guo, Yueyuan Ma, Yutao Zhu, Zhanliang Liu, Zhicheng Dou, and Ji-Rong Wen. 2021. Pchatbot: A large-scale dataset for personalized chatbot. In *Proceedings of the 44th International ACM SIGIR Conference on Research and Development in Information Retrieval*, page 2470–2477, New York, NY, USA. Association for Computing Machinery.

Lianhui Qin, Michel Galley, Chris Brockett, Xiaodong Liu, Xiang Gao, W. Dolan, Yejin Choi, and Jianfeng Gao. 2019. Conversing by reading: Contentful neural conversation with on-demand machine reading. *ArXiv*, abs/1906.02738.

Alec Radford, Karthik Narasimhan, Tim Salimans, and Ilya Sutskever. 2018. Improving language understanding by generative pre-training.

Alec Radford, Jeffrey Wu, Rewon Child, David Luan, Dario Amodei, and Ilya Sutskever. 2019. Language models are unsupervised multitask learners. *OpenAI Blog*, 1(8):9.

A. Ram, Rohit Prasad, C. Khatri, Anu Venkatesh, R. Gabriel, Q. Liu, J. Nunn, Behnam Hedayatnia, Ming Cheng, Ashish Nagar, E. King, Kate Bland, Amanda Wartick, Yi Pan, Han Song, Sk Jayadevan, Gene Hwang, and Art Pettigrue. 2018a. Conversational ai: The science behind the alexa prize. *ArXiv*, abs/1801.03604.

Ashwin Ram, Rohit Prasad, Chandra Khatri, Anu Venkatesh, Raefer Gabriel, Qing Liu, Jeff Nunn, Behnam Hedayatnia, Ming Cheng, Ashish Nagar, et al. 2018b. Conversational AI: The science behind the Alexa prize. *arXiv preprint arXiv:1801.03604*.

Hannah Rashkin, Eric Michael Smith, Margaret Li, and Y-Lan Boureau. 2019. Towards empathetic open-domain conversation models: A new benchmark and dataset. In *Proceedings of the 57th Annual Meeting of the Association for Computational Linguistics*, pages 5370–5381, Florence, Italy. Association for Computational Linguistics.

Alan Ritter, Colin Cherry, and Bill Dolan. 2010. Unsupervised modeling of Twitter conversations. In *Human Language Technologies: The 2010 Annual Conference of the North American Chapter of the Association for Computational Linguistics*, pages 172–180, Los Angeles, California. Association for Computational Linguistics.

Alan Ritter, Colin Cherry, and William B. Dolan. 2011. Data-driven response generation in social media. In *Proceedings of the 2011 Conference on Empirical Methods in Natural Language Processing*, pages 583–593, Edinburgh, Scotland, UK. Association for Computational Linguistics.

Anna Rogers, Olga Kovaleva, and Anna Rumshisky. 2020. A primer in BERTology: What we know about how BERT works. *Transactions of the Association for Computational Linguistics*, 8:842–866.

Stephen Roller, Emily Dinan, Naman Goyal, Da Ju, Mary Williamson, Yinhan Liu, Jing Xu, Myle Ott, Eric Michael Smith, Y-Lan Boureau, and Jason Weston. 2021. Recipes for building an open-domain chatbot. In *Proceedings of the 16th Conference of the European Chapter of the Association for Computational Linguistics: Main Volume*, pages 300–325, Online. Association for Computational Linguistics.

Abdelrhman Saleh, Tovly Deutsch, Stephen Casper, Yonatan Belinkov, and Stuart Shieber. 2020. Probing neural dialog models for conversational understanding. In *Proceedings of the 2nd Workshop on Natural Language Processing for Conversational AI*, pages 132–143, Online. Association for Computational Linguistics.

Chinnadhurai Sankar and Sujith Ravi. 2019. Deep reinforcement learning for modeling chit-chat dialog with discrete attributes. *arXiv preprint arXiv:1907.02848*.

Sashank Santhanam, Behnam Hedayatnia, Spandana Gella, Aishwarya Padmakumar, Seokhwan Kim, Yang Liu, and Dilek Hakkani-Tur. 2021. Rome was built in 1776: A case study on factual correctness in knowledge-grounded response generation. *arXiv preprint arXiv:2110.05456*.

William Schallock, Daniel Agress, Yao Du, Dheeru Dua, Lyuyang Hu, Yoshitomo Matsubara, and Sameer Singh. 2020. Zotbot: Using reading comprehension and commonsense reasoning in conversational agents. *Alexa prize proceedings*.

Thijs Scheepers. 2017. *Improving the compositionality of word embeddings*. Ph.D. thesis, Master's thesis, Universiteit van Amsterdam.

Abigail See and Christopher Manning. 2021. Understanding and predicting user dissatisfaction in a neural generative chatbot. In *Proceedings of the 22nd Annual Meeting of the Special Interest Group on Discourse and Dialogue*, pages 1–12, Singapore and Online. Association for Computational Linguistics.

Joseph Seering, Michal Luria, Geoff Kaufman, and Jessica Hammer. 2019. Beyond dyadic interactions: Considering chatbots as community members. In *Proceedings of the 2019 CHI Conference on Human Factors in Computing Systems*, pages 1–13.

Iulian Serban, Alessandro Sordoni, Ryan Lowe, Laurent Charlin, Joelle Pineau, Aaron Courville, and Yoshua Bengio. 2017. A hierarchical latent variable encoder-decoder model for generating dialogues. *Proceedings of the AAAI Conference on Artificial Intelligence*, 31(1).

Iulian Vlad Serban, Ryan Lowe, Peter Henderson, Laurent Charlin, and Joelle Pineau. 2015. A survey of available corpora for building data-driven dialogue systems. *arXiv preprint arXiv:1512.05742*.

Deven Santosh Shah, H. Andrew Schwartz, and Dirk Hovy. 2020. Predictive biases in natural language processing models: A conceptual framework and overview. In *Proceedings of the 58th Annual Meeting of the Association for Computational Linguistics*, pages 5248–5264, Online. Association for Computational Linguistics.

Lifeng Shang, Zhengdong Lu, and Hang Li. 2015. Neural responding machine for short-text conversation. In *Proceedings of the 53rd Annual Meeting of the Association for Computational Linguistics and the 7th International Joint Conference on Natural Language Processing (Volume 1: Long Papers)*, pages 1577–1586, Beijing, China. Association for Computational Linguistics.

Mingyue Shang, Zhenxin Fu, Nanyun Peng, Yansong Feng, Dongyan Zhao, and Rui Yan. 2018. Learning to converse with noisy data: Generation with calibration. In *Proceedings of the Twenty-Seventh International Joint Conference on Artificial Intelligence, IJCAI-18*, pages 4338–4344. International Joint Conferences on Artificial Intelligence Organization.

Nuobei Shi, Qin Zeng, and Raymond Lee. 2020. The design and implementation of language learning chatbot with xai using ontology and transfer learning.

Kurt Shuster, Samuel Humeau, Antoine Bordes, and Jason Weston. 2020. Image-chat: Engaging grounded conversations. In *Proceedings of the 58th Annual Meeting of the Association for Computational Linguistics*, pages 2414–2429, Online. Association for Computational Linguistics.

Kurt Shuster, Eric Michael Smith, Da Ju, and Jason Weston. 2021. Multi-modal open-domain dialogue. In *Proceedings of the 2021 Conference on Empirical Methods in Natural Language Processing*, pages 4863–4883, Online and Punta Cana, Dominican Republic. Association for Computational Linguistics.

Haoyu Song, Yan Wang, Wei-Nan Zhang, Zhengyu Zhao, Ting Liu, and Xiaojiang Liu. 2020. Profile consistency identification for open-domain dialogue agents. In *Proceedings of the 2020 Conference on Empirical Methods in Natural Language Processing (EMNLP)*, pages 6651–6662, Online. Association for Computational Linguistics.

Alessandro Sordoni, Michel Galley, Michael Auli, Chris Brockett, Yangfeng Ji, Margaret Mitchell, Jian-Yun Nie, Jianfeng Gao, and Bill Dolan. 2015. A neural network approach to context-sensitive generation of conversational responses. In *Proceedings of the 2015 Conference of the North American Chapter of the Association for Computational Linguistics: Human Language Technologies*, pages 196–205, Denver, Colorado. Association for Computational Linguistics.

Jianheng Tang, Tiancheng Zhao, Chenyan Xiong, Xiaodan Liang, Eric Xing, and Zhiting Hu. 2019. Target-guided open-domain conversation. In *Proceedings of the 57th Annual Meeting of the Association for Computational Linguistics*, pages 5624–5634, Florence, Italy. Association for Computational Linguistics.

Chongyang Tao, Wei Wu, Can Xu, Wenpeng Hu, Dongyan Zhao, and Rui Yan. 2019. One time of interaction may not be enough: Go deep with an interaction-over-interaction network for response selection in dialogues. In *Proceedings of the 57th Annual Meeting of the Association for Computational Linguistics*, pages 1–11, Florence, Italy. Association for Computational Linguistics.

Rahul Tripathi, Balaji Dhamodharaswamy, Srinivasan Jagannathan, and Abhishek Nandi. 2019. Detecting sensitive content in spoken language. In *2019 IEEE International Conference on Data Science and Advanced Analytics (DSAA)*, pages 374–381. IEEE.

Yi-Lin Tuan, Yun-Nung Chen, and Hung-yi Lee. 2019. DyKgChat: Benchmarking dialogue generation grounding on dynamic knowledge graphs. In *Proceedings of the 2019 Conference on Empirical Methods in Natural Language Processing and the 9th International Joint Conference on Natural Language Processing (EMNLP-IJCNLP)*, pages 1855–1865, Hong Kong, China. Association for Computational Linguistics.

Ashish Vaswani, Noam Shazeer, Niki Parmar, Jakob Uszkoreit, Llion Jones, Aidan N Gomez, Lukasz Kaiser, and Illia Polosukhin. 2017. Attention is all you need. In *Advances in Neural Information Processing Systems 30*, pages 5998–6008.

Oriol Vinyals and Quoc Le. 2015. A neural conversational model. *arXiv preprint arXiv:1506.05869*.

Richard Wallace. 1995. Alice - artificial linguistic internet computer entity. https://web.archive.org/web/20171227223848/http://www.alicebot.org/.

Hao Wang, Zhengdong Lu, Hang Li, and Enhong Chen. 2013. A dataset for research on short-text conversations. In *Proceedings of the 2013 Conference on Empirical Methods in Natural Language Processing*, pages 935–945, Seattle, Washington, USA. Association for Computational Linguistics.

J. Wang, Junhao Liu, Wei Bi, Xiaojiang Liu, Kejing He, Ruifeng Xu, and Min Yang. 2020a. Improving knowledge-aware dialogue generation via knowledge base question answering. In *AAAI*.

Mingxuan Wang, Zhengdong Lu, Hang Li, and Qun Liu. 2015. Syntax-based deep matching of short texts. *arXiv preprint arXiv:1503.02427*.

Xuewei Wang, Weiyan Shi, Richard Kim, Yoojung Oh, Sijia Yang, Jingwen Zhang, and Zhou Yu. 2020b. Persuasion for good: Towards a personalized persuasive dialogue system for social good.

Joseph Weizenbaum. 1966. Eliza—a computer program for the study of natural language communication between man and machine. *Communications of the ACM*, 9(1):36–45.

Jason Weston, Emily Dinan, and Alexander Miller. 2018. Retrieve and refine: Improved sequence generation models for dialogue. In *Proceedings of the 2018 EMNLP Workshop SCAI: The 2nd International Workshop on Search-Oriented Conversational AI*, pages 87–92, Brussels, Belgium. Association for Computational Linguistics.

Taesun Whang, Dongyub Lee, Dongsuk Oh, Chanhee Lee, Kijong Han, Dong hun Lee, and Saebyeok Lee. 2020. Do response selection models really know what's next? utterance manipulation strategies for multi-turn response selection.

Lucas Wright, Derek Ruths, Kelly P Dillon, Haji Mohammad Saleem, and Susan Benesch. 2017. Vectors for counterspeech on Twitter. In *Proceedings of the First Workshop on Abusive Language Online*, pages 57–62, Vancouver, BC, Canada. Association for Computational Linguistics.

Wenquan Wu, Zhen Guo, Xiangyang Zhou, Hua Wu, Xiyuan Zhang, Rongzhong Lian, and Haifeng Wang. 2019. Proactive human-machine conversation with explicit conversation goal. In *Proceedings of the 57th Annual Meeting of the Association for Computational Linguistics*, pages 3794–3804, Florence, Italy. Association for Computational Linguistics.

Yu Wu, Wei Wu, Chen Xing, Ming Zhou, and Zhoujun Li. 2017. Sequential matching network: A new architecture for multi-turn response selection in retrieval-based chatbots. In *Proceedings of the 55th Annual Meeting of the Association for Computational Linguistics (Volume 1: Long Papers)*, pages 496–505, Vancouver, Canada. Association for Computational Linguistics.

Jing Xu, Da Ju, Margaret Li, Y-Lan Boureau, Jason Weston, and Emily Dinan. 2020. Recipes for safety in open-domain chatbots. *arXiv preprint arXiv:2010.07079*.

Rui Yan, Yiping Song, and Hua Wu. 2016. Learning to respond with deep neural networks for retrieval-based human-computer conversation system. In *Proceedings of the 39th International ACM SIGIR conference on Research and Development in Information Retrieval*, pages 55–64.

Chunyuan Yuan, Wei Zhou, Mingming Li, Shangwen Lv, Fuqing Zhu, Jizhong Han, and Songlin Hu. 2019. Multi-hop selector network for multi-turn response selection in retrieval-based chatbots. In *Proceedings of the 2019 Conference on Empirical Methods in Natural Language Processing and the 9th International Joint Conference on Natural Language Processing (EMNLP-IJCNLP)*, pages 111–120.

Hainan Zhang, Yanyan Lan, Jiafeng Guo, Jun Xu, and Xueqi Cheng. 2018a. Reinforcing coherence for sequence to sequence model in dialogue generation. In *Proceedings of the Twenty-Seventh International Joint Conference on Artificial Intelligence, IJCAI-18*, pages 4567–4573. International Joint Conferences on Artificial Intelligence Organization.

Hainan Zhang, Yanyan Lan, Liang Pang, Hongshen Chen, Zhuoye Ding, and Dawei Yin. 2020a. Modeling topical relevance for multi-turn dialogue generation. In *Proceedings of the Twenty-Ninth International Joint Conference on Artificial Intelligence, IJCAI-20*, pages 3737–3743. International Joint Conferences on Artificial Intelligence Organization.

Rongsheng Zhang, Yinhe Zheng, Jianzhi Shao, Xiaoxi Mao, Yadong Xi, and Minlie Huang. 2020b. Dialogue distillation: Open-domain dialogue augmentation using unpaired data. In *Proceedings of the 2020 Conference on Empirical Methods in Natural Language Processing (EMNLP)*, pages 3449–3460, Online. Association for Computational Linguistics.

Saizheng Zhang, Emily Dinan, Jack Urbanek, Arthur Szlam, Douwe Kiela, and Jason Weston. 2018b. Personalizing dialogue agents: I have a dog, do you have pets too? In *Proceedings of the 56th Annual Meeting of the Association for Computational Linguistics (Volume 1: Long Papers)*, pages 2204–2213, Melbourne, Australia. Association for Computational Linguistics.

Yizhe Zhang, Siqi Sun, Michel Galley, Yen-Chun Chen, Chris Brockett, Xiang Gao, Jianfeng Gao, Jingjing Liu, and Bill Dolan. 2020c. DIALOGPT: Large-scale generative pre-training for conversational response generation. In *Proceedings of the 58th Annual Meeting of the Association for Computational Linguistics: System Demonstrations*, pages 270–278, Online. Association for Computational Linguistics.

Zhuosheng Zhang, Jiangtong Li, Pengfei Zhu, Hai Zhao, and Gongshen Liu. 2018c. Modeling multi-turn conversation with deep utterance aggregation. In *Proceedings of the 27th International Conference on Computational Linguistics*, pages 3740–3752, Santa Fe, New Mexico, USA. Association for Computational Linguistics.

Tianyu Zhao and Tatsuya Kawahara. 2020. Multi-referenced training for dialogue response generation. *arXiv preprint arXiv:2009.07117*.

Yinhe Zheng, Guanyi Chen, Minlie Huang, Song Liu, and Xuan Zhu. 2019. Personalized dialogue generation with diversified traits. *arXiv preprint arXiv:1901.09672*.

Yinhe Zheng, Guanyi Chen, Xin Liu, and Ke Lin. 2021a. MMChat: Multi-modal chat dataset on social media. *arXiv preprint arXiv:2108.07154*.

Yinhe Zheng, Zikai Chen, Rongsheng Zhang, Shilei Huang, Xiaoxi Mao, and Minlie Huang. 2021b. Stylized dialogue response generation using stylized unpaired texts. *Proceedings of the AAAI Conference on Artificial Intelligence*, 35(16):14558–14567.

Kangyan Zhou, Shrimai Prabhumoye, and Alan W Black. 2018. A dataset for document grounded conversations. In *Proceedings of the 2018 Conference on Empirical Methods in Natural Language Processing*, pages 708–713, Brussels, Belgium. Association for Computational Linguistics.

Li Zhou, Jianfeng Gao, Di Li, and Heung-Yeung Shum. 2020. The design and implementation of xiaoice, an empathetic social chatbot. *Computational Linguistics*, 46(1):53–93.

Xiangyang Zhou, Daxiang Dong, Hua Wu, Shiqi Zhao, Dianhai Yu, Hao Tian, Xuan Liu, and Rui Yan. 2016. Multi-view response selection for human-computer conversation. In *Proceedings of the 2016 Conference on Empirical Methods in Natural Language Processing*, pages 372–381, Austin, Texas. Association for Computational Linguistics.

A Overview of Existing Datasets

Dataset Name	Paper	Language	Method	Source
KvPI	Song et al. (2020)	zh	Scraped	Weibo
PChatbot	Qian et al. (2021)	zh	Scraped	Weibo, Judicial
Douban	Wu et al. (2017)	zh	Scraped	Douban, Weibo
E-commerce	Zhang et al. (2018c)	zh	Scraped	Taobao
Weibo	Wang et al. (2013)	zh	Scraped	Weibo
PersonalDialog	Zheng et al. (2019)	zh	Scraped	Weibo
DuConv	Wu et al. (2019)	zh	Human-Human	-
Short Text Conversation	Shang et al. (2015)	zh	Scraped	Weibo
Switchboard	Godfrey et al. (1992)	en	Human-Human	-
Twitter Dataset	Ritter et al. (2010)	en	Scraped	Twitter
Twitter Triples	Sordoni et al. (2015)	en	Scraped	Twitter
Reddit Dataset	Al-Rfou et al. (2016)	en	Scraped	Reddit
PersonaChat	Zhang et al. (2018b)	en	Human-Human	-
Wizard of Wikipedia	Dinan et al. (2019)	en	Human-Human	-
EmphateticDialogues	Rashkin et al. (2019)	en	Human-Human	-
Meena	Adiwardana et al. (2020)	en	Scraped	Social Media
AntiScam	Li et al. (2020c)	en	Human-Human	-
Dailydialogue	Li et al. (2017b)	en	Scraped	-
Persuasion for Social Good	Wang et al. (2020b)	en	Human-Human	-
CMU Document Grounded Dataset	Zhou et al. (2018)	en	Human-Human	-
Grounded Conversation Dataset	Qin et al. (2019)	en	Scraped	Reddit
Topical Chats	Gopalakrishnan et al. (2019)	en	Human-Human	-
OpenDialKG	Moon et al. (2019)	en	Human-Human	-
Target Guided Conversation Dataset	Tang et al. (2019)	en	Human-Human	-
Image-Chat	Shuster et al. (2020)	en	Human-Human	-
OpenViDial	Meng et al. (2020)	en	Scraped	Movies/TV
MMChat	Zheng et al. (2021a)	en	Sraped	Weibo
NUS SMS	Chen and Kan (2013)	en,zh	Human-Human	SMS
Korean Wizard of Wikipedia	Kim et al. (2021)	ko	MT Human-Human	-
XPersona	Lin et al. (2020a)	zh,fr,ind,it,ko,ja	MT Human-Human	-

Table 2: Overview of existing dialogue datasets. *Human–Human* denotes datasets where two people converse with each other. *Scraped* marks datasets which are gathered from an existing online resource.

Relevance in Dialogue: Is Less More? An Empirical Comparison of Existing Metrics, and a Novel Simple Metric

Ian Berlot-Attwell
University of Toronto
Vector Institute
ianberlot@cs.toronto.edu

Frank Rudzicz
University of Toronto
Vector Institute
Unity Health Toronto
frank@cs.toronto.edu

Abstract

In this work, we evaluate various existing dialogue relevance metrics, find strong dependency on the dataset, often with poor correlation with human scores of relevance, and propose modifications to reduce data requirements and domain sensitivity while improving correlation. Our proposed metric achieves state-of-the-art performance on the HUMOD dataset (Merdivan et al., 2020) while reducing measured sensitivity to dataset by 37%-66%. We achieve this without fine-tuning a pretrained language model, and using only $3,750$ unannotated human dialogues and a single negative example. Despite these limitations, we demonstrate competitive performance on four datasets from different domains. Our code, including our metric and experiments, is open sourced[1].

1 Introduction

The automatic evaluation of generative dialogue systems remains an important open problem, with potential applications from tourism (Şimşek and Fensel, 2018) to medicine (Fazzinga et al., 2021). In recent years, there has been increased focus on interpretable approaches (Deriu et al., 2021; Chen et al., 2021) often through combining various sub-metrics, each for a specific aspect of dialogue (Berlot-Attwell and Rudzicz, 2021; Phy et al., 2020; Mehri and Eskenazi, 2020b). One of these key aspects is "relevance" (sometimes called "context coherence"), commonly defined as whether "[r]esponses are on-topic with the immediate dialogue history" (Finch and Choi, 2020).

These interpretable approaches have motivated measures of dialogue relevance that are not reliant on expensive human annotations. Such measures have appeared in many recent papers on dialogue evaluation, including USR (Mehri and Eskenazi, 2020b), USL-H (Phy et al., 2020), and others (Pang et al., 2020; Merdivan et al., 2020). Additionally, dialogue relevance has been used directly in training dialogue models (Xu et al., 2018).

Despite this work, comparison between these approaches has been limited. Aggravating this problem is that authors often collect human annotations on their own datasets with varying amounts and types of non-human responses. Consequently, direct comparisons are not possible. It is known that metrics of dialogue *quality* often perform poorly on new test sets of quality ratings (Yeh et al., 2021), but it remains an open question whether poor generalization also plagues the much simpler dialogue relevance task. We address this problem by evaluating and comparing six prior approaches on four publicly available datasets of dialogue annotated with human ratings of relevance. We find poor correlation with human ratings across various methods, with high sensitivity to dataset.

Based on our observations, we propose a simple metric of logistic regression trained on pretrained BERT NSP features (Devlin et al., 2019), using "i don't know." as the only negative example. With this metric, we achieve state-of-the-art correlation on the HUMOD dataset (Merdivan et al., 2020). We release our metric and evaluation code to encourage comparable results in future research.

Our primary contributions are: (i) empirical evidence that current dialogue relevance metrics for English are sensitive to dataset, and often have poor correlation with human ratings, (ii) a simple relevance metric that exhibits good correlation and reduced domain sensitivity, and (iii) the counter-intuitive result that a single negative example can be equally effective as random negative sampling.

2 Prior metrics

Prior metrics of relevance in dialogue can generally be divided into more traditional approaches that are token-based, and more current approaches based on large pretrained models. These metrics are given

[1] https://github.com/ikb-a/idk-dialogue-relevance

Proceedings of the 4th Workshop on NLP for Conversational AI, pages 166 - 183
May 27, 2022 ©2022 Association for Computational Linguistics

the *context* (i.e., the two-person conversation up to a given point in time), as well as a *response* (i.e., the next speaker's response, also known as the 'next turn' in the conversation). From these, they produce a measure of the response's relevance to the context. The ground-truth response (i.e., the 'gold response') may or may not be available.

2.1 n-gram approaches

There have been attempts to use metrics based on n-grams from machine-translation and summarization, such as BLEU (Papineni et al., 2002), ROUGE (Lin, 2004), and METEOR (Banerjee and Lavie, 2005) in dialogue. However, we discard these approaches due to their limitations: they require a ground-truth response, and correlate poorly with dialogue relevance (Merdivan et al., 2020).

2.2 Average-embedding cosine similarity

Xu et al. (2018) proposed to measure the cosine similarity of a vector representation of the context and the response. Specifically, the context and response are represented via an aggregate (typically an average) of the uncontextualized word embeddings. This approach can be modified to exploit language models by instead using contextualized word embeddings.

2.3 Fine-tuned embedding model for Next Utterance Prediction (NUP)

This family of approaches combines a word embedding model (typically max- or average-pooled BERT word embeddings) with a simple 1-3 layer MLP, trained for next utterance prediction (typically using negative sampling) (Mehri and Eskenazi, 2020b; Phy et al., 2020). The embedding model is then fine-tuned to the domain of interest. In some variants, the model is provided with information in addition to the context and response; e.g., Mehri and Eskenazi (2020b) appended a topic string to the context. This approach has also been directly used as a metric of overall dialogue quality (Ghazarian et al., 2019). In this paper, we focus on the specific implementation by Phy et al. (2020): max-pooled BERT embeddings passed into a single-layer MLP followed by two-class softmax, trained with binary cross-entropy (BCE) loss and random sampling of negative samples.

Note that, for methods that are fine-tuned or otherwise require training, it will often be the case that annotated relevance data is not available on the domain of interest. As a result, model performance cannot be measured on a validation set during training. Therefore, either the method must be trained to convergence on the training set, or a different method other than validation set performance must be employed to reduce the risk of halting training on a model with poor performance.

Another concern with using trained metrics to evaluate trained dialogue systems is that they may both learn the same patterns in the training data. An extreme example would be a dialogue model that learns only to reproduce responses from the training data verbatim, and a relevance metric that learns to only accept verbatim responses from the training data. We believe that this risk can be reduced by training the metric on separate data from the model. However, this approach is only practical if the metric can be trained with a relatively small amount of data and therefore does not compete with the dialogue model for training examples. Alternatively, a sufficiently generalizable metric may be trained on data from a different domain.

2.4 Normalized conditional probability

Pang et al. (2020) also exploited pretrained models, however they instead relied on a generative language model (specifically GPT-2). Their proposed metric is the conditional log-probability of the response given the context, normalized to the range $[0, 1]$ (see Appendix D.1 for details).

Mehri and Eskenazi (2020a) also relied on a generative language model (specifically, DialoGPT (Zhang et al., 2020)), however their approach measured the probability of followup-utterances, e.g., "Why are you changing the topic?" to indicate irrelevance. Their relevance and correctness scores are defined as $c(q \mid r) = -\sum_{i=1}^{|n|} \log P(n_i \mid r, q)$, where $n_i \in n$ is a negative response suggesting irrelevance or incorrectness. Note that positive utterances can be used, however the author's measures of correctness and relevance only used negative utterances.

3 Datasets used for analysis

A literature review reveals that many of these methods have never been evaluated on the same datasets. As such, it is unclear both how these approaches compare, and how well they generalize to new data. For this reason, we consider four publicly available English datasets of both human and synthetic dialogue with human relevance annotations. All datasets are annotated with Likert ratings of rele-

Dataset	Superset	Contexts	Turns per Context	Responses per Context	Response types	Relevance Annotation
HUMOD (Merdivan et al., 2020)	Cornell movie dialogue (Danescu-Niculescu-Mizil and Lee, 2011)	4, 750	2-7	2	Human, Random Human	Likert 1-5
USR-TC (Mehri and Eskenazi, 2020b)	Topical Chat (Gopalakrishnan et al., 2019)	60	1-19	6	Human (x2), Transformer (x4)	Likert 1-3
P-DD (Pang et al., 2020)	DailyDialogue (Li et al., 2017)	200	1	1	LSTM	Likert 1-5
FED (Mehri and Eskenazi, 2020a)	N/A	375	3-33	1	Human, Meena (Adiwardana et al., 2020), or Mitsuku	Likert 1-3 (relevance and correctness)

Table 1: Summary of datasets used.

vance from multiple reviewers; following Merdivan et al. (2020), we average these ratings over all reviewers. Due to variations in data collection procedures, as well as anchoring effects (Li et al., 2019), Likert ratings from different datasets may not be directly comparable. Consequently, we keep the datasets separate. This also allows us to observe generalization across datasets.

Altogether, our selected datasets cover a wide variety of responses, including human, LSTM, Transformer, Meena (Adiwardana et al., 2020), and Mitsuku[2] generated responses, and random distractors. See Table 1 for an overview.

3.1 HUMOD Dataset

The HUMOD dataset (Merdivan et al., 2020) is an annotated subset of the Cornell movie dialogue dataset (Danescu-Niculescu-Mizil and Lee, 2011). The Cornell dataset consists of 220, 579 conversations from 617 films. The HUMOD dataset is a subset of 4, 750 contexts, each consisting of between two and seven turns. Every context is paired with both the original human response, and a randomly sampled human response. Each response is annotated with crowd-sourced ratings of relevance from 1-5. The authors measured inter-annotator agreement via Cohen's kappa score (Cohen, 1968), and it was found to be 0.86 between the closest ratings, and 0.42 between randomly selected ratings. Following the authors, we split the dataset into a training set consisting of the first 3, 750 contexts, a validation set of the next 500 contexts, and a testset of the remaining 500 contexts. As it is unclear how HUMOD was subsampled from the Cornell movie dialogue dataset, we do not use the Cornell movie dialogue dataset as training data.

3.2 USR Topical-Chat Dataset (USR-TC)

The USR-TC dataset is a subset of the Topical-Chat (TC) dialogue dataset (Gopalakrishnan et al., 2019) created by Mehri and Eskenazi (2020b). The Topical-Chat dataset consists of approximately 11, 000 conversations between Amazon Mechanical Turk workers, each grounding their conversation in a provided reading set. The USR-TC dataset consists of 60 contexts taken from the TC frequent test set, each consisting of 1-19 turns. Every context is paired with six responses: the original human response, a newly created human response, and four samples taken from a Transformer dialog model (Vaswani et al., 2017). Each sample follows a different decoding strategy, namely: argmax sampling, and nucleus sampling (Holtzman et al., 2020) at the rates $p = 0.3, 0.5, 0.7$, respectively. Each response is annotated with a human 1-3 score of relevance, produced by one of six dialogue researchers. The authors reported an inter-annotator agreement of 0.56 (Spearman's correlation). We divide the dataset evenly into a validation and test set, each containing 30 contexts. We use the TC train set as the training set.

3.3 Pang et al. (2020) Annotated DailyDialogue Dataset (P-DD)

The P-DD dataset (Pang et al., 2020) is a subset of the DailyDialogue (DD) dataset (Li et al., 2017). The DailyDialogue dataset consists of 13, 118 conversations scraped from websites where English language learners could practice English conversation. The P-DD dataset contains 200 contexts, each of a single turn and paired with a single synthetic response, generated by a 2-layer LSTM (Bahdanau et al., 2015). Responses are sampled using top-K sampling for $k \in \{1, 10, 100\}$; note that k varies by context. Each response is annotated with ten crowdsourced 1-5 ratings of relevance with a reported inter-annotator Spearman's correlation between 0.57 and 0.87. Due to the very small size of the dataset (only 200 dialogues in total), and the lack of information on how the contexts were sampled, we use this dataset exclusively for testing.

[2] 2019 Loebner prize winning system

3.4 FED Dataset

The FED dataset (Mehri and Eskenazi, 2020a), consists of 375 annotated dialogue turns taken from 40 human-human, 40 human-Meena (Adiwardana et al., 2020), and 40 human-Mitsuku conversations. We use a subset of the annotations, specifically turnwise relevance, and turnwise correctness (the latter defined by the authors as whether there was a "a misunderstanding of the conversation"). As the authors note, their definition of correctness is often encapsulated within relevance; we thus evaluate on both annotations. Due to the small size, we used this dataset only for testing.

4 Evaluating Prior Metrics

For each of the aforementioned datasets, we evaluate the following relevance metrics:

- COS-FT: average fastText [3] embedding cosine similarity. Code by Csáky et al. (2019)
- COS-MAX-BERT: Cosine similarity with max-pooled BERT contextualized word embeddings, inspired by BERT-RUBER (Ghazarian et al., 2019)
- COS-NSP-BERT: Cosine similarity using the pretrained features extracted from the [CLS] token used by next-sentence-prediction head.
- NUP-BERT: Fine-tuned BERT next-utterance prediction approach. Implementation by Phy et al. (2020). We experiment with fine-tuning BERT to the HUMOD train set (3750 dialogues), the full TC train set, and TC-S (a subset of the TC training set containing $3,750$ dialogues).
- NORM-PROB: GPT-2 based normalized conditional-probability; approach and implementation by Pang et al. (2020); note that the P-DD dataset was released in the same paper.
- FED-RELEVANT & FED-CORRECT: DialoGPT based normalized conditional-probability; approach and implementation by Mehri and Eskenazi (2020a)

In all cases, we use hugging-face `bert-base-uncased` as the pretrained BERT model. Only NUP-BERT was fine-tuned. To prevent an unfair fitting to any specific dialogue model, and to better reflect the evaluation of a new dialogue model, only human responses were used at train time. All hyperparameters were left at their recommended values. NUP-BERT performance is averaged over 3 runs.

Note that we also evaluate GRADE (Huang et al., 2020) and DYNA-EVAL (Zhang et al., 2021); however these do not measure relevance, but rather *dialogue coherence*: "whether a piece of text is in a consistent and logical manner, as opposed to a random collection of sentences" (Zhang et al., 2021). As relevance is a major aspect of dialogue coherence, we include these baselines for completeness. As both metrics are graph neural networks intended for larger train sets, we use checkpoints provided by the authors. GRADE is trained on DailyDialogue (Li et al., 2017), and DynaEval on Empathetic Dialogue (Rashkin et al., 2019). Both are trained with negative sampling, with GRADE constructing more challenging negative samples.

A summary of the authors' stated purpose for each metric can be found in the Appendix C.

4.1 Analysis

Table 2 makes it clear that the normalized probability and cosine similarity approaches do not generalize well across datasets. Although NORM-PROB excels on the P-DD dataset, it has weak performance on HUMOD and a significant *negative* correlation on USR-TC. Likewise the FED metrics perform well on the FED data, but are negatively correlated on all other datasets. Consequently, we believe that the NORM-PROB and FED metrics are overfitted to their corresponding datasets. Similarly, although COS-FT has the best performance on the USR-TC dataset, it performs poorly on HUMOD, and has negative correlation on P-DD. As such, it is clear that, while both cosine-similarity and normalized probability approaches can perform well, they have serious limitations. They are very sensitive to the domain and models under evaluation, and are capable of becoming negatively correlated with human ratings under suboptimal conditions.

Looking at the *dialogue coherence* metrics, DYNA-EVAL performs strongly on FED, and weakly on all other datasets. GRADE performs very strongly on HUMOD and P-DD (the latter, likely in part as it was trained on DailyDialogue), but is uncorrelated on USR-TC. Given that these metrics were not intended to measure relevance, uneven performance is to be expected as relevance and *dialogue coherence* will not always align.

The final baseline, NUP-BERT, is quite com-

[3] `https://fasttext.cc/`

	HUMOD		USR-TC		P-DD		FED-Correctness		FED-Relevance	
Prior Metric	S	P	S	P	S	P	S	P	S	P
COS-FT	0.09	0.10	*0.26	*0.24	−0.02	−0.04	0.08	0.04	0.11	0.07
COS-MAX-BERT	*0.13	*0.10	*0.20	0.14	0.03	0.02	0.03	0.01	0.06	0.04
COS-NSP-BERT	0.08	0.06	0.08	0.09	*0.30	*0.23	−0.03	−0.01	−0.04	−0.02
NORM-PROB	*0.19	*0.16	*−0.24	*−0.26	*0.65	*0.59	0.05	0.06	0.07	0.07
FED-CORRECT	−0.06	−0.04	−0.08	−0.12	*−0.25	*−0.26	*0.17	*0.17	*0.15	*0.15
FED-RELEVANT	−0.06	−0.05	−0.08	−0.12	*−0.26	*−0.27	*0.17	*0.17	*0.15	*0.15
GRADE	*0.61	*0.61	0.00	0.03	*0.70	*0.68	0.12	0.12	*0.15	*0.15
DYNA-EVAL	*0.09	*0.10	0.10	0.10	0.00	-0.02	*0.26	*0.27	*0.32	*0.31
NUP-BERT (H)	*0.33 (0.02)	*0.37 (0.02)	0.10 (0.02)	*0.22 (0.01)	*0.62 (0.04)	*0.54 (0.02)	†0.14 (0.04)	*0.21 (0.03)	*0.22 (0.01)	*0.30 (0.01)
NUP-BERT (TC-S)	*0.29 (0.02)	*0.35 (0.03)	†0.17 (0.03)	†0.20 (0.04)	*0.58 (0.05)	*0.56 (0.04)	0.05 (0.04)	0.12 (0.01)	†0.16 (0.04)	*0.21 (0.01)
NUP-BERT (TC)	*0.30 (0.01)	*0.38 (0.00)	0.16 (0.02)	*0.21 (0.02)	*0.62 (0.05)	*0.58 (0.04)	0.06 (0.01)	†0.12 (0.02)	*0.18 (0.02)	*0.23 (0.01)

Table 2: Spearman (S) and Pearson (P) correlations of baseline models with average human ratings on the test sets. BERT-NUP is averaged over three runs, with the standard deviation reported in brackets. Training data is specified in brackets: (H) signifies HUMOD, (TC) signifies the Topical Chat training set, and (TC-S) signifies a subset of TC containing 3,750 dialogues (same size as the HUMOD train set). '*' indicates all trials were significant at the $p < 0.01$ level. '†' indicates at least one trial was significant. Note that most cosine and language-model based metrics attain negative correlation with human scores.

	HUMOD		USR-TC		P-DD		FED-Correctness		FED-Relevance	
Prior Metric	S	P	S	P	S	P	S	P	S	P
NUP-BERT (H)	*0.33 (0.02)	*0.37 (0.02)	0.10 (0.02)	*0.22 (0.01)	***0.62** (0.04)	*0.54 (0.02)	†0.14 (0.04)	*0.21 (0.03)	*0.22 (0.01)	***0.30** (0.01)
NUP-BERT (TC-S)	*0.29 (0.02)	*0.35 (0.03)	†0.17 (0.03)	†0.20 (0.04)	*0.58 (0.05)	*0.56 (0.04)	0.05 (0.04)	0.12 (0.01)	†0.16 (0.04)	*0.21 (0.01)
NUP-BERT (TC)	*0.30 (0.01)	*0.38 (0.00)	0.16 (0.02)	*0.21 (0.02)	***0.62** (0.05)	***0.58** (0.04)	0.06 (0.01)	†0.12 (0.02)	*0.18 (0.02)	*0.23 (0.01)
IDK (H)	***0.58** (0.00)	***0.58** (0.00)	**0.18** (0.00)	***0.24** (0.00)	*0.53 (0.00)	*0.48 (0.01)	***0.15** (0.00)	***0.23** (0.00)	***0.24** (0.00)	*0.29 (0.00)
IDK (TC-S)	***0.58** (0.00)	***0.58** (0.00)	**0.18** (0.00)	*0.22 (0.00)	*0.54 (0.01)	*0.49 (0.01)	***0.15** (0.00)	***0.23** (0.00)	***0.24** (0.00)	*0.29 (0.00)

Table 3: Comparison of our proposed metric (IDK) against the NUP-BERT baseline on the test set. Note the strong improvement on HUMOD and equivalent, or slightly improved performance on USR-TC, at the cost of performance loss on P-DD. Note IDK (H) and IDK (TC-S) performance is almost identical, suggesting that IDK performance is largely independent of training data.

petitive, outperforming each of the other baselines on at least 2 of the datasets. Despite this, we can see that performance on HUMOD, USR-TC, and FED is still fairly weak. We can also observe that NUP-BERT has some sensitivity to the domain of the training data; fine-tuning on HUMOD data results in lower Spearman's correlation on USR-TC, and fine-tuning on USR-TC performs worse on the FED datasets. However, the amount of training data (TC vs TC-S) has little impact.

Overall, the results of Table 2 are concerning as they suggest that at least five current approaches generalize poorly across either dialogue models or domains. The absolute performance of all metrics studied vary considerably by dataset, and the relative performance of closely related metrics such as COS-FT and COS-NSP-BERT, or NUP-BERT with different training data, varies considerably between datasets. As a result, research into new dialogue relevance metrics is required. Furthermore, it is clear that the area's evaluation methodology must be updated to use various dialogue models in various different domains.

5 IDK: A metric for dialogue relevance

Based on these results, we propose a number of modifications to the NUP-BERT metric to produce a novel metric that we call IDK ("I Don't Know"). The architecture is mostly unchanged, however the training procedure and the features used are altered.

First, based on the observation that the amount of training data has little impact, we freeze BERT features and do not fine-tune to the domain. Additionally, whereas the NUP-BERT baseline uses max-pooled BERT word embeddings, we use the pre-trained next sentence prediction (NSP) features: "(classification token) further processed by a Linear layer and a Tanh activation function [...] trained from the next sentence prediction (classification) objective during pre-training"[4].

Second, to improve generalization and reduce variation in training (particularly important as the practitioner typically has no annotated relevance data), and operating on the assumption that relevance is captured by a few key dimensions of the NUP features, we add L1 regularization to our regression weights ($\lambda = 1$). Note that experiments with L2 regularization yielded similar validation

[4] https://huggingface.co/transformers/v2.11.0/model_doc/bert.html

set performance (see Appendix, Table 10).

Third, in place of random sampling we use a fixed negative sample, "i don't know". This allows us to train the model on less data.

Additionally, we simplify the model, using logistic regression in place of 2-class softmax. We train for 2 epochs using BCE loss – the same as the NUP-BERT baseline. We use the Adam optimizer (Kingma and Ba, 2015) with an initial learning rate of 0.001, and batch size 6.

Table 3 reports the correlation between the metric's responses and the average human rating. We achieve a Pearson's correlation on HUMOD of 0.58, surpassing HUMOD baselines (Merdivan et al., 2020), and achieving parity with GRADE (0.61). Examples of the our metric's output on the HUMOD dataset, and a scatter plot of IDK vs human scores are in Appendices A and F, respectively.

Compared to NUP-BERT, our proposed metric provides strong improvement on the HUMOD dataset and equivalent or stronger performance on USR-TC and FED, at a cost of performance on P-DD. In particular, IDK (TC-S) performance on the FED datasets is considerably stronger than NUP-BERT (TC-S). As the performance drop on P-DD is less than the performance gain on HUMOD, and as HUMOD is human data rather than LSTM data, we consider this tradeoff to be a net benefit.

Compared to GRADE in particular, we have reduced performance on P-DD, equivalent performance on HUMOD, and stronger performance on USR-TC and FED (in particular, correlation on the USR-TC dataset is non-zero). It is worth noting that, in general, our approach does not out-perform the baselines in *all* cases – only the *majority* of cases. As such, when annotated human data is not available for testing, it would appear that our approach is the preferred choice.

Our metric is also preferable, as it is less sensitive to domain. To numerically demonstrate this, we measure the domain sensitivity of the evaluated metrics as the ratio of best Spearman's correlation to worst Spearman's correlation – this value should be positive (i.e., there is no dataset where the metric becomes negatively correlated), and as close to 1 as possible (i.e., there is no difference in performance). Looking at Table 10, we find IDK strongly outperforms all prior metrics, reducing this ratio by more than 37%-66% compared to the best baseline.

Prior Metric	Ratio
FED-CORRECT	−0.7
FED-RELEVANT	−0.7
NORM-PROB	−2.7
COS-NSP-BERT	−7.5
COS-FT	−13
GRADE	∞
DYNA-EVAL	∞
NUP-BERT (TC-S)	11.6
NUP-BERT (TC)	10.3
COS-MAX-BERT	6.7
NUP-BERT (H)	6.2
IDK (H)	**3.9**
IDK (TC-S)	**3.9**

Table 4: Ratio of best Spearman correlation to worst on all datasets for all metrics. Sorted in improving order.

5.1 Testing NSP feature dimensionality

As a followup experiment, we tested our assumption that only a fraction of the BERT-NSP features are needed. Plotting the weights learned by IDK on HUMOD, we found a skewed distribution with a small fraction of weights with magnitude above 0.01 (See Appendix, Figure 1). Hypothesizing that the largest weights correspond to the relevant dimensions, we modified the pretrained huggingface NSP BERT to zero all dimensions of the NSP feature, except for the 7 dimensions corresponding to the largest IDK HUMOD weights. We then evaluated NSP accuracy on three NLTK (Bird et al., 2009) corpora: Brown, Gutenburg, and Webtext. As expected, we found that reducing the dimensionality from 768 to 7 had no negative impact (see Appendix, Table 7). Again, note that the mask was created using IDK trained on HUMOD data, and the weights of BERT and the NSP prediction head were in no way changed. Therefore, it is clear that (at least on these datasets) over 99% of the BERT NSP feature dimensions can be safely discarded.

5.2 Ablation tests

Table 5 outlines correlation when ablating the L1 regularization, or when using randomly sampled negative samples in place of "i don't know". Random samples are produced by shuffling the responses of the next 3, 750 dialogues in the dataset.

Overall, it appears that the majority of the performance gains come from the combination of L1 regularization with pretrained BERT NSP features. The clearest observation is that L1 regularization is critical to good performance when using "i don't know" in place of random samples – otherwise, the model presumably overfits. Second, using "i don't know" in place of random samples has a mixed, but relatively minor effect. Thirdly, the effect of L1 regularization is quite positive when training on

			HUMOD		USR-TC		P-DD		FED-Correctness		FED-Relevance	
Data	L1	idk	S	P	S	P	S	P	S	P	S	P
H	✓	✓	*0.58 (0.00)	*0.58 (0.00)	0.18 (0.00)	*0.24 (0.00)	*0.53 (0.00)	*0.48 (0.01)	*0.15 (0.00)	*0.23 (0.00)	*0.24 (0.00)	*0.29 (0.00)
H		✓	*0.42 (0.06)	*0.42 (0.05)	*0.24 (0.00)	*0.25 (0.00)	*0.29 (0.06)	*0.32 (0.03)	*0.14 (0.00)	*0.17 (0.01)	*0.21 (0.01)	*0.19 (0.02)
H	✓		*0.61 (0.00)	*0.61 (0.00)	0.12 (0.00)	*0.21 (0.01)	*0.55 (0.00)	*0.52 (0.01)	0.09 (0.00)	*0.19 (0.01)	*0.17 (0.00)	*0.26 (0.01)
H			*0.60 (0.00)	*0.61 (0.00)	0.18 (0.00)	*0.26 (0.01)	*0.54 (0.00)	*0.50 (0.01)	0.10 (0.02)	†0.11 (0.02)	†0.14 (0.02)	0.09 (0.03)
TC-S	✓	✓	*0.58 (0.00)	*0.58 (0.00)	0.18 (0.00)	*0.22 (0.00)	*0.54 (0.01)	*0.49 (0.01)	*0.15 (0.00)	*0.23 (0.00)	*0.24 (0.00)	*0.29 (0.00)
TC-S		✓	*0.36 (0.04)	*0.34 (0.05)	0.17 (0.01)	0.11 (0.01)	*0.34 (0.03)	*0.32 (0.04)	*0.14 (0.00)	*0.15 (0.01)	*0.21 (0.00)	*0.17 (0.01)
TC-S	✓		*0.59 (0.01)	*0.54 (0.03)	†0.18 (0.04)	*0.27 (0.02)	*0.52 (0.03)	*0.43 (0.05)	†0.14 (0.01)	*0.21 (0.00)	*0.22 (0.01)	*0.29 (0.01)
TC-S			*0.35 (0.07)	*0.41 (0.01)	†0.13 (0.10)	*0.21 (0.03)	†0.23 (0.10)	†0.27 (0.11)	0.05 (0.06)	0.11 (0.03)	†0.12 (0.12)	†0.18 (0.04)

Table 5: Test correlation of various ablations of the proposed metric. The L1 column signifies whether L1 regularization is used ($\lambda = 1$), and the "idk" column indicates whether the negative samples are "i don't know", or a random shuffle of $3,750$ other human responses. Note that L1 regularization is beneficial when training on TC-S.

TC data (regardless of the negative samples), and mixed but smaller when training on HUMOD data. Overall, this suggests that when a validation set of domain-specific annotated relevance data is not available, then L1 regularization may be helpful. Its effect varies by domain, but appears to have a much stronger positive effect than a negative effect.

The result that L1 regularization allows us to use "i don't know" in place of random negatives samples is quite interesting, as it seems to counter work in contrastive representation learning (Robinson et al., 2021), and dialogue quality evaluation (Lan et al., 2020) suggesting that "harder" negative examples are better. We believe that the reason for this apparent discrepancy is that *we are not performing feature learning*; the feature space is fixed, pretrained, BERT NSP. Furthermore, we've shown that this feature space is effectively 7 dimensional. As a result, we believe that the L1 regularization causes an effective projection to 7D. Consequently, as our model is low-capacity, "i don't know" is sufficient to find the separating hyperplane. Having said this, it is still unclear why we see *improved* performance on FED when training on HUMOD data. Comparing the histograms of learned weight magnitudes (see Appendix, Figure 2) we find that the ablated model has larger number of large weights – we speculate that the random negative samples' variation in irrelevant aspects such as syntactic structure is responsible.

5.3 Additional Experiments

We repeated our IDK experiments with two different fixed negative samples; performance and domain sensitivity are generally comparable, although unexpectedly more sensitive to the choice of training data (see Appendix J). We also experimented with using the pretrained BERT NSP predictor as a measure of relevance, however performance is considerably worse on the longer-context FED dataset (see Appendix I). Finally, we observed that BCE loss encourages the model to always map "i don't know" to zero; yet, the relevance of "i don't know" varies by context. Unfortunately, experiments with a modified triplet loss did not yield improvements (see Appendix H).

6 Related Work

In addition to the prior metrics already discussed, the area of dialogue relevance is both motivated by, and jointly developed with, the problem of automatic dialogue evaluation. As relevance is a major component of good dialogue, there is a bidirectional flow of innovations. The NUP-BERT relevance metric is very similar to BERT-RUBER (Ghazarian et al., 2019); both train a small MLP to perform the next-utterance-prediction task based on aggregated BERT features. Both of these share a heritage with earlier self-supervised methods, such as adversarial approaches to dialogue evaluation that train a classifier to distinguish human from generated samples (Kannan and Vinyals, 2017). Another example of shared development is the use of word-overlap metrics such as BLEU (Papineni et al., 2002) and ROUGE (Lin, 2004) that have been imported wholesale into both dialogue relevance and overall quality from the fields of machine-translation and summarization, respectively.

Simultaneously, metrics of dialogue evaluation have been motivated by dialogue relevance. There is a long history of evaluating dialogue models on specific aspects; Finch and Choi (2020) performed a meta-analysis of prior work, and proposed dimensions of: grammaticality, relevance, informativeness, emotional understanding, engagingness, consistency, proactivity, and satisfaction. New approaches to dialogue evaluation have emerged from this body of work, seeking to aggregate individual measures of various dimensions of dialogue, often including relevance (Mehri and Eskenazi, 2020b; Phy et al., 2020; Berlot-Attwell and Rudzicz, 2021).

These approaches also share heritage with earlier ensemble measures of dialogue evaluation such as RUBER (Tao et al., 2018) – although in the case of RUBER, it combined a referenced and unreferenced metric rather than separate aspects.

Metrics of dialogue relevance and quality also share common problems such as the diversity of valid responses. Our findings that existing relevance metrics generalize poorly to new domains is consistent with previous findings about metrics of dialogue quality (Lowe, 2019; Yeh et al., 2021). Thus, our work suggests that this challenge extends to the subproblem of dialogue relevance as well.

At the same time, it must be remembered that measuring holistic dialogue quality is a very different task from measuring dialogue relevance – it is well established that aspects of dialogue such as fluency, and interestingness are major components of quality (Mehri and Eskenazi, 2020b,a), and these should have no impact on relevance.

With respect to prior work comparing relevance metrics, we are aware of only one tangential work. Yeh et al. (2021) performed a comparison of various metrics of dialogue *quality*; within this work they dedicated three paragraphs to a brief comparison of how these *quality* metrics performed at predicting various dialogue qualities, including relevance. They reported results on only two of the datasets we used (P-DD and FED). Interestingly, the authors found that the FED metric performs well on P-DD (reporting a Spearman's correlation of 0.507), however our results demonstrate that the *components* of FED that are meant to measure relevance (i.e. FED-REL and FED-COR) are significantly *negatively* correlated with human relevance scores. Additionally, as Yeh et al. (2021) focus on quality, they do not compare performance between the two relevance datasets. Instead they compare performance on quality against performance on relevance, and use the discrepancy to conclude that measuring relevance alone (as done by NORM-PROB) is insufficient to determine quality. Although we agree that relevance alone is insufficient for dialogue quality evaluation, our work provides a richer understanding. Our finding that NORM-PROB performs poorly across a range of relevance datasets suggests that the poor performance of NORM-PROB in the quality-prediction task is also caused by the *poor relevance generalization* in addition to the insufficiency of relevance to measure overall quality.

7 Discussion

Our experiments demonstrate that several published measures of dialogue relevance have poor, or even negative, correlation when evaluated on new datasets of dialogue relevance, suggesting overfitting to either model or domain. As such, it is clear that further research into new measures of dialogue relevance is required, and that care must be taken in their evaluation to compare against a number of different models in a number of domains. Furthermore, it is also clear that for the current practitioner who requires a measure of relevance, there are no guarantees that current methods will perform well on a given domain. As such, it is wise to collect a validation dataset of human-annotated relevance data for use in selecting a relevance metric. If this is not possible, then our metric, IDK, appears to be the best option – achieving both good correlation and the lowest domain sensitivity, even when trained on different domains. Furthermore, when training data is scarce, our results suggest that the use of strong regularization allows for the use of a single negative example, "i don't know", in the place of randomly sampled negative samples. If that is still too data intensive, then our results suggest that our metric is fairly agnostic to the domain of the training data; therefore training data can be used from a different dialogue domain in place of the domain of interest.

Having said this, it is clear that further research into what exactly these metrics are measuring, and why they fail to generalize, is merited. The results are often counter-intuitive; our demonstration that 99% of the BERT NSP features can be safely discarded is just one striking example. Similarly, although our empirical results suggest that use of a single negative example generalizes across domains, there is no compelling theoretical reason why this should be so. More generally, all the metrics outlined are complex, dependent on large corpora, and created without ground truth annotations. As a result, they are all dependent on either surrogate tasks (i.e., NUP), or unsupervised learning (e.g., FastText embeddings). Consequently, it is especially difficult to conclude what exactly these metrics are measuring. At present, the only strong justification that these metrics are indeed measuring relevance is good correlation with human judgements – poor generalization across similar domains is not an encouraging result.

Although the metric outlined is not appropriate for final model evaluation (as it risks unfairly favouring dialogue models based on the same pre-trained BERT, or similar architectures), our aim is to provide a useful metric for rapid prototyping and hyperparameter search. Additionally, we hope that our findings on the domain sensitivity of existing metrics will spur further research into both the cause of – and solutions to – this problem.

8 Conclusion

Our work demonstrates that several existing metrics of dialogue relevance are problematic as their performance varies wildly between test-domains. We take a first step towards resolving this issue by proposing IDK: a simple metric that is less sensitive to test domain and trainable with minimal data. We reduce IDK's data requirements through the novel use of a fixed negative example, provide evidence that the underlying BERT NSP features are low-dimensional, and propose that this fact (combined with IDK's lack of feature learning) allows for the counter-intuitive use of a single negative example. Beyond this, we call for better evaluation of future relevance metrics, and thus release our code for processing four diverse, publicly available, relevance-annotated data sets.

9 Acknowledgements

Resources used in preparing this research were provided, in part, by the Province of Ontario, the Government of Canada through CIFAR, and companies sponsoring the Vector Institute `https://vectorinstitute.ai/partners/`. Ian Berlot-Attwell is funded by an Ontario Graduate Scholarship and a Vector Institute Research Grant. Frank Rudzicz is supported by a CIFAR Chair in AI. We would also like to thank the various reviewers who helped to shape and improve this work; without them it would not be what it is today.

References

Daniel Adiwardana, Minh-Thang Luong, David R. So, Jamie Hall, Noah Fiedel, Romal Thoppilan, Zi Yang, Apoorv Kulshreshtha, Gaurav Nemade, Yifeng Lu, and Quoc V. Le. 2020. Towards a human-like open-domain chatbot. *CoRR*, abs/2001.09977.

Dzmitry Bahdanau, Kyunghyun Cho, and Yoshua Bengio. 2015. Neural machine translation by jointly learning to align and translate. In *3rd International Conference on Learning Representations, ICLR 2015, San Diego, CA, USA, May 7-9, 2015, Conference Track Proceedings*.

Satanjeev Banerjee and Alon Lavie. 2005. METEOR: An automatic metric for MT evaluation with improved correlation with human judgments. In *Proceedings of the ACL Workshop on Intrinsic and Extrinsic Evaluation Measures for Machine Translation and/or Summarization*, pages 65–72, Ann Arbor, Michigan. Association for Computational Linguistics.

Ian Berlot-Attwell and Frank Rudzicz. 2021. On the use of linguistic features for the evaluation of generative dialogue systems. *CoRR*, abs/2104.06335.

Steven Bird, Ewan Klein, and Edward Loper. 2009. *Natural Language Processing with Python*. O'Reilly.

Zhang Chen, João Sedoc, Luis Fernando D'Haro, Rafael Banchs, and Alexander Rudnicky. 2021. DSTC10: Track 5: Automatic evaluation and moderation of open-domain dialogue systems. Accessed: 9-7-2021 `https://drive.google.com/file/d/1B2YBtWaLJU5X3uudSZEaOyNWQ_QoTZLG/view`.

Jacob Cohen. 1968. Weighted kappa: nominal scale agreement provision for scaled disagreement or partial credit. *Psychological bulletin*, 70(4):213.

Richárd Csáky, Patrik Purgai, and Gábor Recski. 2019. Improving neural conversational models with entropy-based data filtering. In *Proceedings of the 57th Annual Meeting of the Association for Computational Linguistics*, pages 5650–5669, Florence, Italy. Association for Computational Linguistics.

Cristian Danescu-Niculescu-Mizil and Lillian Lee. 2011. Chameleons in imagined conversations: A new approach to understanding coordination of linguistic style in dialogs. In *Proceedings of the 2nd Workshop on Cognitive Modeling and Computational Linguistics*, pages 76–87, Portland, Oregon, USA. Association for Computational Linguistics.

Jan Deriu, Alvaro Rodrigo, Arantxa Otegi, Guillermo Echegoyen, Sophie Rosset, Eneko Agirre, and Mark Cieliebak. 2021. Survey on evaluation methods for dialogue systems. *Artificial Intelligence Review*, 54(1):755–810.

Jacob Devlin, Ming-Wei Chang, Kenton Lee, and Kristina Toutanova. 2019. BERT: Pre-training of deep bidirectional transformers for language understanding. In *Proceedings of the 2019 Conference of the North American Chapter of the Association for Computational Linguistics: Human Language Technologies, Volume 1 (Long and Short Papers)*, pages 4171–4186, Minneapolis, Minnesota. Association for Computational Linguistics.

Bettina Fazzinga, Andrea Galassi, and Paolo Torroni. 2021. An argumentative dialogue system for covid-19 vaccine information. In *Logic and Argumentation*, pages 477–485, Cham. Springer International Publishing.

Sarah E. Finch and Jinho D. Choi. 2020. Towards unified dialogue system evaluation: A comprehensive analysis of current evaluation protocols. In *Proceedings of the 21th Annual Meeting of the Special Interest Group on Discourse and Dialogue*, pages 236–245, 1st virtual meeting. Association for Computational Linguistics.

Sarik Ghazarian, Johnny Wei, Aram Galstyan, and Nanyun Peng. 2019. Better automatic evaluation of open-domain dialogue systems with contextualized embeddings. In *Proceedings of the Workshop on Methods for Optimizing and Evaluating Neural Language Generation*, pages 82–89, Minneapolis, Minnesota. Association for Computational Linguistics.

Karthik Gopalakrishnan, Behnam Hedayatnia, Qinlang Chen, Anna Gottardi, Sanjeev Kwatra, Anu Venkatesh, Raefer Gabriel, and Dilek Hakkani-Tür. 2019. Topical-Chat: Towards Knowledge-Grounded Open-Domain Conversations. In *Proc. Interspeech 2019*, pages 1891–1895.

Ari Holtzman, Jan Buys, Li Du, Maxwell Forbes, and Yejin Choi. 2020. The curious case of neural text degeneration. In *International Conference on Learning Representations*.

Lishan Huang, Zheng Ye, Jinghui Qin, Liang Lin, and Xiaodan Liang. 2020. GRADE: Automatic graph-enhanced coherence metric for evaluating open-domain dialogue systems. In *Proceedings of the 2020 Conference on Empirical Methods in Natural Language Processing (EMNLP)*, pages 9230–9240, Online. Association for Computational Linguistics.

Anjuli Kannan and Oriol Vinyals. 2017. Adversarial evaluation of dialogue models. *CoRR*, abs/1701.08198.

Diederik P. Kingma and Jimmy Ba. 2015. Adam: A method for stochastic optimization. In *3rd International Conference on Learning Representations, ICLR 2015, San Diego, CA, USA, May 7-9, 2015, Conference Track Proceedings*.

Tian Lan, Xian-Ling Mao, Wei Wei, Xiaoyan Gao, and Heyan Huang. 2020. PONE: A novel automatic evaluation metric for open-domain generative dialogue systems. *ACM Trans. Inf. Syst.*, 39(1):7:1–7:37.

Jiwei Li, Michel Galley, Chris Brockett, Jianfeng Gao, and Bill Dolan. 2016. A diversity-promoting objective function for neural conversation models. In *Proceedings of the 2016 Conference of the North American Chapter of the Association for Computational Linguistics: Human Language Technologies*, pages 110–119, San Diego, California. Association for Computational Linguistics.

Margaret Li, Jason Weston, and Stephen Roller. 2019. ACUTE-EVAL: improved dialogue evaluation with optimized questions and multi-turn comparisons. *CoRR*, abs/1909.03087.

Yanran Li, Hui Su, Xiaoyu Shen, Wenjie Li, Ziqiang Cao, and Shuzi Niu. 2017. DailyDialog: A manually labelled multi-turn dialogue dataset. In *Proceedings of the Eighth International Joint Conference on Natural Language Processing (Volume 1: Long Papers)*, pages 986–995, Taipei, Taiwan. Asian Federation of Natural Language Processing.

Chin-Yew Lin. 2004. ROUGE: A package for automatic evaluation of summaries. In *Text Summarization Branches Out*, pages 74–81, Barcelona, Spain. Association for Computational Linguistics.

Ryan Lowe. 2019. A retrospective for "Towards an automatic Turing test - learning to evaluate dialogue responses". *ML Retrospectives*.

Shikib Mehri and Maxine Eskenazi. 2020a. Unsupervised evaluation of interactive dialog with DialoGPT. In *Proceedings of the 21th Annual Meeting of the Special Interest Group on Discourse and Dialogue*, pages 225–235, 1st virtual meeting. Association for Computational Linguistics.

Shikib Mehri and Maxine Eskenazi. 2020b. USR: An unsupervised and reference free evaluation metric for dialog generation. In *Proceedings of the 58th Annual Meeting of the Association for Computational Linguistics*, pages 681–707, Online. Association for Computational Linguistics.

Erinc Merdivan, Deepika Singh, Sten Hanke, Johannes Kropf, Andreas Holzinger, and Matthieu Geist. 2020. Human annotated dialogues dataset for natural conversational agents. *Applied Sciences*, 10(3).

Bo Pang, Erik Nijkamp, Wenjuan Han, Linqi Zhou, Yixian Liu, and Kewei Tu. 2020. Towards holistic and automatic evaluation of open-domain dialogue generation. In *Proceedings of the 58th Annual Meeting of the Association for Computational Linguistics*, pages 3619–3629, Online. Association for Computational Linguistics.

Kishore Papineni, Salim Roukos, Todd Ward, and Wei-Jing Zhu. 2002. BLEU: a method for automatic evaluation of machine translation. In *Proceedings of the 40th Annual Meeting of the Association for Computational Linguistics*, pages 311–318, Philadelphia, Pennsylvania, USA. Association for Computational Linguistics.

Vitou Phy, Yang Zhao, and Akiko Aizawa. 2020. Deconstruct to reconstruct a configurable evaluation metric for open-domain dialogue systems. In *Proceedings of the 28th International Conference on Computational Linguistics*, pages 4164–4178, Barcelona, Spain (Online). International Committee on Computational Linguistics.

Hannah Rashkin, Eric Michael Smith, Margaret Li, and Y-Lan Boureau. 2019. Towards empathetic open-domain conversation models: A new benchmark and dataset. In *Proceedings of the 57th Annual Meeting of the Association for Computational Linguistics*, pages 5370–5381, Florence, Italy. Association for Computational Linguistics.

Joshua David Robinson, Ching-Yao Chuang, Suvrit Sra, and Stefanie Jegelka. 2021. Contrastive learning with hard negative samples. In *International Conference on Learning Representations*.

Chongyang Tao, Lili Mou, Dongyan Zhao, and Rui Yan. 2018. Ruber: An unsupervised method for automatic evaluation of open-domain dialog systems.

Ashish Vaswani, Noam Shazeer, Niki Parmar, Jakob Uszkoreit, Llion Jones, Aidan N Gomez, Ł ukasz Kaiser, and Illia Polosukhin. 2017. Attention is all you need. In *Advances in Neural Information Processing Systems*, volume 30. Curran Associates, Inc.

Xinnuo Xu, Ondřej Dušek, Ioannis Konstas, and Verena Rieser. 2018. Better conversations by modeling, filtering, and optimizing for coherence and diversity. In *Proceedings of the 2018 Conference on Empirical Methods in Natural Language Processing*, pages 3981–3991, Brussels, Belgium. Association for Computational Linguistics.

Yi-Ting Yeh, Maxine Eskenazi, and Shikib Mehri. 2021. A comprehensive assessment of dialog evaluation metrics. In *The First Workshop on Evaluations and Assessments of Neural Conversation Systems*, pages 15–33, Online. Association for Computational Linguistics.

Chen Zhang, Yiming Chen, Luis Fernando D'Haro, Yan Zhang, Thomas Friedrichs, Grandee Lee, and Haizhou Li. 2021. DynaEval: Unifying turn and dialogue level evaluation. In *Proceedings of the 59th Annual Meeting of the Association for Computational Linguistics and the 11th International Joint Conference on Natural Language Processing (Volume 1: Long Papers)*, pages 5676–5689, Online. Association for Computational Linguistics.

Yizhe Zhang, Siqi Sun, Michel Galley, Yen-Chun Chen, Chris Brockett, Xiang Gao, Jianfeng Gao, Jingjing Liu, and Bill Dolan. 2020. DIALOGPT : Large-scale generative pre-training for conversational response generation. In *Proceedings of the 58th Annual Meeting of the Association for Computational Linguistics: System Demonstrations*, pages 270–278, Online. Association for Computational Linguistics.

Umutcan Şimşek and Dieter Fensel. 2018. Now we are talking! Flexible and open goal-oriented dialogue systems for accessing touristic services. *e-Review of Tourism Research*.

A Example Evaluations

Dialogue Turn	Human	IDK
Mommy –	-	-
Yes, darling.	-	-
Did you ever make a wish?	-	-
Oh, lots of times.	-	-
Did your wishes ever come true?	5.00	4.97
What's your real name?	1.00	3.81
Sometimes.	4.67	4.60
From high school Mary? Yeah, I saw her about six months ago at a convention in Las Vegas.	1.00	1.13
I made a wish today, and it came true just like Edward said it would.	5	4.9
When I am sure I am among friends.	2.33	3.01
Yes, Albert?	-	-
John, we're going huntin'.	-	-
Who's goin?	-	-
We're all going.	-	-
Nick's going?	4.67	4.65
I will keep you safe. We are both older.	2.00	1.09
Nick , Vince , Albert and John.	4.00	4.95
A ride? Hell, that's a good idea. Okay, let's go. Hey, let's go.	2.33	4.68
No women?	4.00	2.39
I guess so	3.00	2.59

Table 6: Two multi-turn examples from HUMOD test set. The randomly sampled distractor turns are italicized, and are not part of the context in subsequent turns. For ease of comparison, the scores generated by our metric (IDK trained on HUMOD) are linearly shifted and rescaled to 1-5.

B NSP Masking Experiment Results

The results of the NSP masking experiment are outlined in Table 7. Note that masking $>99\%$ of the NSP feature had no impact on the pretrained model, and actually improved accuracy by 2.8% on the Webtext corpus.

C Exact objectives of prior metrics

In this section, we briefly outline the stated purpose of each of our relevance metrics evaluated:

Masked	Brown	Gutenburg	Webtext
	85.7%	75.3%	65.4%
✓	85.6%	**75.5%**	**68.2%**

Table 7: Next Sentence Prediction (NSP) performance on various NLTK (Bird et al., 2009) corpora using a pre-trained BERT and NSP head. When masked, we zero-out the 768-dim BERT NSP feature, leaving only the 7 dimensions corresponding to the largest magnitude weights in IDK (H) (i.e., we zero out $>99\%$ of the feature vector).

- COS-FT: "In this work, given a dialogue history, we regard as a coherent response an utterance that is thematically correlated and naturally continuing from the previous turns, as well as lexically diverse." (Xu et al., 2018)
- NUP-BERT: "Maintains Context: Does the response serve as a valid continuation of the preceding conversation?" (Mehri and Eskenazi, 2020b)
- NORM-PROB: "context coherence of a dialogue: the meaningfulness of a response within the context of prior query" (Pang et al., 2020)
- FED-REL: "Is the response relevant to the conversation?" (Mehri and Eskenazi, 2020a)
- FED-COR: "Is the response correct or was there a misunderstanding of the conversation? [...] No one has specifically used Correct, however its meaning is often encapsulated in Relevant." (Mehri and Eskenazi, 2020a)

We also outline the stated purpose of the *dialogue coherence* metrics evaluated:

- GRADE: "Coherence, what makes dialogue utterances unified rather than a random group of sentences" (Huang et al., 2020)
- DYNA-EVAL: "dialogue coherence: considers whether a piece of text is in a consistent and logical manner, as opposed to a random collection of sentences" (Zhang et al., 2021)

D Details for Prior work

D.1 NORM-PROB

Pang et al. (2020) relied on a pretrained generative language model (specifically GPT-2). Their proposed metric is the conditional log-probability of the response given the context, normalized to the range $[0,1]$. Specifically, for a context q with candidate response r, their proposed relevance score is defined as: $c(q \mid r) = -\frac{\max(c_{5th}, \frac{1}{|r|} \log P(r \mid q)) - c_{5th}}{c_{5th}}$, where $|r|$ is the number of tokens in the response, $P(r \mid q)$ is the conditional probability of the response given the context under the language model, and c_{5th} is the 5th percentile of the distribution of $\frac{1}{|r|} \log P(r \mid q)$ over the examples being evaluated.

E Learned HUMOD-IDK Weights

Figure 1 depicts the distribution of weight-magnitudes learned by IDK on the HUMOD training set. Notably, there is a very small subset of weights which is an order of magnitude larger than the others. Figure 2 demonstrates that the use of random sampling in place of "i don't know" when training on the HUMOD dataset causes a larger number of large weights.

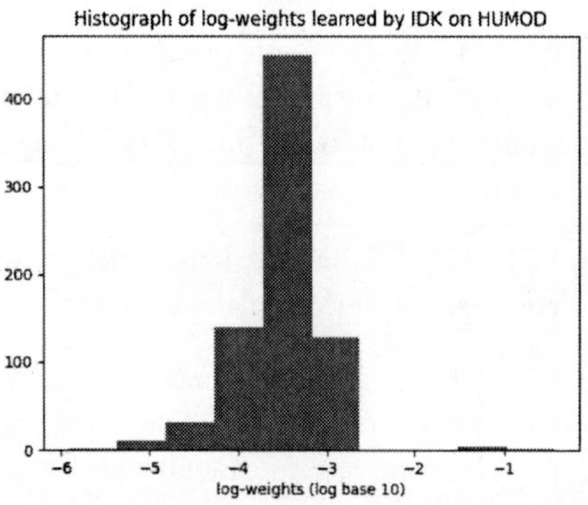

Figure 1: Histogram of log weight magnitudes learned by IDK on HUMOD. Note the small number of weights that are an order of magnitude larger.

F Scatter Plots

Figures 3, 4, 5, 6, and 7 illustrate IDK vs human scores of relevance, where the IDK training data is HUMOD. A regression line is fitted to highlight the trend.

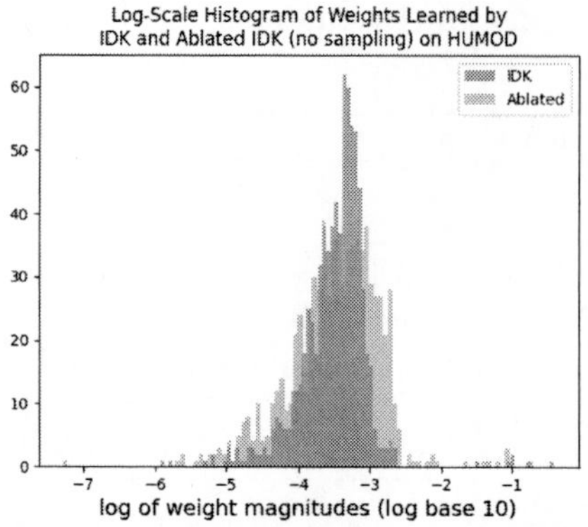

Figure 2: Histogram of log weight magnitudes learned by IDK and Ablated IDK on HUMOD. The specific ablation is the use of random negative samples in place of "i don't know". Note that Ablated IDK has a larger number of large weights than normal IDK.

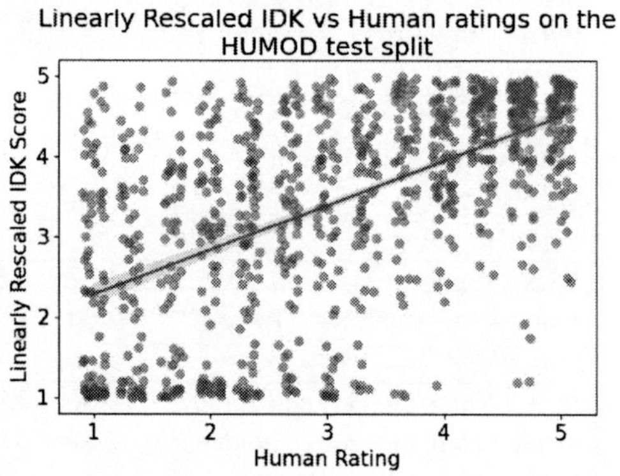

Figure 3: IDK scores, linearly re-scaled to the range 1-5, versus human scores of relevance, on the HUMOD test set.

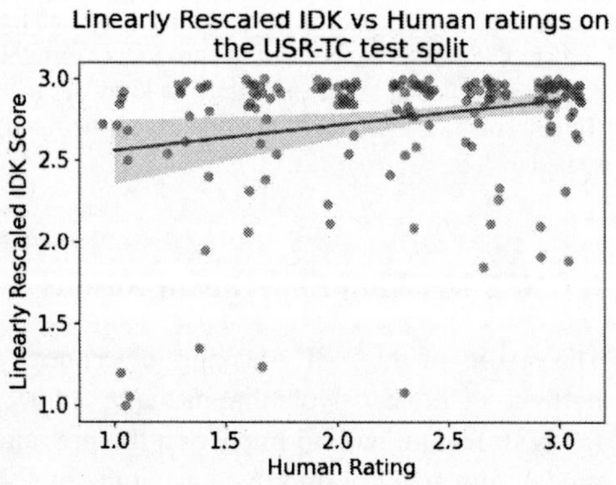

Figure 4: IDK scores, linearly re-scaled to the range 1-3, versus human scores of relevance, on the USR-TC test set.

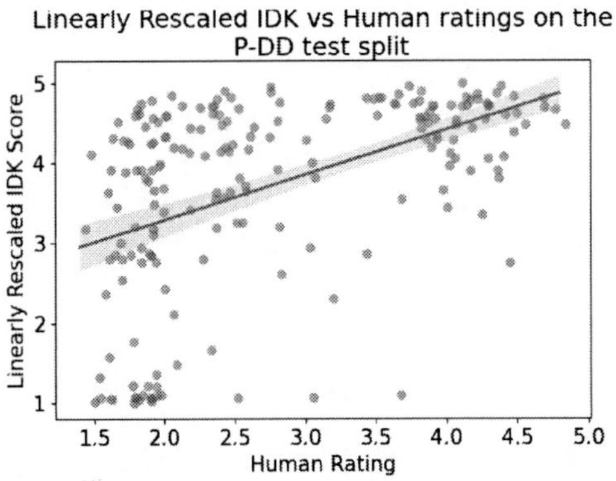

Figure 5: IDK scores, linearly re-scaled to the range 1-5, versus human scores of relevance, on the P-DD test set.

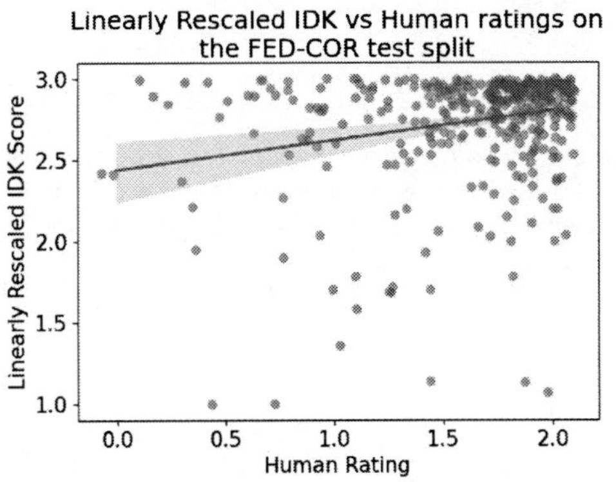

Figure 6: IDK scores, linearly re-scaled to the range 1-3, versus human scores of relevance, on the FED-CORRECT test set.

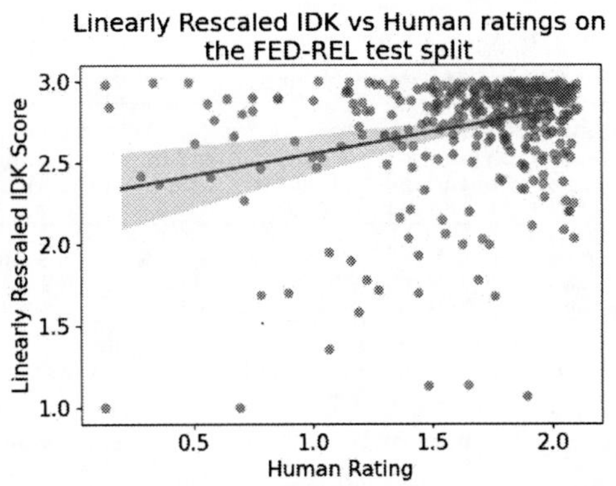

Figure 7: IDK scores, linearly re-scaled to the range 1-3, versus human scores of relevance, on the FED-RELEVANT test set.

G Performance on validation data split

Correlations of the models on the validation set are outlined in Table 8 for prior metrics, and in Table 10 for all ablations and variants of our model.

	HUMOD		USR-TC	
Prior Metric	S	P	S	P
COS-FT	0.08	0.08	*0.27	0.17
COS-MAX-BERT	0.08	0.05	0.18	*0.19
COS-NSP-BERT	0.06	*0.09	*0.23	*0.25
NORM-PROB	*0.27	*0.25	*−0.29	*−0.30
FED-CORRECT	*−0.10	*−0.09	−0.14	−0.15
FED-RELEVANT	*−0.10	*−0.09	−0.14	−0.16
GRADE	*0.64	*0.64	0.02	0.00
DYNA-EVAL	*0.14	*0.15	−0.05	−0.06
NUP-BERT (H)	*0.37 (0.01)	*0.38 (0.00)	*0.38 (0.02)	*0.39 (0.01)
NUP-BERT (TC-S)	*0.32 (0.01)	*0.36 (0.02)	*0.38 (0.04)	*0.41 (0.04)
NUP-BERT (TC)	*0.33 (0.02)	*0.37 (0.02)	*0.45 (0.07)	*0.44 (0.02)

Table 8: Spearman (S) and Pearson (P) correlations of prior metrics with human ratings on the validation splits of all provided dataset. As NUP-BERT is trained we perform 3 runs, reporing the mean and standard deviation. (*) denotes $p < 0.01$ accross all trials. Underline indicates a negative correlation. NOTE: USR scores are human only for COS-FT, NORM-PROB and NUP-BERT

			HUMOD		USR-TC		P-DD		FED-Correctness		FED-Relevance	
Data	L1	idk	S	P	S	P	S	P	S	P	S	P
H	✓	✓	*0.59 (0.01)	*0.55 (0.02)	0.17 (0.01)	*0.28 (0.01)	*0.54 (0.03)	*0.44 (0.02)	†0.13 (0.02)	*0.21 (0.01)	*0.21 (0.01)	*0.30 (0.00)
H		✓	*0.15 (0.05)	*0.19 (0.06)	†0.19 (0.01)	*0.25 (0.02)	0.10 (0.04)	†0.17 (0.05)	0.10 (0.02)	†0.11 (0.02)	†0.14 (0.02)	0.09 (0.03)
H	✓		*0.45 (0.24)	*0.42 (0.21)	0.14 (0.04)	†0.23 (0.10)	†0.39 (0.21)	*0.34 (0.14)	0.11 (0.02)	†0.18 (0.06)	*0.20 (0.02)	*0.25 (0.08)
H			*0.61 (0.00)	*0.60 (0.01)	0.17 (0.00)	*0.23 (0.01)	*0.55 (0.01)	*0.53 (0.01)	†0.14 (0.00)	*0.20 (0.02)	*0.22 (0.00)	*0.27 (0.02)
TC-S	✓	✓	*0.32 (0.44)	*0.25 (0.55)	0.12 (0.06)	†0.10 (0.24)	*0.24 (0.47)	*0.21 (0.46)	0.10 (0.04)	†0.10 (0.14)	†0.17 (0.07)	†0.14 (0.21)
TC-S		✓	*0.27 (0.11)	*0.26 (0.10)	0.16 (0.02)	0.14 (0.03)	†0.22 (0.12)	†0.22 (0.09)	†0.13 (0.01)	*0.15 (0.01)	*0.19 (0.02)	*0.17 (0.02)
TC-S	✓		*-0.20 (0.69)	*-0.20 (0.65)	-0.03 (0.17)	†-0.05 (0.29)	*-0.18 (0.62)	*-0.19 (0.54)	†-0.05 (0.18)	*-0.07 (0.26)	*-0.08 (0.27)	*-0.09 (0.35)
TC-S			†0.18 (0.20)	*0.18 (0.06)	0.04 (0.07)	0.09 (0.17)	0.10 (0.07)	0.07 (0.06)	0.02 (0.10)	†0.08 (0.07)	0.00 (0.10)	†0.12 (0.10)

Table 9: Repeat of ablation experiments, instead using modified triplet loss ($m = 0.4$) in place of BCE. Contrary to our intuition, we do not find any improvement in performance. Comparing against Table 5, we find either equivalent or degraded performance, with an additional tendency to converge to a degenerate solution (e.g., see high variances in TC-S with L1 and idk).

Name	HUMOD Spear	HUMOD Pear	TC Spear	TC Pear
H_Rand3750_bce	*0.58 (0.00)	*0.57 (0.01)	*0.46 (0.00)	*0.43 (0.02)
H_Rand3750	*0.58 (0.00)	*0.58 (0.00)	*0.46 (0.00)	*0.45 (0.02)
H_IDK_L1	*0.56 (0.01)	*0.53 (0.02)	*0.45 (0.03)	*0.44 (0.02)
H_IDK_L2	*0.55 (0.00)	*0.55 (0.01)	*0.44 (0.00)	*0.44 (0.00)
H_Rand3750_L1	*0.42 (0.22)	*0.40 (0.20)	*0.44 (0.00)	*0.45 (0.01)
H_Rand3750_L2	*0.56 (0.00)	*0.55 (0.01)	*0.45 (0.00)	*0.44 (0.02)
H_Rand3750_bce_L1	*0.58 (0.00)	*0.58 (0.00)	*0.45 (0.00)	*0.46 (0.00)
H_Rand3750_bce_L2	*0.57 (0.00)	*0.56 (0.00)	*0.45 (0.00)	*0.42 (0.00)
H_IDK_bce_L1	*0.57 (0.00)	*0.56 (0.00)	*0.42 (0.01)	*0.41 (0.00)
H_IDK_bce_L2	*0.50 (0.01)	*0.51 (0.01)	*0.39 (0.00)	*0.42 (0.00)
H_IDK_bce	*0.39 (0.05)	*0.40 (0.05)	*0.36 (0.02)	*0.34 (0.00)
H_IDK	*0.15 (0.05)	*0.19 (0.06)	0.09 (0.05)	†0.21 (0.05)
TC-S_IDK_L1	*0.29 (0.43)	*0.23 (0.53)	*0.39 (0.07)	*0.41 (0.07)
TC-S_IDK_L2	*0.54 (0.01)	*0.55 (0.01)	*0.43 (0.01)	*0.44 (0.00)
TC-S_IDK_bce_L1	*0.57 (0.00)	*0.56 (0.00)	*0.43 (0.00)	*0.40 (0.00)
TC-S_IDK_bce_L2	*0.47 (0.02)	*0.48 (0.01)	*0.41 (0.00)	*0.39 (0.01)
TC-S_IDK_bce	*0.35 (0.04)	*0.33 (0.05)	*0.40 (0.01)	*0.31 (0.01)
TC-S_IDK	*0.25 (0.10)	*0.24 (0.10)	*0.34 (0.05)	*0.36 (0.03)
TC-S_Rand3750_L1	*-0.19 (0.67)	*-0.20 (0.63)	*-0.13 (0.52)	*-0.14 (0.50)
TC-S_Rand3750_L2	†-0.33 (0.27)	†-0.32 (0.26)	*-0.45 (0.02)	*-0.43 (0.02)
TC-S_Rand3750_bce_L1	*0.56 (0.01)	*0.52 (0.03)	*0.44 (0.03)	*0.40 (0.02)
TC-S_Rand3750_bce_L2	*0.04 (0.55)	*0.09 (0.56)	†-0.26 (0.27)	†-0.23 (0.31)
TC-S_Rand3750_bce	*0.31 (0.05)	*0.36 (0.03)	†0.16 (0.29)	†0.18 (0.26)
TC-S_Rand3750	†0.15 (0.17)	*0.11 (0.02)	†-0.14 (0.24)	†-0.06 (0.27)

Table 10: Validation correlation of all of tested variants and ablations of our model. H vs. TC-S indicates training set (HUMOD or subset of TopicalChat respectively). IDK vs. Rand3750 indicates whether negative examples are "i don't know" or random. If bce is present, then BCE was used as the loss, otherwise our modified triplet loss is used. If L1 or L2 is present, then L1 or L2 regularization with $\lambda = 1$ is used respectively, otherwise no regularization is used. Again, standard deviation over three trials is reported in parentheses, and '*' is used to indicate that all trials were significant at $p < 0.01$. '†' indicates at least one trial was significantly different from zero at $p < 0.01$. Note that L1 and L2 regularization have similar effects, with the exception of worse performance between TC-S_Rand2750_bce_L1 and TC-S_Rand2750_bce_L2; we suspect this could be overcome with hyperparameter tuning.

	HUMOD		USR-TC		P-DD		FED-Correctness		FED-Relevance	
Prior Metric	S	P	S	P	S	P	S	P	S	P
NUP-BERT (H)	*0.33 (0.02)	*0.37 (0.02)	0.10 (0.02)	*0.22 (0.01)	***0.62** (0.04)	*0.54 (0.02)	†0.14 (0.04)	*0.21 (0.03)	*0.22 (0.01)	***0.30** (0.01)
NUP-BERT (TC-S)	*0.29 (0.02)	*0.35 (0.03)	†0.17 (0.03)	†0.20 (0.04)	*0.58 (0.05)	*0.56 (0.04)	0.05 (0.04)	0.12 (0.01)	†0.16 (0.04)	*0.21 (0.01)
NUP-BERT (TC)	*0.30 (0.01)	*0.38 (0.00)	0.16 (0.02)	*0.21 (0.02)	***0.62** (0.05)	***0.58** (0.04)	0.06 (0.01)	†0.12 (0.02)	*0.18 (0.02)	*0.23 (0.01)
IDK (H)	*0.58 (0.00)	*0.58 (0.00)	0.18 (0.00)	*0.24 (0.00)	*0.53 (0.00)	*0.48 (0.01)	*0.15 (0.00)	***0.23** (0.00)	***0.24** (0.00)	*0.29 (0.00)
IDK (TC-S)	*0.58 (0.00)	*0.58 (0.00)	0.18 (0.00)	*0.22 (0.00)	*0.54 (0.01)	*0.49 (0.01)	*0.15 (0.00)	***0.23** (0.00)	***0.24** (0.00)	*0.29 (0.00)
IDK-ICS (H)	*0.55 (0.01)	*0.53 (0.00)	***0.25** (0.01)	***0.27** (0.00)	*0.44 (0.01)	*0.39 (0.00)	***0.16** (0.00)	*0.22 (0.00)	*0.22 (0.00)	***0.30** (0.00)
IDK-ICS (TC-S)	*0.58 (0.00)	*0.47 (0.00)	0.17 (0.00)	***0.27** (0.00)	*0.52 (0.00)	*0.36 (0.00)	*0.14 (0.00)	*0.16 (0.00)	*0.22 (0.00)	*0.24 (0.00)
IDK-OK (H)	*0.58 (0.00)	***0.59** (0.00)	0.15 (0.00)	*0.23 (0.00)	*0.49 (0.00)	*0.47 (0.00)	0.11 (0.00)	*0.19 (0.00)	*0.19 (0.00)	*0.26 (0.00)
IDK-OK (TC-S)	***0.59** (0.00)	***0.59** (0.00)	0.18 (0.00)	*0.24 (0.00)	*0.52 (0.00)	*0.46 (0.00)	*0.15 (0.00)	***0.23** (0.00)	*0.23 (0.00)	*0.29 (0.00)
BERT NSP	***0.59**	*0.40	0.17	*0.25	*0.53	*0.31	0.12	0.10	*0.21	*0.18

Table 11: Comparison of our proposed metric (IDK) against the pretrained BERT NSP predictor on the test set. We also trained IDK with different fixed negative examples, "i couldn't say" (IDK-ICS) and "i'm ok." (IDK-OK). Note BERT NSP tends to have comparable Spearman's performance and worse Pearson's correlation. The only exception is FED where BERT NSP has inferior performance. In general, IDK with different fixed negative samples outperforms NUP-BERT, and is less sensitive to training data, although not to the same extent as baseline IDK.

H Additional Experiments: Triplet Loss

An intuitive limitation of using "i don't know" as a negative example with BCE loss is that this encourages the model to always map "i don't know" to exactly zero. However, the relevance of "i don't know" evidently varies by context. Clearly, it is a far less relevant response to "I was interrupted all week and couldn't get anything done, it was terrible!" than it is to "what is the key to artificial general intelligence?" Motivated by this intuition, we experimented with a modified triplet loss, $\mathcal{L}(c, r) = -\log(1 + m - f_t(c, r))$ where $f_t(c, r) = \max(y(c, r) - y(c, r') + m, 0)$.

Intuitively, a triplet loss would allow for the relevance of "i don't know" to shift, without impacting the loss as long as the ground-truth responses continue to score sufficiently higher. Note that the loss is modified to combat gradient saturation due to the sigmoid non-linearity. However, the results (see Table 9) suggest equivalence, at best. Often, this loss performs equivalently to BCE but it can also produce degenerate solutions (note the high variance when training on TC data). Furthermore, it does not appear to produce superior correlations.

For this reason, we believe that, although adapting triplet loss for next-utterance prediction in place of BCE could be made to work, it does not appear to provide any advantages. If validation data is available, it can be used to confirm whether the model has reached a degenerate solution, and thus this loss could be used interchangeably with BCE. However, there does not appear to be any advantage in doing so.

I Additional Experiments: BERT NSP

As a followup experiment we compared IDK against directly using the pretrained BERT NSP predictor. In general, Spearman's correlation was comparable on all datasets *except for FED*, and Pearson's correlation was degraded. Performance on FED was inferior to IDK. We speculate that the reason for this is that the FED datasets has longer contexts, which is problematic for the NSP predictor as it was trained with sentences rather than utterances. Results are summarized in Table 11.

J Additional Experiments: IDK with other fixed negative samples

As a followup experiment we trained IDK using two different fixed negative samples: "i couldn't say" (simply chosen as a synonym for "i don't know"), and "i'm ok." (chosen as an example of a generic response from Li et al. (2016)). Results are reported in Table 11; in general we still see an performance improvement over NUP-BERT, and in some cases we exceed the performance of baseline IDK. We also see that performance remains consistent between runs, maintaining a lower standard deviation than NUP-BERT.

However, it is also clear that changing the fixed negative sample has some unexpected consquences: specifically, we see variation based on training data that is not observed when using "i don't know" as the fixed negative sample (although the variation due to training data appears to be less than NUP-BERT).

We retain the reduced sensitivity to test set. Specically, our ratios of best-to-worst Spearman's correlation are 3.44 for IDK-ICS (H), 4.14 for IDK-ICS (TC-S), 5.27 for IDK-OK (H), and 3.93; most are very close to the baseline IDK ratio of 3.9, and all are an improvement on the best prior work; 6.2 on NUP-BERT (H) – it is worth noting that NUP-BERT (TC-S) attains a ratio of 11.6, considerably worse than when trained on HUMOD data.

RetroNLU: Retrieval Augmented Task-Oriented Semantic Parsing

Vivek Gupta[1,2*], **Akshat Shrivastava**[2], **Adithya Sagar**[2], **Armen Aghajanyan**[2], **Denis Savenkov**[2]
[1]School of Computing, University of Utah
[2] Facebook Conversational AI, Menlo Park
vgupta@cs.utah.edu ; {akshats, adithyasagar, armenag, denxx}@fb.com

Abstract

While large pre-trained language models accumulate a lot of knowledge in their parameters, it has been demonstrated that augmenting it with non-parametric retrieval-based memory has a number of benefits ranging from improved accuracy to data efficiency for knowledge-focused tasks such as question answering. In this work, we apply retrieval-based modeling ideas to the challenging complex task of multi-domain task-oriented semantic parsing for conversational assistants. Our technique, RetroNLU, extends a sequence-to-sequence model architecture with a retrieval component, which is used to retrieve existing similar samples and present them as an additional context to the model. In particular, we analyze two settings, where we augment an input with (a) retrieved nearest neighbor utterances (utterance-nn), and (b) ground-truth semantic parses of nearest neighbor utterances (semparse-nn). Our technique outperforms the baseline method by 1.5% absolute macro-F1, especially at the low resource setting, matching the baseline model accuracy with only 40% of the complete data. Furthermore, we analyse the quality, model sensitivity, and performance of the nearest neighbor retrieval component's for semantic parses of varied utterance complexity.

1 Introduction

Roberts et al. (2020) demonstrated that neural language models quite effectively store factual knowledge in their parameters without any external information source. However, such implicit knowledge is hard to update, i.e. remove certain information (Bourtoule et al., 2021), change or add new data and labels. Additionally, parametric knowledge may perform worse for less frequent facts, which don't appear often in the training set, and "hallucinate" responses. On the other hand, memory-augmented models (Sukhbaatar et al., 2015) decouple knowledge source and task-specific "business logic", which allows updating memory index directly without model retraining. Recent studies showed their potential for knowledge-intensive NLP tasks, such as question answering (Khandelwal et al., 2020; Lewis et al., 2020c).

In this work, we explore RetroNLU: retrieval-based modeling approach for task-oriented semantic parsing problem, where explicit memory provides examples of semantic parses, which model needs to learn to transfer to a given input utterance. An example semantic parse for task-oriented dialog utterance and its corresponding hierarchical representation are presented in Figure 1.

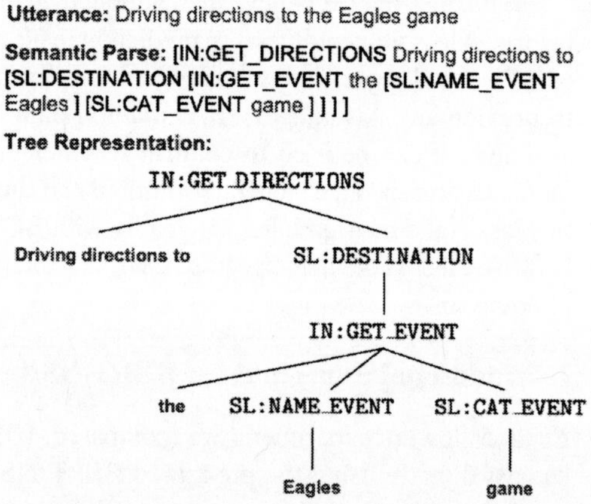

Figure 1: An intent-slot based compositional semantic parsing example(coupled) from TOPv2 (Chen et al., 2020).

In this paper we are focusing on the following questions: (a) *Data Efficiency*: Can retrieval based on non-parametric external knowledge alleviate reliance on parametric knowledge typically acquired via supervised training on large labeled datasets?[1] We examine how different training settings, depending on the amount of supervision data available,

*Work done by author while interning at Facebook Conversational AI.

[1]Parametric knowledge is information stored in model parameters. Non-parametric knowledge refers to external data sources that the model uses to infer.

Proceedings of the 4th Workshop on NLP for Conversational AI, pages 184 - 196
May 27, 2022 ©2022 Association for Computational Linguistics

impact model prediction, i.e. fully supervised vs. limited supervised training. (b) *Semi-supervised Setting*: Can we enhance models by using abundant and inexpensive unlabeled external non-parametric knowledge rather than structurally labeled knowledge? We examine the effect of utilizing unlabeled similar utterances instead of labelled semantic parses as external non-parametric knowledge on model performance. (c) *Robustness to Noise*: Can a model opt to employ parametric knowledge rather than non-parametric knowledge in a resilient manner, for example, when the non-parametric information is unreliable? We examine the model's resilience and its reliance on non-parametric external information. External knowledge is not always precisely labeled and reliable for all examples/utterances. (d) *Utterance Complexity*: Is non-parametric external knowledge addition effective for both uncommon and complex structured (hierarchical) examples? We examine whether external knowledge addition is more beneficial in certain cases than others, or if it supports accurate predictions for all situations equally. It would be fascinating to investigate if external information could also help enhance difficult and complex examples/utterances. Finally, we examine the upper limit on the utility of external information. We examine structural redundancy concerns in nearest neighbor retrieval. (e) *Knowledge Efficiency*: Is it beneficial to continue adding external information, or are there certain boundaries and challenges? Our contribution are as follows:

1. We demonstrate that combining parametric and non-parametric knowledge enhance model performance on the complex structured task of task-oriented semantic parsing.

2. We illustrate the effectiveness of our approach in a critical situation of learning with sparse labeled data (i.e. limited parametric knowledge).

3. We establish the efficacy of retrieval-based method in semi-supervised settings, where model's input is supplemented with unannotated instances (i.e. unlabeled examples).

4. By comparing predictions on clean vs. noisy neighbours, we establish the model's resilience to external non-parametric knowledge quality.

5. Finally, we examine performance gains with inputs of varying complexity: semantic structure composition and it's frequency (i.e. frequent/rare).

Overall, we demonstrate that retrieval enhanced method can improve performance on complicated structured prediction tasks like task oriented semantic parsing without extra supervision. Furthermore, the augmentation approach is data efficient and performs well in low resource settings with limited label data. The dataset, and associated scripts, will be available at `https://retronlu.github.io`.

2 Proposed Approach

Our proposed approach consists of four main steps: (a) **index construction** by embedding training examples and computing cosine similarity; (b) **retrieval**, where we extract the nearest neighbor utterances from the index given an example utterance; (c) **augmentation**, in which we append the nearest-neighbor utterance ground truth semantic parse (semparse-nn) or the utterance itself (utterance-nn) to the original input via a special separator token (such as '|'); and (d) **semantic parsing**, in which we train the parsing model using the retrieval-augmented input with output ground truth. Figure 2 illustrates the Retrieval Augmented Semantic Parsing (RETRONLU) approach.

Indexing: To build an index we use a pre-trained BART model to get training utterance embeddings. More specifically, we get sentence embedding for all the training utterances. These sentence embeddings are obtained as average of token embeddings from last model layers of the BART models.[2] We then used the cosine similarity between embeddings to build a fast and efficient retrieval index with efficient FAISS library (Johnson et al., 2019).

Retrieval: Next, given a new input (training or test row), we obtain embeddings by running it through same pre-trained BART, and then query the index with it to retrieve nearest neighbors text and their ground truth semantic parses based on cosine similarity. For training data, we exclude an example itself from the retrieved list. For example, for input utterance *"please add 20 minutes on the lasagna timer"*, we retrieve the nearest neighbour *"add ten minutes to the oven timer"* along

[2]extract_features function `https://github.com/pytorch/fairseq/tree/main/examples/bart`

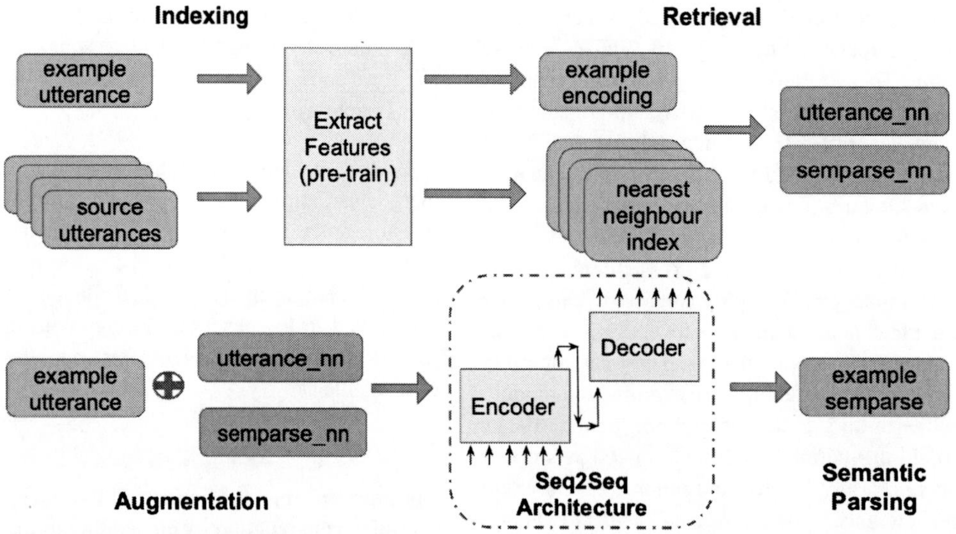

Figure 2: High level flowchart for retrieval augmented semantic parsing (RETRONLU) approach.

with the semantic parse as *"[in:add_ time_ timer add [sl:date_ time ten minutes] to the [sl:timer_ name oven] [sl:method_ timer timer]]"*.

Augmentation: Once we got a list of nearest neighbors, we can append either utterance text or semantic parse to the input, following the left to right order.[3] The closest neighbor appears to the immediate left of the input example utterance. One can also directly append the nearest neighbor utterance rather than the semparse, refer as utterance-nn. For the last example the final input would after augmentation would be *"[in:add_ time_ timer add [sl:date_ time ten minutes] to the [sl:timer_ name oven] [sl:method_ timer timer]] | please add 20 minutes on the lasagna timer"* for semparse-nn, and *"add ten minutes to the oven timer | please add 20 minutes on the lasagna timer"* for utterance-nn. Here, the token '|' act as a separator between the input utterance and the neighbour's.

Semantic Parsing: The final step is to train a sequence-to-sequence model such as LSTM or Transformer. We fine-tune a BART model with copy mechanism (Aghajanyan et al., 2020), which incorporates benefits of pre-trained language model (BART) and sequence copy mechanism (copy-ptr), and most importantly obtain state-of-the-art results on the TOPv2 (Chen et al., 2020), a challenging task oriented semantic parsing dataset with hierarchical compositional instances. The retrieval augmented example is an input to the encoder and the corresponding ground-truth semantic parse as the labeled decoded sequence. At test time, we simply pass the augmented input to the trained RETRONLU model, and take it's output as the predicted semantic parse for the input utterance.

[3]We followed GPT-3 and other generation model, where task examples are pre-pended to the input. Hence, utterance is always nearest to the decoder followed by the first nearest neighbour inorder.

3 Experiment and Analysis

Our experiments examines how our knowledge retrieval-based augmentation technique impacts model performance indicators such as accuracy and data efficiency. We study the following questions:

RQ1. Can today's pre-trained models leverage non-parametric information in manner as described in §2 to enhance task-oriented semantic parsing?

RQ2. If only part of the dataset has semantic parses, i.e. limited supervision setting, can augmentation with unannotated instances (utterance_nn) enhance semantic parsing accuracy?

RQ3. How efficient is a retrieval-augmented model in terms of data? Is it more accurate even with less training data than the baseline seq2seq model?

RQ4. Does non-parametric memory benefit instances equally, e.g., do we notice greater benefits for (a) more complex (i.e. compositional) or (b) less frequent semantic frames (i.e. tail over head)?

RQ5. (a) Does augmentation with more nearest neighbors benefits? (b) How sensitive is the model to retrieval noise? Can the model predict right intent/slots for low-quality retrieve instances?

Our experiments are designed to demonstrate how non-parametric external information can be beneficial to a parametric model and to undertake an in-depth assessment of the impact.[4]

3.1 Experimental setup

In this section, we discuss the datasets, preprocessing, and the model used in the experiments.

Datasets. For our experiments, we used the multi-domain complex compositional queries based popular TOPv2 (Chen et al., 2020) dataset for task-oriented semantic parsing. We concentrated our efforts on task-oriented parsing because of the commercial importance of data efficiency requirements in conversational AI assistants dialogues.[5] The TOPv2 dataset contains utterances and their semantic representations for 8 domains: source domains - 'alarm', 'messaging', 'music', 'navigation', 'timer', and 'event', and target domains: 'reminder' and 'weather', designed especially to test the zero-shot setting. For our experiments we chose source domains, which has a good mixture of simple (flat) and complex (compositional) semantic frames. For dataset statistics refer Table 1 in Chen et al. (2020).

Data Processing. To build a retrieval index we used the training split of the dataset. Each utterance was represented by its BART-based embedding and indexed using FAISS library (Johnson et al., 2019). [6] With FAISS computation cost of updating indexing was kept to bare minimum. The only additional cost will be increase in inference time due to augmented neighbor. To produce augmented examples, we retrieved nearest neighbors for each training and test examples from the training set, except excluding all training instances with exact utterance matches. In the augmented examples, we use the special token '|' to separate the nearest neighbors, as well as utterance with the first neighbor.[7] We used only one neighbor for most experiments except when we analyse multiple neighbors effects on performance.

In nearest neighbor augmented input, we followed right to left order, where the actual model input comes last, and its highest ranked neighbor is appended to the left of the utterance, followed by other neighbors in the left based on their ranking. [8] For input data pre-processing, we follow (Chen et al., 2020) procedure, we obtain BPE tokens of all tokens, except ontology tokens (intents and slot labels), which are treated as atomic tokens and appended to the BPE vocabulary. Furthermore, we use the decoupled canonical form of semparse for all our experiments. For decoupling, phrases irrelevant to slot values are removed from semparse, and for canonicality, slots are arranged in alphabetic order (Aghajanyan et al., 2020).

Models. For fair comparison with the earlier baseline, we use the state-of-the-art BART based Seq2Seq-CopyPtr model for task-oriented semantic parsing. [9] The BART based Seq2Seq-CopyPtr model initialize both the encoder and decoder with pre-trained BART (Lewis et al., 2020b) model and also use the copy mechanism similar to See et al. (2017), refer Chen et al. (2020) for details. We choose the BART based Seq2Seq-CopyPtr model for the task because it's a strong baseline, the performance of the other language model such as RoBERTa without augmentation was inferior (Chen et al., 2020; Aghajanyan et al., 2020). On out-of-domain instances, RoBERTa-CopyPtr performs 0.6 % worse than BART-CopyPtr.[10] The model is using the copy mechanism (See et al., 2017), which enables it to directly copy tokens from the input utterance (or from example semantic parses from nearest neighbors).

Hyperparameters. We use the same default hyper-parameters for all models training , i.e. baseline (without-nn) and RETRONLU models (utternce-nn, semparse-nn). For training we use 100 epochs, Adam optimizer (Kingma and Ba, 2014) with learning rate α of $1e-4$ and decay rate β_1 and β_2 of 0.9 and 0.98 respectively in all our experiments. Also, we didn't added any left or right padding and rely on variable length encoding in our experiments. We use warm-up steps of 4000,

[4]We did not seek to modify the architecture which ensure the augmentation methodology is flexible.

[5]Regardless of augmented neighbors structure the approach remain consistent.

[6]We use L2 over unit norm BART embedding for indexing.

[7]Using different separator tokens for neighbor-neighbor pair and utterance-neighbor pair didn't improve performance.

[8]Similar performance is obtained by ordering utterances left to right, followed by their neighbors in index order.

[9]We prefer transformer-based language model over non-transformer models, such as LSTM, because the later does not capture extended context as well as the former.

[10]Our findings, however, we believe, are universal and can be applied to different models, including RoBERTa.

dropout ratio of 0.4, and weight decay 0.0001, but no clip normalization as regularization during the training. We use batch size of 128 and maximum token size of 2048. Furthermore, to ensure both encoder and decoder BART, can utilise the extra nearest neighbour information, we increase the embedding dimension to 1024.

3.2 Results and Analysis

This section summarizes our findings in relation to the aforementioned research questions.

Full Training Setting. To answer RQ1, we compare performance of original baseline (without-nn) with our retrieval augmented models, i.e. augmenting first neighbour utterance (utterance-nn) and augmenting first neighbour semantic parse (semparse-nn). Table 1 compares the frame accuracy of retrieval augmented (a) top nearest neighbour utterance (utterance-nn), (b) top nearest neighbour ground-truth semantic parse (semparse-nn) with original baseline (without-nn) with model train on complete training data.

Domains	without-nn	utterance-nn	semparse-nn
Alarm	86.67	87.17	**88.57**
Event	83.83	**85.03**	84.77
Music	79.80	**80.73**	**80.71**
Timer	81.21	**81.75**	81.01
Messaging	93.50	94.52	**94.65**
Navigation	82.96	84.16	**85.20**
micro-avg	84.43	85.28	**85.74**
macro-avg	84.66	85.56	**85.82**

Table 1: Performance of RETRONLU w.r.t original baseline (without-nn) with full training.

Analysis: We observe performance improvements with retrieval-augmented models for most domains compared to the original baseline (without-nn) in both cases. The increase in performance (micro-avg) is more substantial 1.4% with semparse-nn compare to 0.85% with utterance-nn. The improvement in utterance-nn augmentation performance is likely due to memorization-based generalization, as explained earlier by (Khandelwal et al., 2019).[11] The results shows the retrieval augmented semantic parsing is overall effective. Furthermore, the performance enhancement can be obtained also with unstructured utterance (utternace-nn) as nearest neighbour. The utterance-nn based augmentation is particularly beneficial in semi-supervised scenarios, where we have a large unlabelled dataset.

[11]The scores are averaged over three runs with std. of 0.3%

Limited Training Setting. To answer RQ2, we compare model performance which are trained with limited training data. Figure 3 shows frame accuracy (micro-avg) when we use only 10% to 50% of the training data. The training datasets are created in an incremental setting so that next set include examples from the former set. Additionally, we use the complete index to retrieve the nearest neighbors.

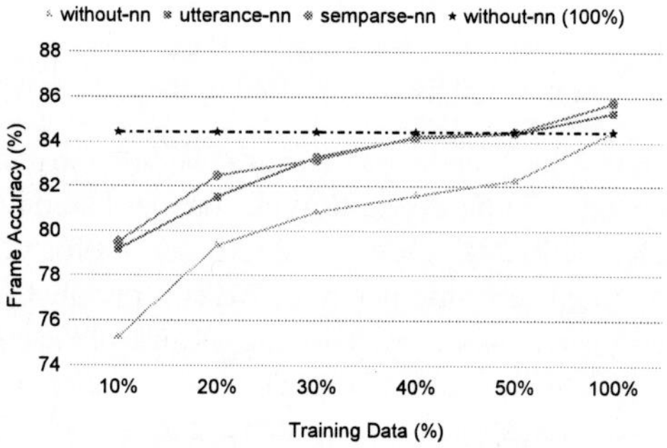

Figure 3: Performance of RETRONLU w.r.t original baseline (without-nn) with limited supervised training. The x-axis is linearly scaled upto 50% data.

Analysis: As expected, the performance of all models increases with training set size. Both retrieval augmented models i.e. utterance-nn and semparse-nn outperform the without-nn baseline for all the training sizes. The improvement via augmentation is more substantial with less training data, i.e. 4.24% at 10% data vs 1.30% at 100% data. Furthermore, the semparse-nn augmented model outperforms the original completely train (without-nn) model with only 40% of the data (i..e RQ3). The results show that the retrieval augmented semantic parsing is more data efficient, i.e. when there is (a) limited labelled training dataset with more unlabelled data for indexing (utterance-nn), and (b) sufficient training data but limited training time (semparse-nn).

The first case is useful when the ground truth label is missing for utterances due to lack of annotation resources. In such a scenario, one can build the index using large amount of unlabeled utterances and use the index for augmentation. The second case helps us train the model faster, while maintaining all annotated examples in the index. In such a case, one can update the retrieval index only, without re-training the model again and again. This is useful when training on full data is not possible due to limited access to model (black-box), a cap on the computation resources, or for saving training time i.e. industries fast deployment need. E.g. There is a constant stream of bugs relating to misclassified examples in production systems. Our RETRONLU approach enables rapid adjustment of the system's behavior without retraining or establishing a new model.

Effect of Utterance Complexity. To answer RQ4(a), we analyse the retrieval augmented model performance improvements (with full training) on simple utterance with only one level in semantic representation (depth-1) vs complex utterance with hierarchical semantic frames (compositional depth-2 and above). Figure 4 shows frame accuracy of without-nn, utterance-nn and semparse-nn model with utterance complexity.

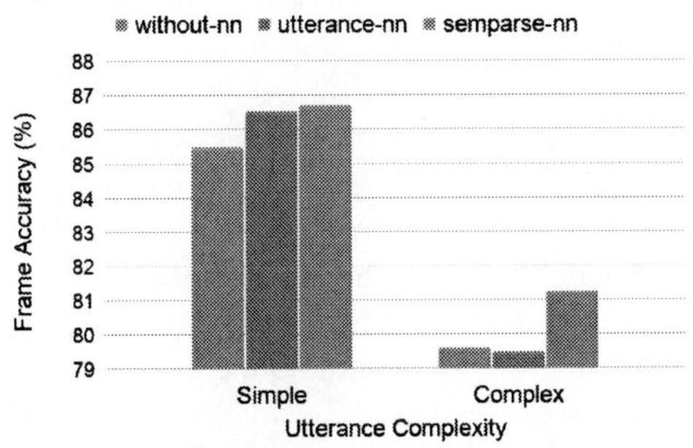

Figure 4: Performance comparison (micro-avg) of RETRONLU w.r.t original baseline (without-nn) with utterance complexity, i.e. simple and complex.

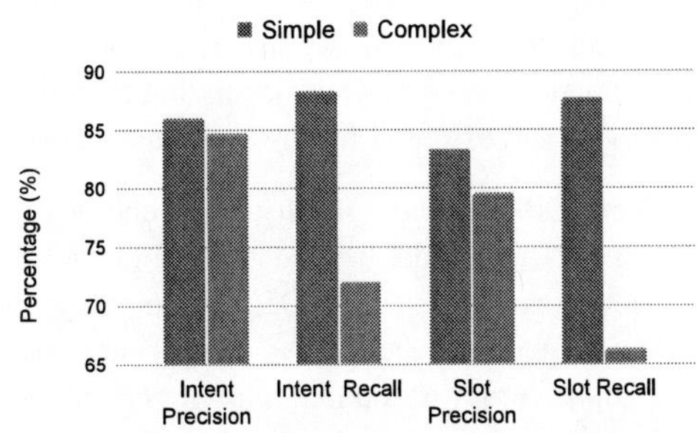

Figure 5: Precision and Recall of intents and slots for semparse-nn nearest neighbour w.r.t to gold semparse.

Analysis: As expected, all models perform relatively poorly on complex utterances (79.5%) in comparison to simple utterances (85.5%). Interestingly, both augmentation models equally improve performance on simple queries. And with semantic-frame based augmentation we observe a substantial performance improvement on complex challenging utterances, of 2%, with respect to the original baseline (without-nn). This suggests, that by retrieving nearest neighbors and providing a model with examples of complex parses, the model learns to apply it to a new request. Figure 5 shows precision and recall for intents and slots in retrieved semantic parses. The recall for intent and slot retrieval is 15% lower for complex utterances. [12] Thus, highlighting one reason for a performance gap between simple and complex frames.

Effect of Frame Rareness. To answer RQ4(b), we analyze the retrieval augmented model performance improvement (with full training data) with frame rareness, as shown in Figure 6.

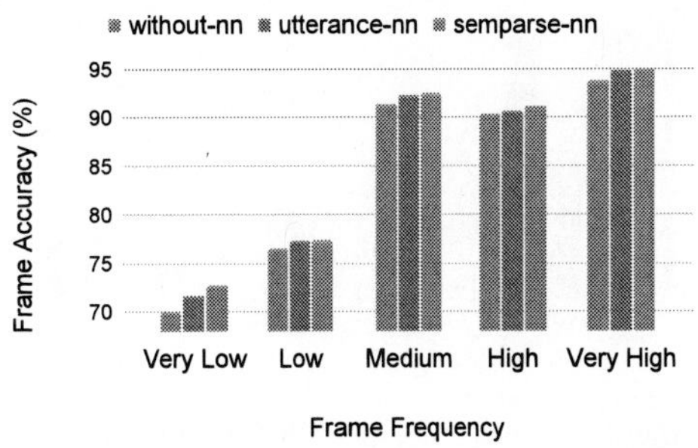

Figure 6: Performance of RETRONLU w.r.t original baseline (without-nn) with varying frame frequency.

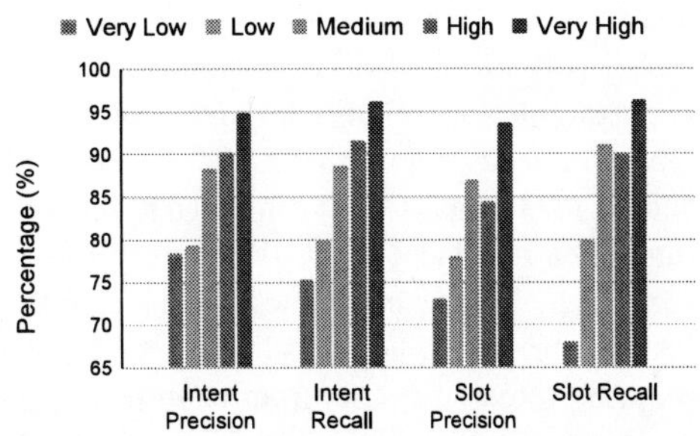

Figure 7: Precision and Recall of intents and slots w.r.t to frame frequency for semparse-nn of the RETRONLU.

Rare or uncommon frames are those example utterances whose ground truth semantic parses without slot value tokens appear infrequently in the training set. To analyze this, we divided the test set into five equal sizes i.e., *Very Low*, *Low*, *Medium*, *High*, and *Very High* sets, based on the frequency of

[12]The precision gap was small 1% (intents) and 4% (slots).

semantic frame structure. The experiment checks if performance improvement is mainly attributed to frequently repeating frames (frequent frames) or for rarely occurring frames (uncommon frames).

Analysis: Figure 6 shows that all models perform worse on rare frames. This is expected as the parametric model gets less data for training on these frames. Furthermore, many of the low-frequency frames are also complex utterances with more than one intent and have more slots too. Moreover, the nearest neighbour will be noisier for less frequent frames. This is evident from the lower values of precision (20% gap) and recall (25% gap) on the intent and slots for nearest neighbors in Figure 7.

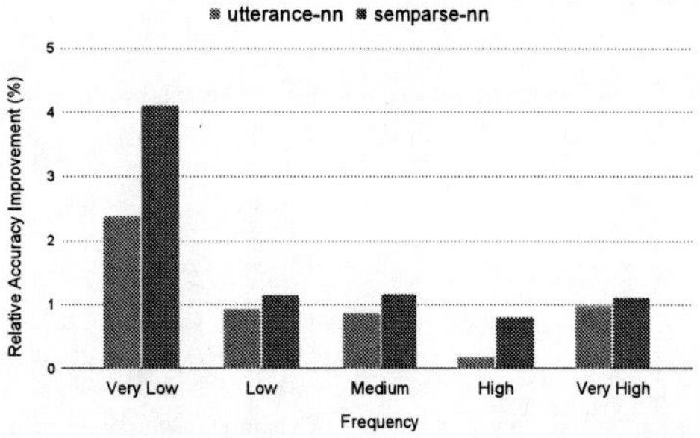

Figure 8: Relative performance improvement of RETRONLU w.r.t original baseline (without-nn) with varying frame frequency.

However, compared to original baseline (without-nn) the relative performance improvement on rare frames with retrieval augmented model is more substantial, as shown in Figure 8. For example, the relative improvement for *Very Low* frequency frames is 2.37% (utterance-nn) and 4.11% (semparse-nn) compared to just 1.01% (utterance-nn) and 1.11 % (semparse-nn)for the *Very High* Frequency frames. We suspect this is because of the model's ability to copy the required intent and slots from nearest neighbors if the parametric knowledge fails to generate it. This shows the retrieval augmented model is even more beneficial for the rare frames. As earlier, semparse-nn outperform utterance-nn.

Effect of the number of neighbors. To answer RQ5(a), we compare k = 1, 2, and 3 nearest neighbours for both utterance-nn and semparse-nn setups[13] The results are reported in Table 2.

[13]Extending beyond 3 neighbors was not useful for many reasons: (a) the BART 512 tokenization limit, (b) exponential rise in training time, and (c) only minimal performance gain.

#neighbors	k = 1	k = 2	k = 3
without-nn	84.43	84.43	84.43
utterance-nn	85.28	85.35	85.40
semparse-nn	**85.74**	**85.81**	**85.80**

Table 2: Performance with increasing nearest neighbors.

Metric	Average Precision		Average Recall	
Intent	**Farthest**	**Closest**	**Farthest**	**Closest**
Train	81.39	**84.84**	81.81	**85.04**
Valid	80.46	**87.59**	81.10	**87.93**
Test	79.09	**86.23**	79.35	**86.22**
Slot	**Farthest**	**Closest**	**Farthest**	**Closest**
Train	75.02	**80.05**	79.56	**83.19**
Valid	73.40	**82.38**	79.77	**85.81**
Test	74.59	**83.21**	79.51	**85.11**

Table 3: Intent-slots precision/recall for RETRONLU semparse-nn with closest/farthest neighbors.

Analysis: As shown in Table 2 the model performance only improves marginally with more nearest neighbors. We attribute this to the following two reasons (a) redundancy - many utterance examples can share the same frame, as evident from the high accuracy for frequent frame Figure 6., and (b) complexity - as k increases, the problem is getting harder for the model with longer inputs, more irrelevant and noisier inputs. To further verify the above reasons, we examine the semparse-nn retrieve nearest neighbors quality by comparing the intent and slot both Precision and Recall score for closest (k=1) and farthest (k=3) neighbor w.r.t to the gold semparse. From Table 3 it is evident that precision and recall for intents and slots decrease as we go down the ranked neighbors list. Adding more nearest neighbour would only be beneficial when added neighbour capture diverse and different semantic structure which is missing from earlier neighbor and essential for the correct semparse.

Effect of Retrieval Quality. To check if our RETRONLU model is robust to the noise in the retrieved examples (i.e. RQ5(b)), we analyse the effect of quality of retrieval by comparing semantic parsing accuracy of top neighbor augmented models on the test data with (a) the top neighbour with random neighbor from domain other than the example domain, and (b) random neighbor selected from the top 100 ranked nearest neighbors in the index. It should be noted that these 100 top rank nearest neighbour can have some redundant semparse-nn structure, only slot values might differ. Figure 9 shows the results of the experiments.

Analysis: From Figure 9 it is clear that quality of nearest neighbor affect the semantic parsing ac-

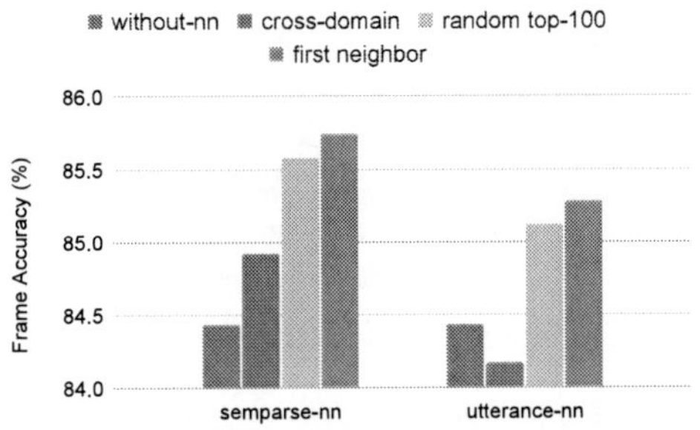

Figure 9: Performance of RETRONLU with varying nearest neighbor quality on test data.

curacy. We observe a 0.4% drop when random neighbor from top 100 nearest neighbors is chosen, instead of first neighbor, the small drop is because of redundancy in intent/slots structure between examples, only slots value could be major difference. However, the performance is still 0.9% to 1.0% better than the one without the nearest neighbor. We suspect this is because of the fact that the data has many utterances with similar semparse output. Upon deeper inspection we found that top-100 still includes many relevant frames, and therefore random examples from top-100 are often still relevant. Furthermore, there is also frame redundancy, many different utterance queries have similar semantic parse frames structure and only differ at the slot values. This is also evident from table 2 which shows adding more neighbors is not beneficial, because of frame redundancy. Surprisingly, we also observe that the model performance with random cross-domain neighbor is better than without-nn for semparse-nn by 0.5%. This shows that the model knows when to ignore the nearest neighbors and when to rely on the parametric model. Furthermore, it also indicates that underlying parametric model parameters is improved by retrieval augmented training for the semparse-nn.

For the utterance-nn the performance drops when testing on cross-domain nearest neighbor augmented example. Thus, underlying the utterance-nn model is more sensitive than semparse-nn to the nearest neighbor quality. In addition, we also conducted an experiment in which we added the best possible neighbor based on the gold parse frame structure. The trained model, though this approach was not robust and relies too heavily on coping frames from neighbors, resulting in poor generalization. Our technique, on the other hand, with embedding-based retrieval, is good at generalization and has enhances the underlying parametric model. Overall, we can conclude that the semparse-nn and utterance-nn model are both quite robust to nearest neighbors quality. We can also conclude that the semparse-nn model was able to capture richer information through additional similar inputs than without-nn. However, to obtain the best performance good quality neighbour is an essential.

4 Comparison with Related Work

Task-oriented Semantic Parsing. Sequence-to-sequence (*seq2seq*) models have recently achieved state of the art results in semantic parsing (Rongali et al., 2020; Gupta et al., 2018), and they also provide a flexible framework for incorporating session-based, complex hierarchical semantic parsing (Sun et al., 2019; Aghajanyan et al., 2020; Cheng et al., 2020; Mehri et al., 2020) and multilingual semantic parsing (Li et al., 2021; Louvan and Magnini, 2020). Architectures, such as T5 and BART (Raffel et al., 2020; Lewis et al., 2020b), with large pre-trained language models pushed the performance even further. Such models are quite capable of storing a lot of knowledge in their parameters (Roberts et al., 2020), and in this work we explore the benefits of additional non-parametric knowledge in a form of nearest neighbor retrieval for the task of semantic parsing. To improve low resource seq2seq parsers Chen et al. (2020) have proposed looking at meta learning methods such as reptile, and Ghoshal et al. (2021) have introduced new fine-tuning objectives. Our approach is focused on non-architecture changes to augment generation with retrieval and thus can be combined with either of these approaches.

Incorporating External Knowledge. An idea to help a model by providing an additional information, relevant to the task at hand is not new. This includes both implicit memory tables (Weston et al., 2014; Sukhbaatar et al., 2015), as well as incorporating this knowledge explicitly as an augmentation to the input. Explicit knowledge are incorporated in one of the following two ways (a) suitable model architecture change to incorporate dedicated extended memory space internally i.e. memory network (Bapna and Firat, 2019; Guu et al., 2020; Lewis et al., 2020a; Tran et al., 2020) or span pointer networks (Desai and Aly, 2021; Shrivastava et al., 2021), and (b) appending example specific extra knowledge externally with the input example directly without modifying model architecture (Papernot and McDaniel, 2018; Weston et al., 2018; Lewis et al., 2020c; Tran et al., 2020; Khandelwal et al., 2021; Fan et al., 2021; Chen et al., 2018; Wang et al., 2019; Neeraja et al., 2021) . Retrieval-augmented approaches have been improving language model pre-training as well (Guu et al., 2020; Lewis et al., 2020a; Tran et al., 2020). The idea here is to decouple memorizing factual knowledge and actual language modeling tasks, which can help mitigate hallucinations, and other common problems.

Multiple works like DkNN (Papernot and McDaniel, 2018), RAG (Lewis et al., 2020c), kNN-LM (Tran et al., 2020), kNN-MT (Khandelwal et al., 2021), and KIF-Transformer (Fan et al., 2021) show that external knowledge is useful for large pre-trained language models, and can help fine-tuning. DkNN shows that nearest neighbour augmented transformer-based neutral network is more robust and interpretable. RAG shows that one can append external knowledge to improve open domian, cloze-style question answering, and even fact verification task such as FEVER. kNN-LM shows that for cloze task for fact completion, one can combine nearest neighbour predictions with original prediction using appropriate weighting to improve model performance. However, these works mostly study knowledge dependent question answering task, while we are exploring a complex task of structural prediction of semantic frame structures for task-oriented dialog.

Very recently, Pasupat et al. (2021) share similar finding of exemplar augmentation and propose ControllAble Semantic Parser via Exemplar Retrieval (CASPER). In their work, the semantic parser gets relevant exemplars from a retrieval index, augments them with the query, and then generates an output parse using a generative seq2seq model. The exemplars serve as a control mechanism for the generic generative model: by modifying the retrieval index or the construction of the augmented query, one may alter the parser's behavior. Compare to them, our study focuses more on the influence of augmentation on the performance of the state-of-the-art Copy Transformer BART model for task-oriented semantic parsing. By design, the copy transformer effectively utilizes it's copy mechanism to get non-parametric information from augmented nearest neighbor semparse/utterances. Additionally, we conduct a detailed investigation of the influence of retrieval quality, utterance and semantic complexity, and the rarity of semantic frames. We anticipate that our findings will shed light on the potential advantages of retrieval enhancing parametric neural networks for the complex structural task of task-oriented semantic parsing.

5 Conclusion and Future Work

We show that task-oriented semantic parsing performance can be enhanced by augmenting neural model-stored parametric information with non-parametric external memory. On the TOPv2 dataset, we demonstrated that adding instances derived from a nearest neighbor index greatly improves the semantic parsing performance of a BART model with copy mechanism. Our RETRONLU model is able to achieve higher accuracy earlier with less training data (limited supervision setting), which allows maintaining a large index with annotated data, while using only a subset to train a model more efficiently. Lastly, we performed an analysis of performance improvements on different slices, and found RETRONLU to be more effective on rarer complex frames, compared to a traditional *seq2seq* model.

RETRONLU extensions, we focus on joint training of retrieval and parsing components. Having task specific utterances representation can benefit i.e. finding utterances with similar semantic parse. Exploring few/zero-shot performance could be interesting direction. Having an easily-updateable index enables you to amend annotations, add new ones, or remove existing ones, without affecting the model. It will be useful to study other approaches of sentence embedding, such as Reimers and Gurevych (2019). Finally, using cross-lingual representations such as mBART (Liu et al., 2020), could help multilingual semantic parsing.

Acknowledgements

We thank members of the Utah NLP group for their valuable insights and suggestions at various stages of the project; and reviewers their helpful comments. Additionally, we would like to express our gratitude to Xilun Chen, Asish Ghoshal, Arash Einolghozati, Shrey Desai, Anchit Gupta, Abhinav Arora, Sonal Gupta, Alexander Zotov, Ahmed Aly, and Luke Zettlemoyer of Meta (Formerly Facebook AI) for their insightful feedback and suggestions.

References

Armen Aghajanyan, Jean Maillard, Akshat Shrivastava, Keith Diedrick, Michael Haeger, Haoran Li, Yashar Mehdad, Veselin Stoyanov, Anuj Kumar, Mike Lewis, and Sonal Gupta. 2020. Conversational semantic parsing. In *Proceedings of the 2020 Conference on Empirical Methods in Natural Language Processing (EMNLP)*, pages 5026–5035, Online. Association for Computational Linguistics.

Ankur Bapna and Orhan Firat. 2019. Non-parametric adaptation for neural machine translation. In *Proceedings of the 2019 Conference of the North American Chapter of the Association for Computational Linguistics: Human Language Technologies, Volume 1 (Long and Short Papers)*, pages 1921–1931, Minneapolis, Minnesota. Association for Computational Linguistics.

Lucas Bourtoule, Varun Chandrasekaran, Christopher A Choquette-Choo, Hengrui Jia, Adelin Travers, Baiwu Zhang, David Lie, and Nicolas Papernot. 2021. Machine unlearning. In *2021 IEEE Symposium on Security and Privacy (SP)*, pages 141–159. IEEE.

Qian Chen, Xiaodan Zhu, Zhen-Hua Ling, Diana Inkpen, and Si Wei. 2018. Neural natural language inference models enhanced with external knowledge. In *Proceedings of the 56th Annual Meeting of the Association for Computational Linguistics (Volume 1: Long Papers)*, pages 2406–2417, Melbourne, Australia. Association for Computational Linguistics.

Xilun Chen, Asish Ghoshal, Yashar Mehdad, Luke Zettlemoyer, and Sonal Gupta. 2020. Low-resource domain adaptation for compositional task-oriented semantic parsing. In *Proceedings of the 2020 Conference on Empirical Methods in Natural Language Processing (EMNLP)*, pages 5090–5100, Online. Association for Computational Linguistics.

Jianpeng Cheng, Devang Agrawal, Héctor Martínez Alonso, Shruti Bhargava, Joris Driesen, Federico Flego, Dain Kaplan, Dimitri Kartsaklis, Lin Li, Dhivya Piraviperumal, Jason D. Williams, Hong Yu, Diarmuid Ó Séaghdha, and Anders Johannsen. 2020. Conversational semantic parsing for dialog state tracking. In *Proceedings of the 2020 Conference on Empirical Methods in Natural Language Processing (EMNLP)*, pages 8107–8117, Online. Association for Computational Linguistics.

Shrey Desai and Ahmed Aly. 2021. Diagnosing transformers in task-oriented semantic parsing. In *Findings of the Association for Computational Linguistics: ACL-IJCNLP 2021*, pages 57–62, Online. Association for Computational Linguistics.

Angela Fan, Claire Gardent, Chloé Braud, and Antoine Bordes. 2021. Augmenting transformers with KNN-based composite memory for dialog. *Transactions of the Association for Computational Linguistics*, 9:82–99.

Asish Ghoshal, Xilun Chen, Sonal Gupta, Luke Zettlemoyer, and Yashar Mehdad. 2021. Learning better structured representations using low-rank adaptive label smoothing. In *International Conference on Learning Representations*.

Sonal Gupta, Rushin Shah, Mrinal Mohit, Anuj Kumar, and Mike Lewis. 2018. Semantic parsing for task oriented dialog using hierarchical representations. In *Proceedings of the 2018 Conference on Empirical Methods in Natural Language Processing*, pages 2787–2792, Brussels, Belgium. Association for Computational Linguistics.

Kelvin Guu, Kenton Lee, Zora Tung, Panupong Pasupat, and Mingwei Chang. 2020. Retrieval augmented language model pre-training. In *Proceedings of the 37th International Conference on Machine Learning*, volume 119 of *Proceedings of Machine Learning Research*, pages 3929–3938. PMLR.

Jeff Johnson, Matthijs Douze, and Hervé Jégou. 2019. Billion-scale similarity search with gpus. *IEEE Transactions on Big Data*.

Urvashi Khandelwal, Angela Fan, Dan Jurafsky, Luke Zettlemoyer, and Mike Lewis. 2021. Nearest neighbor machine translation. In *International Conference on Learning Representations*.

Urvashi Khandelwal, Omer Levy, Dan Jurafsky, Luke Zettlemoyer, and Mike Lewis. 2019. Generalization through memorization: Nearest neighbor language models. In *International Conference on Learning Representations*.

Urvashi Khandelwal, Omer Levy, Dan Jurafsky, Luke Zettlemoyer, and Mike Lewis. 2020. Generalization through memorization: Nearest neighbor language models. In *International Conference on Learning Representations*.

Diederik P Kingma and Jimmy Ba. 2014. Adam: A method for stochastic optimization. *arXiv preprint arXiv:1412.6980*.

Mike Lewis, Marjan Ghazvininejad, Gargi Ghosh, Armen Aghajanyan, Sida Wang, and Luke Zettlemoyer. 2020a. Pre-training via paraphrasing. In *Advances in Neural Information Processing Systems*, volume 33, pages 18470–18481. Curran Associates, Inc.

Mike Lewis, Yinhan Liu, Naman Goyal, Marjan Ghazvininejad, Abdelrahman Mohamed, Omer Levy, Veselin Stoyanov, and Luke Zettlemoyer. 2020b. BART: Denoising sequence-to-sequence pre-training for natural language generation, translation, and comprehension. In *Proceedings of the 58th Annual Meeting of the Association for Computational Linguistics*, pages 7871–7880, Online. Association for Computational Linguistics.

Patrick Lewis, Ethan Perez, Aleksandra Piktus, Fabio Petroni, Vladimir Karpukhin, Naman Goyal, Heinrich Küttler, Mike Lewis, Wen-tau Yih, Tim Rocktäschel, Sebastian Riedel, and Douwe Kiela. 2020c.

Retrieval-augmented generation for knowledge-intensive nlp tasks. In *Advances in Neural Information Processing Systems*, volume 33, pages 9459–9474. Curran Associates, Inc.

Haoran Li, Abhinav Arora, Shuohui Chen, Anchit Gupta, Sonal Gupta, and Yashar Mehdad. 2021. MTOP: A comprehensive multilingual task-oriented semantic parsing benchmark. In *Proceedings of the 16th Conference of the European Chapter of the Association for Computational Linguistics: Main Volume*, pages 2950–2962, Online. Association for Computational Linguistics.

Chunxi Liu, Qiaochu Zhang, Xiaohui Zhang, Kritika Singh, Yatharth Saraf, and Geoffrey Zweig. 2020. Multilingual graphemic hybrid ASR with massive data augmentation. In *Proceedings of the 1st Joint Workshop on Spoken Language Technologies for Under-resourced languages (SLTU) and Collaboration and Computing for Under-Resourced Languages (CCURL)*, pages 46–52, Marseille, France. European Language Resources association.

Samuel Louvan and Bernardo Magnini. 2020. Recent neural methods on slot filling and intent classification for task-oriented dialogue systems: A survey. In *Proceedings of the 28th International Conference on Computational Linguistics*, pages 480–496, Barcelona, Spain (Online). International Committee on Computational Linguistics.

Shikib Mehri, Mihail Eric, and Dilek Hakkani-Tur. 2020. Dialoglue: A natural language understanding benchmark for task-oriented dialogue. *arXiv preprint arXiv:2009.13570*.

J. Neeraja, Vivek Gupta, and Vivek Srikumar. 2021. Incorporating external knowledge to enhance tabular reasoning. In *Proceedings of the 2021 Conference of the North American Chapter of the Association for Computational Linguistics: Human Language Technologies*, pages 2799–2809, Online. Association for Computational Linguistics.

Nicolas Papernot and Patrick McDaniel. 2018. Deep k-nearest neighbors: Towards confident, interpretable and robust deep learning. *arXiv preprint arXiv:1803.04765*.

Panupong Pasupat, Yuan Zhang, and Kelvin Guu. 2021. Controllable semantic parsing via retrieval augmentation. In *Proceedings of the 2021 Conference on Empirical Methods in Natural Language Processing*, pages 7683–7698, Online and Punta Cana, Dominican Republic. Association for Computational Linguistics.

Colin Raffel, Noam Shazeer, Adam Roberts, Katherine Lee, Sharan Narang, Michael Matena, Yanqi Zhou, Wei Li, and Peter J. Liu. 2020. Exploring the limits of transfer learning with a unified text-to-text transformer. *Journal of Machine Learning Research*, 21(140):1–67.

Nils Reimers and Iryna Gurevych. 2019. Sentence-bert: Sentence embeddings using siamese bert-networks. In *Proceedings of the 2019 Conference on Empirical Methods in Natural Language Processing*. Association for Computational Linguistics.

Adam Roberts, Colin Raffel, and Noam Shazeer. 2020. How much knowledge can you pack into the parameters of a language model? In *Proceedings of the 2020 Conference on Empirical Methods in Natural Language Processing (EMNLP)*, pages 5418–5426, Online. Association for Computational Linguistics.

Subendhu Rongali, Luca Soldaini, Emilio Monti, and Wael Hamza. 2020. *Don't Parse, Generate! A Sequence to Sequence Architecture for Task-Oriented Semantic Parsing*, page 2962–2968. Association for Computing Machinery, New York, NY, USA.

Abigail See, Peter J. Liu, and Christopher D. Manning. 2017. Get to the point: Summarization with pointer-generator networks. In *Proceedings of the 55th Annual Meeting of the Association for Computational Linguistics (Volume 1: Long Papers)*, pages 1073–1083, Vancouver, Canada. Association for Computational Linguistics.

Akshat Shrivastava, Pierce Chuang, Arun Babu, Shrey Desai, Abhinav Arora, Alexander Zotov, and Ahmed Aly. 2021. Span pointer networks for non-autoregressive task-oriented semantic parsing. In *Findings of the Association for Computational Linguistics: EMNLP 2021*, pages 1873–1886, Punta Cana, Dominican Republic. Association for Computational Linguistics.

Sainbayar Sukhbaatar, arthur szlam, Jason Weston, and Rob Fergus. 2015. End-to-end memory networks. In *Advances in Neural Information Processing Systems*, volume 28. Curran Associates, Inc.

Yibo Sun, Duyu Tang, Jingjing Xu, Nan Duan, Xiaocheng Feng, Bing Qin, Ting Liu, and Ming Zhou. 2019. Knowledge-aware conversational semantic parsing over web tables. In *Natural Language Processing and Chinese Computing*, pages 827–839, Cham. Springer International Publishing.

Chau Tran, Yuqing Tang, Xian Li, and Jiatao Gu. 2020. Cross-lingual retrieval for iterative self-supervised training. In *Advances in Neural Information Processing Systems*, volume 33, pages 2207–2219. Curran Associates, Inc.

Xiaoyan Wang, Pavan Kapanipathi, Ryan Musa, Mo Yu, Kartik Talamadupula, Ibrahim Abdelaziz, Maria Chang, Achille Fokoue, Bassem Makni, Nicholas Mattei, and Michael Witbrock. 2019. Improving natural language inference using external knowledge in the science questions domain. volume 33, pages 7208–7215.

Jason Weston, Sumit Copra, and Antoine Bordes. 2014. Memory networks. *arXiv preprint arXiv:1410.3916*.

Jason Weston, Emily Dinan, and Alexander Miller. 2018. Retrieve and refine: Improved sequence generation models for dialogue. In *Proceedings of the 2018 EMNLP Workshop SCAI: The 2nd International Workshop on Search-Oriented Conversational AI*, pages 87–92, Brussels, Belgium. Association for Computational Linguistics.

A Qualitative Examples

Below, we provide some qualiative example from the TOPv2 datasets, in the first box, we shows the input utterance, nearest neighbour utterance i.e. nearest-nn utterance and it corresponding semantic parse i.e. semparse-nn (from the training set). In the second box we showed expected gold semantic parse (expected-sparse) and the semantic parse prediction with baseline i.e. without nearest neighbor (without-nn), and our models utterance only nearest neighbor, where the input is appending with nearest-nn utterance (utterance-nn) and semantic augmented model i.e. (semparse-nn), where the input is augmented with semantic parse of first nearest neighbor. We can clearly see from the examples that augmented nearest neighbor enhance models in identifying correct intent and slots.

example 1 input
utterance : message just lizzie and trent from my group if they have any updates yet ?

nearest-nn utterance : message kira and lena saying want to get drinks this week ?
nearest-nn semparse : [in:send_message message [sl:recipient kira] and [sl:recipient lena] saying [sl:content_exact want to get drinks this week]?]

example 1 output
expected-parse : [in:send_message [sl:recipient lizzie] [sl:recipient trent] [sl:content_exact they have any updates yet]]
without-nn : [in:get_message [sl:content_exact they have any updates yet] [sl:group lizzie] [sl:group trent]]
semparse-nn : [in:send_message [sl:recipient lizzie] [sl:recipient trent] [sl:content_exact they have any updates yet]]
utterance-nn : [in:send_message [sl:recipient lizzie] [sl:recipient trent] [sl:content_exact they have any updates yet]]

In example 1, the model misses the correct intent and corresponding slots completely, the correct intent is sending a message rather than receiving a message is correctly identified by both semparse-nn and utterance-nn.

example 2 input
utterance : no more country
nearest-nn utterance : no more music
nearest-nn semparse : [in:stop_music [sl:music_type music]]

example 2 output
expected-parse : [in:remove_from_playlist_music [sl:music_genre country]]
without-nn : [in:play_music [sl:music_genre country]]
semparse-nn : [in:remove_from_playlist_music [sl:music_genre country]]
utterance-nn : [in:remove_from_playlist_music [sl:music_genre country]]

In example 2, the baseline model without nearest neighbour did the exact opposite of intended task of removing music of genre country from the playlist. However, after augmenting nearest neighbor context the model quickly correct the expected intent and slot. It should also be noted the both the correct intent and slot (i.e. in:remove_from_playlist_music and sl:music_genre) are not present in the nearest-nn semparse but it do contain similar intent and slot (i.e. in:stop_music. and sl:music_type), which help retrieval augmented model in correct prediction. As earlier the model is able to predict correct even with utterance only augmentation too.

example 3 input
utterance : block all songs of mariah carey
nearest-nn utterance : delete mariah carey songs
nearest-nn semparse : [in:remove_from_playlist_music delete [sl:music_artist_name mariah carey] [sl:music_type songs]]

example 3 output
expected-parse : [in:remove_from_playlist_music [sl:music_artist_name mariah carey]]
without-nn : [in:unsupported_music [sl:music_type songs]]
semparse-nn : [in:remove_from_playlist_music [sl:music_type songs] [sl:music_artist_name mariah carey]]
utterance-nn : [in:remove_from_playlist_music [sl:music_type songs] [sl:music_artist_name mariah carey]]

In example 3 the model without nearest neighbor augmentation struggle to identify the intent from utterance text token "block" therefore prediction unsupported music as the intent and the music type as songs, however the model with augmented nearest neighbour example with "delete" intended slot

Percentage	10 %			20 %			30 %		
Domain	**w/o nn**	**uttr-nn**	**sem-nn**	**w/o nn**	**uttr-nn**	**sem-nn**	**w/o nn**	**uttr-nn**	**sem-nn**
Alarm	80.50	84.05	83.60	83.71	84.89	85.76	84.22	85.93	82.92
Event	68.56	78.33	79.38	75.01	80.85	82.32	77.64	81.91	82.92
Music	69.12	75.74	73.23	74.09	77.53	77.34	75.6	78.01	78.13
Timer	71.63	76.76	76.27	75.51	76.18	79.28	77.21	79.68	79.84
Navigation	74.30	73.86	76.44	77.89	79.40	79.96	80.11	81.79	81.61
Messaging	84.38	87.30	89.44	88.39	91.31	91.50	89.53	92.78	92.25

Table 4: Limited training setting results on various domain with original baseline (without-nn), RETRONLU model utterance-nn and semparse-nn, shown here as w/o nn, utter-nn and sem-nn respectively.

#neighbour's	one			two			three		
Domain	**w/o nn**	**uttr-nn**	**sem-nn**	**w/o nn**	**uttr-nn**	**sem-nn**	**w/o nn**	**uttr-nn**	**sem-nn**
Alarm	86.67	87.17	88.57	86.67	87.77	87.87	86.67	87.68	87.90
Event	83.83	85.03	84.77	83.83	84.92	85.26	83.83	85.26	85.34
Music	79.80	80.73	80.71	79.80	80.71	81.50	79.80	80.52	81.11
Timer	81.21	81.75	81.01	81.21	81.04	82.29	81.21	81.44	82.10
Messaging	93.50	94.52	94.65	93.50	94.92	95.05	93.50	94.88	94.92
Navigation	82.96	84.16	85.20	82.96	84.12	84.46	82.96	84.59	84.79

Table 5: Effect of number of nearest neighbours of RETRONLU performance across domains

correct identified both the intent and slots. Furthermore, using nearest neighbor augmentation, the model resolves the active passive voice confusion.

B Domain based Limited Training Setting

In Table 4 shows the performance of model for each domain on original baseline (without-nn), and RetroNLU model utterance-nn and semparse-nn with varying amount of supervised training data. Overall, semparse-nn outperform utterance-nn over most of the domains. Surprising, we also found that for few domain (with large number of samples) utterance-nn perform marginally better than semparse-nn, need to investigate exact reason for that. As expected both model utternace-nn and semparse-nn perform much better than original baseline which is without any nearest neighbour augmentation.

C Domain Specific Effect of Nearest Neighbours

In Table 5 we shows the performance of model for each domain on original baseline (without-nn), and RetroNLU model utterance-nn and semparse-nn with varying number of nearest neighbour augmented. We found the utternace-nn performance increases with increasing number of neighbours where semparse performance remain mostly constant after the first neighbour augmentation for many domains. We suspect this is due to the fact that the data contains a large number of utterances with identical semparse output.. There is also frame redundancy, since many unique utterance inquiries have comparable semantic parse frames structure with differences only on slot values.

Stylistic Response Generation by Controlling Personality Traits and Intent

Sougata Saha, Souvik Das, Rohini Srihari
State University of New York at Buffalo
Department of Computer Science and Engineering
{sougatas, souvikda, rohini}@buffalo.edu

Abstract

Personality traits influence human actions and thoughts, which is manifested in day to day conversations. Although glimpses of personality traits are observable in existing open domain conversation corpora, leveraging generic language modelling for response generation overlooks the interlocutor idiosyncrasies, resulting in non-customizable personality agnostic responses. With the motivation of enabling stylistically configurable response generators, in this paper we experiment with end-to-end mechanisms to ground neural response generators based on both (i) interlocutor Big-5 personality traits, and (ii) discourse intent as stylistic control codes. Since most of the existing large scale open domain chat corpora do not include Big-5 personality traits and discourse intent, we employ automatic annotation schemes to enrich the corpora with noisy estimates of personality and intent annotations, and further assess the impact of using such features as control codes for response generation using automatic evaluation metrics, ablation studies and human judgement. Our experiments illustrate the effectiveness of this strategy resulting in improvements to existing benchmarks. Additionally, we yield two silver standard annotated corpora with intents and personality traits annotated, which can be of use to the research community.

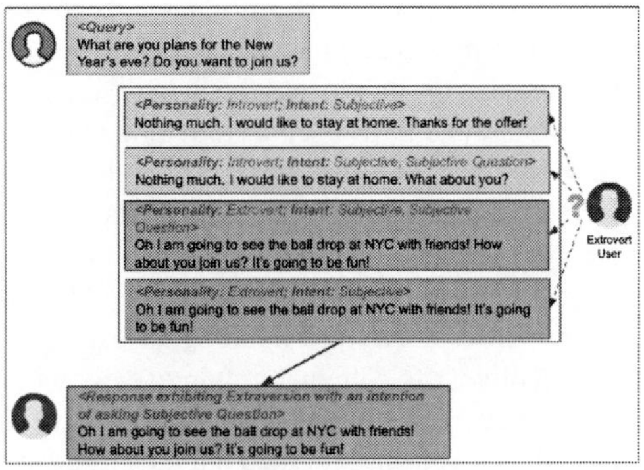

Figure 1: Sample conversation between two users, depicting the influence of personality trait and dialogue intent.

1 Introduction

Recent years have witnessed a growth in neural methods for language modelling, specifically in the domain of open domain dialogue and interactive systems. Large neural language models with billions of parameters, trained on one or more dialogue corpora, have accomplished state-of-the-art results in response generation tasks (Roller et al., 2020; Xu et al., 2021). Incorporating such generators in their pipelines, end-to-end dialogue systems in Alexa Prize (Saha et al., 2021; Chi et al., 2021; Konrád et al., 2021) have demonstrated capabilities of engaging in prolonged live conversations with humans on a multitude of real world topics, thus bettering human-computer interaction, and paving a way for more human centered NLP applications. Although such language models are capable of generating human-like responses, they often come with their own set of predicaments. Leveraging only textual data sans any other explicit control mechanism for training, such models often engender undesirable responses, diminishing the trust of users in such systems. Rashkin et al. (2021) discusses the issue of knowledge hallucinations in response generation and the importance of grounding factual responses to the correct knowledge, Nie et al. (2021) elucidates the inconsistent and self-contradictory nature of such models, and Saha et al. (2021) discusses the impact of such undesirable responses in production grade human centered systems. However, in many applications it is also desirable for generators to control the style of an utterance along with its content, which is difficult to achieve using vanilla language modelling. With the motivation of incorporating more stylistic control in conversational systems, we experiment with ways of enhancing language modelling by incorporating personality and dialogue intent for controlling the

Proceedings of the 4th Workshop on NLP for Conversational AI, pages 197 - 211

mannerism and intention of the response.

Personality is the most fundamental dimension of variation between humans (Mairesse et al., 2007). Not only does it play a crucial role in how humans react to different scenarios, but also reflects characteristic patterns of thoughts, feelings, expressions, and behaviors. Speech being the ultimate form of expression is influenced by a person's personality trait (Sanford, 1942). For example, the response to the query inquiring about New Year's eve plans in Figure 1 is not only subjective, but also dependent on the personality of the interlocutor. Had the interlocutor been introverted, the response could have been different. Apart from personality, the response to a query is also greatly influenced by the intentions of the interlocutors. In the same example, responding with the intention of asking subjective question would yield a different response, albeit still exhibiting the extroverted personality trait. Although relying solely on language modelling might engender informative and factual response, the style and intention exuded by such generated responses are often generic and unpredictable. For controlling the response style in terms of personality and intent, we utilize control codes based on the well established Big 5 personality traits taxonomy (Soto, 2018; Costa Jr, 1992) and diverse locutionary acts (Barbara, 2017).

2 Related Work

Personality Trait from Text: Research in automatic personality detection from text is still nascent, and can be attributed to the lack of publicly available large scale personality annotated datasets. Mairesse et al. (2007) explored the usage of statistical models for detecting personality traits from text, which inspired Majumder et al. (2017) to implement a document modeling technique based on a CNN features extractor for identifying Big-5 traits from the Essays dataset. Using the PersIA corpus (Dix et al., 2003) for training, Ivanov et al. (2011) experimented with statistical models to automatically detect Big-5 personality traits. Ren et al. (2021) experimented with leveraging BERT for detecting Big-5 and Myers-Briggs Type Indicator (Myers, 1962) personality traits from social media text. Recently, Gjurković et al. (2021) published the first large-scale dataset of Reddit comments labeled with 3 personality models, which we leverage for out experiments, along with the Essays dataset.
Controllable Text Generation: Considerable amount of work has been done for controllable text generation. Mairesse and Walker (2007, 2008a) proposed Personage: the first highly parametrizable language generator for modelling extraversion. Mairesse and Walker (2008b) experimented with statistical models, that can produce recognisable variation along the personality dimension. Oraby et al. (2018) and Harrison et al. (2019) explored with neural generators capable of generating language that exhibits variation in personality, for task-oriented dialogue systems. Leveraging myPersonality dataset, Wanqi and Sakai (2020) annotated the Cornell Movie-dialogs corpus (Danescu-Niculescu-Mizil and Lee, 2011) with personality trait identifier, and experimented with GRU-based seq2seq model with attention mechanism to generate personality conditioned responses. Keskar et al. (2019) introduced the concept of leveraging control codes for stylized text generation in CTRL, and Dathathri et al. (2020) proposed Plug and Play Language Models (PPLM), which combines a pretrained language model with an attribute classifiers for guiding text generation, without training the language model. Inspired by CTRL and PPLM, Smith et al. (2020) leveraged 200 distinct style based control codes, for stylized response generation. Madotto et al. (2020) further demonstrated plug-and-play methods for controllable response generation, which neither require dialogue specific datasets, nor rely on fine-tuning a large model. Rashkin et al. (2021) explored tackling knowledge hallucination by incorporating control codes, which act as stylistic controls that encourage the model to generate responses that are faithful to the provided evidence. Hedayatnia et al. (2020) proposed a policy driven neural response generator, which generates a response policy, and adheres to it for faithful generation. Our work is primarily inspired by CTRL (Keskar et al., 2019), PD-NRG (Hedayatnia et al., 2020), and the latest work by Rashkin et al. (2021).

3 Task

Our goal is to experiment with ways of controlling the style of language model generated responses, using personality trait and dialogue intent based control codes. For our purpose, we utilize the Big-5 personality traits listed in table 1 as stylistic control codes. Further, as pointed out by Saha et al. (2021), for practically incorporate factual response generators in real world conversational systems,

Type	Control Code	Abbreviation	Description	Possible Levels
Big-5 Personality Traits	Agreeableness	Agr	Level of critical and rational nature.	Strong/Weak
	Openness	Opn	Level of imagination and insight.	Strong/Weak
	Conscientiousness	Con	Level of self-discipline and efficiency.	Strong/Weak
	Extraversion	Ext	Level of outgoing nature.	Strong/Weak
	Neuroticism	Neu	Tendency to experience negative emotions.	Strong/Weak
Corpus Based Traits	Attitude		Overall pre-dominant stance of an interlocutor.	Positive/Negative/Neutral
	Tone		Overall pre-dominant intention of an interlocutor.	Subjective/Objective/Both
	Length		Response length preference of an interlocutor.	Talkative/Reserved
Intent	Subjectivity	Subj	Intention of sharing personal anecdotes or opinions.	Present/Absent
	Objectivity	Obj	Intention of sharing factual knowledge.	Present/Absent
	Subjective Question	Subj Q	Intention of seeking personal anecdotes or opinions.	Present/Absent
	Objective Question	Obj Q	Intention of seeking factual knowledge.	Present/Absent

Table 1: Description of different types of control codes.

it is important to control the usage of facts in response, in order to prevent the bot from entering a recurrent fact telling mode and hurting the colloquialism of the bot. Hence, we propose leveraging dialogue intents to control the nature of the generated response. For our use case, we re-purpose the intent taxonomy defined by Saha et al. (2021), and derive four intent categories based on subjectivity and objectivity, as listed in table 1. Further, we experiment with controlling the intensities of each personality and intent based stylistic control codes by defining levels, and use combinations of multiple control codes during response generation.

4 Data

We leverage the publicly available multi-turn, large scale Wizard of Wikipedia (Dinan et al., 2019), and Topical chat (Gopalakrishnan et al., 2019; Hedayatnia et al., 2020) corpora for our experiments, which we further enrich with turn wise intent and personality trait annotations.

4.1 Conversation Corpus

Wizard of Wikipedia (WOW): It is an asymmetric chat corpus comprising of conversations between a wizard who has access to Wikipedia knowledge, and an apprentice, who does not have access to external knowledge. The apprentice has the goal of diving deep into a conversation, and the wizard is assigned the role of being knowledgeable. The conversation continues until one of the conversation partners ends the chat after a minimum of 4 or 5 turns, randomly chosen beforehand.

Topical Chat (TC): It is a more symmetric chat corpus consisting of conversations between two human interlocutors, where both the agents have access to diverse external knowledge sources. The conversation continues for at least 20 turns, before either interlocutor can end the conversation. With 21.8 average turns per conversation in TC compared to 9.0 in WOW, TC reflects real world conversations better, with lengthier conversations.

4.2 Corpus Enrichment using Annotations

Employing automatic annotation schemes, we enrich both WOW and TC with discourse features like intent, and interlocutor personality traits.

4.2.1 Dialogue Intent Annotation

Leveraging the BERT (Devlin et al., 2019) based intent classifier by Saha et al. (2021), we automatically annotate each turn with interlocutor intent. Since our objective is to control the subjectivity and objectivity of the response, we disregard the intent classes 'acknowledgement', 'rejection', 'clarification', 'topic suggestion', 'general chat' and 'others'. Further, on evaluating 60 random annotations by the author spanning both the WOW and TC datasets, we observed an overall agreement of 95% between the model predicted and human assigned labels. Table 10 (in appendix A) further illustrates the class wise annotation agreement. Further, we noticed that the classifier mostly confused between the subjective intent of sharing personal anecdotes and opinions. Hence, we combine the intent categories into four distinct classes: (i) Subjectivity: The intention of sharing personal anecdotes or opinions; (ii) Objectivity: The intention of sharing factual knowledge; (iii) Subjective Question: The intention of seeking personal anecdotes or opinions; (iv) Objective Question: The intention of seeking factual knowledge.

4.2.2 Personality Trait Annotation

Big-5 Personality Traits We make the following assumptions for personality annotation: (i) The personality of an interlocutor can be best judged after observing all their responses. Fewer turns will result in partially observable and noisy traits. (ii) By definition, people who exhibit openness are intellectually curious. Hence, leveraging factual knowledge in a turn is considered as high for openness. Leveraging the Pandora (Gjurković et al., 2021) and the Essays (Pennebaker and King, 2000) datasets, we train models for automatically detecting Big-5 personality traits from text. Pandora is the first large-scale dataset of Reddit comments labeled with intensities of Big-5 traits, and the Essays dataset is a smaller collection of stream-of-consciousness texts written by psychology students, with binary labels denoting the presence or absence of each of the Big-5 traits, which are converted to continuous intensities to maintain parity between the two datasets. We fine tune RoBERTa (Liu et al., 2019) with a regression head on both the personality datasets separately and automatically annotate each cumulative interlocutor turns in the WOW and TC corpora with 2 sets of Big-5 trait intensities. The regression model attains a Pearson correlation of 0.266 on the Essays dataset, and a correlation of 0.806 on the Pandora dataset. More details about the training and evaluation of each regression model are provided in appendix A. Post annotation, we convert the intensities to strong and weak classes, where intensities above 0.5 standard deviation (SD) from the mean intensity for a trait are considered strong, lower than -0.5 SD are considered weak, and the rest are considered not significant and ignored. Further, in order to evaluate the accuracy of the automatic annotation we sampled 40 random examples, and calculated the agreement between the automatic annotations and our judgement. Overall we observed 50% agreement for the Pandora based traits and 58% agreement for the Essays based traits, which is warranted given the complex nature of the task of determining personality traits from written conversation. Table 11 further illustrates the class wise annotation agreement for both the personality datasets.

Corpus Based Traits We also define 3 interlocutor specific universal traits (table 1), derived using corpus statistics. (i) **Attitude**: Captures the predominant interlocutor stance (Jaffe et al., 2009) in a conversation. Leveraging AllenNLP (Gardner et al., 2017) textual entailment classifier trained on the MNLI (Williams et al., 2018) dataset, we calculate the frequency of contradicting turns between the interlocutors, and classify an interlocutor as positive if no contradictions are found, negative if more than 1 contradictions are found, and neutral otherwise. (ii) **Tone**: Captures the predominant interlocutor voice. Post intent annotation, we compute the distribution of subjective and objective voice from an interlocutor's turns, and assign the majority class with a margin of 10% as the preferred tone, else both. (iii) **Length**: Captures the length of interlocutor responses. An interlocutor is tagged as talkative, if the average number of tokens used by the interlocutor in a turn is greater than the median number of tokens per turn from the entire corpus, else reserved.

5 Modelling

Mathematically, given a response Y consisting of tokens $(y_1, ..., y_n)$, and the conversation context till the current turn C, language modelling for response generation estimates $p(Y|C)$. Employing personality trait P, intent control codes I, and the relevant facts F, we model the posterior probability distribution $p(Y|C, P, I, F)$. Further, in order to facilitate learning we incorporate a multi-task learning framework, where along with generating the response Y, we perform fact selection and target personality P and intent control code I prediction. We employ parameterized neural networks, and train end-to-end leveraging encoder-decoder transformers (Vaswani et al., 2017) BART (Lewis et al., 2020) and Blenderbot (Roller et al., 2020) as the base architectures of our model. Figure 2 illustrates the end-to-end system, and below we detail each component. [1]

5.1 Encoder

The encoding step utilizes the context encoder f_c and the fact encoder f_k to encode the conversation context till the current turn C, along with the golden fact required in the current turn F^j, to generate the final hidden representation $\mathbf{C_{emb}} = [\mathbf{C_h};\mathbf{F_h}]$ for the decoder, where $\mathbf{C_h} = f_c(C)$, and $\mathbf{F_h} = f_k(F^j)$.

In order to facilitate learning, we devise a multi-task learning framework, where along with generating the response, we also perform fact selection, and target personality trait and intent prediction. We input the personality traits and intent based stylistic features of each turn in the context C as additional input features S, along with a set of four random facts as distractors F. Encoding the feature S using a feature encoder f_s, followed by an alignment with the context hidden representation C_h

[1]The code and datasets are publicly available at: `https://github.com/sougata-ub/personality-response-generation`.

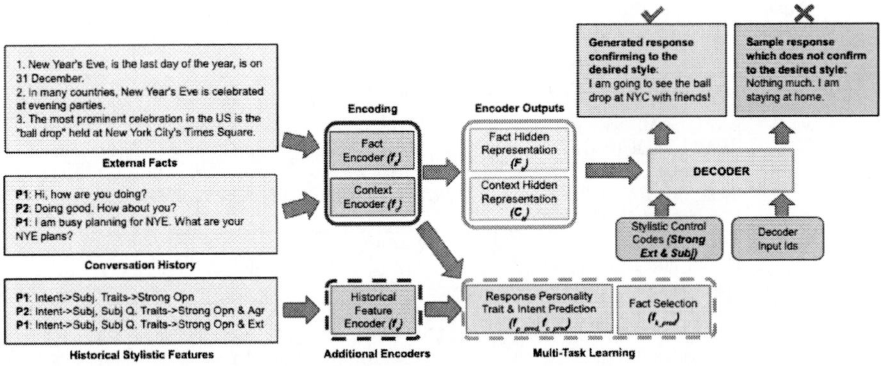

Figure 2: Proposed end-to-end system architecture for configurable stylistic response generation.

using multi-headed attention and feed forward layers $f_{s'}$, we get the feature hidden representation S_h, which is further concatenated with the context hidden representation into a joint representation $\vec{H_{cs}}$. Employing two fully connected neural networks f_{i_pred} and f_{p_pred}, we predict the target response intent I_{tgt} and personality control codes P_{tgt}, and minimise the loss between the actual response intent I and personality P respectively.

$$\mathbf{S_{h'}} = f_s(S),\ \mathbf{S_h} = f_{s'}([\text{MultiHead}(\mathbf{S_{h'}}, \mathbf{C_h});\mathbf{S_{h'}}])$$
$$\mathbf{H_{cs}} = [\mathbf{C_h};\mathbf{S_h}],\ \vec{H_{cs}} = \text{avg}(\mathbf{H_{cs}})$$
$$\mathbf{I_{tgt}} = f_{i\_pred}(\vec{H_{cs}}),\ \mathbf{P_{tgt}} = f_{p\_pred}(\vec{H_{cs}})$$

Deciding the most relevant fact not only depends on the conversation context, but also on the intent. For example, if the intention is to share a personal anecdote, then most probably none of the available facts should be relevant for generating the response. Each of the fact distractors F^i along with the golden fact F^j are encoded using the fact encoder f_k to the initial encoding $\mathbf{F^i_{h'}} = f_k(F^i)$, which is followed by an alignment with the joint context and feature hidden representation $\mathbf{F^i_h} = f_{k'}([\text{MultiHead}(\mathbf{F^i_{h'}}, \mathbf{H_{cs}});\mathbf{F^i_{h'}}])$. Finally, each fact encoding is average pooled and concatenated with the predicted intent logits I_{tgt}, followed by a fully connected neural network f_{k_pred} to predict relevancy $F^i_{pred} = f_{k\_pred}([\text{avg}(\mathbf{F^i_h});I_{tgt}])$, which is trained by minimizing the loss between the prediction and the true label.

5.2 Decoder

Apart from the hidden encoder representation $\mathbf{C_{emb}}$, we also condition the response generation on the response personality and intent control codes, which enables the model to adapt to the required style. Similar to Rashkin et al. (2021), the control codes are prepended to the decoder input ids, and passed to the decoder, which generates the response by conditioning on the encoder context $\mathbf{C_{emb}}$, and the control codes. The entire system is trained end-to-end by minimizing the weighted sum of the language modelling cross entropy loss, the binary cross entropy fact selection loss, binary cross entropy intent prediction loss, and the cross entropy trait prediction loss.

6 Experiments and Results

6.1 Experiment Set-up

We used the pre-trained 139M parameters (base) version of BART (Lewis et al., 2020), and the 400M parameters distilled BlenderBot (Roller et al., 2020) from the Huggingface library (Wolf et al., 2020) as our base models, and added 24 new tokens comprising of speaker identifiers (agent_1, agent_2), traits and intent control codes to the embedding layer. Similar to Transfertransfo (Wolf et al., 2019), we introduce a token type embedding layer to demarcate turns. We utilized a learning rate of 2E-5, and batch size of 32 and 16 per GPU for BART and BlenderBot respectively, with gradient accumulation (Lin et al., 2018) for 2 steps, for BlenderBot. We clipped (Pascanu et al., 2013) the gradients to unit norm, and used AdamW (Loshchilov and Hutter, 2019) with default PyTorch parameters for optimization. Beam search was used during decoding with a beam length of 5, with penalty for trigram repetitions within the generated text, and between the context and generated text. The corpus based codes are only input to the encoder to aid in trait and intent predictions, and are not used as stylistic control codes.

Corpus	Model	Perplexity	BLEU 4	Rouge L	BLEURT
WOW	E2E (Dinan et al., 2019)	23.1/32.8	1.5 / 0.3		
	GPT2 (Rashkin et al., 2021)		8.9 / 8.4		
	T5 (Rashkin et al., 2021)		8.4 / 8.7		
	BART	9.74 / 10.53	8.44 / 8.24	0.341 / 0.342	0.491 / 0.488
	BART + All (P-Traits)	**9.37 / 10.13**	9.01 / 8.60	**0.349 / 0.349**	0.502 / **0.502**
	BART + All (E-Traits)	9.43 / 10.23	**9.20 / 8.79**	0.348 / 0.347	**0.506** / 0.501
	BlenderBot	7.48 / 8.54	**6.31** / 4.77	0.302 / 0.282	**0.462 / 0.444**
	BlenderBot + All (P-Traits)	7.38 / 8.39	6.22 / **4.90**	**0.305 / 0.294**	0.450 / 0.437
	BlenderBot + All (E-Traits)	**7.37 / 8.38**	6.22 / 4.77	0.304 / 0.294	0.451 / 0.441
TC	NRG (Gopalakrishnan et al., 2019)	26.30 / 36.30			
	PD-NRG (Hedayatnia et al., 2020)	12.25 / 12.62	1.9 / 2.0	0.113 / 0.108	
	Proto (Saha et al., 2021)	11.55 / 10.87			
	BART	13.81 / 14.71	3.62 / 4.10	0.235 / 0.250	0.365 / 0.388
	BART + All (P-Traits)	**13.21** / 14.10	3.72 / **4.37**	0.242 / **0.259**	0.370 / 0.400
	BART + All (E-Traits)	13.22 / **14.02**	**3.73** / 4.28	**0.246** / 0.258	**0.376 / 0.403**
	BlenderBot	11.09 / 10.75	3.13 / **3.75**	0.223 / 0.240	0.367 / 0.390
	BlenderBot + All (P-Traits)	10.75 / 10.39	**3.22** / 3.65	0.232 / 0.247	0.367 / 0.389
	BlenderBot + All (E-Traits)	**10.72 / 10.35**	3.20 / 3.62	**0.234 / 0.247**	**0.369 / 0.391**

Table 2: Language modelling results on the seen/unseen and frequent/rare topic portions of WOW and TC test sets.

6.2 Evaluating Language Modelling

For automatically evaluating the language modelling capabilities of our proposed model we compute and compare language modelling perplexity, BLEU-4 (Papineni et al., 2002) and ROUGE-L (Lin, 2004) scores. Since BLEU and ROUGE are known to be incomplete metrics, as they don't completely capture sentence semantics, we also compare the BLEURT (Sellam et al., 2020) scores. We report our results and compare with baselines in Table 2. For both WOW and TC, we consider the models void of any control codes, using only conversation context and facts as the internal baseline (underlined), and compare against variations containing both the Pandora and Essays based personality and intent based control codes, All (P-Traits), and All (E-Traits) respectively. As reference, we also include results of the end-to-end generative model (E2E) with gold knowledge that was introduced in the original WOW paper (Dinan et al., 2019), and the GPT-2 and T5 based knowledge grounded models proposed by (Rashkin et al., 2021) for WOW. For TC, we include results from the neural response generator (NRG) model introduced in the original paper (Gopalakrishnan et al., 2019), the follow up work using policy driven approach (PD-NRG) (Hedayatnia et al., 2020), and the recent work by Proto (Saha et al., 2021). For each dataset and model type in Table 2, we highlight in bold the best performing model by each metric, and underline the metric wise best performing models for a dataset. We observe: (i) In comparison to both the internal and external baselines, conditioning on intent and personality trait based control codes consistently yields better automatic evaluation scores. We reason that the introduction of control codes not only provides additional supervision signals, but also helps the language model to better factorize the probability distributions of the words. (ii) Using BlenderBot yields better perplexity scores, at the cost of precision/recall based metrics. We reason that although the extensive pre-training of BlenderBot on the BST dataset (Smith et al., 2020) helps in language modelling, its low vocabulary size of 8,008 tokens compared to 50,265 of BART, hinders adapting to the new datasets. (iii) Both the Essays and Pandora based codes work well; The Pandora based codes seem to work slightly better for WOW, while the Essays based codes perform better for TC. We reason that as depicted in Table 12, the Pandora based personality classifier identifies more instances of openness compared to the Essays based classifier. Since being objective is associated with the trait of openness, and the WOW dataset has 71% objective exchanges, which is more compared to 51% in the TC dataset (Table 7), it works better for WOW.

6.3 Evaluating Stylistic Control

We introduce two automatic metrics for comparing the intent and personality traits exhibited by the generated response and the golden response: (i) **Intent F1:** Re-using the intent classifier used for automatic annotation from section 4.2.2, we predict the intents exhibited by each of the the generated responses, and calculate the F1 score between the exhibited intents and the actual desired intent. We further derive a single metric by averaging the F1 score for all classes. (ii) **Trait Correlation:** Re-using the Big-5 personality trait intensity prediction models from section 4.2.2, we predict the intensity of each trait exhibited by the generated response, and compute the Pearson's correlation between the actual intensity from the golden response. We further average the correlation score across all the 5 traits to derive a single metric. Table 3 reports the results; For each dataset and model type we highlight the best performing model by each metric in bold, and underline the metric wise best performing models for each dataset. We observe: (i) Models that utilize the stylistic control codes during response generation yield better results, compared to the baseline versions which don't use any control codes. This indicates the effectiveness of our proposed method of controlling the response generation using stylistic control codes. (ii) Compared to using Pandora based personality codes, responses from models incorporating the Essays based control codes correlate more to the desired response trait. (iii) In majority cases, responses from models incorporating the Pandora and intent based control codes confirm more to the desired response intent, compared to models using the Essays based control codes along with intent for controlling personality. This hints towards possible synergic relationships between the personality and intent based codes.

Corpus	Model	Intent F1	Trait Correl.
WOW	BART	0.300 / 0.319	0.850 / 0.824
	BART + All (P-Traits)	<u>**0.669 / 0.683**</u>	0.858 / 0.836
	BART + All (E-Traits)	0.634 / 0.639	<u>**0.870 / 0.848**</u>
	BlenderBot	0.316 / 0.321	0.825 / 0.804
	BlenderBot + All (P-Traits)	0.466 / 0.469	0.828 / 0.810
	BlenderBot + All (E-Traits)	**0.480 / 0.491**	**0.835 / 0.818**
TC	BART	0.264 / 0.256	0.726 / 0.763
	BART + All (P-Traits)	**0.505 / <u>0.523</u>**	0.731 / 0.765
	BART + All (E-Traits)	0.465 / 0.468	<u>**0.748 / 0.782**</u>
	BlenderBot	0.267 / 0.261	0.691 / 0.733
	BlenderBot + All (P-Traits)	**<u>0.518</u> / 0.517**	0.720 / 0.749
	BlenderBot + All (E-Traits)	0.517 / 0.513	**0.737 / 0.768**

Table 3: Stylistic control results on the seen/unseen and frequent/rare topic portions of WOW and TC.

6.4 Ablation Study

We further perform the following ablation study with diverse combinations of the stylistic control codes for observing the effect of each type of code independently: (i) Intent: Using only intent based control codes in the decoder. (ii) C-Traits: Using only corpus based traits in the encoder, without any control codes in the decoder. (iii) P / E-Traits: Using only Pandora or Essays based personality control codes in the decoder. (iv) Intent + P / E-Traits: Using both intent and personality control codes in the decoder. (v) All: Using both intent and personality control codes in the decoder, along with corpus traits in the encoder. Table 9 reports the results of the ablation study. We observe: (i) Using intent as stylistic control code mostly yields better results for all metrics, compared to the baseline. (ii) Leveraging the corpus traits in the encoder alone, without incorporating any control codes in the decoder mostly yields poor results for all metrics. (iii) Incorporating both intent and personality codes in the decoder mostly yields best results across all metrics. The addition of corpus based traits in the encoder further improves the results in some cases.

6.5 Human Evaluation for Relevance

Since the ultimate desired impact of our model is to find use in human facing systems, we further perform human evaluation to qualitatively compare the responses generate by the trained models. Considering only the BART based models as they resulted in better BLEU and ROUGE scores in table 2, we sampled 100 examples from the test sets of each dataset, and utilized Amazon Mechanical Turk for performing human evaluation. An initial manual evaluation by us revealed that almost all the generated candidates were fluent, which can be attributed to the extensive pre-training of the state-of-the-art base language models. This is further corroborated by the human evaluations performed by Rashkin et al. (2021), where they observed fluency to be the least dimension of variation. Hence, employing 2 evlauators per sample, we evaluated the relevance of each candidate responses to the conversation context on a Likert scale from 1 to 5, where a rating of 1 signifies low relevance and 5 signifies high relevance. More details about the annotation framework is presented in the appendix A.4. Table 5 includes the averaged results from the human evaluation. We highlight the best scoring model per dataset in bold, and perform Welch's t-test to mark models which perform significantly lower than the best score with asterisks. Further, we calculate the inter annotator agreement using Krippendorff's alpha and find that the agreement to be > 0.90, indicating a high agreement. The results indicate that responses generated by controlling the personality traits were deemed more relevant to the conversation. Additionally, incorporating intent based stylistic codes along with personality achieves best results for the WOW dataset.

ID	Conversation Context	Generated Stylistic Response	Generated Variation Response	Style
1	**Agent 1**: Fred missed the penalty, and was dropped from the team. I wonder what he is going through.	i'm sorry to hear that. i'm sure he's going through some tough times. i hope he's ok.	i'm not sure what he's going through right now. i'm sure he is struggling.	Strong Agr
2	**Agent 1**: do you want to go on a hike this weekend? **Agent 2**: sure. where are we going? **Agent 1**: how about Yosemite?	yosemite national park. it's surrounded on the southeast by the Sierra national forest and on the northwest by the Stanislaus national forest. i've never been there.	yosemite is a beautiful place. i would love to hike there.	Objectivity
3	**Agent 1**: do you like to party?	i love to party! do you?	i do not. do you?	Strong Agr Strong Ext Weak Neu
4	**Agent 1**: how's it going, do you follow football? depending on the country it could refer to rugby or soccer.	i do follow football. it's one of the four major professional sports leagues in north america and the highest professional level of american football in the world. how about you?	i don't really follow football. i do know that the nfl is one of the four major professional sports leagues in north america and the highest professional level of american football in the world.	Strong Agr Strong Ext Weak Neu
5	**Agent 2**: i know! and brady won the super bowl in the first year he was a starter! **Agent 1**: wasn't the only other quarterback to do that kurt warner?	yes, he was! i think he was the first to win a super bowl. i wonder if he ever played in the nfl? did you know those huge american flags at football stadiums weigh 1,100 pounds and cost $50,000 to make?	no, i'm not sure, but i do know that those huge american flags at football stadiums weigh 1,100 pounds and cost $50,000 to make!	Strong Agr Strong Opn Strong Ext
6	**Agent 2**: congrats! that's awesome! when i fish in my local lake, i usually use lures instead of bait. it's easier and the fish seem to respond just as well. **Agent 1**: well we definitely got our money's worth, but it was so long just to get out there, and it was cold.	that's true. some hobbyists even make handmade tackle themselves, using plastic lures and artificial flies. that's pretty cool!	that's a shame! i'm glad you didn't have to use plastic lures or artificial flies to catch the red fish.	Strong Agr Strong Opn Strong Con Strong Ext Weak Neu Objectivity

Table 4: Generated samples with different combinations of stylistic control codes.

Model	TC	WOW
BART	3.54*	3.44**
BART + Intent	3.51*	3.61
BART + Big-5 Traits	**3.73**	3.58
BART + Intent + Big-5 Traits	3.47*	3.45**
BART + All	3.5**	**3.71**

Table 5: Human evaluation results: *, ** indicates that this result is significantly different from the best result in that column with p-value < 0.05 and < 0.02 respectively.

6.6 Discussion

Table 4 showcases a few style controlled responses generated by our proposed models. For each conversation context, we leverage the control code in the style column and generate the stylistic response. We further contrast the stylistic response against a variation response generated either using randomly selected control codes or the baseline model without any stylistic codes. Example 1 demonstrates how incorporating strong agreeableness as stylistic code results in the response exuding empathy, in comparison to the variation response. Example 2 demonstrates the model's capability of generating objective response, by leveraging external facts. Through examples 3-6 we demonstrate the model's capability of simultaneously incorporating multiple stylistic codes during generation. Examples 3-6 demonstrate how increasing agreeableness results in a positive stance in the response. We also notice in examples 4 and 5 how increasing extraversion results in the model asking open-ended questions, thus portraying an extroverted and outgoing personality. Further, in examples 4 and 6 we notice the effect of controlling neuroticism, where the variant response is not consistent compared to the stylistic controlled response. Overall, we observe that utilizing our proposed method, it is possible to control the style of the response using stylistic control codes, and further combine different codes to generate compounded stylistic responses.

7 Conclusion

Here we experiment with training end-to-end methods for controlling the response style in generative conversational models. We believe incorporating such methods in human facing dialogue systems should benefit the system by providing it with more control. Using combinations of Big-5 personality traits and dialogue intent based stylistic control codes during language modelling, we are able to successfully control the style of a response as desired, the efficacy of which is further established by the achieved results. Additionally, we engender two annotated dialogue corpora with intents and personality traits for use by the community.

References

Johnstone Barbara. 2017. *Discourse Analysis.*, volume Third edition of *Introducing Linguistics*. Wiley-Blackwell.

Ethan A. Chi, Chetanya Rastogi, Alexander Iyabor, Hari Sowrirajan, Avanika Narayan, and Ashwin Paranjape. 2021. Neural, neural everywhere: Controlled generation meets scaffolded, structured dialogue.

Paul T Costa Jr. 1992. Revised neo personality inventory and neo five-factor inventory. *Professional manual.*

Cristian Danescu-Niculescu-Mizil and Lillian Lee. 2011. Chameleons in imagined conversations: A new approach to understanding coordination of linguistic style in dialogs. In *Proceedings of the Workshop on Cognitive Modeling and Computational Linguistics, ACL 2011.*

Sumanth Dathathri, Andrea Madotto, Janice Lan, Jane Hung, Eric Frank, Piero Molino, Jason Yosinski, and Rosanne Liu. 2020. Plug and play language models: A simple approach to controlled text generation. In *International Conference on Learning Representations.*

Jacob Devlin, Ming-Wei Chang, Kenton Lee, and Kristina Toutanova. 2019. *Proceedings of the 2019 Conference of the North.*

Emily Dinan, Stephen Roller, Kurt Shuster, Angela Fan, Michael Auli, and Jason Weston. 2019. Wizard of Wikipedia: Knowledge-powered conversational agents. In *Proceedings of the International Conference on Learning Representations (ICLR).*

Alan Dix, Janet Finlay, Gregory D Abowd, and Russell Beale. 2003. *Human-computer interaction.* Pearson Education.

Matt Gardner, Joel Grus, Mark Neumann, Oyvind Tafjord, Pradeep Dasigi, Nelson F. Liu, Matthew Peters, Michael Schmitz, and Luke S. Zettlemoyer. 2017. Allennlp: A deep semantic natural language processing platform.

Matej Gjurković, Mladen Karan, Iva Vukojević, Mihaela Bošnjak, and Jan Snajder. 2021. PANDORA talks: Personality and demographics on Reddit. In *Proceedings of the Ninth International Workshop on Natural Language Processing for Social Media*, pages 138–152, Online. Association for Computational Linguistics.

Karthik Gopalakrishnan, Behnam Hedayatnia, Qinlang Chen, Anna Gottardi, Sanjeev Kwatra, Anu Venkatesh, Raefer Gabriel, and Dilek Hakkani-Tür. 2019. Topical-Chat: Towards Knowledge-Grounded Open-Domain Conversations. In *Proc. Interspeech 2019*, pages 1891–1895.

Vrindavan Harrison, Lena Reed, Shereen Oraby, and Marilyn Walker. 2019. Maximizing stylistic control and semantic accuracy in NLG: Personality variation and discourse contrast. In *Proceedings of the 1st Workshop on Discourse Structure in Neural NLG*, pages 1–12, Tokyo, Japan. Association for Computational Linguistics.

Behnam Hedayatnia, Karthik Gopalakrishnan, Seokhwan Kim, Yang Liu, Mihail Eric, and Dilek Hakkani-Tur. 2020. Policy-driven neural response generation for knowledge-grounded dialogue systems.

Alexei V. Ivanov, Giuseppe Riccardi, Adam J. Sporka, and Jakub Franc. 2011. Recognition of personality traits from human spoken conversations. In *INTERSPEECH.*

Alexandra Jaffe et al. 2009. *Stance: sociolinguistic perspectives.* Oup Usa.

Nitish Shirish Keskar, Bryan McCann, Lav Varshney, Caiming Xiong, and Richard Socher. 2019. CTRL - A Conditional Transformer Language Model for Controllable Generation. *arXiv preprint arXiv:1909.05858.*

Jakub Konrád, Jan Pichl, Petr Marek, Petr Lorenc, Van Duy Ta, Ondřej Kobza, Lenka Hýlová, and Jan Šedivý. 2021. Alquist 4.0: Towards social intelligence using generative models and dialogue personalization.

Mike Lewis, Yinhan Liu, Naman Goyal, Marjan Ghazvininejad, Abdelrahman Mohamed, Omer Levy, Veselin Stoyanov, and Luke Zettlemoyer. 2020. BART: Denoising sequence-to-sequence pre-training for natural language generation, translation, and comprehension. In *Proceedings of the 58th Annual Meeting of the Association for Computational Linguistics*, pages 7871–7880, Online. Association for Computational Linguistics.

Chin-Yew Lin. 2004. ROUGE: A package for automatic evaluation of summaries. In *Text Summarization Branches Out*, pages 74–81, Barcelona, Spain. Association for Computational Linguistics.

Yujun Lin, Song Han, Huizi Mao, Yu Wang, and Bill Dally. 2018. Deep gradient compression: Reducing the communication bandwidth for distributed training. In *International Conference on Learning Representations.*

Yinhan Liu, Myle Ott, Naman Goyal, Jingfei Du, Mandar Joshi, Danqi Chen, Omer Levy, Mike Lewis, Luke Zettlemoyer, and Veselin Stoyanov. 2019. Roberta: A robustly optimized bert pretraining approach.

Ilya Loshchilov and Frank Hutter. 2019. Decoupled weight decay regularization. In *International Conference on Learning Representations.*

Andrea Madotto, Etsuko Ishii, Zhaojiang Lin, Sumanth Dathathri, and Pascale Fung. 2020. Plug-and-play conversational models. In *Proceedings of the 2020 Conference on Empirical Methods in Natural Language Processing: Findings*, pages 2422–2433.

François Mairesse and Marilyn Walker. 2007. Personage: Personality generation for dialogue. In *Proceedings of the 45th annual meeting of the association of computational linguistics*, pages 496–503.

François Mairesse, Marilyn A Walker, Matthias R Mehl, and Roger K Moore. 2007. Using linguistic cues for the automatic recognition of personality in conversation and text. *Journal of artificial intelligence research*, 30:457–500.

François Mairesse and Marilyn A. Walker. 2008a. A personality-based framework for utterance generation in dialogue applications. In *AAAI Spring Symposium: Emotion, Personality, and Social Behavior.*

François Mairesse and Marilyn A. Walker. 2008b. Trainable generation of big-five personality styles through data-driven parameter estimation. In *ACL.*

Navonil Majumder, Soujanya Poria, Alexander Gelbukh, and Erik Cambria. 2017. Deep learning-based document modeling for personality detection from text. *IEEE Intelligent Systems*, 32(2):74–79.

Isabel Briggs Myers. 1962. The myers-briggs type indicator: Manual (1962).

Yixin Nie, Mary Williamson, Mohit Bansal, Douwe Kiela, and Jason Weston. 2021. I like fish, especially dolphins: Addressing contradictions in dialogue modeling. In *Proceedings of the 59th Annual Meeting of the Association for Computational Linguistics and the 11th International Joint Conference on Natural Language Processing (Volume 1: Long Papers)*, pages 1699–1713, Online. Association for Computational Linguistics.

Shereen Oraby, Lena Reed, Shubhangi Tandon, Sharath T.S., Stephanie Lukin, and Marilyn Walker. 2018. Controlling personality-based stylistic variation with neural natural language generators. In *Proceedings of the 19th Annual SIGdial Meeting on Discourse and Dialogue*, pages 180–190, Melbourne, Australia. Association for Computational Linguistics.

Kishore Papineni, Salim Roukos, Todd Ward, and Wei-Jing Zhu. 2002. Bleu: a method for automatic evaluation of machine translation. In *Proceedings of the 40th Annual Meeting of the Association for Computational Linguistics*, pages 311–318, Philadelphia, Pennsylvania, USA. Association for Computational Linguistics.

Razvan Pascanu, Tomas Mikolov, and Yoshua Bengio. 2013. On the difficulty of training recurrent neural networks. In *ICML.*

James Pennebaker and Laura King. 2000. Linguistic styles: Language use as an individual difference. *Journal of personality and social psychology*, 77:1296–312.

Hannah Rashkin, David Reitter, Gaurav Singh Tomar, and Dipanjan Das. 2021. Increasing faithfulness in knowledge-grounded dialogue with controllable features. In *Proceedings of the 59th Annual Meeting of the Association for Computational Linguistics and the 11th International Joint Conference on Natural Language Processing (Volume 1: Long Papers)*, pages 704–718, Online. Association for Computational Linguistics.

Zhancheng Ren, Qiang Shen, Xiaolei Diao, and Hao Xu. 2021. A sentiment-aware deep learning approach for personality detection from text. *Information Processing Management*, 58(3):102532.

Stephen Roller, Emily Dinan, Naman Goyal, Da Ju, Mary Williamson, Yinhan Liu, Jing Xu, Myle Ott, Kurt Shuster, Eric M. Smith, Y-Lan Boureau, and Jason Weston. 2020. Recipes for building an open-domain chatbot.

Sougata Saha, Souvik Das, Elizabeth Soper, Erin Pacquetet, and Rohini K. Srihari. 2021. Proto: A neural cocktail for generating appealing conversations.

Fillmore H Sanford. 1942. Speech and personality. *Psychological Bulletin*, 39(10):811.

Thibault Sellam, Dipanjan Das, and Ankur P Parikh. 2020. Bleurt: Learning robust metrics for text generation. In *Proceedings of ACL.*

Eric Michael Smith, Mary Williamson, Kurt Shuster, Jason Weston, and Y-Lan Boureau. 2020. Can you put it all together: Evaluating conversational agents' ability to blend skills. In *Proceedings of the 58th Annual Meeting of the Association for Computational Linguistics*, pages 2021–2030, Online. Association for Computational Linguistics.

Christopher Soto. 2018. *Big Five personality traits*, pages 240–241.

Ashish Vaswani, Noam Shazeer, Niki Parmar, Jakob Uszkoreit, Llion Jones, Aidan N Gomez, Łukasz Kaiser, and Illia Polosukhin. 2017. Attention is all you need. In *Advances in neural information processing systems*, pages 5998–6008.

WU Wanqi and Tetsuya Sakai. 2020. Response generation based on the big five personality traits.

Adina Williams, Nikita Nangia, and Samuel Bowman. 2018. A broad-coverage challenge corpus for sentence understanding through inference. In *Proceedings of the 2018 Conference of the North American Chapter of the Association for Computational Linguistics: Human Language Technologies, Volume 1 (Long Papers)*, pages 1112–1122. Association for Computational Linguistics.

Thomas Wolf, Lysandre Debut, Victor Sanh, Julien Chaumond, Clement Delangue, Anthony Moi, Pierric Cistac, Tim Rault, Remi Louf, Morgan Funtowicz, Joe Davison, Sam Shleifer, Patrick von Platen, Clara Ma, Yacine Jernite, Julien Plu, Canwen Xu, Teven Le Scao, Sylvain Gugger, Mariama Drame, Quentin Lhoest, and Alexander Rush. 2020. Transformers: State-of-the-art natural language processing. In *Proceedings of the 2020 Conference on Empirical Methods in Natural Language Processing: System Demonstrations*, pages 38–45, Online. Association for Computational Linguistics.

Thomas Wolf, Victor Sanh, Julien Chaumond, and Clement Delangue. 2019. Transfertransfo: A transfer learning approach for neural network based conversational agents.

Jing Xu, Arthur Szlam, and Jason Weston. 2021. Beyond goldfish memory: Long-term open-domain conversation.

A Appendix

A.1 Big-5 Personality Trait Annotation

We utilized the Pandora and Essays datasets to train automatic personality predictors. The Pandora dataset consists of multiple Reddit posts for a user, along with the actual Big-5 trait intensities for the user, whereas the Essays dataset consist of essays written by psychology students, with actual Big-5 trait labels, which we converted to intensities, for maintaining parity between the datasets. For both the datasets, we tokenized the text into sentences, and maintained a list of sentences for each user. We further cleansed and normalised the sentence lists, and preserved sentences containing ASCII characters with 3 to 50 tokens. In order to make the length distribution of the training examples similar to conversation datasets, for each user we derived m non-overlapping samples by randomly selecting and concatenating k sentences, where k was randomly selected to vary between 2 and 30. The target intensities for each of the Big-5 traits were kept same for the m samples, and were scaled to vary between -1 and 1. Overall, we derived 7,230 train and 804 validation examples from Essays, and 75,172 training, and 39,447 validation examples from the Pandora dataset. We incorporated fully connected layers followed by Tanh activation on top of RoBERTa base, to predict all the 5 trait intensities simultaneously, and trained the models to minimize mean squared error loss. With the intention of comparing the quality and usefulness of the automatic personality annotations, we trained 2 versions of the models, one for each personality dataset. In order to leverage pre-training, the model trained on Essays dataset was initialized from a checkpoint of the Pandora model. Both the models were trained with a batch size of 32, and learning rate of 2E-5, till validation loss ceased improving. We leveraged AdamW optimizer for optimizing the model parameters, and resorted to mixed precision training to reduce the training time. In Table 6, for each trait we report Pearson correlation between the predicted intensity and the actual values for both the datasets. Using 0 as a threshold, we further binarize the predicted intensities and actual labels, and report classification F1.

Trait	Essays Pearson Correl.	Essays F1	Pandora Pearson Correl.	Pandora F1
Agr	0.228	0.640	0.813	0.832
Opn	0.321	0.620	0.813	0.902
Con	0.276	0.578	0.797	0.776
Ext	0.255	0.568	0.808	0.799
Neu	0.249	0.658	0.799	0.848

Table 6: Correlation and F1 metrics on the respective validation dataset for the Pandora based and Essays based model.

A.2 Fact Selection Example Creation

During fact selection, for both the Topical Chat and Wizard of Wikipedia we presented 5 external facts per example to choose from, for each interlocutor turn. The 5 facts comprised of the golden fact(s) required for generating the current response, and the remaining were randomly sampled from the facts which are available to the interlocutor. Table 7 contains the percentage distribution of the positive class for fact selection, and for each dialogue intent.

Corpus	Split	Subj	Obj	Subj Q	Obj Q	Fact
WOW	Seen	46%	71%	6%	2%	18%
WOW	Unseen	43%	71%	6%	2%	18%
TC	Frequent	68%	51%	12%	6%	5%
TC	Rare	70%	52%	13%	4%	7%

Table 7: Percentage distribution of positive class for each intent type, and fact selection in Wizard of Wikpedia and Topical Chat.

A.3 Additional Results

Table 8 reports the F1 scores of the best performing models for predicting each of the additional tasks in the multi-task learning framework. Table 9

Type	Model (WOW)	F1 (WOW)	Model (TC)	F1 (TC)
Fact	BART + Intent / BART + All (P-Traits)	0.50 / 0.44	BlenderBot / BlenderBot	0.13 / 0.12
Subj	BART + All (E-Traits) / BART + All (E-Traits)	0.75 / 0.73	BART + All (E-Traits) / BART + Intent + E-Traits	0.83 / 0.84
Obj	BART + All (P-Traits) / BART + All (P-Traits)	0.86 / 0.86	BART + Intent / BlenderBot + All (E-Traits)	0.69 / 0.70
Subj Q	BlenderBot + E-Traits / BlenderBot + E-Traits	0.58 / 0.59	BART + E-Traits / BART + E-Traits	0.63 / 0.63
Obj Q	BlenderBot + E-Traits / BlenderBot + E-Traits	0.58 / 0.60	BART + E-Traits / BART + E-Traits	0.61 / 0.64
Agr	BART + All (E-Traits) / BART + All (E-Traits)	0.61 / 0.58	BART + Intent + E-Traits / BART + E-Traits	0.64 / 0.66
Opn	BART + All (E-Traits) / BART + All (E-Traits)	0.46 / 0.44	BlenderBot + All (E-Traits) / BlenderBot + All (E-Traits)	0.47 / 0.46
Con	BART + All (E-Traits) / BART + All (E-Traits)	0.61 / 0.62	BART + Intent + E-Traits / BART + Intent + E-Traits	0.63 / 0.63
Ext	BART + All (E-Traits) / BART + All (E-Traits)	0.61 / 0.62	BART + All (E-Traits) / BART + Intent + E-Traits	0.62 / 0.65
Neu	BART + All (E-Traits) / BART + All (E-Traits)	0.62 / 0.61	BART + Intent + E-Traits / BART + All (E-Traits)	0.61 / 0.66

Table 8: F1 scores of the best performing planning models for each policy component, in both the seen/unseen splits of Wizard of Wikipedia (WOW), and frequent/rare splits of Topical Chat (TC) test sets.

Corpus	Model	Perplexity	BLEU 4	RougeL	BLEURT	Intent F1	Trait Correl.
WOW	BART	9.74 / 10.53	8.44 / 8.24	0.341 / 0.342	0.491 / 0.488	0.300 / 0.319	0.85 / 0.824
	BART + Intent	9.43 / 10.23	8.69 / 7.96	0.338 / 0.335	0.495 / 0.492	0.469 / 0.486	0.848 / 0.824
	BART + C-Traits	9.76 / 10.52	8.32 / 8.11	0.338 / 0.338	0.487 / 0.486	0.297 / 0.300	0.849 / 0.826
	BART + P-Traits	9.53 / 10.27	8.72 / 8.45	0.344 / 0.347	0.496 / 0.492	0.402 / 0.406	0.855 / 0.827
	BART + E-Traits	9.52 / 10.27	8.99 / 8.58	0.345 / **0.349**	0.496 / 0.494	0.395 / 0.397	0.866 / 0.844
	BART + Intent + P-Traits	9.41 / 10.21	9.22 / 8.44	0.345 / 0.342	0.502 / 0.496	0.618 / 0.636	0.856 / 0.833
	BART + Intent + E-Traits	**9.37** / 10.14	**9.25** / 8.51	0.346 / 0.345	0.502 / 0.500	0.654 / 0.656	0.866 / **0.849**
	BART + All (P-Traits)	**9.37 / 10.13**	9.01 / 8.60	**0.349** / **0.349**	0.502 / **0.502**	**0.669** / **0.683**	0.858 / 0.836
	BART + All (E-Traits)	9.43 / 10.23	9.20 / **8.79**	0.348 / 0.347	**0.506** / 0.501	0.634 / 0.639	**0.870** / 0.848
	BlenderBot	7.48 / 8.54	6.31 / 4.77	0.302 / 0.282	**0.462** / 0.444	0.316 / 0.321	0.825 / 0.804
	BlenderBot + Intent	**7.35** / 8.38	**6.52 / 5.29**	**0.311 / 0.297**	**0.462 / 0.449**	**0.570 / 0.564**	0.834 / 0.809
	BlenderBot + C-Traits	7.49 / 8.54	6.33 / 5.00	0.301 / 0.286	0.460 / 0.447	0.320 / 0.329	0.825 / 0.801
	BlenderBot + P-Traits	7.42 / 8.44	6.24 / 4.90	0.306 / 0.293	0.456 / 0.445	0.369 / 0.370	0.831 / 0.809
	BlenderBot + E-Traits	7.41 / 8.42	6.37 / 4.89	0.309 / 0.293	0.459 / 0.445	0.359 / 0.369	0.840 / **0.818**
	BlenderBot + Intent + P-Traits	7.37 / 8.38	6.26 / 5.01	0.307 / 0.295	0.455 / 0.442	0.472 / 0.485	0.833 / 0.811
	BlenderBot + Intent + E-Traits	7.36 / **8.37**	6.29 / 5.04	0.308 / 0.295	0.457 / 0.444	0.508 / 0.500	**0.841** / 0.817
	BlenderBot + All (P-Traits)	7.38 / 8.39	6.22 / 4.90	0.305 / 0.294	0.450 / 0.437	0.466 / 0.469	0.828 / 0.810
	BlenderBot + All (E-Traits)	7.37 / 8.38	6.22 / 4.77	0.304 / 0.294	0.451 / 0.441	0.480 / 0.491	0.835 / **0.818**
TC	BART	13.81 / 14.71	3.62 / 4.10	0.235 / 0.250	0.365 / 0.388	0.264 / 0.256	0.726 / 0.763
	BART + Intent	13.25 / 14.12	3.62 / 4.30	0.234 / 0.251	0.373 / 0.399	0.359 / 0.377	0.723 / 0.767
	BART + C-Traits	13.73 / 14.68	3.49 / 4.13	0.233 / 0.251	0.361 / 0.390	0.263 / 0.267	0.725 / 0.759
	BART + P-Traits	13.59 / 14.57	3.60 / 4.12	0.236 / 0.253	0.363 / 0.390	0.286 / 0.317	0.731 / 0.766
	BART + E-Traits	13.57 / 14.53	3.52 / 4.08	0.237 / 0.252	0.364 / 0.390	0.290 / 0.299	0.733 / 0.771
	BART + Intent + P-Traits	13.25 / 14.14	3.69 / 4.20	0.239 / 0.252	0.364 / 0.392	0.461 / 0.471	0.729 / 0.773
	BART + Intent + E-Traits	**13.21** / 14.10	**3.75** / **4.38**	**0.246** / **0.259**	**0.377** / **0.403**	0.459 / 0.470	0.747 / **0.783**
	BART + All (P-Traits)	**13.21** / 14.10	3.72 / 4.37	0.242 / **0.259**	0.370 / 0.400	**0.505 / 0.523**	0.731 / 0.765
	BART + All (E-Traits)	13.22 / **14.02**	3.73 / 4.28	**0.246** / 0.258	0.376 / **0.403**	0.465 / 0.468	**0.748** / 0.782
	BlenderBot	11.09 / 10.75	3.13 / 3.75	0.223 / 0.240	0.367 / 0.390	0.267 / 0.261	0.691 / 0.733
	BlenderBot + Intent	10.79 / 10.45	**3.41 / 3.85**	0.230 / **0.247**	**0.373 / 0.396**	0.472 / 0.480	0.713 / 0.747
	BlenderBot + C-Traits	11.09 / 10.75	3.22 / 3.75	0.222 / 0.240	0.365 / 0.390	0.273 / 0.268	0.695 / 0.737
	BlenderBot + P-Traits	11.01 / 10.65	3.16 / 3.66	0.227 / 0.243	0.366 / 0.390	0.326 / 0.336	0.710 / 0.745
	BlenderBot + E-Traits	10.98 / 10.61	3.18 / 3.66	0.229 / 0.246	0.369 / 0.391	0.329 / 0.334	0.732 / 0.766
	BlenderBot + Intent + P-Traits	10.76 / 10.41	3.19 / 3.64	0.232 / **0.247**	0.368 / 0.390	**0.524** / **0.531**	0.715 / 0.753
	BlenderBot + Intent + E-Traits	10.73 / 10.37	3.13 / 3.66	**0.234 / 0.247**	0.370 / 0.392	0.513 / 0.525	0.733 / **0.770**
	BlenderBot + All (P-Traits)	10.75 / 10.39	3.22 / 3.65	0.232 / **0.247**	0.367 / 0.389	0.518 / 0.517	0.720 / 0.749
	BlenderBot + All (E-Traits)	**10.72** / **10.35**	3.20 / 3.62	**0.234 / 0.247**	0.369 / 0.391	0.517 / 0.513	**0.737** / 0.768

Table 9: Ablation study on the seen/unseen and frequent/rare topic portions of the Wizard of Wikipedia (WOW), and Topical Chat (TC) test sets. Best performing models are highlighted in bold.

contains the ablation study results. For each conversation corpus, and personality dataset combination, Table 12 lists the percentage distribution of strong and weak categories (seperated by '/') for each Big-5 trait, by each split of the dataset. Table 13 contains results without access to the golden policy consisting of control codes during inference. The model leverages the predicted control codes as policy for response generation. Figure 3 plots the context length wise style adaptation of the generated response, which hints lengthier context facilitates better adaptation to the desired response style.

A.4 Amazon Mechanical Turk for Evaluation

We leveraged Amazon Mechanical Turk (AMT) in order to perform human evaluations on our model

Intent	Percentage Occurance	Annotator Agreement
State Knowledge Fact	0.33	0.95
State Opinion	0.30	0.81
State Personal Fact	0.13	1.00
Request (Opinion/Knowledge Fact/Personal Fact)	0.13	1.00
Others	0.11	1.00

Table 10: Intent Automatic Annotation Evaluation.

Personality Trait	Pandora Occurance	Pandora Agreement	Essays Occurance	Essays Agreement
agreeableness	0.195	0.696	0.197	0.760
openness	0.229	0.630	0.252	0.563
conscientiousness	0.169	0.550	0.181	0.391
extraversion	0.186	0.364	0.189	0.750
neuroticism	0.220	0.308	0.181	0.435

Table 11: Personality Trait Automatic Annotation Evaluation.

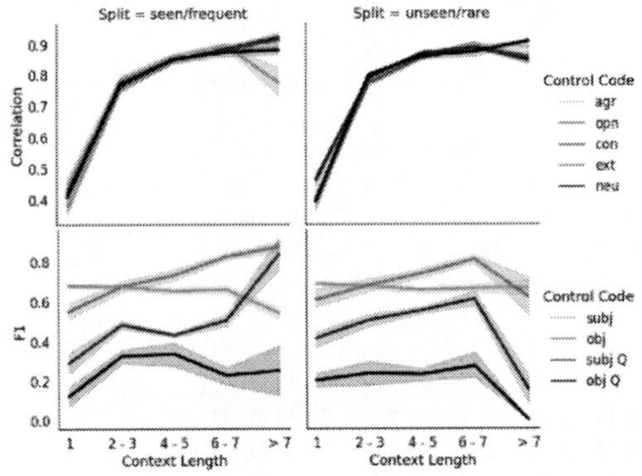

Figure 3: Turn length wise adaptation to the desired response style, collated from all the full version models.

response. We set up human intelligence task (HIT) in the AMT platform, with two evaluators per example and each task worth $0.01. The evaluators were provided with clear instructions on what to annotate and how to annotate the examples. The task comprised of reading a conversation context, and rating 5 different responses on a Likert scale of 1 to 5, where the responses were generated by different models, unknown to the annotator. Figure 4 illustrates a sample screenshot of the HIT interface along with the instructions used for collecting the evaluations.

Corpus	Personality Corpus	Seen/ Frequent Topic Agr	Opn	Con	Ext	Neu	Unseen/ Rare Topic Agr	Opn	Con	Ext	Neu
WOW	Pandora	19/20	80/8	19/19	17/20	19/20	20/18	81/8	17/20	12/24	22/15
	Essays	22/15	78/10	20/17	21/15	16/20	21/12	79/10	15/18	20/16	14/20
TC	Pandora	47/18	72/10	29/25	39/19	20/33	20/38	67/16	22/37	12/46	37/18
	Essays	40/12	61/23	38/14	49/8	7/49	22/29	65/17	14/41	11/45	40/17

Table 12: Percentage of Strong/Weak categories for all traits in each chat corpus, split by each personality corpus.

Corpus	Model	BLEU 4	RougeL	BLEURT
WOW	BART	8.44 / 8.24	0.341 / 0.342	0.491 / 0.488
	BART + Intent	8.63 / 7.87	0.334 / 0.332	0.495 / 0.491
	BART + C-Traits	8.32 / 8.11	0.338 / 0.338	0.487 / 0.486
	BART + P-Traits	8.69 / 8.42	0.343 / 0.342	0.494 / 0.489
	BART + E-Traits	8.94 / 8.60	0.342 / 0.344	0.495 / 0.490
	BART + Intent + P-Traits	9.41 / 8.47	0.342 / 0.336	0.499 / 0.490
	BART + Intent + E-Traits	8.86 / 8.12	0.337 / 0.332	0.497 / 0.491
	BART + All (P-Traits)	9.09 / 8.60	0.343 / 0.343	0.496 / 0.498
	BART + All (E-Traits)	9.26 / 8.82	0.340 / 0.343	0.499 / 0.495
	BlenderBot	6.31 / 4.77	0.302 / 0.282	0.462 / 0.444
	BlenderBot + Intent	6.36 / 5.20	0.301 / 0.287	0.457 / 0.446
	BlenderBot + C-Traits	6.33 / 5.00	0.301 / 0.286	0.460 / 0.447
	BlenderBot + P-Traits	6.28 / 4.98	0.306 / 0.289	0.453 / 0.441
	BlenderBot + E-Traits	6.34 / 4.90	0.305 / 0.288	0.457 / 0.441
	BlenderBot + Intent + P-Traits	6.32 / 4.99	0.301 / 0.289	0.450 / 0.440
	BlenderBot + Intent + E-Traits	6.21 / 4.99	0.300 / 0.288	0.452 / 0.441
	BlenderBot + All (P-Traits)	6.29 / 4.75	0.301 / 0.287	0.443 / 0.430
	BlenderBot + All (E-Traits)	6.18 / 4.77	0.299 / 0.286	0.448 / 0.433
TC	BART	3.62 / 4.10	0.235 / 0.250	0.365 / 0.388
	BART + Intent	3.40 / 4.00	0.228 / 0.243	0.369 / 0.397
	BART + C-Traits	3.49 / 4.13	0.233 / 0.251	0.361 / 0.390
	BART + P-Traits	3.54 / 4.10	0.233 / 0.250	0.362 / 0.389
	BART + E-Traits	3.40 / 4.01	0.233 / 0.248	0.363 / 0.388
	BART + Intent + P-Traits	3.32 / 3.92	0.227 / 0.240	0.361 / 0.389
	BART + Intent + E-Traits	3.29 / 4.00	0.229 / 0.243	0.371 / 0.397
	BART + All (P-Traits)	3.36 / 3.96	0.227 / 0.242	0.366 / 0.396
	BART + All (E-Traits)	3.54 / 4.14	0.231 / 0.245	0.372 / 0.397
	BlenderBot	3.13 / 3.75	0.223 / 0.240	0.367 / 0.390
	BlenderBot + Intent	3.12 / 3.73	0.215 / 0.233	0.363 / 0.387
	BlenderBot + C-Traits	3.22 / 3.75	0.222 / 0.240	0.365 / 0.390
	BlenderBot + P-Traits	3.18 / 3.71	0.222 / 0.240	0.363 / 0.387
	BlenderBot + E-Traits	3.11 / 3.52	0.221 / 0.239	0.364 / 0.385
	BlenderBot + Intent + P-Traits	3.03 / 3.59	0.214 / 0.228	0.361 / 0.382
	BlenderBot + Intent + E-Traits	3.04 / 3.69	0.213 / 0.230	0.362 / 0.384
	BlenderBot + All (P-Traits)	3.06 / 3.50	0.214 / 0.229	0.359 / 0.382
	BlenderBot + All (E-Traits)	3.03 / 3.52	0.213 / 0.229	0.359 / 0.385

Table 13: Experimental results and ablation study on the seen/unseen and frequent/rare topic portions of the Wizard of Wikipedia (WOW), and Topical Chat (TC) test sets, using golden facts and model predicted stylistic control codes.

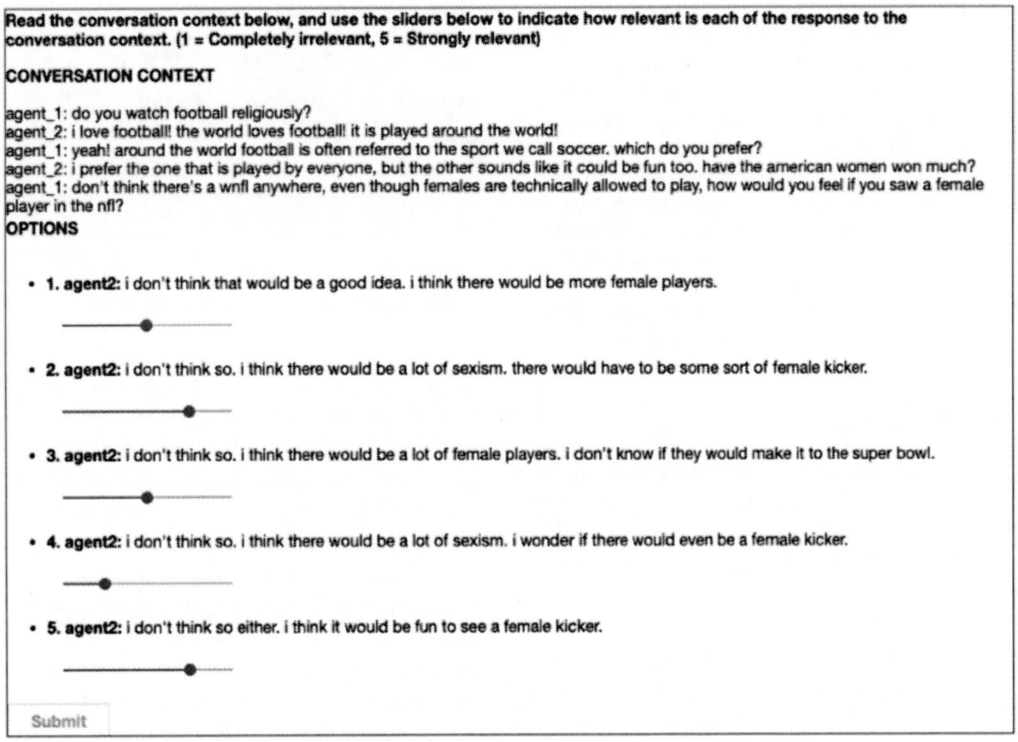

Read the conversation context below, and use the sliders below to indicate how relevant is each of the response to the conversation context. (1 = Completely irrelevant, 5 = Strongly relevant)

CONVERSATION CONTEXT

agent_1: do you watch football religiously?
agent_2: i love football! the world loves football! it is played around the world!
agent_1: yeah! around the world football is often referred to the sport we call soccer. which do you prefer?
agent_2: i prefer the one that is played by everyone, but the other sounds like it could be fun too. have the american women won much?
agent_1: don't think there's a wnfl anywhere, even though females are technically allowed to play, how would you feel if you saw a female player in the nfl?

OPTIONS

- **1. agent2:** i don't think that would be a good idea. i think there would be more female players.
- **2. agent2:** i don't think so. i think there would be a lot of sexism. there would have to be some sort of female kicker.
- **3. agent2:** i don't think so. i think there would be a lot of female players. i don't know if they would make it to the super bowl.
- **4. agent2:** i don't think so. i think there would be a lot of sexism. i wonder if there would even be a female kicker.
- **5. agent2:** i don't think so either. i think it would be fun to see a female kicker.

Submit

Figure 4: Sample screenshot from AMT HIT task.

Toward Knowledge-Enriched Conversational Recommendation Systems

Tong Zhang[1], Yong Liu[2, 3], Boyang Li[1, 2], Peixiang Zhong[2, 3],
Chen Zhang[4], Hao Wang[4] and Chunyan Miao[1, 2, 3]

[1]School of Computer Science and Engineering, Nanyang Technological University (NTU), Singapore
[2]Alibaba-NTU Singapore Joint Research Institute, NTU, Singapore
[3]Joint NTU-UBC Research Centre of Excellence in Active Living for the Elderly, NTU, Singapore
[4]Alibaba Group, China

{tong24, stephenliu, boyang.li, peixiang001, ascymiao}@ntu.edu.sg,
zhangchen010295@163.com, cashenry@126.com

Abstract

Conversational Recommendation Systems recommend items through language based interactions with users. In order to generate naturalistic conversations and effectively utilize knowledge graphs (KGs) containing background information, we propose a novel Bag-of-Entities loss, which encourages the generated utterances to mention concepts related to the item being recommended, such as the genre or director of a movie. We also propose an alignment loss to further integrate KG entities into the response generation network. Experiments on the large-scale REDIAL dataset demonstrate that the proposed system consistently outperforms state-of-the-art baselines.

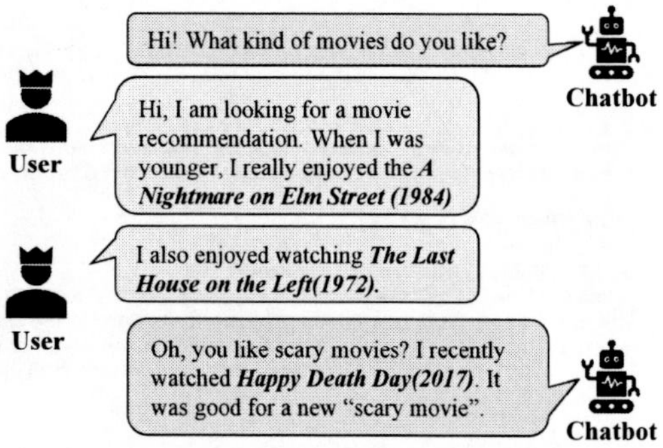

Figure 1: An example of a conversation between a user and the Chatbot for movie recommendation.

1 Introduction

Conversational recommendation systems (CRS) have received increasing attention from the Natural Language Processing community (Li et al., 2018; Chen et al., 2019; Zhou et al., 2020a; Sarkar et al., 2020; Liu et al., 2020; Zhou et al., 2020b; Hayati et al., 2020). CRS aims to recommend items, such as movies or songs, in naturalistic interactive conversations with the user. This interactive form allows the system to provide recommendations tailored to preferences provided by the user at the moment.

A crucial issue of CRS is to extract user preferences from the conversation, which often requires background information provided by knowledge graphs (KGs). As an example, in Figure 1, the user mentions two movies that belong to the horror genre. To this end, some existing studies (Chen et al., 2019; Zhou et al., 2020a) leverage knowledge graphs to understand user intentions.

We observe that when humans recommend items to friends, they usually describe attributes of the item. For example, to recommend a movie, they may mention the director or actors. Such information can be easily extracted from the knowledge graph, but has not been well utilized by existing approaches. To emulate naturalistic conversations, we propose a Bag-of-Entities (BOE) loss, which encourages the generated utterances to mention concepts related to the item. Moreover, we propose an alignment loss that ties the word embeddings to the entity embeddings.

Experiments demonstrate that the proposed two losses improve model performance. The proposed the Knowledge-Enriched Conversational Recommendation System (KECRS) consistently outperforms state-of-the-art CRSs on the large-scale REDIAL dataset (Li et al., 2018).

2 Related work

We briefly review work on conversational recommendation systems and conversational characters in e-commerce settings. A number of works on conversational recommendation systems focus solely on interactive recommendation rather than language understanding (Christakopoulou et al., 2016, 2018; Sun and Zhang, 2018; Zhang et al., 2018; Lei et al., 2020a,b; Zou et al., 2020; Xu et al., 2021; Zhang et al., 2022). In contrast, a second category of works aims to provide both accurate interactive recommendations and generate natural

Proceedings of the 4th Workshop on NLP for Conversational AI, pages 212 - 217
May 27, 2022

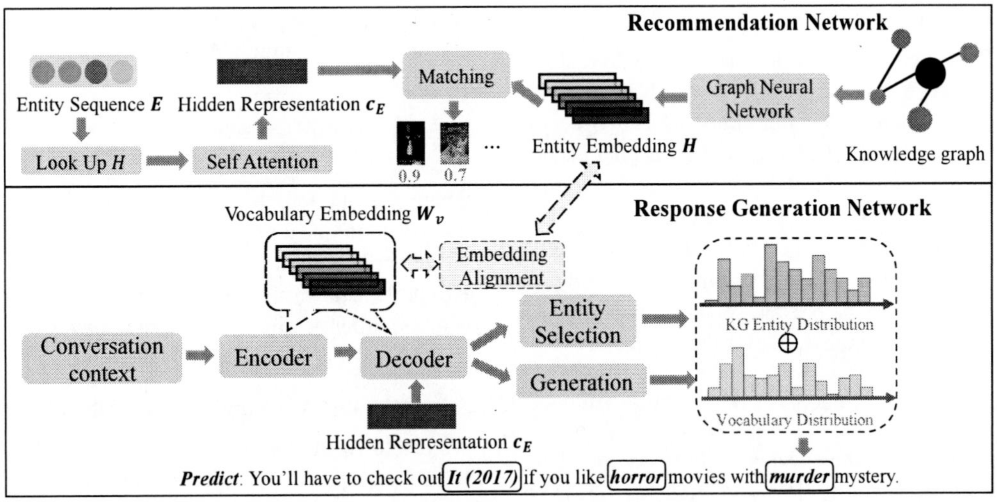

Figure 2: The overall framework of the proposed KECRS model.

and human-like responses (Li et al., 2018; Chen et al., 2019; Zhou et al., 2020a; Sarkar et al., 2020; Liu et al., 2020; Zhou et al., 2020b; Hayati et al., 2020). Finally, research on conversational characters for e-commerce has the broad goal of building a complete shopping assistant that can answer a variety of questions in addition to recommendation (Li et al., 2017; Yang et al., 2018; Fu et al., 2020; Song et al., 2021).

3 Approach

The overall goal of a conversational recommendation system is to identify an item (e.g., a movie, a song, or a piece of merchandise) that the user will likely interact with and suggest the item to the user in the form of natural language conversations.

Formally, we represent the historic conversation $X = \langle x_1, x_2, ..., x_n \rangle$ as a sequence of n utterances x_i. The knowledge graph $\mathcal{G} = \{(v_h, r, v_t)\}$ is a set of entities E and a set of relationships r between the head entity $v_h \in E$ and the tail entity $v_t \in E$.

The conversational recommendation task is to predict the next utterance x_{n+1} using the recommendation network $f(X, \mathcal{G})$ and the response generation network $g(X, \mathcal{G}, f(X, \mathcal{G}))$. $f(X, \mathcal{G})$ predicts the next item to recommend to the user, whereas $g(X, \mathcal{G}, f(X, \mathcal{G}))$ predicts the utterance x_{n+1} one word at a time.

Figure 2 shows the overall structure of our proposed method, the Knowledge-Enriched Conversational Recommendation System (KECRS).

3.1 Recommendation Network

First, we exhaustively match each word in the conversational history X with the name of each entity in the KG. In this way, we identify K entities from the history and sequence them according to their original positions. Next, we apply a graph convolutional network, R-GCN (Schlichtkrull et al., 2017) to encode the entire KG and obtain embeddings for each KG entity node. The D-dimensional entity embeddings of the K entity form the matrix $\boldsymbol{H}_E \in \mathbb{R}^{K \times D}$. Subsequently, we apply an attention operation where the attention vector $\boldsymbol{\alpha}$ is computed by 2 fully connected (FC) layers.

$$\begin{aligned} \boldsymbol{\alpha} &= \text{softmax}\big(\mathbf{W}_k \tanh(\mathbf{W}_q \mathbf{H}_E^\top)\big), \\ \mathbf{c}_E &= \boldsymbol{\alpha} \mathbf{H}_E, \end{aligned} \tag{1}$$

where $\mathbf{W}_q$ and $\mathbf{W}_k$ are learnable parameters. The resulting $\mathbf{c}_E \in \mathbb{R}^D$ is a condensed representation of entities appearing in the conversational history.

The recommendation module classifies $\boldsymbol{c}_E$ directly into one of the items. We directly take the entity embedding $\boldsymbol{e}_i$ from the R-GCN network as the representation of the item. The probability of recommending item i is computed with softmax:

$$P_{rec}(i) \propto \exp(\boldsymbol{c}_E^\top \boldsymbol{e}_i). \tag{2}$$

The module is trained using the cross-entropy loss. To avoid the model recommending the same movie that the user might have just mentioned, we only consider as a ground-truth recommendation the movie that is first time to be mentioned by the recommender in the conversation.

3.2 Response Generation Network

The response generation module predicts the utterance to the user word by word. We use the classic encoder-decoder Transformer architecture (Vaswani et al., 2017), where the encoder encodes the entire conversational history word by word.

At decoding time step j, the output of the Transformer decoder s_j is concatenated with the entity representation c_E and goes through two fully connected layers before the softmax function. The probability distribution over the vocabulary is

$$P_{res} = \text{softmax}\big(\mathbf{W}_v \boldsymbol{W}_a[\mathbf{s}_j; \mathbf{c}_E] + \boldsymbol{b}\big), \quad (3)$$

where $\mathbf{W}_v$ is the word embedding matrix shared with the encoder. $\mathbf{W}_a$ is a trainable linear projection to align the dimensions, and $\boldsymbol{b}$ is the bias. We train the module using cross-entropy at every decoder time step.

To separate movie names from other words in the conversation, for every movie name we create specialized tokens in the vocabulary. For example, the token for the movie name *It* is separate from the word token *it*. This is feasible as the dataset, REDIAL, has explicitly represented movie names with special strings.

3.3 Bag-of-Entities Loss

Although the response generation module trained using per-step cross-entropy is capable of recommending items, it rarely mentions concepts related to the recommended item. We postulate that mentioning related entities will produce natural conversations. For example, when recommending the movie *It*, one may want to mention that it is a horror movie based on a book by Stephen King.

For this purpose, we introduce the Bag-of-Entity (BOE) loss, which encourages the decoder state $[\mathbf{s}_j; \mathbf{c}_E]$ to contain additional information about first-order neighbors of the ground-truth recommendation on the KG.

First, at every time step, we compute a score $\boldsymbol{r}_j \in \mathbb{R}^M$ for all M entities in the knowledge graph,

$$\boldsymbol{r}_j = \mathbf{H}\mathbf{W}_b[\mathbf{s}_j; \mathbf{c}_E] + \mathbf{b}_{ent}, \quad (4)$$

where $\mathbf{H}$ contains the embeddings of all KG entities, as produced by the R-GCN. $\mathbf{W}_b$ is a trainable matrix for dimension alignment and $\mathbf{b}_{ent}$ the bias.

As we do not constrain exactly which word in the response should contain the information, we sum up the word-level scores and then apply the component-wise sigmoid function. The probability that entity m is mentioned in the response is thus

$$P_{\text{BOE}}(m) = \text{sigmoid}(\sum_{j=1}^{L} r_{jm}), \quad (5)$$

where L is the length of the response and r_{jm} is the mth component of $\boldsymbol{r}_j$.

We apply a binary cross-entropy loss for each KG entity. The ground-truth label is 1 if the entity is a first-order neighbor of the recommended item on the knowledge graph and 0 otherwise.

3.4 Aligning Word and Entity Embeddings

We create two types of tokens in the vocabulary V of the response generation network. The first type corresponds to a plain word appearing in the conversation text. The second type represents an entity that appears in the conversation and in the knowledge graph.

To tie the token embeddings of the second type to the R-GCN encoding of the knowledge graph, we propose the alignment loss. For a conversation, we use the entity representation $\mathbf{c}_E$ in Eq. (1) to represent all entities in the conversation and calculate the similarity score between $\mathbf{c}_E$ and each word embedding,

$$\mathbf{s} = \mathbf{W}_{v[E]}\mathbf{W}_c\mathbf{c}_E + \mathbf{b}_{align}, \quad (6)$$

where $\mathbf{W}_{v[E]}$ is the matrix resulting from selecting the rows of $\mathbf{W}_v$ corresponding to entity tokens only. $\mathbf{W}_c$ is a trainable matrix and $\mathbf{b}_{align}$ is the bias. The alignment loss is the mean square error between the s and an indicator vector $\mathbf{q} \in \{0,1\}^{|E|}$.

$$L_{align} = ||\boldsymbol{s} - \boldsymbol{q}||^2 \quad (7)$$

Specifically, if an entity e exists in the conversation, the corresponding component of $\mathbf{q}$ is set to 1. Otherwise, the component is 0.

Finally, to learn the parameters of generation module, we minimize the following objective function:

$$L_{total} = L_{gen} + \lambda_1 L_{\text{BOE}} + \lambda_2 L_{align}, \quad (8)$$

where λ_1 and λ_2 are two hyperparameters. In the testing procedure, the probability distribution over the vocabulary at time step j is calculated as follows,

$$P_{all} = P_{res} + \lambda_3 P_{boe}, \quad (9)$$

where λ_3 is a hyperparameter.

Model	Automatic			Human		
	Dist-2	Dist-3	Dist-4	Fluency	Relevancy	Informativeness
HRED-CRS	0.10	0.18	0.24	1.92	1.62	1.05
Transformer	0.15	0.31	0.46	2.03	1.73	1.36
KBRD	0.31	0.38	0.52	2.10	1.72	1.32
KGSF	0.38	0.61	0.73	2.32	2.11	1.56
KECRS(Ours)	**0.48***	**0.91***	**1.23***	**2.56***	**2.29***	**2.18***

Table 1: Automatic and human evaluation results of the response generation achieved by different methods. Human evaluation scores are from 0-3. Dist-2,3,4 is short for Distinct-2,3,4. * indicates that the improvement over the best baseline method is statistically significant with $p < 0.01$ using student *t-test*

4 Experiments

4.1 Dataset

We use the REDIAL dataset (Li et al., 2018), which includes 10,006 conversations and 182,150 utterances related to 51,699 movies. Following (Li et al., 2018; Chen et al., 2019; Zhou et al., 2020a), we split REDIAL into training, validation, and testing sets with the ratio 8:1:1. We build the knowledge graph, TMDKG, from The Movie Database[1], which contains 15822 entities and 15 types of relations.

4.2 Evaluation Metrics

Following (Chen et al., 2019; Zhou et al., 2020a), we use Distinct n-gram (n=2, 3, 4) to measure the diversity of generated responses. To better evaluate the performance of generated responses, we adopt human evaluation. We randomly sample 100 multi-turn conversations from the test set and invite three annotators to score responses generated by different models from the following aspects: 1) **Fluency**: whether responses are fluent;2) **Relevancy**: whether responses are correlated with contexts;3) **Informativeness**: whether responses contain rich information of recommended items. Each aspect is rated in $[0, 3]$, and final scores are the average of all annotators. For all evaluation metrics, the higher value indicates better performances.

4.3 Baseline Methods

We compare KECRS with the following baseline methods: 1) **HRED-CRS** (Li et al., 2018): This is a basic CRS based on HRED(Serban et al., 2016); 2) **Transformer** (Vaswani et al., 2017): This is a basic transformer model that generates responses only from utterance text and does not contain a separate recommendation module; 3) **KBRD** (Chen et al., 2019):This is a knowledge-based CRS that employs DBpedia to understand the user's intentions and leverage KG information as a bias for generation; 4) **KGSF** (Zhou et al., 2020a): This method exploits both entity-oriented and word-oriented KGs to enrich the data representations. It adopts two KG-enriched decoder layers for the generation.

[1]https://www.themoviedb.org/

Model	Dist-2	Dist-3	Dist-4
KGSF	0.38	0.61	0.73
$\text{KECRS}_{\text{w/o BOE}}$	0.31	0.64	0.87
$\text{KECRS}_{\text{w/o align}}$	0.36	0.69	0.95
KECRS	**0.48***	**0.91***	**1.23***

Table 2: Response generation performances of KGSF and different variants of KECRS. * indicates that the improvement over the best baseline method is statistically significant with $p < 0.01$ using student *t-test*

4.4 Results and Discussion

The automatic and human evaluation results of different methods are shown in Table 1. We note that Transformer performs better than HRED-CRS, which demonstrates that Transformer is powerful to understand and generate natural language. KBRD performs better than Transformer, because it adds a vocabulary bias to fuse knowledge from KG into the generated responses. Among all the baseline models, KGSF generates the most diverse responses, by exploiting both TMDKG and ConceptNet (Speer et al., 2017). The potential reason is that KGSF employs two additional KG-based attention layers to make the generative model focus more on items and relevant entities in TMDKG and ConceptNet. Moreover, the proposed KECRS model outperforms all baseline methods with a large margin in terms of all evaluation metrics. This demonstrates that the proposed BOE loss and alignment loss can work jointly to better leverage KG and generate more diverse and informative responses.

For human evaluation, we note that *Fluency* is relatively higher compared to *Informativeness* and *Relevancy* for all models. This indicates that responses generated by these models are fluent and can be understood by human judges. However, responses generated by baseline models are more likely to be generic responses (*e.g.,* "I haven't seen that one"). By including additional supervision signals and aligning embeddings of word and entities, the proposed KECRS model alleviates this issue. Overall, KECRS can understand the dialogue context and generate fluent, relevant, and informative responses.

4.5 Ablation Study

To better understand effectiveness of each component in KECRS, we study the performances of following two variants of KECRS: 1) **KECRS$_{\text{w/o BOE}}$**, which removes the BOE loss, and 2) **KECRS$_{\text{w/o align}}$**, which removes the infusion loss.

Table 2 summarizes the response generation performance in terms of Distinct n-gram (n=2,3,4). Distinct n-gram measures the diversity of sentences by calculating the number of distinct n-gram in generated responses. KECRS outperforms KECRS$_{\text{w/o BOE}}$, which indicates the proposed BOE loss can help the model learn to generate responses not only from conversations but also from the knowledge graph. Moreover, KECRS$_{\text{w/o align}}$ performs poorer than KECRS. This indicates that aligning the the word embeddings and entity embeddings also helps improve the model performances. Compared with KGSF, both ablated versions of KECRS can achieve better performances in terms of most metrics. This again demonstrates that encouraging model to mention concept related to the recommended items and aligning word embeddings with KG entity embeddings both can help model generate more diverse responses.

4.6 Case Study

In Table 3, we present a qualitative comparison of the responses generated by different models. The conversation is selected from the dataset REDIAL. When the user expresses preferences on "*There's Something About Mary*", KECRS infers the user may like romantic comedy movie. Thus, KECRS recommends another romantic comedy movie "*Meet the Parents*" and provides an informative and natural response *"It 's a classic. It's a little older , but still funny and romantic"*.

User:	Hi there, how are you?
Recommender:	I'm doing great, how about you?
User:	Fine thanks. I 'd love to see something similar to ***There's Something About Mary***. That movie always cracks me up !
Transformer:	I haven't seen that one.
KBRD:	I haven't seen that one. What about ***My Best Friend's Wedding***?
KGSF:	I recommend ***The Other Woman***?
KECRS (Ours):	I love ***Meet the Parents***. It 's a ***classic***. It's a little ***older*** , but still ***funny*** and ***romantic***.

Table 3: Case Study.

5 Conclusions

In this paper, we propose a novel Knowledge-Enriched Conversational Recommendation System (KECRS). Specifically, we develop the Bag-of-Entity (BOE) loss and the alignment loss to improve the response generation performances. The experimental results on REDIAL demonstrate that the proposed BOE loss can guide the model to generate more knowledge-enriched responses by selecting entities in KG, and the alignment loss can ties the word embeddings to the entity embeddings. Overall, KECRS achieves superior response quality than state-of-the-art baselines.

For future work, we would like to investigate how to use keywords to conduct the conversation from chit-chat to the recommendation (Zhou et al., 2020b; Liu et al., 2020). Moreover, we are also interested in using external knowledge (*e.g.,* KG) to modify the REDIAL dataset and make responses more relevant to the recommended items (Jannach and Manzoor, 2020).

6 Acknowledgments

The authors gratefully acknowledge the support from the Alibaba-NTU Joint Research Institute, Nanyang Associate Professorship, and the National Research Foundation, Singapore (NRF-NRFF13-2021-0006). Any opinions, findings, conclusions, or recommendations expressed in this paper are those of the authors and do not necessarily reflect the view of the funding agencies.

References

Qibin Chen, Junyang Lin, Yichang Zhang, Ming Ding, Yukuo Cen, Hongxia Yang, and Jie Tang. 2019. Towards knowledge-based recommender dialog system. *arXiv preprint arXiv:1908.05391.*

Konstantina Christakopoulou, Alex Beutel, Rui Li, Sagar Jain, and Ed H. Chi. 2018. Q&R: A two-stage approach toward interactive recommendation. In *SIGKDD*, pages 139–148.

Konstantina Christakopoulou, Filip Radlinski, and Katja Hofmann. 2016. Towards conversational recommender systems. In *SIGKDD*, pages 815–824.

Min Fu, Jiwei Guan, Xi Zheng, Jie Zhou, Jianchao Lu, Tianyi Zhang, Shoujie Zhuo, Lijun Zhan, and Jian Yang. 2020. ICS-Assist: Intelligent customer inquiry resolution recommendation in online customer service for large E-commerce businesses. *arXiv preprint arXiv:2008.13534.*

Shirley Anugrah Hayati, Dongyeop Kang, Qingxiaoyang Zhu, Weiyan Shi, and Zhou Yu. 2020. INSPIRED: Toward sociable recommendation dialog systems. *arXiv preprint arXiv:2009.14306.*

Dietmar Jannach and Ahtsham Manzoor. 2020. End-to-End learning for conversational recommendation: A long way to go? In *RecSys*, pages 72–76.

Wenqiang Lei, Xiangnan He, Yisong Miao, Qingyun Wu, Richang Hong, Min-Yen Kan, and Tat-Seng Chua. 2020a. Estimation-action-reflection: Towards deep interaction between conversational and recommender systems. In *WSDM*, pages 304–312.

Wenqiang Lei, Gangyi Zhang, Xiangnan He, Yisong Miao, Xiang Wang, Liang Chen, and Tat-Seng Chua. 2020b. Interactive path reasoning on graph for conversational recommendation. In *SIGKDD*, pages 2073–2083.

Feng-Lin Li, Minghui Qiu, Haiqing Chen, Xiongwei Wang, Xing Gao, Jun Huang, Juwei Ren, Zhongzhou Zhao, Weipeng Zhao, and Lei Wang. 2017. Alime assist: An intelligent assistant for creating an innovative e-commerce experience. In *CIKM*.

Raymond Li, Samira Ebrahimi Kahou, Hannes Schulz, Vincent Michalski, Laurent Charlin, and Chris Pal. 2018. Towards deep conversational recommendations. In *NeurIPS*, pages 9725–9735.

Zeming Liu, Haifeng Wang, Zheng-Yu Niu, Hua Wu, Wanxiang Che, and Ting Liu. 2020. Towards conversational recommendation over multi-type dialogs. *arXiv preprint arXiv:2005.03954.*

Rajdeep Sarkar, Koustava Goswami, Mihael Arcan, and John Philip McCrae. 2020. Suggest me a movie for tonight: Leveraging knowledge graphs for conversational recommendation. In *COLING*, pages 4179–4189.

Michael Schlichtkrull, Thomas N. Kipf, Peter Bloem, Rianne Van Den Berg, Ivan Titov, and Max Welling. 2017. Modeling relational data with graph convolutional networks. *arXiv preprint arXiv:1703.06103.*

Iulian Vlad Serban, Alessandro Sordoni, Ryan Lowe, Laurent Charlin, Joelle Pineau, Aaron Courville, and Yoshua Bengio. 2016. A hierarchical latent variable encoder-decoder model for generating dialogues. *arXiv preprint arXiv:1605.06069.*

Shuangyong Song, Chao Wang, Haiqing Chen, and Huan Chen. 2021. An emotional comfort framework for improving user satisfaction in E-commerce customer service chatbots. In *NAACL*, pages 130–137.

Robyn Speer, Joshua Chin, and Catherine Havasi. 2017. Conceptnet 5.5: An open multilingual graph of general knowledge. In *AAAI*.

Yueming Sun and Yi Zhang. 2018. Conversational recommender system. In *SIGIR*, pages 235–244.

Ashish Vaswani, Noam Shazeer, Niki Parmar, Jakob Uszkoreit, Llion Jones, Aidan N. Gomez, Lukasz Kaiser, and Illia Polosukhin. 2017. Attention is all you need. *arXiv preprint arXiv:1706.03762.*

Kerui Xu, Jingxuan Yang, Jun Xu, Sheng Gao, Jun Guo, and Ji-Rong Wen. 2021. Adapting user preference to online feedback in multi-round conversational recommendation. In *WSDM*, page 364–372.

Liu Yang, Minghui Qiu, Chen Qu, Jiafeng Guo, Yongfeng Zhang, W Bruce Croft, Jun Huang, and Haiqing Chen. 2018. Response ranking with deep matching networks and external knowledge in information-seeking conversation systems. In *SIGIR*, pages 245–254.

Yinan Zhang, Boyang Li, Yong Liu, Yuan You, and Chunyan Miao. 2022. Minimalist and high-performance conversational recommendation with uncertainty estimation for user preference.

Yongfeng Zhang, Xu Chen, Qingyao Ai, Liu Yang, and W. Bruce Croft. 2018. Towards conversational search and recommendation: System ask, user respond. In *CIKM*, pages 177–186.

Kun Zhou, Wayne Xin Zhao, Shuqing Bian, Yuanhang Zhou, Ji-Rong Wen, and Jingsong Yu. 2020a. Improving conversational recommender systems via knowledge graph based semantic fusion. In *SIGKDD*.

Kun Zhou, Yuanhang Zhou, Wayne Xin Zhao, Xiaoke Wang, and Ji-Rong Wen. 2020b. Towards topic-guided conversational recommender system. *arXiv preprint arXiv:2010.04125.*

Jie Zou, Yifan Chen, and Evangelos Kanoulas. 2020. Towards question-based recommender systems. *arXiv preprint arXiv:2005.14255.*

Understanding and Improving the Exemplar-based Generation for Open-domain Conversation

Seungju Han[†], Beomsu Kim[†], Seokjun Seo[†], Enkhbayar Erdenee[†], Buru Chang[*]
Hyperconnect
{seungju.han,beomsu.kim,seokjun.seo,enkhbayar.erdenee,buru.chang}@hpcnt.com

Abstract

Exemplar-based generative models for open-domain conversation produce responses based on the exemplars provided by the retriever, taking advantage of generative models and retrieval models. However, due to the one-to-many problem of the open-domain conversation, they often ignore the retrieved exemplars while generating responses or produce responses over-fitted to the retrieved exemplars. To address these advantages, we introduce a training method selecting exemplars that are semantically relevant to the gold response but lexically distanced from the gold response. In the training phase, our training method first uses the gold response instead of dialogue context as a query to select exemplars that are semantically relevant to the gold response. And then, it eliminates the exemplars that lexically resemble the gold responses to alleviate the dependency of the generative models on that exemplars. The remaining exemplars could be irrelevant to the given context since they are searched depending on the gold response. Thus, our training method further utilizes the relevance scores between the given context and the exemplars to penalize the irrelevant exemplars. Extensive experiments demonstrate that our proposed training method alleviates the drawbacks of the existing exemplar-based generative models and significantly improves the performance in terms of appropriateness and informativeness.

1 Introduction

Exemplar-based generative models (Wu et al., 2019; Weston et al., 2018; Cai et al., 2019b; Gupta et al., 2021) for open-domain conversation combine a retrieval model (Humeau et al., 2019; Mazare et al., 2018; Kim et al., 2021) and a generative model (Adiwardana et al., 2020; Roller et al., 2021;

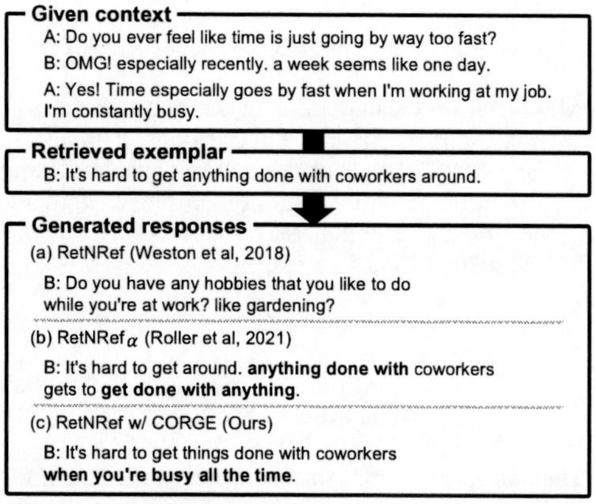

Figure 1: Responses generated by the three exemplar-based generative models. *RetNRef* ignores the exemplar during response generation, *RetNRef*$_\alpha$ generates the response highly over-fitted to the exemplar, and *RetNRef* trained with our training method (CORGE) well utilizes the exemplar to produce a more fluent response than that of the others.

Zhang et al., 2020; Brown et al., 2020) into a single framework to generate responses in two steps: (1) the retriever searches an exemplar using the given context as a query, and (2) the generator produces a response based on the given context and the retrieved exemplar. Exemplar-based generative models produce more specific responses than vanilla generative models while being more fluent than retrieval models.

Despite their success, exemplar-based generative models have two major shortcomings. Primitive exemplar-based generative models (Weston et al., 2018; Cai et al., 2019a) tend to ***entirely ignore the exemplars*** and produce responses similar to those of vanilla generative models. This is due to the *one-to-many problem* (Li et al., 2016) where there are many possible responses for each dialogue context. During the training phase, the retrieved exemplar is not helpful for generating the gold response when the exemplar retrieved for the given context is significantly different from the gold response.

[†] Equal contribution
[*] Corresponding author

Proceedings of the 4th Workshop on NLP for Conversational AI, pages 218 - 230
May 27, 2022 ©2022 Association for Computational Linguistics

This leads exemplar-based generative models to ignore the exemplar while generating responses, as shown in Figure 1(a). To address this issue, recent exemplar-based generative models utilize the gold response (Roller et al., 2021) or the slightly perturbed gold response (Cai et al., 2019b) as an exemplar in the training phase. However, these training methods cause the generator to ***rely heavily on the retrieved exemplar***, i.e. the generator resorts to copying the provided tokens, as shown in Figure 1(b). These two disadvantages of existing exemplar-based generative models can adversely affect the quality of the generated response.

Therefore, we introduce ***CORGE*** (COnnecting Retriever and GEnerator), a simple training method of exemplar-based generative models considering the one-to-many problem of the open-domain conversation. As inspired by Wu et al. (2019), CORGE first utilizes the gold response instead of dialogue context as the query for the retriever to select exemplars that are similar to the gold response. The retrieved exemplars ensure that exemplar-based generative models utilize their semantics while generating the gold response at the training phase. Since the exemplars are retrieved by the gold response, some of them are lexically identical or too similar to the gold response. These exemplars lead exemplar-based generative models to be trained to depend on the exemplar heavily. Thus, CORGE then eliminates the exemplars based on the distance between the exemplars and the gold response to alleviate the dependency of the generative models on the exemplars. Here, we employ Jaccard similarity to measure the distance (Guu et al., 2018; Cai et al., 2019a; Wu et al., 2019). However, as the selected exemplars solely depend on the gold response, some of them may be irrelevant to the given context, which results in exemplar-based generative models still ignoring the retrieved exemplar. To solve this, CORGE utilizes the relevance scores between the context and the exemplar to weight the relevant exemplars and penalizes irrelevant exemplars to the given context. Extensive experiments show that CORGE is generally applicable to the existing exemplar-based generative models and improves the quality of generated responses regarding appropriateness and informativeness.

Our main contributions: (1) We analyze the shortcomings of existing exemplar-based generative models derived from the nature of the open-domain conversation, the one-to-many problem. (2) We introduce a training method (CORGE) to improve the quality of generated responses by selecting useful exemplars and weighting the exemplars by relevance scores assessed by the retriever. (3) Through the human evaluation, we demonstrate that CORGE significantly improves the performance of exemplar-based generative models in terms of appropriateness and informativeness.

2 Related Work

2.1 Exemplar-based Generation

While generative models have shown remarkable performance on the open-domain conversation, it is well-known that generative models tend to yield uninformative and bland responses (Li et al., 2016; Liu et al., 2016; Serban et al., 2017; Li et al., 2020; Holtzman et al., 2019; Welleck et al., 2019). Exemplar-based generative models are introduced to overcome the aforementioned problem generative models suffer. Wu et al. (2019) introduce an exemplar-based generative model for open-domain conversation, which retrieves a context-exemplar pair conditioned by the input context and encodes the lexical difference between the input context and the retrieved context to the edit vector. The response is produced by feeding the exemplar and the edit vector to the generator. Weston et al. (2018); Roller et al. (2021) also retrieve the exemplar using the given context as a query and concatenate the exemplar with the context, then feed the concatenated exemplar into the generator to produce the final response for the open-domain conversation. Cai et al. (2019a,b) propose a method that removes the irrelevant information from the exemplar, then uses the masked exemplar to inform the generator to produce the response. Gupta et al. (2021) condition the generator with the retrieved exemplars and the extracted semantic frames of the exemplars, which improves the coherence of generated responses. We do not consider this model as a baseline because their model requires an additional semantic frame extractor, and it can be mutually complemented with our proposed training method.

2.2 Knowledge-grounded Generation

Knowledge-grounded generation models that utilize retrieved results (e.g., relevant documents from Wikipedia) to generate informative responses have been proposed to perform knowledge-intensive NLP tasks (e.g., open-domain question answering). The knowledge-grounded generation has a

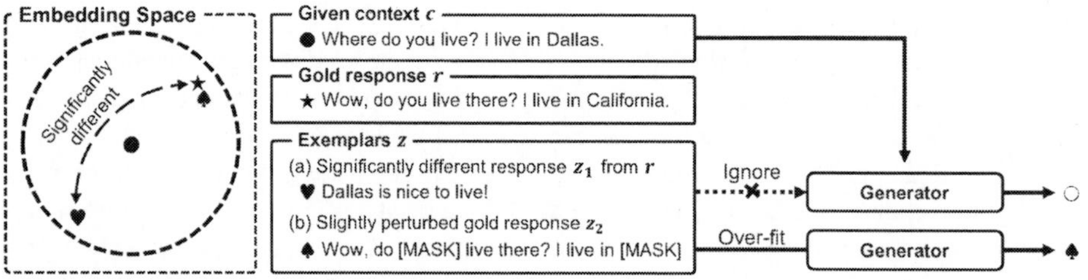

Figure 2: Illustration of the drawbacks of existing exemplar-based generative models. The black dotted line indicates the boundary of the relevant exemplars to the given context.

similar form with the exemplar-based generation. However, the main difference is that knowledge-grounded generative models extract the knowledge from external resources to generate the informative response. Guu et al. (2020) show the effectiveness of pre-training a knowledge retriever with the large-scale language model for open-domain question answering, and Lewis et al. (2020) demonstrate that knowledge-grounded generative models produce more informative and diverse sentences than vanilla generative models on a wide range of knowledge-intensive NLP tasks. Fan et al. (2021) similarly propose a knowledge-grounded generative model for response generation, but they do not focus on the open-domain conversation. In *Method Section*, we demonstrate the difference between our approach and knowledge-grounded generative models, and we show that existing knowledge-grounded generative models are not directly applicable to the open-domain conversation in *Experiments Section*.

3 Preliminaries

3.1 Exemplar-based Generation

Let $D = \{(c_i, r_i) \mid 1 \leq i \leq n\}$ denote the dialogue dataset, which consists of n pairs of context c and response r. Exemplar-based generative models are composed of two components: a retriever $\mathcal{R}$ and a generator $\mathcal{G}$. For a given context c_i, the retriever finds the top-scoring exemplar based on the relevance score $S_{\mathcal{R}}(z, c_i)$ of the exemplar $z \in R$, where R is a pre-defined response set. The generator computes the probability of the response for the context c_i while utilizing the exemplar z as $P_{\mathcal{G}}(r|c_i, z)$.

3.2 Drawbacks of Existing Exemplar-based Generative models

As mentioned in Roller et al. (2021), the primitive exemplar-based generative model (Weston et al., 2018) tends to ignore the retrieved exemplar during response generation due to the one-to-many problem in open-domain conversation (Li et al., 2016). Since its retriever searches an exemplar based on a given context, the retrieved exemplar is often significantly different from a gold response of the generator, although both of the retrieved exemplar and gold response are relevant to the given context, which is shown in Figure 2(a). As the retrieved exemplar is not helpful for generating the gold response, the generator is trained to ignore the retrieved exemplar and to produce a response using only the given context.

To induce the generator to utilize retrieved exemplars more actively, Roller et al. (2021) make use of the gold response, and Cai et al. (2019b) use perturbed gold response as an exemplar rather than using retrieved exemplars during the model training. However, since the exemplar z_i and the gold response r_i are too similar (as shown in Figure 2(b)), the exemplar-based generative model learns to rely overly on the exemplar. Eventually, the generator produces a highly over-fitted response to the exemplar by directly copying the tokens of the exemplar.

4 Method

We hypothesize that selecting semantically relevant but lexically distanced exemplars from the gold response could solve the drawbacks above. To validate this hypothesis, we introduce a training method of exemplar-based generative models, called CORGE. Our proposed training method is illustrated in Figure 3, and the illustrative examples about the exemplars selected by CORGE are described in Table 1.

4.1 Selecting Exemplars Semantically Relevant but Lexically Distanced to the Gold Response

We describe how CORGE selects semantically relevant but lexically distanced exemplars to the gold response. Conventionally, the retriever selects the exemplars z based on the relevance score $S_{\mathcal{R}}(z, c_i)$ for the given context c_i. However, this searching process could return a significantly different exemplar z from the gold response r_i, and it induces the generator $\mathcal{G}$ to ignore the retrieved exemplar during response generation. Therefore, we select exemplars based on the gold response r_i to ensure that the generator $\mathcal{G}$ utilizes the exemplars inspired by Wu et al.. We select top-k scoring exemplars based on the score $S_{\mathcal{R}'}(z, r_i)$, which we call *k-Nearest Exemplars (kNE)*.[1] These kNE are more semantically related to the gold response r_i than the exemplar obtained by using $S_{\mathcal{R}}(z, c_i)$.

However, some of the selected kNE are lexically identical or too close to the gold response r unintentionally since the retriever searches the exemplars based on the gold response. We observe that using these exemplars also causes the over-fitting problem of generated responses; therefore, the generator excessively copies tokens from the exemplars. From this, we are motivated to filter out the exemplars which are lexically too close to the gold response and preserve the exemplars properly distanced to the gold response to mitigate the over-fitting problem. Here, we employ *Jaccard similarity* to measure the lexical similarity (Guu et al., 2018; Cai et al., 2019a; Wu et al., 2019) between the exemplar and the gold response. Exemplars are filtered out when their Jaccard distance with the gold response r is larger than 0.6, and we replace them with the randomly chosen responses from the pre-defined response set R. The threshold of filtering is empirically chosen as 0.6. The set of the final exemplars z obtained through these steps is referred to as $Z_i = \{z_{i,1}, z_{i,2}, \cdots, z_{i,k}\}$.

4.2 Weighting the Selected Exemplars based on the Relevance Score

As we select the exemplar totally based on the gold response, some of kNE could be relevant to the gold response r_i but irrelevant to the given context c_i. Therefore, we condition the generator with the relevance score of kNE to reward the relevant exemplars and penalize irrelevant exemplars. Using the retriever $\mathcal{R}$, we calculate the relevance score $S_{\mathcal{R}}(z_{i,j}, c_i)$ per each selected exemplar $z_{i,j}$, then apply the softmax function to the relevance score to

[1] Note that $S_{\mathcal{R}}(z, c)$ and $S_{\mathcal{R}'}(z, r_i)$ use the same retriever, but they are computed differently. Please refer to how we calculate the score $S_{\mathcal{R}'}(z, r_i)$ and $S_{\mathcal{R}}(z, c)$ in the Supplementary Materials.

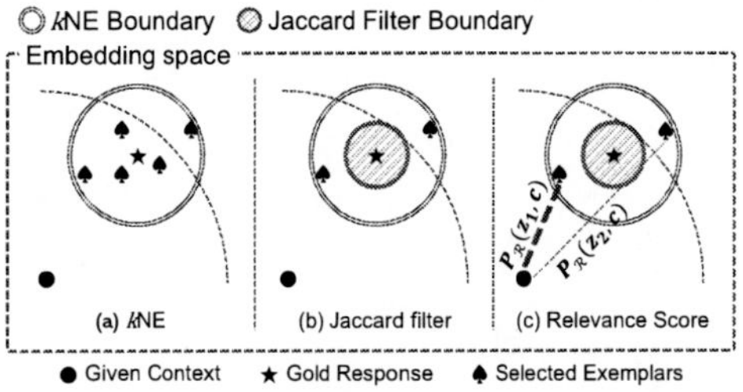

Figure 3: The procedure of our proposed training method, CORGE. (a): Selecting kNE of the gold response r based on $S_{\mathcal{R}'}(z, r)$. (b): Filtering out the exemplars which are too close to the gold response r. (c): Weighting the exemplars z depending on their normalized relevance scores $P_{\mathcal{R}}(z, c)$.

obtain the normalized relevance score $P_{\mathcal{R}}(z_{i,j}, c_i)$. Then we replace the traditional likelihood with the weighted likelihood using the normalized score. Our final training objective is to minimize the loss function $L = \sum_{i=1}^{n} L(r_i, c_i)$ where:

$$L(r_i, c_i) = -\log \sum_{z \in Z_i} P_{\mathcal{R}}(z, c_i) P_{\mathcal{G}}(r_i | c_i, z) \quad (1)$$

The gradient of the generator $\mathcal{G}$ is calculated as follows:

$$\nabla_{\mathcal{G}} L(r_i, c_i) = -\alpha \cdot \sum_{z \in Z_i} P_{\mathcal{R}}(z, c_i) \nabla_{\mathcal{G}}(P_{\mathcal{G}}(r_i | c_i, z)), \quad (2)$$

where $\alpha^{-1} = \sum_{z \in Z_i} P_{\mathcal{R}}(z, c_i) P_{\mathcal{G}}(r_i | c_i, z)$. This equation demonstrates that the gradient of the generator $\mathcal{G}$ is scaled by the normalized relevance score $P_{\mathcal{R}}(z, c_i)$, which indicates that the generator is less updated when the retrieved exemplar z is not relevant to the given context c_i. This procedure helps the model ignore the irrelevant exemplars. Thus, the generator learns to fetch tokens from the exemplar more easily, which is relevant to the gold response.

Difference between CORGE and Knowledge-grounded generative models The way of leveraging the relevance scores is already employed by knowledge-grounded generative models (Lewis et al., 2020; Sachan et al., 2021) in open-domain question answering. However, there is a significant difference between our CORGE and knowledge-grounded generative models. CORGE uses the relevance score $P_{\mathcal{R}}(z, c_i)$ to penalize the irrelevant exemplars z to the given context c_i since the exemplars are retrieved by $S_{\mathcal{R}'}(z, r_i)$. Knowledge-grounded generative models use it as the latent variable to jointly train the retriever $\mathcal{R}$ and generator $\mathcal{G}$. Especially, knowledge-grounded generative models also tend to ignore the retrieved exemplars due

Input Context		
What kind of animals you take care of?		
Gold Response		
I work with a variety of animals. I sometimes work with lions and monkeys.		
Context Retrieval	**Sim**	$P_{\mathcal{R}}(z,c)$
I raise two dogs.	0.1	0.9
***k*NE**	**Sim**	$P_{\mathcal{R}}(z,c)$
I work with a variety of animals.	**0.9**	0.2
He works with various people.	0.3	**0.0**
I work with lots of different animals.	0.5	0.3
I do some work with animals they're amazing creatures.	0.3	0.3

Table 1: Samples of the exemplars selected by CORGE. **Context Retrieval** indicates the exemplar retrieved by using the context as a query, and ***k*NE** shows the exemplars selected by using the gold response as a query. **Sim** measures the lexical similarity between the gold response and the exemplar and $P_{\mathcal{R}}(z,c)$ indicates the normalized relevance score calculated by retriever.

to the one-to-many nature in open-domain conversation when the retriever and generator are jointly trained. On the other hand, we do not perform the joint learning of the retriever and the generator, but freeze the retriever while training the generator.

5 Experiments

5.1 Dataset

We utilize the following four datasets used in Roller et al. (2021), which are Blended Skill Talk (BST) (Smith et al., 2020), ConvAI2 (Zhang et al., 2018), Empathetic Dialogues (ED) (Rashkin et al., 2019), and Wizard of Wikipedia (WoW) (Dinan et al., 2018). To simplify the notation, we denote the concatenated version of these four datasets as ***BST+***. We split BST+ into train, validation, and test sets following Smith et al. (2020).

5.2 Baselines

Retrieval and Generative Models *Bi-encoder 256M* (Mazare et al., 2018) and *Blender 90M* (Roller et al., 2021) are considered as a baseline retrieval model and a baseline generative model. Further, they are also employed as a retriever and a generator of the following exemplar-based generative baselines, respectively.

Exemplar-based Generative Models Since our proposed training method is for training exemplar-based generation models, we first consider recent exemplar-based generation models, *RetNRef* (Weston et al., 2018), *RetNRef*$_\alpha$ (Roller et al., 2021), and *MatToGen* (Cai et al., 2019b), as baselines. *RetNRef* concatenates the retrieved exemplar with the given context as the input of the generator to produce the response. *RetNRef*$_\alpha$ is the dialogue retrieval version of *RetNRef*, which adopts α-blending to escape from simply ignoring the retrieved exemplars ($\alpha = 0.5$). *MatToGen* extracts the meaningful tokens from the exemplar to provide them to the generator.

To verify the effectiveness of our training method, we apply CORGE to *RetNRef* and *MatToGen* instead of their training method. They are denoted as *RetNRef+CORGE* and *MatToGen+CORGE*, respectively.

Knowledge-grounded Generative Models Although *RAG* (Lewis et al., 2020) and *KIF* (Fan et al., 2021) are proposed to perform knowledge-grounded generation tasks, we employ *RAG* and *KIF* as baselines since they have a similar form with exemplar-based generative models. Our experiments demonstrate that these knowledge-grounded generative models cannot be directly applied to the open-domain conversation.

5.3 Evaluation Metrics

To verify the effectiveness of our training method CORGE, we conduct a pair-wise comparison through the human evaluation following Weston et al. (2018). We use two criteria: **Appropriateness** and **Informativeness**. Appropriateness measures how the generated response is fluent, logical, and appropriate to the given context. Informativeness measures how the generated response has meaningful information relevant to the given context. We use Amazon Mechanical Turk to collect the annotations, and more details are described in the Supplementary Material.

We also employ the automatic evaluation metrics, **Perplexity** (PPL), **Dist-n**, and **BLEU** (Papineni et al., 2002), to analyze the generated responses of each model. PPL measures how well the model predicts a response based on the given input context, and lower PPL indicates that the model predicts the response better. To analyze how much the exemplar-based generative model leverages the retrieved exemplar, we introduce two variants of PPL by utilizing conditional probability when exemplars are given: (1) PPL$_{gold}$ uses the

Model Names (A vs. B)	Appropriateness (%)				Informativeness (%)			
	Win Rate	A win	Tie	B win	Win Rate	A win	Tie	B win
RetNRef$_\alpha$ vs. Bi-encoder 256M	44.9	32.0	28.7	**39.3**	47.5	31.3	34.0	**34.7**
RetNRef$_\alpha$ vs. Blender 90M	50.2	**37.3**	25.7	37.0	53.3	**40.3**	24.3	35.4
RetNRef + CORGE vs. Bi-encoder 256M	52.6	**34.0**	35.3	30.7	51.9	**35.7**	31.3	33.0
RetNRef + CORGE vs. Blender 90M	57.7*	**33.7***	41.7*	24.6*	54.6	**30.0**	45.0	25.0
RetNRef + CORGE vs. RetNRef$_\alpha$	53.2	**30.3**	43.0	26.7	51.6	**27.7**	46.3	26.0
RetNRef + CORGE vs. RetNRef	54.4	**41.0**	24.7	34.3	53.4	**37.0**	30.7	32.3
RetNRef + CORGE vs. KIF	57.5*	**37.0***	35.7*	27.3*	50.0	30.0	40.0	30.0
RetNRef + CORGE vs. RAG	53.5	**37.7**	29.7	32.6	52.1	**29.7**	43.0	27.3
MatToGen vs. Bi-encoder 256M	47.1	33.3	29.3	**37.4**	50.9	**36.7**	28.0	35.3
MatToGen vs. Blender 90M	48.1	34.0	29.3	**36.7**	46.3	31.6	31.7	**36.7**
MatToGen + CORGE vs. Bi-encoder 256M	54.2	**43.0**	20.7	36.3	54.4	**41.3**	24.0	34.7
MatToGen + CORGE vs. Blender 90M	58.0*	**35.0***	39.7*	25.3*	58.1*	**36.0***	38.0*	26.0*
MatToGen + CORGE vs. MatToGen	52.6	**33.3**	36.7	30.0	53.3	**32.7**	38.7	28.6
MatToGen + CORGE vs. KIF	57.1*	**44.0***	23.0*	33.0*	52.5	**39.0**	25.7	35.3
MatToGen + CORGE vs. RAG	51.6	**38.3**	25.7	36.0	55.6	**41.3**	25.7	33.0

Table 2: Pair-wise human evaluation results show that our proposed training method improves the performance against the existing exemplar-based generation approaches in terms of appropriateness and informativeness. The win rate is calculated by excluding the tie. * indicates statistical significance (two-tailed binomial test, $p < 0.05$).

conditional probability $P_{\mathcal{G}}(r|c, r)$, which assumes the situation when the gold response is given as an exemplar, and (2) PPL$_{ret}$ uses the conditional probability $P_{\mathcal{G}}(r|c, z)$ where z is the retrieved exemplar by using $S_{\mathcal{R}'}(z, r)$. Lower PPL$_{gold}$ denotes that the exemplar-based generative model predicts the gold response well when the gold response is given as an exemplar. Lower PPL$_{ret}$ indicates that the exemplar-based generative model well leverages the provided exemplar to predict the gold response. Dist-n (Li et al., 2016) is the ratio of distinct n-grams to a total number of n-grams for all the generated responses, which measures the degree of the diversity of the generated responses. BLEU$_{(z,r)}$ is adopted to measure the degree of the token overlap between the provided exemplar and the generated response pair (z, r). A higher BLEU$_{(z,r)}$ score indicates that the generator copies more from the provided exemplar while generating the response.

5.4 Implementation Details

We provide the details of our implementation in the Supplementary Material. We will the source codes of CORGE for the reproducibility of the conducted experiments.

6 Experimental Results

6.1 Pair-wise Comparison Results

Table 2 shows the pair-wise comparison results through the human evaluation. When *RetNRef* and *MatToGen* adopt our proposed CORGE as their training method, they outperform all baselines except for a case of *RetNRef+CORGE* vs. *KIF* on the informativeness. In detail, *RetNRef+CORGE* and *MatToGen+CORGE* show better performance than *RetNRef*$_\alpha$ and *MatToGen*, respectively, in both metrics. Especially, *MatToGen+CORGE* outperforms *Bi-encoder 256M* and exceeds *Blender 90M*, while *MatToGen* performs worse than *Bi-encoder 256M* and *Blender 90M*. Furthermore, CORGE enlarges the win rate of *RetNRef*$_\alpha$ for *Blender 90M*. These evaluation results demonstrate that CORGE leads the existing exemplar-based generative models to produce more fluent and informative responses.

6.2 Investigating the Exemplar-based Generative Models with Automatic Metrics

Through the automatic evaluation, we verify that existing exemplar-based generative models ignore the provided exemplar or generate responses overfitted to the provided exemplar. As shown in Table 3, *RetNRef+CORGE* and *MatToGen+CORGE* show lower PPL$_{ret}$ than *Blender 90M*, which means that the exemplar-based generative models trained with CORGE make a better prediction of the gold response than *Blender 90M* by utilizing the provided exemplar. *RetNRef+CORGE* has a smaller degree of PPL$_{gold}$ and PPL$_{ret}$ than those of *RetNRef*, which infers *RetNRef+CORGE* leverages the provided exemplar better than *RetNRef*. *RetNRef*$_\alpha$ has lower PPL$_{gold}$ than *RetNRef+CORGE*, however, *RetNRef*$_\alpha$ has higher

Models	PPL_{gold}	PPL_{ret}	Dist-2	Dist-3	$\text{BLEU}_{(z,r)}$-2	$\text{BLEU}_{(z,r)}$-3
Blender 90M	13.79	13.79	0.236	0.372	-	-
Bi-encoder 256M	-	-	0.681	0.881	-	-
RetNRef	8.518	13.37	0.256	0.386	0.030	0.009
RetNRef_{α}	3.061	16.99	0.530	0.778	0.319	0.201
RetNRef + CORGE	4.863	11.53	0.349	0.520	0.102	0.048
MatToGen	5.291	17.71	0.362	0.567	0.169	0.095
MatToGen + CORGE	5.651	13.45	0.313	0.474	0.069	0.028
RAG	11.84	14.91	0.257	0.390	0.015	0.003
KIF	12.11	15.18	0.238	0.363	0.002	0.000

Table 3: Automatic evaluation results. Since *Blender 90M* can not utilize the exemplar, we report PPL calculated from $P_{\mathcal{G}}(r|c)$ in the place of PPL_{gold} and PPL_{ret}.

PPL_{ret} than *RetNRef+CORGE*. This result demonstrates that *RetNRef*$_{\alpha}$ does not make good use of the retrieved exemplar except when the gold response is given as the retrieved exemplar. From this observation, we claim that *RetNRef*$_{\alpha}$ generates a response highly over-fitted to the selected exemplar, which is caused by utilizing the gold response as an exemplar in the training phase. The same goes for *MatToGen*, where applying CORGE mitigates the over-fitting issue.

Higher Dist-n of *RetNRef+CORGE* and *MatToGen+CORGE* compared to *Blender 90M* shows that our exemplar-based generative models produce more diverse responses than the vanilla generative model. Moreover, *RetNRef+CORGE* has higher Dist-n than *RetNRef*, which shows that utilizing the exemplars helps the generator diversify the responses. Although *RetNRef*$_{\alpha}$ is the only one that achieves comparable Dist-n to that of the vanilla retrieval model, *Bi-encoder 256M*, it is derived from an over-fitting to the exemplar considering the gap between PPL_{gold} and PPL_{ret}, resulting in the degradation of appropriateness and informativeness in human evaluation.

Average $\text{BLEU}_{(z,r)}$ scores implicitly measure the overlap between the retrieved exemplar and the generated response; thus, a higher degree of $\text{BLEU}_{(z,r)}$ indicates that the generator depends more on the retrieved exemplar. *RetNRef* shows a negligible $\text{BLEU}_{(z,r)}$ score, which reaffirms that the model is almost not utilizing the retrieved exemplar. *RetNRef*$_{\alpha}$ and *MatToGen* have higher $\text{BLEU}_{(z,r)}$ scores compared to *RetNRef+CORGE* and *MatToGen+CORGE*, respectively, which verifies that the former depends more on the retrieved exemplar than the latter.

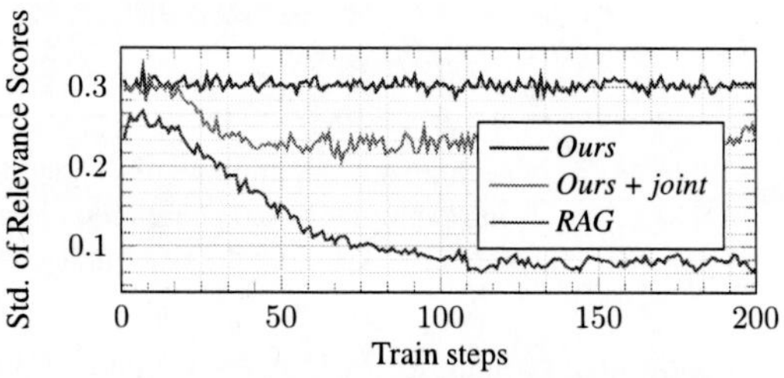

Figure 4: The standard deviation of the normalized retriever score gets smaller when we jointly train the retriever for exemplar-based generative models. *Ours* stands for *RetNRef+CORGE*, and *joint* indicates jointly training the retriever with the generator.

6.3 Incapability of Knowledge-grounded Generative Models in Open-domain Conversation

The automatic evaluation results in Table 3 confirm that knowledge-grounded generative models are ignoring the exemplar. PPL_{gold}, PPL_{ret}, and Dist-n of *RAG* and *KIF* have a similar degree to those of *Blender 90M*, which implies that the exemplars are not providing useful information while generating the response. The average $\text{BLEU}_{(z,r)}$ score also has a poor degree, indicating almost no overlap between the retrieved exemplars and the generated responses. We explain that these results are originated from the difference between the open-domain conversation and knowledge-grounded generation tasks. While training knowledge-grounded generative models, they use $P_{\mathcal{R}}(z,c)$ to fetch the external knowledge. However, the generator also ignores the retrieved exemplar due to the one-to-many nature of the open-domain conversation.

In addition, we observe that jointly training the retriever with the generator causes the retriever stuck in the local minima. As shown in Figure 4, the standard deviation of normalized relevance scores $P_{\mathcal{R}}(z,c)$ computed by the retriever

Input Context	A: No way i do it a lot, at least when i am feeling well enough. B: Awesome. That's the only thing i'll never do. I do like the outdoors though. A: I'm a thrill seaker. Do you like extreme sports?
Bi-encoder 256M	I love extreme sports. Its the only real way I can get the adrenaline boost I need.
Blender 90M	No, I don 't think I' ve ever done that. I' d love to though.
Exemplar	I love extreme sports. Its the only real way I can get the adrenaline boost I need.
RetNRef	I don' t really have a lot of time for sports. I spend most of my free time working.
Exemplar	I love extreme sports. Its the only real way I can get the adrenaline boost I need.
RetNRef$_\alpha$	I love extreme sports I need the adrenaline boost. Its the only way I can get the real adrenaline.
Exemplar	I love extreme sports. Its the only real way I can get the adrenaline boost I need.
RetNRef + CORGE	I love extreme sports as well. It' s a great way to get out and enjoy life.
Exemplar	nicde.
KIF	I don' t really have a lot of time for sports. I spend most of my time working.
Exemplar	Do you like sports?
RAG	I don' t really have a lot of time for sports. I spend most of my time working.

Table 4: Examples for model responses and provided exemplars corresponding to given input contexts.

Models	**PPL$_{\text{gold}}$**	**PPL$_{\text{ret}}$**	**Dist-2**	**Dist-3**	**BLEU$_{(z,r)}$-2**	**BLEU$_{(z,r)}$-3**
RetNRef + CORGE	4.863	11.53	0.349	0.520	0.102	0.048
RetNRef + CORGE − RS	6.482	11.75	0.316	0.478	0.074	0.031
RetNRef + CORGE − kNE	8.657	13.82	0.250	0.380	0.034	0.010
RetNRef + CORGE − JF	1.698	32.91	0.537	0.785	0.332	0.207

Table 5: Results of the ablation study. −RS, −kNE, and −JF denote that relevance score (RS), kNE, and Jaccard filter (JF) are removed from CORGE, respectively.

almost gets near zero when the retriever of RAG is jointly trained. A smaller standard deviation means the relevance scores are getting flattened. Although knowledge-grounded generative models empirically have shown that jointly training the retriever and generator improves the performance in knowledge-intensive NLP tasks (Lewis et al., 2020), in open-domain conversation, the retrieved exemplars are ignored. Thus, the retriever learns to produce an uninformative relevance score. As a result, the retriever collapses, which means the retriever may return inappropriate exemplars to the generator (also shown in the example of KIF and RAG in Table 4). Intriguingly, jointly training the retriever with CORGE also causes the retriever scores to be flattened, as shown in Figure 4, and we empirically observe the minor collapse of the retriever as we experienced in RAG as well. Thus, CORGE does not jointly train the retriever.

6.4 Ablation Study

To verify the effectiveness of each component in CORGE, we conduct the ablation study. In Table 5, PPL$_{ret}$ from *RetNRef+CORGE* is lower than any other ablation counterparts, which confirms each component contributes to predicting the responses. *RetNRef+CORGE*−RS and *RetNRef+CORGE*−kNE have a higher degree of PPL$_{ret}$ and PPL$_{gold}$, which indicates *RS* and *kNE* help the generator to utilize the exemplar while generating the response. *RetNRef+CORGE*−JF provides a strong signal of over-fitting, where it has extremely low PPL$_{gold}$ but exceptionally high PPL$_{ret}$. Dist-n shows our model produces the most diverse responses among the models except *RetNRef+CORGE*−JF, where *RetNRef+CORGE*−JF excessively copies the tokens from the retrieved exemplar. The average BLEU$_{(z,r)}$ scores also show the same trend, where reaffirms the effect of the components of CORGE.

7 Conclusion

In this paper, we introduce a generally applicable training method for exemplar-based generative models to alleviate their disadvantages derived from the one-to-many problem. Our training method selects exemplars that are semantically relevant but lexically distanced from the gold response and weights those exemplars with the relevance score measured by the retriever. Through the extensive analysis, including pair-wise human evaluation, we verify that our method improves the performance of existing exemplar-based generative models in terms of appropriateness and informativeness.

References

Daniel Adiwardana, Minh-Thang Luong, David R So, Jamie Hall, Noah Fiedel, Romal Thoppilan, Zi Yang, Apoorv Kulshreshtha, Gaurav Nemade, Yifeng Lu, et al. 2020. Towards a human-like open-domain chatbot. *arXiv preprint arXiv:2001.09977*.

Tom Brown, Benjamin Mann, Nick Ryder, Melanie Subbiah, Jared D Kaplan, Prafulla Dhariwal, Arvind Neelakantan, Pranav Shyam, Girish Sastry, Amanda Askell, Sandhini Agarwal, Ariel Herbert-Voss, Gretchen Krueger, Tom Henighan, Rewon Child, Aditya Ramesh, Daniel Ziegler, Jeffrey Wu, Clemens Winter, Chris Hesse, Mark Chen, Eric Sigler, Mateusz Litwin, Scott Gray, Benjamin Chess, Jack Clark, Christopher Berner, Sam McCandlish, Alec Radford, Ilya Sutskever, and Dario Amodei. 2020. Language models are few-shot learners. In *Advances in Neural Information Processing Systems*, volume 33, pages 1877–1901. Curran Associates, Inc.

Deng Cai, Yan Wang, Wei Bi, Zhaopeng Tu, Xiaojiang Liu, Wai Lam, and Shuming Shi. 2019a. Skeleton-to-response: Dialogue generation guided by retrieval memory. In *Proceedings of the 2019 Conference of the North American Chapter of the Association for Computational Linguistics: Human Language Technologies, Volume 1 (Long and Short Papers)*, pages 1219–1228.

Deng Cai, Yan Wang, Wei Bi, Zhaopeng Tu, Xiaojiang Liu, and Shuming Shi. 2019b. Retrieval-guided dialogue response generation via a matching-to-generation framework. In *Proceedings of the 2019 Conference on Empirical Methods in Natural Language Processing and the 9th International Joint Conference on Natural Language Processing (EMNLP-IJCNLP)*, pages 1866–1875.

Emily Dinan, Stephen Roller, Kurt Shuster, Angela Fan, Michael Auli, and Jason Weston. 2018. Wizard of wikipedia: Knowledge-powered conversational agents. In *International Conference on Learning Representations*.

Angela Fan, Claire Gardent, Chloé Braud, and Antoine Bordes. 2021. Augmenting transformers with knn-based composite memory for dialog. *Transactions of the Association for Computational Linguistics*, 9:82–99.

Alex Graves. 2012. Sequence transduction with recurrent neural networks. *arXiv preprint arXiv:1211.3711*.

Prakhar Gupta, Jeffrey P Bigham, Yulia Tsvetkov, and Amy Pavel. 2021. Controlling dialogue generation with semantic exemplars. In *Proceedings of the 2021 Conference of the North American Chapter of the Association for Computational Linguistics: Human Language Technologies*, pages 3018–3029.

Kelvin Guu, Tatsunori B Hashimoto, Yonatan Oren, and Percy Liang. 2018. Generating sentences by editing prototypes. *Transactions of the Association for Computational Linguistics*, 6:437–450.

Kelvin Guu, Kenton Lee, Zora Tung, Panupong Pasupat, and Ming-Wei Chang. 2020. Realm: Retrieval-augmented language model pre-training. *arXiv preprint arXiv:2002.08909*.

Ari Holtzman, Jan Buys, Li Du, Maxwell Forbes, and Yejin Choi. 2019. The curious case of neural text degeneration. In *International Conference on Learning Representations*.

Samuel Humeau, Kurt Shuster, Marie-Anne Lachaux, and Jason Weston. 2019. Poly-encoders: Architectures and pre-training strategies for fast and accurate multi-sentence scoring. In *International Conference on Learning Representations*.

Beomsu Kim, Seokjun Seo, Seungju Han, Enkhbayar Erdenee, and Buru Chang. 2021. Distilling the knowledge of large-scale generative models into retrieval models for efficient open-domain conversation. In *Findings of the Association for Computational Linguistics: EMNLP 2021*, pages 3357–3373.

Patrick Lewis, Ethan Perez, Aleksandra Piktus, Fabio Petroni, Vladimir Karpukhin, Naman Goyal, Heinrich Küttler, Mike Lewis, Wen-tau Yih, Tim Rocktäschel, Sebastian Riedel, and Douwe Kiela. 2020. Retrieval-augmented generation for knowledge-intensive nlp tasks. In *Advances in Neural Information Processing Systems*, volume 33, pages 9459–9474. Curran Associates, Inc.

Jiwei Li, Michel Galley, Chris Brockett, Jianfeng Gao, and William B Dolan. 2016. A diversity-promoting objective function for neural conversation models. In *Proceedings of the 2016 Conference of the North American Chapter of the Association for Computational Linguistics: Human Language Technologies*, pages 110–119.

Margaret Li, Stephen Roller, Ilia Kulikov, Sean Welleck, Y-Lan Boureau, Kyunghyun Cho, and Jason Weston. 2020. Don't say that! making inconsistent dialogue unlikely with unlikelihood training. In *Proceedings of the 58th Annual Meeting of the Association for Computational Linguistics*, pages 4715–4728.

Raymond Li, Samira Kahou, Hannes Schulz, Vincent Michalski, Laurent Charlin, and Chris Pal. 2018. Towards deep conversational recommendations. *arXiv preprint arXiv:1812.07617*.

Chia-Wei Liu, Ryan Lowe, Iulian Vlad Serban, Mike Noseworthy, Laurent Charlin, and Joelle Pineau. 2016. How not to evaluate your dialogue system: An empirical study of unsupervised evaluation metrics for dialogue response generation. In *Proceedings of the 2016 Conference on Empirical Methods in Natural Language Processing*, pages 2122–2132.

Edward Loper and Steven Bird. 2002. Nltk: The natural language toolkit. In *In Proceedings of the ACL Workshop on Effective Tools and Methodologies for*

Teaching Natural Language Processing and Computational Linguistics. Philadelphia: Association for Computational Linguistics.

Pierre-Emmanuel Mazare, Samuel Humeau, Martin Raison, and Antoine Bordes. 2018. Training millions of personalized dialogue agents. In *Proceedings of the 2018 Conference on Empirical Methods in Natural Language Processing*, pages 2775–2779.

A. H. Miller, W. Feng, A. Fisch, J. Lu, D. Batra, A. Bordes, D. Parikh, and J. Weston. 2017. Parlai: A dialog research software platform. *arXiv preprint arXiv:1705.06476.*

Kishore Papineni, Salim Roukos, Todd Ward, and Wei-Jing Zhu. 2002. Bleu: a method for automatic evaluation of machine translation. In *Proceedings of the 40th annual meeting of the Association for Computational Linguistics*, pages 311–318.

Hannah Rashkin, Eric Michael Smith, Margaret Li, and Y-Lan Boureau. 2019. Towards empathetic open-domain conversation models: A new benchmark and dataset. In *Proceedings of the 57th Annual Meeting of the Association for Computational Linguistics*, pages 5370–5381.

Stephen Roller, Emily Dinan, Naman Goyal, Da Ju, Mary Williamson, Yinhan Liu, Jing Xu, Myle Ott, Eric Michael Smith, Y-Lan Boureau, et al. 2021. Recipes for building an open-domain chatbot. In *Proceedings of the 16th Conference of the European Chapter of the Association for Computational Linguistics: Main Volume*, pages 300–325.

Devendra Singh Sachan, Mostofa Patwary, Mohammad Shoeybi, Neel Kant, Wei Ping, William L Hamilton, and Bryan Catanzaro. 2021. End-to-end training of neural retrievers for open-domain question answering. *arXiv preprint arXiv:2101.00408.*

Iulian Serban, Tim Klinger, Gerald Tesauro, Kartik Talamadupula, Bowen Zhou, Yoshua Bengio, and Aaron Courville. 2017. Multiresolution recurrent neural networks: An application to dialogue response generation. In *Proceedings of the AAAI Conference on Artificial Intelligence*, volume 31.

Eric Michael Smith, Mary Williamson, Kurt Shuster, Jason Weston, and Y-Lan Boureau. 2020. Can you put it all together: Evaluating conversational agents' ability to blend skills. In *Proceedings of the 58th Annual Meeting of the Association for Computational Linguistics*, pages 2021–2030.

Sean Welleck, Ilia Kulikov, Stephen Roller, Emily Dinan, Kyunghyun Cho, and Jason Weston. 2019. Neural text generation with unlikelihood training. In *International Conference on Learning Representations.*

Jason Weston, Emily Dinan, and Alexander Miller. 2018. Retrieve and refine: Improved sequence generation models for dialogue. In *Proceedings of the 2018 EMNLP Workshop SCAI: The 2nd International Workshop on Search-Oriented Conversational AI*, pages 87–92.

Yu Wu, Furu Wei, Shaohan Huang, Yunli Wang, Zhoujun Li, and Ming Zhou. 2019. Response generation by context-aware prototype editing. In *Proceedings of the AAAI Conference on Artificial Intelligence*, volume 33, pages 7281–7288.

Saizheng Zhang, Emily Dinan, Jack Urbanek, Arthur Szlam, Douwe Kiela, and Jason Weston. 2018. Personalizing dialogue agents: I have a dog, do you have pets too? In *Proceedings of the 56th Annual Meeting of the Association for Computational Linguistics (Volume 1: Long Papers)*, pages 2204–2213.

Yizhe Zhang, Siqi Sun, Michel Galley, Yen-Chun Chen, Chris Brockett, Xiang Gao, Jianfeng Gao, Jingjing Liu, and William B Dolan. 2020. Dialogpt: Large-scale generative pre-training for conversational response generation. In *Proceedings of the 58th Annual Meeting of the Association for Computational Linguistics: System Demonstrations*, pages 270–278.

A Implementation Details

A.1 How the Retriever Calculates the Scores

Our retriever follows the architecture of Bi-encoder (Mazare et al., 2018), and the score $S_{\mathcal{R}}(z, c)$ and $S_{\mathcal{R}'}(z, r)$ are calculated as follows:

$$\begin{aligned} S_{\mathcal{R}}(z, c) &= d(z) \cdot q(c), \\ S_{\mathcal{R}'}(z, r) &= d(z) \cdot d(r), \\ d(z) &= \mathbf{BERT}_r(z), \\ d(r) &= \mathbf{BERT}_r(r), \\ q(c) &= \mathbf{BERT}_c(c), \end{aligned} \tag{3}$$

where $d(z)$ and $d(r)$ are encoded vectors produced by response encoder $\mathbf{BERT}_r$ and $q(c)$ is an encoded vector produced by context encoder $\mathbf{BERT}_c$. The notation $\mathcal{R}'$ indicates that it only uses the response encoder instead of using the context encoder together. CORGE is not limited to use Bi-encoder as a retriever and can be applied to other types of a retriever (e.g. Poly-encoder (Humeau et al., 2019)).

A.2 Model Details

As we mentioned in Section 5.2, we employ Bi-encoder 256M and Blender 90M as a retriever and a generator of each exemplar-based generative model, respectively. For MatToGen, additional MLP layers are added to the retriever, as follows the details in Cai et al. (2019b). When training the models, weights of the retriever and the generator are initialized with the pre-trained Bi-encoder 256M and Blender 90M, respectively, For Blender 90M, we use the model released by ParlAI (Miller et al., 2017), which is fine-tuned on the BST+ dataset. For Bi-encoder 256M, we fine-tune the model released by ParlAI on the BST+ dataset, and we follow the hyperparameter settings of Humeau et al. (2019), which are implemented in the ParlAI library. The pre-defined response set is constructed from the BST+ training set, which contains about 400K responses. We use NVIDIA DGX Station A100 for training the models.

A.3 Hyperparameters

When training exemplar-based generative models with CORGE, five (k=5) exemplars are utilized for each training instance. The exemplar-based generators are trained with a batch size of 32 and an initial learning rate of 7e-6, and the learning rate is decayed in half when the training loss meets the plateau. The model is trained until there is no progress in the validation PPL.

A.4 Generation Strategy

When we generate samples using generative model, exemplar-based generative models, and knowledge-grounded generative models, we adopt a beam decoding strategy which is widely used in generative models (Graves, 2012). Following (Roller et al., 2021), we choose a minimum beam length and a beam size as 20 BPE tokens and 10, respectively, and use tri-gram beam blocking on context and response blocks. During the inference phase, both exemplar-based generative models and knowledge-grounded generative models use the top-1 scoring candidate as an exemplar chosen from utilizing the relevance score $S_{\mathcal{R}}(z, c)$.

B Evaluation Details

We prepare dialogue cases that have three-turn input contexts and the gold response from the BST and evaluate them by human pair-wise comparison and automatic evaluation. There are 980 test cases, and we randomly choose 100 test cases for the human evaluation.

B.1 Pair-wise Human Evaluation

As we described in Section 5.3, we use Amazon Mechanical Turk to collect the annotations. Each test case is rated by three annotators to improve the robustness of the evaluation result. We set a maximum number of annotations per worker in order to reduce the potential bias. To control the quality of the annotations, we only allowed annotators who satisfy the following requirements to evaluate our results: (1) HITs approval rate greater than 95%, (2) Location is one of Australia, Canada, New Zealand, United Kingdom, and the United States, (3) Lifetime number of HITs approved greater than 1000, following Li et al. (2018). Figure 5 shows the instructions and the interface for the human evaluation. To mitigate the bias from the annotator, we randomly shuffle the order of the model and the corresponding response.

B.2 Automatic Evaluation

For automatic metrics, we calculate the metric for each case and take the average of those values. When calculating BLEU, we use `sentence_bleu` function in `nltk` python package (Loper and Bird, 2002).

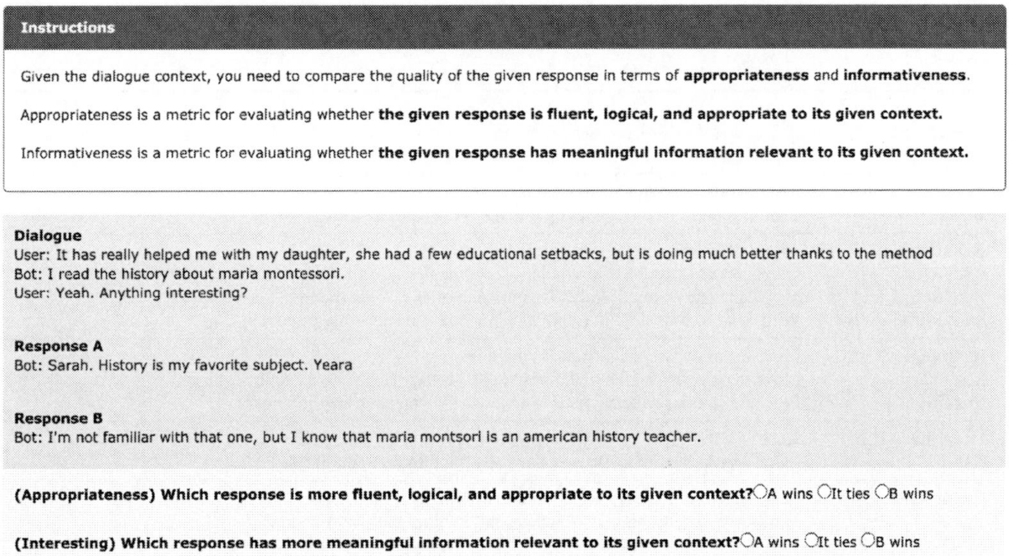

Figure 5: The interface of pairwise human evaluation for appropriateness and informativeness.

C Measuring Inference Time

We measure how much time spend when the model generates the responses. When generating the response, *Blender 90M* takes 0.481 seconds, and *RetNRef+CORGE* takes 0.523 seconds per instance. There is only an 8.7% amount of inference time gap between *Blender 90M* and *RetNRef+CORGE*. This tells us that exemplar-based generation can significantly improve the quality of responses regarding appropriateness, informativeness, and diversity without increasing the amount of time to generate answers. We test our model on NVIDIA DGX Station A100 with PyTorch 1.7.1, CUDA 11.0, CuDNN 8.0, and here we adopt the generation strategy we describe above. When we measure the inference time, we only use a single GPU (NVIDIA A100 GPU, 40GB Memory), and the inference time is measured as the average inference time of 100 response generations.

D Additional Results

We provide additional samples for the retrieved exemplar and the model response from the baselines and our models in Table 6.

Input Context	A: I crash around 230 to 300. I don't have much of a social life. B: Neither do I, you are not alone A: I am alone but I'm not lonely. I have a dog who's great company.
Bi-encoder 256M	Any friends? My dog is one of mine.
Blender 90M	That 's good to hear, I 've a dog too, he' s my best friend.
Exemplar	Any friends? My dog is one of mine.
RetNRef	I am sorry to hear that. Do you have any hobbies that you like to do?
RetNRef$_\alpha$	My dog is one of my friends? Is yours one of any of his friends? lol.
RetNRef + CORGE	What kind of dog is it? I' ve got a chihuahua and she' s my best friend.
Exemplar	I love dogs too. My best friend is my dog.
MatToGen	I love my best friend, he' s the best dog I've ever had. What is your best friend?
MatToGen + CORGE	I love dogs too, my best friend is my dog. Do you have any hobbies?
Exemplar	nicde.
KIF	I am sorry to hear that. Do you have any hobbies that you like to do?
Exemplar	I'm usually alone because I don't like my family.
RAG	I am sorry to hear that. Do you have any hobbies that you like to do?
Input Context	A: Sounds like a horror movie, my favorite kind B: Haha, yeah he melts my heart. A: Did you do anything fun for Halloween?
Bi-encoder 256M	I enjoy Halloween, it's fun to dress up. Do you like it?
Blender 90M	I went to a halloween party with my friends. It was a lot of fun. What about you?
Exemplar	I enjoy Halloween, it's fun to dress up. Do you like it?
RetNRef	No, I don 't think I could do it. I' m not a big fan of halloween.
RetNRef$_\alpha$	I like it, it' s fun to dress up. Do you like halloween? I enjoy dressing up.
RetNRef + CORGE	I like to dress up as a clown, but I don' t think I' ll be doing that this year.
Exemplar	No we went to a haunted house and I got chased often.
MatToGen	No we never got to go to the haunted house we went to once and got chased by a ghost.
MatToGen + CORGE	No, I don 't like to go to haunted houses. I' m scared of them.
Exemplar	nicde.
KIF	Yes, I went to a haunted house and watched all the horror movies. It was so scary!
Exemplar	Are you doing anything cool for halloween
RAG	No, I don' t think I' m going to. I' ve never been a fan of halloween.
Input Context	A: Oh God no! I can't stay tied down to one woman. Why would you want to do that? B: I know right? Most people consider marriage to be involving 2 people but in certain parts of the world that varies between cultures and religions, so it doesn't seem so bad A: Marriage is very good.
Bi-encoder 256M	I agree, but in some cultures, marriage is recommended and unmarried folks are frowned upon!
Blender 90M	I agree! I' m not sure if i could do it though. I don' t think I could.
Exemplar	I agree, but in some cultures, marriage is recommended and unmarried folks are frowned upon!
RetNRef	I agree. I think it' s important for people to have a healthy relationship with each other.
RetNRef$_\alpha$	I agree, but some folks are recommended to marry in some cultures, and some are frown upon!
RetNRef + CORGE	I agree! In some cultures marriage is recommended, but in some countries it' s not recommended.
Exemplar	I agree. I think it' s important for people to have a healthy relationship with each other.
MatToGen	I agree, some cultures are more strict than others, but i agree that some religions are more lenient.
MatToGen + CORGE	I agree! In some cultures marriage is recommended by some religions, but I don' t believe in it!
Exemplar	nicde.
KIF	I agree! I think it' s important to remember that marriage is a legal, social, and financial union.
Exemplar	That is good and great
RAG	I agree! I think it' s important for people to have a healthy relationship with each other.

Table 6: Additional examples for model responses and provided exemplars corresponding to given input contexts.

Author Index

Association for Computational Linguistics
209 N. Eighth Street
Stroudsburg, Pennsylvania 18360

ISBN 978-1-7138-6748-7

9 781713 867487

CURRAN ASSOCIATES INC.
proceedings
.com